BATTLES
MAP BY MAP

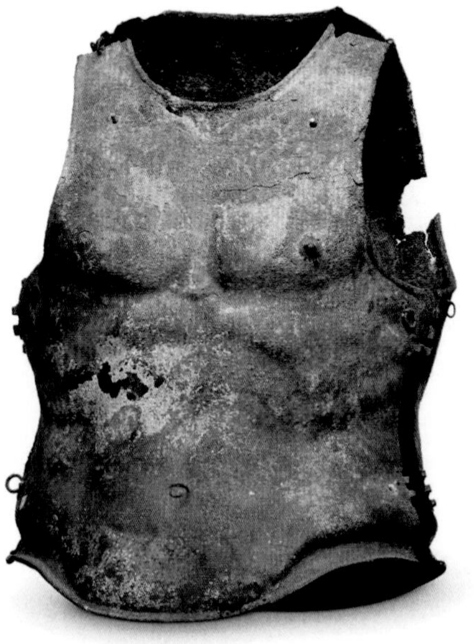

BATTLES
MAP BY MAP

FOREWORD BY

PETER SNOW

10

BEFORE 1000 CE

CONTENTS

DK | Penguin Random House

DK LONDON

Senior Editor Hugo Wilkinson
Editors Tom Booth, Polly Boyd
Assistant Editor Michael Clark
Managing Editor Angeles Gavira Guerrero
Associate Publishing Director Liz Wheeler
Publishing Director Jonathan Metcalf

Lead Senior Art Editor Duncan Turner
Senior Art Editor Sharon Spencer
Design Development Manager Sophia MTT
Jacket Designer Surabhi Wadhwa-Gandhi
Production Editor Gillian Reid
Senior Production Controller Meskerem Berhane
Managing Art Editor Michael Duffy
Art Director Karen Self
Design Director Phil Ormerod

54

1000–1500

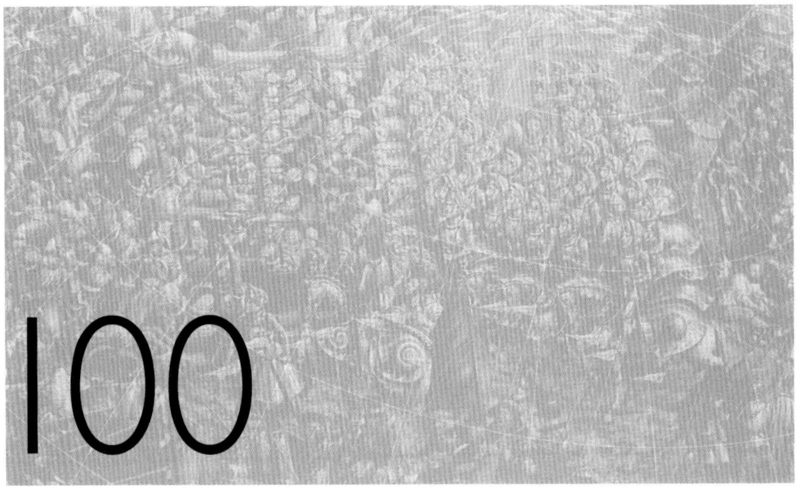
100

1500–1700

DK INDIA

Senior Editor Dharini Ganesh
Editors Ishita Jha, Priyanjali Narain
Picture Research Coordinator Sumita Khatwani
Picture Research Manager Taiyaba Khatoon
Senior Editorial Manager Rohan Sinha
Managing Art Editor Sudakshina Basu
Production Manager Pankaj Sharma
Pre-production Manager Balwant Singh
Editorial Head Glenda Fernandes
Design Head Malavika Talukder
Senior Art Editor Vaibhav Rastogi
Project Art Editor Anjali Sachar
Art Editors Mridushmita Bose, Rabia Ahmad
Senior Cartographers Subhashree Bharati, Mohammad Hassan
Cartographer Ashif
Cartography Manager Suresh Kumar
Senior Jackets Designer Suhita Dharamjit
Senior DTP Designers Harish Aggarwal, Vishal Bhatia
DTP Designer Nityanand Kumar

COBALT ID

Designer Darren Bland
Art Director Paul Reid
Editorial Director Marek Walisiewicz

CONTRIBUTORS

FOREWORD
Peter Snow CBE

CONSULTANT
Professor Philip Sabin, Professor of Strategic Studies, Kings College, London

WRITERS
Tony Allan, Kay Celtel, R.G. Grant, Philip Parker, Dr Arrigo Velicogna

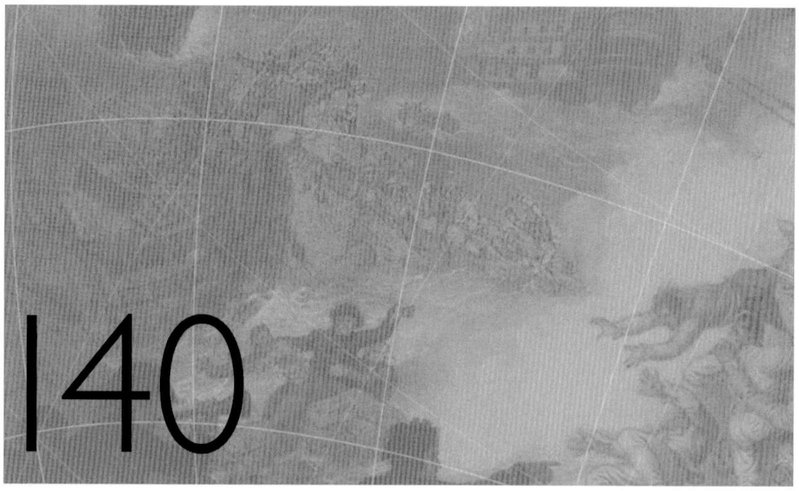
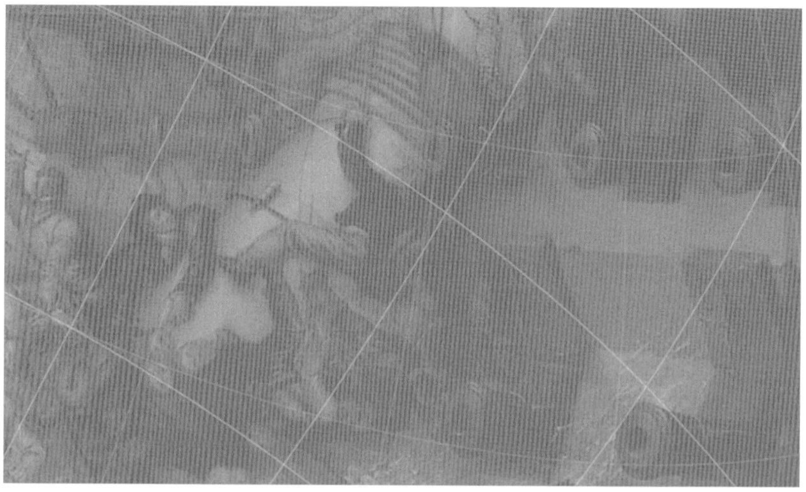

140

1700–1900

First published in Great Britain in 2021 by
Dorling Kindersley Limited, DK, One Embassy Gardens, 8 Viaduct Gardens, London SW11 7BW

The authorised representative in the EEA is Dorling Kindersley Verlag GmbH. Arnulfstr. 124, 80636 Munich, Germany.

10 9 8 7 6 5 4 3 2 1

001–319134–May/2021

A CIP catalogue record for this book is available from the British Library.

ISBN 978-0-2414-4634-8

FSC www.fsc.org MIX Paper from responsible sources FSC™ C018179

This book was made with Forest Stewardship Council TM certified paper—one small step in DK's commitment to a sustainable future. For more information go to www.dk.com/our-green-pledge

Printed and bound in United Arab Emirates

For the curious
www.dk.com

200

1900–PRESENT

FOREWORD

Wars and the battles that punctuate them are a timeless feature of human experience. Fighting is our ultimate means of resolving conflict when all else fails. Bloody though battles are, history cannot ignore them. This exceptional book illuminates the stories of the most important of those battles with a clarity I've never seen before. Only a map, the bird's eye view of a battle, can explain and illustrate the twists and turns of each contest.

All the battles in this meticulously designed volume are in their own way decisive. Some change the shape of the world map by shifting frontiers or deciding the rise and fall of nations. Others erupt within frontiers, marking the transformative moments in civil wars and revolutions. Marathon thwarted the awesome westward sweep of the Persians in 490 BCE; Ain Jalut blocked the Mongols in 1260; Tenochtitlan destroyed the Aztec empire and launched Mexico in 1521; Mohacs – in 1526 – left most of Hungary under Ottoman domination until their defeat at Vienna in 1683. The Battle of Britain and Stalingrad were two key deciding moments of World War II. Cromwell's victory at Naseby in 1645 changed England's government; Tokugawa Ieyasu's triumph at Sekigahara in 1600 propelled the Tokugawa shogunate into power in Japan for more than 250 years. Japan's defeat in World War II was decisively hastened by America's victory of Midway in 1942. Other battles light a different torch – the flare of great symbolic victories that become legends. Ethiopia's defeat of Italy at Adowa in 1896 lit the beacon of African resistance to colonialism. Kosovo Polje in 1389, although a defeat, is still celebrated in Serbia as a proud national symbol of resistance to a foreign invader.

This book also describes in unparalleled detail several key features of each battle. The arrows depicting movement on each map show how commanders responded to the chaos that soon ripped up carefully laid plans. German chief of staff Helmuth von

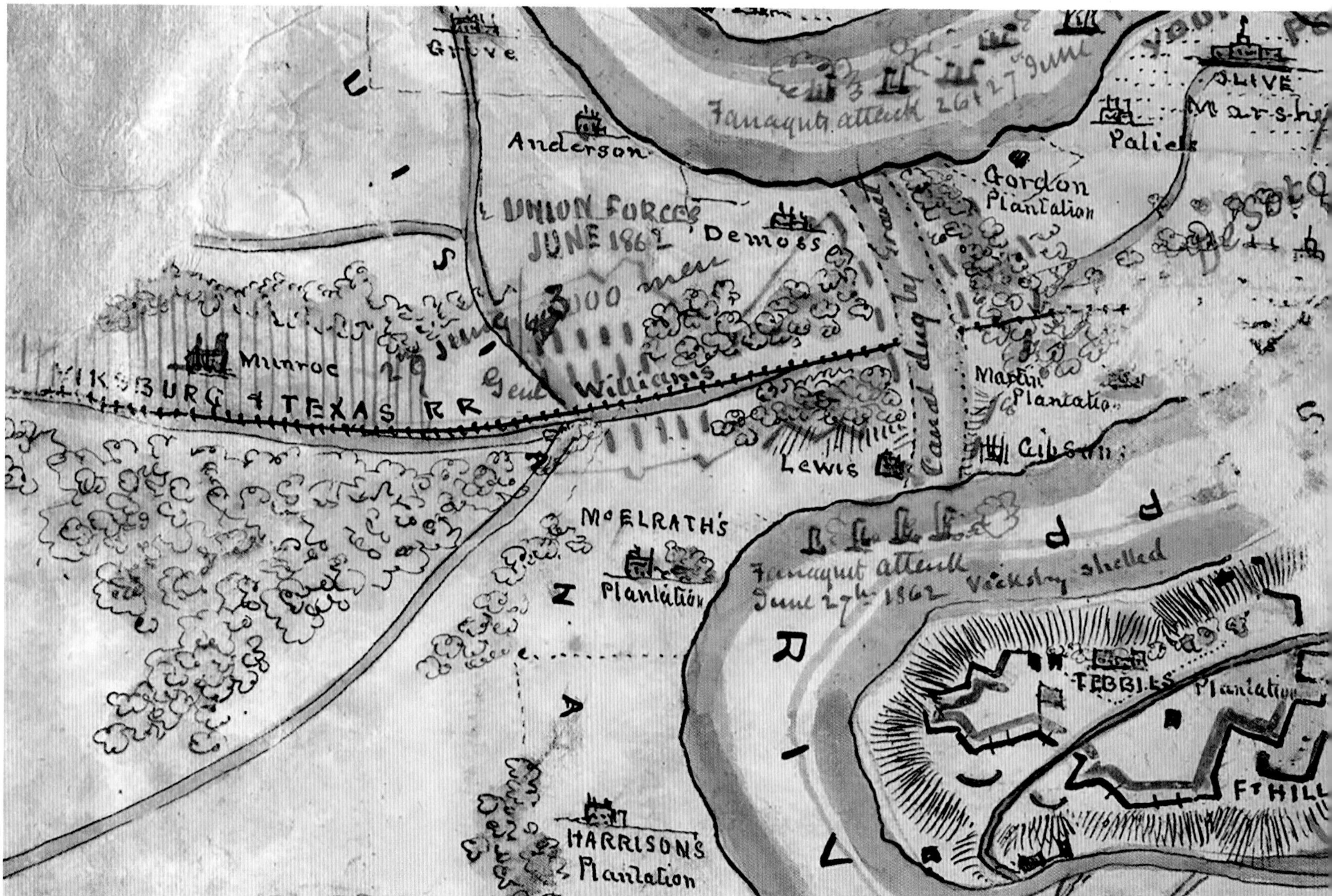
Grove
Anderson
UNION FORCES
JUNE 1862
Demoss
Munroe
VIKSBURG & TEXAS RR
Genl Williams
Gordon
Plantation
Martin
Plantation
Lewis
McELRATH'S
Plantation
Vicksburg shelled
TEBBILS
Plantation
Ft HILL
HARRISON'S
Plantation

Moltke observed in 1871 that no plan for battle survives first contact with the enemy. Here we can see how great leadership by Frederick the Great at Leuthen in 1757 seized the opportunity to send a large force around his enemy's left flank and roll up the Austrian army. It's also easy to make out how the arrival of Gebhard Leberecht von Blücher's Prussian troops swooping down on Napoleon's right at Waterloo in 1815 helped decide one of the most pivotal battles in history. You can see the ridge at Crécy in 1346 that gave King Edward III of England the commanding view of the field that enabled him to tailor his tactics to achieve victory. At Austerlitz in 1805, the strategic importance of the Pratzen heights stormed by Napoleon's generals Vandamme and Saint-Hilaire is unmistakable.

Another striking feature of this parade of maps from century to century is how they describe the changing face of battle. For two millennia the battles are close fought with sword, spear, and bow. Then, around the 14th century, we begin to discern how gunpowder widens the conflict. Babur's cannon were more than a match for the Indian elephants at Panipat in 1526. And finally the invention of the motor engine has tanks and armoured cars dragging warfare out of the World War I trenches at Amiens in 1918 and unleashing them into the vast mobile battles at El Alamein in 1942 and Desert Storm in 1991 .

If, as I fear, war persists as a permanent feature in the ebb and flow of civilization, this book will remain an essential guide to how its battles are won and lost.

PETER SNOW, 2020

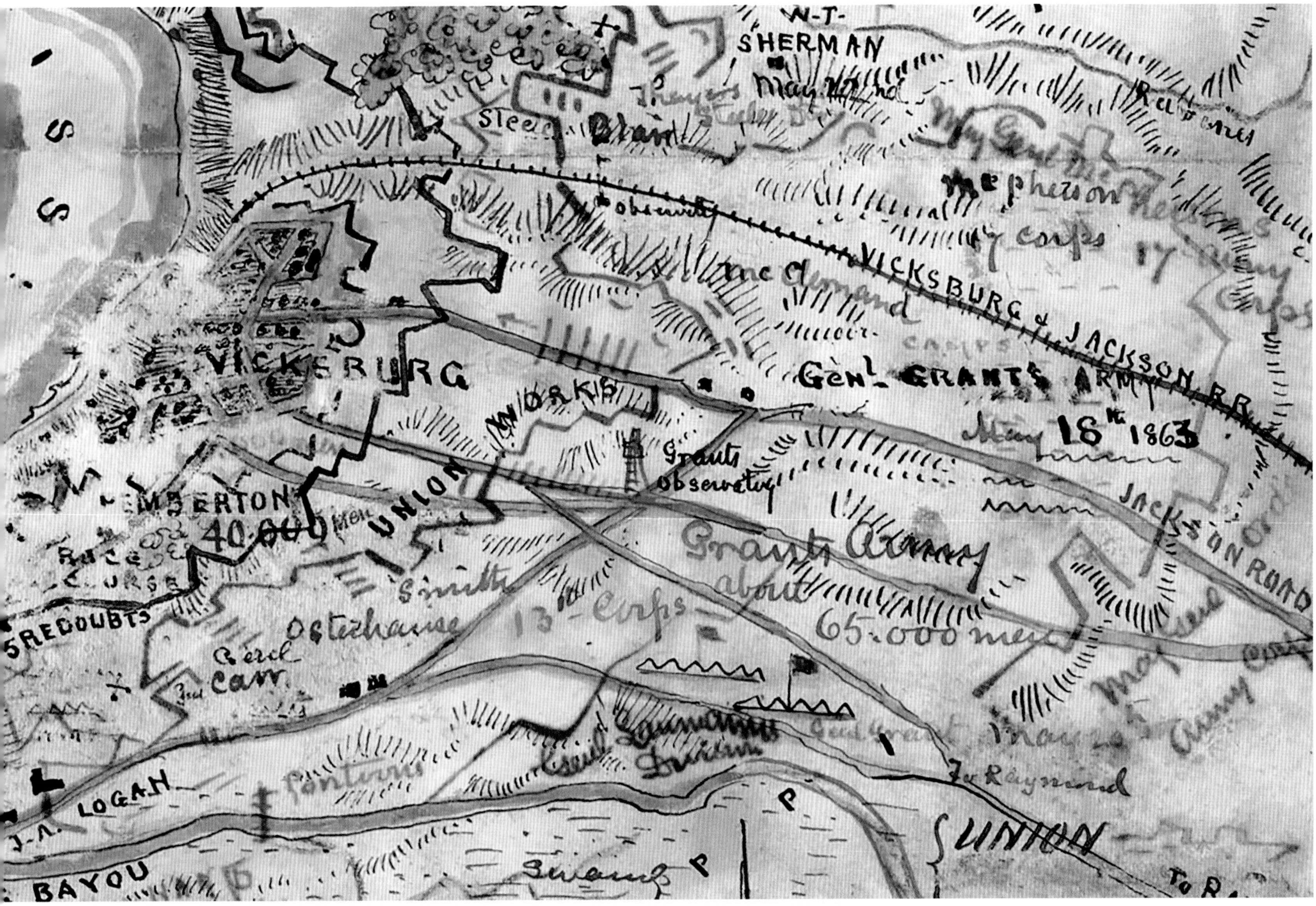
SHERMAN
VICKSBURG
VICKSBURG & JACKSON R.R.
GEN.L GRANT'S ARMY
May 18th 1863
UNION WORKS
JACKSON ROAD
Grants Army about 65.000 men
13th Corps
5 REDOUBTS
LOGAN
BAYOU
UNION

▽ **The civil war that founded a nation**
Drawn in 1864, this map shows the western theatre during the American Civil War (see pp.182–87), around the town of Vicksburg, Mississippi. The map shows railways, fortifications, and Union and Confederate forces. By the time it ended in 1865, the war had claimed an estimated total of over 600,000 lives.

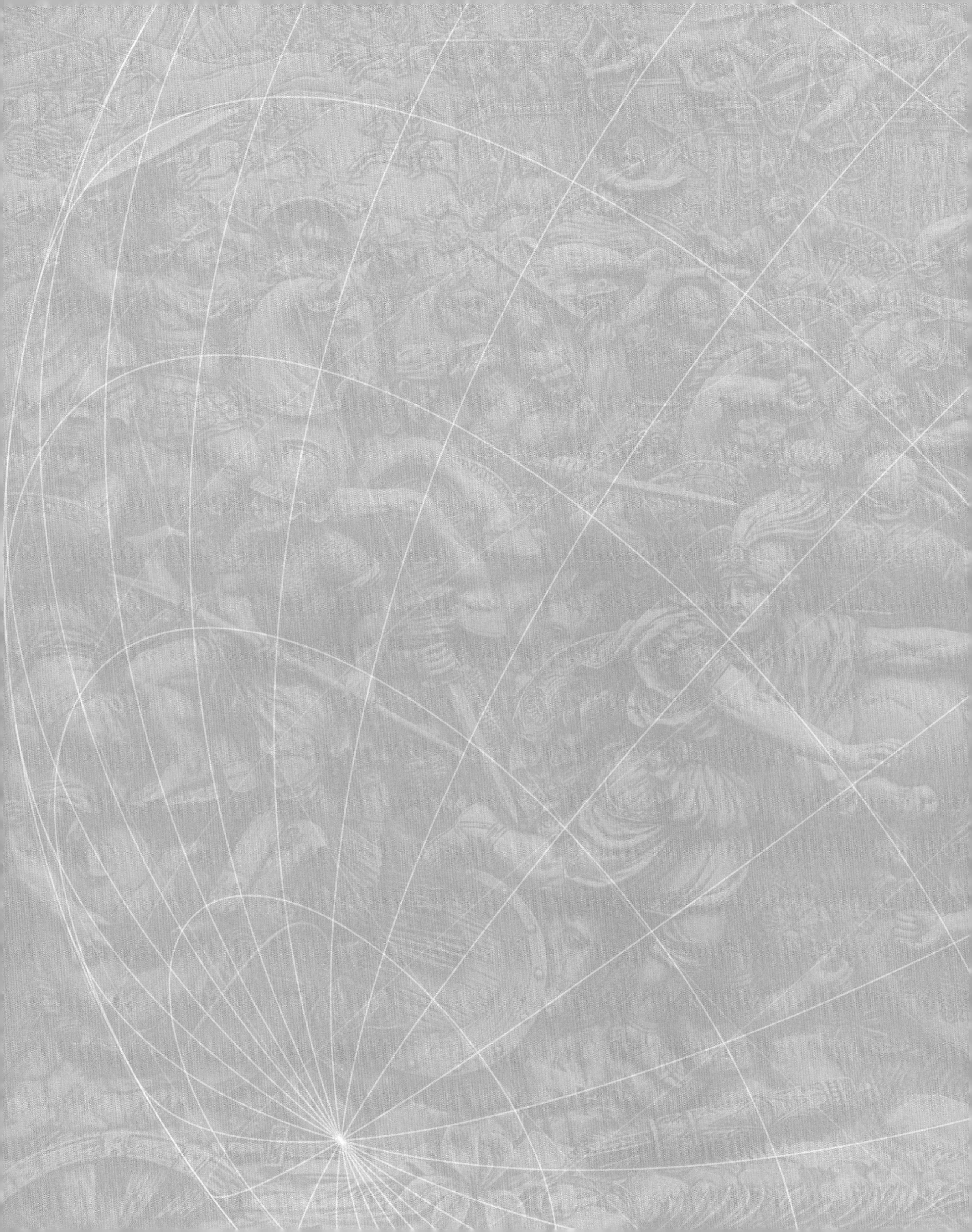

BEFORE 1000 CE

AS HUMAN CIVILIZATIONS GREW, SO ORGANIZED MILITARY FORCES BEGAN TO DEVELOP. EMPIRES WERE WON AND LOST ON THE BATTLEFIELD, WHILE SPECIALIZED TROOPS SUCH AS CAVALRY AND CHARIOTEERS EMERGED TO FIGHT ALONGSIDE INFANTRY.

△ **Egyptian sphinx**
The Sphinx is from the reign of Ramesses II (r.1279–1213 BCE), whose battle against the Hittites at Kadesh in 1274 BCE involved large chariot forces on each side.

BEFORE 1000 CE

The period up to 1000 CE saw the dawn of organized warfare. Armies gradually grew larger, and foot soldiers were complemented by cavalry and other arms. The largest states developed professional armies, but they were constantly challenged by newer forces who employed new weaponry, tactics, and modes of organization in battle.

The rise of cities in Mesopotamia by 3000 BCE created a need for specialized warriors to defend them against outsiders. By 1500 BCE, some city-states had become empires, and began to fight for territorial expansion. The Egyptians and Hittites, for example, vied for supremacy. They used chariots in battles, which provided greater mobility. Several centuries later, advances in metallurgy saw the spread of iron weaponry which was more lethal than bronze swords. The Assyrians developed siege engines by around 800 BCE, rendering even the most sturdy city walls vulnerable.

Citizen militia to professional soldiers

Empires grew larger, but the largest of them all, the Persian Achaemenid empire, found itself outmatched by smaller Greek city-states. The Greek hoplites – heavily armed infantry made up of citizens – wielded long spears in tightknit rectangular formations known as phalanxes to defeat two Persian invasions in the 5th century BCE. This tactic set the pattern for warfare in the eastern Mediterranean for 300 years. Perfected by the Macedonian king Alexander the Great, phalanxes were skilfully combined with cavalry and light infantry to conquer the Persian Empire in a series of campaigns from 334 to 323 BCE. However, the Macedonian phalanx, despite its improvements, proved unwieldy, falling victim to the latest Mediterranean military power, the Roman army.

From the 4th century BCE, the Romans combined political aggression with close-combat infantry tactics, conquering first Italy and then the entire Mediterranean region. The Roman legions were not unbeatable, but over the centuries they became increasingly well trained and professional, annexing new provinces as far north as Britain and as far east as Syria, and overcoming almost all opposition. Gradually it became clear, however, that defending their long frontiers against barbarian raiders would not be sustainable.

▷ **Death of a Roman emperor**
This Coptic icon depicts a vision of the 3rd century Christian martyr Saint Mercurius killing the pagan emperor Julian, portraying his death as divine justice.

Changing battlefields

China became a unified state in 221 BCE and faced a similar evolution. Internal warfare in the preceding years had led to large armies including many infantry and crossbowmen, significant naval forces, and a focus on clever strategy. The Chinese faced pressure along their northern borders from nomadic Xiongnu tribes, whose horse-mounted archers made them formidable foes.

BIRTH OF WARFARE

Organized warfare has its origins in Africa and the ancient Near East, where the Egyptians fought to expand their empire and quash rebellious states. Subsequently, the rise of iron weaponry saw warfare become ever-more efficient. Large-scale infantry formations were perfected by the Romans, birthing an empire that would only fall at the hands of Germanic tribes in 476 CE. The 8th century CE saw both Chinese and Frankish expansion, and the first Viking invasions of Britain.

WARFARE
POLITICS
TECHNOLOGY

1500 BCE · 1300 BCE · 1100 BCE · 900 BCE · 700 BCE

c.1500 BCE Horse-drawn war chariots are used commonly throughout the Middle East

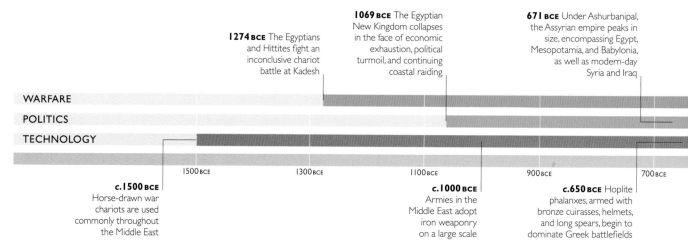

1274 BCE The Egyptians and Hittites fight an inconclusive chariot battle at Kadesh

1069 BCE The Egyptian New Kingdom collapses in the face of economic exhaustion, political turmoil, and continuing coastal raiding

c.1000 BCE Armies in the Middle East adopt iron weaponry on a large scale

671 BCE Under Ashurbanipal, the Assyrian empire peaks in size, encompassing Egypt, Mesopotamia, and Babylonia, as well as modern-day Syria and Iraq

c.650 BCE Hoplite phalanxes, armed with bronze cuirasses, helmets, and long spears, begin to dominate Greek battlefields

◁ **Viking longships**
The seafaring Vikings used swift longships to transport their armies along wide stretches of coastline or to sail upriver. Besides using the ships for raiding and invasions, the Vikings often fought sea battles among themselves.

> *"I have come not to make war on the Italians, but to aid the Italians against Rome."*
>
> HANNIBAL BARCA, 217 BCE

In the 620s, the Byzantine Empire, Rome's successor state in the east, lost much territory to the Arab armies united by the new religion of Islam. Highly mobile and experienced in hit-and-run raids, these Arab forces soon adapted to the tactics required of larger armed formations. The peoples they conquered, such as the Persians and some Turkic tribes, became a source of military manpower for the Arab states, giving them an edge over their rivals.

While the Byzantine Empire managed to survive, the Roman Empire in the West deteriorated, giving way to a series of Germanic successor states by the 6th century. Initially these states retained the ethos of a nomadic warband, conceptualizing warfare as a clash of axes and spears until one side fled. However, they gradually cultivated sophisticated semi-permanent forces.

The adoption of stirrups in Western Europe around 800 CE gave riders greater stability and reinforced the emerging dominance of heavily armoured cavalry now that disciplined infantry had become scarce. They were the predecessors of the knights who would make up the backbone of armies by the 11th century.

Armies continued to face new waves of invaders, such as the Magyars in Hungary and the Vikings from Scandinavia. However, by 1000 CE, more centralized states, capable of resisting most invaders, began to consolidate in Europe.

▷ **Striking fear into Rome**
This 16th-century fresco shows the Carthaginians crossing the Alps in 218 BCE during the Second Punic War against Rome. Carthaginian leader Hannibal used war elephants to intimidate Roman soldiers and their horses.

490 BCE Athenian hoplites defeat a much larger Persian army at Marathon, ending the first Persian invasion of Greece

331 BCE Macedonian King Alexander the Great decisively defeats the Persian ruler Darius III at Gaugamela

c.200 BCE Roman legions adopt the improved *gladius hispaniensis* short sword

216 BCE Carthaginian general Hannibal defeats the Roman legions at Cannae during the Second Punic War

27 BCE Julius Caesar's adopted heir Octavian becomes the first Roman emperor

476 CE After a period of invasions, a Germanic general in Roman employ deposes the last Roman emperor in the West

622 CE The prophet Mohammed moves from Mecca to Medina, beginning the Islamic era and a period of Arab conquests

581 CE The Sui dynasty reunites China after a period of fragmentation

634 CE Muslim armies defeat the Byzantine empire at Yarmuk, leading to the conquest of Syria and Palestine, and paving the way for the Arab conquest of north Africa

751 CE Tang armies from China are defeated by the Abbasid army at the River Talas, ending Chinese expansion westward of Central Asia

771 CE Charlemagne becomes the Frankish ruler, and during his reign the kingdom expands to cover a large part of Western Europe

793 CE The first Viking raiders attack England, beginning a 250-year long period of attacks on the coastlines of northwestern Europe

c.900 CE Gunpowder is discovered by Chinese alchemists. It is later utilized for fireworks and primitive firearms

500 BCE · 300 BCE · 100 BCE · 100 CE · 300 CE · 500 CE · 700 CE · 900 CE

A CLASH OF EMPIRES

The Egyptian New Kingdom and the Hittite Empire had been vying for control of the eastern Mediterranean for the past two centuries. In 1274 BCE, Ramses II set out to reassert Egyptian dominance of the region.

KEY

EGYPTIANS: Camp; Chariots; Forces

HITTITES: Camp; Chariots; Forces

TIMELINE

MAY 1274 BCE — JUN 1274 BCE

1 HITTITES LAY AN AMBUSH MAY 1274 BCE

Muwatallis set a trap for the Egyptians. Two of his agents fed Ramses with false information, claiming the Hittite army was nowhere near Kadesh. As a result, the pharaoh confidently advanced to establish a camp outside the city, while his army marched to join him in loose order. Hidden by the hills, the Hittites moved to attack the marching Egyptians' unprotected flank.

Arrival of the Egyptians

2 HITTITE CHARIOTS CHARGE

A Hittite force, estimated to number more than 2,500 chariots, forded the Orontes River and charged into the flank of the Re division, the second formation in the Egyptian line of march. Unprepared for this shock attack, the division was routed and scattered. The Hittites failed to take full advantage of their initial success, lingering to plunder the Egyptians' baggage.

Hittite chariot attack — Re division scatters

3 RAMSES HEADS THE COUNTER-ATTACK

Even before the Hittite blow was struck, Ramses had received information of the proximity of the enemy. Ramses issued orders for the rear divisions to hasten their march, and prepared himself to enter battle. As the Hittites attacked the Amun division and threatened Ramses' camp, the pharaoh mounted a chariot and led his troops in a counter-charge. The agile Egyptian chariots outmanoeuvred their Hittite opponents and turned the tide of the battle.

Egyptian chariot attack

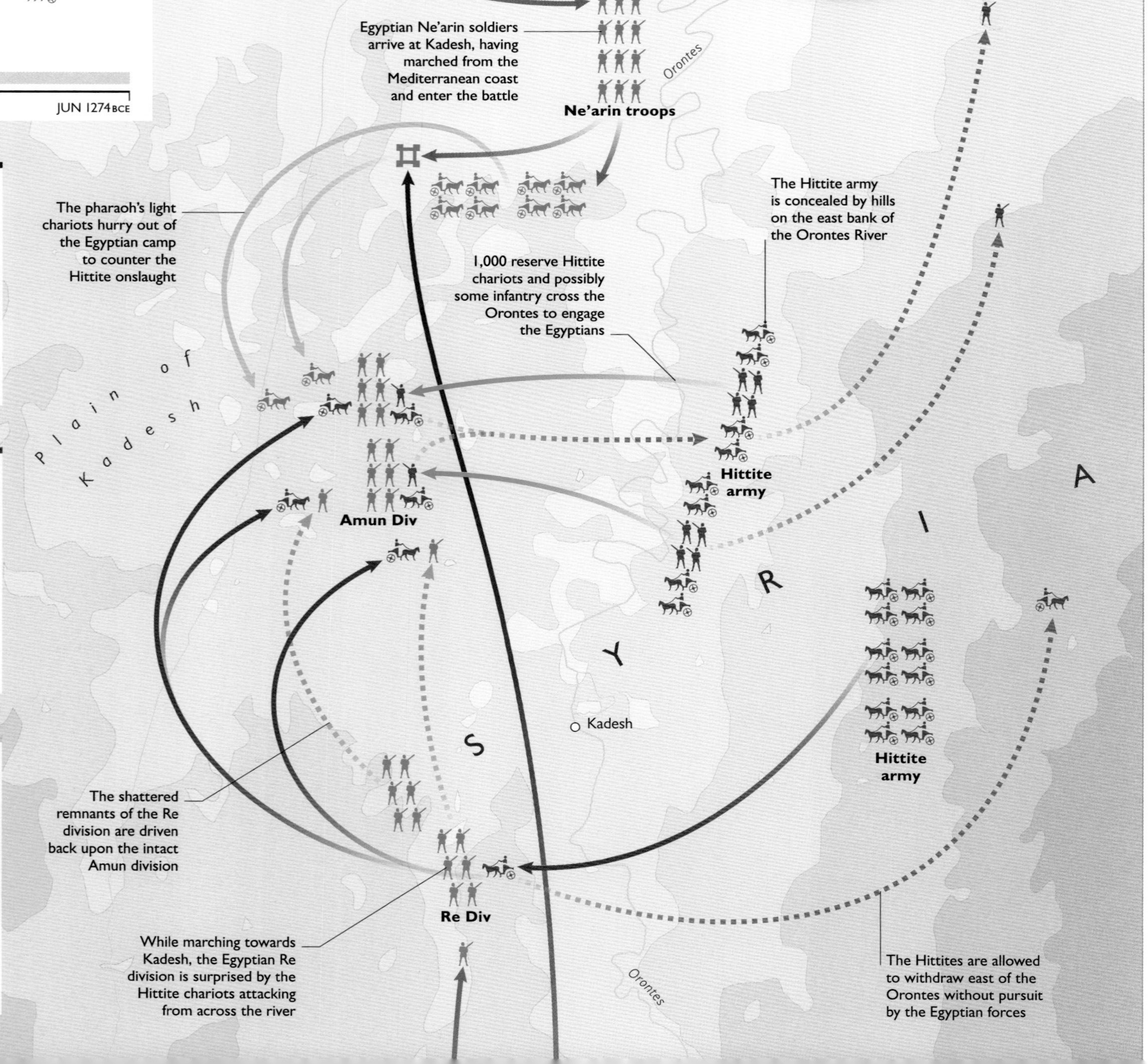
From the Mediterranean coast
Egyptian Ne'arin soldiers arrive at Kadesh, having marched from the Mediterranean coast and enter the battle
Ne'arin troops
Orontes
The pharaoh's light chariots hurry out of the Egyptian camp to counter the Hittite onslaught
1,000 reserve Hittite chariots and possibly some infantry cross the Orontes to engage the Egyptians
The Hittite army is concealed by hills on the east bank of the Orontes River
Plain of Kadesh
Amun Div
Hittite army
S Y R I A
Kadesh
Hittite army
The shattered remnants of the Re division are driven back upon the intact Amun division
Re Div
While marching towards Kadesh, the Egyptian Re division is surprised by the Hittite chariots attacking from across the river
Orontes
The Hittites are allowed to withdraw east of the Orontes without pursuit by the Egyptian forces

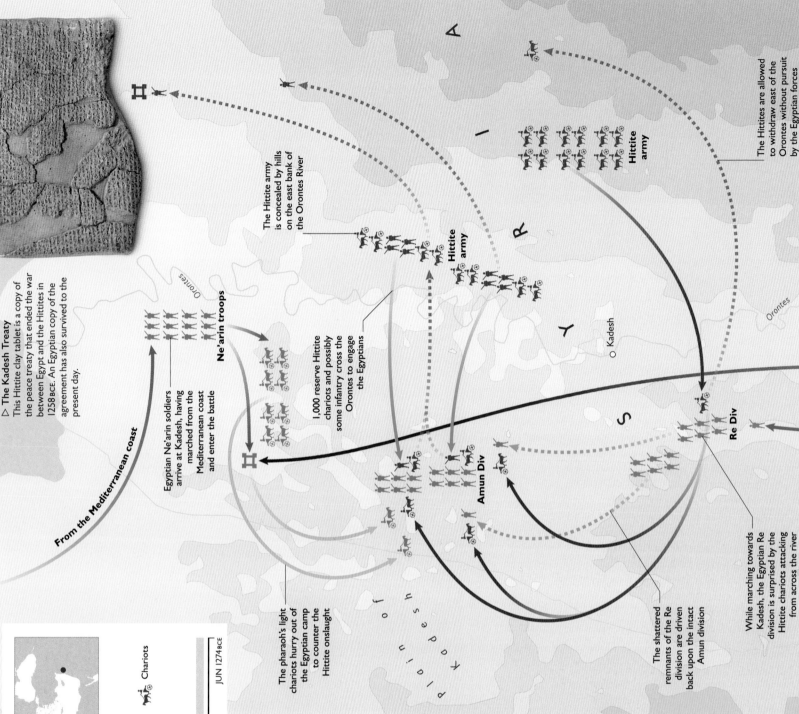

▷ **The Kadesh Treaty**
This Hittite clay tablet is a copy of the peace treaty that ended the war between Egypt and the Hittites in 1258 BCE. An Egyptian copy of the agreement has also survived to the present day.

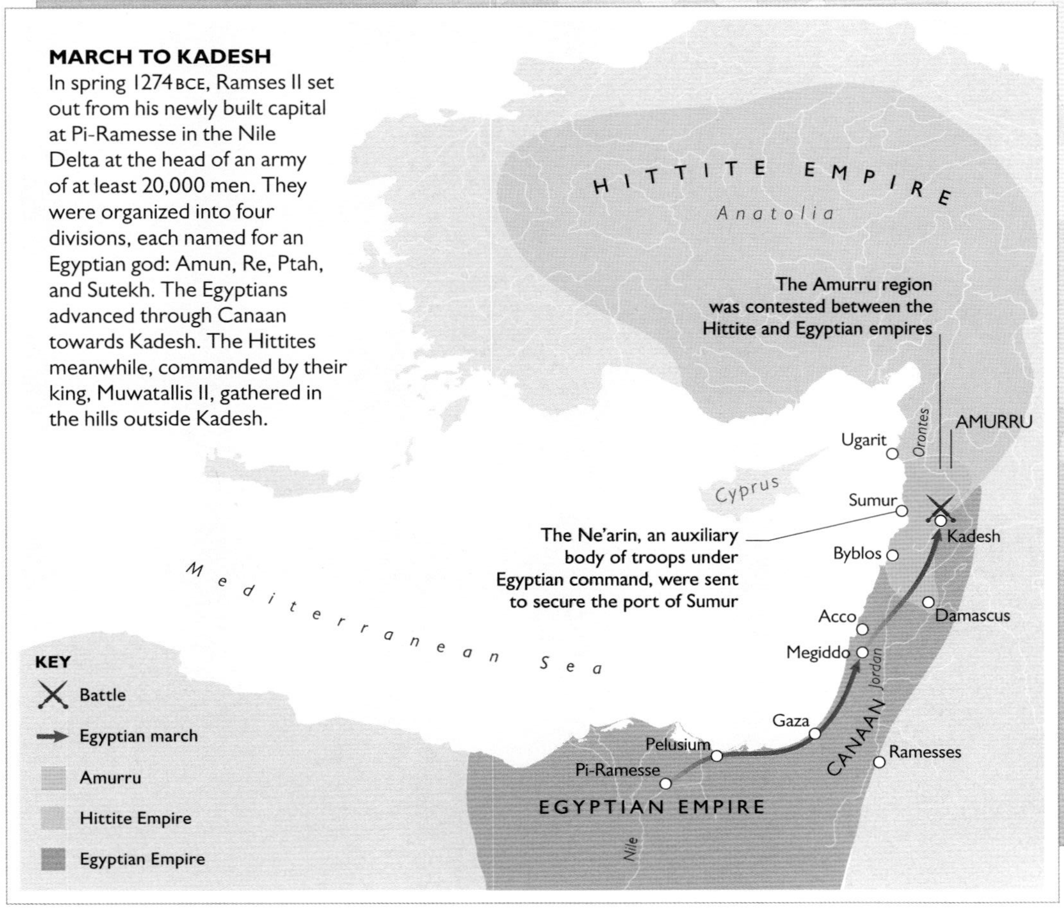
HITTITE EMPIRE
Anatolia
The Amurru region was contested between the Hittite and Egyptian empires
AMURRU
Orontes
Ugarit
Cyprus
Sumur
Kadesh
The Ne'arin, an auxiliary body of troops under Egyptian command, were sent to secure the port of Sumur
Byblos
Mediterranean Sea
Acco
Damascus
Megiddo
Jordan
Gaza
CANAAN
Pelusium
Ramesses
Pi-Ramesse
EGYPTIAN EMPIRE
Nile
KEY
Battle
Egyptian march
Amurru
Hittite Empire
Egyptian Empire

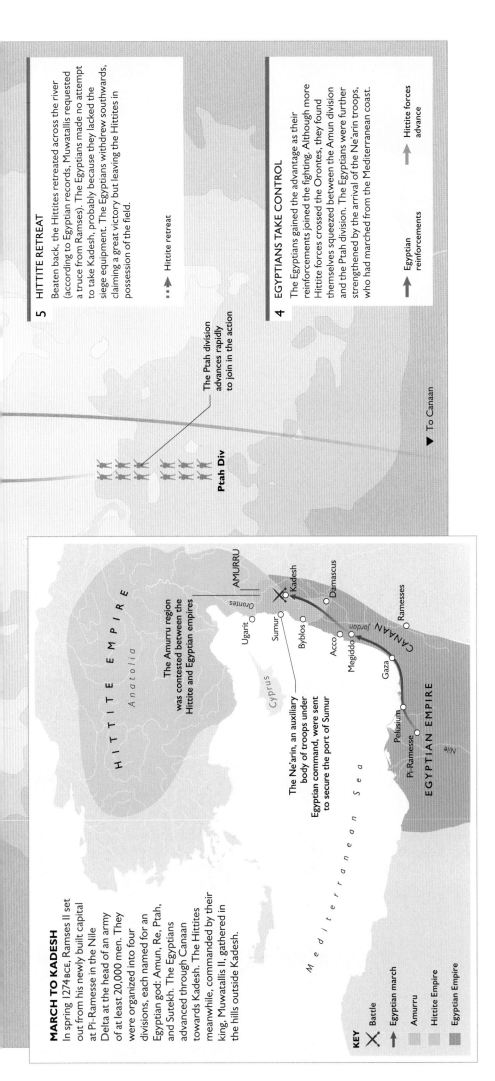

MARCH TO KADESH
In spring 1274 BCE, Ramses II set out from his newly built capital at Pi-Ramesse in the Nile Delta at the head of an army of at least 20,000 men. They were organized into four divisions, each named for an Egyptian god: Amun, Re, Ptah, and Sutekh. The Egyptians advanced through Canaan towards Kadesh. The Hittites meanwhile, commanded by their king, Muwatallis II, gathered in the hills outside Kadesh.

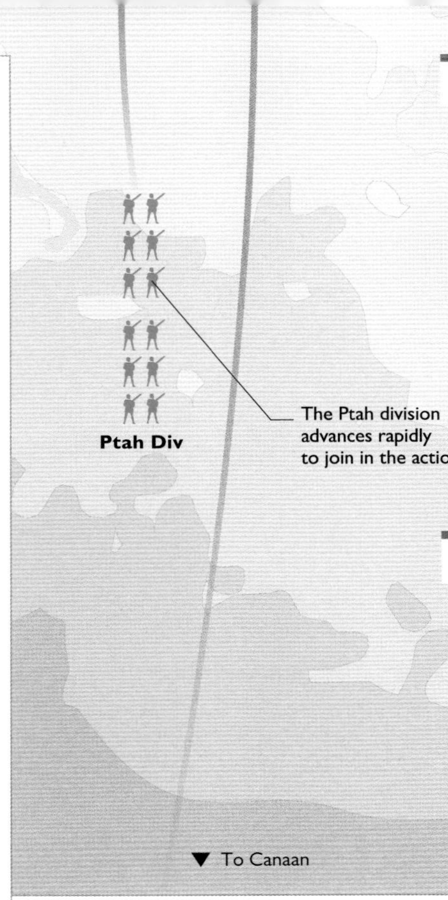
Ptah Div
The Ptah division advances rapidly to join in the action
▼ To Canaan

5 HITTITE RETREAT
Beaten back, the Hittites retreated across the river (according to Egyptian records, Muwatallis requested a truce from Ramses). The Egyptians made no attempt to take Kadesh, probably because they lacked the siege equipment. The Egyptians withdrew southwards, claiming a great victory but leaving the Hittites in possession of the field.

Hittite retreat

4 EGYPTIANS TAKE CONTROL
The Egyptians gained the advantage as their reinforcements joined the fighting. Although more Hittite forces crossed the Orontes, they found themselves squeezed between the Amun division and the Ptah division. The Egyptians were further strengthened by the arrival of the Ne'arin troops, who had marched from the Mediterranean coast.

Egyptian reinforcements
Hittite forces advance

KADESH

More than 3,000 years ago, the Egyptian pharaoh Ramses II led an army into an area of Syria long contested with the Hittite Empire. The resulting clash between Egyptian and Hittite chariot forces, fought outside the city of Kadesh, is the earliest battle for which detailed information has survived.

Ramses II succeeded his father Seti I as ruler of the Egyptian New Kingdom in 1279 BCE. He inherited a long-running dispute with the Hittite Empire (based in Anatolia) over the possession of Amurru, a region in what is present-day northern Syria. Ramses conducted a successful offensive against the Hittites' allies in Amurru in 1275 BCE. The following year, he sought to repeat this exploit, taking as his target the walled city of Kadesh. But on this occasion, the Hittite ruler Muwatallis II responded by fielding an army that, in the words of an Egyptian chronicler, "covered the mountains and the valleys and were like locusts in their numbers".

Both the Egyptians and the Hittites depended on chariots for their elite shock force on the battlefield – the Hittites employing three-man chariots, the Egyptians lighter vehicles crewed by a horse driver and an archer. With about 5,000 chariots deployed, the fight that took place outside Kadesh in 1274 BCE is the largest chariot battle known to history. The most vivid account of the battle was written by the Egyptians, who claimed a heroic victory. Other evidence suggests it should be regarded as an inconclusive draw. Amurru remained in Hittite hands and fighting over the region intermittently continued. Sixteen years later, the border dispute between the two empires was settled by the world's earliest recorded international peace treaty, which was originally inscribed on a silver tablet. A period of relative peace would be maintained between the two powers for the following century.

RAMSES II
R.1279–1213 BCE

Known by later Egyptians as the "Great Ancestor", Ramses II became ruler of the Egyptian New Kingdom in 1279 BCE. As well as fighting the Hittites, he launched successful campaigns against the Nubians to the south, and the Sherden sea pirates. Many of Ancient Egypt's finest temples were built during his 66-year-long reign, including Abu Simbel in southern Egypt.

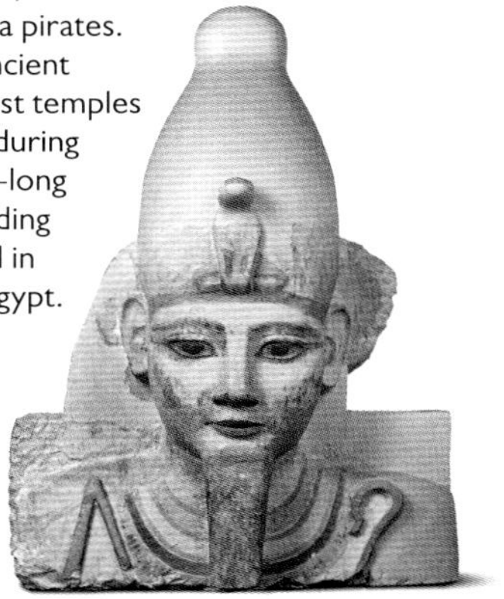

CHARIOT WARFARE

Chariots dominated warfare across cultures from around 1800 to 600 BCE, and continued in use in cultures ranging from the Celtic world and Carthage to India and China for many centuries, especially until the 3rd century BCE.

△ **Assyrian forces**
This 7th-century BCE relief depicts a scene from the Battle of Til-Tuba (c.650 BCE). Elite warriors of the Assyrian army can be seen on board a chariot.

Carts pulled by onagers (Asian wild asses) and oxen were first used in what is today Europe and the Middle East in around 2500 BCE, and with them came early chariots. However, it was not until around 1800 BCE, with the domestication of horses and the invention of the spoked wheel, that war chariots became truly effective. Probably originating in Central Asia, they became a constant feature of wars fought in China, India, the Middle East, and also in the Aegean region and central Europe.

Chariot warfare reached its peak in the late Bronze (*c.*1550–1200 BCE) and early Iron (*c.*1200 BCE–550 BCE) ages. The Hittites, Mitanni, Egyptians, Canaanites, Assyrians, and Babylonians, all fielded armies that included thousands of chariots. The Egyptians and Canaanites tended to favour light, two-horse chariots that were easier to manoeuvre, but could only accommodate the driver and an archer. In contrast, other cultures such as Assyria, Carthage, India, and China used heavier, three- or four-horse chariots that could carry bigger crews, often including spearmen. War Chariots usually constituted the elite striking force of any army, and were supported by infantry, and later, by cavalry.

Cavalry on the rise

Towards the 8th century BCE, the use of war chariots declined as cavalry gained in popularity on the battlefield. Cavalry units were cheaper to recruit, equip, and train as well as easier to maintain. The Battle of Qarqar in the 9th century BCE, is possibly the last time war chariots dominated the battlefield. Nevertheless chariots (including the infamous scythed version) appeared in battles for centuries after, and chariot racing later grew in popularity as a sport.

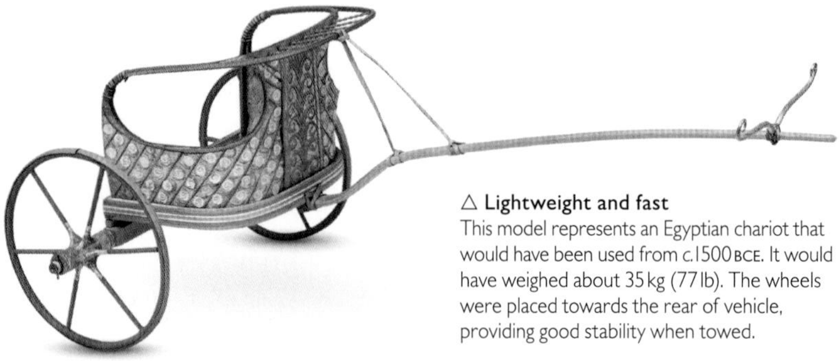

△ **Lightweight and fast**
This model represents an Egyptian chariot that would have been used from c.1500 BCE. It would have weighed about 35 kg (77 lb). The wheels were placed towards the rear of vehicle, providing good stability when towed.

The pharaoh in battle
This scene from a casket in the tomb of Egyptian king Tutankhamun (r.1334–1325 BCE) shows the king shooting arrows at his enemies from his two-horse chariot. He is accompanied by an infantry escort.

THE PERSIAN CAMPAIGN

The Persians set out to invade Greece in 492 BCE, but this expedition was abandoned after a storm destroyed their fleet. In 490 BCE, a second attempt was made under Datis and Artaphernes. The Persians sailed by a southerly route towards Eretria and Athens. Eretria was swiftly destroyed. The Persian army then re-embarked and landed at Marathon, 42 km (26 miles) northeast of Athens.

KEY

- Main battle
- Persian Empire
- Persian fleet and army, 492 BCE
- Persian fleet, 490 BCE

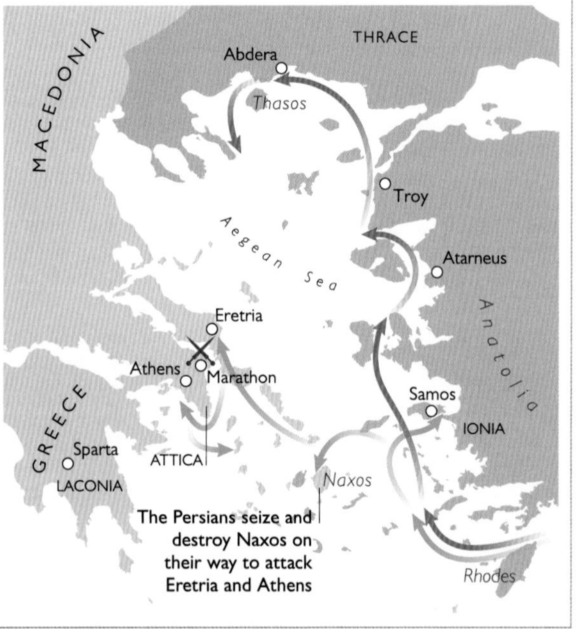

MACEDONIA
THRACE
Abdera
Thasos
Troy
Aegean Sea
Atarneus
Anatolia
Eretria
Athens
Marathon
Samos
IONIA
GREECE
Sparta
LACONIA
ATTICA
Naxos
The Persians seize and destroy Naxos on their way to attack Eretria and Athens
Rhodes

SWIFT VICTORY

Marathon was not a large battle. Fought in a single day, it involved some 10,000 Greeks fighting 25,000 Persian troops. The victorious Greeks were hoplites, armoured foot soldiers who fought at close quarters in a tight formation called the phalanx. Their tactics surprised the Persians, who preferred to fight at a distance with bows and javelins. The battle made the reputation of the Greek hoplites as fearsome infantry.

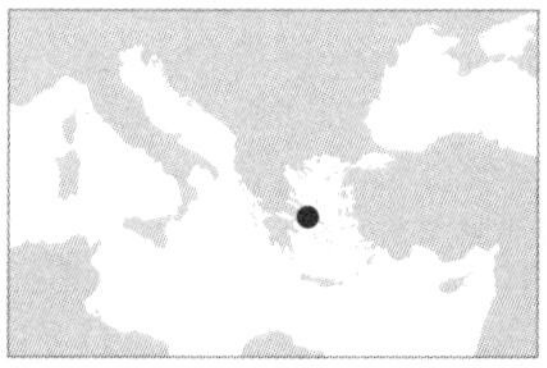

KEY

- Greek troops

PERSIAN FORCES

- Camp
- Troops
- Cavalry
- Fleet

TIMELINE

12 SEP 490 BCE — 13 SEP 490 BCE

1 THE GREEKS ATTACK 12 SEPTEMBER 490 BCE

The Athenians and their allies took up a position blocking the Persians on the coastal plain. After a standoff of several days, Miltiades decided to attack. His troops, all hoplites armed with spears and shields, ran in tight formation towards the Persian army, a diverse force including javelin throwers, archers, and horsemen.

- Greek advance

2 CHARGE AND COUNTER-CHARGE

The hoplites in the centre of the Greek line became disorganized, stumbling over rough ground under a rain of arrows. Seeing their enemy falter, the Persian infantry launched a counter-charge. Struggling to reform their phalanx formations, the Greek hoplites retreated.

- Persian advance
- Greek retreat

3 GREEK ADVANCE ON THE FLANKS

The Persians pushed the hoplites back in the centre. On the flanks, however, the dense masses of armoured Greek infantry charged the inferior Persian foot soldiers who had been relegated to the wings. Overwhelmed, the Persian infantry on the flanks fled the field.

- Greek advance
- Persian flight

BATTLE IS JOINED

The Athenians and their allies took the offensive, charging their more numerous enemy. The Persians counter-attacked in the centre, but on both flanks they were routed.

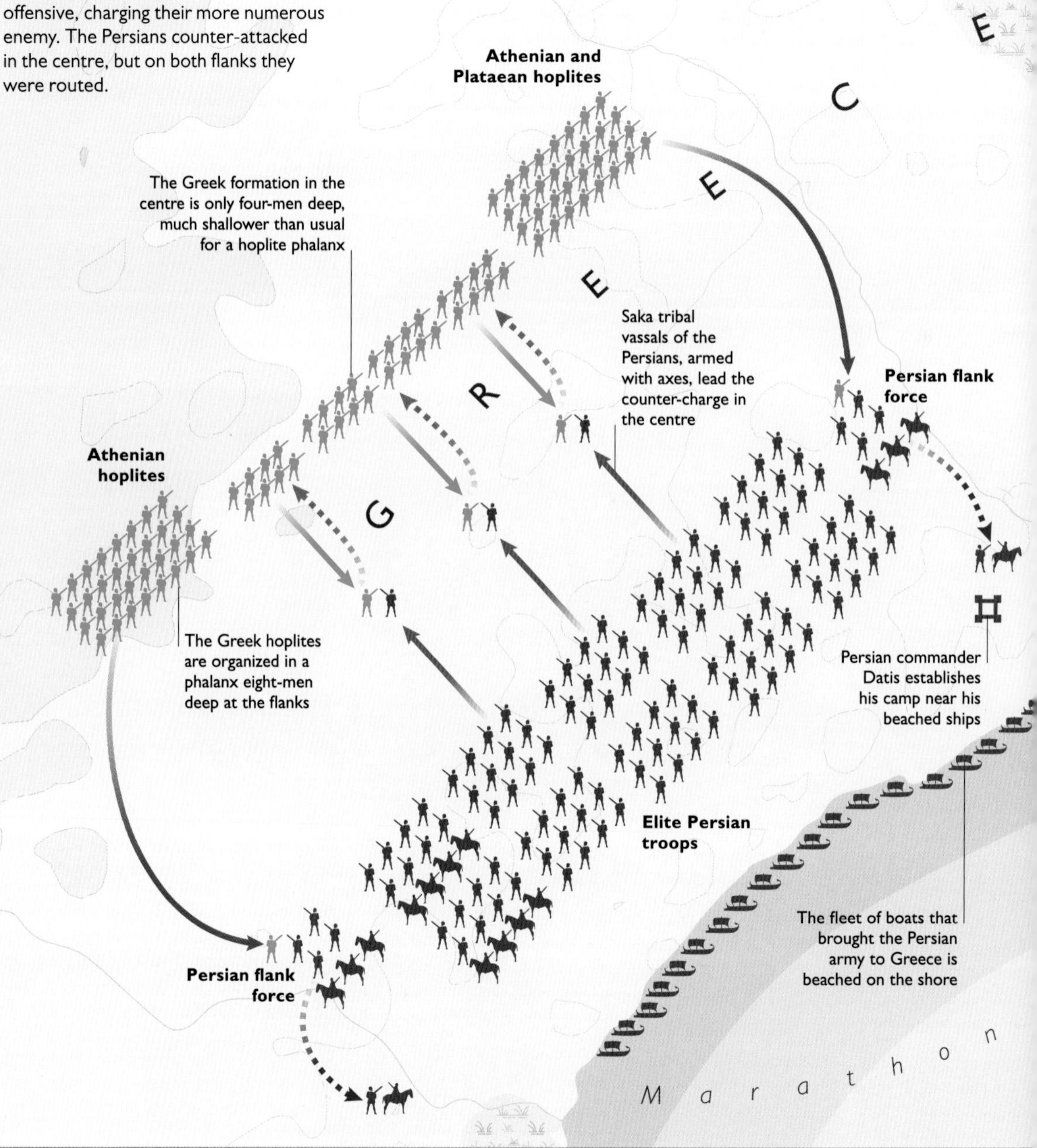

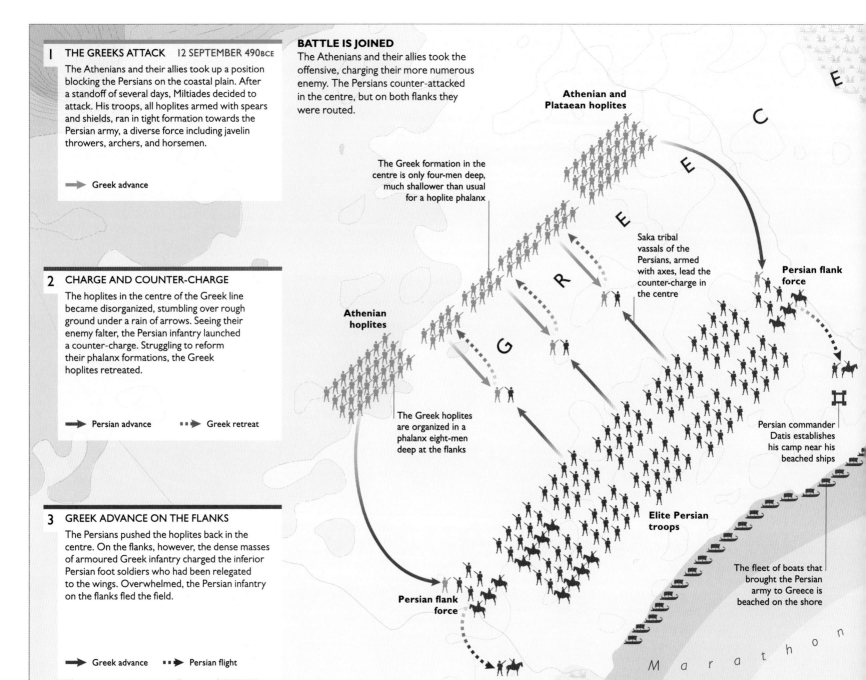

Athenian and Plataean hoplites
GREECE
The Greek formation in the centre is only four-men deep, much shallower than usual for a hoplite phalanx
Saka tribal vassals of the Persians, armed with axes, lead the counter-charge in the centre
Persian flank force
Athenian hoplites
The Greek hoplites are organized in a phalanx eight-men deep at the flanks
Persian commander Datis establishes his camp near his beached ships
Elite Persian troops
The fleet of boats that brought the Persian army to Greece is beached on the shore
Persian flank force
Marathon

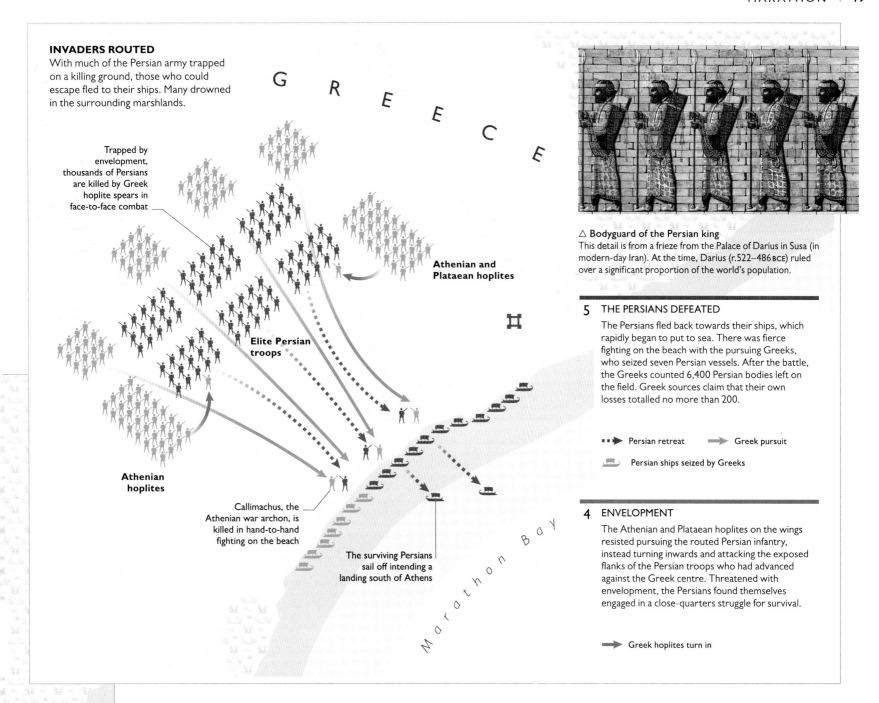

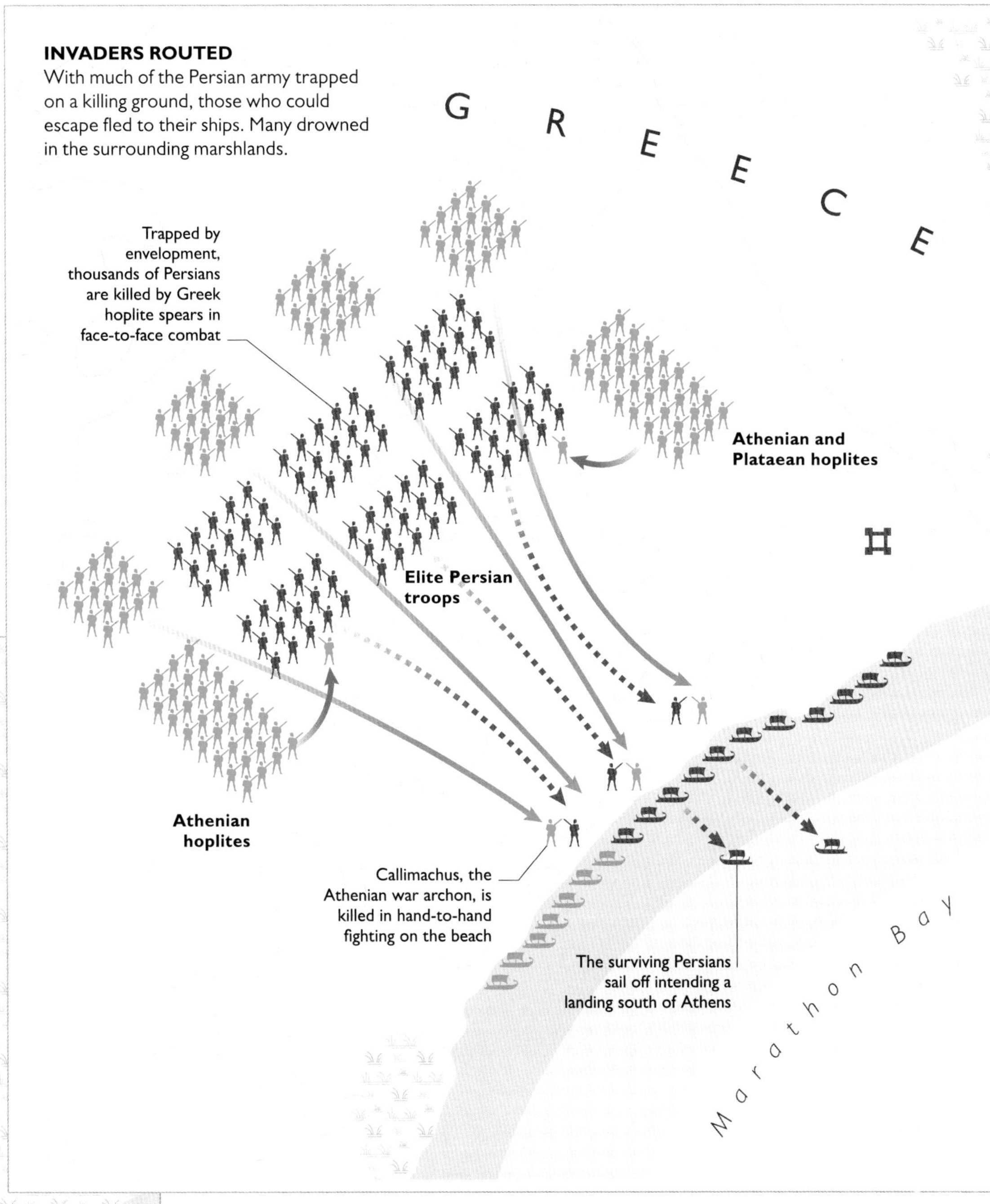
INVADERS ROUTED
With much of the Persian army trapped on a killing ground, those who could escape fled to their ships. Many drowned in the surrounding marshlands.
GREECE
Trapped by envelopment, thousands of Persians are killed by Greek hoplite spears in face-to-face combat
Athenian and Plataean hoplites
Elite Persian troops
Athenian hoplites
Callimachus, the Athenian war archon, is killed in hand-to-hand fighting on the beach
The surviving Persians sail off intending a landing south of Athens
Marathon Bay

△ **Bodyguard of the Persian king**
This detail is from a frieze from the Palace of Darius in Susa (in modern-day Iran). At the time, Darius (r.522–486 BCE) ruled over a significant proportion of the world's population.

5 THE PERSIANS DEFEATED

The Persians fled back towards their ships, which rapidly began to put to sea. There was fierce fighting on the beach with the pursuing Greeks, who seized seven Persian vessels. After the battle, the Greeks counted 6,400 Persian bodies left on the field. Greek sources claim that their own losses totalled no more than 200.

Persian retreat — Greek pursuit

Persian ships seized by Greeks

4 ENVELOPMENT

The Athenian and Plataean hoplites on the wings resisted pursuing the routed Persian infantry, instead turning inwards and attacking the exposed flanks of the Persian troops who had advanced against the Greek centre. Threatened with envelopment, the Persians found themselves engaged in a close-quarters struggle for survival.

Greek hoplites turn in

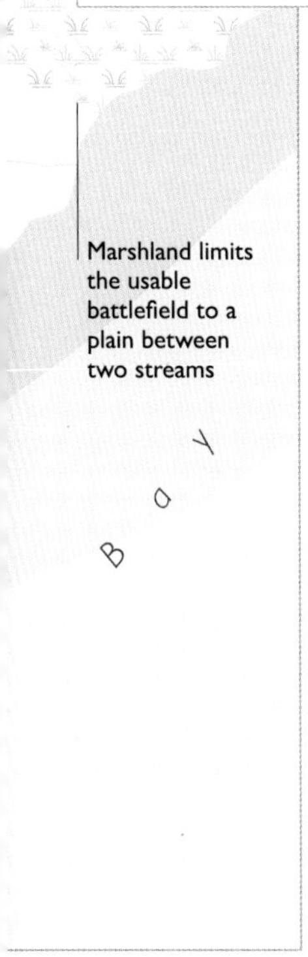
Marshland limits the usable battlefield to a plain between two streams
Bay

MARATHON

In 490 BCE, an army sent by Persian emperor Darius I invaded mainland Greece, going ashore at Marathon. Despite being heavily outnumbered, the soldiers of the Greek city-state of Athens and its allies from Plataea boldly engaged the Persian invasion force.

In the early 5th century BCE, the expanding Persian Achaemenid Empire controlled a vast area from Northern India to southeast Europe, and included among its subjects Ionian Greeks in western Anatolia (present-day western Turkey). The Greek city-states of Athens and Eretria supported an Ionian revolt against Persian rule that was crushed by Emperor Darius I in 494 BCE. It was Darius's resolve to punish the Athenians and Eretrians that motivated the Persian invasion of Greece in 490 BCE.

When the seaborne Persian army landed at Marathon, the Athenians marched out under leaders including Miltiades to confront the invaders at their landing ground. The Spartans, the most militaristic of the Greeks, were urged to join the war but insisted they could not come immediately because they were engaged in sacred ceremonies. Only the small city of Plataea at the last moment sent troops to aid Athens.

The battle is known chiefly through the account of the Greek historian Herodotus, in which many details are obscure and some mythologized. News of the Greek victory is said to have been carried to Athens by the messenger Pheidippides, who ran 42 km (26 miles), giving the name to the modern marathon. A setback rather than a disaster for the Persians, the defeat delayed a full-scale invasion of Greece for another ten years.

THERMOPYLAE

Celebrated for acts of heroism and self-sacrifice, Thermopylae was a delaying action fought in Greece by a small body of Spartan-led Greek hoplites against a vast invading army of the Persian Empire. The Spartans held a mountain pass for three days against superior forces before being betrayed and overwhelmed.

In 480 BCE, the Persian Empire resumed its bid to conquer Greece, having temporarily abandoned its attempt ten years earlier, after the defeat of Darius I at the Battle of Marathon (see pp.18–19). Xerxes I (r. 486-465 BCE), his son and successor, led an army from Asia into Europe across the Hellespont (the Dardenelles Strait, in modern-day Turkey) on a bridge of boats, and advanced down the Greek coast accompanied by a large offshore fleet (see p.22). The Greek city-states, usually divided, agreed to co-operate in the face of this common threat. The city of Sparta sent 300 hoplites northwards under King Leonidas to block the Persian advance, and other city-states sent contingents to join the Spartans. An army of about 7,000 Greeks took up position in the Thermopylae pass, a narrow stretch of land between Mount Kallidromo and the sea on the east coast of central Greece. The Persian army they faced was huge; exact figures are unknown, but it is thought the army numbered over 100,000 men.

Whether the fighting at Thermopylae significantly delayed the progress of the Persian invasion is open for debate. After the conflict, the Persian army occupied Athens and was overcome only when the naval defeat at Salamis (see pp.22–23) forced some of it to withdraw, with the remainder defeated at Plataea the following year. However, Thermopylae has legendary status in Greece as well as in wider European culture, where it became a symbol of supposed European moral superiority.

> *"Eat your breakfast as if you are to eat your dinner in the other world."*
>
> LEONIDAS OF SPARTA TO HIS MEN ON THE EVE OF BATTLE

SPARTAN HOPLITES

In ancient Greece, Sparta was the only city-state with full-time soldiers. Male Spartan citizens dedicated their lives to training for war, following an austere regime of exercise and military drills, while civilian work was carried out by slaves. Other Greeks, whose soldiers were part-time militia, were in awe of the abilities of the Spartan warriors. Their hardiness and discipline, as demonstrated at Thermopylae, made Sparta the dominant Greek city-state in land warfare, as Athens was at sea.

5th-century BCE drinking cup showing a hoplite fighting a Persian

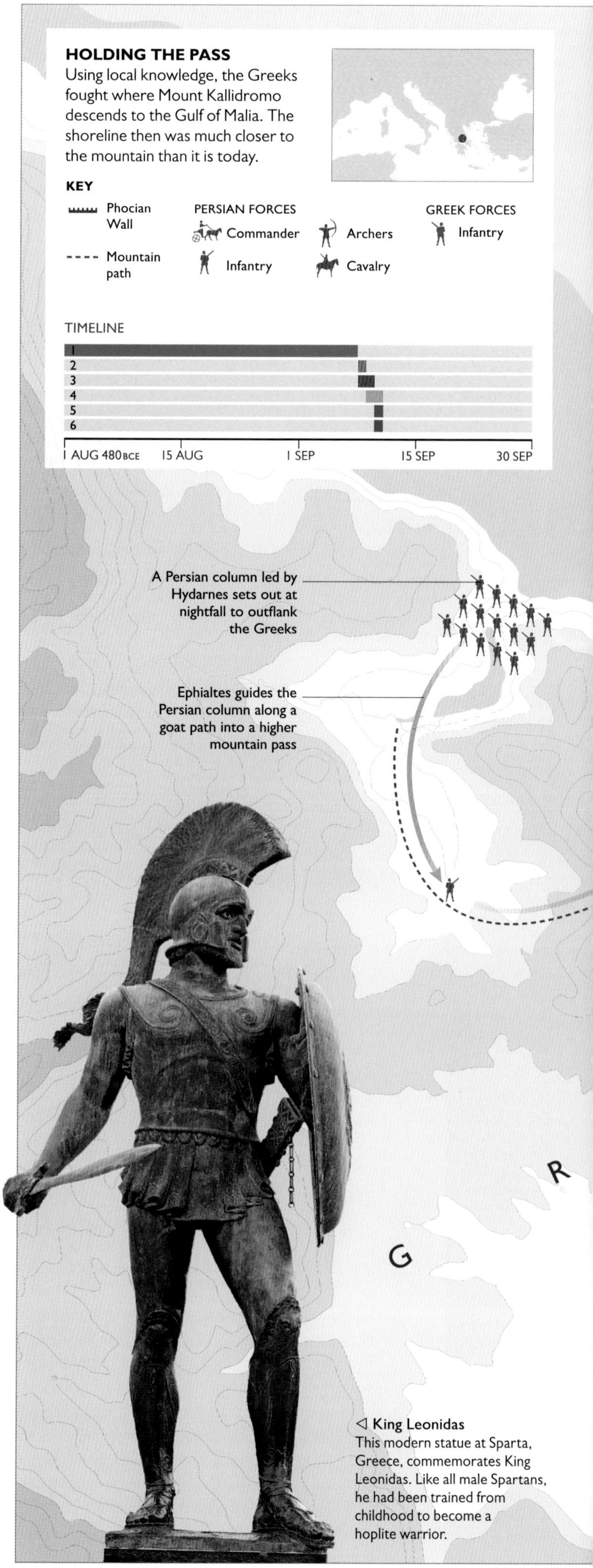
HOLDING THE PASS
Using local knowledge, the Greeks fought where Mount Kallidromo descends to the Gulf of Malia. The shoreline then was much closer to the mountain than it is today.
KEY
Phocian Wall
Mountain path
PERSIAN FORCES
Commander
Infantry
Archers
Cavalry
GREEK FORCES
Infantry
TIMELINE
1
2
3
4
5
6
1 AUG 480 BCE
15 AUG
1 SEP
15 SEP
30 SEP
A Persian column led by Hydarnes sets out at nightfall to outflank the Greeks
Ephialtes guides the Persian column along a goat path into a higher mountain pass
R
G

◁ **King Leonidas** This modern statue at Sparta, Greece, commemorates King Leonidas. Like all male Spartans, he had been trained from childhood to become a hoplite warrior.

1 PREPARING FOR BATTLE
AUGUST–EARLY SEPTEMBER 480 BCE

Knowing they would be heavily outnumbered by the Persians, the Greeks took up position at the narrowest point in the Thermopylae pass, the Middle Gate, where only a limited number of soldiers from either side would be able to engage at any one time. Nonetheless, when they saw the Persian army arrive, many of the Greek commanders argued for withdrawal.

Greeks take up position

2 OPENING CLASHES 8 SEPTEMBER

After a four-day delay, Xerxes launched his army in a frontal attack. Thousands of archers delivered an opening barrage, which had little impact on the armoured hoplites. Then Xerxes' infantry, the Medes and Cissians, swarmed forward but were slaughtered by the Greeks, drawn up in phalanx formation in front of the Phocian Wall. Reluctantly, Xerxes resolved to commit the Immortals, his crack troops, to the battle in the pass.

Persian advance · Persian barrage

3 FIGHTING TO A STANDSTILL
8–9 SEPTEMBER

The 10,000 Persian Immortals attacked in waves. Leonidas rotated his troops, successively placing contingents from different cities in the frontline. At moments he staged fake retreats, drawing the Persians forward so the Greeks could punish them with counter-attacks. Xerxes assumed that he must be wearing down Greek resistance, but renewed Persian attacks the following day were again repulsed with heavy losses.

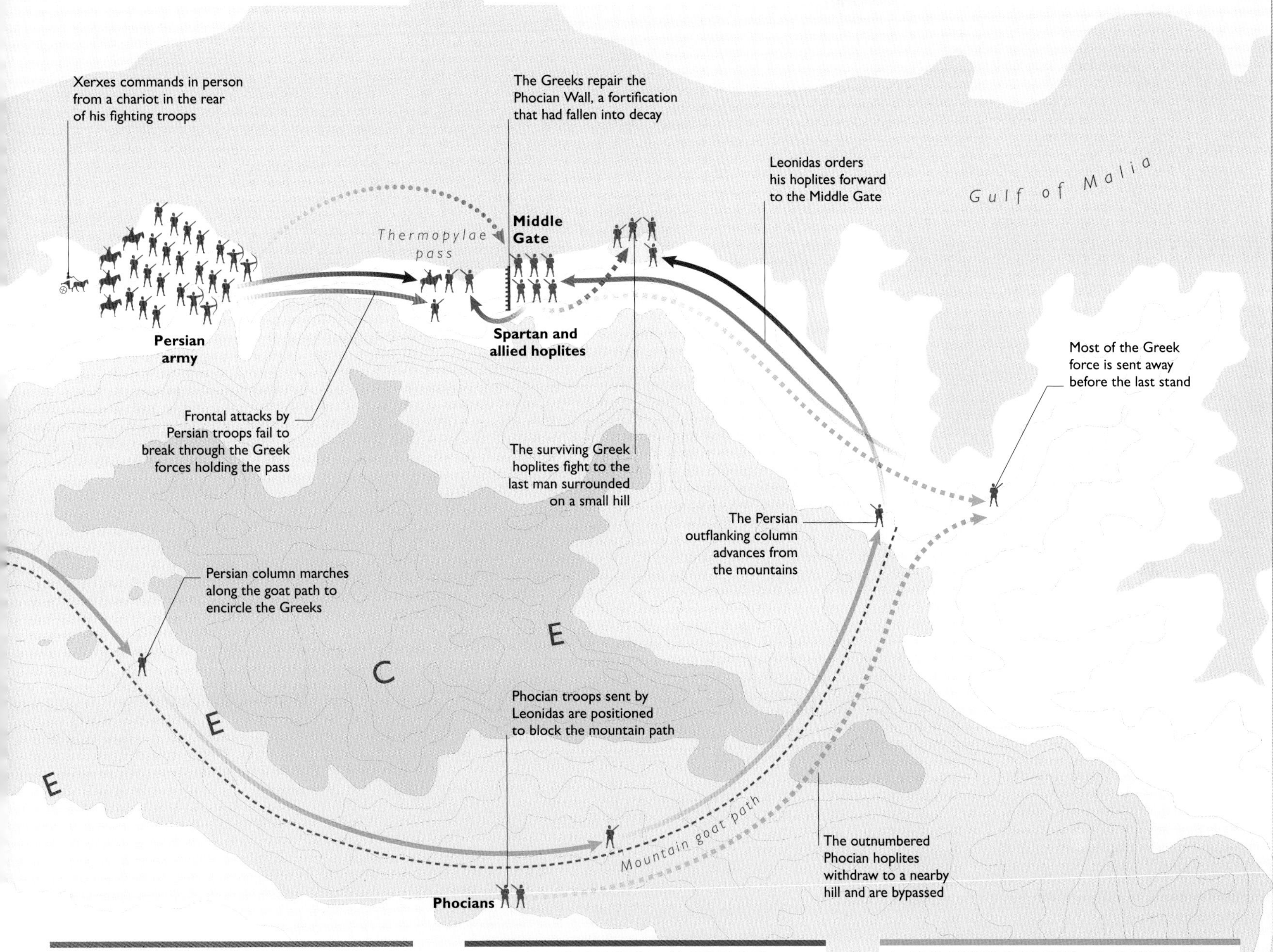

Xerxes commands in person from a chariot in the rear of his fighting troops
The Greeks repair the Phocian Wall, a fortification that had fallen into decay
Leonidas orders his hoplites forward to the Middle Gate
Gulf of Malia
Thermopylae pass
Middle Gate
Persian army
Spartan and allied hoplites
Most of the Greek force is sent away before the last stand
Frontal attacks by Persian troops fail to break through the Greek forces holding the pass
The surviving Greek hoplites fight to the last man surrounded on a small hill
The Persian outflanking column advances from the mountains
Persian column marches along the goat path to encircle the Greeks
E
C
E
E
Phocian troops sent by Leonidas are positioned to block the mountain path
Mountain goat path
The outnumbered Phocian hoplites withdraw to a nearby hill and are bypassed
Phocians

6 LAST STAND AND AFTERMATH
10 SEPTEMBER

The surviving Spartans and Thespians carried Leonidas' body to a hill behind the Phocian Wall, where they fought to the death against the Persians. Only the Thebans surrendered. When the fighting was over, Xerxes had Leonidas' corpse decapitated and crucified as revenge for the losses he had inflicted. The Phocian Wall was dismantled and the Persian army continued their advance.

Spartans' and Thespians' last stand

5 DEATH OF LEONIDAS 10 SEPTEMBER

Informed of the Persian outflanking move, Leonidas knew the battle was lost. Ordering most of his army to withdraw, he remained at the pass with his 300 Spartans, supported by 700 Thespians and 400 Thebans, to cover the retreat. At dawn he led his men out to meet the Persians on open ground. As Xerxes sent forward his cavalry and light infantry, Leonidas was killed by an arrow.

Main Greek force withdrawal · Last stand of Leonidas · Persian attacks

4 THE GREEKS BETRAYED 9–10 SEPTEMBER

The betrayal of the Greeks by a local man called Ephialtes gave Xerxes new hope. Ephialtes offered to guide the Persians along a goat path through the mountains leading to the rear of the Greek position. The Spartan King Leonidas had positioned 1,000 Phocian troops to defend it. Faced with 20,000 Persian infantry, however, the Phocians decided not to engage, and later withdrew.

Route of Persian outflanking manoeuvre · Phocian retreat

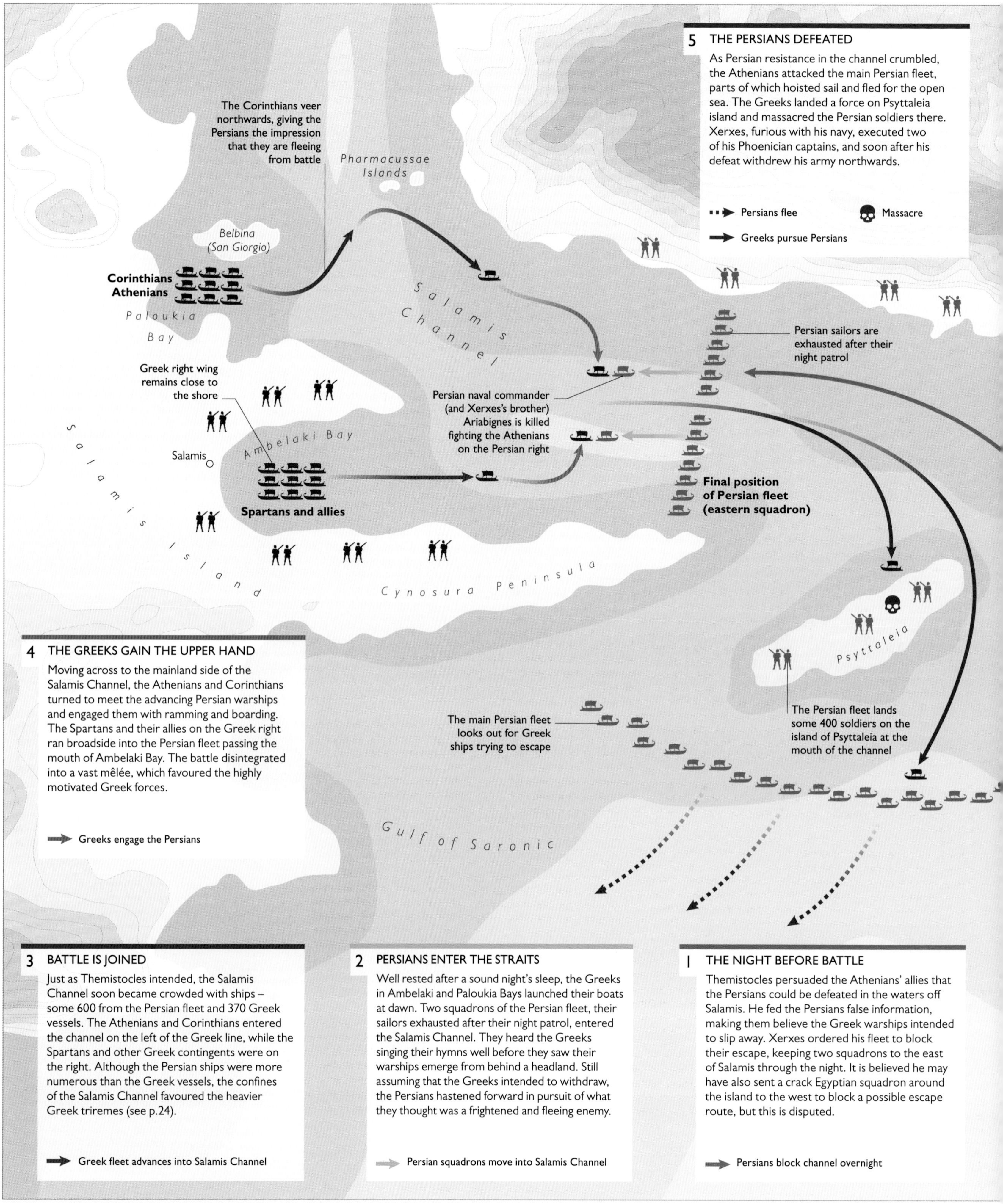

The Corinthians veer northwards, giving the Persians the impression that they are fleeing from battle
Pharmacussae Islands
Belbina (San Giorgio)
Corinthians
Athenians
Paloukia Bay
Salamis Channel
Greek right wing remains close to the shore
Ambelaki Bay
Salamis
Salamis Island
Spartans and allies
Persian naval commander (and Xerxes's brother) Ariabignes is killed fighting the Athenians on the Persian right
Persian sailors are exhausted after their night patrol
Final position of Persian fleet (eastern squadron)
Cynosura Peninsula
Psyttaleia
The Persian fleet lands some 400 soldiers on the island of Psyttaleia at the mouth of the channel
The main Persian fleet looks out for Greek ships trying to escape
Gulf of Saronic

1 THE NIGHT BEFORE BATTLE

Themistocles persuaded the Athenians' allies that the Persians could be defeated in the waters off Salamis. He fed the Persians false information, making them believe the Greek warships intended to slip away. Xerxes ordered his fleet to block their escape, keeping two squadrons to the east of Salamis through the night. It is believed he may have also sent a crack Egyptian squadron around the island to the west to block a possible escape route, but this is disputed.

Persians block channel overnight

2 PERSIANS ENTER THE STRAITS

Well rested after a sound night's sleep, the Greeks in Ambelaki and Paloukia Bays launched their boats at dawn. Two squadrons of the Persian fleet, their sailors exhausted after their night patrol, entered the Salamis Channel. They heard the Greeks singing their hymns well before they saw their warships emerge from behind a headland. Still assuming that the Greeks intended to withdraw, the Persians hastened forward in pursuit of what they thought was a frightened and fleeing enemy.

Persian squadrons move into Salamis Channel

3 BATTLE IS JOINED

Just as Themistocles intended, the Salamis Channel soon became crowded with ships – some 600 from the Persian fleet and 370 Greek vessels. The Athenians and Corinthians entered the channel on the left of the Greek line, while the Spartans and other Greek contingents were on the right. Although the Persian ships were more numerous than the Greek vessels, the confines of the Salamis Channel favoured the heavier Greek triremes (see p.24).

Greek fleet advances into Salamis Channel

4 THE GREEKS GAIN THE UPPER HAND

Moving across to the mainland side of the Salamis Channel, the Athenians and Corinthians turned to meet the advancing Persian warships and engaged them with ramming and boarding. The Spartans and their allies on the Greek right ran broadside into the Persian fleet passing the mouth of Ambelaki Bay. The battle disintegrated into a vast mêlée, which favoured the highly motivated Greek forces.

Greeks engage the Persians

5 THE PERSIANS DEFEATED

As Persian resistance in the channel crumbled, the Athenians attacked the main Persian fleet, parts of which hoisted sail and fled for the open sea. The Greeks landed a force on Psyttaleia island and massacred the Persian soldiers there. Xerxes, furious with his navy, executed two of his Phoenician captains, and soon after his defeat withdrew his army northwards.

Persians flee

Massacre

Greeks pursue Persians

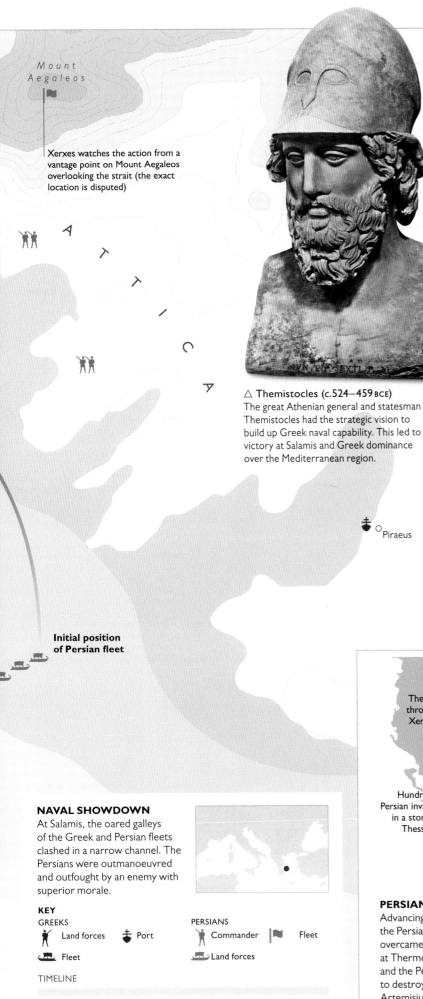

Mount Aegaleos
Xerxes watches the action from a vantage point on Mount Aegaleos overlooking the strait (the exact location is disputed)
ATTICA
Piraeus
Initial position of Persian fleet

△ **Themistocles (*c.*524–459 BCE)**
The great Athenian general and statesman Themistocles had the strategic vision to build up Greek naval capability. This led to victory at Salamis and Greek dominance over the Mediterranean region.

SALAMIS

The huge naval battle fought off the island of Salamis in 480 BCE is considered a turning point in world history. A decisive victory for the city-states of Greece over the invading forces of the Persian ruler Xerxes I, it secured the survival of Ancient Greek civilization.

The Greek victory at Marathon in 490 BCE (see pp.18–19) had been a dire insult to the Persian Empire. Ten years later, the Persian ruler Xerxes led a second invasion of Greece, this time commanding far larger land and sea forces. The Persians were able to assemble a powerful navy from their subject peoples around the Mediterranean, including the Phoenicians, the Egyptians, and the Ionian Greeks. Anticipating an attack, the Greek city-states had made plans for joint defence, but relations between them were quarrelsome and unity was precarious. In 482 BCE, Athens, inspired by the leadership of Themistocles, embarked on a major shipbuilding programme that made the city the leading Greek power at sea.

Xerxes' power on land proved irresistible when he launched his invasion in 480 BCE, but the battle at Salamis demonstrated the clear superiority of the Athenians and their allies at sea. After the battle, Xerxes withdrew from Greece with part of his army, leaving a reduced force under Mardonius to complete the Persian conquest. However, he was defeated the following year and the attempt to rule Greece was abandoned. The following century was the golden age of Greek civilization, centred on Athens, with high achievements in philosophy, the arts, and political thought.

NAVAL SHOWDOWN

At Salamis, the oared galleys of the Greek and Persian fleets clashed in a narrow channel. The Persians were outmanoeuvred and outfought by an enemy with superior morale.

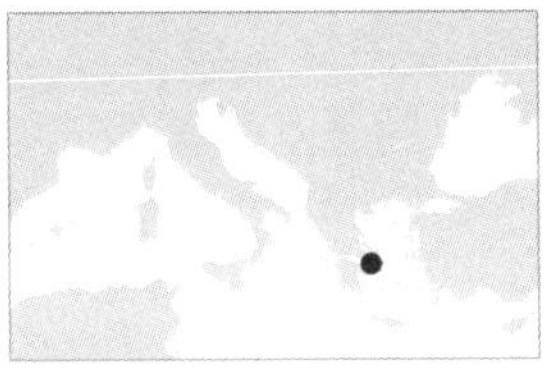

KEY

GREEKS
Land forces
Port
Fleet

PERSIANS
Commander
Fleet
Land forces

TIMELINE

SEP 480 BCE — OCT 480 BCE

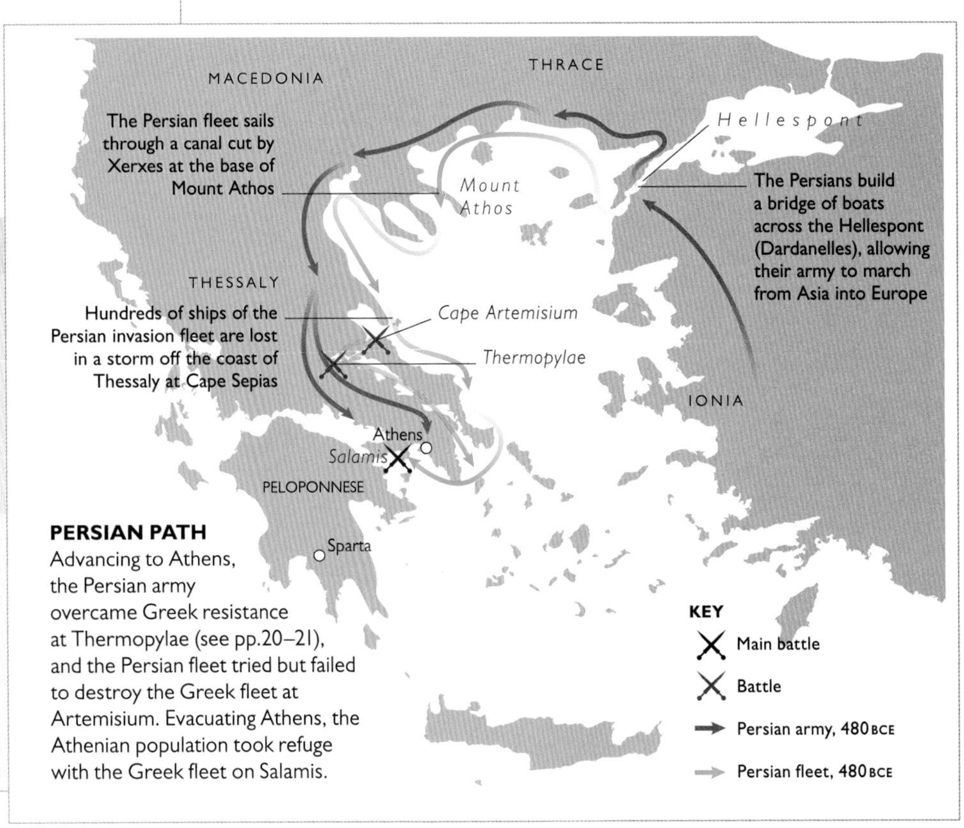
MACEDONIA
THRACE
The Persian fleet sails through a canal cut by Xerxes at the base of Mount Athos
Hellespont
Mount Athos
The Persians build a bridge of boats across the Hellespont (Dardanelles), allowing their army to march from Asia into Europe
THESSALY
Hundreds of ships of the Persian invasion fleet are lost in a storm off the coast of Thessaly at Cape Sepias
Cape Artemisium
Thermopylae
IONIA
Athens
Salamis
PELOPONNESE
Sparta
KEY
Main battle
Battle
Persian army, 480 BCE
Persian fleet, 480 BCE

PERSIAN PATH
Advancing to Athens, the Persian army overcame Greek resistance at Thermopylae (see pp.20–21), and the Persian fleet tried but failed to destroy the Greek fleet at Artemisium. Evacuating Athens, the Athenian population took refuge with the Greek fleet on Salamis.

ANCIENT GREEKS AT WAR

The Greek city-states of the Classical era developed a unique style of fighting, both on land and at sea. Their citizen-soldiers were widely regarded to be the finest infantry of their day, excelling in close-quarter combat.

△ **Hoplite helmet**
This 4th-century BCE bronze helmet would most likely have been ceremonial. It is decorated with a griffin, a mythical creature that is part-lion, part-eagle.

Greek armies in the 5th and 4th centuries BCE centred around heavily armoured foot soldiers known as hoplites. Wearing a bronze helmet, a cuirass (to protect the upper body), and greaves (to protect the legs), hoplites carried a large shield and used a spear as their primary weapon. Hoplites fought shoulder-to-shoulder in a phalanx, a tight formation usually eight ranks deep, with each man's shield covering the exposed side of his neighbour to the left.

Often at war with one another, Greek city-states differed in military organization. In Sparta, all men underwent rigorous training from an early age, resulting in a hardened, disciplined infantry. In democratic Athens, however, military service was a part-time duty of free male citizens, and hoplites received little formal training. Athenian citizens were expected to provide their own equipment, and those too poor to afford it volunteered to serve as oarsmen in the fleet instead. Slaves were used as light infantry skirmishers, supported by professional archers, slingers, and javelinmen.

All Greek citizen soldiers were highly motivated by attachment to their home city. When Greek cities fought one another, as in the Peloponnesian Wars (431–404 BCE), phalanx clashed with phalanx, shield to shield, in murderous close-quarter battles. The quality of Greek foot soldiers was widely appreciated and they were recruited as mercenaries by other countries, including Persia.

ATHENIAN TRIREMES

The Athenian trireme – shown here in a later illustration – was a swift, nimble warship rowed by about 170 oarsmen in three tiers. It carried a handful of fighting men, and mainly depended on the bronze-sheathed ram at its prow to sink enemy vessels by driving holes in them below the waterline.

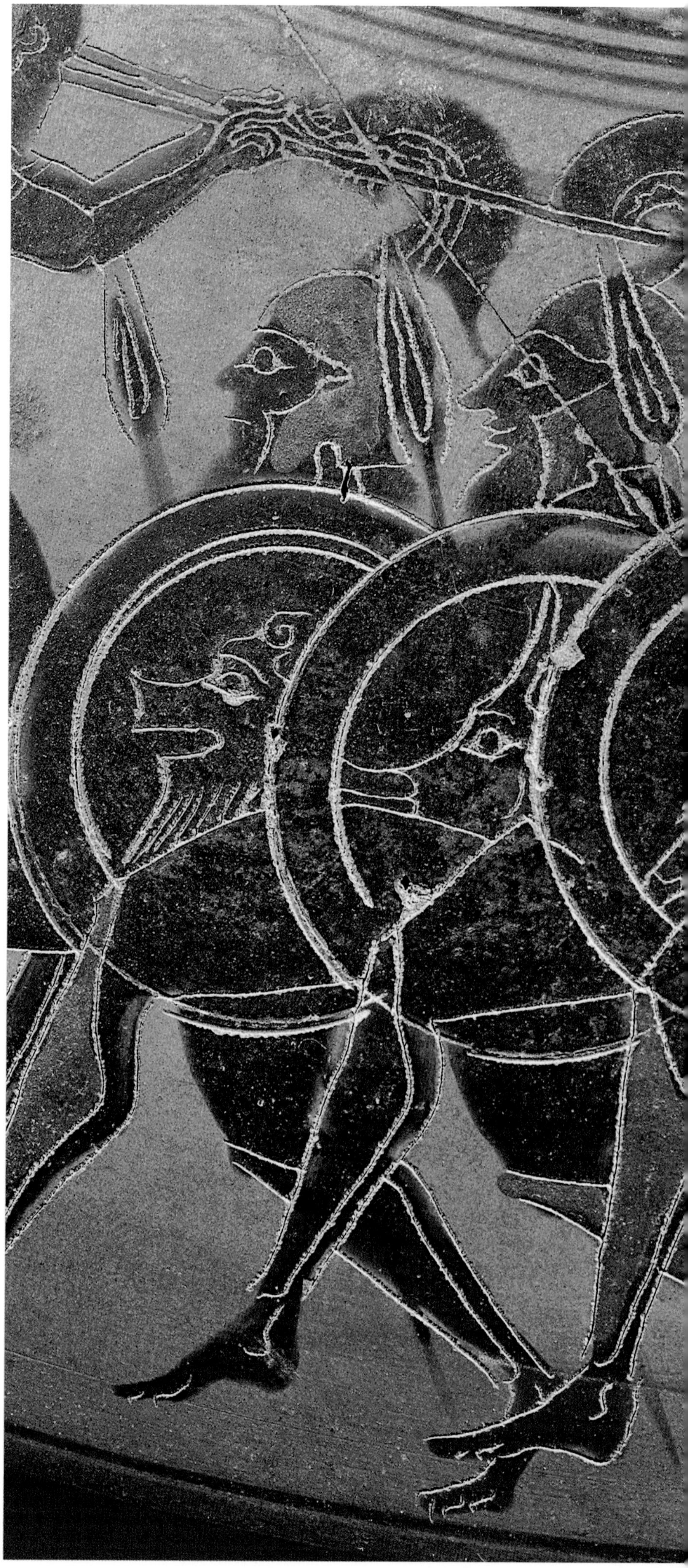

Close formation
This painting on a 6th-century BCE vase shows hoplites wearing helmets adorned with horsehair crests as they enter battle. They would have fought in a tightknit phalanx, stabbing with spears from behind a wall of shields.

ISSUS

Fought in northern Syria in 333 BCE, the battle of Issus was a major victory for Alexander the Great over the larger forces of the Persian Empire. It allowed him to seize control of the eastern Mediterranean in preparation for an invasion of Persia itself.

In the 4th century BCE, Macedonia was a kingdom on Greece's northern border. Under King Philip II (r. 359–336 BCE), the Macedonians conquered Athens and the other city-states of Greece. Claiming leadership of the Greek world, Philip planned an attack on the Achaemenid Persian Empire, Greece's enemy. Philip's son Alexander inherited this project. Since its defeat in the Greco-Persian Wars of the 5th century BCE (see pp.18–25), the Persians had regained control of the Greek city-states of Anatolia. Alexander set out to liberate these cities and draw the Persian Great King, Darius III, into a major battle.

At the heart of Alexander's army were elite Macedonian cavalry and foot soldiers – the "Companions" – supported by horsemen from Macedonia's neighbour, Thessaly. Greeks from the city-states played a minor role – indeed, more Greeks fought in the Persian army, where they were employed as mercenary infantry. Alexander nonetheless saw himself as a crusader for the cause of Greek civilization. Instead of sating his ambitions, his victory at Issus stimulated him to envisage further ventures, which would eventually take him as far as India.

"We of Macedon for generations past have been trained in the hard school of danger and war."

ALEXANDER THE GREAT, ADDRESSING HIS TROOPS AT ISSUS

ALEXANDER OF MACEDON
356–323 BCE

Shown here in a mosaic depicting him at Issus, Alexander inherited the Macedonian throne from his father at the age of 20. He stamped his authority on the Greek city-states and pursued the conquest of the Persian Empire, which he achieved by 331 BCE. His military exploits continued in Central Asia and Northern India. He fell ill and died in Babylon aged only 33.

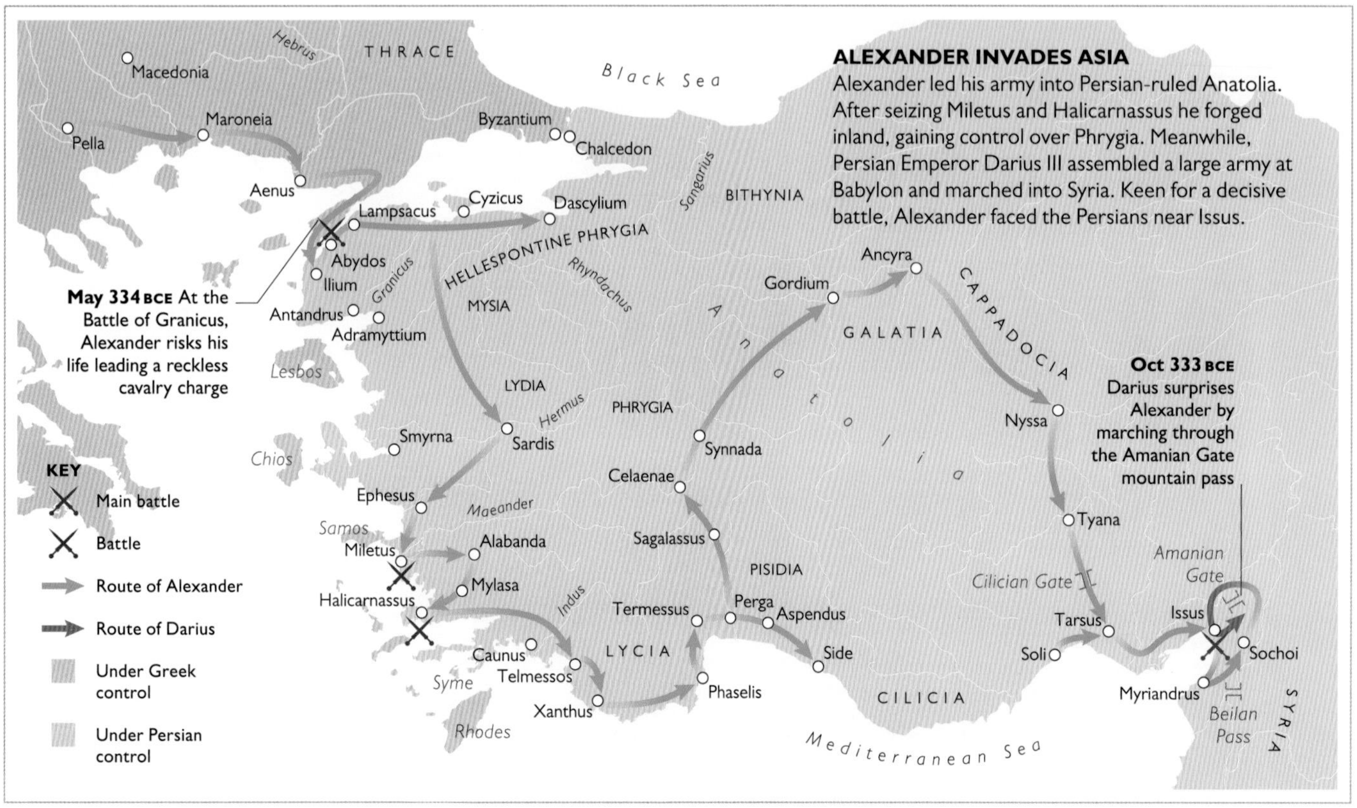
ALEXANDER INVADES ASIA
Alexander led his army into Persian-ruled Anatolia. After seizing Miletus and Halicarnassus he forged inland, gaining control over Phrygia. Meanwhile, Persian Emperor Darius III assembled a large army at Babylon and marched into Syria. Keen for a decisive battle, Alexander faced the Persians near Issus.
May 334 BCE At the Battle of Granicus, Alexander risks his life leading a reckless cavalry charge
Oct 333 BCE Darius surprises Alexander by marching through the Amanian Gate mountain pass
KEY
Main battle
Battle
Route of Alexander
Route of Darius
Under Greek control
Under Persian control
THRACE
Hebrus
Macedonia
Pella
Maroneia
Aenus
Black Sea
Byzantium
Chalcedon
Sangarius
BITHYNIA
Cyzicus
Dascylium
Lampsacus
Abydos
Ilium
Granicus
Antandrus
Adramyttium
HELLESPONTINE PHRYGIA
Rhyndachus
MYSIA
Lesbos
Chios
Samos
Smyrna
Sardis
LYDIA
Hermus
PHRYGIA
Ephesus
Maeander
Miletus
Alabanda
Halicarnassus
Mylasa
Indus
Caunus
Telmessos
Syme
Xanthus
Rhodes
LYCIA
Termessus
Phaselis
Perga
Aspendus
Side
PISIDIA
Sagalassus
Celaenae
Synnada
Gordium
Ancyra
GALATIA
Anatolia
CAPPADOCIA
Nyssa
Tyana
Cilician Gate
Tarsus
Soli
CILICIA
Mediterranean Sea
Amanian Gate
Issus
Sochoi
Myriandrus
Beilan Pass
SYRIA

PERSIAN EMP
Gulf of Issus

1 THE ARMIES LINE UP 5 NOVEMBER 333 BCE

The rival armies met on a plain between the mountains and the sea, a restricted area that made it difficult for Darius to bring his superior numbers into play. The Persians took up a defensive position behind the River Pinarus, reinforced by a palisade. Darius commanded from a chariot at the rear, protected by his elite guard, the Immortals. Alexander, in contrast, led from the front, positioned at the head of his Companion cavalry on the Macedonian right.

2 BATTLE IS JOINED

Persian skirmishers tried to pass around the Macedonian right flank, but were blocked by Alexander's light infantry. Near the sea, Thessalian horsemen under Parmenion were attacked by Persian cavalry but held. The Macedonian phalanx crossed the river in the centre, but became disordered and was outmatched by nimbler Greek mercenary hoplites.

Persian advance Macedonian advance

3 MACEDONIAN BREAKTHROUGH

With the battle going against him, Alexander launched a devastating charge on the Persian left. Riding at the head of his elite Companions, he shattered the Persian flank, scattering horsemen and light infantry. Turning inwards, the Companion cavalry threatened to fight through to Darius himself.

Alexander's cavalry charge

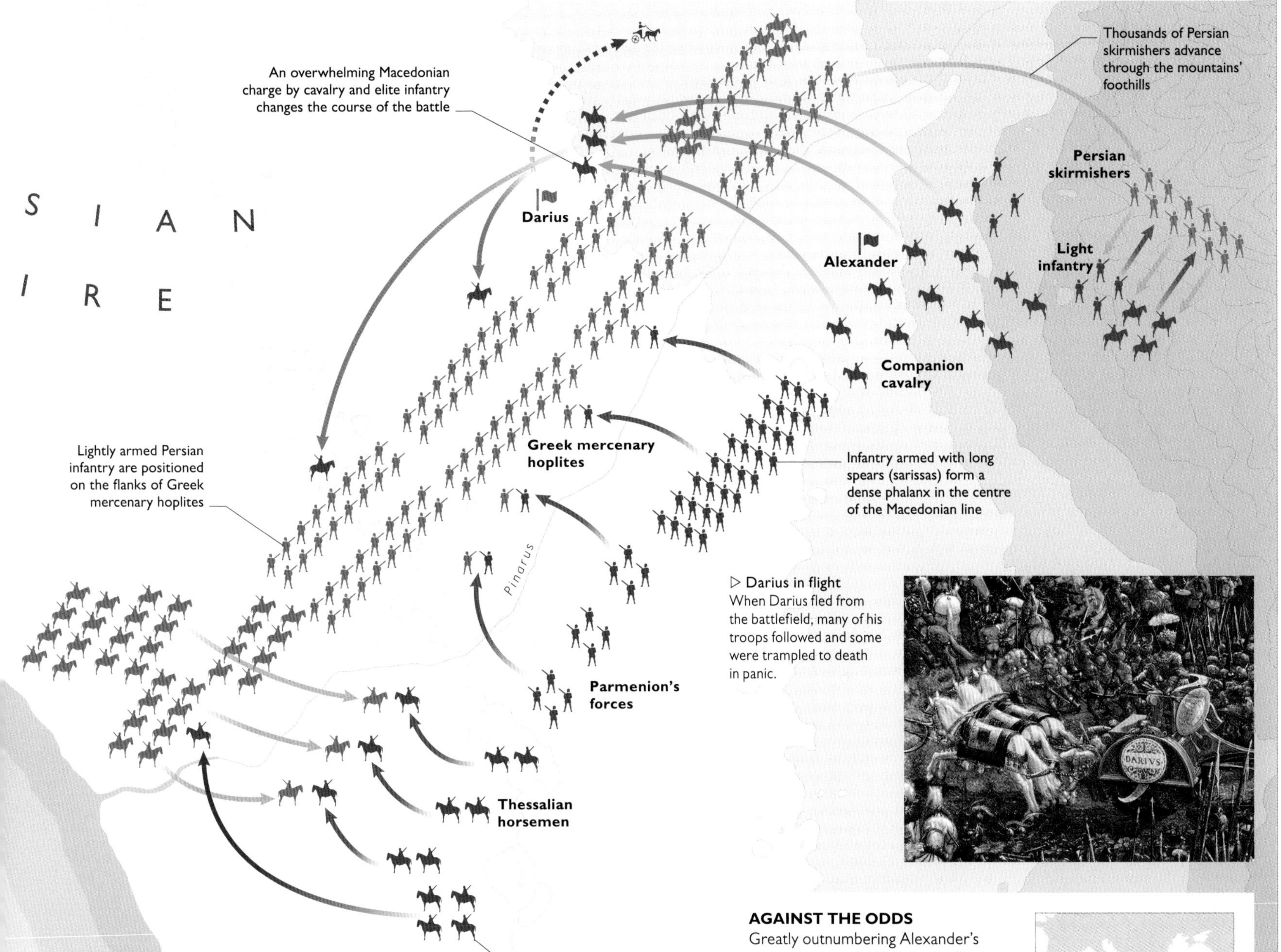

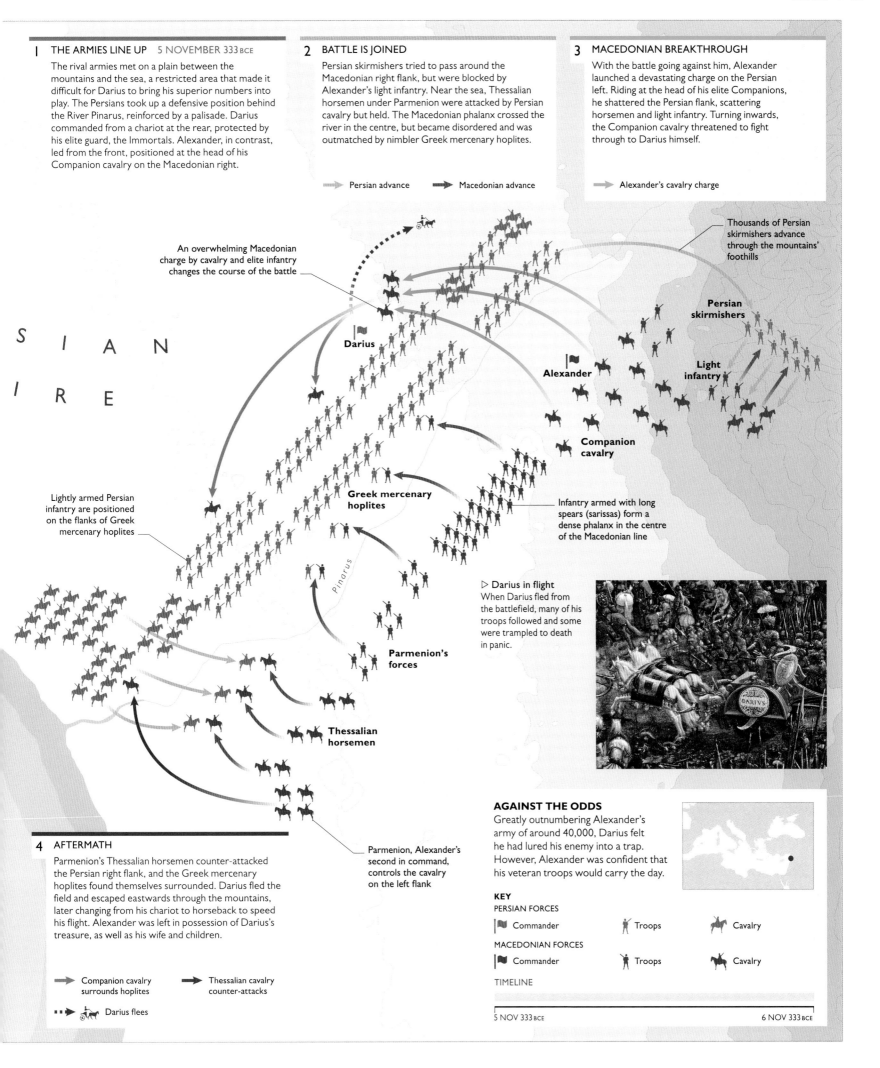

An overwhelming Macedonian charge by cavalry and elite infantry changes the course of the battle
Thousands of Persian skirmishers advance through the mountains' foothills
Persian skirmishers
S I A N
I R E
Darius
Alexander
Light infantry
Companion cavalry
Greek mercenary hoplites
Lightly armed Persian infantry are positioned on the flanks of Greek mercenary hoplites
Infantry armed with long spears (sarissas) form a dense phalanx in the centre of the Macedonian line
Pinarus
Parmenion's forces
Thessalian horsemen
Parmenion, Alexander's second in command, controls the cavalry on the left flank

▷ **Darius in flight**
When Darius fled from the battlefield, many of his troops followed and some were trampled to death in panic.

4 AFTERMATH

Parmenion's Thessalian horsemen counter-attacked the Persian right flank, and the Greek mercenary hoplites found themselves surrounded. Darius fled the field and escaped eastwards through the mountains, later changing from his chariot to horseback to speed his flight. Alexander was left in possession of Darius's treasure, as well as his wife and children.

Companion cavalry surrounds hoplites
Thessalian cavalry counter-attacks
Darius flees

AGAINST THE ODDS

Greatly outnumbering Alexander's army of around 40,000, Darius felt he had lured his enemy into a trap. However, Alexander was confident that his veteran troops would carry the day.

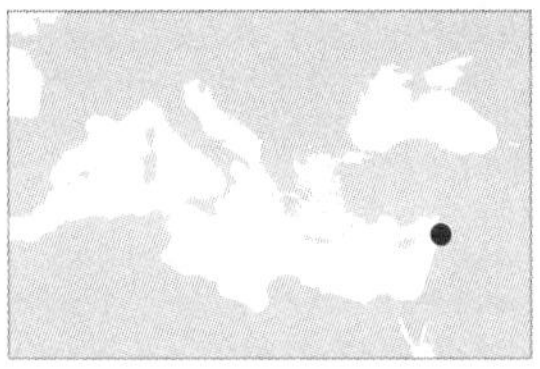

KEY

PERSIAN FORCES

Commander Troops Cavalry

MACEDONIAN FORCES

Commander Troops Cavalry

TIMELINE

5 NOV 333 BCE 6 NOV 333 BCE

FRONTAL CONFLICT

Rejecting the option of a night attack, Alexander chose to confront the far larger Persian army in a set-piece battle on open ground. His confidence was justified.

KEY

MACEDONIAN FORCES

- Infantry
- Cavalry
- Camp and baggage train

PERSIAN FORCES

- Infantry
- Cavalry
- Chariots

TIMELINE

29 SEP 331 BCE — 1 OCT 331 BCE

ROUTE TO BATTLE

After his victory at Issus in 333 BCE, Alexander took the Persian-held cities of Tyre and Gaza. Occupying Egypt, he founded the new city of Alexandria as a base for Macedonian rule. In 331 BCE, he assembled an army at Tyre and marched east to meet Darius in battle at Gaugamela.

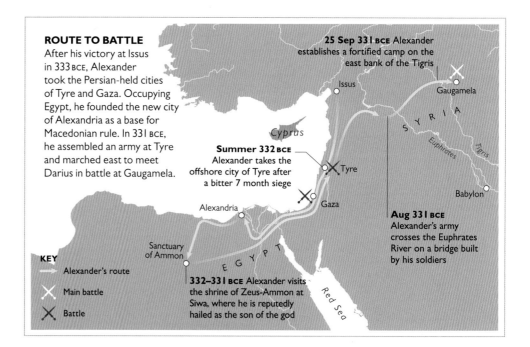

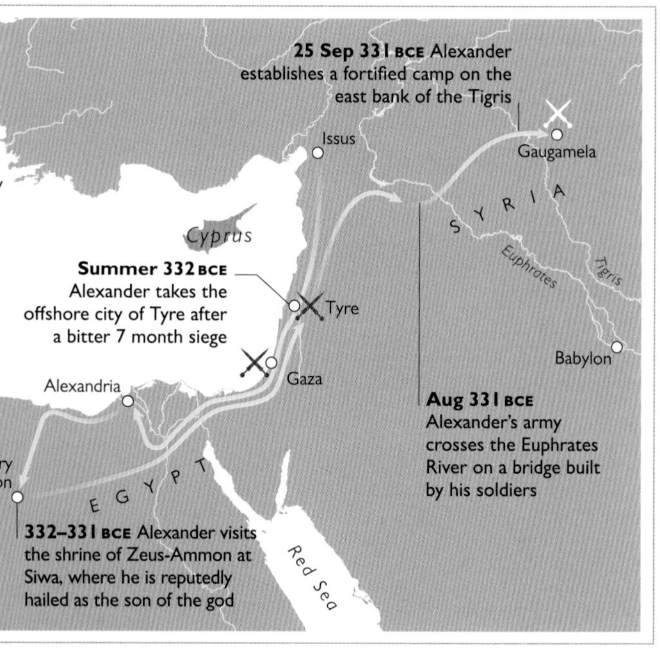
25 Sep 331 BCE Alexander establishes a fortified camp on the east bank of the Tigris
Issus
Gaugamela
SYRIA
Euphrates
Tigris
Cyprus
Summer 332 BCE Alexander takes the offshore city of Tyre after a bitter 7 month siege
Tyre
Gaza
Babylon
Alexandria
Aug 331 BCE Alexander's army crosses the Euphrates River on a bridge built by his soldiers
Sanctuary of Ammon
EGYPT
KEY
Alexander's route
Main battle
Battle
332–331 BCE Alexander visits the shrine of Zeus-Ammon at Siwa, where he is reputedly hailed as the son of the god
Red Sea

DARIUS ATTACKS

Before battle, Emperor Darius III had the ground cleared of rocks so he could deploy his war chariots to best effect, but Alexander's forces parried the initial chariot and cavalry onslaughts.

1 BATTLE IS JOINED
29 SEPTEMBER–1 OCTOBER 331 BCE

Darius had drawn up his 100,000-strong forces on a broad plain as Alexander led his 47,000 men toward Gaugamela. On the morning of 1 October, Alexander marched his army to meet Darius. The battle began with a charge by the Persian chariots, which were equipped with scythes on their wheels. They were repelled by Alexander's light troops armed with bows and javelins.

- Persian chariot attack

2 FLANKING MANOEUVRE 1 OCTOBER

Darius ordered the Persian cavalry to outflank Alexander's forces, and instructed Bessus, the satrap of Bactria, to round the Macedonian right wing and attack its phalanx from the back. However, Alexander's outnumbered forces resisted the Persian advance. Meanwhile, Alexander ordered his infantry, accompanied by the elite Companion cavalry, to advance on Darius's line at an oblique angle.

- Persian cavalry advance
- Macedonians counter-attacks
- Macedonian main advance

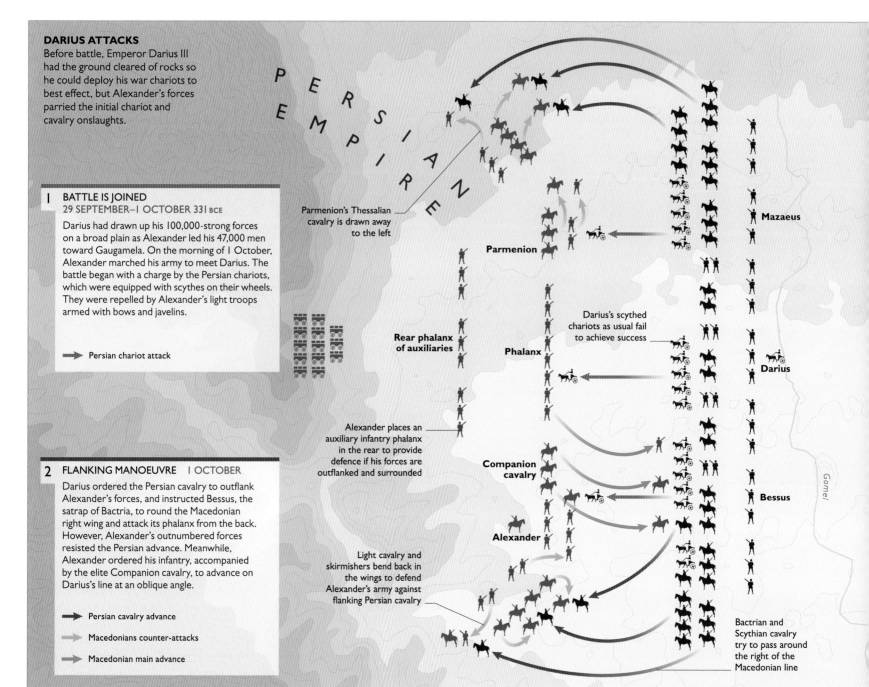

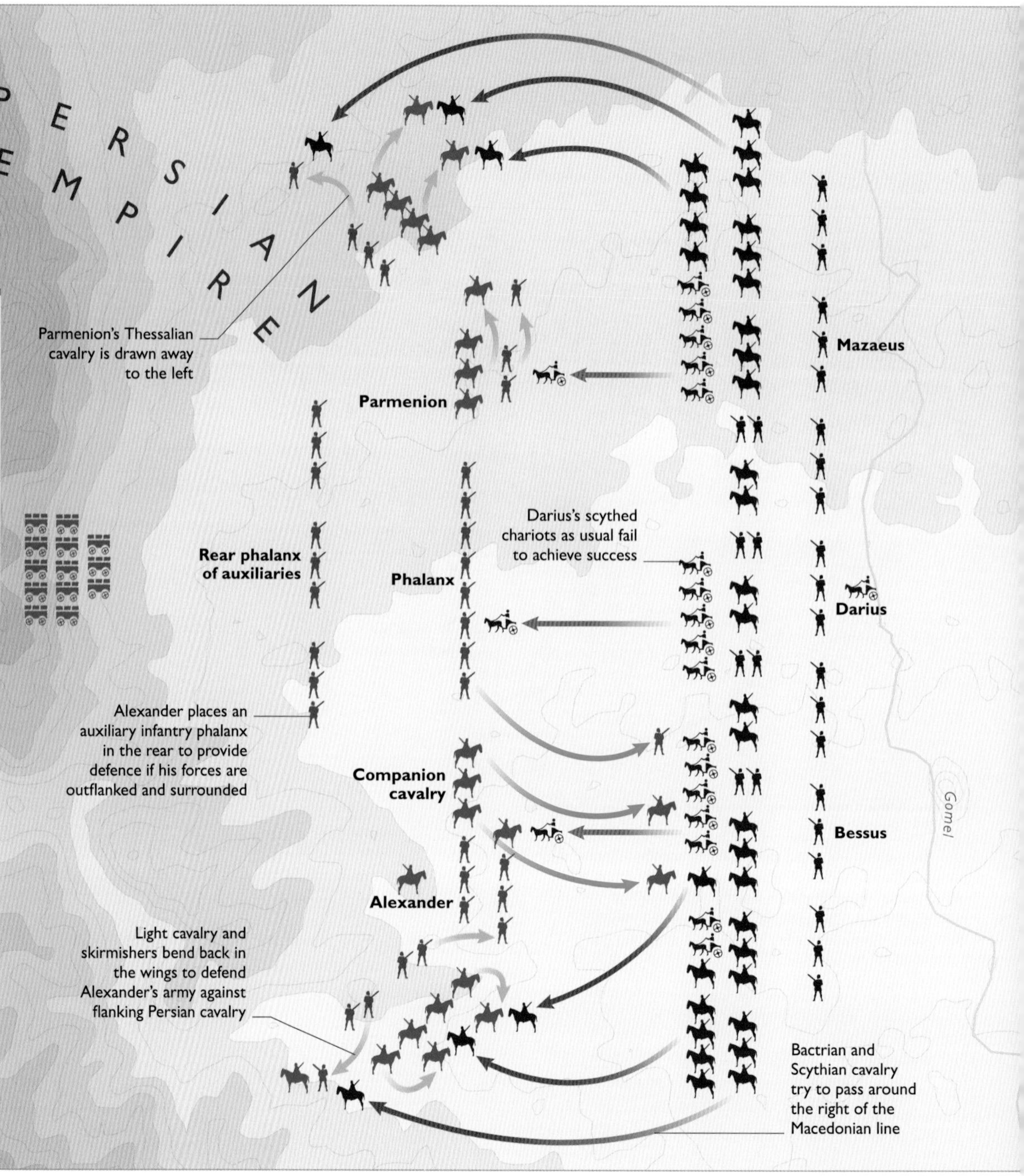
PERSIAN EMPIRE
Parmenion's Thessalian cavalry is drawn away to the left
Parmenion
Mazaeus
Darius's scythed chariots as usual fail to achieve success
Rear phalanx of auxiliaries
Phalanx
Darius
Alexander places an auxiliary infantry phalanx in the rear to provide defence if his forces are outflanked and surrounded
Companion cavalry
Bessus
Gomel
Alexander
Light cavalry and skirmishers bend back in the wings to defend Alexander's army against flanking Persian cavalry
Bactrian and Scythian cavalry try to pass around the right of the Macedonian line

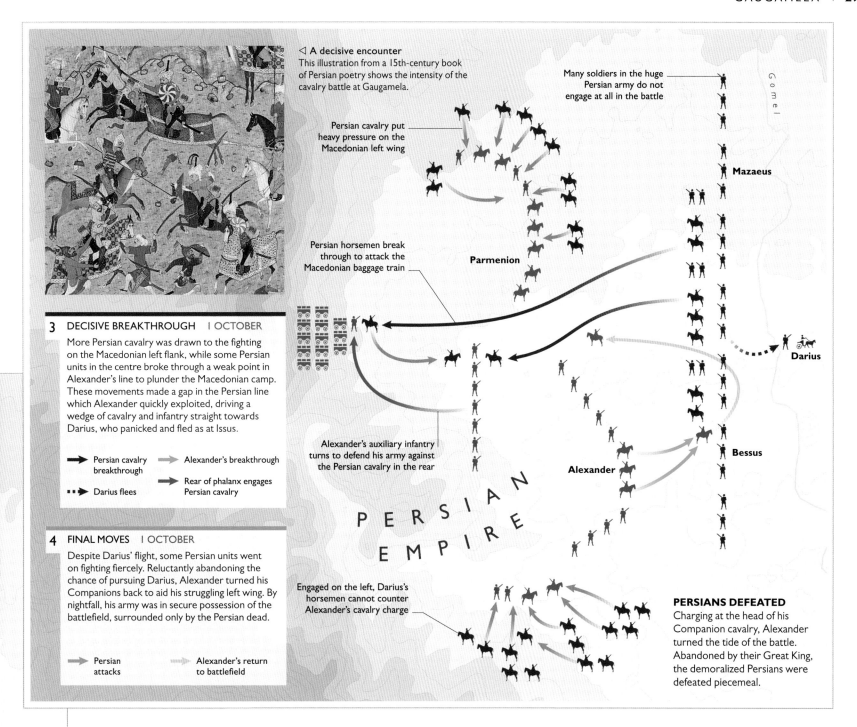

◁ **A decisive encounter**
This illustration from a 15th-century book of Persian poetry shows the intensity of the cavalry battle at Gaugamela.

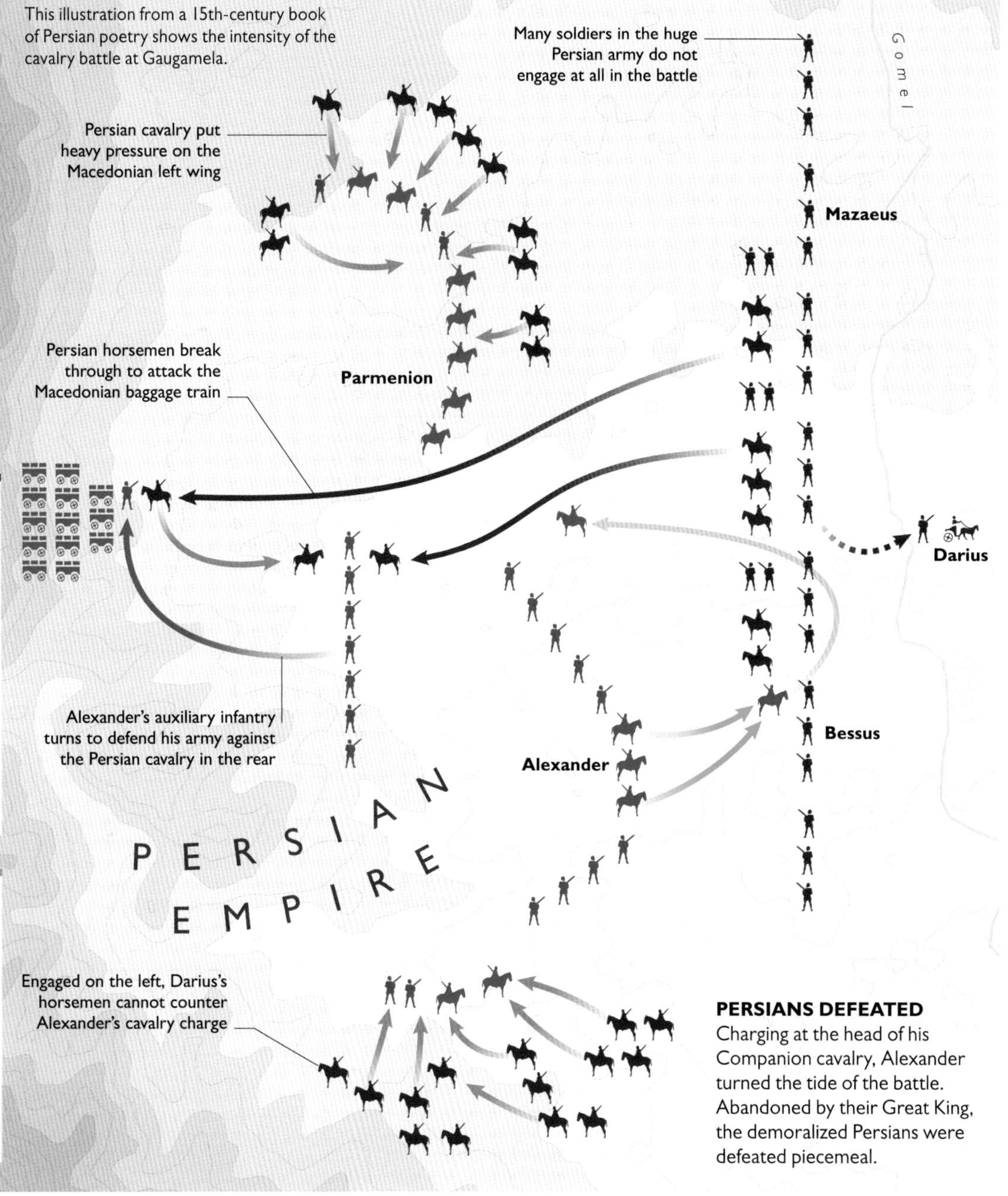
Many soldiers in the huge Persian army do not engage at all in the battle
Gomel
Persian cavalry put heavy pressure on the Macedonian left wing
Mazaeus
Persian horsemen break through to attack the Macedonian baggage train
Parmenion
Darius
Alexander's auxiliary infantry turns to defend his army against the Persian cavalry in the rear
Bessus
Alexander
PERSIAN EMPIRE
Engaged on the left, Darius's horsemen cannot counter Alexander's cavalry charge

PERSIANS DEFEATED
Charging at the head of his Companion cavalry, Alexander turned the tide of the battle. Abandoned by their Great King, the demoralized Persians were defeated piecemeal.

3 DECISIVE BREAKTHROUGH | OCTOBER

More Persian cavalry was drawn to the fighting on the Macedonian left flank, while some Persian units in the centre broke through a weak point in Alexander's line to plunder the Macedonian camp. These movements made a gap in the Persian line which Alexander quickly exploited, driving a wedge of cavalry and infantry straight towards Darius, who panicked and fled as at Issus.

- Persian cavalry breakthrough
- Darius flees
- Alexander's breakthrough
- Rear of phalanx engages Persian cavalry

4 FINAL MOVES | OCTOBER

Despite Darius' flight, some Persian units went on fighting fiercely. Reluctantly abandoning the chance of pursuing Darius, Alexander turned his Companions back to aid his struggling left wing. By nightfall, his army was in secure possession of the battlefield, surrounded only by the Persian dead.

- Persian attacks
- Alexander's return to battlefield

GAUGAMELA

The Battle of Gaugamela was a momentous victory for Macedonian conqueror Alexander the Great. Fought in 331 BCE in what is now Iraq, it completed the destruction of the powerful Achaemenid Persian Empire, which was brought under Alexander's rule.

After his defeat of the Persians at Issus in 333 BCE (see pp.26–27) and his occupation of Egypt (which had previously been conquered by the Persians), Alexander claimed to be successor to the pharaohs and became further persuaded of his own divine origins. Convinced of his superiority to the Persians in battle, he rejected generous peace offers from Emperor Darius III and sought a decisive showdown with his Persian foe. Alexander marched northeast to cross the headwaters of the Euphrates and Tigris, avoiding the predictability of the direct route along the Euphrates. Darius meanwhile raised another vast army from all parts of his Asian domains and marched to meet Alexander. To make the most of his huge cavalry, he chose to fight on an open plain near the village of Gaugamela (in modern-day Dohuk, in Iraqi Kurdistan). He was routed. Pursuing the defeated Persian army, Alexander occupied Babylon and the ceremonial capital, Persepolis, which was destroyed by fire. After Darius was killed by his own satrap, Bessus, Alexander claimed the succession to the Persian throne, extending his empire through further campaigns into Central Asia and Northern India before his death in 323 BCE.

Mounted warfare
The detailed marble reliefs on the Alexander Sarcophagus were thought to have been carved in around the late 4th century BCE, and here show a horseman from Alexander's triumphant battle at Issus (see pp.26–27) in what is now Turkey.

ALEXANDER'S ARMY

The Macedonian commander Alexander the Great (356–323 BCE) led one of the most successful armies in history, conquering the vast Persian Empire and campaigning deep into Central Asia and Northern India.

The strength of Alexander's army lay in its fusion of martial traditions from his native Macedonia with those of the Ancient Greek city-states (see pp.22–23). The Macedonians were a rough warrior people, whose horse-riding aristocracy regarded personal courage and individual prowess in battle as supreme values. From the Greeks, they learned the importance of disciplined infantry – foot soldiers fighting as a unified mass formation.

△ **Tribute to a legend**
Sculptors made many posthumous depictions of Alexander. This one dates from about two centuries after his death in 323 BCE.

Battle formation

Alexander led from the front, riding into battle at the head of his Companion cavalry, a mounted war band drawn from the Macedonian nobility. Numbering a few thousand, the Companions fought with a lance and a short, curved sword – the *kopis*. Always deployed on the right of the line – considered the place of honour – they acted as a shock attack force, charging into the heart of the enemy. Cavalry recruited from Thessaly, Macedonia's southern neighbour, rode on the left flank. The centre of the battle line was occupied by trained, professional infantry in phalanxes of 256 men wielding long spears. Alexander's army also included foot soldiers with flexible roles, from the elite Macedonian *hypaspists* (shield-bearers) who were part of the right flank striking force along with the Companions, to various lightly equipped archers and skirmishers. This hybrid force, galvanized by its aggressive and charismatic leader, proved formidable on the battlefield.

MACEDONIAN PHALANX FORMATION

The Macedonian infantry fought in dense formations, up to 16 ranks deep and 16 wide. Each soldier in this phalanx was armed with a sarissa, a pike up to 6 m (20 ft) long, wielded with both hands. The raised sarissas of the rear ranks helped to deflect incoming arrows.

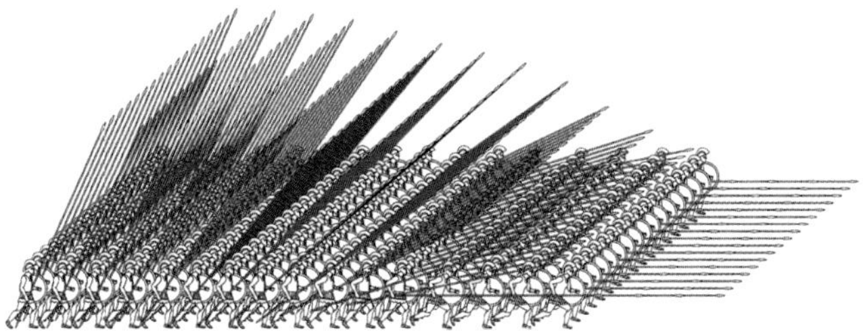

NAVAL TACTICS

Most warships of the Roman navy were cumbersome quinqueremes with three banks of oars, requiring a crew of 300 oarsmen. Armed with catapults hurling rocks or darts, each vessel carried more than 100 soldiers, whose objective was to board and capture enemy ships. The Carthaginians, better seamen in lighter quinqueremes, manoeuvred to sink their opponents with the long rams at their prows.

Roman quinquereme

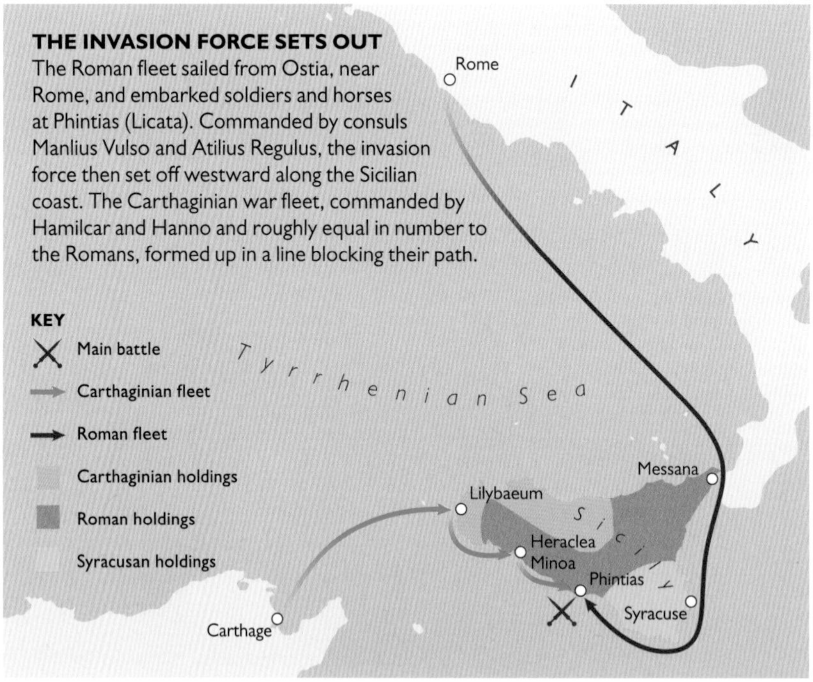
THE INVASION FORCE SETS OUT
The Roman fleet sailed from Ostia, near Rome, and embarked soldiers and horses at Phintias (Licata). Commanded by consuls Manlius Vulso and Atilius Regulus, the invasion force then set off westward along the Sicilian coast. The Carthaginian war fleet, commanded by Hamilcar and Hanno and roughly equal in number to the Romans, formed up in a line blocking their path.
KEY
Main battle
Carthaginian fleet
Roman fleet
Carthaginian holdings
Roman holdings
Syracusan holdings
Rome
ITALY
Tyrrhenian Sea
Messana
Lilybaeum
SICILY
Heraclea Minoa
Phintias
Syracuse
Carthage

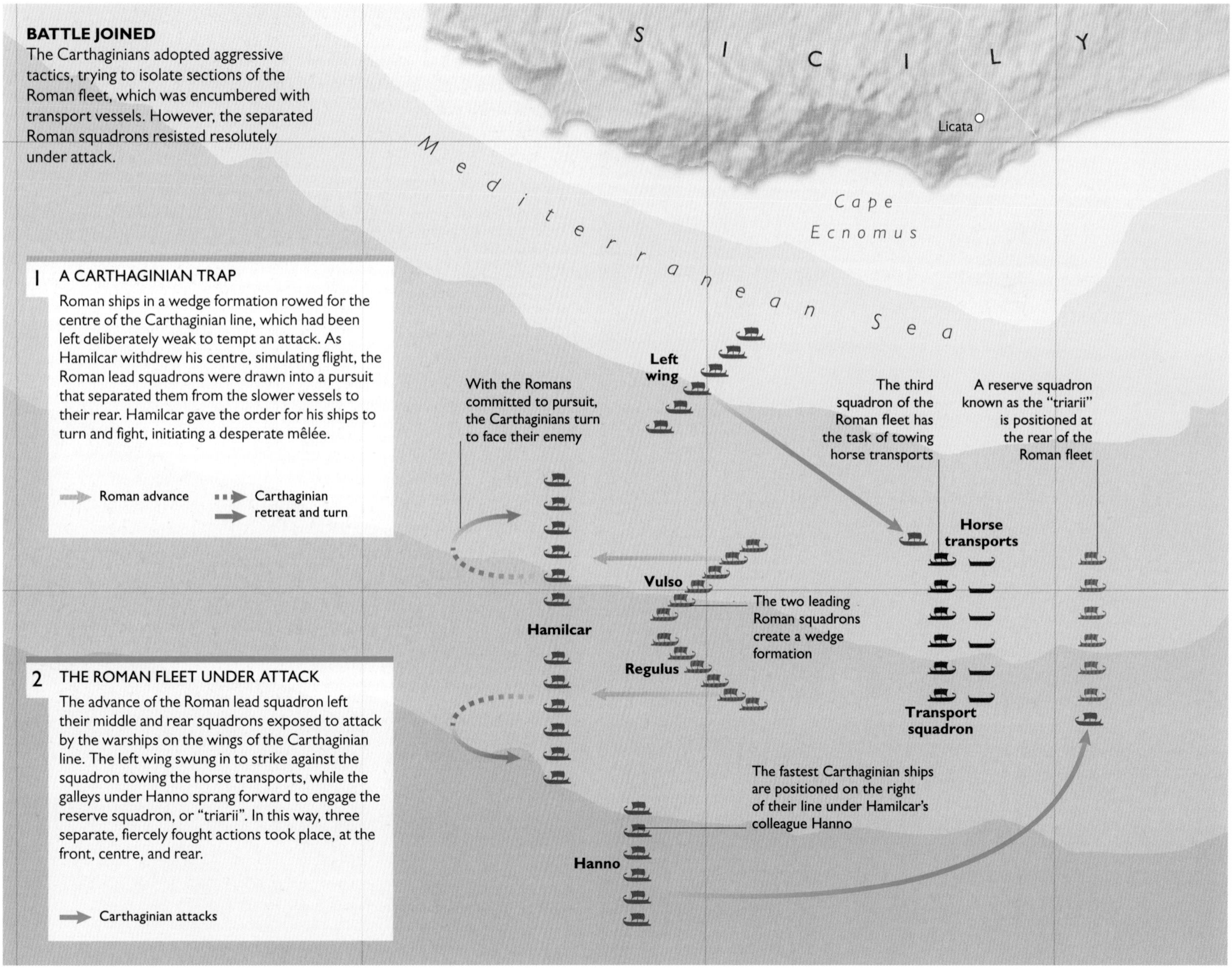
BATTLE JOINED
The Carthaginians adopted aggressive tactics, trying to isolate sections of the Roman fleet, which was encumbered with transport vessels. However, the separated Roman squadrons resisted resolutely under attack.
SICILY
Licata
Mediterranean Sea
Cape Ecnomus
1 A CARTHAGINIAN TRAP
Roman ships in a wedge formation rowed for the centre of the Carthaginian line, which had been left deliberately weak to tempt an attack. As Hamilcar withdrew his centre, simulating flight, the Roman lead squadrons were drawn into a pursuit that separated them from the slower vessels to their rear. Hamilcar gave the order for his ships to turn and fight, initiating a desperate mêlée.
Roman advance
Carthaginian retreat and turn
2 THE ROMAN FLEET UNDER ATTACK
The advance of the Roman lead squadron left their middle and rear squadrons exposed to attack by the warships on the wings of the Carthaginian line. The left wing swung in to strike against the squadron towing the horse transports, while the galleys under Hanno sprang forward to engage the reserve squadron, or "triarii". In this way, three separate, fiercely fought actions took place, at the front, centre, and rear.
Carthaginian attacks
Left wing
With the Romans committed to pursuit, the Carthaginians turn to face their enemy
The third squadron of the Roman fleet has the task of towing horse transports
A reserve squadron known as the "triarii" is positioned at the rear of the Roman fleet
Horse transports
Vulso
The two leading Roman squadrons create a wedge formation
Hamilcar
Regulus
Transport squadron
The fastest Carthaginian ships are positioned on the right of their line under Hamilcar's colleague Hanno
Hanno

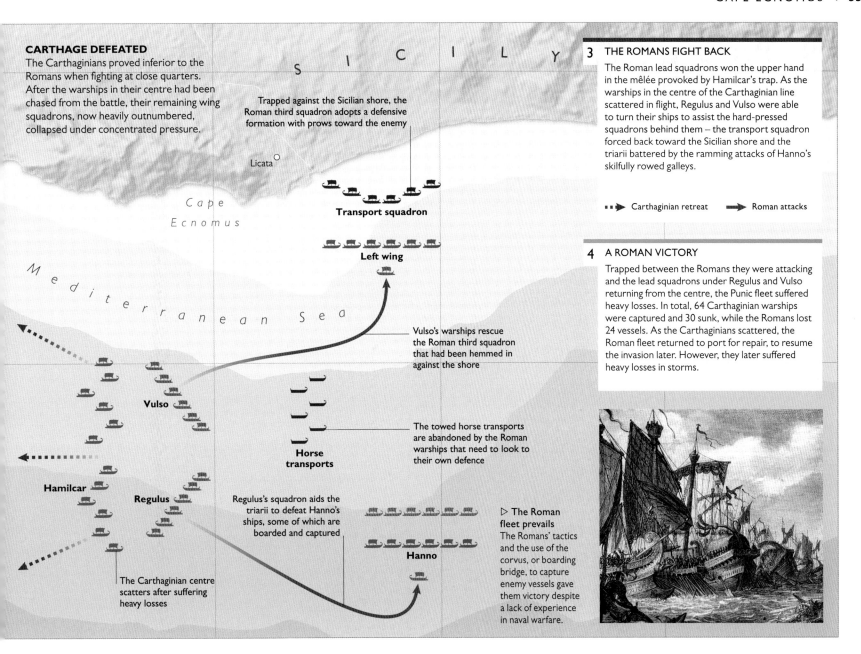

CARTHAGE DEFEATED
The Carthaginians proved inferior to the Romans when fighting at close quarters. After the warships in their centre had been chased from the battle, their remaining wing squadrons, now heavily outnumbered, collapsed under concentrated pressure.

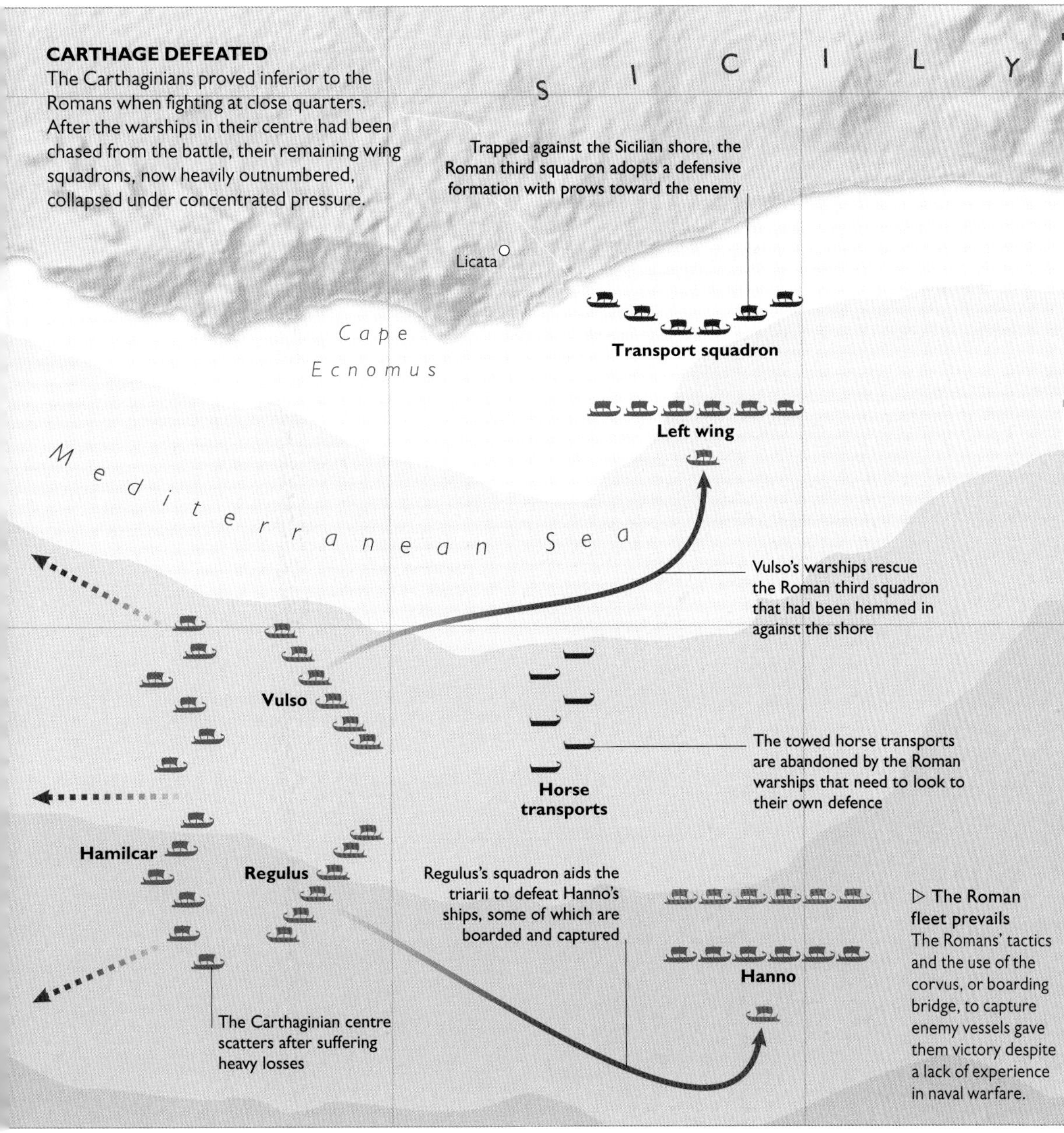
S I C I L Y
Trapped against the Sicilian shore, the Roman third squadron adopts a defensive formation with prows toward the enemy
Licata
Cape Ecnomus
Transport squadron
Left wing
Mediterranean Sea
Vulso's warships rescue the Roman third squadron that had been hemmed in against the shore
Vulso
The towed horse transports are abandoned by the Roman warships that need to look to their own defence
Horse transports
Hamilcar
Regulus
Regulus's squadron aids the triarii to defeat Hanno's ships, some of which are boarded and captured
Hanno
The Carthaginian centre scatters after suffering heavy losses

3 THE ROMANS FIGHT BACK
The Roman lead squadrons won the upper hand in the mêlée provoked by Hamilcar's trap. As the warships in the centre of the Carthaginian line scattered in flight, Regulus and Vulso were able to turn their ships to assist the hard-pressed squadrons behind them – the transport squadron forced back toward the Sicilian shore and the triarii battered by the ramming attacks of Hanno's skilfully rowed galleys.

Carthaginian retreat — Roman attacks

4 A ROMAN VICTORY
Trapped between the Romans they were attacking and the lead squadrons under Regulus and Vulso returning from the centre, the Punic fleet suffered heavy losses. In total, 64 Carthaginian warships were captured and 30 sunk, while the Romans lost 24 vessels. As the Carthaginians scattered, the Roman fleet returned to port for repair, to resume the invasion later. However, they later suffered heavy losses in storms.

▷ **The Roman fleet prevails**
The Romans' tactics and the use of the corvus, or boarding bridge, to capture enemy vessels gave them victory despite a lack of experience in naval warfare.

CAPE ECNOMUS

Fought in 256 BCE between the fleets of Carthage and the Roman Republic, Cape Ecnomus was one of the largest naval battles in history, with almost 700 ships and 300,000 men engaged. The Romans emerged victorious, winning overall command of the western Mediterranean Sea.

In the mid-3rd century BCE, the North African city of Carthage ruled an empire in the western Mediterranean based on trade and naval power. Its ascendancy was challenged by the rising Roman Republic, which had won control of Italy through the strength of its army. In the First Punic War (264–241 BCE) Carthage and Rome fought over Sicily, which had great strategic and economic value. Realising that superiority on land would not suffice, the Romans built a navy almost from scratch. Knowing that they would never match Carthaginian seamanship, they packed their ships with soldiers, devising a spiked wooden drawbridge known as a corvus to grapple and board enemy vessels.

In 256 BCE, with the war on Sicily stalemated, the Romans sent an army by sea to invade north Africa and attack Carthage. Attempting to block this invasion force off Cape Ecnomus, the Carthaginians suffered a crushing defeat. Although the invasion of north Africa proved a failure, the Romans had won naval superiority and as a result were eventually able to win control of Sicily.

BATTLE FOR THE MEDITERRANEAN
At Ecnomus, the Carthaginians deployed all available naval resources to intercept the Roman force. Their defeat shifted the balance of regional power to Rome.

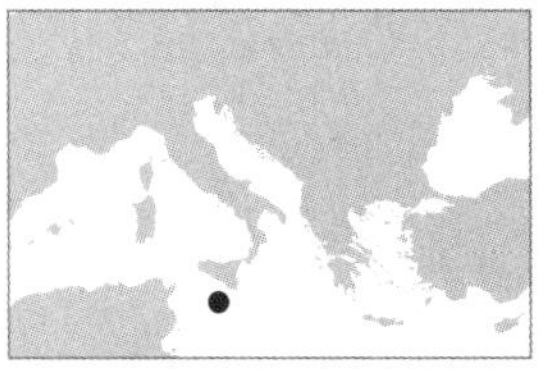

KEY
ROMAN: Lead squadrons; Triarii; Transports
CARTHAGINIAN: Carthaginian force

TIMELINE
256 BCE — 257 BCE

CANNAE

At the start of the Second Punic War (218–201 BCE), Carthaginian general Hannibal Barca led an army across the Alps to invade the territory of the Roman Republic. His invasion culminated in the annihilation of a Roman army at Cannae in 216 BCE, a masterpiece of battlefield tactics.

Carthage's defeat in the First Punic War (see pp.32–33) left the Roman Republic in control of Italy and Sicily; Carthage remained a major power in north Africa and southern Spain. In 221 BCE, 26-year-old Hannibal took command of the Carthaginian army in Spain and sought to avenge the defeat of his father, Hamilcar, in the First Punic War. In 219 BCE, Hannibal captured the Spanish city Saguntum, with which Rome had an alliance, prompting Rome to declare war. Hannibal led an invasion of Roman-ruled Italy, and won several battles culminating at Cannae, but did not risk attacking Rome itself. Led by consuls including Fabius Maximus, the Romans refused to make peace and conducted a war of attrition, denying Hannibal any further battlefield triumphs. The Carthaginians remained in Italy for 15 years without a decisive battle. In 204 BCE, a Roman invasion of north Africa forced the Carthaginians to recall Hannibal's army; their defeat at Zama in 202 BCE forced Carthage into peace. Hannibal killed himself in exile in 182 BCE and Carthage was destroyed by the Romans after the Third Punic War in 149–146 BCE.

> *"Hannibal excelled as a tactician. No battle in history is a finer sample of tactics than Cannae."*
>
> THEODORE AYRAULT DODGE, US HISTORIAN, 1893

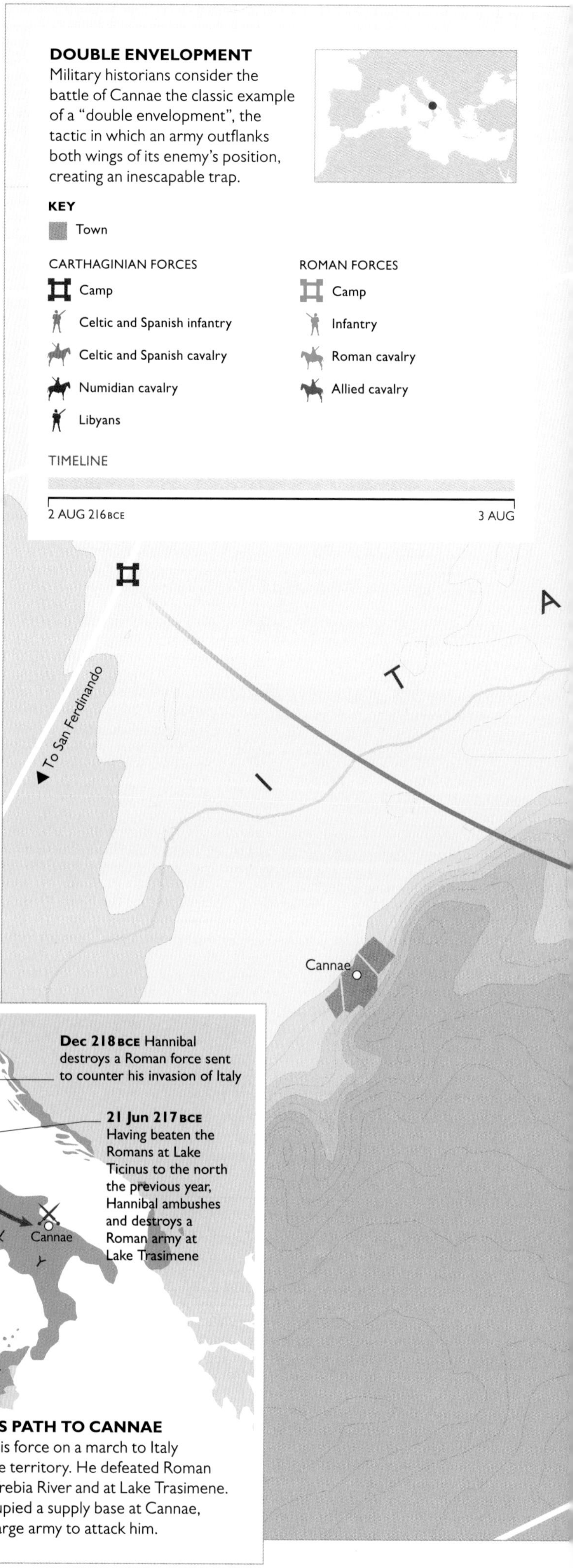

DOUBLE ENVELOPMENT
Military historians consider the battle of Cannae the classic example of a "double envelopment", the tactic in which an army outflanks both wings of its enemy's position, creating an inescapable trap.
KEY
Town
CARTHAGINIAN FORCES
Camp
Celtic and Spanish infantry
Celtic and Spanish cavalry
Numidian cavalry
Libyans
ROMAN FORCES
Camp
Infantry
Roman cavalry
Allied cavalry
TIMELINE
2 AUG 216 BCE
3 AUG
To San Ferdinando
I T A
Cannae

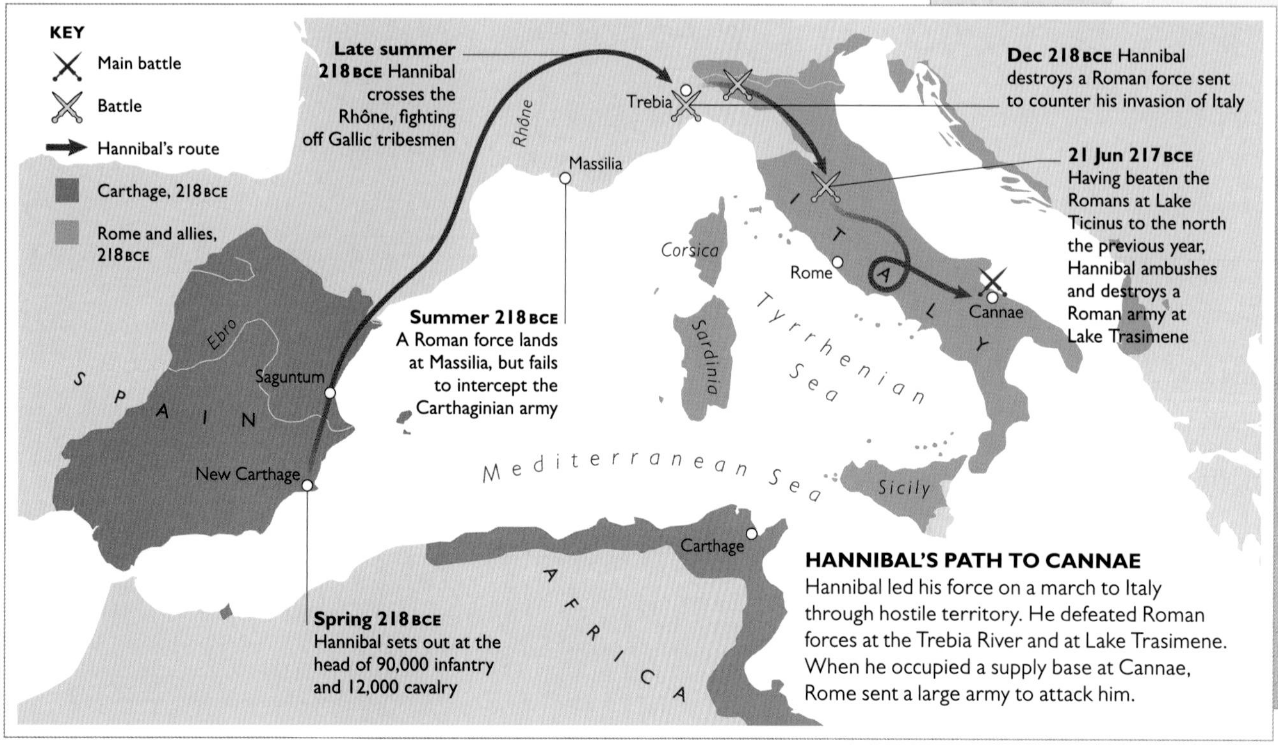

KEY
Main battle
Battle
Hannibal's route
Carthage, 218 BCE
Rome and allies, 218 BCE
Late summer 218 BCE Hannibal crosses the Rhône, fighting off Gallic tribesmen
Rhône
Massilia
Trebia
Dec 218 BCE Hannibal destroys a Roman force sent to counter his invasion of Italy
21 Jun 217 BCE Having beaten the Romans at Lake Ticinus to the north the previous year, Hannibal ambushes and destroys a Roman army at Lake Trasimene
Corsica
Rome
Cannae
I T A L Y
Tyrrhenian Sea
Sardinia
Ebro
Saguntum
S P A I N
Summer 218 BCE A Roman force lands at Massilia, but fails to intercept the Carthaginian army
New Carthage
Mediterranean Sea
Sicily
Carthage
A F R I C A
Spring 218 BCE Hannibal sets out at the head of 90,000 infantry and 12,000 cavalry

HANNIBAL'S PATH TO CANNAE
Hannibal led his force on a march to Italy through hostile territory. He defeated Roman forces at the Trebia River and at Lake Trasimene. When he occupied a supply base at Cannae, Rome sent a large army to attack him.

1 DEPLOYING FOR BATTLE

2 AUGUST 216 BCE

The Roman and Carthaginian armies camped on a plain alongside the River Aufidus. Early on the morning of 2 August, the Romans, commanded by the consuls Aemilius Paullus and Terentius Varro, crossed the river to form a battle line in the constrained space between the river and the hills to the south. Hannibal, accepting the challenge, followed suit.

- Carthaginians move into battle formation
- Romans move into battle formation

2 HANNIBAL'S CRESCENT

Hannibal's force was made up of soldiers from different parts of the Carthaginian empire, including Celts, Spanish tribesmen, Numidians, and Libyans. While his cavalry was strong, his infantry was greatly outnumbered by the Romans. Hannibal arranged his infantry in a shallow crescent hoping to tempt the massed Roman infantry to attack at its centre, where he had deployed his Spanish and his more expendable Celtic foot soldiers.

3 BATTLE JOINED

After some initial skirmishes, the Roman infantry pressed forward. The Celtic and Spanish centre drew back, drawing the Roman infantry with them, while the heavy Libyan infantry to the left and right held its ground. Meanwhile, Hasdrubal's horsemen got the upper hand over the Roman heavy cavalry on the left flank, putting them to flight.

- Roman infantry push forward
- Roman cavalry flee
- Carthaginian cavalry advance
- Celtic and Spanish infantry draw back

4 ROMANS TRAPPED

The Roman infantry were surrounded on three sides as Hannibal's Libyan troops turned in against their flanks. As the Numidian horsemen on the right chased the Roman allied cavalry from the field, Hasdrubal's cavalry swung round to attack the Roman foot soldiers from the rear. The Roman infantry were destroyed, with few escaping.

- Romans push forward
- Libyans push forward
- Numidians push forward
- Celts and Spanish push forward
- Romans fall back

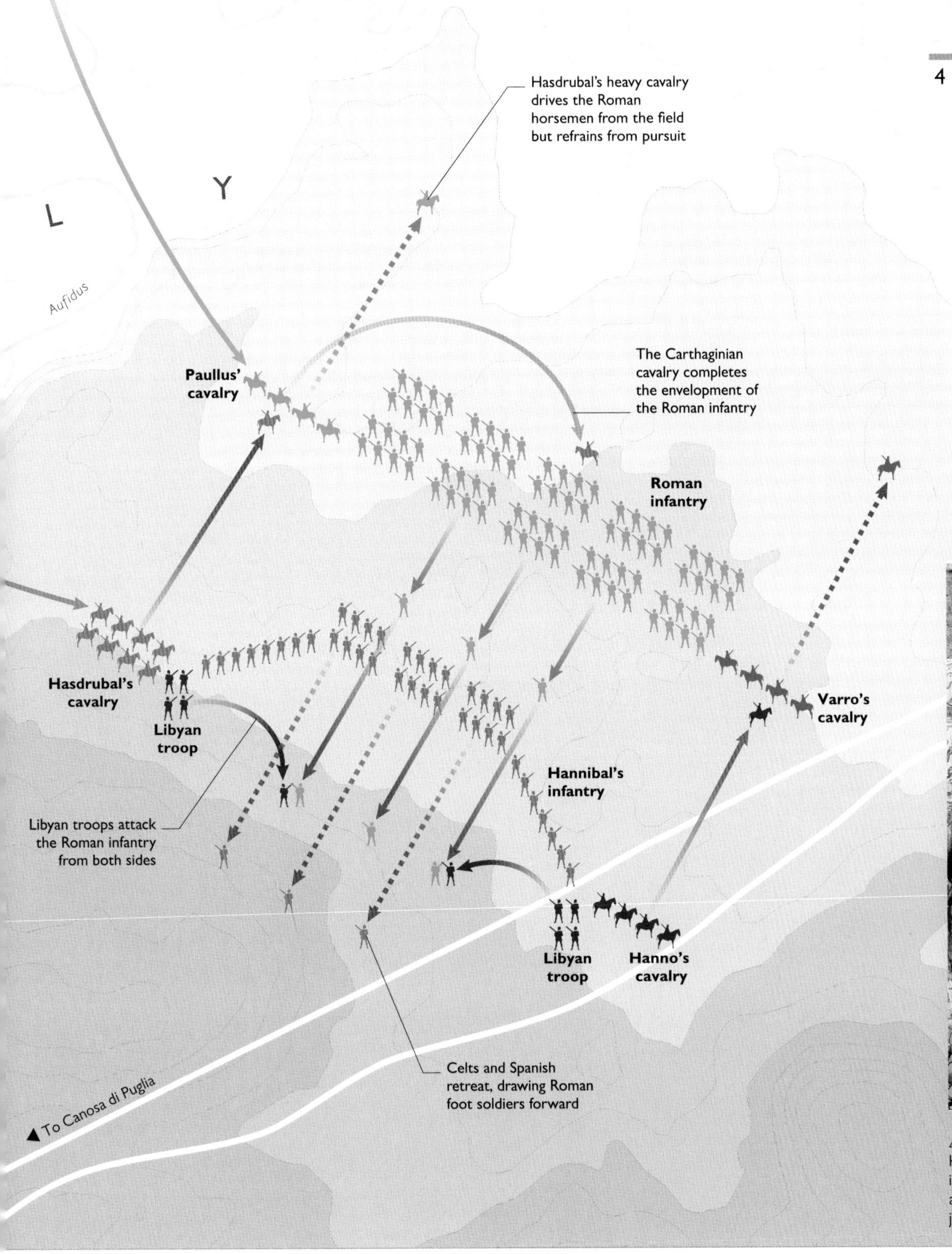
L
Y
Aufidus
Hasdrubal's heavy cavalry drives the Roman horsemen from the field but refrains from pursuit
Paullus' cavalry
The Carthaginian cavalry completes the envelopment of the Roman infantry
Roman infantry
Hasdrubal's cavalry
Libyan troop
Varro's cavalry
Hannibal's infantry
Libyan troops attack the Roman infantry from both sides
Libyan troop
Hanno's cavalry
Celts and Spanish retreat, drawing Roman foot soldiers forward
To Canosa di Puglia
To Barletta

△ **Crossing the Alps**
Hannibal's epic crossing of the Alps, accompanied by his infantry, cavalry, mules, and an estimated 37 elephants allowed him to avoid hostile land and naval forces on his journey to attack the Roman Republic.

ALESIA

The siege of Alesia in 52 BCE was the climax of Roman general Julius Caesar's campaign to conquer Gaul. Caesar encircled and destroyed an army of rebel Gallic tribesmen led by Vercingetorix, fighting off an attack by a relief force. As a result of Caesar's victory, Gaul fell under Roman domination for the following 500 years.

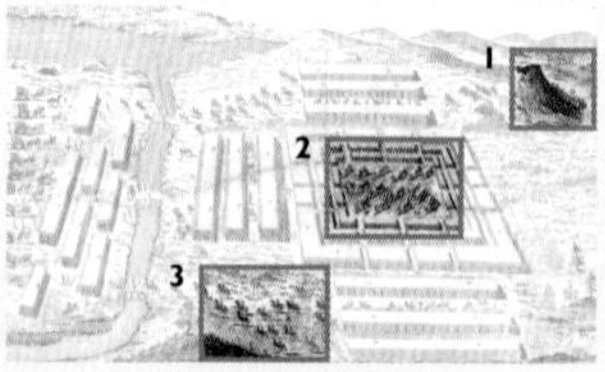
1
2
3

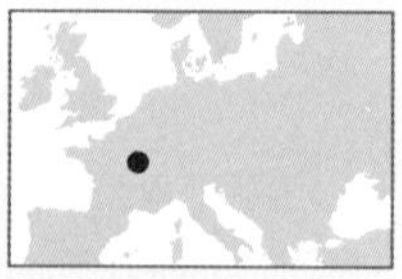

LOCATOR

Covering present-day France, Belgium, Switzerland, and neighbouring areas, Gaul was home to a number of Celtic tribes. Beginning in 58 BCE, Julius Caesar conquered these tribes in a series of campaigns, but his brutal treatment of the defeated provoked discontent. In the winter of 53–52 BCE, Vercingetorix, leader of the Arverni tribe, won the support of other Gallic tribes for an uprising. Caesar alleviated his supply shortage by seizing the fortified town of Avaricum, but when he attacked the Arverni capital of Gergovia, he was repelled. Vercingetorix attacked Caesar's marching army, but his cavalry were beaten back. Vercingetorix harassed the retreating Romans, but was defeated when he committed to a full-scale attack. He withdrew to a strong defensive position at the hill settlement of Alesia in eastern France.

Caesar knew, especially after Gergovia, that it would be foolish to assault the strong Gallic army in this hill position. Instead, he planned a siege to starve the Gauls. The legionaries enclosed Alesia in a 16-km (10-mile) siege line of ditches and ramparts of timber and earth. Before it was completed, Vercingetorix dispatched horsemen to seek aid from other Gallic tribal leaders. Anticipating a counter-attack from the rear, Caesar had a second circle of fortifications built outside the first, so his troops were defended from both sides. With forces of up to 80,000 men, the Gauls were soon short of food. To save supplies, Vercingetorix ordered the elderly, women, and children to leave. Caesar refused to allow them through Roman lines, letting them starve to death between the armies. In late September, a huge Gallic relief force arrived outside Alesia. The Romans were outnumbered, but their fortifications allowed them to repel successive Gallic assaults. The battle ended in a desperate all-out effort by the Gauls, which Caesar held off by inspiring his troops and sending his Germanic mercenary cavalry to attack from behind. The relief force was driven off and Vercingetorix surrendered.

THE FINAL BATTLE

The Gauls tried to lift the siege by co-ordinating a breakout attempt with an attack by the relief force outside. They identified a weak point in a Roman camp at the foot of Mount Réa. Seeing the Gauls threatening this position, Caesar led a counter-attack and ordered his Germanic cavalry to strike the Gauls from the rear. The relief army dispersed in disarray.

KEY

ROMAN FORCES
- Roman siege lines
- Defensive trench
- Roman camps
- Roman forces
- Caesar's movement
- Germanic cavalry
- Germanic counter-attack

GALLIC FORCES
- Gallic relief force camp
- Gallic forces
- Gallic advance

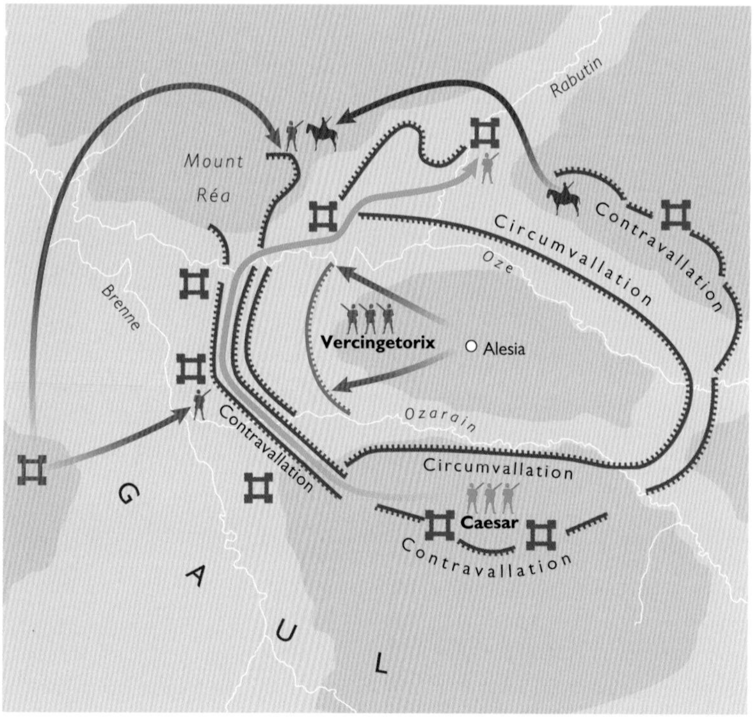
Rabutin
Mount
Réa
Circumvallation
Contravallation
Oze
Brenne
Vercingetorix
Alesia
Ozarain
Contravallation
Circumvallation
Caesar
Contravallation
G
A
U
L

Tome II.
A

△ **The prelude to Alesia**
This 18th-century map shows an anachronistically formal portrayal of the failed attack on Caesar's marching army. The Gauls withdrew to Alesia, where they were besieged by Caesar's army.

▽ **Germanic cavalry**
Caesar made effective use of his Germanic horsemen during the campaign. Here, they prepare to counter-attack the Gallic cavalry.

1
G

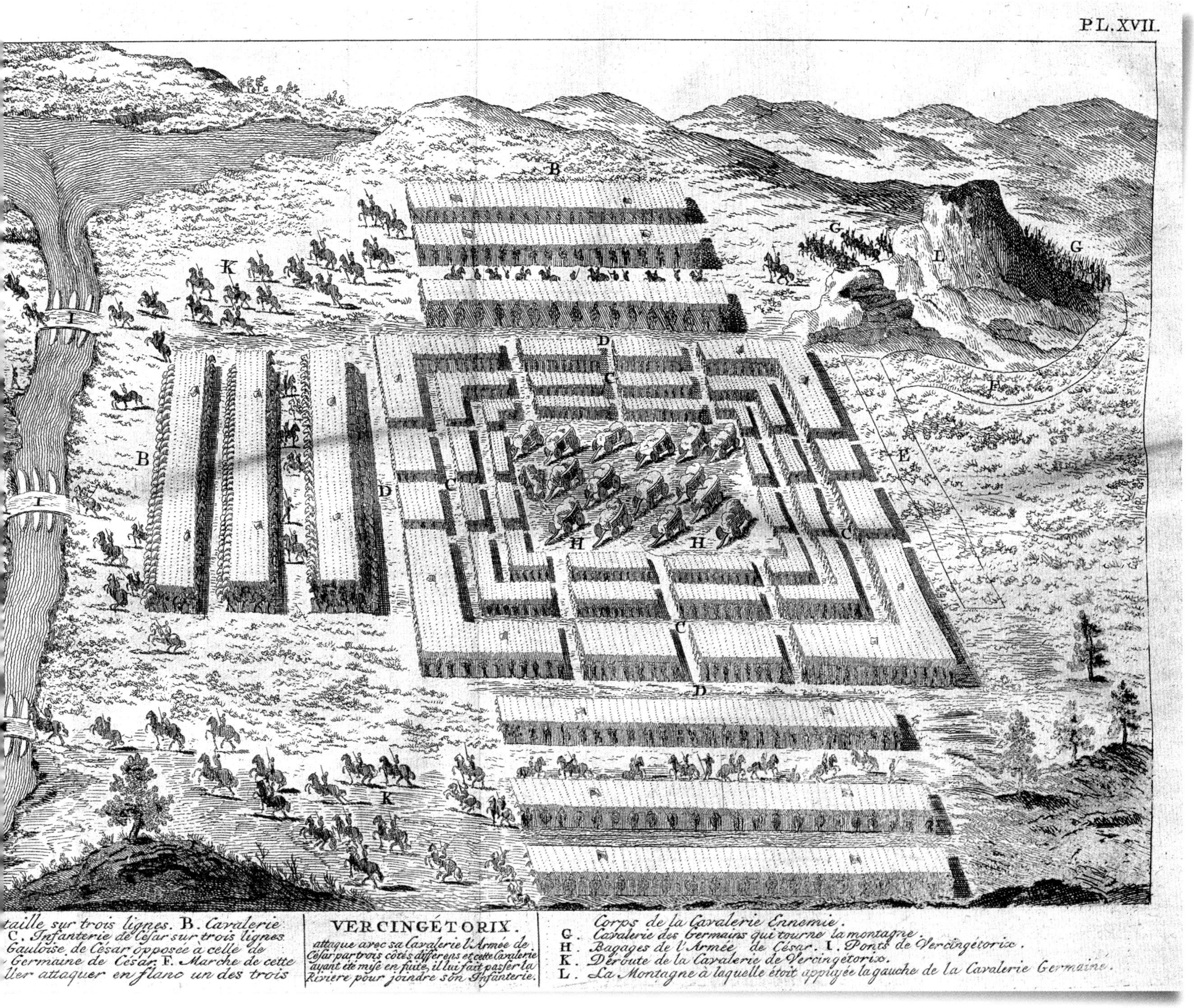
PL. XVII.
B
K
I
B
D
C
C
C
D
C
H
H
C
D
K
G
L
G
F
E
taille sur trois lignes. B. Cavalerie
C. Infanterie de César sur trois lignes.
Gauloise de César opposée à celle de
Germaine de César. F. Marche de cette
ller attaquer en flanc un des trois
VERCINGÉTORIX.
attaque avec sa Cavalerie l'Armée de César par trois côtés differens et cette Cavalerie ayant été mise en fuite, il lui fait passer la Riviere pour joindre son Infanterie.
Corps de la Cavalerie Ennemie.
G. Cavalerie des Germains qui tourne la montagne.
H. Bagages de l'Armée de César. I. Ponts de Vercingétorix.
K. Déroute de la Cavalerie de Vercingétorix.
L. La Montagne à laquelle étoit appuyée la gauche de la Cavalerie Germaine.

2

H
H

3

K

◁ **Defensive formation**
Caesar's army is shown in a defensive square with its baggage train at the centre.

△ **The Gauls flee**
Following their defeat by the Romans, the Gallic cavalry fled back to their own lines.

Trajan's column
Erected in Rome in 113 CE to celebrate Emperor Trajan's victories on the Danube, Trajan's Column displays vivid images of life in the Roman army while on campaigns. Much of a legion's time was spent building walls, roads, and bridges.

ROMAN LEGIONS

Ancient Rome created and sustained one of the world's greatest empires through the power and efficiency of its army. Formidable in battle, Roman legionaries were also outstanding military engineers.

The Roman army was divided into legions of around 5,000 legionaries, and from the 1st century BCE became a fully professional force. Its soldiers were mostly men with Roman citizenship who signed up for 20 years of active service. Legionaries tended to come from the poorer classes, attracted by regular pay and the prospect of a grant of farmland when they retired. A legionary could rise up to the rank of centurion and command 80 legionaries (a century). Each legion consisted of ten cohorts, each made up of six centuries. Legions were also supported by auxiliaries without Roman citizenship recruited from subjects of the empire. These non-citizens provided additional cavalry, supporting the legions' own 300 cavalry.

NERO CAESAR AVGVSTVS

△ **Roman coin**
Augustus, the first Roman emperor, is seen above. During his reign, legionaries were paid 225 denarii a year.

Skilled force

Roman legionaries excelled as disciplined foot soldiers. Armed with two heavy javelins and a short sword, and well protected by a large shield, helmet, and cuirass, they were trained to fight flexibly in a variety of formations, and used various torsion catapults, from small "scorpions" to larger ballistae and one-armed onagers. Legionaries were not unbeatable in battle – they were especially vulnerable to mounted archers – but they were unmatched as engineers. Some of the siege works they built were remarkable in scale, including a spur and ramp to capture the mountain fortress of Masada in 73 CE. Legionaries also built most of the Roman road network as well as some great frontier fortifications, such as Hadrian's Wall in Britain.

THE *TESTUDO*

Named after the Latin word for tortoise, the *testudo* was a formation that Roman legionaries used when under attack by projectiles. Some of the men in the closely packed body raised their long shields to create a protective roof, like a tortoise's shell, while others formed a shield wall at the front and sides. The *testudo* was especially useful when facing massed enemy archers, allowing legionaries to approach the enemy through an otherwise deadly hail of arrows.

ACTIUM

The naval battle at Actium in 31 BCE was the climactic event in the struggle for power that followed the assassination of Roman dictator Julius Caesar by a group of senators in 44 BCE. At Actium, Caesar's adopted son Octavian defeated his rivals Mark Antony and Cleopatra, and was able to make himself the sole ruler of the Roman world.

In 43 BCE, Mark Antony, once Julius Caesar's most trusted general, set up a triumvirate (a political alliance) with Caesar's adopted son Octavian and the statesman Lepidus to rule over the Roman Republic. Over the following decade, this unstable arrangement was torn apart by rivalries. While Octavian held sway in Rome, Antony established a power base in the rich lands of the eastern Mediterranean, forming a political (and sexual) relationship with Egyptian ruler Cleopatra VII. In 32 BCE, Antony and Cleopatra assembled 19 legions and a large fleet at Actium, on the west coast of Greece. Antony was probably planning an invasion of Italy, but Octavian seized the initiative. The two forces confronted one another over the summer of 31 BCE, and Antony and Cleopatra finally opted for a naval battle to decide the issue, or to break out if this failed. They escaped, but their fates were sealed. The eastern Mediterranean fell to Octavian's forces, and in 30 BCE both Antony and Cleopatra committed suicide. Egypt came under Roman rule, and three years later Octavian was recognized as sole ruler of Rome.

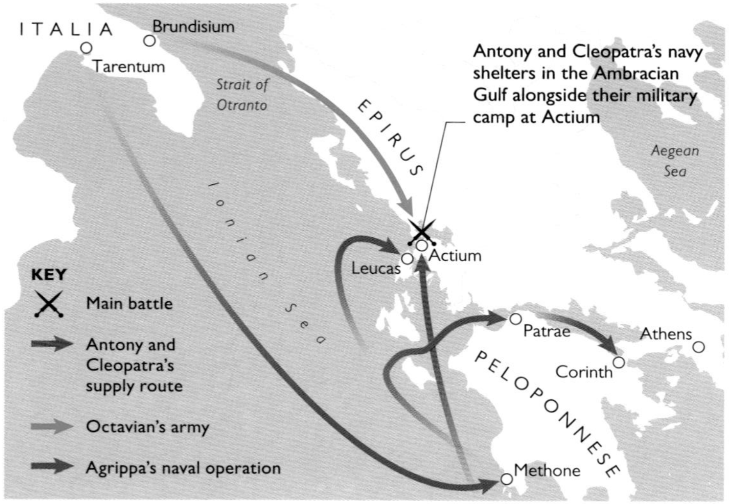
ITALIA
Brundisium
Tarentum
Strait of Otranto
EPIRUS
Antony and Cleopatra's navy shelters in the Ambracian Gulf alongside their military camp at Actium
Aegean Sea
Ionian Sea
Actium
Leucas
Patrae
Athens
Corinth
PELOPONNESE
Methone
KEY
Main battle
Antony and Cleopatra's supply route
Octavian's army
Agrippa's naval operation

THREATENED FROM LAND AND SEA

Antony and Cleopatra established their army and navy at Actium and other Greek bases in autumn 32 BCE. In 31 BCE, Octavian's aggressive naval commander Marcus Vipsanius Agrippa raided key locations on the Greek coast with some success, and attempted to disrupt maritime supply shipments to Antony and Cleopatra's forces. Meanwhile, Octavian ferried an army from Italy to Epirus, and established his own camp opposite Actium.

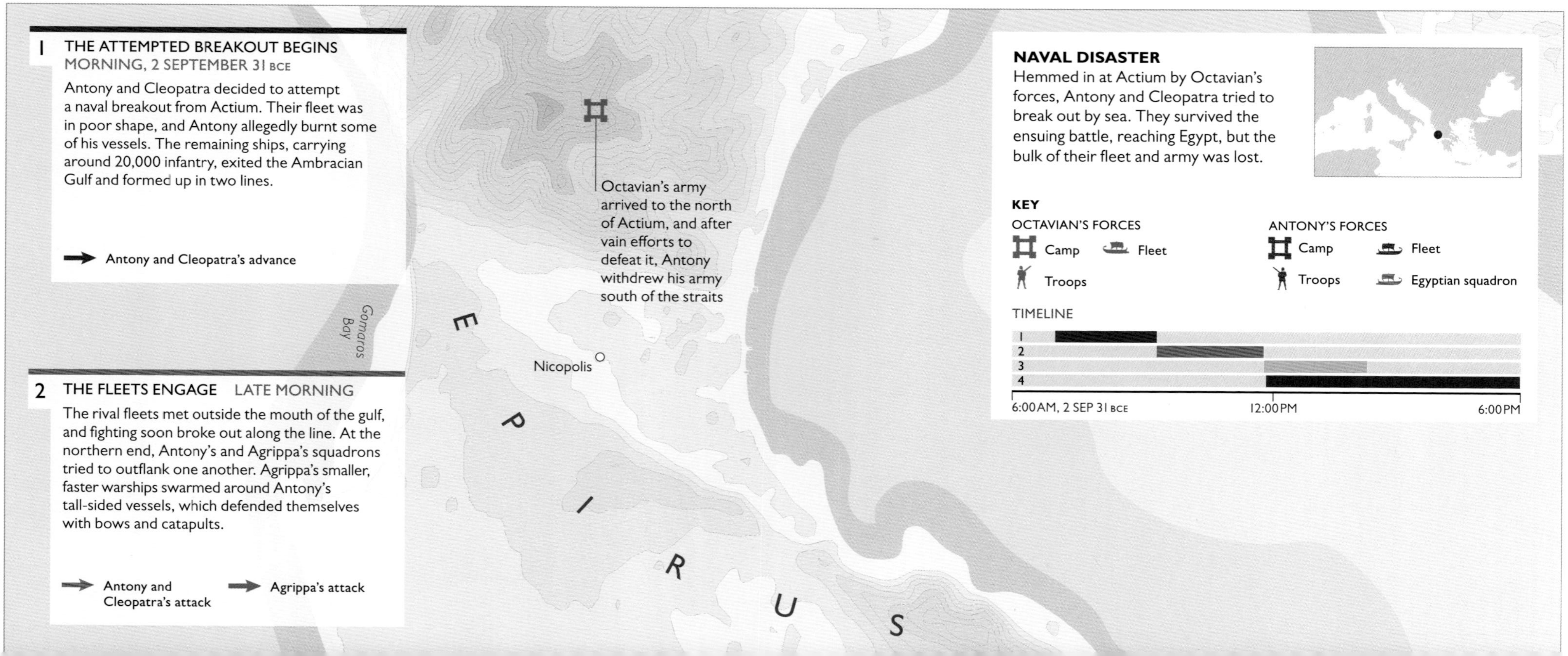
Octavian's army arrived to the north of Actium, and after vain efforts to defeat it, Antony withdrew his army south of the straits
Gomaros Bay
Nicopolis
EPIRUS
Antony and Cleopatra's advance
Antony and Cleopatra's attack
Agrippa's attack
KEY
OCTAVIAN'S FORCES
Camp
Fleet
Troops
ANTONY'S FORCES
Camp
Fleet
Troops
Egyptian squadron
TIMELINE
1
2
3
4
6:00AM, 2 SEP 31 BCE
12:00PM
6:00PM

1 THE ATTEMPTED BREAKOUT BEGINS
MORNING, 2 SEPTEMBER 31 BCE

Antony and Cleopatra decided to attempt a naval breakout from Actium. Their fleet was in poor shape, and Antony allegedly burnt some of his vessels. The remaining ships, carrying around 20,000 infantry, exited the Ambracian Gulf and formed up in two lines.

2 THE FLEETS ENGAGE LATE MORNING

The rival fleets met outside the mouth of the gulf, and fighting soon broke out along the line. At the northern end, Antony's and Agrippa's squadrons tried to outflank one another. Agrippa's smaller, faster warships swarmed around Antony's tall-sided vessels, which defended themselves with bows and catapults.

NAVAL DISASTER

Hemmed in at Actium by Octavian's forces, Antony and Cleopatra tried to break out by sea. They survived the ensuing battle, reaching Egypt, but the bulk of their fleet and army was lost.

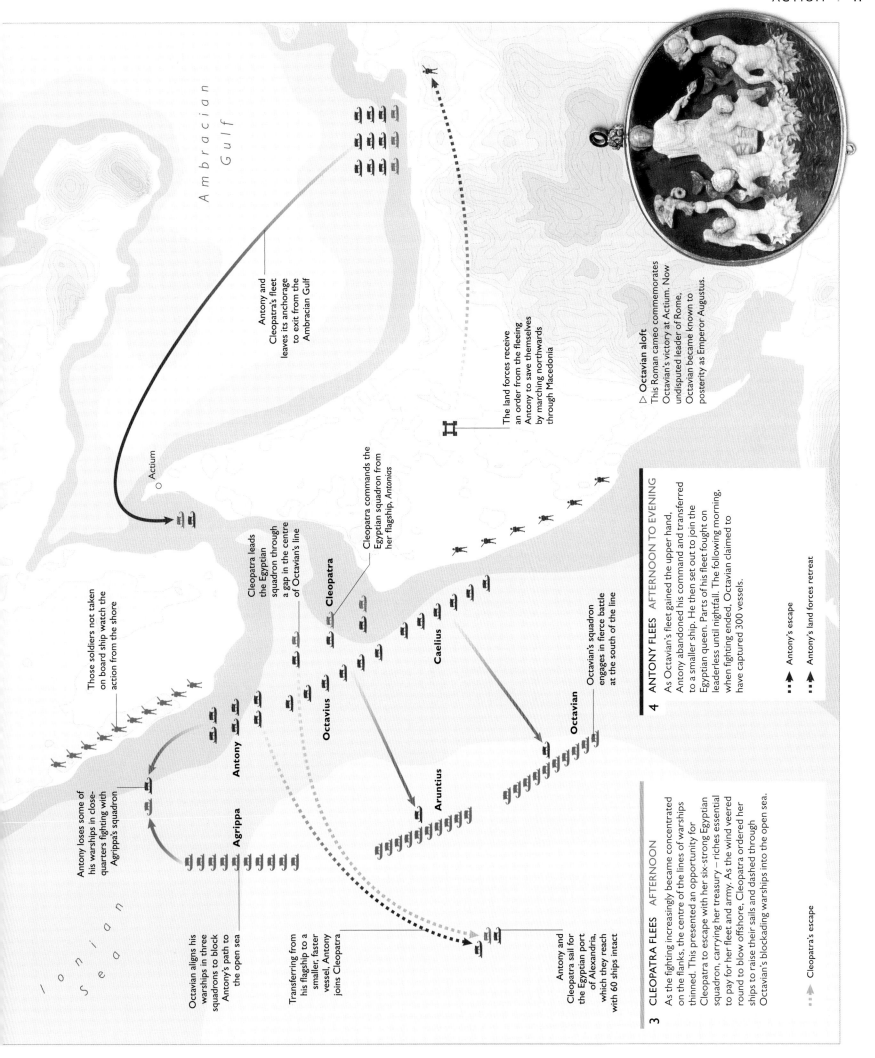

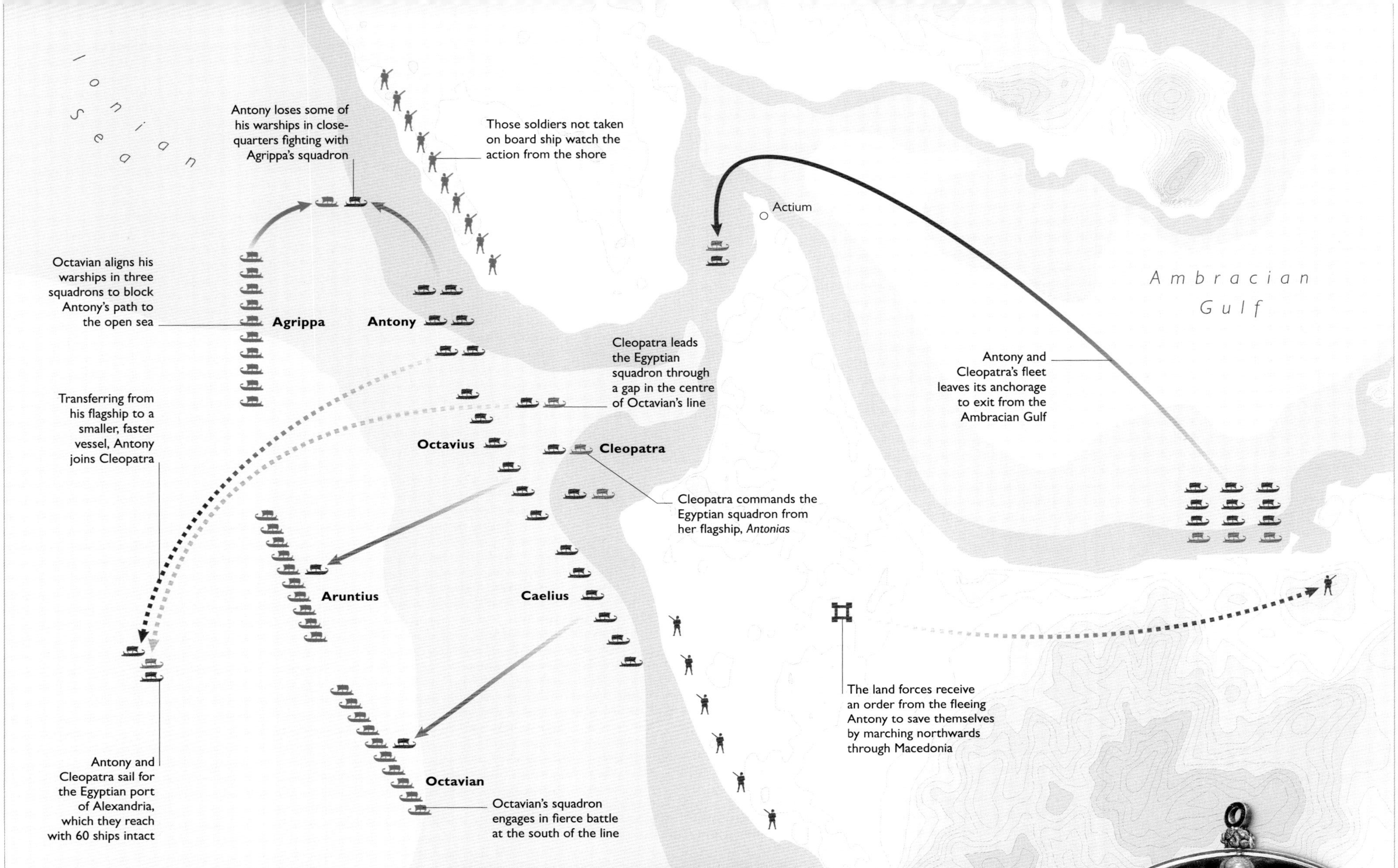
Ionian Sea
Antony loses some of his warships in close-quarters fighting with Agrippa's squadron
Those soldiers not taken on board ship watch the action from the shore
Actium
Ambracian Gulf
Octavian aligns his warships in three squadrons to block Antony's path to the open sea
Agrippa
Antony
Cleopatra leads the Egyptian squadron through a gap in the centre of Octavian's line
Antony and Cleopatra's fleet leaves its anchorage to exit from the Ambracian Gulf
Transferring from his flagship to a smaller, faster vessel, Antony joins Cleopatra
Octavius
Cleopatra
Cleopatra commands the Egyptian squadron from her flagship, *Antonias*
Aruntius
Caelius
The land forces receive an order from the fleeing Antony to save themselves by marching northwards through Macedonia
Antony and Cleopatra sail for the Egyptian port of Alexandria, which they reach with 60 ships intact
Octavian
Octavian's squadron engages in fierce battle at the south of the line

3 CLEOPATRA FLEES AFTERNOON

As the fighting increasingly became concentrated on the flanks, the centre of the lines of warships thinned. This presented an opportunity for Cleopatra to escape with her six-strong Egyptian squadron, carrying her treasury – riches essential to pay for her fleet and army. As the wind veered round to blow offshore, Cleopatra ordered her ships to raise their sails and dashed through Octavian's blockading warships into the open sea.

Cleopatra's escape

4 ANTONY FLEES AFTERNOON TO EVENING

As Octavian's fleet gained the upper hand, Antony abandoned his command and transferred to a smaller ship. He then set out to join the Egyptian queen. Parts of his fleet fought on leaderless until nightfall. The following morning, when fighting ended, Octavian claimed to have captured 300 vessels.

Antony's escape

Antony's land forces retreat

▷ **Octavian aloft**
This Roman cameo commemorates Octavian's victory at Actium. Now undisputed leader of Rome, Octavian became known to posterity as Emperor Augustus.

TEUTOBURG FOREST

In September 9 CE, an army of Roman legionaries led by Publius Quinctilius Varus was ambushed and annihilated by Germanic tribal warriors in the forests of Saxony. This military disaster ensured that the Roman Empire never succeeded in extending its rule over Germany east of the Rhine.

In the early 1st century CE, during the reign of Emperor Augustus, the Romans embarked upon the conquest of northern Germany. By summer 9 CE, the legate Quinctilius Varus was campaigning in what is now Lower Saxony with an army of three legions, plus cavalry and tribal auxiliaries – German warriors recruited to fight for Rome. Varus was accompanied by the chief of the Cherusci tribe, Arminius, a German who was considered trustworthy and had been given Roman citizenship. Arminius had secretly organized a plot with other tribal leaders to destroy Varus's army. As the Romans marched westwards towards their winter quarters, Arminius falsely informed Varus that a rebellion had broken out nearby. Turning to take action against the supposed rebels, the Romans were led into an ambush. Their massacre was soon avenged, but the Germanic tribes kept their independence and their devastating raids would eventually contribute to the collapse of the Roman Empire.

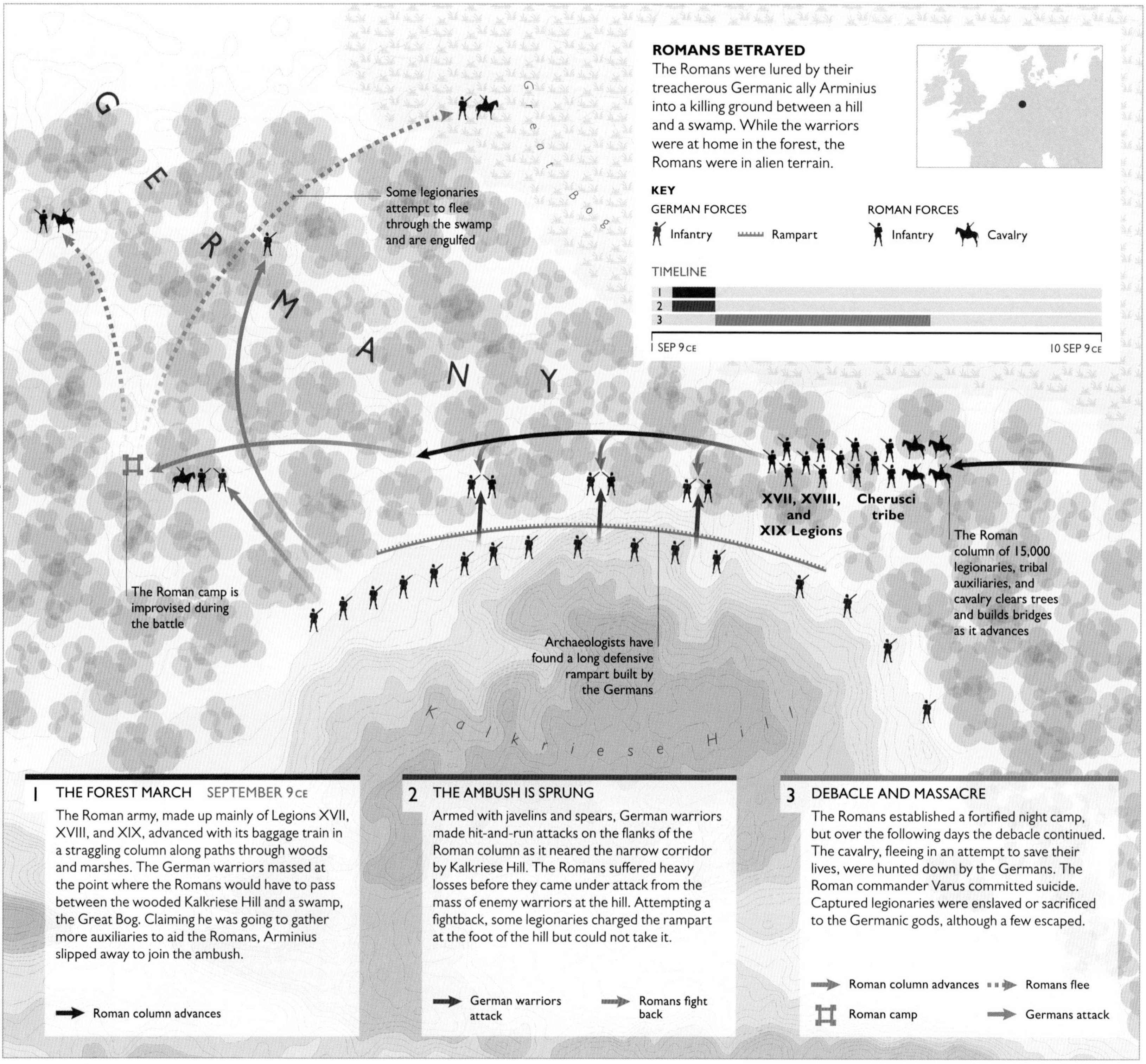
ROMANS BETRAYED
The Romans were lured by their treacherous Germanic ally Arminius into a killing ground between a hill and a swamp. While the warriors were at home in the forest, the Romans were in alien terrain.
KEY
GERMAN FORCES
Infantry
Rampart
ROMAN FORCES
Infantry
Cavalry
TIMELINE
1
2
3
1 SEP 9 CE
10 SEP 9 CE
GERMANY
Great Bog
Some legionaries attempt to flee through the swamp and are engulfed
XVII, XVIII, and XIX Legions
Cherusci tribe
The Roman column of 15,000 legionaries, tribal auxiliaries, and cavalry clears trees and builds bridges as it advances
The Roman camp is improvised during the battle
Archaeologists have found a long defensive rampart built by the Germans
Kalkriese Hill

1 THE FOREST MARCH SEPTEMBER 9 CE

The Roman army, made up mainly of Legions XVII, XVIII, and XIX, advanced with its baggage train in a straggling column along paths through woods and marshes. The German warriors massed at the point where the Romans would have to pass between the wooded Kalkriese Hill and a swamp, the Great Bog. Claiming he was going to gather more auxiliaries to aid the Romans, Arminius slipped away to join the ambush.

Roman column advances

2 THE AMBUSH IS SPRUNG

Armed with javelins and spears, German warriors made hit-and-run attacks on the flanks of the Roman column as it neared the narrow corridor by Kalkriese Hill. The Romans suffered heavy losses before they came under attack from the mass of enemy warriors at the hill. Attempting a fightback, some legionaries charged the rampart at the foot of the hill but could not take it.

German warriors attack

Romans fight back

3 DEBACLE AND MASSACRE

The Romans established a fortified night camp, but over the following days the debacle continued. The cavalry, fleeing in an attempt to save their lives, were hunted down by the Germans. The Roman commander Varus committed suicide. Captured legionaries were enslaved or sacrificed to the Germanic gods, although a few escaped.

Roman column advances

Romans flee

Roman camp

Germans attack

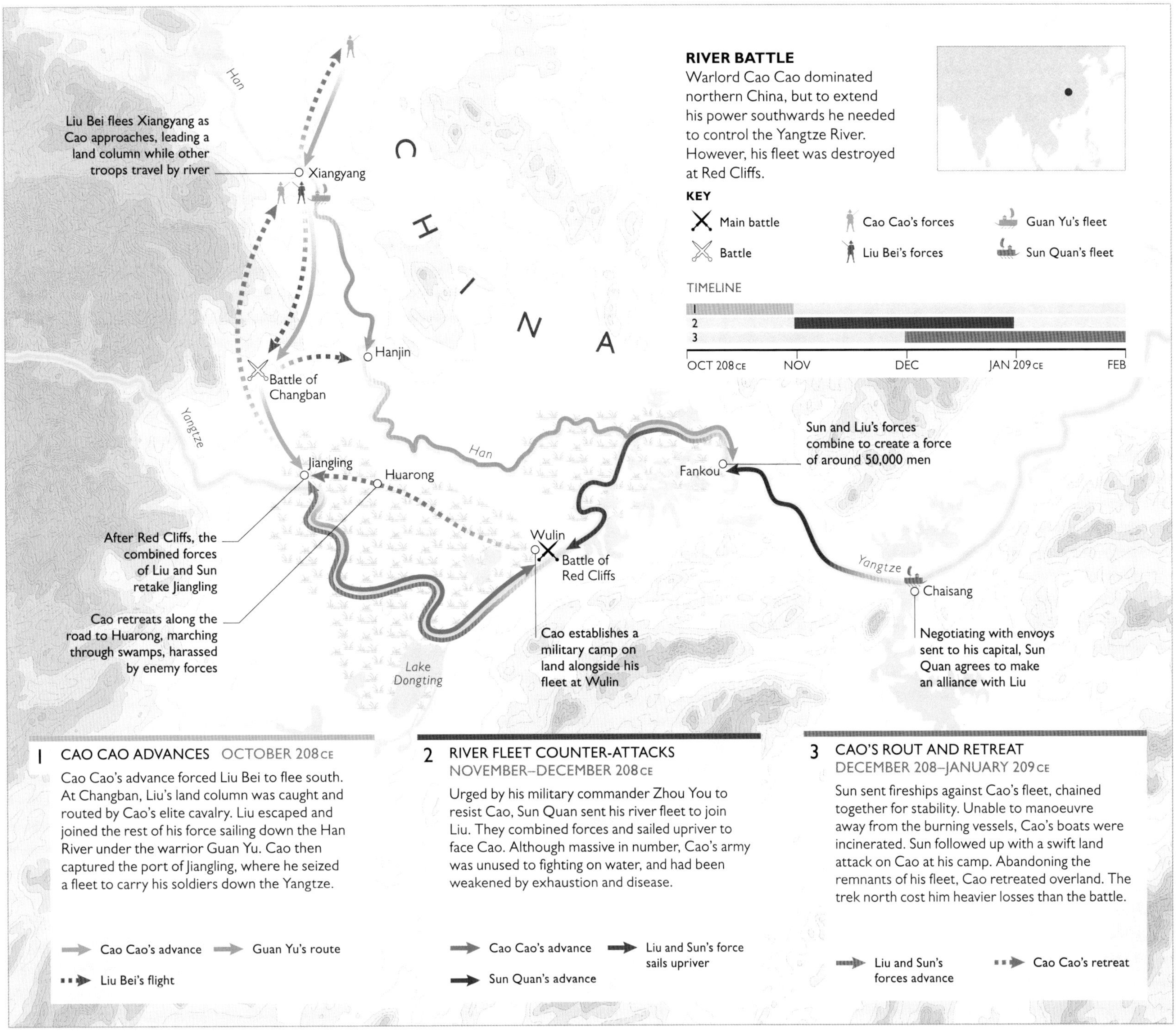
Han
Liu Bei flees Xiangyang as Cao approaches, leading a land column while other troops travel by river
Xiangyang
C H I N A
Hanjin
Battle of Changban
Yangtze
Han
Jiangling
Huarong
Fankou
Sun and Liu's forces combine to create a force of around 50,000 men
After Red Cliffs, the combined forces of Liu and Sun retake Jiangling
Cao retreats along the road to Huarong, marching through swamps, harassed by enemy forces
Wulin
Battle of Red Cliffs
Yangtze
Chaisang
Cao establishes a military camp on land alongside his fleet at Wulin
Lake Dongting
Negotiating with envoys sent to his capital, Sun Quan agrees to make an alliance with Liu
RIVER BATTLE
Warlord Cao Cao dominated northern China, but to extend his power southwards he needed to control the Yangtze River. However, his fleet was destroyed at Red Cliffs.
KEY
Main battle
Battle
Cao Cao's forces
Liu Bei's forces
Guan Yu's fleet
Sun Quan's fleet
TIMELINE
1
2
3
OCT 208 CE
NOV
DEC
JAN 209 CE
FEB

1 CAO CAO ADVANCES OCTOBER 208 CE

Cao Cao's advance forced Liu Bei to flee south. At Changban, Liu's land column was caught and routed by Cao's elite cavalry. Liu escaped and joined the rest of his force sailing down the Han River under the warrior Guan Yu. Cao then captured the port of Jiangling, where he seized a fleet to carry his soldiers down the Yangtze.

Cao Cao's advance · Guan Yu's route · Liu Bei's flight

2 RIVER FLEET COUNTER-ATTACKS NOVEMBER–DECEMBER 208 CE

Urged by his military commander Zhou You to resist Cao, Sun Quan sent his river fleet to join Liu. They combined forces and sailed upriver to face Cao. Although massive in number, Cao's army was unused to fighting on water, and had been weakened by exhaustion and disease.

Cao Cao's advance · Liu and Sun's force sails upriver · Sun Quan's advance

3 CAO'S ROUT AND RETREAT DECEMBER 208–JANUARY 209 CE

Sun sent fireships against Cao's fleet, chained together for stability. Unable to manoeuvre away from the burning vessels, Cao's boats were incinerated. Sun followed up with a swift land attack on Cao at his camp. Abandoning the remnants of his fleet, Cao retreated overland. The trek north cost him heavier losses than the battle.

Liu and Sun's forces advance · Cao Cao's retreat

RED CLIFFS

A decisive episode in the civil war that split China in the final years of the Han dynasty, the battle of Red Cliffs was fought on and around the Yangtze River. The defeat of the feared warlord Cao Cao foiled his bid to unify China under his rule.

In 184 CE the Han dynasty, which had ruled China for almost 400 years, was undermined by a peasant revolt, the Yellow Turban rebellion. China became divided between warlords, the most successful of whom was the ruthless Cao Cao, who held sway in northern China. In 208 CE, he led an army reputed to be over 200,000 strong southwards in pursuit of Liu Bei, a rival with a following of Han dynasty loyalists. Unable to match Cao's forces, Liu formed an alliance with Sun Quan, a southern regional strongman who controlled much of the Yangtze River from Chaisang. Sun's military commander, Zhou Yu, masterminded the defeat of Cao at Red Cliffs, near modern-day Wuhan. The consequence of the battle, after further fighting, was the division of China in 220 CE into the "Three Kingdoms": Wei (north of the Yangtze), Shu (in the southwest), and Wu (in the southeast).

△ **Cao Cao before the battle**
Cao Cao was an accomplished poet. Before the battle, he wrote *Short Song Style*, illustrated in this 19th-century Japanese woodblock print.

WAR IN ANCIENT CHINA

Organized warfare in China traces its roots to the Shang dynasty (c.1600 BCE–1046 BCE) and Zhou dynasty (1046–256 BCE). Wars were either fought between rival Chinese states, or for territorial expansion.

Shang and Zhou armies were built around a core of nobles on chariots and lightly armed slave-conscripts, continuing up to the Spring and Autumn Period (771–476 BCE). The bow was the main early weapon. Trained infantry with bows, dagger-axes, and crossbows, appeared in the Warring States Period (476–221 BCE) alongside charioteers.

The age of horsemen

Cavalry began to replace chariots after the Warring States period. References to horse armour appeared in literary sources from the 3rd century, although it is thought to have been used centuries earlier than this. Non-chinese mounted auxiliaries began to support Chinese cavalry in increasing numbers. By 306 CE, the central authority of the Jin dynasty had collapsed with the War of the Eight Princes, and the steppe tribes Xiongnu and Xianbei established kingdoms in Northern China. Armoured lancer cavalry and horse archers became the dominant strike force of their armies, and this dominance continued in the Sui and Tang dynasties (581–907 CE).

Records suggest Chinese armies were larger than contemporary European ones, and were made up of semi-independent corps. Battle lines stretched for kilometres with extensive field fortifications. Rulers rarely took to battle, as defeat was associated with divine wrath.

◁ **Bronze sword**
Weapons such as this cast bronze sword from the Warring States Period were not just effective battlefield tools, but were also a status symbol for the bearer.

THE TERRACOTTA ARMY

When Qin Shi Huang, the first Qin emperor, died in September 210 BCE, he was interred in a grand mausoleum near modern-day Xian. Along with him, a massive army of possibly tens of thousands of terracotta soldiers was buried in battle array. Several thousand of these figures have been unearthed by archaeologists. The terracotta army gives a rare glimpse at the uniform and equipment of Chinese armies of the time.

Tang tombs cavalry mural
The murals in the corridors and chambers of the subterranean tombs at the Qianling Mausoleum in modern-day Xian have remained mostly intact since 700–800 CE. This painting depicts armed men on horses, possibly in a hunting scene.

CTESIPHON

In 363 CE, Roman emperor Julian led an expedition against the Sassanid Persians in Mesopotamia (modern-day Iraq). Despite his victory at Ctesiphon, the overall campaign was disastrous. Julian was killed, and Rome was forced to accept a humiliating peace treaty. Julian's death ensured the continued dominance of Christianity in the Roman Empire.

The drawn-out conflict between the Roman and Persian empires flared up again in 359 CE, when the Persian ruler, Shapur II, set out to contest Roman control of Armenia and northern Mesopotamia. Aspiring to glory, the young Roman emperor, Julian, decided to strike back at the heart of Shapur's domains. Despite a victory at Ctesiphon, Julian's campaign failed and he was killed as his forces retreated. Shapur gained Mesopotamia for the Persian Empire and forced Rome to recognize Persian suzerainty over Armenia.

In 313 CE Julian's predecessor, Emperor Constantine, had accepted Christianity as a legitimate religion within the Roman Empire. Julian wished to reverse the growing dominance of Christianity and restore pagan polytheism and neoplatonism. His death ended that mission and helped cement Christianity as the official state religion of Rome.

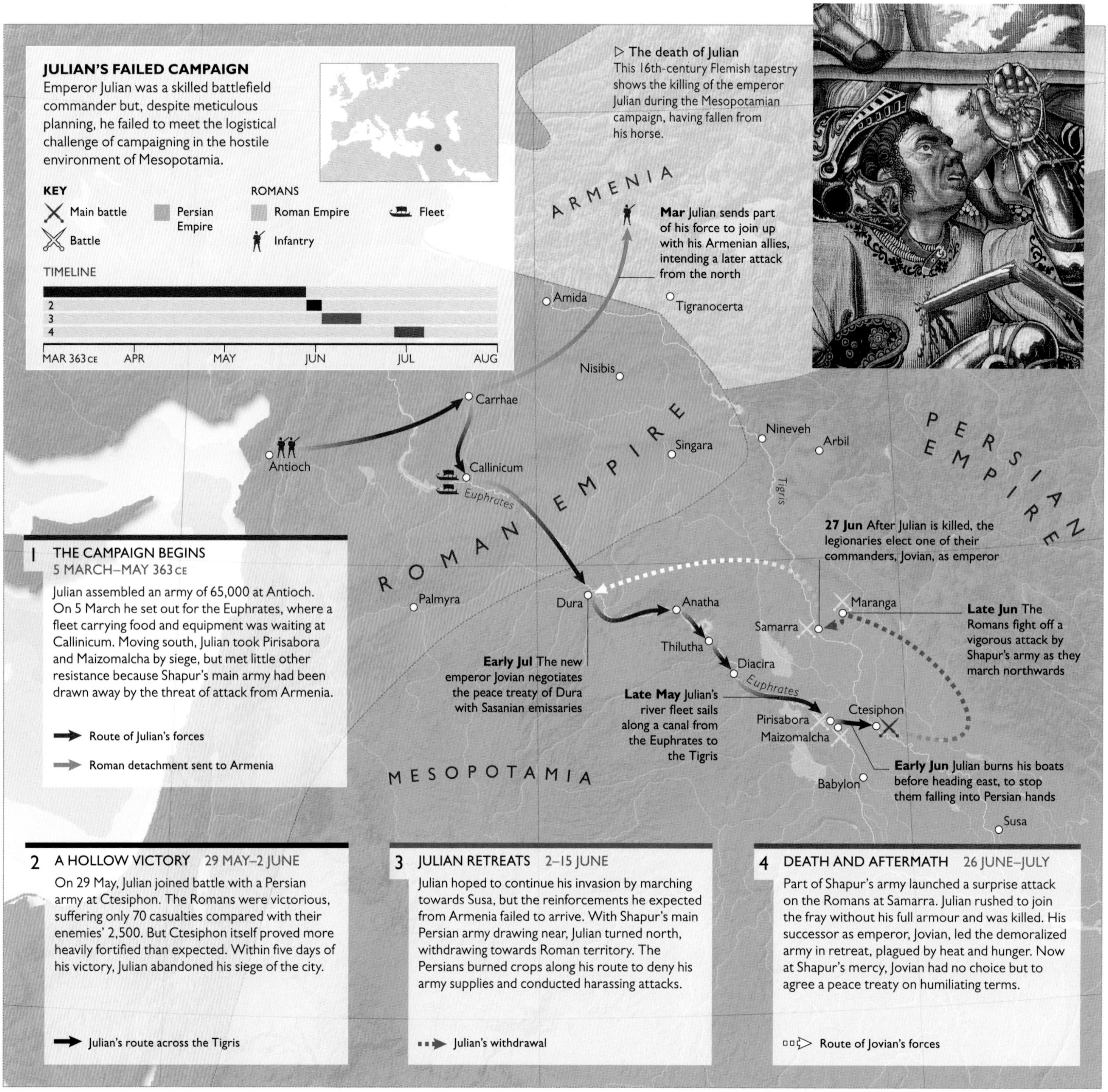
KEY
Main battle
Battle
Persian Empire
ROMANS
Roman Empire
Infantry
Fleet
TIMELINE
2
3
4
MAR 363 CE
APR
MAY
JUN
JUL
AUG
ARMENIA
ROMAN EMPIRE
PERSIAN EMPIRE
MESOPOTAMIA
Amida
Tigranocerta
Nisibis
Carrhae
Antioch
Callinicum
Euphrates
Singara
Nineveh
Arbil
Tigris
Palmyra
Dura
Anatha
Thilutha
Diacira
Samarra
Maranga
Ctesiphon
Pirisabora
Maizomalcha
Babylon
Susa
Mar Julian sends part of his force to join up with his Armenian allies, intending a later attack from the north
27 Jun After Julian is killed, the legionaries elect one of their commanders, Jovian, as emperor
Late Jun The Romans fight off a vigorous attack by Shapur's army as they march northwards
Early Jul The new emperor Jovian negotiates the peace treaty of Dura with Sasanian emissaries
Late May Julian's river fleet sails along a canal from the Euphrates to the Tigris
Early Jun Julian burns his boats before heading east, to stop them falling into Persian hands

JULIAN'S FAILED CAMPAIGN
Emperor Julian was a skilled battlefield commander but, despite meticulous planning, he failed to meet the logistical challenge of campaigning in the hostile environment of Mesopotamia.

▷ **The death of Julian**
This 16th-century Flemish tapestry shows the killing of the emperor Julian during the Mesopotamian campaign, having fallen from his horse.

1 THE CAMPAIGN BEGINS 5 MARCH–MAY 363 CE

Julian assembled an army of 65,000 at Antioch. On 5 March he set out for the Euphrates, where a fleet carrying food and equipment was waiting at Callinicum. Moving south, Julian took Pirisabora and Maizomalcha by siege, but met little other resistance because Shapur's main army had been drawn away by the threat of attack from Armenia.

Route of Julian's forces
Roman detachment sent to Armenia

2 A HOLLOW VICTORY 29 MAY–2 JUNE

On 29 May, Julian joined battle with a Persian army at Ctesiphon. The Romans were victorious, suffering only 70 casualties compared with their enemies' 2,500. But Ctesiphon itself proved more heavily fortified than expected. Within five days of his victory, Julian abandoned his siege of the city.

Julian's route across the Tigris

3 JULIAN RETREATS 2–15 JUNE

Julian hoped to continue his invasion by marching towards Susa, but the reinforcements he expected from Armenia failed to arrive. With Shapur's main Persian army drawing near, Julian turned north, withdrawing towards Roman territory. The Persians burned crops along his route to deny his army supplies and conducted harassing attacks.

Julian's withdrawal

4 DEATH AND AFTERMATH 26 JUNE–JULY

Part of Shapur's army launched a surprise attack on the Romans at Samarra. Julian rushed to join the fray without his full armour and was killed. His successor as emperor, Jovian, led the demoralized army in retreat, plagued by heat and hunger. Now at Shapur's mercy, Jovian had no choice but to agree a peace treaty on humiliating terms.

Route of Jovian's forces

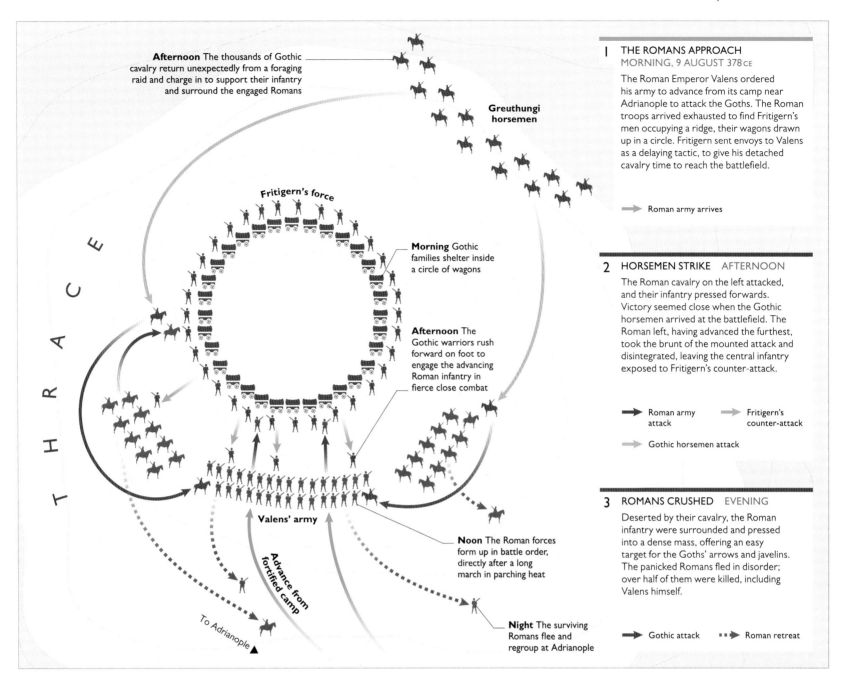

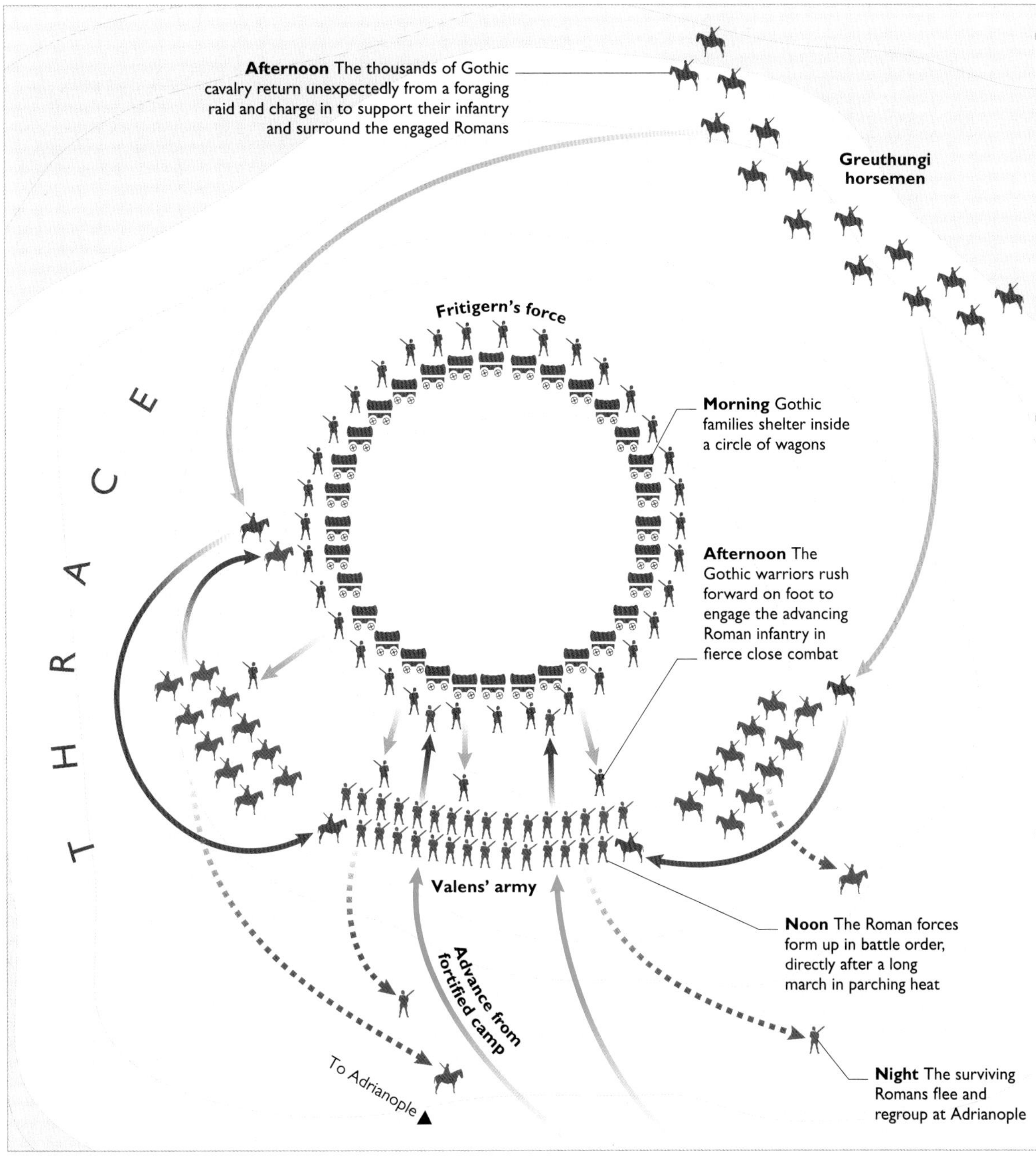
Afternoon The thousands of Gothic cavalry return unexpectedly from a foraging raid and charge in to support their infantry and surround the engaged Romans
Greuthungi horsemen
Fritigern's force
THRACE
Morning Gothic families shelter inside a circle of wagons
Afternoon The Gothic warriors rush forward on foot to engage the advancing Roman infantry in fierce close combat
Valens' army
Advance from fortified camp
Noon The Roman forces form up in battle order, directly after a long march in parching heat
To Adrianople
Night The surviving Romans flee and regroup at Adrianople

1 THE ROMANS APPROACH
MORNING, 9 AUGUST 378 CE

The Roman Emperor Valens ordered his army to advance from its camp near Adrianople to attack the Goths. The Roman troops arrived exhausted to find Fritigern's men occupying a ridge, their wagons drawn up in a circle. Fritigern sent envoys to Valens as a delaying tactic, to give his detached cavalry time to reach the battlefield.

Roman army arrives

2 HORSEMEN STRIKE AFTERNOON

The Roman cavalry on the left attacked, and their infantry pressed forwards. Victory seemed close when the Gothic horsemen arrived at the battlefield. The Roman left, having advanced the furthest, took the brunt of the mounted attack and disintegrated, leaving the central infantry exposed to Fritigern's counter-attack.

Roman army attack | Fritigern's counter-attack | Gothic horsemen attack

3 ROMANS CRUSHED EVENING

Deserted by their cavalry, the Roman infantry were surrounded and pressed into a dense mass, offering an easy target for the Goths' arrows and javelins. The panicked Romans fled in disorder; over half of them were killed, including Valens himself.

Gothic attack | Roman retreat

ADRIANOPLE

Gothic tribal warriors, led by the chieftain Fritigern, crushed a Roman army outside Adrianople (in modern northwest Turkey) in 378 CE. The battle foreshadowed the decline of the Roman Empire, which would later see the "barbarian" tribes take control of Rome itself.

END OF ROMAN DOMINANCE
Valens was overconfident in his ability to conquer the "barbarians", advancing with inadequate preparation and reconnaissance. The battle was another stage in the gradual decline of the once dominant Roman infantry.

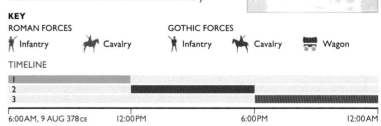

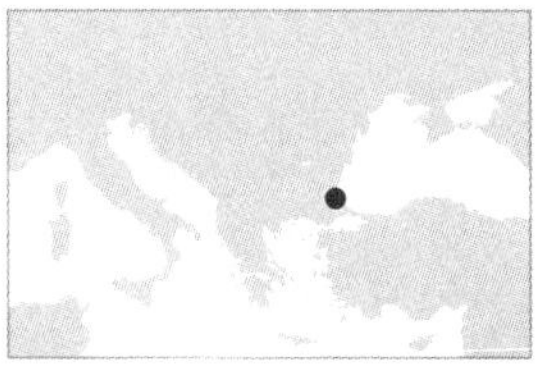

KEY

ROMAN FORCES: Infantry, Cavalry
GOTHIC FORCES: Infantry, Cavalry, Wagon

TIMELINE

1
2
3
6:00 AM, 9 AUG 378 CE
12:00 PM
6:00 PM
12:00 AM

In the 4th century CE, the Roman Empire faced pressure on its borders from migrants regarded as "barbarians". In 376 CE the Thervingi, a Germanic tribe of the group later known as Visigoths, were given permission to cross the border and settle in Thrace. However, the Thervingi were persecuted by local military authorities and together with the Greuthungi, another Gothic tribe, they rose up in revolt and were soon threatening Constantinople (formerly Byzantium), the capital of the Eastern Roman Empire. After two years of running battles, the Roman eastern emperor Valens decided to take command himself and seek glory by crushing the Goths, without waiting for promised reinforcements from the western emperor Gratian. The defeat shook the Romans, but it had only limited consequences. Peace was restored in 382, with the Goths granted land in return for service in the Roman army. However, the battle prefigured later disaster – the sack of Rome by Visigoths in 410.

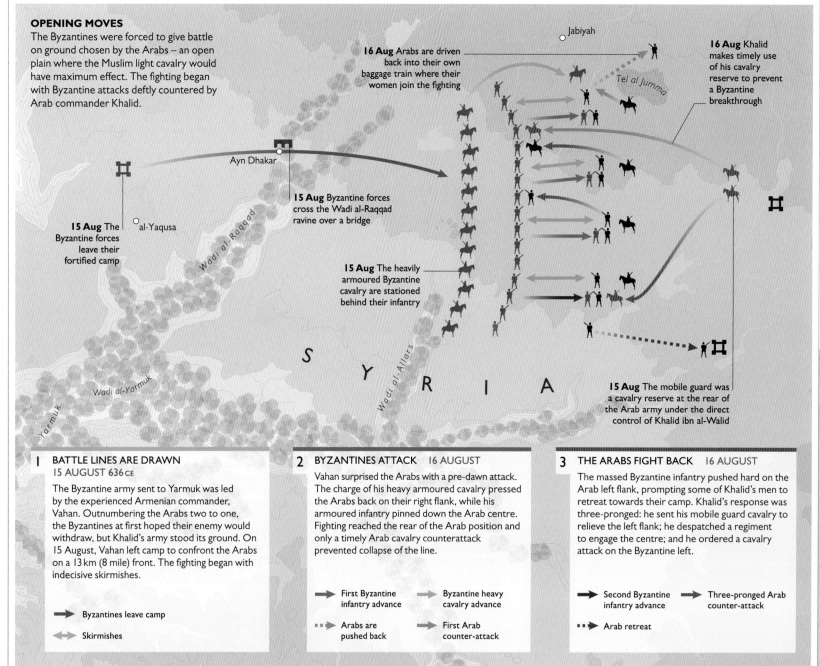

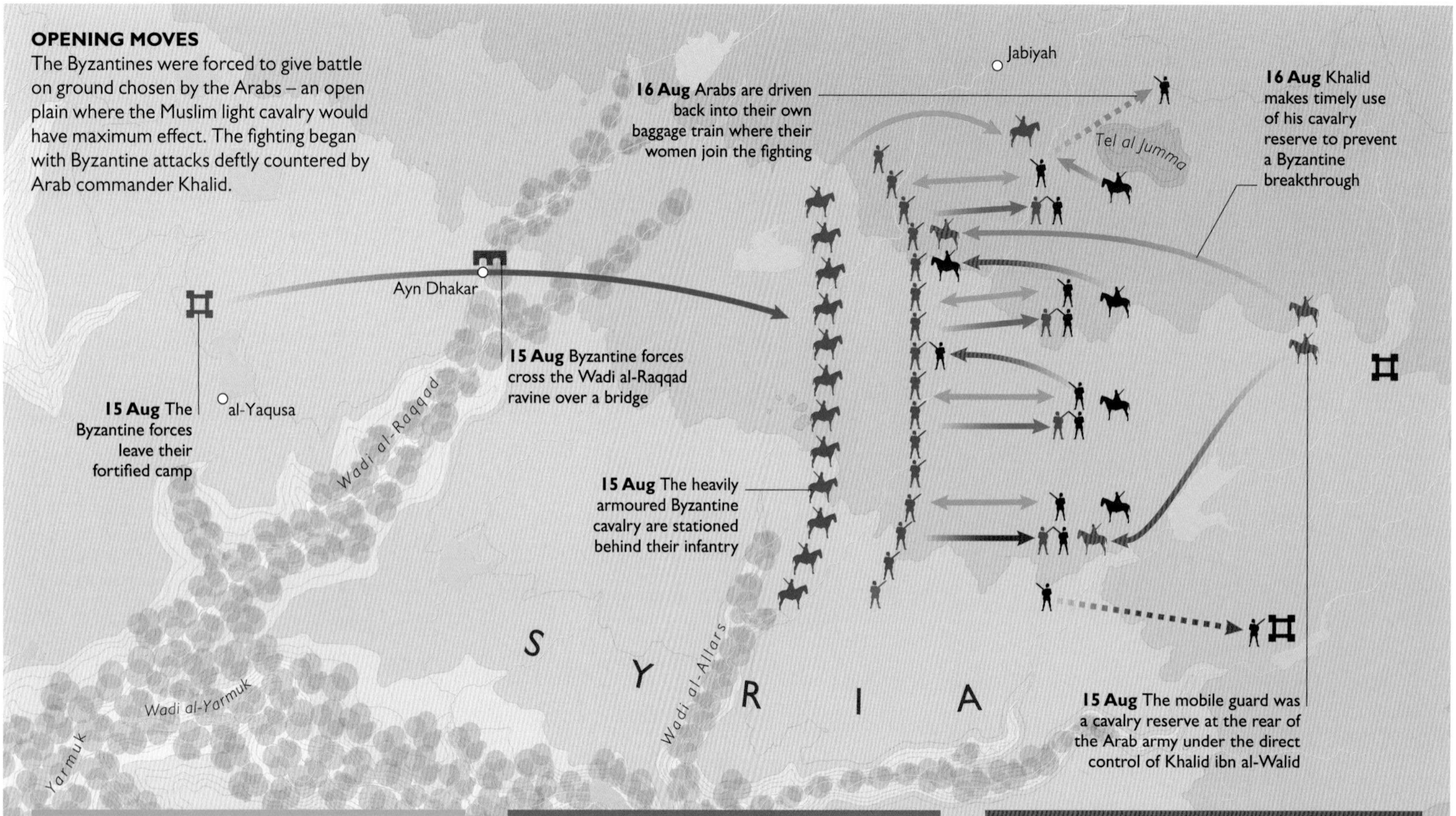
OPENING MOVES
The Byzantines were forced to give battle on ground chosen by the Arabs – an open plain where the Muslim light cavalry would have maximum effect. The fighting began with Byzantine attacks deftly countered by Arab commander Khalid.
Jabiyah
16 Aug Arabs are driven back into their own baggage train where their women join the fighting
Tel al Jumma
16 Aug Khalid makes timely use of his cavalry reserve to prevent a Byzantine breakthrough
Ayn Dhakar
15 Aug Byzantine forces cross the Wadi al-Raqqad ravine over a bridge
15 Aug The Byzantine forces leave their fortified camp
al-Yaqusa
Wadi al-Raqqad
15 Aug The heavily armoured Byzantine cavalry are stationed behind their infantry
S Y R I A
Wadi al-Yarmuk
Yarmuk
Wadi al-Allars
15 Aug The mobile guard was a cavalry reserve at the rear of the Arab army under the direct control of Khalid ibn al-Walid

1 BATTLE LINES ARE DRAWN
15 AUGUST 636 CE

The Byzantine army sent to Yarmuk was led by the experienced Armenian commander, Vahan. Outnumbering the Arabs two to one, the Byzantines at first hoped their enemy would withdraw, but Khalid's army stood its ground. On 15 August, Vahan left camp to confront the Arabs on a 13 km (8 mile) front. The fighting began with indecisive skirmishes.

Byzantines leave camp
Skirmishes

2 BYZANTINES ATTACK 16 AUGUST

Vahan surprised the Arabs with a pre-dawn attack. The charge of his heavy armoured cavalry pressed the Arabs back on their right flank, while his armoured infantry pinned down the Arab centre. Fighting reached the rear of the Arab position and only a timely Arab cavalry counterattack prevented collapse of the line.

First Byzantine infantry advance
Byzantine heavy cavalry advance
Arabs are pushed back
First Arab counter-attack

3 THE ARABS FIGHT BACK 16 AUGUST

The massed Byzantine infantry pushed hard on the Arab left flank, prompting some of Khalid's men to retreat towards their camp. Khalid's response was three-pronged: he sent his mobile guard cavalry to relieve the left flank; he despatched a regiment to engage the centre; and he ordered a cavalry attack on the Byzantine left.

Second Byzantine infantry advance
Three-pronged Arab counter-attack
Arab retreat

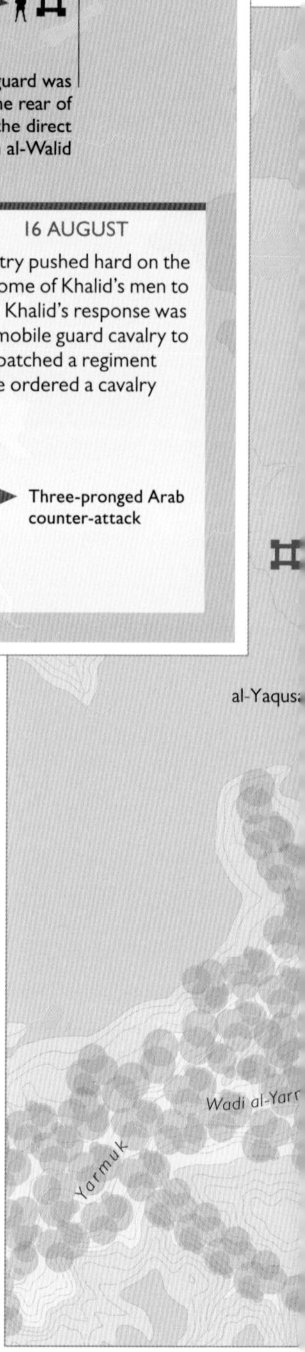
al-Yaqusa
Wadi al-Yarr
Yarmuk

YARMUK

The defeat of a Christian Byzantine Empire army in Syria in 636 CE marked the ascendancy of Arab forces inspired by the new religion of Islam. Over the following century, Muslim armies triumphed from Central Asia to the Atlantic.

At Nineveh in 627 CE, the Byzantine emperor, Heraclius, won a crushing victory over the Sasanid Persian Empire, apparently heralding a new era of Byzantine dominance in the Middle East. However, unnoticed by these warring empires, the tribes of Arabia were uniting under the banner of Islam, a religion based on the teachings of the prophet Mohammed. After Mohammed's death in 632, Arab armies left Arabia with a mission to spread their faith. Led by the gifted general Khalid ibn al-Walid, they seized Damascus from the Byzantines in 634. Heraclius responded to this challenge by assembling a large army at Antioch in northern Syria. As this force marched south, Khalid concentrated his smaller army by the Yarmuk River, preparing for a pitched battle.

Defeat at Yarmuk had a devastating effect on the Byzantine Empire. Although it endured for another eight centuries, much of its subsequent history is the record of a struggle for survival. The Sasanians suffered a decisive defeat at Qadisiyah later in 636. By 750, Arab armies had given the Damascus-based Umayyad Caliphate control of an empire that stretched from modern-day Pakistan to the Iberian peninsula.

EXPANSION OF ISLAM

By the start of the Umayyad Caliphate in 661 CE, Arab armies controlled Persia, the Levant, and Egypt. Later conquests took them to Constantinople. North African Berbers, converted to Islam, invaded Iberia and threatened the kingdom of the Franks.

KEY
- Main battle
- Muslim forces
- Frankish Kingdom
- Byzantine Empire
- Up to the death of Mohammed, 632
- The early caliphs, 632–61
- The Umayyads, 661–750

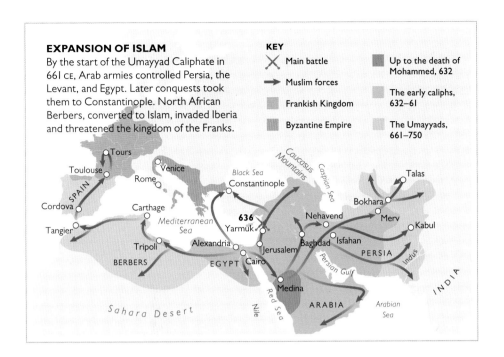

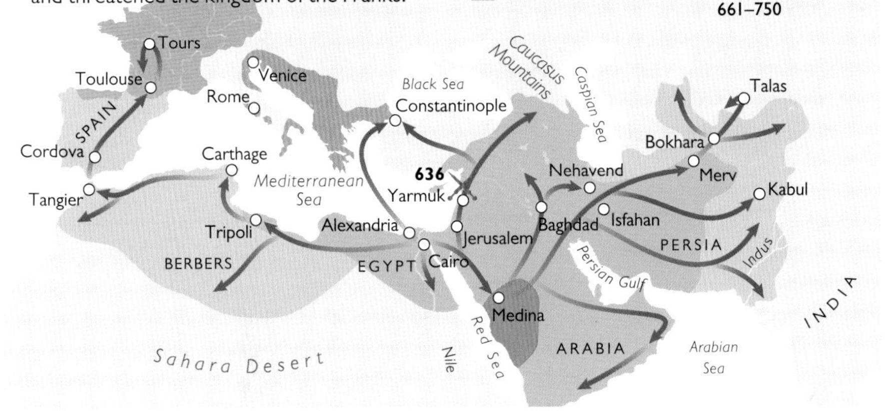
Tours
Toulouse
SPAIN
Cordova
Tangier
Venice
Rome
Carthage
Mediterranean Sea
Tripoli
BERBERS
Alexandria
EGYPT
Cairo
Black Sea
Constantinople
636
Yarmuk
Jerusalem
Caucasus Mountains
Caspian Sea
Nehavend
Baghdad
Isfahan
PERSIA
Persian Gulf
Medina
ARABIA
Red Sea
Nile
Sahara Desert
Arabian Sea
Bokhara
Merv
Talas
Kabul
Indus
INDIA

PITCHED BATTLE

At Yarmuk, the Arab commander Khalid ibn al-Walid drew the Byzantines into a pitched battle, which they preferred to avoid. His tactical skill and the quality of Arab cavalry won the six-day battle.

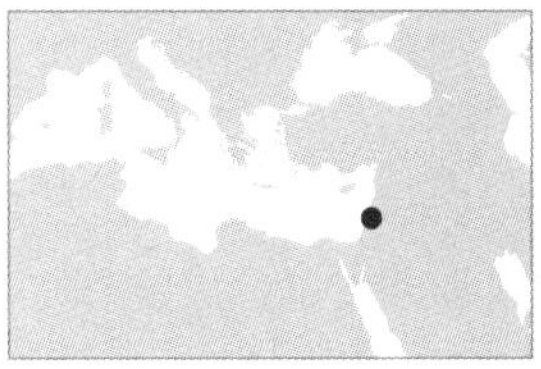

KEY

Bridge

BYZANTINE
- Camp
- Infantry
- Cavalry

MUSLIM
- Camp
- Infantry
- Cavalry
- Cavalry reserve

TIMELINE

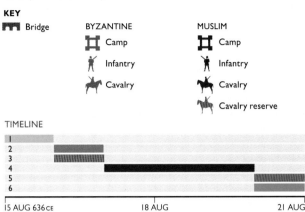

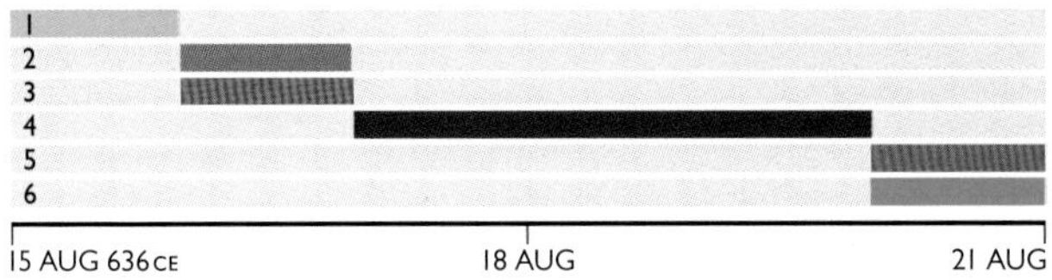
1
2
3
4
5
6
15 AUG 636 CE
18 AUG
21 AUG

ARAB VICTORY

After the Byzantines had been worn down and demoralized by the failure of their repeated attacks, the Arabs routed them through a massed cavalry assault.

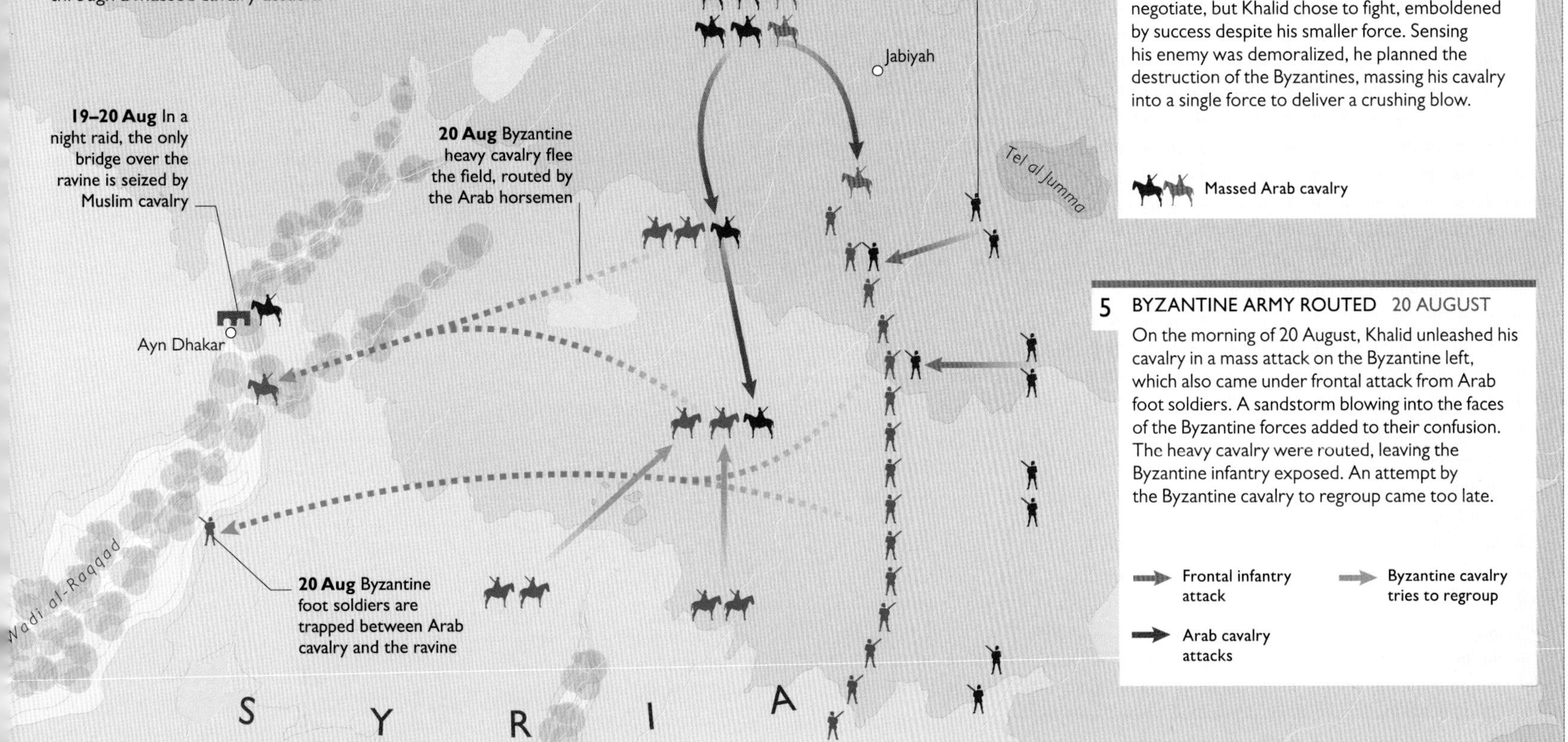
20 Aug Arab foot soldiers drive back the Byzantine flank
Jabiyah
Tel al Jumma
19–20 Aug In a night raid, the only bridge over the ravine is seized by Muslim cavalry
20 Aug Byzantine heavy cavalry flee the field, routed by the Arab horsemen
Ayn Dhakar
Wadi al-Raqqad
20 Aug Byzantine foot soldiers are trapped between Arab cavalry and the ravine
S Y R I A
Wadi al-Allan

4 FIGHTING TO STALEMATE 17–19 AUGUST

The Byzantines repeatedly tried to break the Arab lines, with heavy casualties on both sides. Unable to achieve a breakthrough, Vahan sought to negotiate, but Khalid chose to fight, emboldened by success despite his smaller force. Sensing his enemy was demoralized, he planned the destruction of the Byzantines, massing his cavalry into a single force to deliver a crushing blow.

Massed Arab cavalry

5 BYZANTINE ARMY ROUTED 20 AUGUST

On the morning of 20 August, Khalid unleashed his cavalry in a mass attack on the Byzantine left, which also came under frontal attack from Arab foot soldiers. A sandstorm blowing into the faces of the Byzantine forces added to their confusion. The heavy cavalry were routed, leaving the Byzantine infantry exposed. An attempt by the Byzantine cavalry to regroup came too late.

- Frontal infantry attack
- Byzantine cavalry tries to regroup
- Arab cavalry attacks

6 BYZANTINE INFANTRY FLEE 20 AUGUST

With their left flank routed, many Byzantine soldiers fled the battlefield. By now, Khalid"s forces had taken control of the sole bridge over the deep Wadi al-Raqqad ravine; some Byzantine soldiers plunged to their deaths down its steep cliffs. Their commander, Vahan, was probably killed in the pursuit after the battle, which carried the Arab forces as far as Damascus.

- Byzantine infantry flee

▷ **Byzantine horsemen**
This 6th-century CE ivory carving depicts Byzantine cavalry and infantry. The armoured horsemen were used to break through the enemy's lines and were typically armed with a bow, lance, and sword.

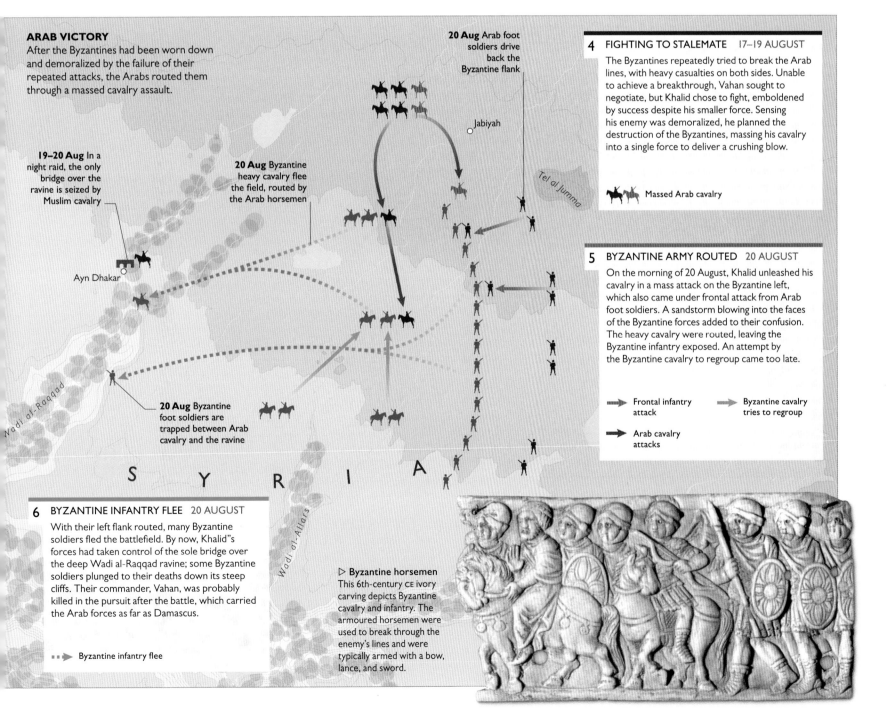

TOURS

Fought in central France in 732 CE, the Battle of Tours (or Poitiers) was a victory for the Christian Franks over the the Umayyad Caliphate. Had the Franks lost, more of Western Europe might have come under the dominance of Islam.

After crossing the straits of Gibraltar from north Africa in 711 CE, the armies of the Muslim Umayyad Caliphate conquered the Iberian peninsula and much of southern France. In 732, Abdul Rahman al-Ghafiqi, the emir of Cordoba, led an army north into the Christian Duchy of Aquitaine. Aquitaine's ruler, Duke Odo, fled and sought help from his old enemy the Franks under the effective leadership of Charles Martel. Martel assembled an army to help Odo in return for Aquitaine accepting Frankish suzerainty. Abdul Rahman met the Frankish army when he was possibly en route to plunder the abbey at Tours; after his defeat, he abandoned campaigning for the year and withdrew. Although the battle was only one episode in the stagnation of Arab expansion, it remains symbolic of the defence of western Christendom.

△ *Grandes Chroniques de France*
This 15th-century depiction of the battle portrays the warriors anachronistically as contemporary knights, including the fleur-de-lys emblem for the Franks

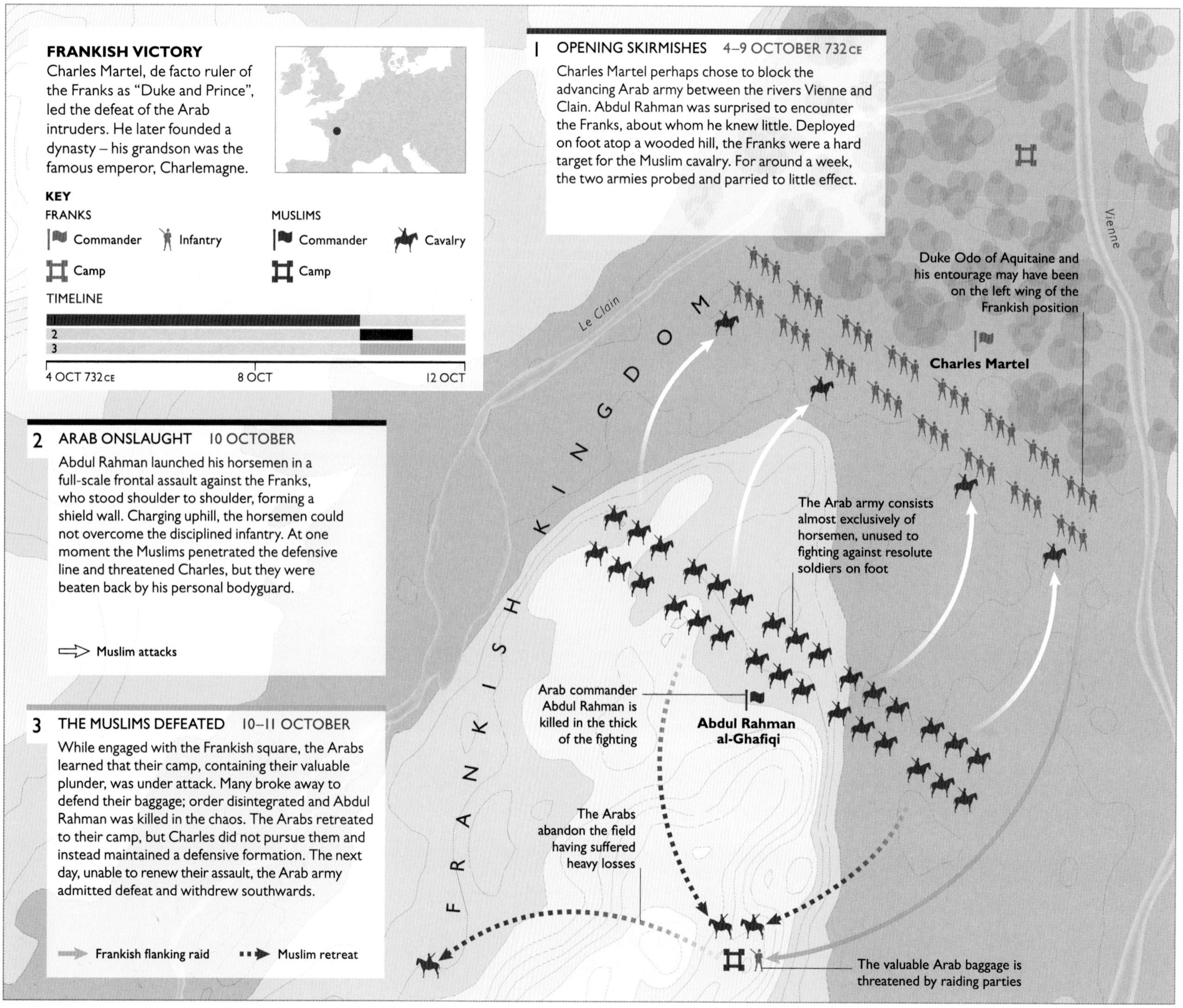

FRANKISH VICTORY
Charles Martel, de facto ruler of the Franks as "Duke and Prince", led the defeat of the Arab intruders. He later founded a dynasty – his grandson was the famous emperor, Charlemagne.
KEY
FRANKS
Commander
Infantry
Camp
MUSLIMS
Commander
Cavalry
Camp
TIMELINE
1
2
3
4 OCT 732 CE
8 OCT
12 OCT
1 OPENING SKIRMISHES 4–9 OCTOBER 732 CE
Charles Martel perhaps chose to block the advancing Arab army between the rivers Vienne and Clain. Abdul Rahman was surprised to encounter the Franks, about whom he knew little. Deployed on foot atop a wooded hill, the Franks were a hard target for the Muslim cavalry. For around a week, the two armies probed and parried to little effect.
2 ARAB ONSLAUGHT 10 OCTOBER
Abdul Rahman launched his horsemen in a full-scale frontal assault against the Franks, who stood shoulder to shoulder, forming a shield wall. Charging uphill, the horsemen could not overcome the disciplined infantry. At one moment the Muslims penetrated the defensive line and threatened Charles, but they were beaten back by his personal bodyguard.
Muslim attacks
3 THE MUSLIMS DEFEATED 10–11 OCTOBER
While engaged with the Frankish square, the Arabs learned that their camp, containing their valuable plunder, was under attack. Many broke away to defend their baggage; order disintegrated and Abdul Rahman was killed in the chaos. The Arabs retreated to their camp, but Charles did not pursue them and instead maintained a defensive formation. The next day, unable to renew their assault, the Arab army admitted defeat and withdrew southwards.
Frankish flanking raid
Muslim retreat
Vienne
Le Clain
FRANKISH KINGDOM
Duke Odo of Aquitaine and his entourage may have been on the left wing of the Frankish position
Charles Martel
The Arab army consists almost exclusively of horsemen, unused to fighting against resolute soldiers on foot
Arab commander Abdul Rahman is killed in the thick of the fighting
Abdul Rahman al-Ghafiqi
The Arabs abandon the field having suffered heavy losses
The valuable Arab baggage is threatened by raiding parties

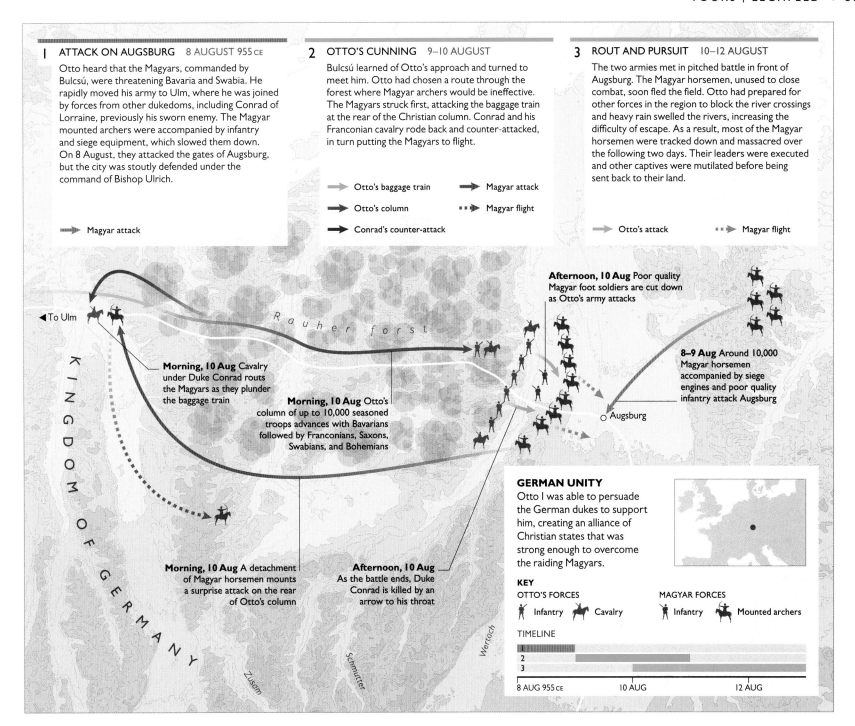

1 ATTACK ON AUGSBURG 8 AUGUST 955 CE

Otto heard that the Magyars, commanded by Bulcsú, were threatening Bavaria and Swabia. He rapidly moved his army to Ulm, where he was joined by forces from other dukedoms, including Conrad of Lorraine, previously his sworn enemy. The Magyar mounted archers were accompanied by infantry and siege equipment, which slowed them down. On 8 August, they attacked the gates of Augsburg, but the city was stoutly defended under the command of Bishop Ulrich.

Magyar attack

2 OTTO'S CUNNING 9–10 AUGUST

Bulcsú learned of Otto's approach and turned to meet him. Otto had chosen a route through the forest where Magyar archers would be ineffective. The Magyars struck first, attacking the baggage train at the rear of the Christian column. Conrad and his Franconian cavalry rode back and counter-attacked, in turn putting the Magyars to flight.

Otto's baggage train
Magyar attack
Otto's column
Magyar flight
Conrad's counter-attack

3 ROUT AND PURSUIT 10–12 AUGUST

The two armies met in pitched battle in front of Augsburg. The Magyar horsemen, unused to close combat, soon fled the field. Otto had prepared for other forces in the region to block the river crossings and heavy rain swelled the rivers, increasing the difficulty of escape. As a result, most of the Magyar horsemen were tracked down and massacred over the following two days. Their leaders were executed and other captives were mutilated before being sent back to their land.

Otto's attack
Magyar flight

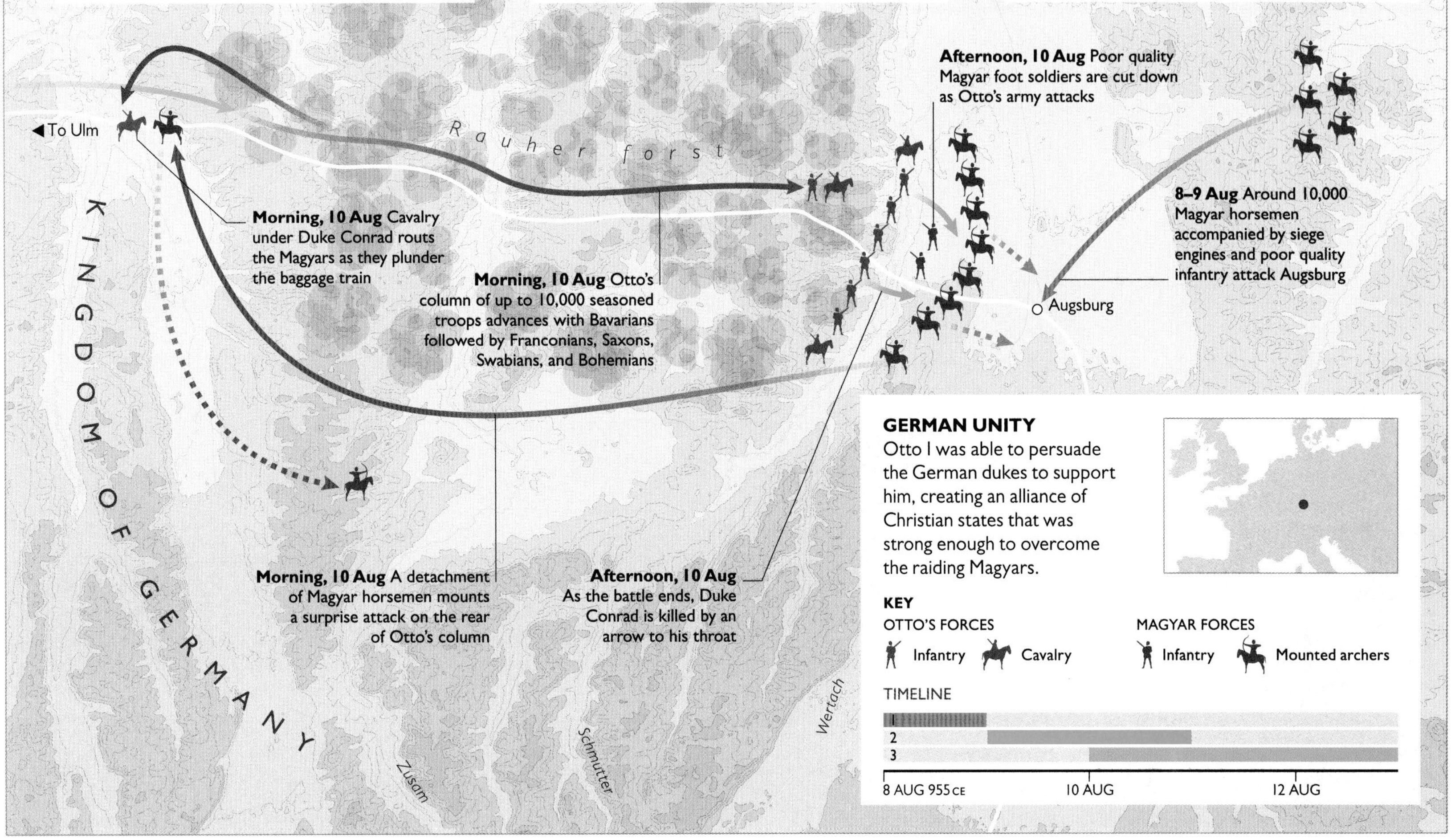

◀ To Ulm
Rauher forst
KINGDOM OF GERMANY
Morning, 10 Aug Cavalry under Duke Conrad routs the Magyars as they plunder the baggage train
Morning, 10 Aug Otto's column of up to 10,000 seasoned troops advances with Bavarians followed by Franconians, Saxons, Swabians, and Bohemians
Afternoon, 10 Aug Poor quality Magyar foot soldiers are cut down as Otto's army attacks
8–9 Aug Around 10,000 Magyar horsemen accompanied by siege engines and poor quality infantry attack Augsburg
Augsburg
Morning, 10 Aug A detachment of Magyar horsemen mounts a surprise attack on the rear of Otto's column
Afternoon, 10 Aug As the battle ends, Duke Conrad is killed by an arrow to his throat
Zusam
Schmutter
Wertach
GERMAN UNITY
Otto I was able to persuade the German dukes to support him, creating an alliance of Christian states that was strong enough to overcome the raiding Magyars.
KEY
OTTO'S FORCES
Infantry
Cavalry
MAGYAR FORCES
Infantry
Mounted archers
TIMELINE
1
2
3
8 AUG 955 CE
10 AUG
12 AUG

LECHFELD

In 955 CE, an army led by German king Otto I defeated nomadic Magyar horsemen, who had been terrorizing Europe. The battle set Otto on course to become Holy Roman Emperor, and eventually led the Magyars to found the Christian kingdom of Hungary.

The Magyars were a nomadic steppe people who migrated to modern-day Hungary around 900 CE. Their horsemen repeatedly swept through Germany and other areas of Christian Europe to plunder towns and villages. The Magyars benefited from the break-up of the Carolingian Empire, which in the late 8th and early 9th century had united France, Germany, and northern Italy. Fragmented, these areas could not field an army capable of defeating the raiding horsemen. In 936 Otto I, Duke of Saxony, was crowned king of Germany. His ambition was to recreate Charlemagne's empire. In 954, while Otto fought to assert his authority over rebellious German dukes, the Magyars raided unchecked. The following year they returned, intending to seize the wealthy city of Augsburg. Otto, who had persuaded the German dukes to follow his banner, was able to crush the invaders at Lechfeld, and went on to impose his rule on Italy as well as Germany. In 962, he was crowned Holy Roman Emperor by the pope. The Magyars, no longer able to mount profitable raids, became a settled people and converted to Christianity, founding the kingdom of Hungary in 1001.

DIRECTORY: BEFORE 1000 CE

SIEGE OF LACHISH

701 BCE

The Assyrian attack on the Judaean walled city of Lachish is the earliest siege about which detailed information is available. As the greatest military power in West Asia, Assyria claimed suzerainty over the Israelite Kingdom of Judah. In 701 BCE, its King Sennacherib (r.705–681) led an army to Judah to punish the Judaean king Hezekiah for rebelling against Assyrian authority.

Friezes carved on the walls of King Sennacherib's palace at Nineveh, in modern-day Iraq, show the siege techniques the Assyrians used against the Judaeans. The carvings portray archers and stone-slingers bombarding the defenders on the battlements as other soldiers were building an earthen ramp against one of the city walls. A wheeled siege engine with a ram was pushed up the ramp in order to break open the fortifications while soldiers scaled ladders to assault the walls. After the city was taken, the Assyrians exacted a fierce vengeance. The Nineveh friezes show Judaeans tortured and massacred, the city looted, and its population led into captivity. In the same year, however, Sennacherib failed to capture the Judaean capital city of Jerusalem.

△ Friezes at the Assyrian royal palace at Nineveh detailing scenes from the siege

THE SICILIAN EXPEDITION

415–413 BCE

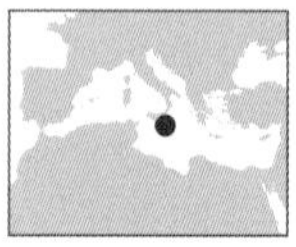

The Athenian seaborne expedition to Sicily set sail in 415 BCE. It proved to be a turning point in the Peloponnesian War (431–404 BCE). The war was a prolonged struggle for supremacy between the two most powerful city-states in Ancient Greece: Athens and Sparta.

The Athenians targeted Syracuse, a Greek city in Sicily, that owed allegiance to the Spartans and provided them with a major part of their grain supply. The cautious Athenian commander Nicias eventually began a lengthy siege, and Athens accepted his request for major reinforcements. The Athenian fleet occupied Syracuse's Grand Harbour and the soldiers began building a surrounding wall to isolate the city. The wall, however, was never completed, and the Spartans succeeded in reinforcing the city's defences. By 413 BCE, the tables had started to turn. The Athenians had begun to face a critical shortage of supplies, and in September, they decided to abandon the siege. However, the Spartans destroyed their fleet and in desperation Nicias attempted – in vain – to withdraw his land forces. Harassed by the enemy, the surviving Athenians finally surrendered. Athens fought on in the Aegean for nine years but was eventually blockaded into surrender.

THE CHANGPING CAMPAIGN

262–260 BCE

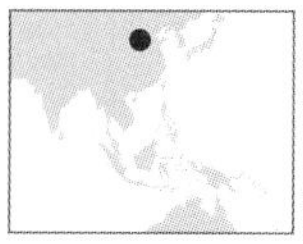

The kingdoms of Qin and Zhao were the strongest of the states into which China was divided in the 3rd century BCE. Both fielded massive armies of foot soldiers and cavalry. In 265 BCE, the Qin ruler Zhaoxiang attacked a town in Shandang, an area controlled by the weaker state of Han; the Zhao ruler Xiaucheng sent his forces to support Han. In 262 BCE, the Zhao army clashed with the Qin forces at Changping, in modern-day Shanxi province, and a stalemate ensued. Xiaucheng replaced his cautious commander Lian Po with the more aggressive Zhao Kuo in 260 BCE. The new general led his army into a rash attack on the Qin's fortified position. The Qin commander Bai Qi used his cavalry to encircle the advancing Zhao army. After a 46-day-long siege and a number of failed breakout attempts, the Zhao army surrendered. Bai Qi massacred almost the entire force. Within 40 years, the Qin unified China under its First Emperor.

ZAMA

202 BCE

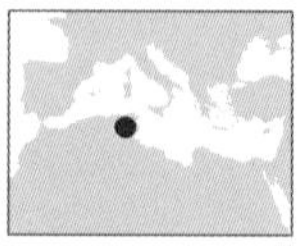

The Battle of Zama, in modern-day Tunisia, was the final encounter of the Second Punic War (218–201 BCE) fought between the Roman Republic and Carthage, a north African city-state. A Carthaginian army led by Hannibal had set out to invade Italy in 218 BCE. Hannibal occupied the south of Italy for more than a decade but failed to subdue Rome.

In 204 BCE, a Roman army under Publius Cornelius Scipio landed in north Africa and threatened Carthage. In desperation the Carthaginians recalled Hannibal's army from Italy. Hannibal advanced to meet Scipio, who confidently accepted battle. The conflict opened with a charge by the Carthaginian war elephants. Harassed by skirmishers, the animals were driven off through corridors deliberately left open in the ranks of the Roman infantry. The foot soldiers then engaged in a brutal contest that resulted in heavy losses on both sides. Meanwhile, the Roman cavalry drove the Carthaginian horsemen far from the field. Returning from the pursuit, they attacked the Carthaginian infantry from the rear, initiating a rout. Hannibal's army was destroyed and Carthage accepted a humiliating peace. Hannibal was driven into exile, and Rome took a major stride towards creating an empire.

△ 17th-century tapestry depicting elephant-riding Carthaginians charging the Romans

PHARSALUS

9 AUGUST 48 BCE

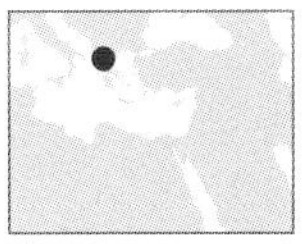

The Battle of Pharsalus was a key step in the quest by Roman general Julius Caesar to achieve supreme power in the Roman Republic. After years of successful campaigning against the Celtic tribes of Gaul (modern France and Belgium) in 49 BCE Caesar led his army across the River Rubicon into Italy and towards Rome, triggering a civil war. Pompey the Great, the most powerful figure in Rome at the time, withdrew to Greece, where he organized a new army. Caesar meanwhile defeated his old army in Spain.

The following year, Caesar sailed across the Adriatic Sea in pursuit of his rival. Pompey fared better than Caesar at an initial confrontation at Dyrrachium, but he failed to capitalize on his success. Short of supplies, Caesar marched into Thessaly, Greece, shadowed by Pompey's army, which outnumbered his forces by two to one. Pompey finally took the risk of engaging Caesar at Pharsalus. He planned to pin Caesar's veteran legionaries with his larger but inexperienced infantry and simultaneously send his superior cavalry, in a flanking move, to attack the legionaries from the rear. However, Caesar deployed skirmishers and infantry reserves to repel the Pompeian cavalry while driving his legionaries relentlessly forward to crush the main body of his enemy's infantry. Pompey fled to Egypt, where he was murdered, and Caesar rose to be dictator of Rome before his assasinantion in 44 BCE.

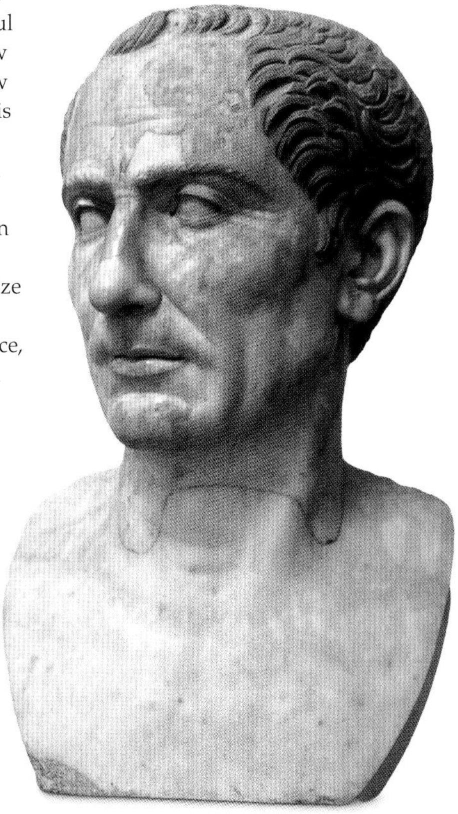

▷ Marble bust of Julius Caesar

WUZHANG PLAINS

234 CE

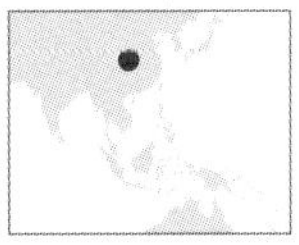

After the fall of the Han dynasty in 220 CE, China was split between the warring kingdoms of Shu Han in the southwest, Sun Wu in the southeast, and Cao Wei in the north. The renowned Shu Han chancellor and general Zhuge Liang led a series of Northern Expeditions to attack Cao Wei. The battle fought on the Wuzhang Plains, in modern-day Shaanxi province, was the climax of his fifth and final northern campaign.

The large Shu Han army advanced to the River Wei, where they were confronted by the massed soldiers of the Cao Wei army already arrayed in defensive positions. After initial raids and skirmishes, the battle settled into a stalemate. Despite the provocations and insults hurled by Zhuge Liang, the Cao Wei emperor Cao Rui prohibited his commander Sima Yi from engaging. Far from their supply base, the Shu Han soldiers turned to farming to keep themselves fed. The standoff continued for more than 100 days until Zhuge Liang died in his camp, exhausted by years of warfare, and the demoralized Shu Han army retreated. However, Sima Yi did not attack even during the withdrawal, fearing that the news of Zhuge Liang's death might be a deception.

The battle at Wuzhang Plains is celebrated by historians as an example of a victory achieved through the refusal to fight. Within 30 years of Cao Wei's bloodless triumph, Sima Yi's grandson founded the Jin Dynasty.

MILVIAN BRIDGE

28 OCTOBER 312 CE

The clash at the Milvian Bridge between Constantine and Maxentius, rivals for power in the Roman Empire, was a key moment in the rise of Christianity as a world religion. In 306 CE, Constantine had been declared emperor in York, England, while in the same year Maxentius was proclaimed emperor in the city of Rome itself.

In 312, Constantine led an army to challenge Maxentius, who somewhat uncharacteristically accepted open battle near Rome. Maxentius's troops had their backs to the River Tiber, which was crossed by the partially dismantled Milvian Bridge and an improvised bridge of boats. Although Constantine was not a Christian at the time, later accounts claim that the night before the battle, he had a vision that convinced him that fighting under the protection of the Christian God would bring him victory on the battlefield.

The battle that took place the following day was relatively brief. Constantine's infantry and cavalry charged, throwing Maxentius's forces into disarray. The latter's panicked soldiers attempted to withdraw to the city walls across the river, but were drowned as the bridge collapsed. Maxentius was among those killed. The next day, Constantine occupied the city of Rome and Maxentius's severed head was paraded through the streets. Constantine converted to Christianity during his subsequent reign, and the religion began its transformation from a repressed minority sect into the dominant religion of the Roman world.

THE SIEGE OF CONSTANTINOPLE

JULY 717–AUGUST 718 CE

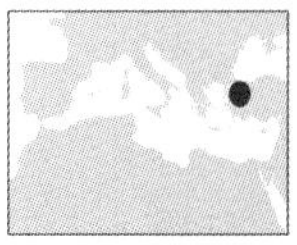

The failure of the siege of Constantinople by the forces of the Arab Umayyad caliphate checked almost a century of Muslim expansion, and ensured the continued survival of the Christian Byzantine Empire for another seven centuries. The defence of the Byzantine capital was led by Emperor Leo the Isaurian, who had only recently usurped the throne in 717 CE (with Arab connivance). The Arab forces were led by the experienced general Maslama ibn Abd al-Malik. The city was besieged both by land and sea: a large army crossed the Hellespont from Asia while a fleet entered the Bosphorus.

However, the naval blockade was crippled by Byzantine ships armed with Greek fire, an early form of flame-throwing weapon, and one against which the Muslims had no defence. As a result, through the hard winter of 717–718 CE, the city was amply supplied by sea, but the Arab besiegers suffered from food shortages, exposure to harsh weather, and the ravages of disease. In the spring, attempts to reinforce the siege failed as fresh Arab land and naval forces were intercepted and defeated by the Byzantines on their way to Constantinople. This, coupled with the intervention of the Bulgar army in the summer of 718, who attacked the Arabs from the north, convinced Maslama that he must withdraw. Constantinople would not finally fall into Muslim hands until much later, in 1453 (see p.96).

△ Illustration from a 12th-century manuscript showing Byzantines in battle using Greek fire against enemy ships

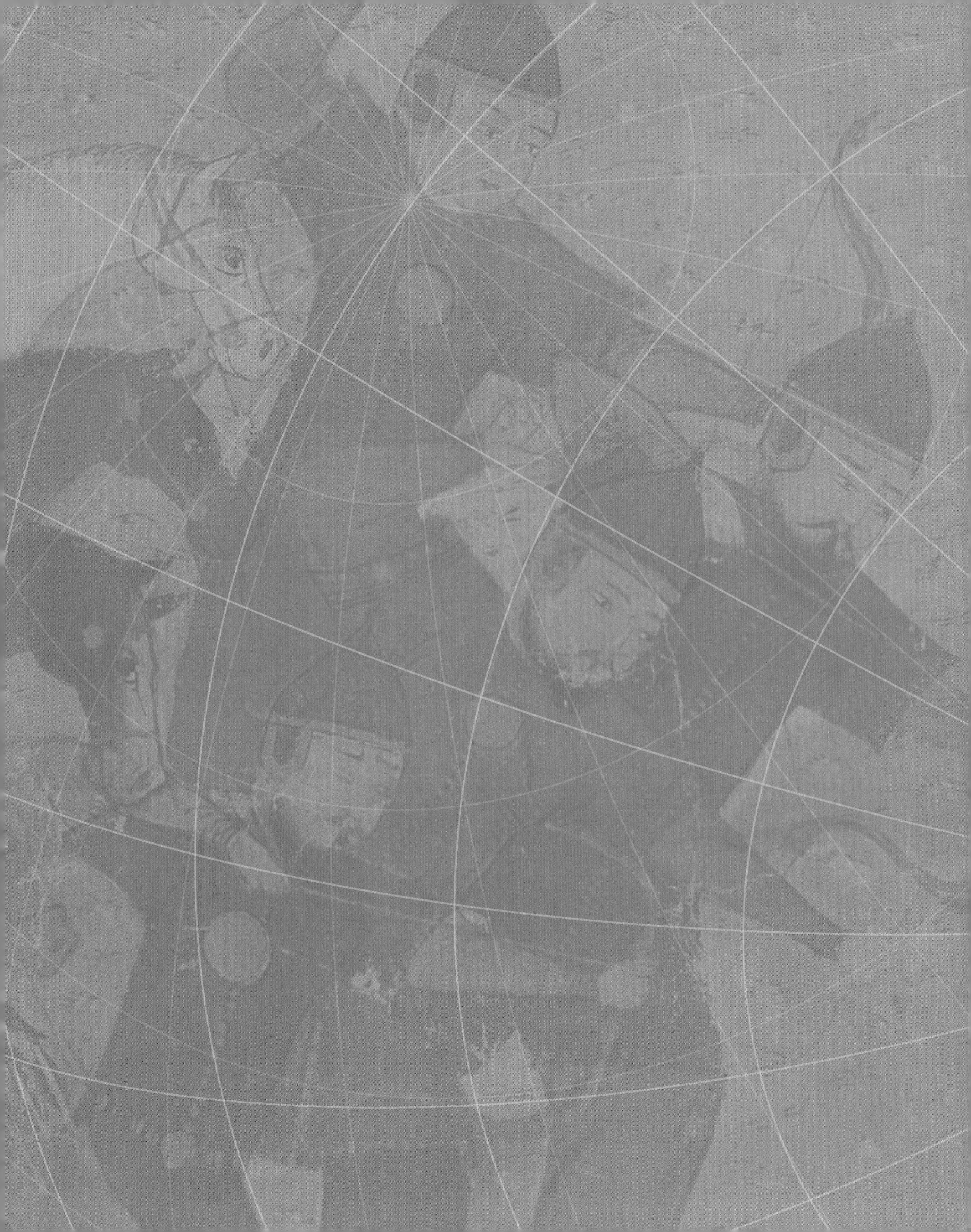

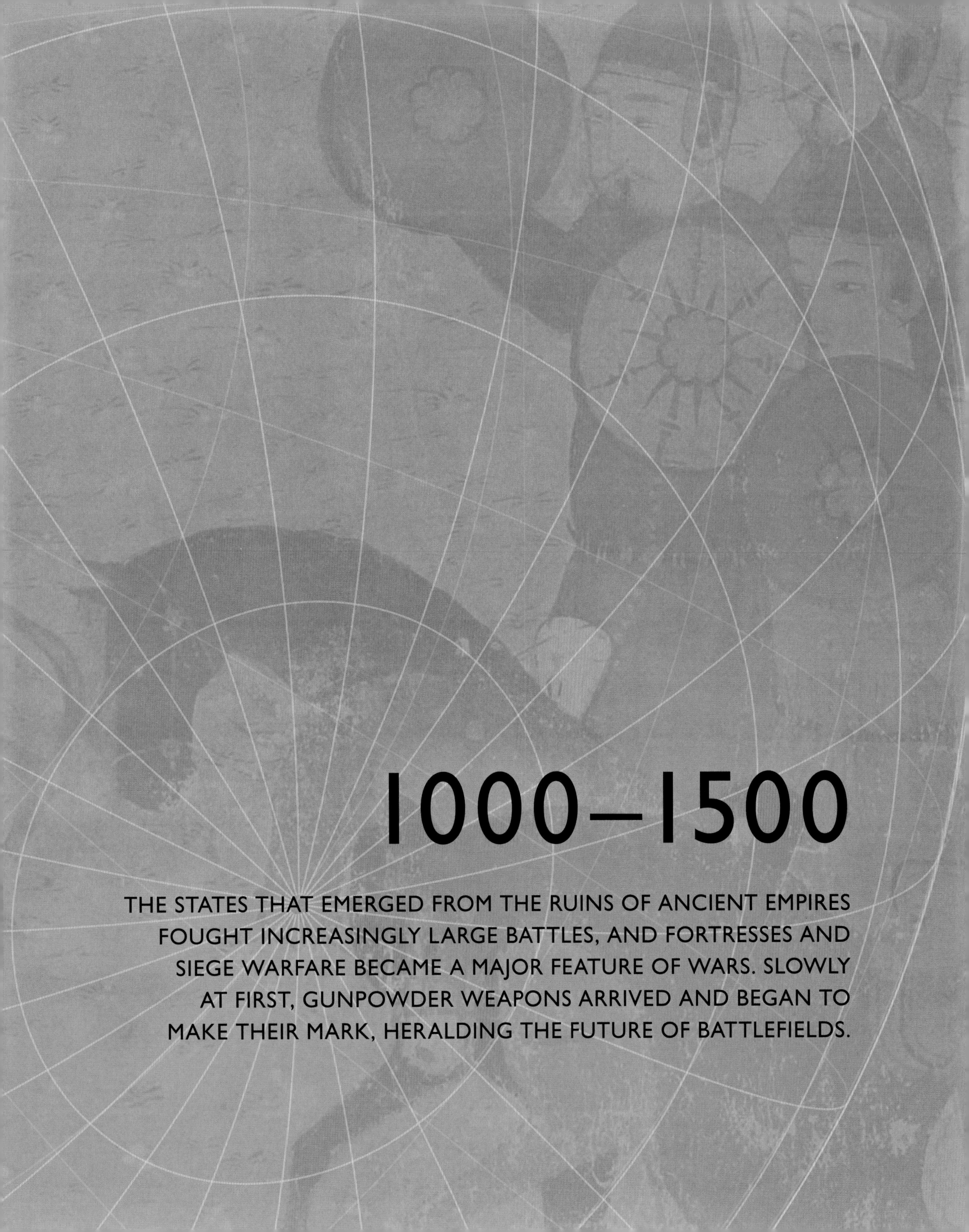

1000–1500

THE STATES THAT EMERGED FROM THE RUINS OF ANCIENT EMPIRES FOUGHT INCREASINGLY LARGE BATTLES, AND FORTRESSES AND SIEGE WARFARE BECAME A MAJOR FEATURE OF WARS. SLOWLY AT FIRST, GUNPOWDER WEAPONS ARRIVED AND BEGAN TO MAKE THEIR MARK, HERALDING THE FUTURE OF BATTLEFIELDS.

1000–1500

From 1000 CE onwards, mounted warriors dominated battlefields, but territorial gains were won more often by siege warfare than field battles. Gradually, the balance shifted as the longbow, the pike, and the first gunpowder weapons made larger infantry-driven armies predominant among more centralized states.

By the 11th century, most European states relied on a central core of household troops for their defence. These troops were supported by a feudal system in which nobles provided the state with a number of mounted warriors in return for holding land, supplemented by peasant levies. Although the mounted knights made for a fearsome sight in battle, the infantry could resist cavalry attacks by presenting a wall of shields, as at the Battle of Hastings (see pp.58–59), or a bristling hedgehog of spears.

Feudal armies were only obliged to serve for periods of around 40 days and found it hard to assault strong fortifications directly. Stone forts and walled cities grew in number, particularly as a means to control newly conquered territory – for example in the Norman conquest of England after 1066. Sieges, using engines such as onagers – catapults that hurled heavy stones – portable siege towers, and battering rams were an essential part of medieval warfare, though starving out the defenders by blockading their supply lines often proved more effective.

The European states saw their first war of expansion during the Crusades, from the late 11th century. They found that the Muslim armies' tactics of harrying the Crusader knights with mounted archers took away the shock induced by the imposing sight of an armoured cavalry charge, and gained the Muslims victories, such as one at Hattin (see p.69) that eventually led to the reconquest of Jerusalem. However, both the Muslim and the Christian European states soon had to face an even more formidable foe in the Mongol empire (see pp.78–79). The Mongols' military organization, mounted archers, and ruthlessness won them a massive Eurasian empire, and devastated both the Muslim Abbasid Caliphate and eastern European states alike.

▽ **Archers at war**
This 15th-century illumination from the *St Albans Chronicle* shows English longbowmen repelling the attack of the French knights at the Battle of Agincourt in 1415 (see pp.90–91).

△ **Siege engine**
Medieval torsion catapults, such as this replica, could inflict serious casualties on the defenders of castles. However, unless striking at a weakened point, they were unlikely to create a breach in the castle's walls.

The rise of the infantry

In Europe, infantry began to assert itself on the battlefield. The spread of the crossbow and longbow (see pp.84–85) in the late 13th century gave foot soldiers greater attacking power as they could now fire arrows capable of penetrating the chain armour of knights. This led to the development of plate armour, which, while stronger, was expensive and

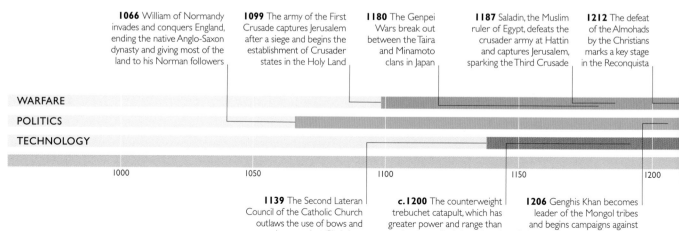

SHIFTING ROLES

Although knights dominated the literature of the Middle Ages, infantry formed a vital part of armies. As states became more organized and new weaponry was developed, the armies came to rely at least as much on infantry as on the previously dominant mounted warriors. With increased resources, states fought larger battles, and civil wars between competing clans and factions became more common.

WARFARE
POLITICS
TECHNOLOGY

1000 | 1050 | 1100 | 1150 | 1200

1066 William of Normandy invades and conquers England, ending the native Anglo-Saxon dynasty and giving most of the land to his Norman followers

1099 The army of the First Crusade captures Jerusalem after a siege and begins the establishment of Crusader states in the Holy Land

1139 The Second Lateran Council of the Catholic Church outlaws the use of bows and crossbows against Christians

1180 The Genpei Wars break out between the Taira and Minamoto clans in Japan

1187 Saladin, the Muslim ruler of Egypt, defeats the crusader army at Hattin and captures Jerusalem, sparking the Third Crusade

c.1200 The counterweight trebuchet catapult, which has greater power and range than torsion catapults, is introduced

1206 Genghis Khan becomes leader of the Mongol tribes and begins campaigns against China and Central Asian powers

1212 The defeat of the Almohads by the Christians marks a key stage in the Reconquista

> *"By the disposition of God who orders all things, the art of war, the flower of knighthood, with horses and chargers of the finest, fell before… the common folk and foot soldiers of Flanders."*
>
> *THE ANNALS OF GHENT*, ACCOUNT OF THE BATTLE OF COURTRAI, 1302

△ **Heavy protection**
The sallet, with extended cheek protection and a flange at the back to guard the neck, became popular in the 15th century, with open face versions also used by archers and crossbowmen.

unwieldy, and did not allow armoured cavalry to regain the dominance in battle that they had once enjoyed. Armies raised by increasingly assertive towns could now win victories with pikes and spears. At Courtrai (see p.98), for example, the townspeople of Flanders defeated an army of French knights.

The Hundred Years War (1337–1453) between England and France saw a new style of mixed armies in which infantry predominated. While the French persisted at first with the old tactics of mounted charges, the English dismounted to meet them and their longbowmen exacted a terrible toll on the French nobility at Crécy (see pp.82–83) and Agincourt (see pp.90–91).

The bow and pike had only newly supplanted the lance and sword in battle when new gunpowder weapons began to appear that would ultimately replace them and revolutionize warfare. By the 1130s, the armies of China's Song dynasty had developed "fire-lances" which shot gunpowder-fuelled projectiles. Their use soon became widespread, with larger versions employed during sieges. Gunpowder weapons appeared in Europe after 1326 as early cannons came in use in Italy. The development of cast-iron barrels and iron cannon balls by the 1450s meant cannons were able, for the first time, to destroy city walls. Although hand-held guns were still primitive and unwieldy, and traditional forms of warfare persisted in regions such as India and Japan, in Europe the battlefield stood on the edge of the gunpowder era.

▷ **Battle at sea**
In this 19th-century painting by Utagawa Kuniyoshi, the ghosts of the Japanese Taira clan defeated at the Battle of Dan-no-ura (see p.68) seek vengeance on a ship carrying the Minamoto clan victor Yoshitsune.

1279 Kublai Khan completes the conquest of southern China, bringing the whole country under the Mongol Yuan dynasty's rule

1314 Scottish king Robert Bruce defeats Edward II of England at Bannockburn to help secure the independence of Scotland

1337 The Hundred Years War breaks out between England and France

1346 The earliest significant use of war cannons in Europe takes place at the Battle of Crécy

1363 A law makes it obligatory for all Englishmen to practice using longbows every Sunday

c.1400 The invention of corned (grained) gunpowder makes cannons more reliable as they ignite more easily

1415 English longbowmen inflict a devastating defeat on the French at Agincourt

1453 Constantinople falls to the Ottoman Sultan Mehmed II, bringing the Byzantine Empire to an end

1492 Granada's capture marks the end of the Reconquista and Spain returns to Christian rule

1250 | 1300 | 1350 | 1400 | 1450 | 1500

HASTINGS

In late September 1066, Duke William of Normandy crossed the English Channel to assert his claim to the throne of England. Two weeks later, near Hastings, he defeated an Anglo-Saxon army that had just repelled another invasion in the north. The death of the English king Harold late in the battle crowned William's victory.

The death of the childless Edward the Confessor in January 1066 ignited a struggle for the succession to the English throne. Duke William of Normandy claimed that the late king had promised him the crown, while Harald Hardrada, king of Norway, maintained he had inherited a right to it from the Danish kings who preceded Edward. When the Anglo-Saxon nobility instead chose Harold Godwinson, Edward's brother-in-law, as king, both the other claimants planned invasions to secure their rights. Hardrada struck first, landing in the north with a force that included Harold's estranged brother Tostig. Although Hardrada won an initial victory at Fulford against the local Anglo-Saxon earls, his death at Stamford Bridge on 25 September ended the threat of a Norwegian conquest.

Harold made a forced march south to resume his guard against the threatened Norman invasion, but learnt that the Norman army had landed on the south coast in his absence. His death at the Battle of Hastings on 14 October (together with his brothers Leofwine and Gyrth, who might have succeeded him) left the English leaderless. An attempt to rally around Edgar the Aetheling, the remaining Anglo-Saxon prince, failed as he was too young to rule, and, after a slow march to London, William entered in triumph and was crowned king on Christmas Day.

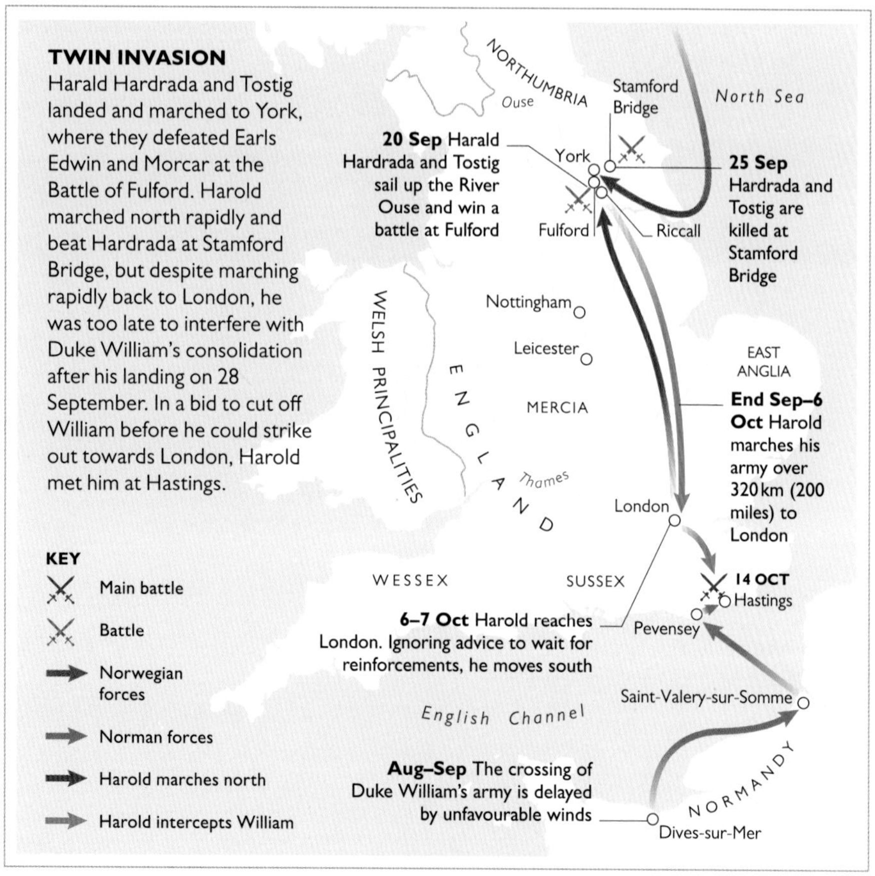
NORTHUMBRIA
Ouse
Stamford Bridge
North Sea
20 Sep Harald Hardrada and Tostig sail up the River Ouse and win a battle at Fulford
York
Fulford
Riccall
25 Sep Hardrada and Tostig are killed at Stamford Bridge
Nottingham
Leicester
WELSH PRINCIPALITIES
ENGLAND
MERCIA
EAST ANGLIA
End Sep–6 Oct Harold marches his army over 320 km (200 miles) to London
Thames
London
WESSEX
SUSSEX
14 OCT Hastings
6–7 Oct Harold reaches London. Ignoring advice to wait for reinforcements, he moves south
Pevensey
Saint-Valery-sur-Somme
English Channel
Aug–Sep The crossing of Duke William's army is delayed by unfavourable winds
NORMANDY
Dives-sur-Mer
KEY
Main battle
Battle
Norwegian forces
Norman forces
Harold marches north
Harold intercepts William

TWIN INVASION
Harald Hardrada and Tostig landed and marched to York, where they defeated Earls Edwin and Morcar at the Battle of Fulford. Harold marched north rapidly and beat Hardrada at Stamford Bridge, but despite marching rapidly back to London, he was too late to interfere with Duke William's consolidation after his landing on 28 September. In a bid to cut off William before he could strike out towards London, Harold met him at Hastings.

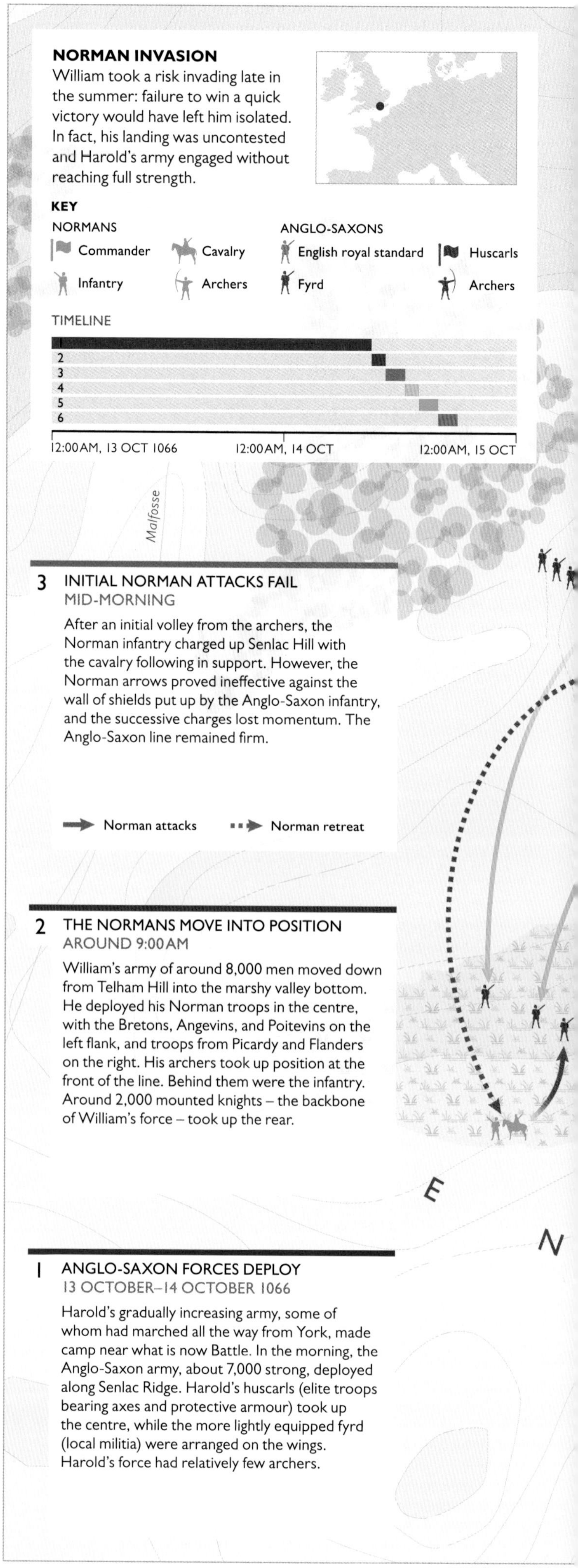
KEY
NORMANS
Commander
Cavalry
Infantry
Archers
ANGLO-SAXONS
English royal standard
Huscarls
Fyrd
Archers
TIMELINE
1
2
3
4
5
6
12:00AM, 13 OCT 1066
12:00AM, 14 OCT
12:00AM, 15 OCT
Malfosse
Norman attacks
Norman retreat
E
N

NORMAN INVASION
William took a risk invading late in the summer: failure to win a quick victory would have left him isolated. In fact, his landing was uncontested and Harold's army engaged without reaching full strength.

3 INITIAL NORMAN ATTACKS FAIL
MID-MORNING
After an initial volley from the archers, the Norman infantry charged up Senlac Hill with the cavalry following in support. However, the Norman arrows proved ineffective against the wall of shields put up by the Anglo-Saxon infantry, and the successive charges lost momentum. The Anglo-Saxon line remained firm.

2 THE NORMANS MOVE INTO POSITION
AROUND 9:00AM
William's army of around 8,000 men moved down from Telham Hill into the marshy valley bottom. He deployed his Norman troops in the centre, with the Bretons, Angevins, and Poitevins on the left flank, and troops from Picardy and Flanders on the right. His archers took up position at the front of the line. Behind them were the infantry. Around 2,000 mounted knights – the backbone of William's force – took up the rear.

1 ANGLO-SAXON FORCES DEPLOY
13 OCTOBER–14 OCTOBER 1066
Harold's gradually increasing army, some of whom had marched all the way from York, made camp near what is now Battle. In the morning, the Anglo-Saxon army, about 7,000 strong, deployed along Senlac Ridge. Harold's huscarls (elite troops bearing axes and protective armour) took up the centre, while the more lightly equipped fyrd (local militia) were arranged on the wings. Harold's force had relatively few archers.

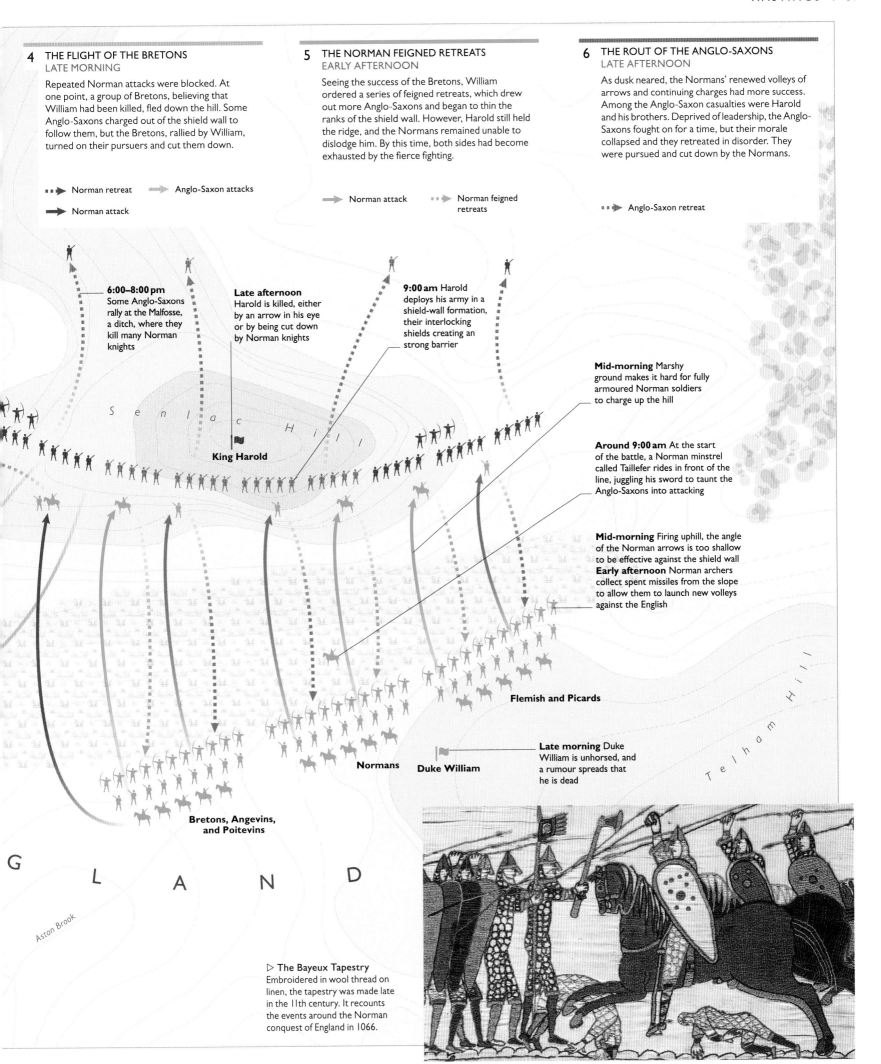

4 THE FLIGHT OF THE BRETONS
LATE MORNING

Repeated Norman attacks were blocked. At one point, a group of Bretons, believing that William had been killed, fled down the hill. Some Anglo-Saxons charged out of the shield wall to follow them, but the Bretons, rallied by William, turned on their pursuers and cut them down.

Norman retreat
Anglo-Saxon attacks
Norman attack

5 THE NORMAN FEIGNED RETREATS
EARLY AFTERNOON

Seeing the success of the Bretons, William ordered a series of feigned retreats, which drew out more Anglo-Saxons and began to thin the ranks of the shield wall. However, Harold still held the ridge, and the Normans remained unable to dislodge him. By this time, both sides had become exhausted by the fierce fighting.

Norman attack
Norman feigned retreats

6 THE ROUT OF THE ANGLO-SAXONS
LATE AFTERNOON

As dusk neared, the Normans' renewed volleys of arrows and continuing charges had more success. Among the Anglo-Saxon casualties were Harold and his brothers. Deprived of leadership, the Anglo-Saxons fought on for a time, but their morale collapsed and they retreated in disorder. They were pursued and cut down by the Normans.

Anglo-Saxon retreat

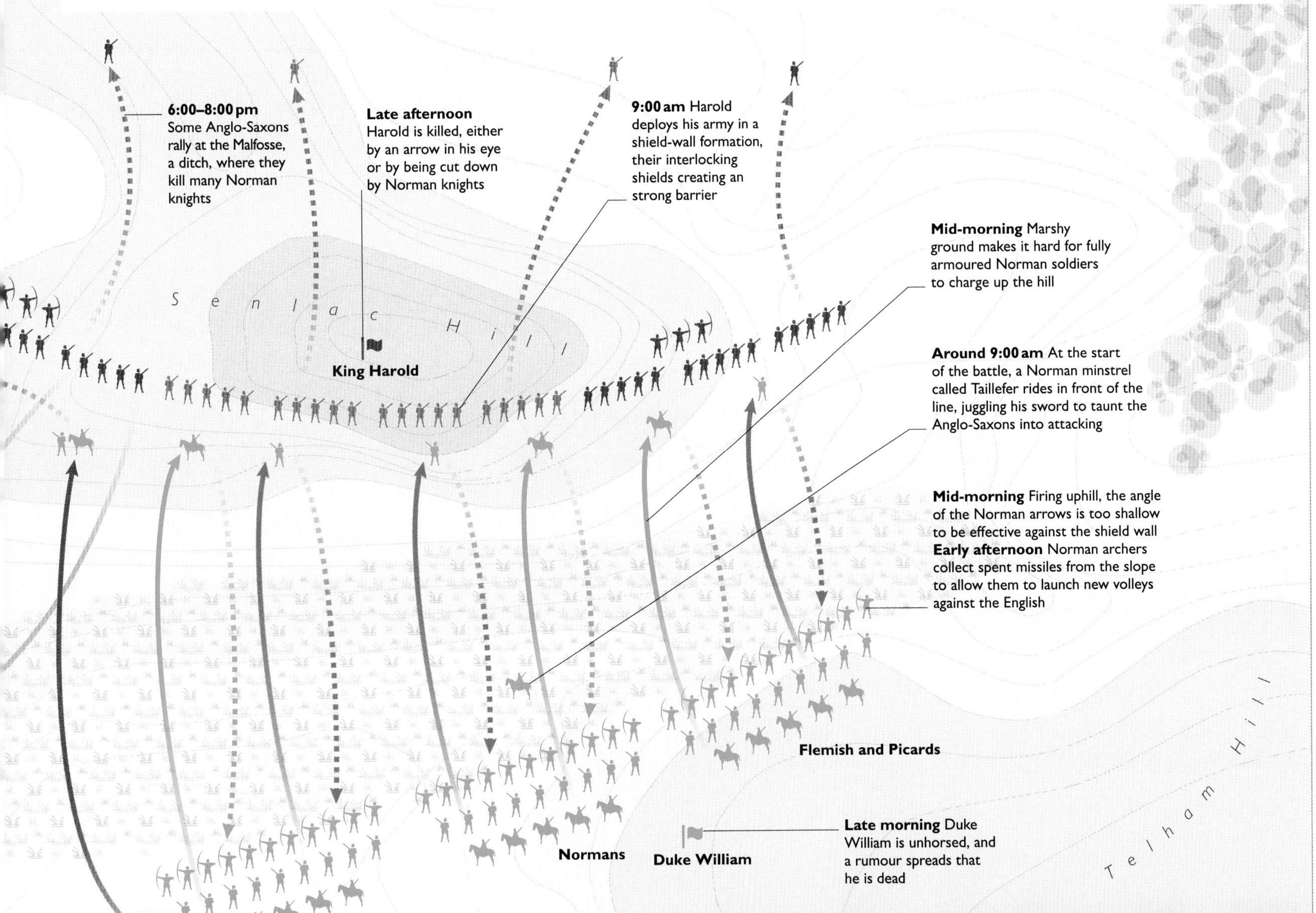

6:00–8:00 pm Some Anglo-Saxons rally at the Malfosse, a ditch, where they kill many Norman knights
Late afternoon Harold is killed, either by an arrow in his eye or by being cut down by Norman knights
9:00 am Harold deploys his army in a shield-wall formation, their interlocking shields creating an strong barrier
Mid-morning Marshy ground makes it hard for fully armoured Norman soldiers to charge up the hill
Senlac Hill
King Harold
Around 9:00 am At the start of the battle, a Norman minstrel called Taillefer rides in front of the line, juggling his sword to taunt the Anglo-Saxons into attacking
Mid-morning Firing uphill, the angle of the Norman arrows is too shallow to be effective against the shield wall
Early afternoon Norman archers collect spent missiles from the slope to allow them to launch new volleys against the English
Flemish and Picards
Telham Hill
Normans
Duke William
Late morning Duke William is unhorsed, and a rumour spreads that he is dead
Bretons, Angevins, and Poitevins
G L A N D
Aston Brook

▷ **The Bayeux Tapestry**
Embroidered in wool thread on linen, the tapestry was made late in the 11th century. It recounts the events around the Norman conquest of England in 1066.

THE NORMANS

In 911 CE, Charles III of France granted the land of Normandy to Rollo, a Norseman, and his followers. Adopting French customs, they became the Normans and emerged as major players in medieval Europe.

△ **Combat helmet**
This is a typical Norman helmet with a nose guard, from the 12–13th centuries. Similar helmets were common in Western and Central Europe.

In the Anglo-Saxon world, the Normans are usually associated with the Norman Conquest, the Battle of Hastings (see pp.58–59), the creation of the medieval kingdom of England, and the English king's claims on a part of France. However, they were also active in southern Italy and the Levant (modern-day western Asia).

Expanding their horizons

The Norsemen went on to adopt Christianity and the French language, and also the French preference for mounted combat. Norman knights, either serving under their lords or as mercenaries, became a common feature of warfare in Europe. The Normans arrived in the Mediterranean as mercenaries for the Byzantine Empire, the Pope, and the local Lombard states. Under Robert Guiscard (*c.*1015–85), they carved out a large empire, at its height spanning southern Italy, Sicily, part of north Africa, and the western coast of Greece and Albania. Guiscard's son, Bohemond of Taranto, took part in the First Crusade (1096–99), claiming the principality of Antioch for himself in Syria.

Despite their fearsome reputation and impressive conquests, the Normans' power did not rest on superior weaponry, inexhaustible manpower, or innovative tactics. Their success stemmed instead from their renowned ferocity, drive and ambition, their determined castle-building, and the Norman princes' cunning and ability to exploit existing power dynamics in the lands they conquered and subsequently administered.

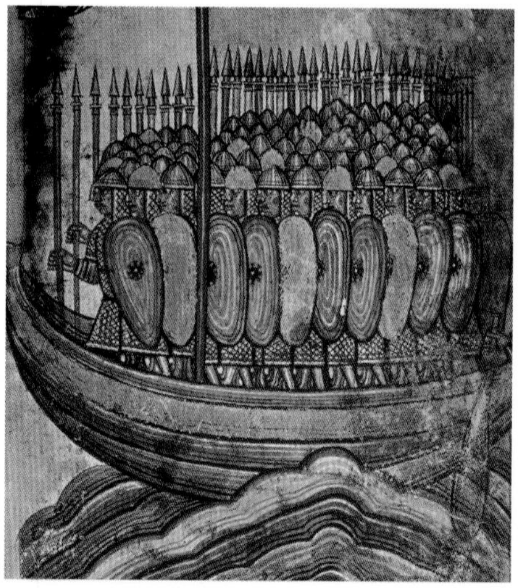

◁ **Crossing the Channel**
This 11th-century French manuscript shows Vikings sailing to attack a Breton town in 919 CE. They wear heavy armour and carry kite shields, as did the Normans who invaded England in the illustrator's century.

▷ **Clashing armies**
This 15th-century scene shows the Battle of Hastings. Although an 11th-century battle, this illustration also shows arms, armour, and troop types contemporary to the illustrator rather than the battle itself, with even the Saxons anachronistically using mounted knights.

MANZIKERT

In 1071, the Byzantine emperor, Romanos IV Diogenes, struck out at the Seljuq Turks who had been harrying his empire's eastern borders. He was defeated and captured at Manzikert, a battle that led to the loss of most of Anatolia to the Seljuqs.

After a military renaissance in the 10th and early 11th century that saw the Byzantine empire consolidate its eastern frontier, a series of weak emperors undermined its position. At the same time, the Seljuq Turks – a Muslim dynasty originating near the Aral Sea – emerged as a potent new threat in Anatolia. In 1068, Romanos Diogenes became emperor and began a series of reforms to strengthen the fractured Byzantine army. He led inconclusive campaigns into Armenia and Syria, and in 1069, made a treaty with the Seljuqs.

During negotiations for the renewal of this treaty in 1071, Romanos took the Seljuq sultan Alp Arslan by surprise, marching across Anatolia to capture territory held by the Seljuqs. On reaching Lake Van, he sent half of his forces – including the feared Varangian guard – under his general Joseph Tarchaneiotes to secure the fortress of Khilat, while he himself took Manzikert from its Turkish garrison.

When Alp Arslan heard of the Byzantine foray, he marched to Manzikert to confront Romanos. Lacking half his force, Romanos was captured. Even though the sultan released him after a week, Romanos's authority was undermined and he was deposed by his former allies, the Doukids. A decade-long civil war followed in Anatolia, allowing much of it to be overrun by the Seljuqs.

"Either I will achieve the goal or I will go as a martyr to Paradise."

ALP ARSLAN BEFORE THE BATTLE OF MANZIKERT

THE BYZANTINE EMPIRE

The Greek-speaking eastern provinces of the Roman empire survived the barbarian invasions of the 5th century CE to become the Byzantine empire, based in Constantinople. Although it lost north Africa to Arab attacks in the 7th century, it regained much of the Balkans from Slav invaders. The rise of new Muslim powers – first the Seljuqs and then the Ottomans – led to large territorial losses, and in 1453 Constantinople fell to the Ottoman sultan Mehmed II.

11th-century ivory panel showing Christ crowning Romanos IV

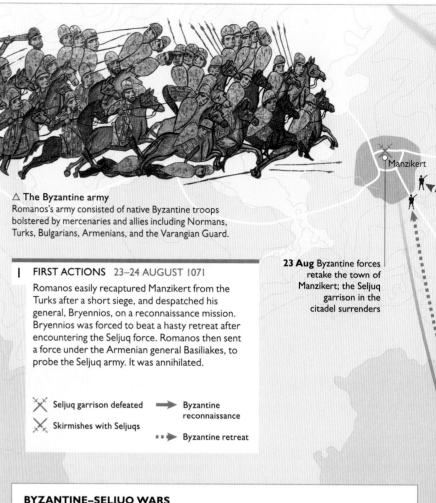

△ **The Byzantine army**
Romanos's army consisted of native Byzantine troops bolstered by mercenaries and allies including Normans, Turks, Bulgarians, Armenians, and the Varangian Guard.

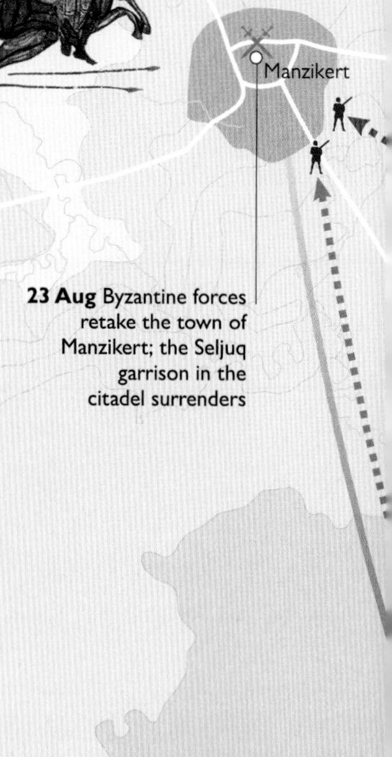
Manzikert
23 Aug Byzantine forces retake the town of Manzikert; the Seljuq garrison in the citadel surrenders

1 FIRST ACTIONS 23–24 AUGUST 1071

Romanos easily recaptured Manzikert from the Turks after a short siege, and despatched his general, Bryennios, on a reconnaissance mission. Bryennios was forced to beat a hasty retreat after encountering the Seljuq force. Romanos then sent a force under the Armenian general Basiliakes, to probe the Seljuq army. It was annihilated.

Seljuq garrison defeated
Skirmishes with Seljuqs
Byzantine reconnaissance
Byzantine retreat

BYZANTINE–SELJUQ WARS

The Seljuqs, a nomadic Turkish group, began raiding the Byzantine empire in 1048, when they attacked the region near Trebizond. Under Sultan Alp Arslan, their attacks grew more severe and in 1064 Arslan captured the Armenian capital of Ani. In 1067–69, he took several key Byzantine towns in Anatolia and – though the Seljuqs were initially forced back – prompted Romanos's Manzikert campaign.

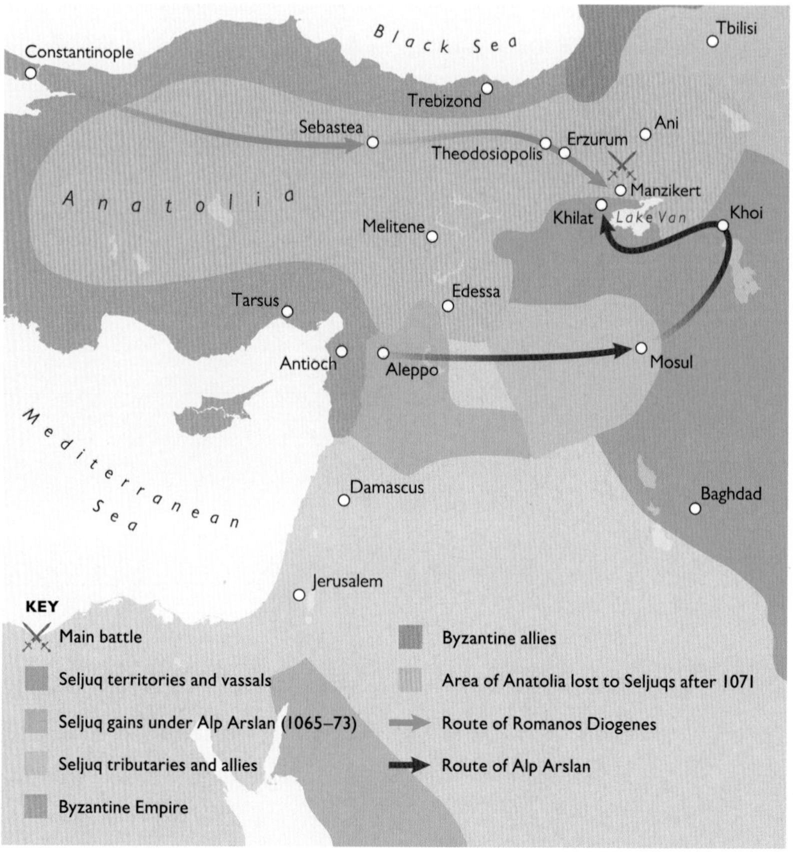
Black Sea
Constantinople
Tbilisi
Trebizond
Sebastea
Ani
Erzurum
Theodosiopolis
Anatolia
Manzikert
Khilat
Lake Van
Khoi
Melitene
Tarsus
Edessa
Antioch
Aleppo
Mosul
Mediterranean Sea
Damascus
Baghdad
Jerusalem
KEY
Main battle
Seljuq territories and vassals
Seljuq gains under Alp Arslan (1065–73)
Seljuq tributaries and allies
Byzantine Empire
Byzantine allies
Area of Anatolia lost to Seljuqs after 1071
Route of Romanos Diogenes
Route of Alp Arslan

IMPERIAL COLLAPSE

Romanus Diogenes's advance into Anatolia to counterattack the Seljuq Turks ended in disaster when his army was destroyed, resulting in the loss of huge swathes of imperial territory.

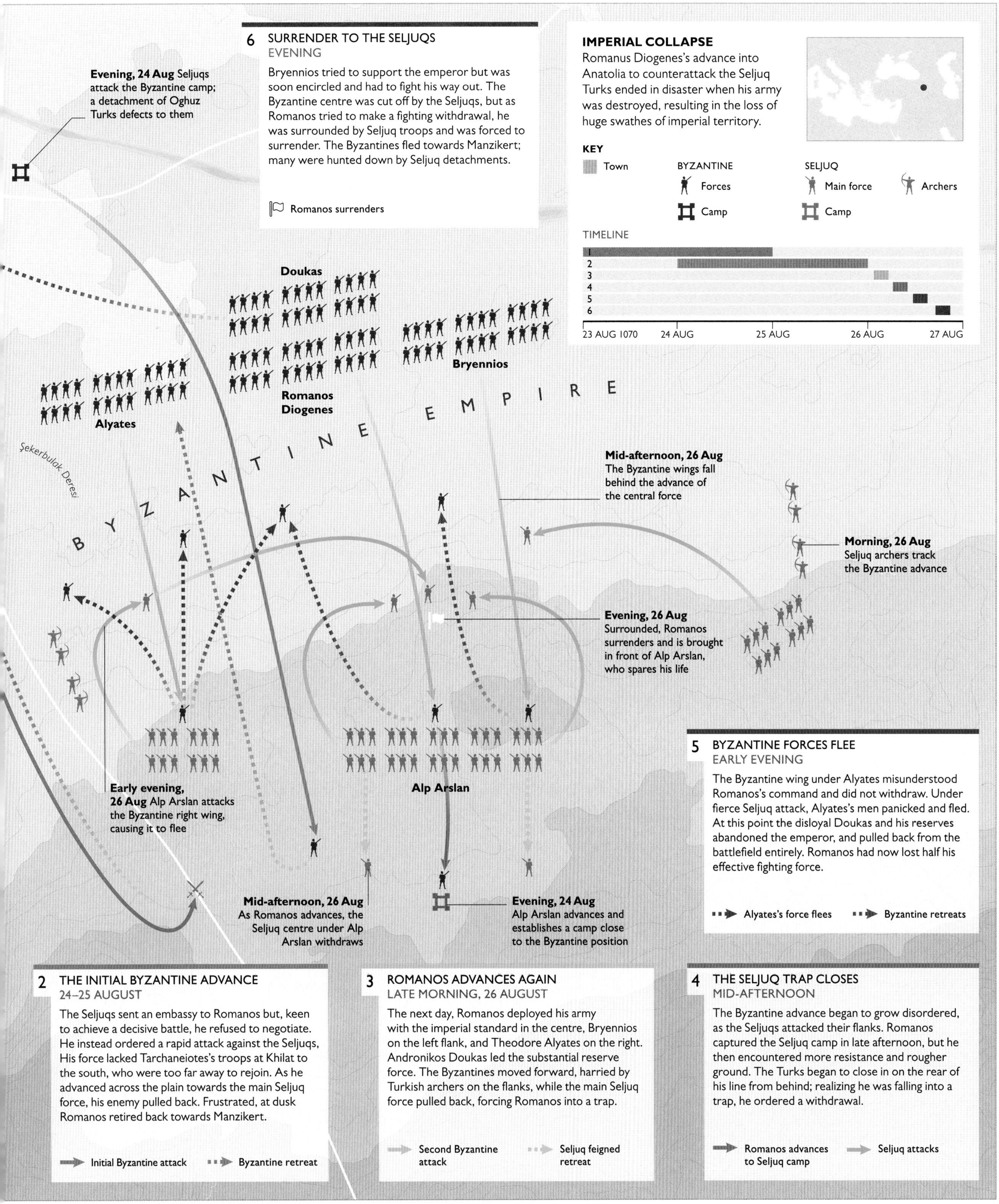
KEY
Town
BYZANTINE
Forces
Camp
SELJUQ
Main force
Camp
Archers
TIMELINE
1
2
3
4
5
6
23 AUG 1070
24 AUG
25 AUG
26 AUG
27 AUG
Evening, 24 Aug Seljuqs attack the Byzantine camp; a detachment of Oghuz Turks defects to them
Doukas
Romanos Diogenes
Bryennios
Alyates
BYZANTINE EMPIRE
Şekerbulak Deresi
Mid-afternoon, 26 Aug The Byzantine wings fall behind the advance of the central force
Morning, 26 Aug Seljuq archers track the Byzantine advance
Evening, 26 Aug Surrounded, Romanos surrenders and is brought in front of Alp Arslan, who spares his life
Early evening, 26 Aug Alp Arslan attacks the Byzantine right wing, causing it to flee
Alp Arslan
Mid-afternoon, 26 Aug As Romanos advances, the Seljuq centre under Alp Arslan withdraws
Evening, 24 Aug Alp Arslan advances and establishes a camp close to the Byzantine position

2 THE INITIAL BYZANTINE ADVANCE
24–25 AUGUST

The Seljuqs sent an embassy to Romanos but, keen to achieve a decisive battle, he refused to negotiate. He instead ordered a rapid attack against the Seljuqs, His force lacked Tarchaneiotes's troops at Khilat to the south, who were too far away to rejoin. As he advanced across the plain towards the main Seljuq force, his enemy pulled back. Frustrated, at dusk Romanos retired back towards Manzikert.

Initial Byzantine attack — Byzantine retreat

3 ROMANOS ADVANCES AGAIN
LATE MORNING, 26 AUGUST

The next day, Romanos deployed his army with the imperial standard in the centre, Bryennios on the left flank, and Theodore Alyates on the right. Andronikos Doukas led the substantial reserve force. The Byzantines moved forward, harried by Turkish archers on the flanks, while the main Seljuq force pulled back, forcing Romanos into a trap.

Second Byzantine attack — Seljuq feigned retreat

4 THE SELJUQ TRAP CLOSES
MID-AFTERNOON

The Byzantine advance began to grow disordered, as the Seljuqs attacked their flanks. Romanos captured the Seljuq camp in late afternoon, but he then encountered more resistance and rougher ground. The Turks began to close in on the rear of his line from behind; realizing he was falling into a trap, he ordered a withdrawal.

Romanos advances to Seljuq camp — Seljuq attacks

5 BYZANTINE FORCES FLEE
EARLY EVENING

The Byzantine wing under Alyates misunderstood Romanos's command and did not withdraw. Under fierce Seljuq attack, Alyates's men panicked and fled. At this point the disloyal Doukas and his reserves abandoned the emperor, and pulled back from the battlefield entirely. Romanos had now lost half his effective fighting force.

Alyates's force flees — Byzantine retreats

6 SURRENDER TO THE SELJUQS
EVENING

Bryennios tried to support the emperor but was soon encircled and had to fight his way out. The Byzantine centre was cut off by the Seljuqs, but as Romanos tried to make a fighting withdrawal, he was surrounded by Seljuq troops and was forced to surrender. The Byzantines fled towards Manzikert; many were hunted down by Seljuq detachments.

Romanos surrenders

△ Crusader siege
This 14th-century painting shows a idealized scene of a siege conducted by Godfrey of Bouillon's forces in the First Crusade. Missiles are exchanged as the crusaders attempt to scale the walls with ladders.

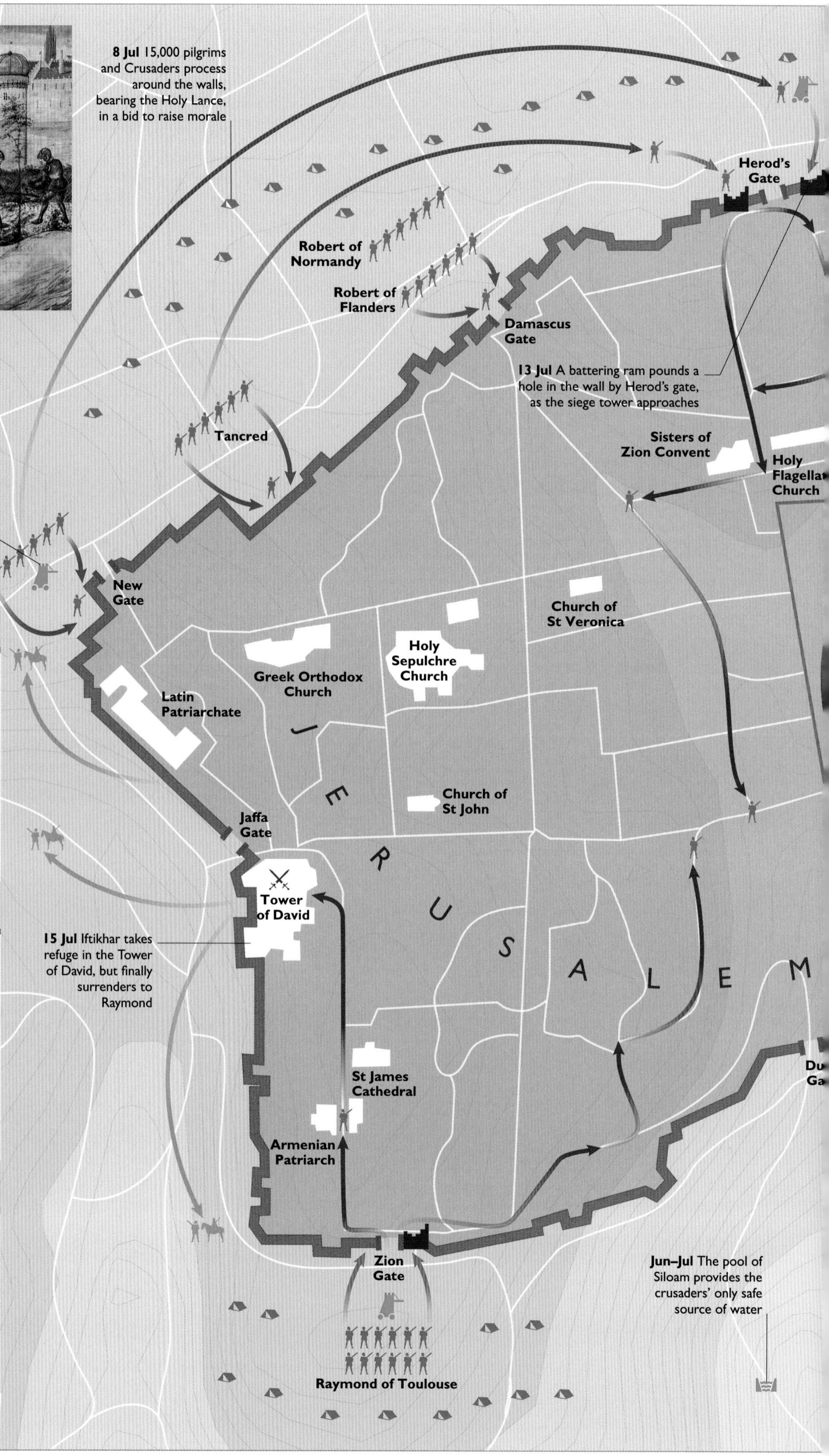

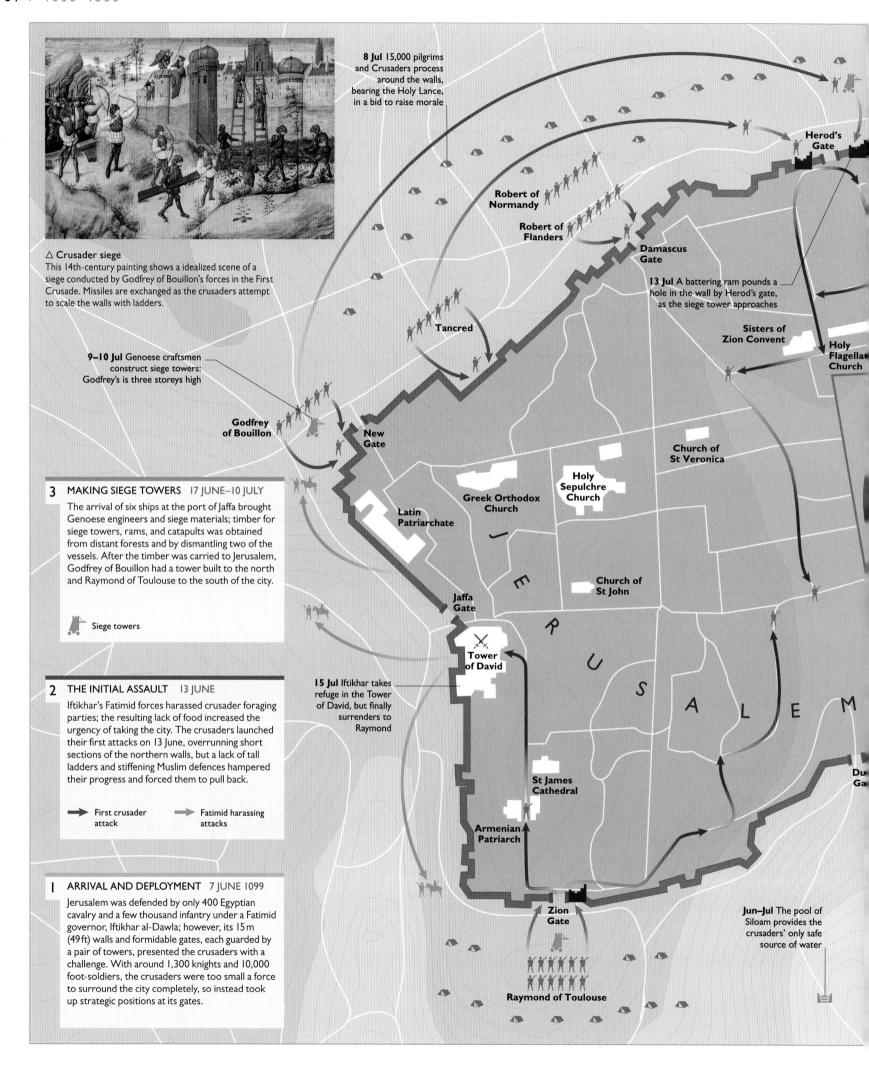

8 Jul 15,000 pilgrims and Crusaders process around the walls, bearing the Holy Lance, in a bid to raise morale
Herod's Gate
Robert of Normandy
Robert of Flanders
Damascus Gate
13 Jul A battering ram pounds a hole in the wall by Herod's gate, as the siege tower approaches
Tancred
Sisters of Zion Convent
Holy Flagella Church
9–10 Jul Genoese craftsmen construct siege towers: Godfrey's is three storeys high
Godfrey of Bouillon
New Gate
Church of St Veronica
Holy Sepulchre Church
Greek Orthodox Church
Latin Patriarchate
JERUSALEM
Church of St John
Jaffa Gate
Tower of David
15 Jul Iftikhar takes refuge in the Tower of David, but finally surrenders to Raymond
St James Cathedral
Armenian Patriarch
Du Ga
Zion Gate
Raymond of Toulouse
Jun–Jul The pool of Siloam provides the crusaders' only safe source of water

3 MAKING SIEGE TOWERS 17 JUNE–10 JULY

The arrival of six ships at the port of Jaffa brought Genoese engineers and siege materials; timber for siege towers, rams, and catapults was obtained from distant forests and by dismantling two of the vessels. After the timber was carried to Jerusalem, Godfrey of Bouillon had a tower built to the north and Raymond of Toulouse to the south of the city.

Siege towers

2 THE INITIAL ASSAULT 13 JUNE

Iftikhar's Fatimid forces harassed crusader foraging parties; the resulting lack of food increased the urgency of taking the city. The crusaders launched their first attacks on 13 June, overrunning short sections of the northern walls, but a lack of tall ladders and stiffening Muslim defences hampered their progress and forced them to pull back.

First crusader attack | Fatimid harassing attacks

1 ARRIVAL AND DEPLOYMENT 7 JUNE 1099

Jerusalem was defended by only 400 Egyptian cavalry and a few thousand infantry under a Fatimid governor, Iftikhar al-Dawla; however, its 15 m (49 ft) walls and formidable gates, each guarded by a pair of towers, presented the crusaders with a challenge. With around 1,300 knights and 10,000 foot-soldiers, the crusaders were too small a force to surround the city completely, so instead took up strategic positions at its gates.

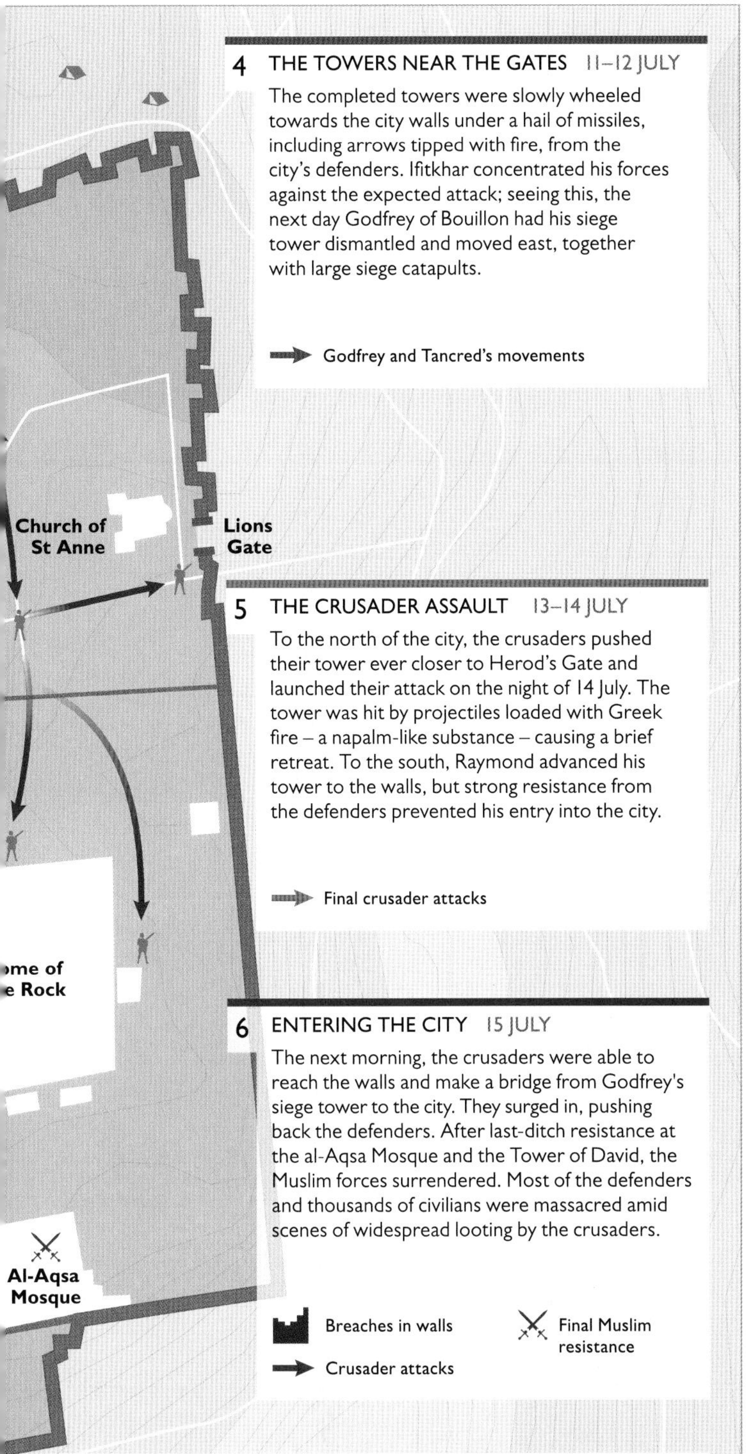
Church of St Anne
Lions Gate
ome of
e Rock
Al-Aqsa Mosque

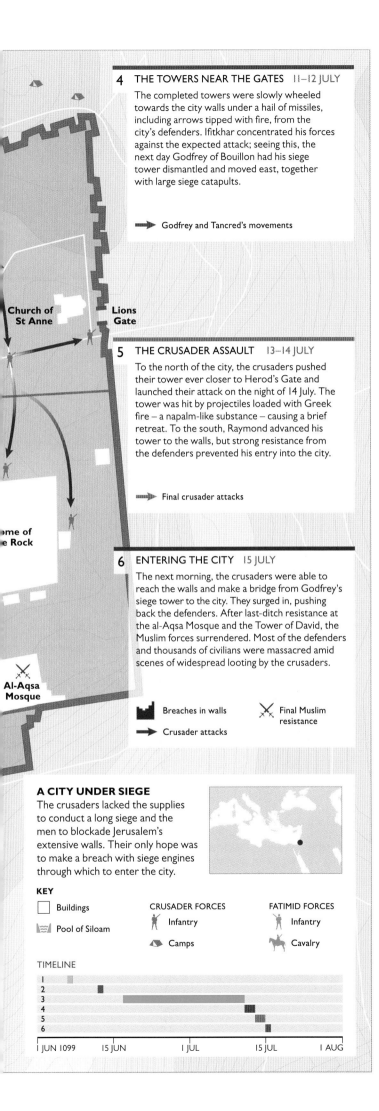

4 THE TOWERS NEAR THE GATES 11–12 JULY

The completed towers were slowly wheeled towards the city walls under a hail of missiles, including arrows tipped with fire, from the city's defenders. Iftikhar concentrated his forces against the expected attack; seeing this, the next day Godfrey of Bouillon had his siege tower dismantled and moved east, together with large siege catapults.

Godfrey and Tancred's movements

5 THE CRUSADER ASSAULT 13–14 JULY

To the north of the city, the crusaders pushed their tower ever closer to Herod's Gate and launched their attack on the night of 14 July. The tower was hit by projectiles loaded with Greek fire – a napalm-like substance – causing a brief retreat. To the south, Raymond advanced his tower to the walls, but strong resistance from the defenders prevented his entry into the city.

Final crusader attacks

6 ENTERING THE CITY 15 JULY

The next morning, the crusaders were able to reach the walls and make a bridge from Godfrey's siege tower to the city. They surged in, pushing back the defenders. After last-ditch resistance at the al-Aqsa Mosque and the Tower of David, the Muslim forces surrendered. Most of the defenders and thousands of civilians were massacred amid scenes of widespread looting by the crusaders.

Breaches in walls
Crusader attacks
Final Muslim resistance

A CITY UNDER SIEGE

The crusaders lacked the supplies to conduct a long siege and the men to blockade Jerusalem's extensive walls. Their only hope was to make a breach with siege engines through which to enter the city.

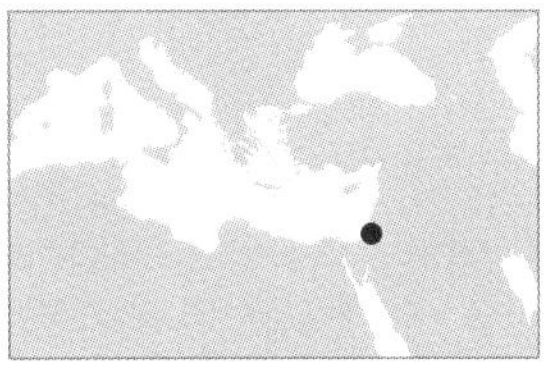

KEY

Buildings
Pool of Siloam

CRUSADER FORCES
Infantry
Camps

FATIMID FORCES
Infantry
Cavalry

TIMELINE

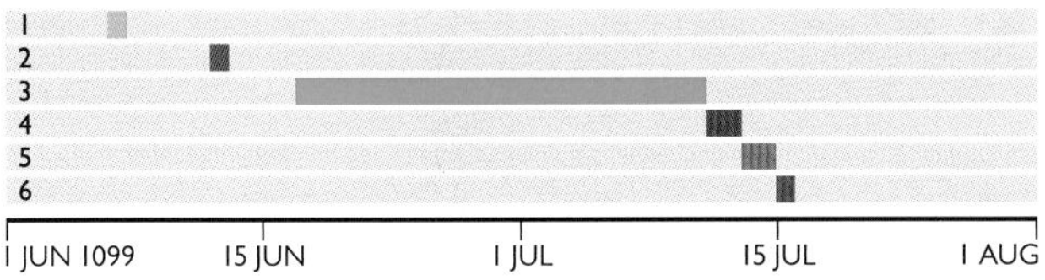
1
2
3
4
5
6
1 JUN 1099
15 JUN
1 JUL
15 JUL
1 AUG

THE SIEGE OF JERUSALEM

The army of the First Crusade, which left its homelands in 1096 to recapture the Holy City of Jerusalem from its Muslim rulers, took nearly three years to reach its objective. Tired and short of supplies, the army succeeded in storming the city's walls, but the massacre of the defenders forever tarnished the crusaders' reputations.

In 1095, the Byzantine Emperor Alexios Komnenos appealed for help to repel the Muslim Seljuq Turks pressing against his borders. Pope Urban II responded, calling for a crusade to free Jerusalem from Muslim control. Thousands of knights under leaders including Godfrey of Bouillon, Bohemond of Taranto, and Count Raymond of Toulouse took up the cause, converging on Constantinople by April 1097. From there, they set out on an arduous journey across Anatolia. Attacks by Seljuqs cost them many men; the prolonged siege of Antioch and the need to garrison the towns they captured drained many more. By the time they reached Jerusalem in June 1099, they were exhausted and demoralized, and Godfrey feared the expedition might collapse. However, in a last-ditch effort they successfully stormed the city walls. With Godfrey elected King of Jerusalem, they shattered an Egyptian army sent to retake the city in August 1099, and consolidated four crusader states based around Antioch, Tripoli, Edessa, and Jerusalem. It took nearly two centuries before Muslim rulers fully dislodged them.

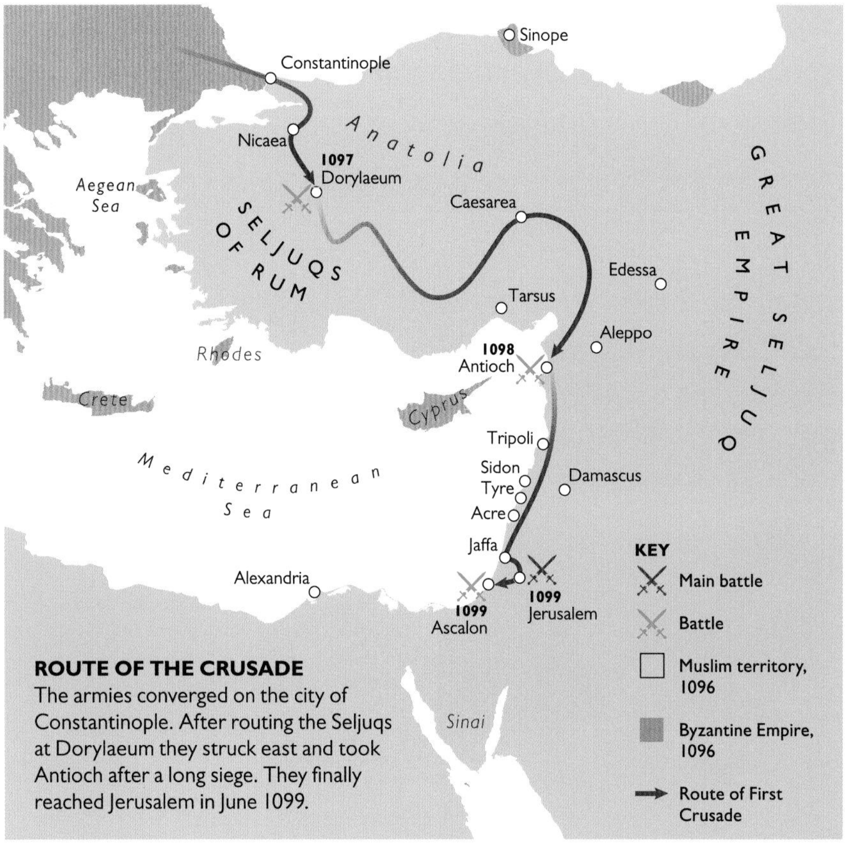
Sinope
Constantinople
Anatolia
Nicaea
1097
Dorylaeum
Aegean Sea
SELJUQS OF RUM
Caesarea
GREAT SELJUQ EMPIRE
Edessa
Tarsus
Aleppo
1098
Antioch
Rhodes
Crete
Cyprus
Tripoli
Sidon
Tyre
Damascus
Acre
Mediterranean Sea
Jaffa
Alexandria
1099
Ascalon
1099
Jerusalem
Sinai
KEY
Main battle
Battle
Muslim territory, 1096
Byzantine Empire, 1096
Route of First Crusade

ROUTE OF THE CRUSADE

The armies converged on the city of Constantinople. After routing the Seljuqs at Dorylaeum they struck east and took Antioch after a long siege. They finally reached Jerusalem in June 1099.

LEGNANO

The Holy Roman Emperor Frederick Barbarossa's struggle to bring the restive towns of northern Italy to obedience came to a head at Legnano, near Milan, in 1176. There, the Italian infantry held firm against Frederick's knights, shattering their charge and dealing a devastating blow to the emperor's ambitions.

Frederick Barbarossa (or "Redbeard"), King of Germany and Holy Roman Emperor (r. 1155–1190), sought for many years to regain control over (and revenues from) the city states of northern Italy. In 1154, he launched the first of six expeditions to bring the cities back into the imperial fold and prevent them from drifting into the orbit of the Papacy. In 1167, with the support of Pope Alexander III, the cities formed an alliance known as the Lombard League. This prompted Frederick to invade Italy for a fifth time in 1174, but his campaign ended in disaster for him at Legnano.

Although he had some initial success with the capture of Susa and Asti, Frederick's siege of Alessandria failed in April 1175, and his campaign became bogged down in fruitless negotiations and abortive appeals for reinforcements from Germany. At long last, in May 1176, a force of only around 2,000 troops (consisting mainly of knights) crossed the Alps, and Frederick rode north with his own knights to meet them and lead them back towards his base at Pavia near Milan.

Unknown to Frederick, the Lombard League had assembled its forces and carroccio (see below) near Legnano. At the ensuing encounter, Frederick was defeated and almost lost his life. He was forced into signing a treaty with Alexander III and, ultimately, into recognizing the autonomy of the north Italian cities. The Italian infantry had not only won a famous victory against the imperial knights, but had secured their independent future.

> *"It is not for the people to give laws to the prince, but to obey his mandate."*
>
> FREDERICK BARBAROSSA, HOLY ROMAN EMPEROR

THE CARROCCIO

First adopted by Milan in the 12th century, the carroccio was a large wooden wagon used by northern Italian cities to carry symbols of their commune, such as battle standards, into combat. Drawn by oxen, it also carried a cross, an altar, and priests to celebrate Mass. A bell (called a martinella) and trumpeters accompanied it to give battle signals to the Lombard troops. The carroccio acted as a rallying point for the troops, and as its capture was regarded as a grave humiliation, it was always bitterly defended.

A 19th-century painting of the defence of the carroccio at Legnano

LOMBARD TRIUMPH

The Lombard League infantry showed what town militias could achieve against mounted knights. Caught between them and the Lombard cavalry, Frederick faced a humiliating defeat.

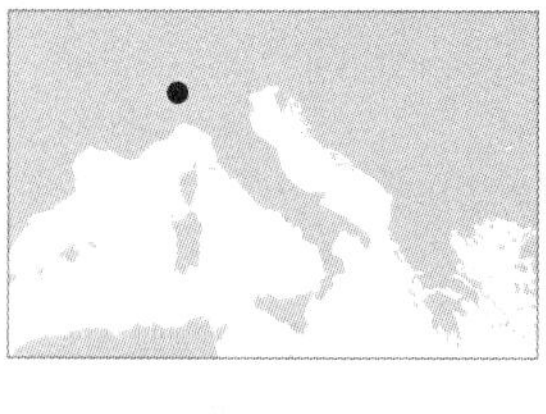

KEY

LOMBARD LEAGUE FORCES: Cavalry, Archers, Infantry

IMPERIAL FORCES: Cavalry

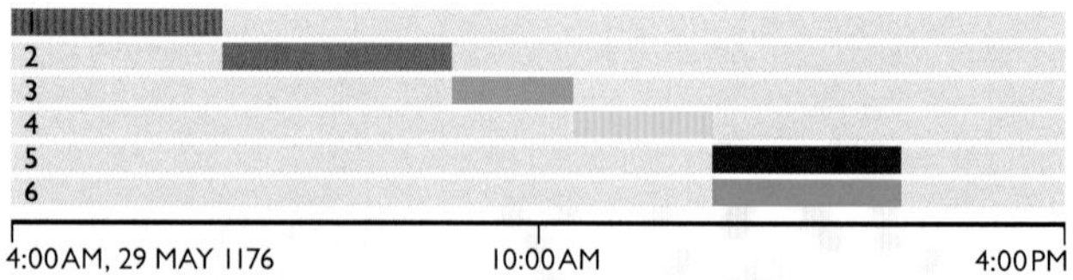
TIMELINE
1
2
3
4
5
6
4:00AM, 29 MAY 1176
10:00AM
4:00PM

1 MILANESE CAVALRY ATTACK THE IMPERIAL FORCE AROUND DAWN, 29 MAY 1176

The Milanese positioned their infantry around their carroccio in a strategic location between Legnano and Borsano. Riding ahead of this position, 700 Milanese knights encountered Frederick's vanguard. The Milanese brushed aside this small imperial force, but Frederick was now aware of the presence of the Lombard League's army.

Lombard vanguard — Imperial vanguard

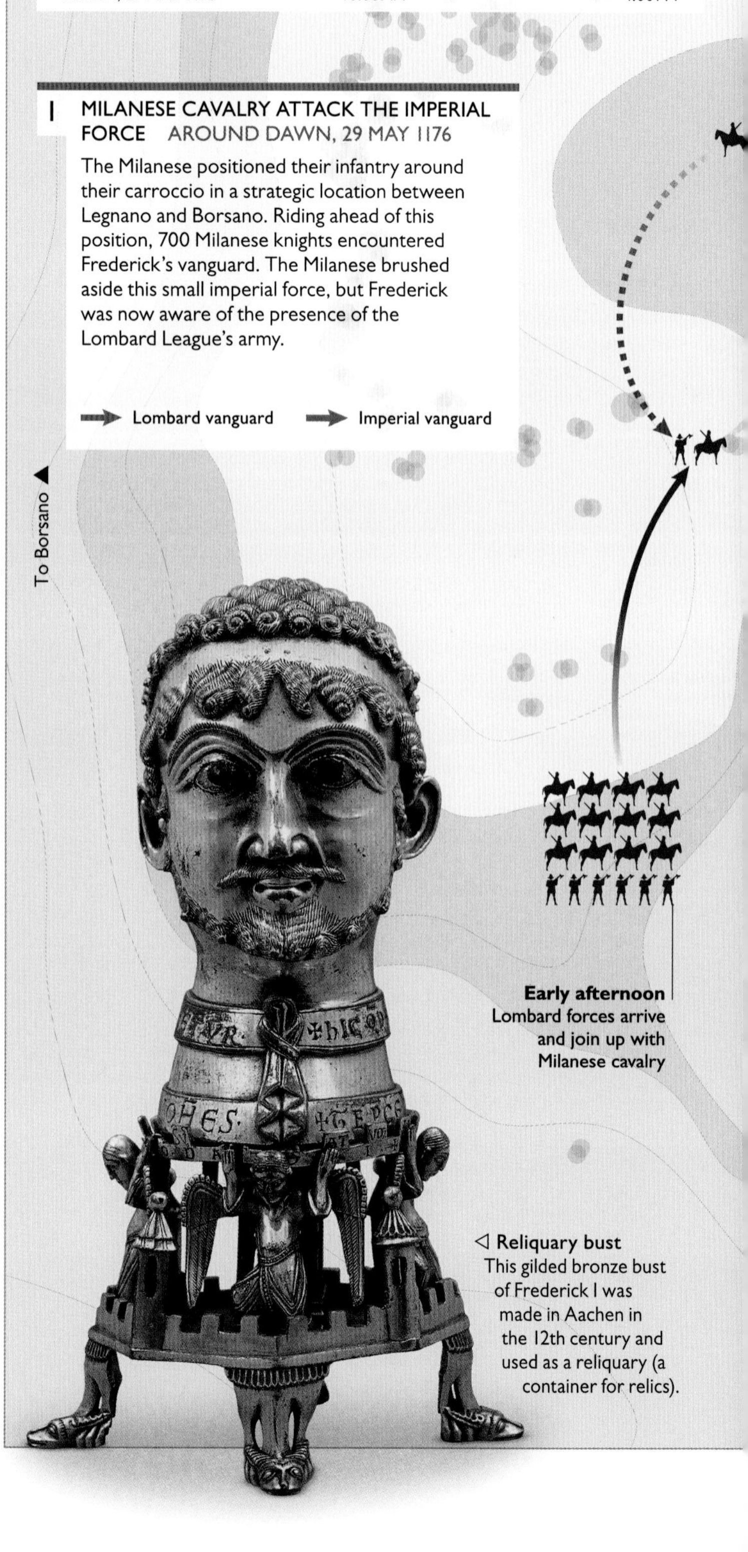
To Borsano
Early afternoon
Lombard forces arrive and join up with Milanese cavalry

◁ **Reliquary bust**
This gilded bronze bust of Frederick I was made in Aachen in the 12th century and used as a reliquary (a container for relics).

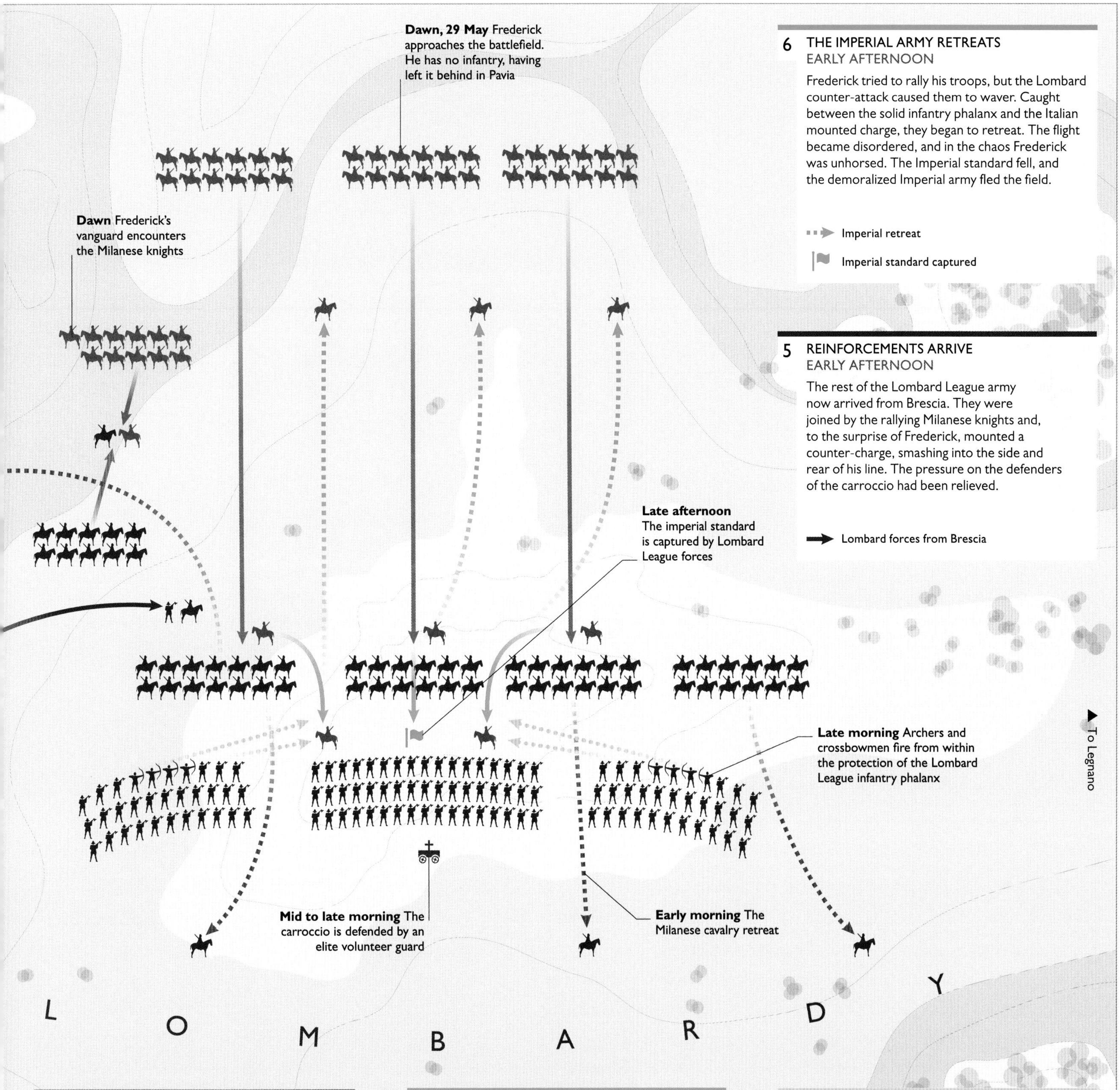

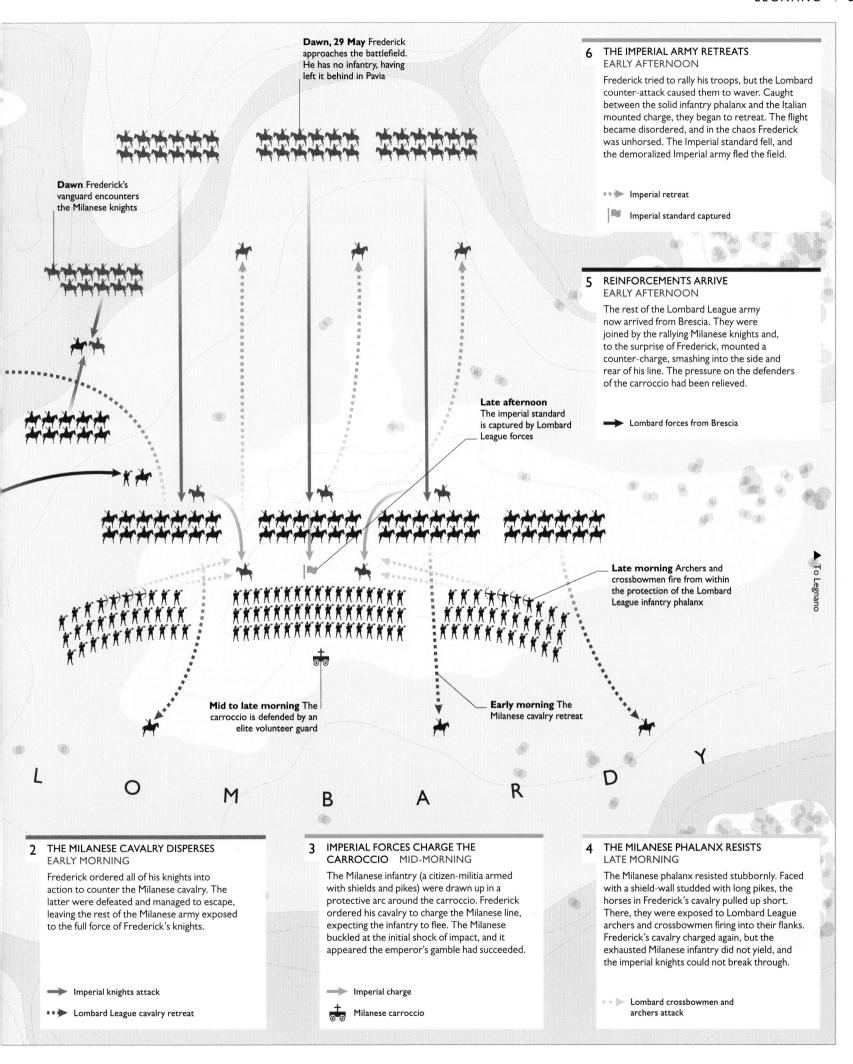

Dawn, 29 May Frederick approaches the battlefield. He has no infantry, having left it behind in Pavia
Dawn Frederick's vanguard encounters the Milanese knights
Late afternoon The imperial standard is captured by Lombard League forces
Late morning Archers and crossbowmen fire from within the protection of the Lombard League infantry phalanx
Mid to late morning The carroccio is defended by an elite volunteer guard
Early morning The Milanese cavalry retreat
To Legnano
LOMBARDY

2 THE MILANESE CAVALRY DISPERSES
EARLY MORNING

Frederick ordered all of his knights into action to counter the Milanese cavalry. The latter were defeated and managed to escape, leaving the rest of the Milanese army exposed to the full force of Frederick's knights.

Imperial knights attack

Lombard League cavalry retreat

3 IMPERIAL FORCES CHARGE THE CARROCCIO
MID-MORNING

The Milanese infantry (a citizen-militia armed with shields and pikes) were drawn up in a protective arc around the carroccio. Frederick ordered his cavalry to charge the Milanese line, expecting the infantry to flee. The Milanese buckled at the initial shock of impact, and it appeared the emperor's gamble had succeeded.

Imperial charge

Milanese carroccio

4 THE MILANESE PHALANX RESISTS
LATE MORNING

The Milanese phalanx resisted stubbornly. Faced with a shield-wall studded with long pikes, the horses in Frederick's cavalry pulled up short. There, they were exposed to Lombard League archers and crossbowmen firing into their flanks. Frederick's cavalry charged again, but the exhausted Milanese infantry did not yield, and the imperial knights could not break through.

Lombard crossbowmen and archers attack

5 REINFORCEMENTS ARRIVE
EARLY AFTERNOON

The rest of the Lombard League army now arrived from Brescia. They were joined by the rallying Milanese knights and, to the surprise of Frederick, mounted a counter-charge, smashing into the side and rear of his line. The pressure on the defenders of the carroccio had been relieved.

Lombard forces from Brescia

6 THE IMPERIAL ARMY RETREATS
EARLY AFTERNOON

Frederick tried to rally his troops, but the Lombard counter-attack caused them to waver. Caught between the solid infantry phalanx and the Italian mounted charge, they began to retreat. The flight became disordered, and in the chaos Frederick was unhorsed. The Imperial standard fell, and the demoralized Imperial army fled the field.

Imperial retreat

Imperial standard captured

1 THE MINAMOTO APPROACH
EARLY MORNING, 25 APRIL 1185

As the Minamoto fleet approached, it deployed in a line blocking the Shimonoseki Strait. The Taira commanders, including Tomomori, divided their ships into three squadrons. They hoped to use the rip tides to launch an attack while the tidal current made it difficult for the Minamoto ships to respond effectively.

Minamoto fleet arrives — Rip tide

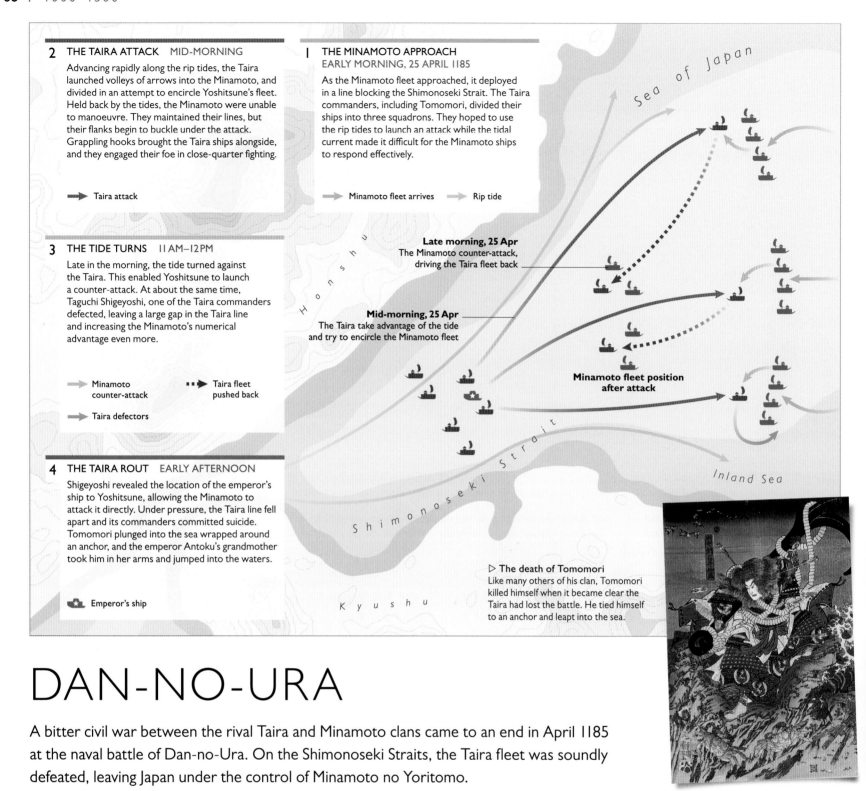

2 THE TAIRA ATTACK MID-MORNING

Advancing rapidly along the rip tides, the Taira launched volleys of arrows into the Minamoto, and divided in an attempt to encircle Yoshitsune's fleet. Held back by the tides, the Minamoto were unable to manoeuvre. They maintained their lines, but their flanks begin to buckle under the attack. Grappling hooks brought the Taira ships alongside, and they engaged their foe in close-quarter fighting.

Taira attack

3 THE TIDE TURNS 11 AM–12 PM

Late in the morning, the tide turned against the Taira. This enabled Yoshitsune to launch a counter-attack. At about the same time, Taguchi Shigeyoshi, one of the Taira commanders defected, leaving a large gap in the Taira line and increasing the Minamoto's numerical advantage even more.

Minamoto counter-attack — Taira fleet pushed back — Taira defectors

4 THE TAIRA ROUT EARLY AFTERNOON

Shigeyoshi revealed the location of the emperor's ship to Yoshitsune, allowing the Minamoto to attack it directly. Under pressure, the Taira line fell apart and its commanders committed suicide. Tomomori plunged into the sea wrapped around an anchor, and the emperor Antoku's grandmother took him in her arms and jumped into the waters.

Emperor's ship

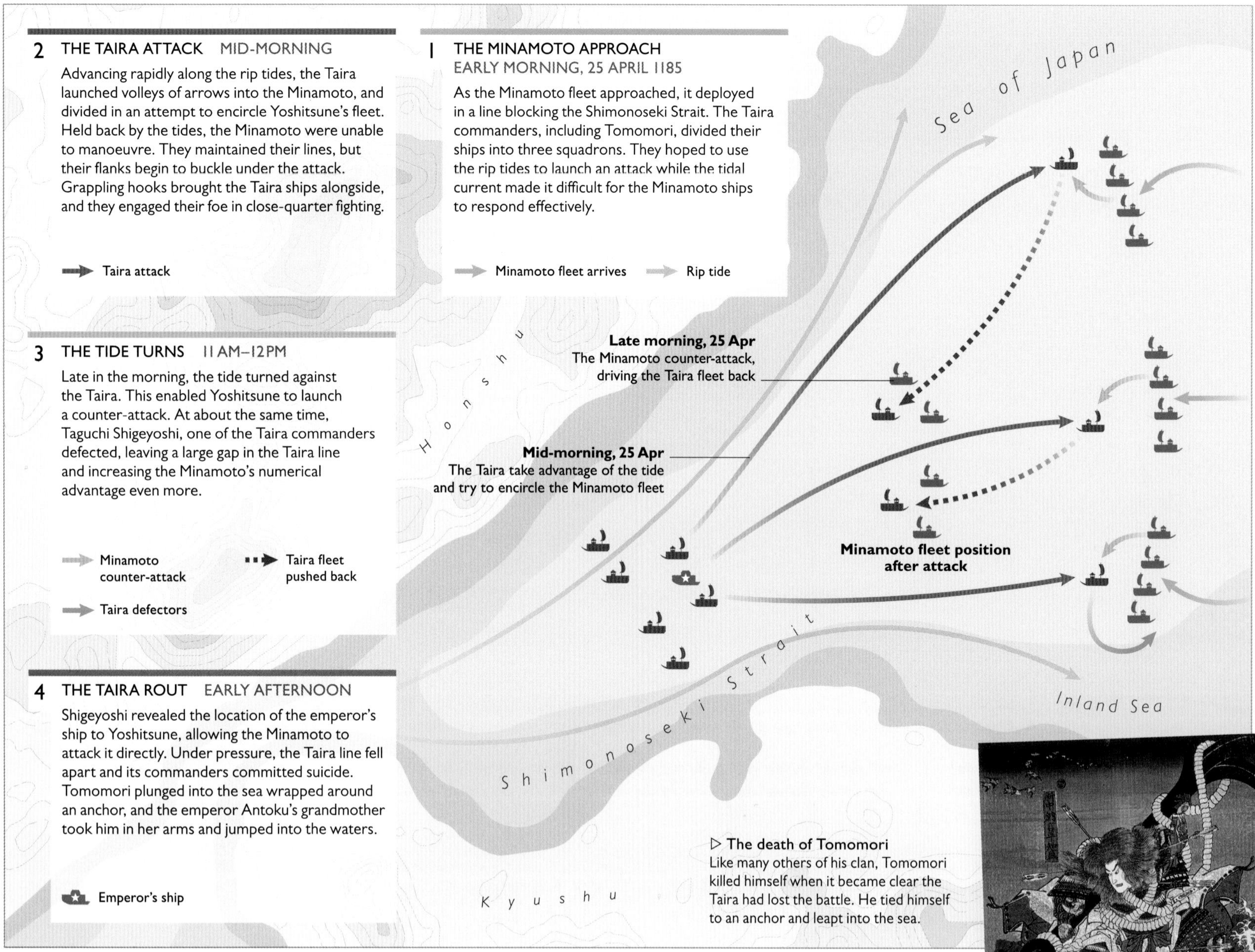
Sea of Japan
Honshu
Late morning, 25 Apr
The Minamoto counter-attack, driving the Taira fleet back
Mid-morning, 25 Apr
The Taira take advantage of the tide and try to encircle the Minamoto fleet
Minamoto fleet position after attack
Shimonoseki Strait
Inland Sea
Kyushu

▷ **The death of Tomomori**
Like many others of his clan, Tomomori killed himself when it became clear the Taira had lost the battle. He tied himself to an anchor and leapt into the sea.

DAN-NO-URA

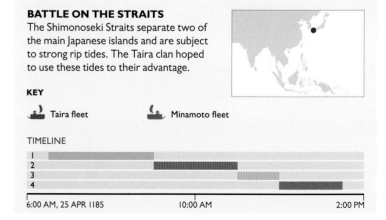

A bitter civil war between the rival Taira and Minamoto clans came to an end in April 1185 at the naval battle of Dan-no-Ura. On the Shimonoseki Straits, the Taira fleet was soundly defeated, leaving Japan under the control of Minamoto no Yoritomo.

In 1180, Japan descended into civil war as the Minamoto clan tried to oust the rival Taira clan from their dominant position in the imperial capital, Kyoto. Three years later, they succeeded in dislodging the Taira, who fled to western Japan, together with five-year-old emperor Antoku. A split in the Minamoto clan between Minamoto no Yoshitsune and his cousin Yoshinaka allowed the Taira brief respite, but Yoshitsune's victory at Uji in early 1184 enabled him to reunite the clan. He pursued the Taira south, storming their fortress of Ichi-no-Tani in March 1184, before forcing them to take to their fleet to escape. With no safe haven on land, the Taira were vulnerable to the pursuing Minamoto fleet, which caught them at Dan-no-Ura, on the narrow Shimonoseki Strait. The Taira suffered a crushing defeat – its fleet was destroyed and the young emperor and senior commanders were killed. In 1185, Minamoto no Yoritomo, Yoshitsune's elder half-brother, became effective ruler of Japan, and later the first shogun of the Kamakura Shogunate (1192–1333).

BATTLE ON THE STRAITS

The Shimonoseki Straits separate two of the main Japanese islands and are subject to strong rip tides. The Taira clan hoped to use these tides to their advantage.

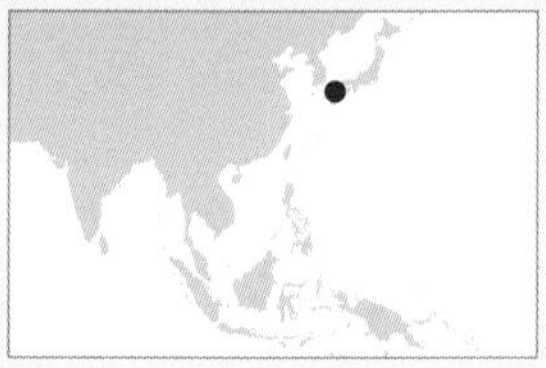

KEY

Taira fleet — Minamoto fleet

TIMELINE

1
2
3
4

6:00 AM, 25 APR 1185 — 10:00 AM — 2:00 PM

HATTIN

In July 1187, Guy de Lusignan, king of Jerusalem, set out to relieve the fortress of Tiberias, held under siege by Saladin. On the arid plain near Hattin, his army was surrounded and destroyed by the Ayyubid forces. Only months later, Saladin's armies would enter Jerusalem itself.

The crusader states of Palestine entered a period of decline in the 1180s. Few fresh recruits were coming from Europe, and Guy de Lusignan, the new king of Jerusalem, was only able to take the throne in 1186 following a damaging succession dispute. A recent truce with Saladin, the Ayyubid sultan of Egypt, broke down in early 1187 after Guy's ally Raynald of Châtillon raided a Muslim caravan travelling from Egypt to Syria. In retaliation, Saladin besieged the fortress at Tiberias on 2 July, aiming to lure the crusaders to its rescue. In response, Guy mustered the crusader host at Sephoria, 30 km (19 miles) to the west of Tiberias, but ignored advice to stand fast and wait for Saladin to come to him. Instead, he headed on across the waterless plains. The resulting destruction of his army at Hattin two days later was a disaster for Guy and his kingdom. One by one, the crusader fortresses fell – Acre, Tiberias, Caesarea, Jaffa, and then on 2 October 1187, the Holy City of Jerusalem. The shock was so profound it led to the calling of the Third Crusade to try to liberate it.

DESERT ENCOUNTER

Against the advice of his allies, Guy led the crusaders across the desert to confront Saladin. Exhausted and short of water, they proved an easy target for Saladin's forces.

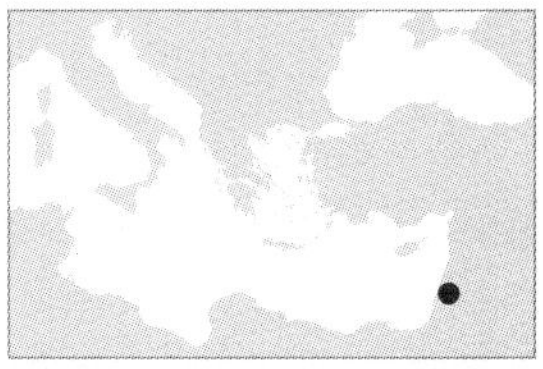

KEY

- Crusader infantry
- Crusader cavalry
- Crusader camp
- Springs
- Ayyubid infantry
- Ayyubid mounted archers
- Ayyubid cavalry

TIMELINE
1
2
3
12:00AM, 3 JUL 1187
12:00PM
12:00AM, 4 JUL
12:00PM

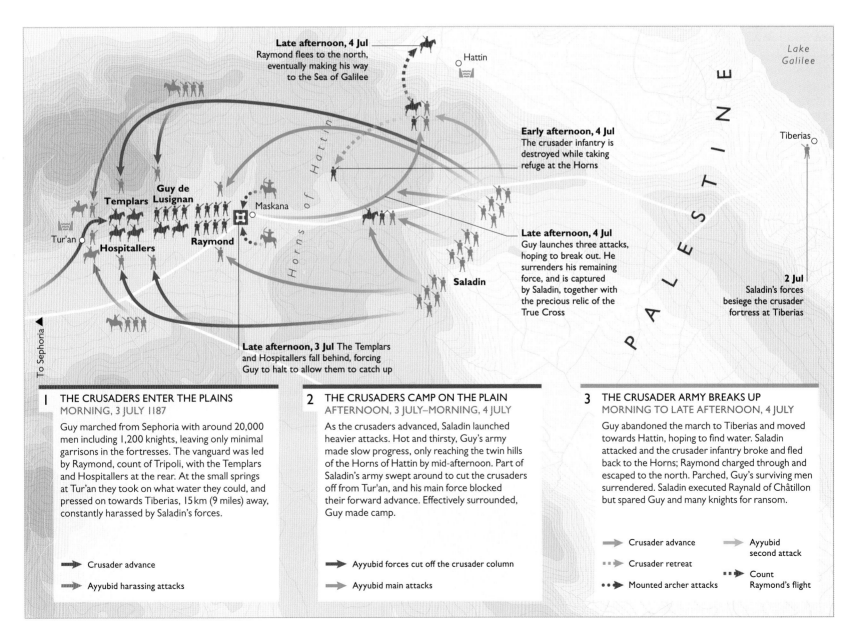

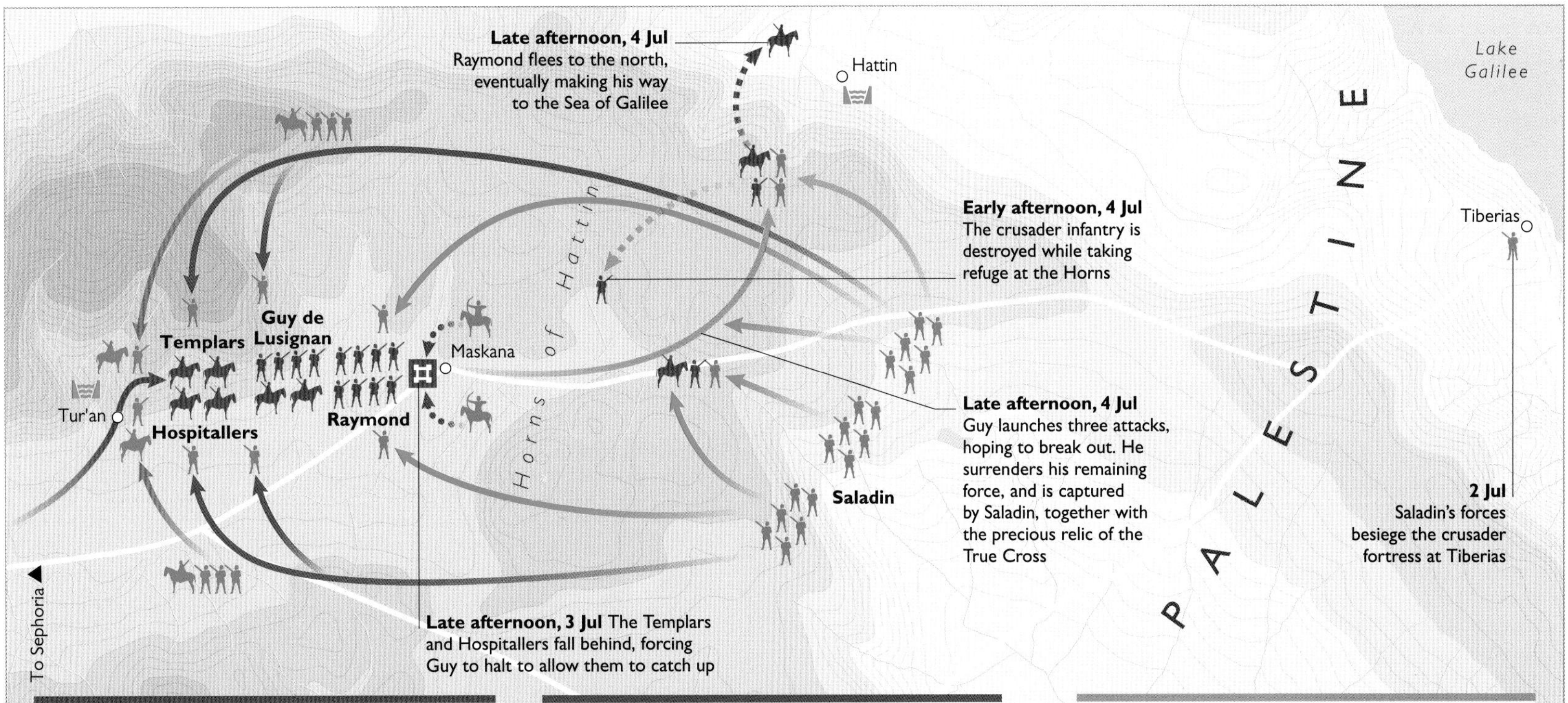
Late afternoon, 4 Jul
Raymond flees to the north, eventually making his way to the Sea of Galilee
Hattin
Lake Galilee
PALESTINE
Tiberias
Early afternoon, 4 Jul
The crusader infantry is destroyed while taking refuge at the Horns
Horns of Hattin
Guy de Lusignan
Templars
Maskana
Tur'an
Hospitallers
Raymond
Late afternoon, 4 Jul
Guy launches three attacks, hoping to break out. He surrenders his remaining force, and is captured by Saladin, together with the precious relic of the True Cross
Saladin
2 Jul
Saladin's forces besiege the crusader fortress at Tiberias
To Sephoria
Late afternoon, 3 Jul The Templars and Hospitallers fall behind, forcing Guy to halt to allow them to catch up

1 THE CRUSADERS ENTER THE PLAINS
MORNING, 3 JULY 1187

Guy marched from Sephoria with around 20,000 men including 1,200 knights, leaving only minimal garrisons in the fortresses. The vanguard was led by Raymond, count of Tripoli, with the Templars and Hospitallers at the rear. At the small springs at Tur'an they took on what water they could, and pressed on towards Tiberias, 15 km (9 miles) away, constantly harassed by Saladin's forces.

- Crusader advance
- Ayyubid harassing attacks

2 THE CRUSADERS CAMP ON THE PLAIN
AFTERNOON, 3 JULY–MORNING, 4 JULY

As the crusaders advanced, Saladin launched heavier attacks. Hot and thirsty, Guy's army made slow progress, only reaching the twin hills of the Horns of Hattin by mid-afternoon. Part of Saladin's army swept around to cut the crusaders off from Tur'an, and his main force blocked their forward advance. Effectively surrounded, Guy made camp.

- Ayyubid forces cut off the crusader column
- Ayyubid main attacks

3 THE CRUSADER ARMY BREAKS UP
MORNING TO LATE AFTERNOON, 4 JULY

Guy abandoned the march to Tiberias and moved towards Hattin, hoping to find water. Saladin attacked and the crusader infantry broke and fled back to the Horns; Raymond charged through and escaped to the north. Parched, Guy's surviving men surrendered. Saladin executed Raynald of Châtillon but spared Guy and many knights for ransom.

- Crusader advance
- Crusader retreat
- Mounted archer attacks
- Ayyubid second attack
- Count Raymond's flight

ARSUF

Saladin appeared invincible to Christian Europe after his capture of Jerusalem in 1187. Four years later, King Richard I of England arrived in the Holy Land as part of the Third Crusade, which aimed to recapture the city. At Arsuf, the crusader armies dealt Saladin's forces a shattering blow and showed he could be defeated.

The capture of Jerusalem by the Muslim Ayyubid leader Saladin in 1187 was greeted with shock and outrage in Christian Europe. It led directly to the Third Crusade (1189–92), the aim of which was to retake the city and reconquer the Holy Land.

Initially, the crusade struggled: Emperor Frederick Barbarossa, the commander of the German contingent, was drowned in June 1190 while crossing Anatolia, and the French crusaders under Philip II had become bogged down in a siege at Acre starting in 1189 – one of the crusaders' first objectives. It took the arrival of King Richard I ("the Lionheart") of England to hasten the final assault on the city, which fell on 12 July 1191. Philip and Leopold went home, along with many French and German crusaders, and the slaughter of prisoners by the crusaders further infuriated Saladin.

Richard pressed south, hoping to take Jaffa as a base from which to assault Jerusalem. When the two forces finally met outside Arsuf, it was their first full encounter on the battlefield. The victory for Richard avenged Saladin's triumph at Hattin four years earlier (see p.69). However, complete victory remained elusive. Under ther terms of a treaty signed in September 1192, Christians would once more be allowed to visit Jerusalem. However, the city itself was to remain in Muslim hands.

"They shouted their shout of battle like one man… and through they rushed in one great charge."

BAHA-AL-DIN, DESCRIBING THE CRUSADERS, *C.*12TH CENTURY

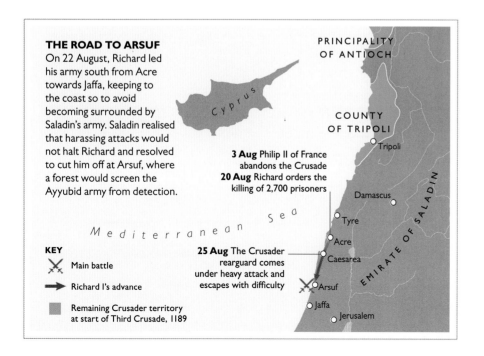

THE ROAD TO ARSUF
On 22 August, Richard led his army south from Acre towards Jaffa, keeping to the coast so to avoid becoming surrounded by Saladin's army. Saladin realised that harassing attacks would not halt Richard and resolved to cut him off at Arsuf, where a forest would screen the Ayyubid army from detection.

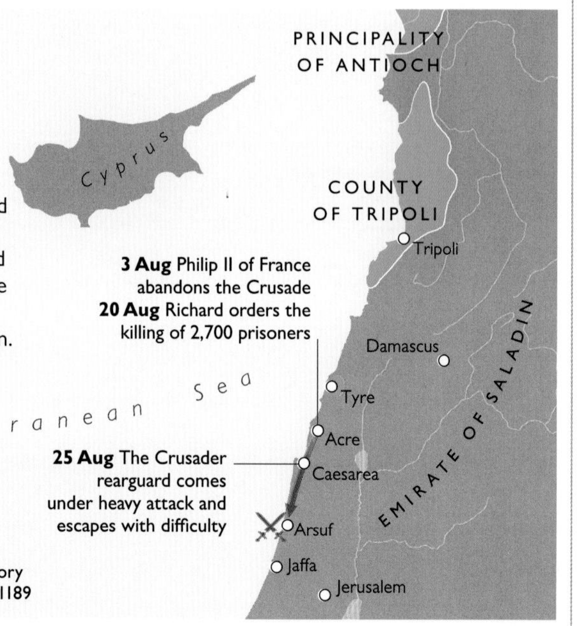
PRINCIPALITY OF ANTIOCH
Cyprus
COUNTY OF TRIPOLI
Tripoli
3 Aug Philip II of France abandons the Crusade
20 Aug Richard orders the killing of 2,700 prisoners
Damascus
Tyre
Mediterranean Sea
EMIRATE OF SALADIN
Acre
Caesarea
25 Aug The Crusader rearguard comes under heavy attack and escapes with difficulty
Arsuf
Jaffa
Jerusalem

KEY
Main battle
Richard I's advance
Remaining Crusader territory at start of Third Crusade, 1189

BETWEEN SEA AND FOREST
As the crusaders continued south, Saladin prepared the Ayyubid forces to confront them on the narrow plain between the Forest of Arsuf and the Mediterranean Sea.

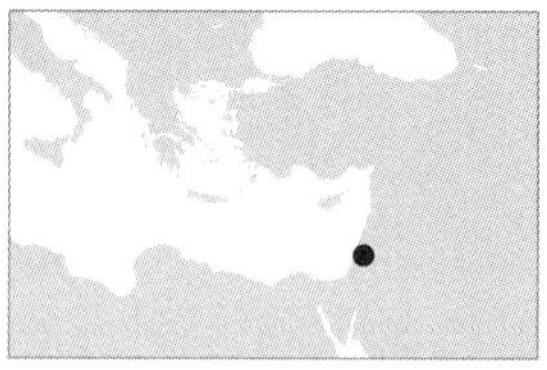

KEY
Town

CRUSADER FORCES
Infantry | Poitevins | English and Normans
Cavalry | Templars | Hospitallers
Crossbowmen | Angevins | Baggage train

AYYUBID FORCES
Camp | Cavalry | Archers and skirmishers

TIMELINE

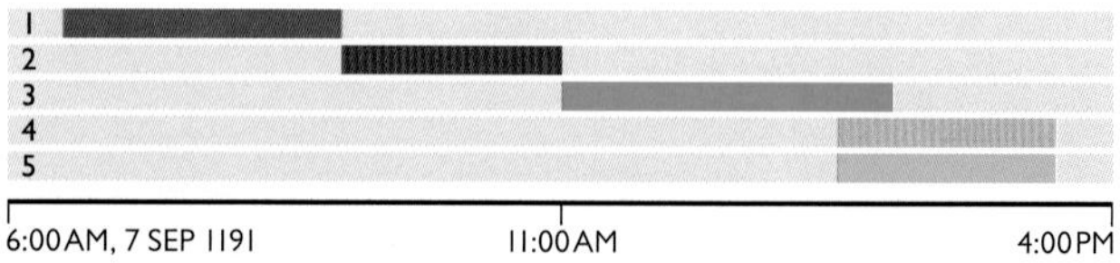
1
2
3
4
5
6:00AM, 7 SEP 1191
11:00AM
4:00PM

1 THE ARMIES PREPARE FOR BATTLE
EARLY MORNING, 7 SEPTEMBER 1191

With scouts reporting the presence of the Ayyubid army in the woodland, Richard formed his army of around 12,000 in a defensive formation, with the Knights Templar in the vanguard, the Poitevins, English and Normans in the centre, and the Knights Hospitaller in the rear. Each group was composed of both knights and protective infantry units.

Crusader arrival

2 SALADIN LAUNCHES HARASSING ATTACKS
9:00–11:00AM

As the crusaders moved onto the plain of Arsuf, hoping to reach the town six miles away, Saladin unleashed a series of harassing attacks. Ayyubid foot archers launched volleys of arrows, while horse archers closed in to fire further volleys, before wheeling away in the hope of enticing some crusaders to break ranks and be cut down.

Ayyubid harassing attacks

3 THE CRUSADER LEFT FLANK BUCKLES
11:00AM–2:00PM

With the crusader line holding firm, Saladin launched heavier attacks against the Hospitallers, in the rear of Richard's army. As they approached, the Ayyubids began to take casualties from Richard's crossbowmen. The Hospitaller Grand Master Garnier de Nablus pleaded with Richard to allow him to attack, but the English king insisted that the crusaders remain in formation until the enemy were exhausted.

Ayyubid attacks

Mediterranean Sea

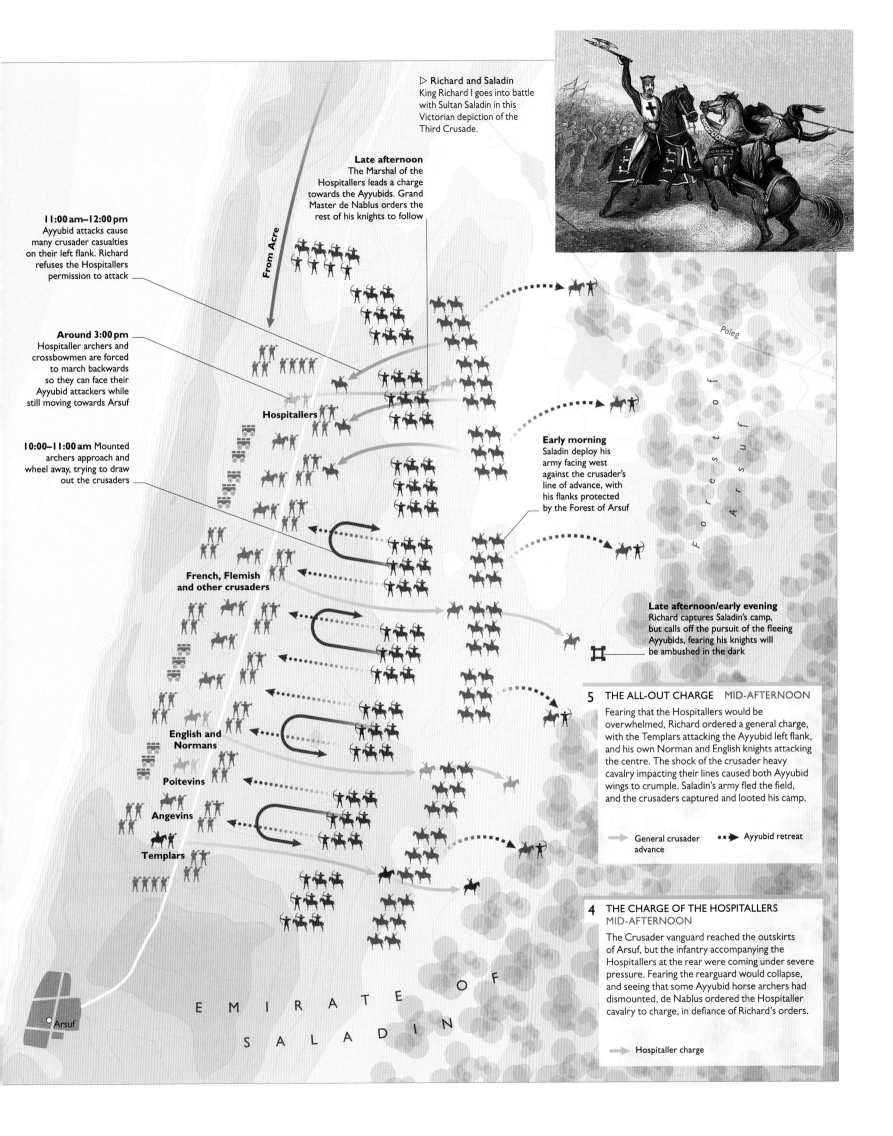

▷ **Richard and Saladin**
King Richard I goes into battle with Sultan Saladin in this Victorian depiction of the Third Crusade.

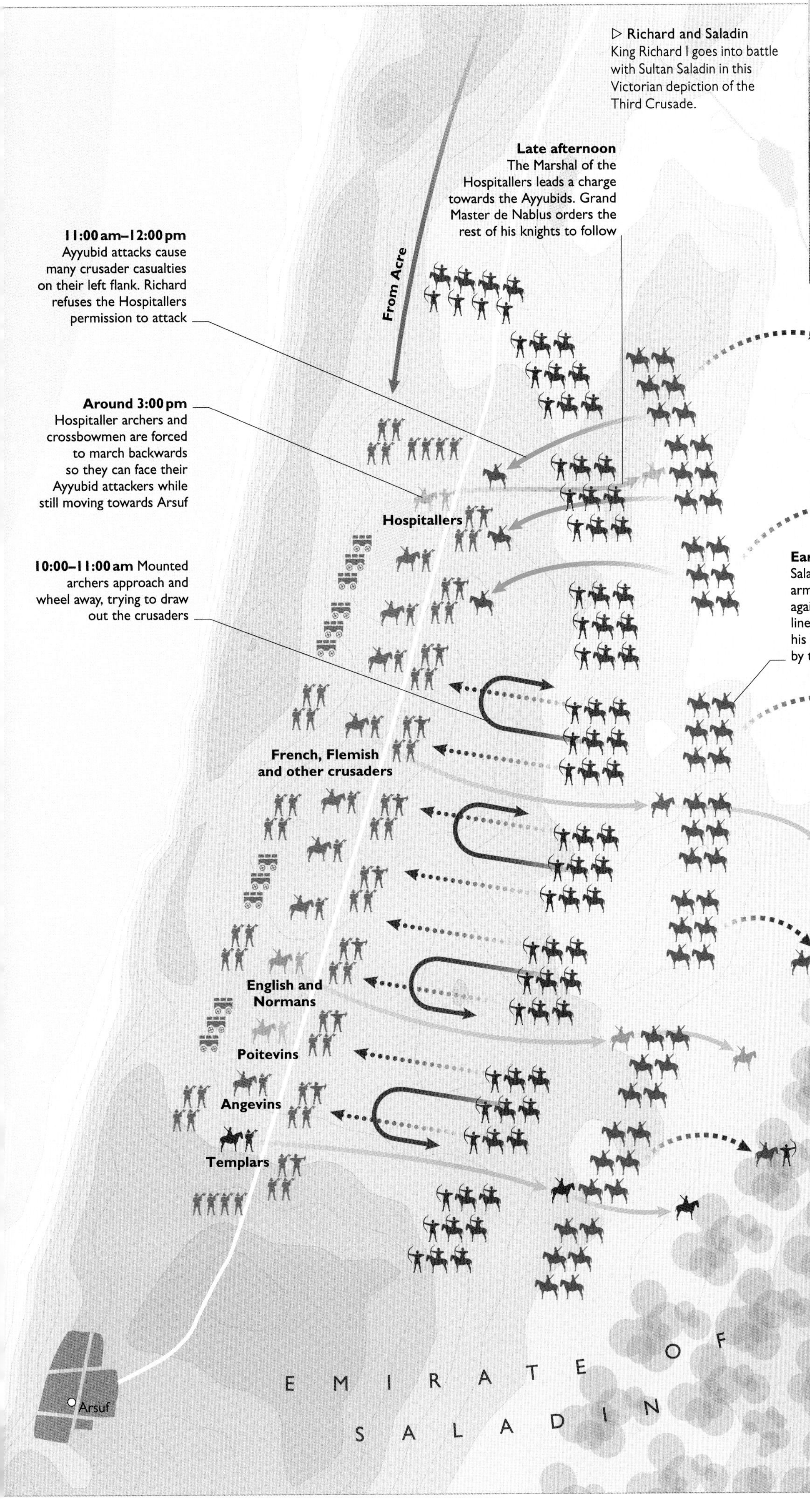

From Acre
Late afternoon
The Marshal of the Hospitallers leads a charge towards the Ayyubids. Grand Master de Nablus orders the rest of his knights to follow
11:00 am–12:00 pm
Ayyubid attacks cause many crusader casualties on their left flank. Richard refuses the Hospitallers permission to attack
Around 3:00 pm
Hospitaller archers and crossbowmen are forced to march backwards so they can face their Ayyubid attackers while still moving towards Arsuf
Hospitallers
10:00–11:00 am Mounted archers approach and wheel away, trying to draw out the crusaders
Poleg
Forest of Arsuf
Early morning
Saladin deploy his army facing west against the crusader's line of advance, with his flanks protected by the Forest of Arsuf
French, Flemish and other crusaders
Late afternoon/early evening
Richard captures Saladin's camp, but calls off the pursuit of the fleeing Ayyubids, fearing his knights will be ambushed in the dark
English and Normans
Poitevins
Angevins
Templars
EMIRATE OF SALADIN
Arsuf
General crusader advance
Ayyubid retreat
Hospitaller charge

5 THE ALL-OUT CHARGE MID-AFTERNOON

Fearing that the Hospitallers would be overwhelmed, Richard ordered a general charge, with the Templars attacking the Ayyubid left flank, and his own Norman and English knights attacking the centre. The shock of the crusader heavy cavalry impacting their lines caused both Ayyubid wings to crumple. Saladin's army fled the field, and the crusaders captured and looted his camp.

4 THE CHARGE OF THE HOSPITALLERS MID-AFTERNOON

The Crusader vanguard reached the outskirts of Arsuf, but the infantry accompanying the Hospitallers at the rear were coming under severe pressure. Fearing the rearguard would collapse, and seeing that some Ayyubid horse archers had dismounted, de Nablus ordered the Hospitaller cavalry to charge, in defiance of Richard's orders.

CRUSADERS AND SARACENS

The invasion of the Muslim-dominated eastern Mediterranean by crusaders from Western Europe led to a clash between two contrasting styles of warfare – Christian armoured knights taking on nimble Muslim horsemen.

Known to the Christians as Saracens, the Muslim armies that resisted the Crusades (1095–1492) were mostly of Central Asian origin. They were fast-moving mounted warriors skilled in manoeuvre and skirmishing. Often armed with composite bows, Saracen horsemen avoided close-quarter fighting until they had worn the enemy down. Only then would they close in to deliver the *coup de grâce*. The crusader knights, wearing heavy armour, could not match the Saracens' mobility. The knights preferred cavalry charges and hand-to-hand fighting, which they prized as a supreme display of valour. The Muslim forces, on the other hand, favoured tricking their enemy with feigned flight.

Clash of cultures

The crusaders partially adapted to Saracen tactics. They deployed foot soldiers to protect the mounted knights and Genoese crossbowmen (see pp.84–85) to counter the Saracen archers. Their heavy armour was unsuited to the heat but offered protection against arrows, and they reinforced the mystique of the knight by creating religious fighting orders such as the Templars. The Saracens also used armoured cavalry in combination with light horse archers. The result was an asymmetric balance, with victories won by generalship and other factors.

◁ **Weapon of choice**
A two-edged sword was standard equipment for a Christian knight. It was an effective weapon whether used for stabbing or slashing.

RICHARD I | 1157–99

Within a year of inheriting the English throne, King Richard I, also known as Richard the Lionheart, set off for Palestine on the Third Crusade (1189–92). He displayed great tactical skill and bravery while fighting the Saracen sultan Saladin at the battles of Arsuf (see pp.70–71) and Jaffa (1192), but failed to retake the city of Jerusalem, which was his primary objective. He returned to England in 1194 and was killed at a siege in France five years later.

Fighting off the enemy
This detail from a 12th-century illuminated manuscript shows Muslim warriors engaging with Christian knights at a siege during the First Crusade (1096–99). Saracen bowmen are seen firing arrows at the heavily armoured crusaders trying to scale the walls of a town.

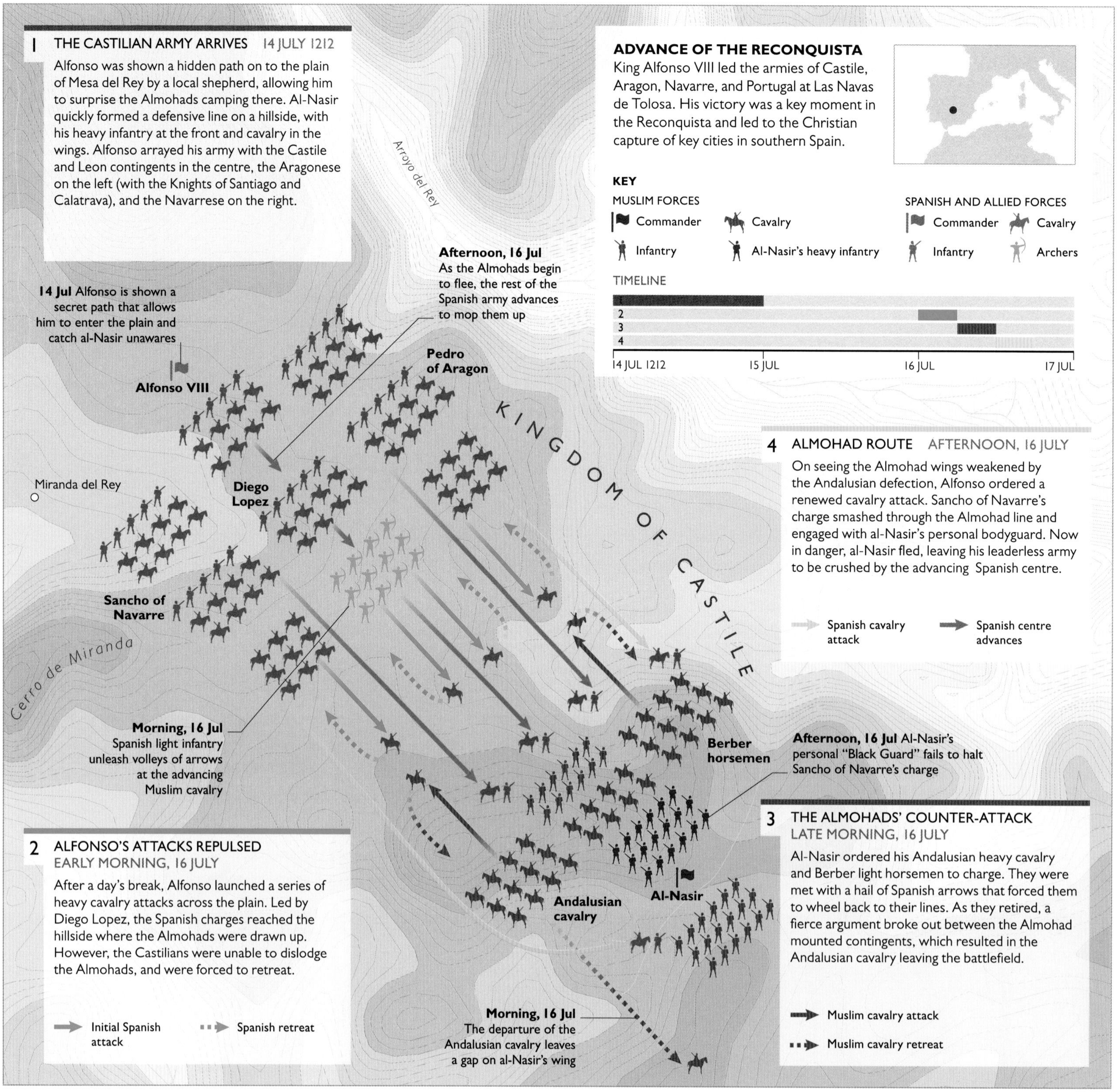
1 THE CASTILIAN ARMY ARRIVES 14 JULY 1212
Alfonso was shown a hidden path on to the plain of Mesa del Rey by a local shepherd, allowing him to surprise the Almohads camping there. Al-Nasir quickly formed a defensive line on a hillside, with his heavy infantry at the front and cavalry in the wings. Alfonso arrayed his army with the Castile and Leon contingents in the centre, the Aragonese on the left (with the Knights of Santiago and Calatrava), and the Navarrese on the right.
ADVANCE OF THE RECONQUISTA
King Alfonso VIII led the armies of Castile, Aragon, Navarre, and Portugal at Las Navas de Tolosa. His victory was a key moment in the Reconquista and led to the Christian capture of key cities in southern Spain.
KEY
MUSLIM FORCES
Commander
Cavalry
Infantry
Al-Nasir's heavy infantry
SPANISH AND ALLIED FORCES
Commander
Cavalry
Infantry
Archers
TIMELINE
1
2
3
4
14 JUL 1212
15 JUL
16 JUL
17 JUL
Arroyo del Rey
Afternoon, 16 Jul As the Almohads begin to flee, the rest of the Spanish army advances to mop them up
14 Jul Alfonso is shown a secret path that allows him to enter the plain and catch al-Nasir unawares
Alfonso VIII
Pedro of Aragon
KINGDOM OF CASTILE
4 ALMOHAD ROUTE AFTERNOON, 16 JULY
On seeing the Almohad wings weakened by the Andalusian defection, Alfonso ordered a renewed cavalry attack. Sancho of Navarre's charge smashed through the Almohad line and engaged with al-Nasir's personal bodyguard. Now in danger, al-Nasir fled, leaving his leaderless army to be crushed by the advancing Spanish centre.
Spanish cavalry attack
Spanish centre advances
Miranda del Rey
Diego Lopez
Sancho of Navarre
Cerro de Miranda
Morning, 16 Jul Spanish light infantry unleash volleys of arrows at the advancing Muslim cavalry
Berber horsemen
Afternoon, 16 Jul Al-Nasir's personal "Black Guard" fails to halt Sancho of Navarre's charge
3 THE ALMOHADS' COUNTER-ATTACK LATE MORNING, 16 JULY
Al-Nasir ordered his Andalusian heavy cavalry and Berber light horsemen to charge. They were met with a hail of Spanish arrows that forced them to wheel back to their lines. As they retired, a fierce argument broke out between the Almohad mounted contingents, which resulted in the Andalusian cavalry leaving the battlefield.
2 ALFONSO'S ATTACKS REPULSED EARLY MORNING, 16 JULY
After a day's break, Alfonso launched a series of heavy cavalry attacks across the plain. Led by Diego Lopez, the Spanish charges reached the hillside where the Almohads were drawn up. However, the Castilians were unable to dislodge the Almohads, and were forced to retreat.
Andalusian cavalry
Al-Nasir
Initial Spanish attack
Spanish retreat
Morning, 16 Jul The departure of the Andalusian cavalry leaves a gap on al-Nasir's wing
Muslim cavalry attack
Muslim cavalry retreat

LAS NAVAS DE TOLOSA

In 1212, a coalition of Christian kings overwhelmed the caliph al-Nasir's Muslim army on the plains of Andalusia in a last-ditch charge. The victory marked a turning point in the Reconquista – the Christian reconquest of the Muslim lands in Spain.

The reign of King Alfonso VIII of Castile (r. 1158–1214) saw new Christian advances against southern Spain's Muslim emirates, which had fallen into disarray after the collapse of the ruling Almoravid dynasty in the 1140s. Alfonso pushed south, but his progress was stalled by the Almohads – a new Muslim power from Morocco. In 1211 Muhammad al-Nasir, the Almohad caliph, marched north from Seville, capturing the key fort of Salvatierra. The following Spring, Alfonso marched south to meet him, joined by the kings of Aragon and Navarre, and Portuguese and French allies. Alfonso waited until July to catch al-Nasir by surprise at Las Navas de Tolosa. The defeat of the Almohads led to rapid Christian gains; eventually Alfonso's grandson, Ferdinand III of Castile, seized Cordoba in 1236 and the Almohad capital of Seville in 1248.

MURET

While leading a crusade against the heretical Cathars in southwestern France in September 1213, the French knight and nobleman Simon de Montfort found himself outnumbered at the fortified town of Muret by a large force from Aragon and Toulouse. His daring sortie unexpectedly routed the Aragonese, killed their king, and dealt a blow to the Cathar cause.

In the 12th century, a heretical Christian movement known as Catharism (or Albigensianism) flourished in southwest France. It was supported by local nobles, who used it to assert independence from the north. In 1208, Pope Innocent III declared a crusade against the Cathars, known as the Albigensian Crusade. Many knights, led by Simon de Montfort, flocked to help. The crusaders captured a string of fortresses and began to crush the Cathars, but met stiffer resistance after Count Raymond VI of Toulouse defected to the Cathars, supported by King Peter II of Aragon. Raymond and Peter were defeated at Muret, but Catharism was not eliminated entirely, and it took the intervention of King Louis VIII of France in 1229 to agree a peace. After a brutal massacre at Montségur in 1244, Catharism disappeared as a significant force in France.

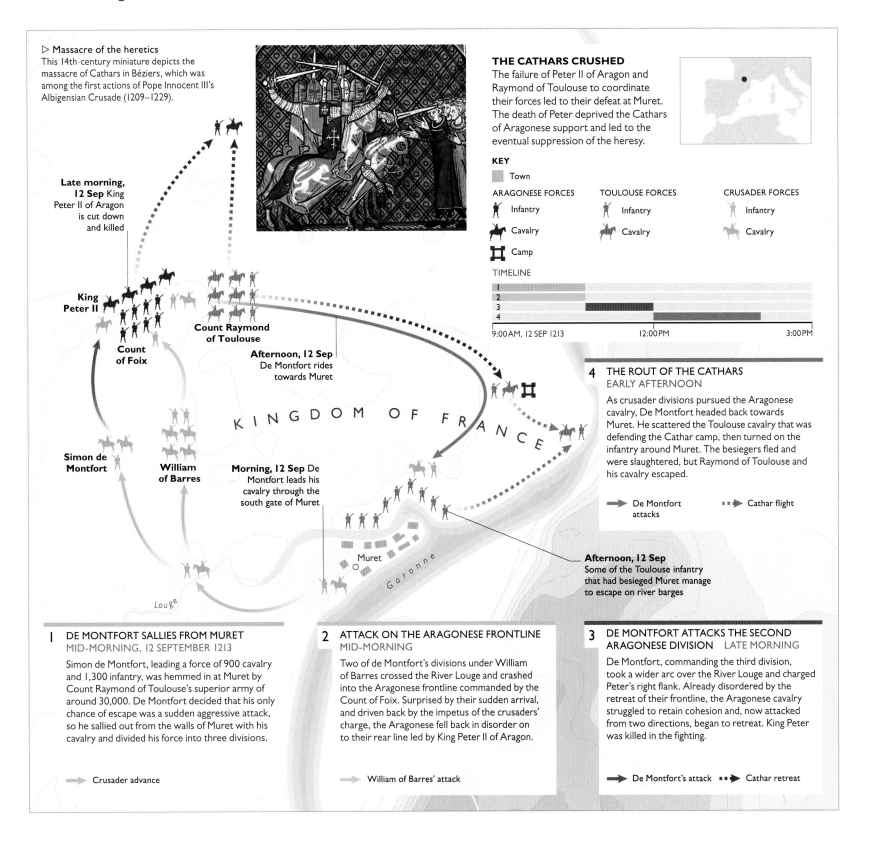

▷ **Massacre of the heretics**
This 14th-century miniature depicts the massacre of Cathars in Béziers, which was among the first actions of Pope Innocent III's Albigensian Crusade (1209–1229).

THE CATHARS CRUSHED
The failure of Peter II of Aragon and Raymond of Toulouse to coordinate their forces led to their defeat at Muret. The death of Peter deprived the Cathars of Aragonese support and led to the eventual suppression of the heresy.

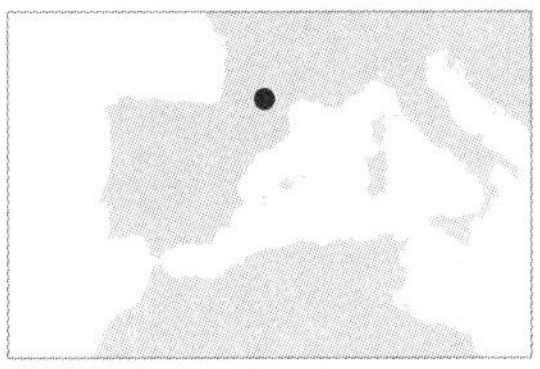

KEY

Town

ARAGONESE FORCES: Infantry, Cavalry, Camp

TOULOUSE FORCES: Infantry, Cavalry

CRUSADER FORCES: Infantry, Cavalry

TIMELINE

1, 2, 3, 4

9:00AM, 12 SEP 1213 — 12:00PM — 3:00PM

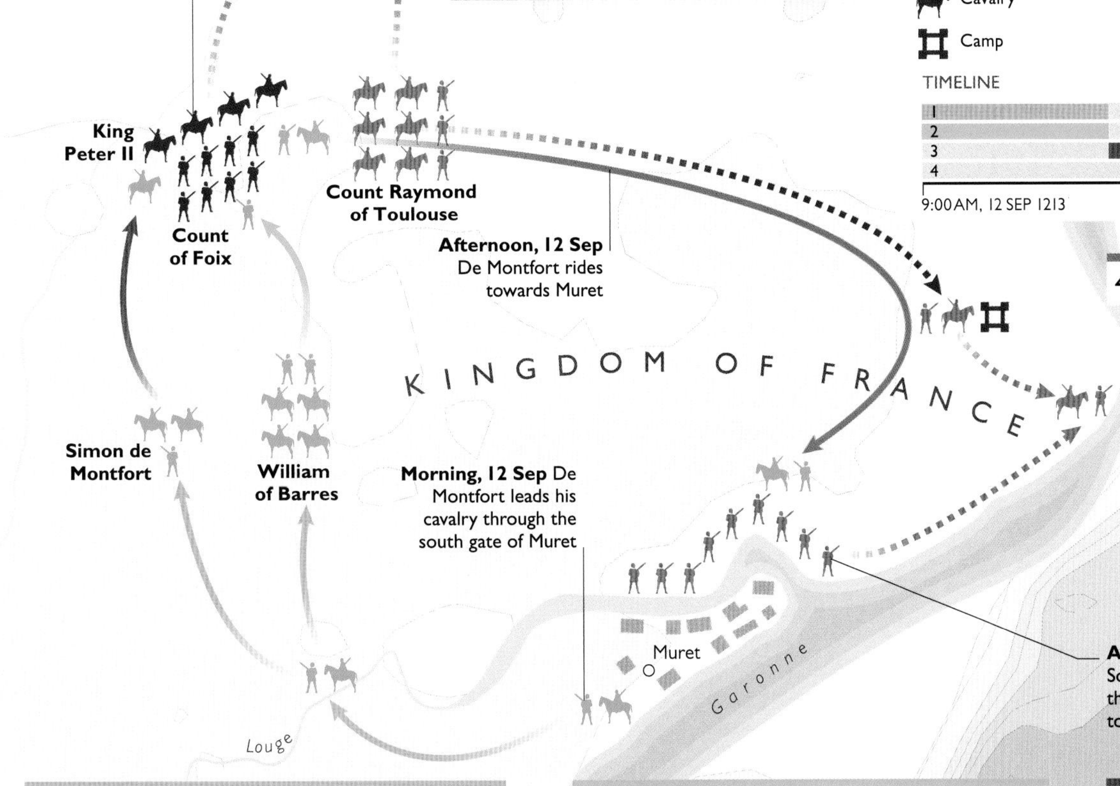

Late morning, 12 Sep King Peter II of Aragon is cut down and killed
King Peter II
Count of Foix
Count Raymond of Toulouse
Afternoon, 12 Sep De Montfort rides towards Muret
KINGDOM OF FRANCE
Simon de Montfort
William of Barres
Morning, 12 Sep De Montfort leads his cavalry through the south gate of Muret
Muret
Garonne
Louge
Afternoon, 12 Sep Some of the Toulouse infantry that had besieged Muret manage to escape on river barges

4 THE ROUT OF THE CATHARS
EARLY AFTERNOON

As crusader divisions pursued the Aragonese cavalry, De Montfort headed back towards Muret. He scattered the Toulouse cavalry that was defending the Cathar camp, then turned on the infantry around Muret. The besiegers fled and were slaughtered, but Raymond of Toulouse and his cavalry escaped.

De Montfort attacks — Cathar flight

1 DE MONTFORT SALLIES FROM MURET
MID-MORNING, 12 SEPTEMBER 1213

Simon de Montfort, leading a force of 900 cavalry and 1,300 infantry, was hemmed in at Muret by Count Raymond of Toulouse's superior army of around 30,000. De Montfort decided that his only chance of escape was a sudden aggressive attack, so he sallied out from the walls of Muret with his cavalry and divided his force into three divisions.

Crusader advance

2 ATTACK ON THE ARAGONESE FRONTLINE
MID-MORNING

Two of de Montfort's divisions under William of Barres crossed the River Louge and crashed into the Aragonese frontline commanded by the Count of Foix. Surprised by their sudden arrival, and driven back by the impetus of the crusaders' charge, the Aragonese fell back in disorder on to their rear line led by King Peter II of Aragon.

William of Barres' attack

3 DE MONTFORT ATTACKS THE SECOND ARAGONESE DIVISION LATE MORNING

De Montfort, commanding the third division, took a wider arc over the River Louge and charged Peter's right flank. Already disordered by the retreat of their frontline, the Aragonese cavalry struggled to retain cohesion and, now attacked from two directions, began to retreat. King Peter was killed in the fighting.

De Montfort's attack — Cathar retreat

LIEGNITZ

In April 1241, Duke Henry II of Silesia faced an invading Mongol army outside the town of Liegnitz. Fooled by the classic mounted nomad tactic of a feigned retreat, his army was cut to pieces and the Duke killed. However, on the brink of conquering Poland and Hungary, the Mongols pulled back, saving Europe from further devastation.

In 1223, Genghis Khan (see p.78) invaded Russia. His horsemen raided towns and defeated the Cumans – a Turkic people who lived in the steppes along the Black Sea. They were granted sanctuary in Hungary by the king, Bela IV, and converted to Christianity.

The new Great Khan Ögodei invaded Russia again in 1237. He demanded the return of the Cumans, and in 1241 used King Bela's refusal as a pretext to invade Hungary. After sweeping through Russia, the Mongol army divided in two: commanders Batu Khan and Subotai were to attack Hungary directly, while a diversionary force under Baidar and Kadan was to strike north into Poland to stop the Hungarians and Poles from uniting.

The Mongols ravaged northern Poland and then turned south, sacking and burning the Polish capital Cracow in March 1241. The last force in Poland capable of stopping the Mongols was the 30,000 strong army of Henry II of Silesia. He decided to attack, unaware that assistance, in the form of 50,000 men under Wenceslas of Bohemia, was just two days' march away.

Henry's army was routed at Liegnitz (Legnica) on 9 April, and two days later southern Mongol forces smashed the Hungarian army at Mohi. Poland and Hungary were only saved by the news of Ögodei's death in December, which ignited a power struggle among the Mongol commanders, causing them to pull their men back to Mongolia.

MONGOL INCURSION
Henry II's army faced the Mongols at Liegnitz, fearing that their enemy would soon be reinforced. They were defeated by Mongol mobility and superior tactics.

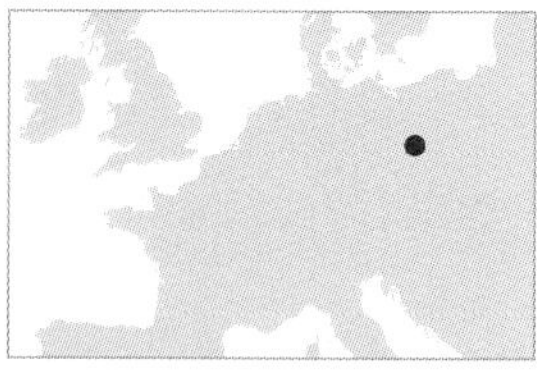

KEY

POLISH FORCES: Commander; Infantry; Cavalry

MONGOL FORCES: Commander; Light cavalry; Heavy cavalry

TIMELINE

9 APR 1241 — 10 APR

△ **Mongol superiority**
This detail from a 14th-century Silesian Codex depicts a scene from the battle, in which the agile mounted Mongol archers face heavy German and Polish cavalry.

THE MONGOL CAMPAIGN, 1237–42
The second Mongol invasion of Europe began in late 1237. Taking the Russian principalities by surprise, the cities of Vladimir, Moscow, and Tver were soon sacked. Then, in early 1241, Batu Khan (commander of the western part of the Mongol empire) sent his army through Kiev and across the Carpathians. In Galicia the force divided: one wing entered Poland to the north, and eventually met Duke Henry of Silesia at Liegnitz; the other wing went south and destroyed the Hungarians at the Battle of Mohi. The Mongol campaign ended with the pursuit by Kadan – the victor of Liegnitz – of King Bela IV of Hungary along the coast of Dalmatia and then through Bulgaria as the Mongols under Batu returned home in 1242.

KEY

- Main battle
- Mongol invasion, winter 1237–38
- Mongol invasion, 1241
- Campaign by Kadan, 1242
- Mongol return route

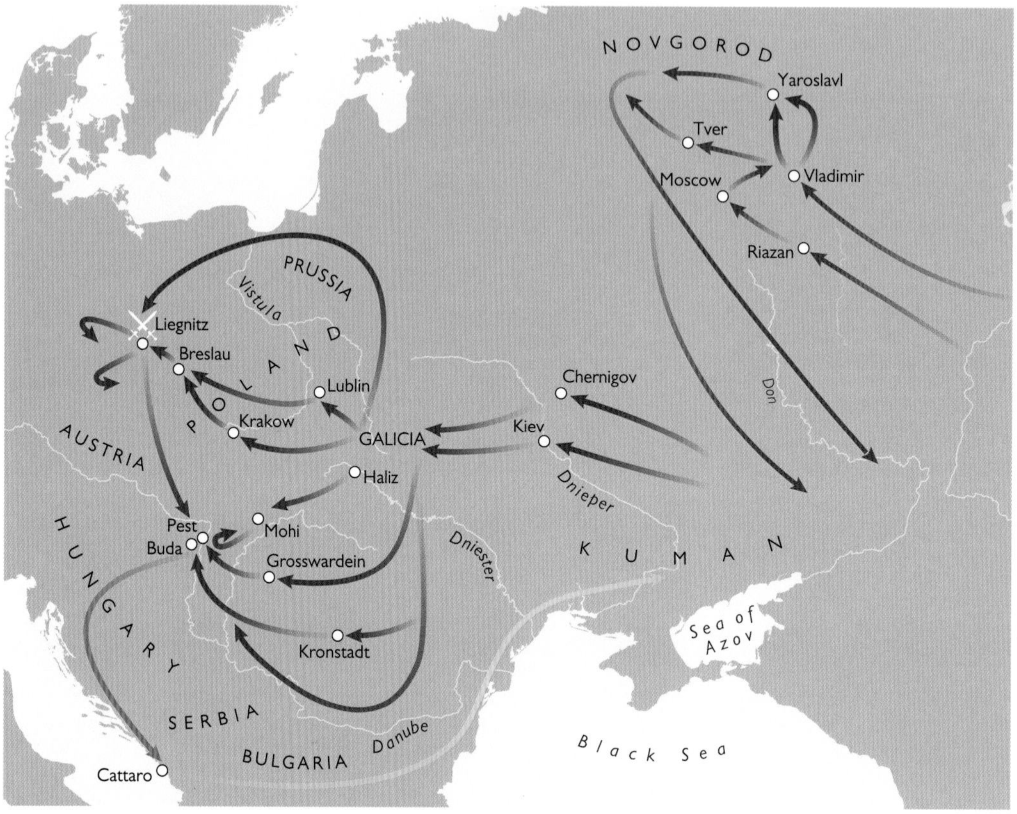
NOVGOROD
Yaroslavl
Tver
Moscow
Vladimir
Riazan
PRUSSIA
Vistula
Liegnitz
Breslau
POLAND
Lublin
Krakow
GALICIA
Chernigov
Kiev
Don
Dnieper
AUSTRIA
Haliz
HUNGARY
Pest
Buda
Mohi
Grosswardein
Dniester
KUMAN
Sea of Azov
Kronstadt
SERBIA
BULGARIA
Danube
Black Sea
Cattaro

1 THE ARMIES DEPLOY 9 APRIL 1241

Henry approached the battlefield from Liegnitz to the northwest. He deployed his army in four squadrons: in the front were the elite German and Templar knights, along with less disciplined Polish levies and a force of Moravian miners. Two further groups of cavalry were commanded by Sulislaw of Cracow and Mieszko of Opole. Henry himself took up the rear. Facing them, Baidar and Kadan drew up their 20,000-strong force in a wide arc, with heavy cavalry at the centre and lighter cavalry on the wings.

2 DUKE HENRY ATTACKS

Duke Henry ordered the cavalry in his first line to charge the Mongol centre. As they surged forward, anticipating fierce close-quarters combat, they were met with a hail of arrows from the Mongol cavalry. The Mongol horsemen were highly skilled archers capable of hitting targets at 300 m (330 yards). As the knights and their mounts crashed to the ground, the charge lost momentum and European cavalry wheeled round and returned to Henry's lines.

Polish attack | Polish retreat

3 THE SECOND ATTACK

Seeing the forward cavalry retreat, Sulislaw and Mieszko launched their attacks, charging towards the Mongol lines. As the Mongol vanguard pulled back, drawing the Poles further forward, the Mongol light cavalry began to close in on the Poles from behind. At one point, a Mongol horseman began to shout in Polish "Run, Run!"; the Poles, taken in by the ruse, turned and began to retreat.

Polish attack | Polish retreat | Mongols' feigned retreat | Mongols close in

4 THE TRAP SPRINGS

Witnessing the confusion in his forces, Duke Henry led his fourth squadron into battle. By this time, the Mongols had set another trap, lighting piles of reeds they had set in front of the Poles. The resulting pall of smoke blinded the Poles and added to their disarray. The Mongol wings closed in still further, cutting off any hope of an organized Polish retreat.

Mongols set fires | Polish attack

5 THE DESTRUCTION OF DUKE HENRY'S ARMY

Continuing to suffer casualties from the Mongol archers, Duke Henry was now engaged at close-quarters by Mongol heavy cavalry. Several of his senior commanders were killed. Realizing he was trapped, the duke tried to break through the Mongol lines, but was struck in the arm with a spear and then beheaded by the jubilant Mongols.

Mongol attack

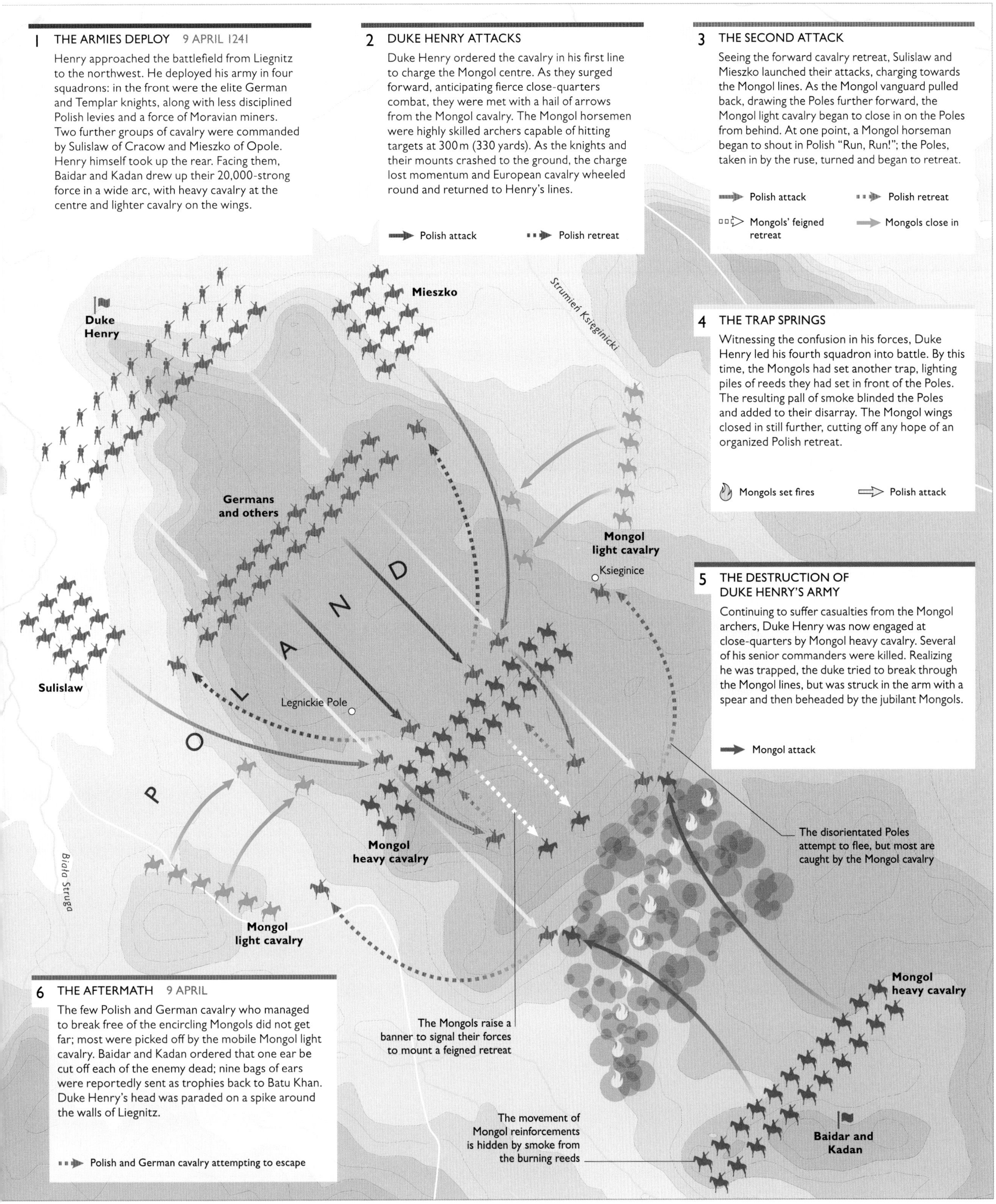

Duke Henry
Mieszko
Strumień Księginicki
Germans and others
Mongol light cavalry
Księginice
Sulislaw
POLAND
Legnickie Pole
Mongol heavy cavalry
Biała Struga
Mongol light cavalry
The disorientated Poles attempt to flee, but most are caught by the Mongol cavalry
The Mongols raise a banner to signal their forces to mount a feigned retreat
Mongol heavy cavalry
Baidar and Kadan
The movement of Mongol reinforcements is hidden by smoke from the burning reeds

6 THE AFTERMATH 9 APRIL

The few Polish and German cavalry who managed to break free of the encircling Mongols did not get far; most were picked off by the mobile Mongol light cavalry. Baidar and Kadan ordered that one ear be cut off each of the enemy dead; nine bags of ears were reportedly sent as trophies back to Batu Khan. Duke Henry's head was paraded on a spike around the walls of Liegnitz.

Polish and German cavalry attempting to escape

THE MONGOL EMPIRE

In 1206 CE Temujin, a Mongol chieftain, took the name of Genghis Khan and united the Mongol tribes of the Central Asian steppes. These tribes, which had been subjects, raiders, interlopers, and mercenaries to imperial China for centuries, went on to create an empire spanning two centuries.

In the early 13th century, China was divided between the southern Song dynasty and the northern Jin Empire. Genghis Khan first allied himself with the Song against the Jin and their puppet Xia dynasty. He then moved west, his army conquering the Khwarazmian empire by the Caspian Sea and defeating a Russian coalition at the Kalka River in 1223. Mongol expansion did not end with the death of Genghis Khan in 1227. When the Song attempted to retake their former capitals from the defeated Jin, the Mongols turned on them and completed their conquest of China. Almost unstoppable, the Mongol armies spread westwards, and in 1294 their empire, at its apex, stretched from the Yellow Sea to the Danube.

Essentially a cavalry force, the Mongol army combined heavily armoured lancer cavalry and more numerous, lightly armoured horsemen with composite bows. The Mongols were masters of mobile warfare and expert tacticians, and were a superior force to other armies of the time. Although the army primarily consisted of Mongol tribal warriors, it was supplemented by local auxiliaries, and the Mongol forces that invaded Japan in 1274 and 1281 included Chinese and Korean troops.

After Genghis Khan died, the sprawling empire had been divided into khanates (sub-empires) between his four sons, with Ögedei, the third son, succeeding his father as the Great Khan (ruler). This tradition of the Great Khans continued until Genghis' grandson Kublai Khan's death in 1294. The various khanates drifted apart, but continued to exert influence until the 15th century.

◁ **Central Asian quiver**
Possibly of Mongol origin, this ornate Central Asian quiver was designed to hold arrows used by mounted Mongol archers. They remained in use for centuries, with examples dating to the Qing Dynasty (1644–1912).

TEMUJIN BORJIGIN
C. 1162–1227

Better known as Genghis Khan ("universal ruler"), Temujin Borjigin was born to a family of minor chieftains. Over the years, he built his reputation as an aggressive warrior and skilled diplomat. With a formidable army, he embarked on a conquest that lasted more than 20 years and resulted in the entire Asian steppe and adjoining territories falling under his rule.

Clashing armies
This reproduction from a 14th-century illustration probably shows Genghis Khan's army besieging a fortress in Western Xia. The Mongols learned siege warfare from the Chinese, and used giant catapults to hurl firebombs over battlements.

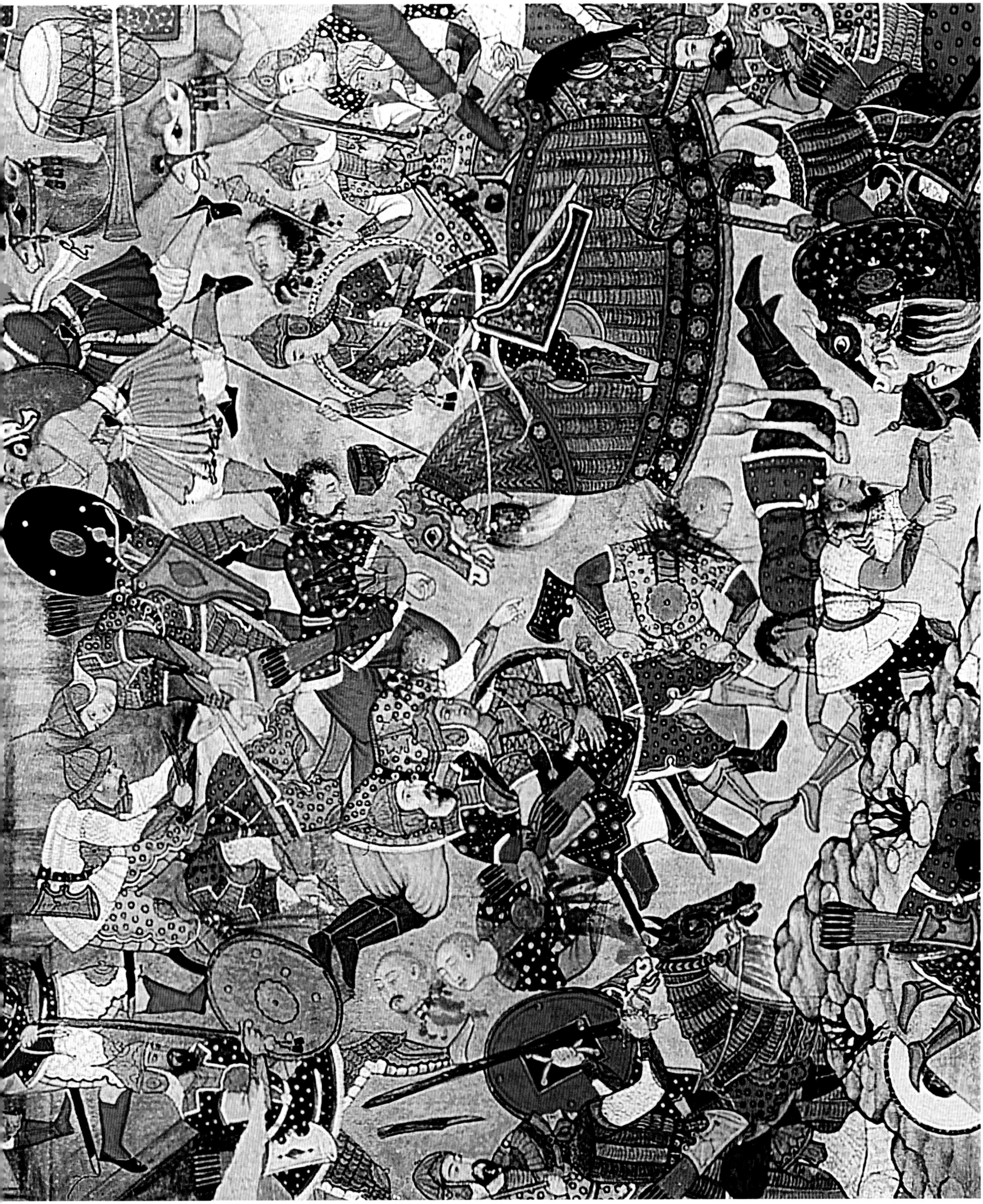

LAKE PEIPUS

The Teutonic Knights' eastward advance into the Novgorod Republic was finally halted on the ice of Lake Peipus in April 1242. There, Prince Alexander Nevsky defeated the invaders, preserving Eastern Orthodoxy from Catholic crusading zeal.

In 1198, Pope Innocent III reiterated his predecessor's call for a crusade against the pagan peoples of the eastern Baltic, marking the beginning of a long series of campaigns to convert them to Christianity. Having secured the Baltic lands, in 1240, the Teutonic Knights turned against the Republic of Novgorod (an Orthodox Christian state in northern Russia) and seized Pskov. It was retaken the following year by the 20-year-old Prince Alexander Nevsky, whom the Novgorodians had earlier banished due to tensions with the nobility. The Knights, led by Prince-Bishop Hermann of Dorpat, renewed the attack in March 1242, heading towards Novgorod. Alexander moved to intercept him, luring the crusaders onto the frozen waters of Lake Peipus, on the present-day Russian-Estonian border. His victory there halted the Teutonic Knights' efforts to absorb Novgorod, although their campaigns in Prussia and Lithuania continued into the early 15th century.

◁ **Battle of the Ice**
With sword aloft, Alexander Nevsky confronts the Teutonic Knights, in this 16th-century depiction of the battle.

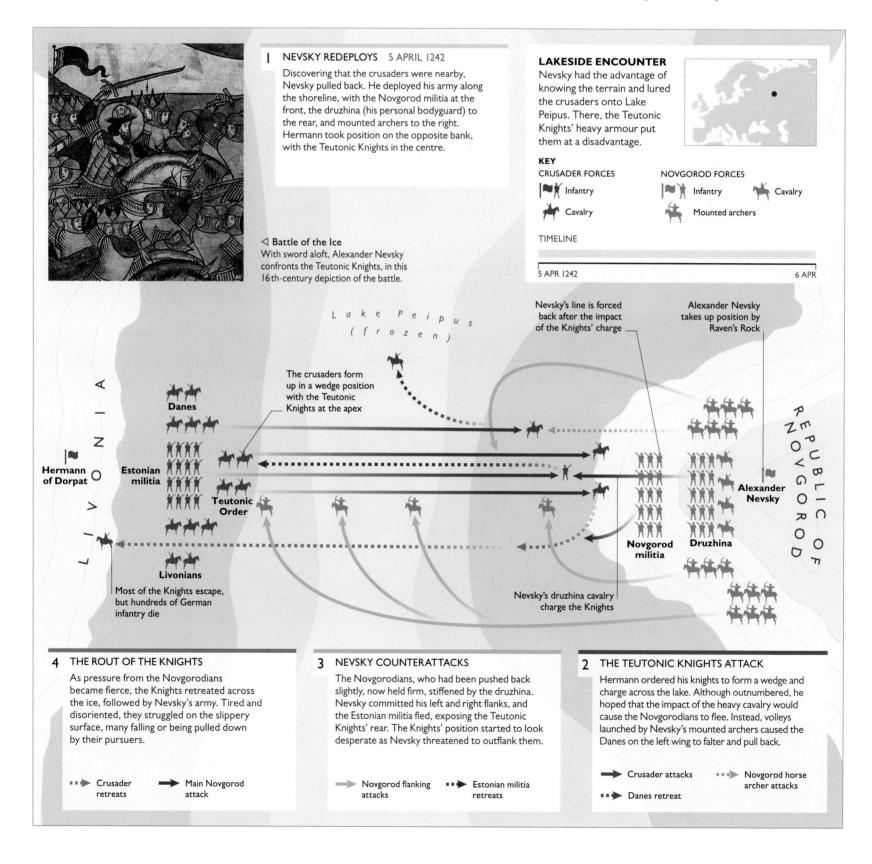

1 NEVSKY REDEPLOYS 5 APRIL 1242

Discovering that the crusaders were nearby, Nevsky pulled back. He deployed his army along the shoreline, with the Novgorod militia at the front, the druzhina (his personal bodyguard) to the rear, and mounted archers to the right. Hermann took position on the opposite bank, with the Teutonic Knights in the centre.

LAKESIDE ENCOUNTER

Nevsky had the advantage of knowing the terrain and lured the crusaders onto Lake Peipus. There, the Teutonic Knights' heavy armour put them at a disadvantage.

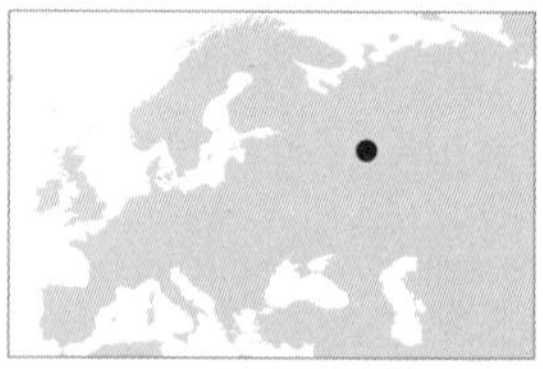

KEY

CRUSADER FORCES
- Infantry
- Cavalry

NOVGOROD FORCES
- Infantry
- Cavalry
- Mounted archers

TIMELINE

5 APR 1242 — 6 APR

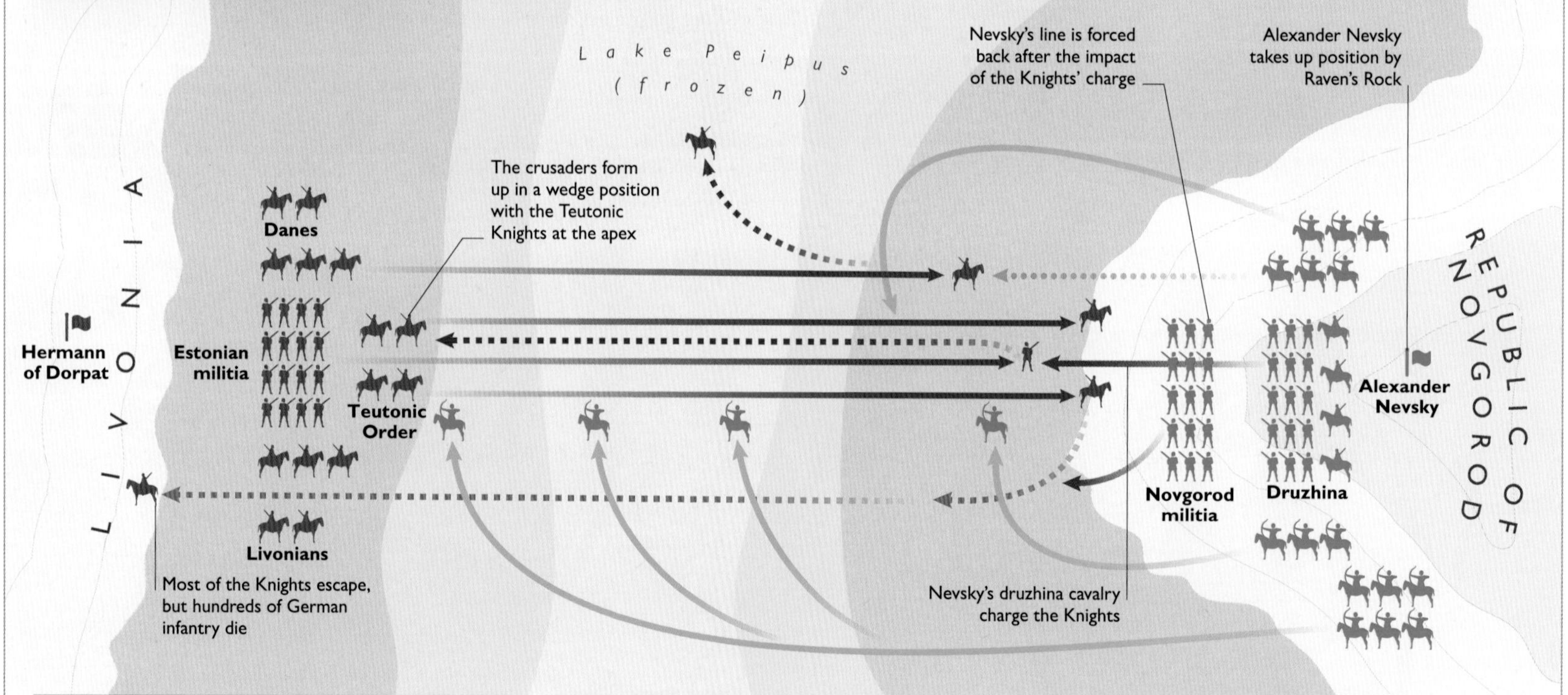

Lake Peipus (frozen)
LIVONIA
REPUBLIC OF NOVGOROD
Danes
Hermann of Dorpat
Estonian militia
Teutonic Order
Livonians
Novgorod militia
Druzhina
Alexander Nevsky
The crusaders form up in a wedge position with the Teutonic Knights at the apex
Nevsky's line is forced back after the impact of the Knights' charge
Alexander Nevsky takes up position by Raven's Rock
Most of the Knights escape, but hundreds of German infantry die
Nevsky's druzhina cavalry charge the Knights

2 THE TEUTONIC KNIGHTS ATTACK

Hermann ordered his knights to form a wedge and charge across the lake. Although outnumbered, he hoped that the impact of the heavy cavalry would cause the Novgorodians to flee. Instead, volleys launched by Nevsky's mounted archers caused the Danes on the left wing to falter and pull back.

- Crusader attacks
- Danes retreat
- Novgorod horse archer attacks

3 NEVSKY COUNTERATTACKS

The Novgorodians, who had been pushed back slightly, now held firm, stiffened by the druzhina. Nevsky committed his left and right flanks, and the Estonian militia fled, exposing the Teutonic Knights' rear. The Knights' position started to look desperate as Nevsky threatened to outflank them.

- Novgorod flanking attacks
- Estonian militia retreats

4 THE ROUT OF THE KNIGHTS

As pressure from the Novgorodians became fierce, the Knights retreated across the ice, followed by Nevsky's army. Tired and disoriented, they struggled on the slippery surface, many falling or being pulled down by their pursuers.

- Crusader retreats
- Main Novgorod attack

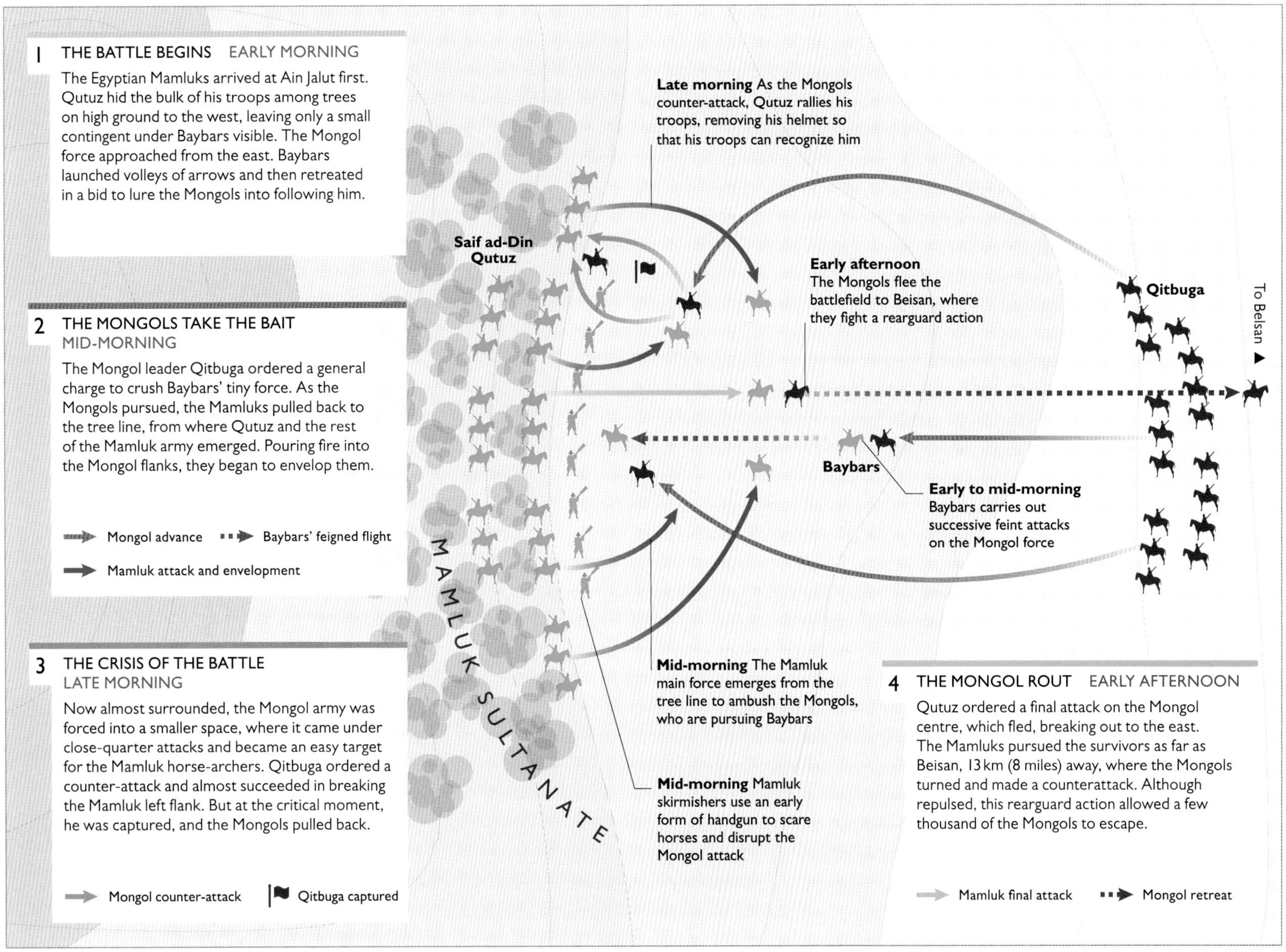
1 THE BATTLE BEGINS EARLY MORNING
The Egyptian Mamluks arrived at Ain Jalut first. Qutuz hid the bulk of his troops among trees on high ground to the west, leaving only a small contingent under Baybars visible. The Mongol force approached from the east. Baybars launched volleys of arrows and then retreated in a bid to lure the Mongols into following him.
2 THE MONGOLS TAKE THE BAIT MID-MORNING
The Mongol leader Qitbuga ordered a general charge to crush Baybars' tiny force. As the Mongols pursued, the Mamluks pulled back to the tree line, from where Qutuz and the rest of the Mamluk army emerged. Pouring fire into the Mongol flanks, they began to envelop them.
Mongol advance
Baybars' feigned flight
Mamluk attack and envelopment
3 THE CRISIS OF THE BATTLE LATE MORNING
Now almost surrounded, the Mongol army was forced into a smaller space, where it came under close-quarter attacks and became an easy target for the Mamluk horse-archers. Qitbuga ordered a counter-attack and almost succeeded in breaking the Mamluk left flank. But at the critical moment, he was captured, and the Mongols pulled back.
Mongol counter-attack
Qitbuga captured
MAMLUK SULTANATE
Saif ad-Din Qutuz
Late morning As the Mongols counter-attack, Qutuz rallies his troops, removing his helmet so that his troops can recognize him
Early afternoon The Mongols flee the battlefield to Beisan, where they fight a rearguard action
Qitbuga
To Belsan ▶
Baybars
Early to mid-morning Baybars carries out successive feint attacks on the Mongol force
Mid-morning The Mamluk main force emerges from the tree line to ambush the Mongols, who are pursuing Baybars
Mid-morning Mamluk skirmishers use an early form of handgun to scare horses and disrupt the Mongol attack
4 THE MONGOL ROUT EARLY AFTERNOON
Qutuz ordered a final attack on the Mongol centre, which fled, breaking out to the east. The Mamluks pursued the survivors as far as Beisan, 13 km (8 miles) away, where the Mongols turned and made a counterattack. Although repulsed, this rearguard action allowed a few thousand of the Mongols to escape.
Mamluk final attack
Mongol retreat

AIN JALUT

In a little over 50 years, the Mongols built a vast empire that dominated much of Asia. In 1260, their seemingly invincible army was defeated in battle at Ain Jalut, around 90 km (56 miles) north of Jerusalem. There, an Egyptian Mamluk army caught the Mongols in an ambush and cut them to pieces.

By 1256, the Mongols had already conquered much of Asia and Eastern Europe. That year, the Mongol Great Khan Möngke directed his brother Hülegü to launch a campaign against the Middle East and the Mamluk rulers of Egypt. His huge army took fortress after fortress, and in February 1258 stormed Baghdad, putting an end to the Abbasid Caliphate. In 1260, he sent an envoy to Qutuz, the Mamluk sultan, demanding Egypt's surrender. Qutuz refused and executed the envoys. At this point, Hülegü received news of Möngke's death, and an assembly was called to elect a new Great Khan. Preoccupied with this (and aware that the Middle East offered little pasture for their horses), Hülegü pulled back most of his forces, leaving the remainder under the command of the general Qitbuga. Hearing of this, Qutuz marched north with his general, Baybars, to confront the Mongols.

The ensuing battle at Ain Jalut destroyed the Mongol reputation for invincibility and shifted the balance of power in favour of the Egyptian Mamluks, who went on to capture Damascus and Aleppo shortly after.

A FATEFUL AMBUSH

The Mamluks made use of hit-and-run tactics to provoke the Mongol troops into battle. The Mamluk general Baybars was familiar with the terrain and used this knowledge to set a fateful trap. Qutuz was later assassinated; Baybars took his place.

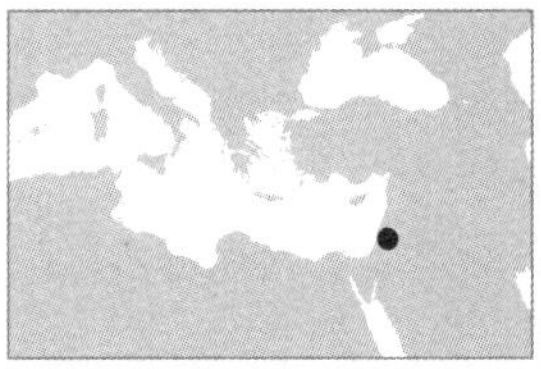

KEY

Mamluk cavalry · Mamluk hand-gunners · Mongol cavalry

TIMELINE

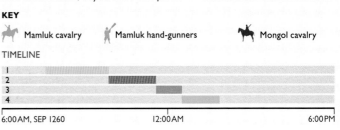

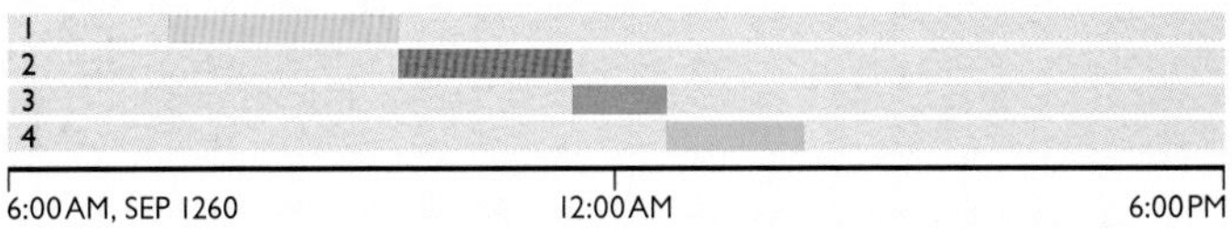
1
2
3
4
6:00AM, SEP 1260
12:00AM
6:00PM

1 THE ARMIES DEPLOY
MORNING–MIDDAY, 26 AUGUST 1346

Edward formed his army along a ridge between Crécy and Wadicourt. His son, Edward the Black Prince, commanded the right flank, the Earl of Northampton the left, with the king in charge of the reserve. The French arrived on the battlefield around mid-day, with Genoese crossbowmen in the vanguard, followed by knights led by the Duke of Alençon, and a rearguard under Philip VI.

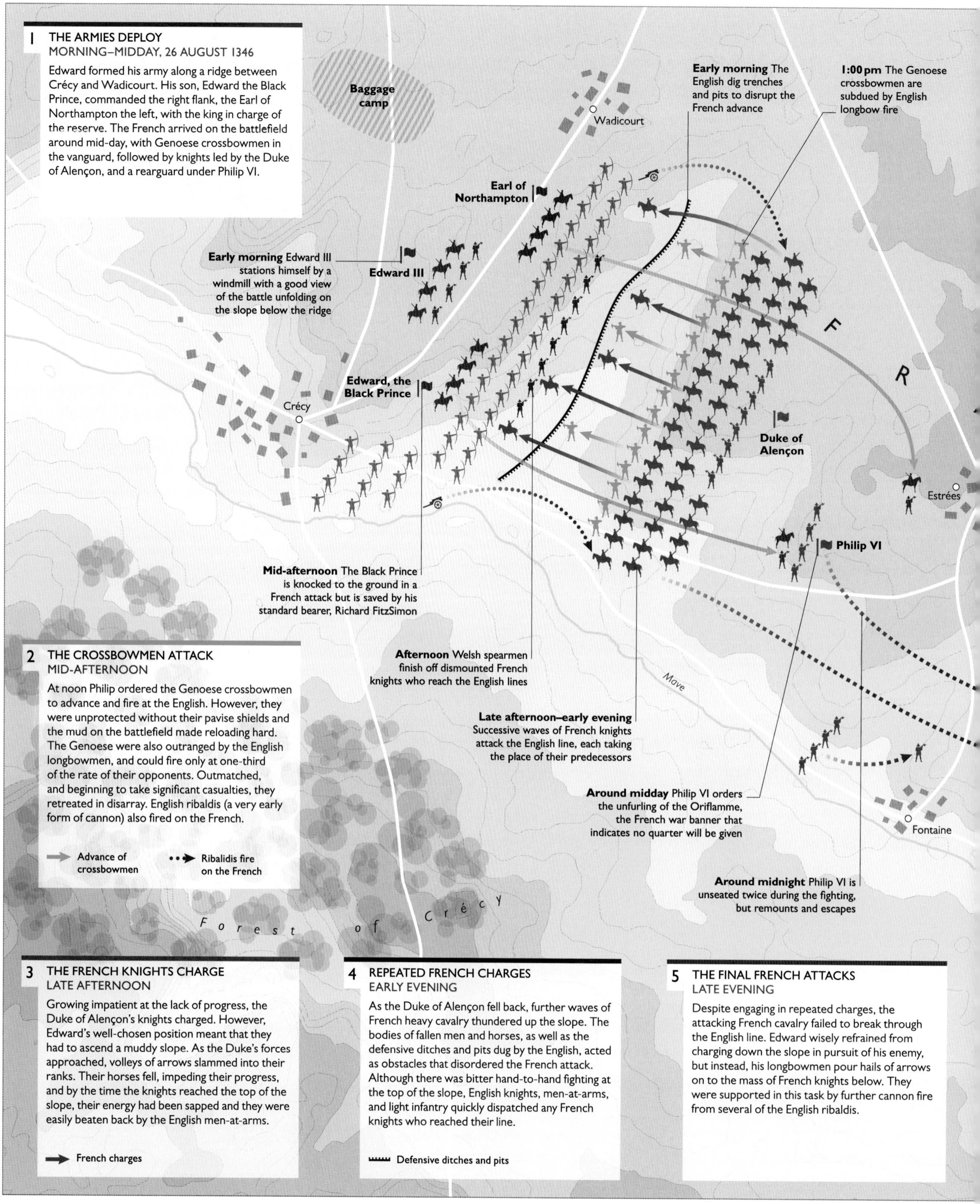

Baggage camp
Wadicourt
Early morning The English dig trenches and pits to disrupt the French advance
1:00 pm The Genoese crossbowmen are subdued by English longbow fire
Earl of Northampton
Early morning Edward III stations himself by a windmill with a good view of the battle unfolding on the slope below the ridge
Edward III
F
R
Edward, the Black Prince
Crécy
Duke of Alençon
Estrées
Philip VI
Mid-afternoon The Black Prince is knocked to the ground in a French attack but is saved by his standard bearer, Richard FitzSimon
Afternoon Welsh spearmen finish off dismounted French knights who reach the English lines
Maye
Late afternoon–early evening Successive waves of French knights attack the English line, each taking the place of their predecessors
Around midday Philip VI orders the unfurling of the Oriflamme, the French war banner that indicates no quarter will be given
Fontaine
Around midnight Philip VI is unseated twice during the fighting, but remounts and escapes
Forest of Crécy

2 THE CROSSBOWMEN ATTACK
MID-AFTERNOON

At noon Philip ordered the Genoese crossbowmen to advance and fire at the English. However, they were unprotected without their pavise shields and the mud on the battlefield made reloading hard. The Genoese were also outranged by the English longbowmen, and could fire only at one-third of the rate of their opponents. Outmatched, and beginning to take significant casualties, they retreated in disarray. English ribaldis (a very early form of cannon) also fired on the French.

Advance of crossbowmen

Ribalidis fire on the French

3 THE FRENCH KNIGHTS CHARGE
LATE AFTERNOON

Growing impatient at the lack of progress, the Duke of Alençon's knights charged. However, Edward's well-chosen position meant that they had to ascend a muddy slope. As the Duke's forces approached, volleys of arrows slammed into their ranks. Their horses fell, impeding their progress, and by the time the knights reached the top of the slope, their energy had been sapped and they were easily beaten back by the English men-at-arms.

French charges

4 REPEATED FRENCH CHARGES
EARLY EVENING

As the Duke of Alençon fell back, further waves of French heavy cavalry thundered up the slope. The bodies of fallen men and horses, as well as the defensive ditches and pits dug by the English, acted as obstacles that disordered the French attack. Although there was bitter hand-to-hand fighting at the top of the slope, English knights, men-at-arms, and light infantry quickly dispatched any French knights who reached their line.

Defensive ditches and pits

5 THE FINAL FRENCH ATTACKS
LATE EVENING

Despite engaging in repeated charges, the attacking French cavalry failed to break through the English line. Edward wisely refrained from charging down the slope in pursuit of his enemy, but instead, his longbowmen pour hails of arrows on to the mass of French knights below. They were supported in this task by further cannon fire from several of the English ribaldis.

CRÉCY

England's victory against France at Crécy in August 1346 was won in large part by the longbow, a quick-firing weapon that decimated Philip VI of France's knights. The battle earned English king Edward III dominance over France in the early phases of the Hundred Years War – a long, intermittent struggle between the two powers.

△ **The fall of the knight**
This Flemish manuscript illumination from 1477 shows the fierce fighting at Crécy. The battle signalled the diminishing usefulness of knights on the battlefield, and marked the rise of England as a significant world power.

Edward III's pursuit of his claim to the French throne led to the outbreak of war against France in 1337. Despite his naval victory at Sluys in 1340, Edward's campaigns were inconclusive until he landed in Normandy in July 1346 with a force of up to 15,000 men. Intent on conducting a *chevauchée* in northern France – terrorizing the region by raiding, burning, and pillaging – Edward attacked a series of northern towns. However, as he neared Paris an approaching French army forced him north, where his forces almost became trapped in the devastated lands south of the Somme river. On 24 August, Edward forced a crossing of the river at Blanchetaque. Only then was he able to turn and face the French on terrain of his choice at Crécy.

Philip wrongly believed that his force's superior numbers – at least double those of the English – would prevail. Instead the battle claimed the lives of thousands of French knights and dozens of nobles, and opened the way to an English advance to Calais, which Edward's forces captured in 1347.

*"Where the pride of the Norman had sway,
The lions lord over the fray."*

FROM "CRÉCY" BY FRANCIS TURNER PALGRAVE, 1881

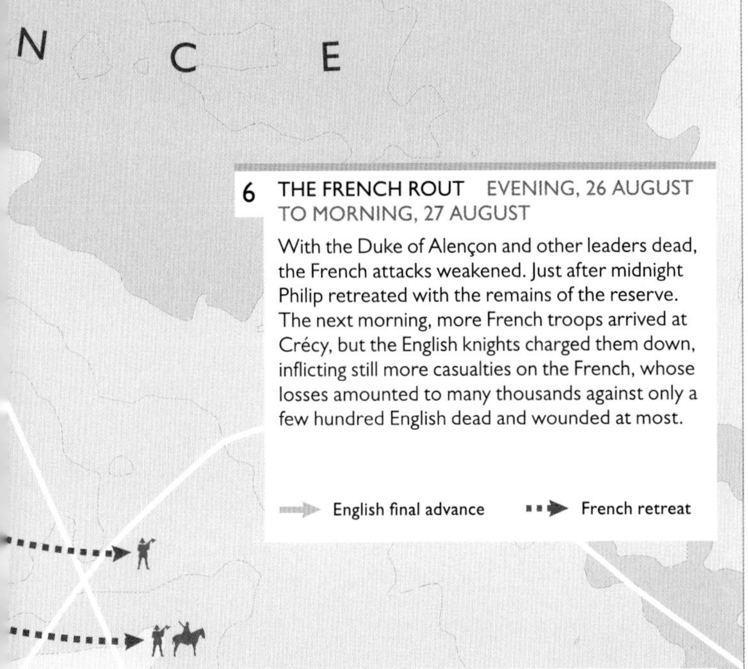
N C E

6 THE FRENCH ROUT EVENING, 26 AUGUST TO MORNING, 27 AUGUST

With the Duke of Alençon and other leaders dead, the French attacks weakened. Just after midnight Philip retreated with the remains of the reserve. The next morning, more French troops arrived at Crécy, but the English knights charged them down, inflicting still more casualties on the French, whose losses amounted to many thousands against only a few hundred English dead and wounded at most.

English final advance · French retreat

VICTORY FOR THE BOW
Edward III's triumph at Crécy was a turning point in the Hundred Years War. It allowed the English to set up a secure base around Calais and cemented the position of the longbow as a key battlefield weapon.

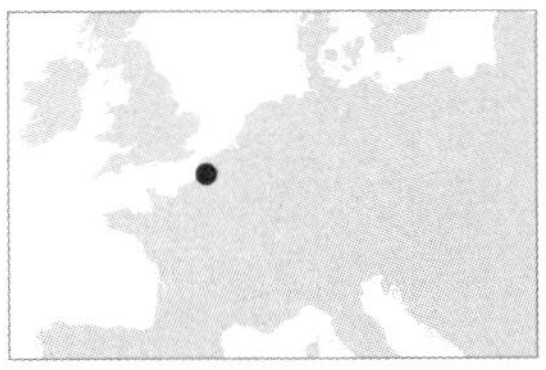

KEY

Towns

ENGLISH FORCES: Commanders; Artillery; Longbowmen; Baggage camp; Infantry; Cavalry

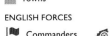

FRENCH FORCES: Commanders; Genoese crossbowmen; Infantry; Cavalry

TIMELINE

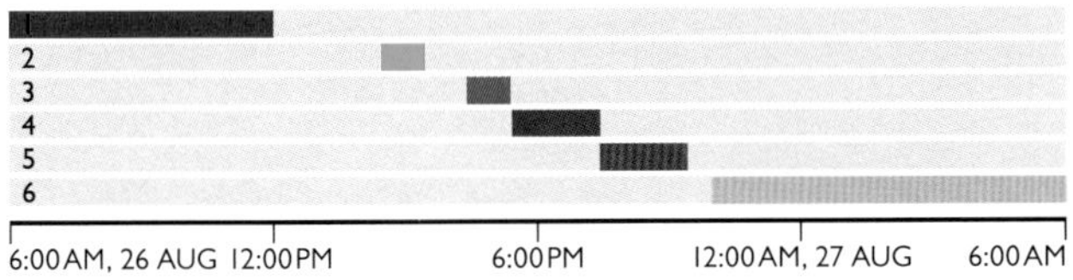
1
2
3
4
5
6
6:00AM, 26 AUG
12:00PM
6:00PM
12:00AM, 27 AUG
6:00AM

THE CRÉCY CAMPAIGN
Edward III's landing at St-Vaast La Hogue on 12 July 1346 took the French by surprise and at first he conducted his *chevauchée* unhindered. As Edward marched towards Paris, Philip VI raised a force to push the English north, where the French had blocked all crossings of the Somme. After overcoming the blockade, Edward met Philip at Crécy.

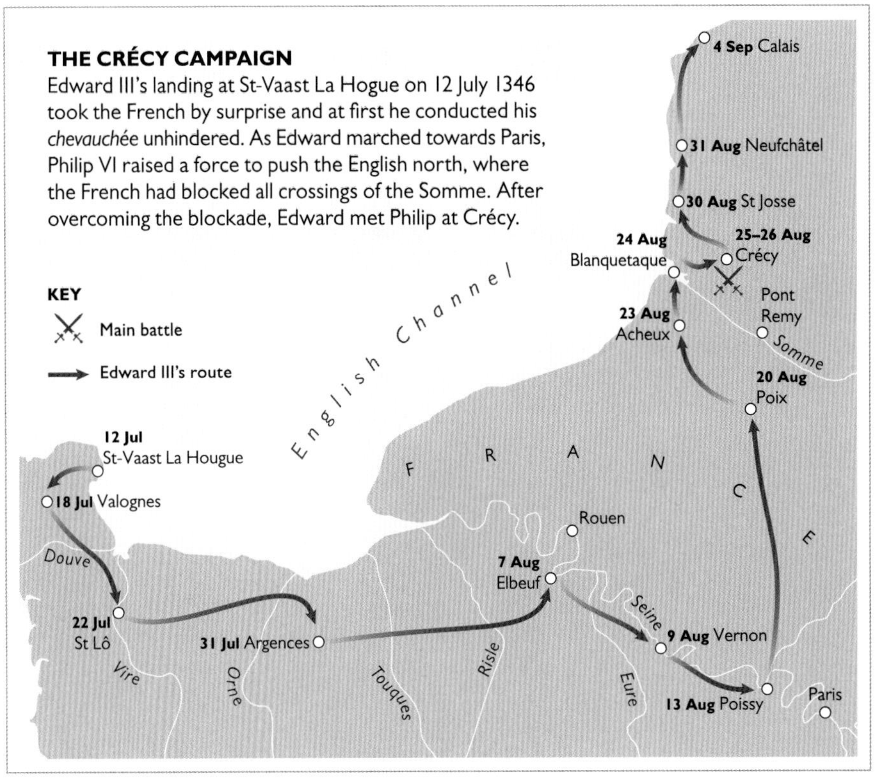
KEY
Main battle
Edward III's route
English Channel
FRANCE
4 Sep Calais
31 Aug Neufchâtel
30 Aug St Josse
24 Aug Blanquetaque
25–26 Aug Crécy
Pont Remy
23 Aug Acheux
Somme
20 Aug Poix
12 Jul St-Vaast La Hougue
18 Jul Valognes
Douve
Rouen
7 Aug Elbeuf
22 Jul St Lô
31 Jul Argences
Seine
9 Aug Vernon
Vire
Orne
Touques
Risle
Eure
13 Aug Poissy
Paris

KNIGHTS AND BOWMEN

Celebrated in chivalric romance, armoured knights had the highest status among warriors in medieval Europe. However, on the battlefield, archers armed with longbows or crossbows often proved more than a match for this military and social elite.

Armed with lances, swords, maces, and poleaxes, knights fought on foot as well as on horseback, and viewed battle as a test of personal courage and strength in close-quarter encounters with a worthy opponent. By contrast archers, who fought largely from a distance, posed a direct threat to this chivalric concept of war. Any archer captured by enemy knights could expect to receive savage treatment. While several medieval popes banned the use of bows in warfare, this had little effect on the battlefield.

In battle, archers typically delivered the opening attack in preparation for a cavalry charge, using either crossbows or longbows. Many of the most accomplished crossbowmen hailed from Genoa, Italy, while Welsh and English longbowmen were the most feared troops in English armies. The crossbow was less successful in defence as it was slow to reload, but required less skill. The longbow was much quicker to arm, but required exceptional skill and strength from the archer. Used in mass formation against a charge by enemy knights, the impact of longbows was similar to machine-gun fire, with each archer shooting at least six arrows per minute. If helmets and plate armour protected knights from the arrows, the longbowmen aimed at their horses. In the 16th century, firearms replaced bows, putting an end to the dominance of knights and bowmen on the battlefield.

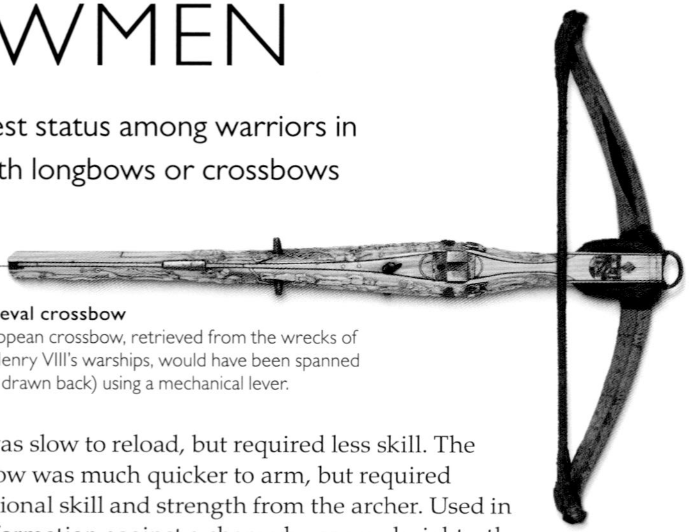

△ **Medieval crossbow**
This European crossbow, retrieved from the wrecks of one of Henry VIII's warships, would have been spanned (its cord drawn back) using a mechanical lever.

△ **Archers at the Battle of Crécy**
At Crécy (see pp.82–83), Genoese crossbowmen clashed with Welsh and English longbowmen. Fought at longer range than shown here in Jean Froissart's *Chronicles*, the duel marked the effectiveness of the longbow, with the crossbowmen hampered by mud and a lack of shields and arrows.

▽ **14th-century painting of siege warfare**
This painting shows longbowmen's feathered arrows taking a heavy toll on the defenders. The crossbow was, in general, a superior siege weapon as it could be aimed more precisely, and bowmen could take cover while reloading.

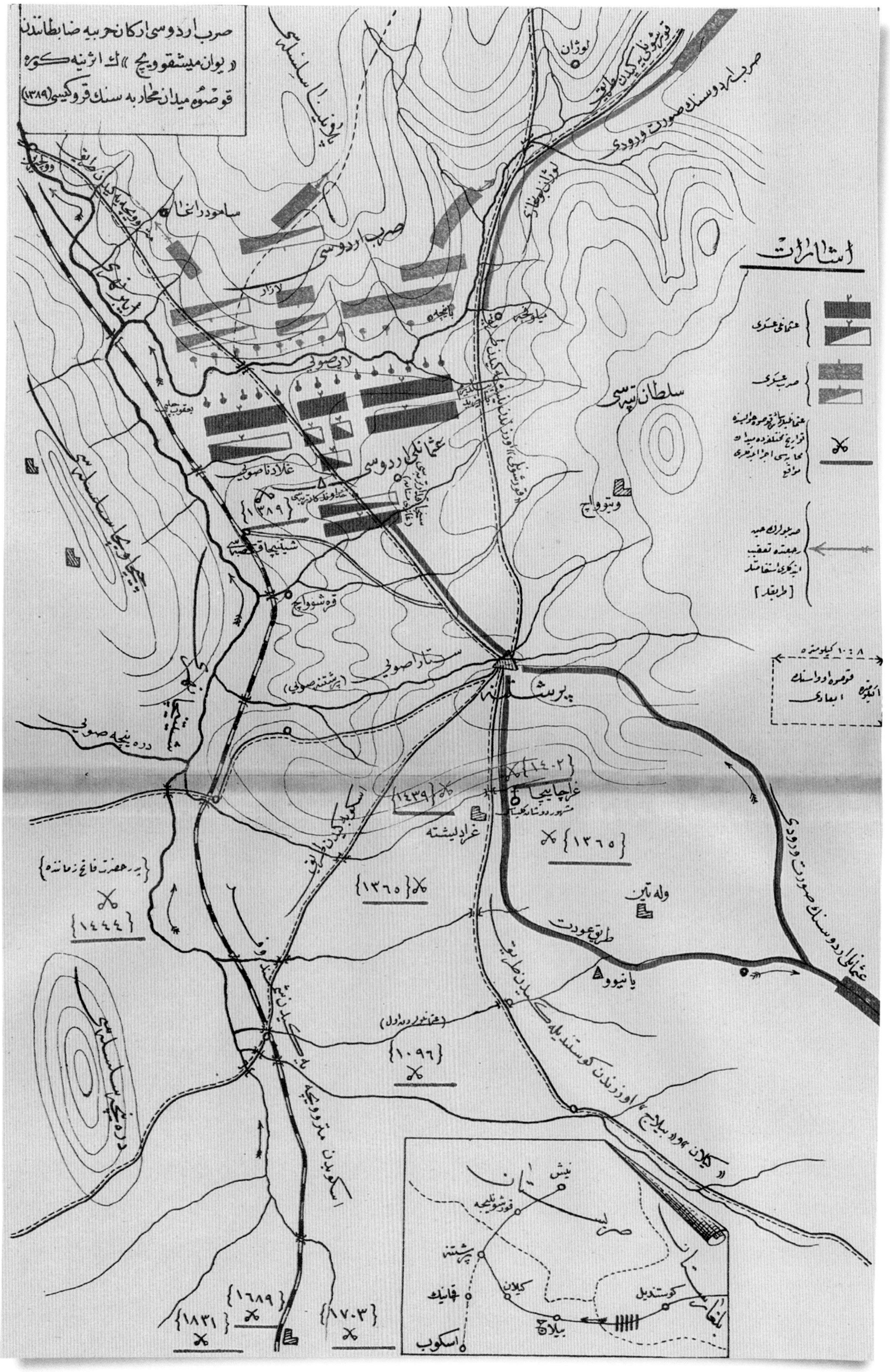
صرب اردوسی ارکان حربیه ضابطاندن
«یوان میشقوویچ» ك اثرینه کوره
قوصوه میدان محاربه سنك قروکیسی (١٣٨٩)
اشارات
صرب اردوسی
عثمانلی اردوسی
سلطان تپه سی
پرشتنه

KOSOVO POLJE

The clash in 1389 between Ottoman Sultan Murad I and the Serb Prince Lazar at Kosovo Polje ended in the death of both leaders. Losses on the Serbian side were so great that Serbia was fatally weakened and ultimately lost its independence to the Ottoman empire in 1459.

In spring 1389, Sultan Murad I, who had steadily expanded Ottoman possessions in the Balkans, gathered an army of up to 40,000 men and moved out of Bulgaria through Sofia into southern Kosovo. On 15 June, Prince Lazar Hrebeljanović, ruler of the largest of Serbia's principalities, drew up his forces (which were significantly outnumbered by Murad's) on the north bank of the River Lub to face the Ottoman threat.

Although the battle began promisingly for the Serbs with an initial cavalry charge, the Ottoman counterattacks were strong. They ended in the death of Lazar, and accusations of treason against Branković, who fled the battle. The killing of Murad by a Serbian noble in the battle marred the Ottoman victory, but Bayezid, now sultan, sealed it by marrying Lazar's daughter and placing his son Stefan Lazarević on the throne as an Ottoman vassal. Gradually the Ottomans annexed parts of Serbia, seizing Skopje in 1392, and putting an end to Serbian independence altogether in 1459.

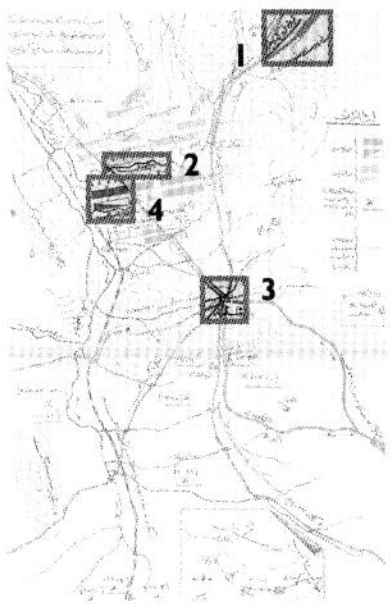
1
2
4
3

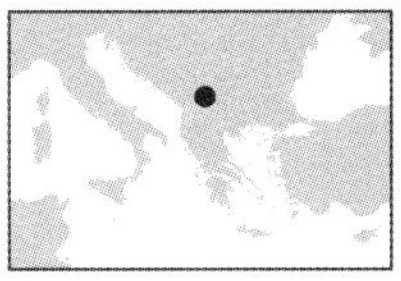

LOCATOR

"When fortune smiles 'tis easy to be good. Adversity reveals the hero's soul."

FROM AN ENGLISH TRANSLATION OF SERBIAN PLAY *THE MOUNTAIN WREATH*, 1847

◁ Rare Ottoman atlas
Extracted from an atlas of Ottoman military maps published in 1908 by the Grand Vizier Ahmed Muhtar Pasha, the map shows the hilly topography around Kosovo Polje, as well as the advance of the two armies towards the battlefield.

▽ Lazar's approach
Lazar advances southwest from Niš, where the Allies had assembled. They include Vuk Branković, a Bosnian contingent sent by Bosnian king Tvrtko I, and smaller groups of Croatian Knights, Hospitallers, and Albanians.

1

2

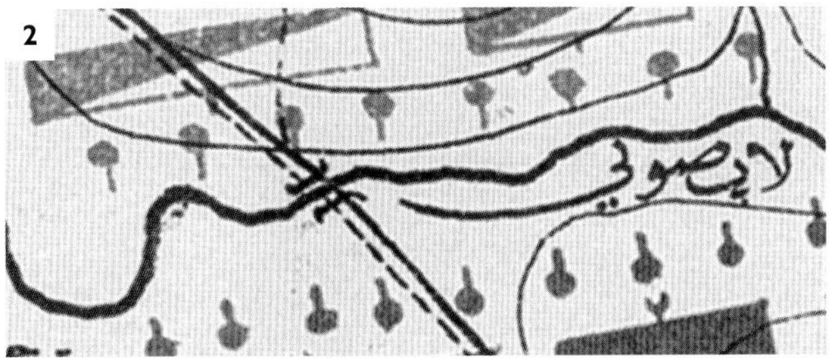

△ Riverside defences
The River Lub, used as a defensive line by Lazar's Allied army. On the right, Lazar placed Brankovic and the main Serb contingent; in the centre, he led the infantry; and on the left, Vukovic commanded the Bosnian allies.

▽ Facing the enemy
Murad and his 40,000-strong army, including elite Janissaries and European levies, arrived at Pristina on 14 June. From there, they began to advance towards Kosovo to face Lazar's forces.

3

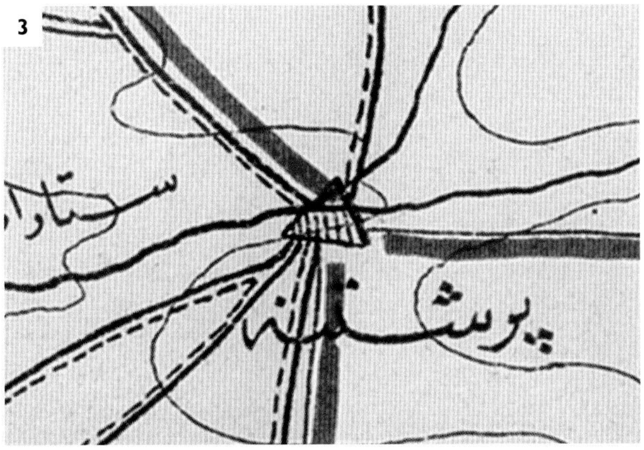

4

◁ Ottoman left wing
Yakub's left wing, made up of Anatolian (Asian) cavalry, faced an initial damaging charge from the Serbian cavalry. Yakub successfully counter-attacked; he was later killed by his brother Bayezid when he inherited the throne.

CHAOTIC BATTLEFIELD
On the Ottoman left, Yakub stemmed Branković's assault. Bayezid meanwhile engaged the Bosnian contingent in bitter fighting. Now severely outnumbered, parts of the main Serbian contingent pulled back, leaving Lazar exposed. There he and many Serbian nobles died in a last stand.

KEY
Town

OTTOMAN FORCES
Cavalry
Retreats
Infantry
Camp
Attacks

ALLIED FORCES
Cavalry
Attacks
Infantry
Retreats

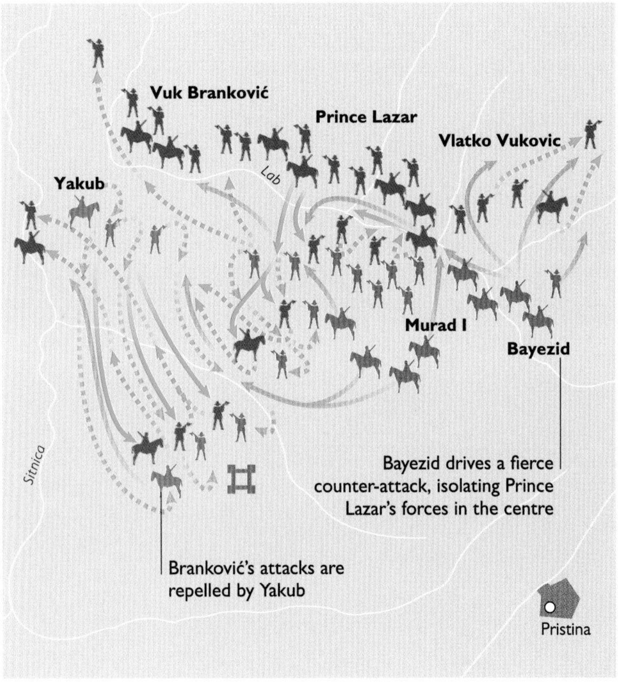
Vuk Branković
Prince Lazar
Vlatko Vukovic
Yakub
Lab
Murad I
Bayezid
Sitnica
Bayezid drives a fierce counter-attack, isolating Prince Lazar's forces in the centre
Branković's attacks are repelled by Yakub
Pristina

THE KNIGHTS' ASCENDANT

The early stages of battle favoured the Teutonic Order, with the weight of its cavalry pushing back its enemy. However, the departure of a force of knights in pursuit of Tatars weakened its line.

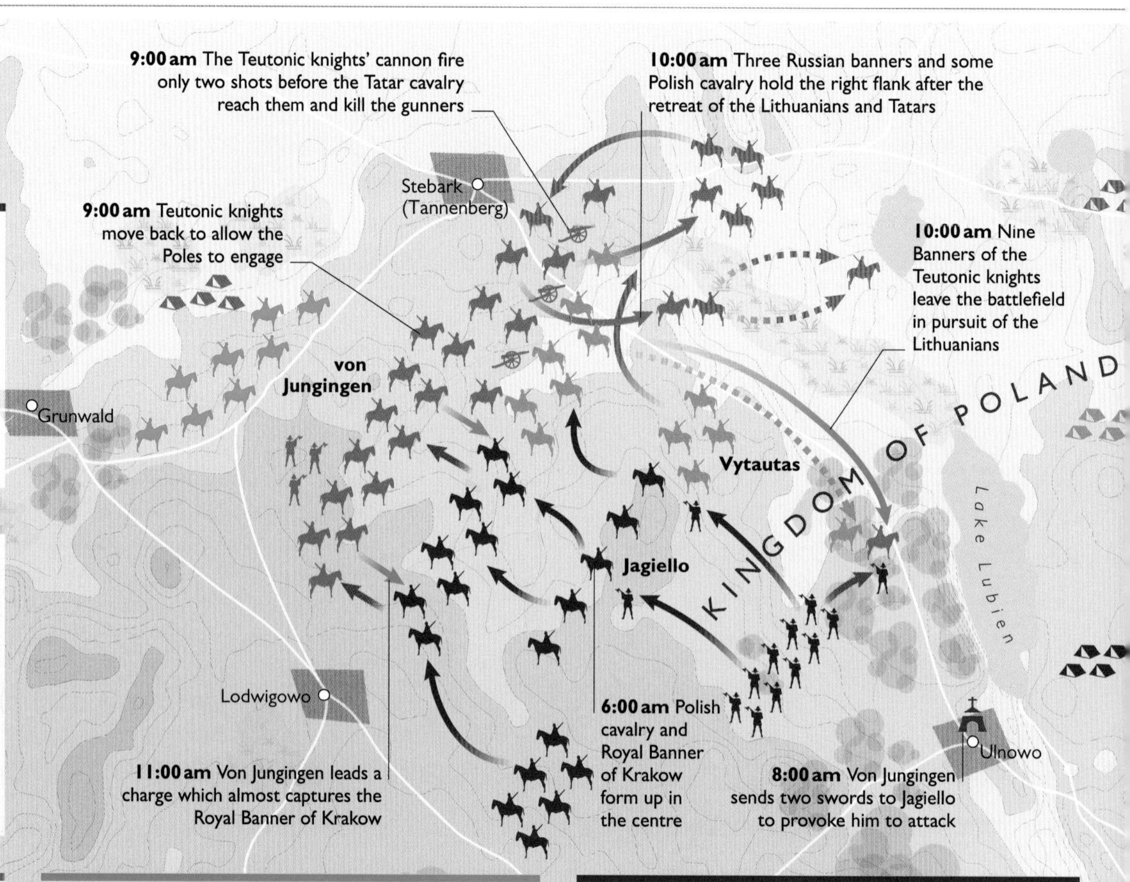

9:00am The Teutonic knights' cannon fire only two shots before the Tatar cavalry reach them and kill the gunners
10:00am Three Russian banners and some Polish cavalry hold the right flank after the retreat of the Lithuanians and Tatars
Stebark (Tannenberg)
9:00am Teutonic knights move back to allow the Poles to engage
10:00am Nine Banners of the Teutonic knights leave the battlefield in pursuit of the Lithuanians
von Jungingen
Grunwald
KINGDOM OF POLAND
Vytautas
Lake Lubien
Jagiello
Lodwigowo
6:00am Polish cavalry and Royal Banner of Krakow form up in the centre
Ulnowo
11:00am Von Jungingen leads a charge which almost captures the Royal Banner of Krakow
8:00am Von Jungingen sends two swords to Jagiello to provoke him to attack

1 THE ARMIES ARRIVE

EVENING, 14 JULY–6:00AM, 15 JULY 1410

The Polish-Lithuanian army arrived the evening before the battle. The Teutonic Order reached the battlefield around 6am the next day, with Grand Master von Jungingen commanding 15 banners (units of roughly 200 men) at the rear. Ahead of him were vassal troops and the Order's artillery.

2 THE BATTLE DELAYED

6:00–9:00AM, 15 JULY

Jagiello delayed beginning the battle while he prayed for success in the chapel tent near the Polish camp. Von Jungingen mockingly sent him two swords as an encouragement to fight, but only in late morning did the Polish forces emerge, forming a left flank near Ludwigsdorf, with Vytautas's Lithuanians to their right, and the Tatars forming the right flank.

3 THE TATAR CHARGE 9:00–10:00AM

Vytautas ordered the Tatars to charge the Order's left flank, and they were followed by his Lithuanian light cavalry. As the Tatars broke through the first rank, the second rank of knights counter-attacked, causing the Tatars to flee. Four banners of the Order chased them off the field.

Tatars and Lithuanians advance — Tatars retreat, pursued by knights — Teutonic cavalry counter-attacks

4 THE ORDER ADVANCES 10:00–11:00AM

The Lithuanian light cavalry were pushed back, and retreated into the woods. Some Teutonic knights broke from their lines in pursuit, only to be decimated by a section of the Polish reserve. Meanwhile, von Jungingen ordered a general advance against the Polish forces, resulting in a hard-fought melee in the centre.

Lithuanians pushed back — Polish resistance — Teutonic forces advance

5 THE POLES RALLY

11:00AM–12:00PM

The battle in the centre was going in favour of the Teutonic Order until Jagiello ordered his cavalry reserves forward; he also deployed the third line of his army to reinforce the centre and support his right wing. The Poles began to make some progress, pushing back the Teutonic knights on the Polish left flank, but with his last reserves deployed, Jagiello's position was still precarious.

Polish cavalry and third line advance

GROWTH OF THE TEUTONIC ORDER

The Teutonic Order established strongholds on the western Baltic and expanded via crusades in Prussia, Lithuania, and Estonia. The marriage of Jagiello, formerly Grand Duke of Lithuania, to the Polish queen in 1386 shifted the power balance in the region, threatening the Order.

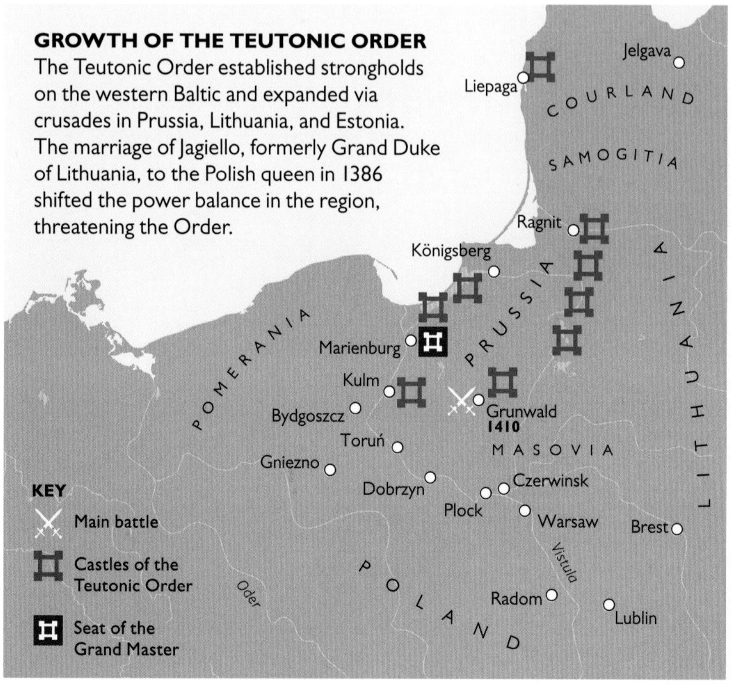

Jelgava
Liepaga
COURLAND
SAMOGITIA
Ragnit
Königsberg
PRUSSIA
LITHUANIA
POMERANIA
Marienburg
Kulm
Grunwald 1410
Bydgoszcz
Toruń
MASOVIA
Gniezno
Dobrzyn
Czerwinsk
Plock
Warsaw
Brest
Oder
Vistula
POLAND
Radom
Lublin
KEY
Main battle
Castles of the Teutonic Order
Seat of the Grand Master

THE END OF THE KNIGHTS

The military might of the Teutonic Order depended on its heavy cavalry. The loss of such a large part of its army at Grunwald compromised the Order's ability to defend its territories. It was forced to rely on expensive mercenaries, which contributed to the state's eventual decline and bankruptcy.

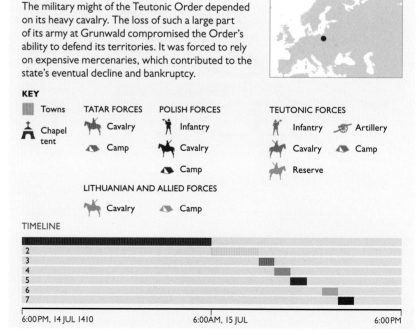

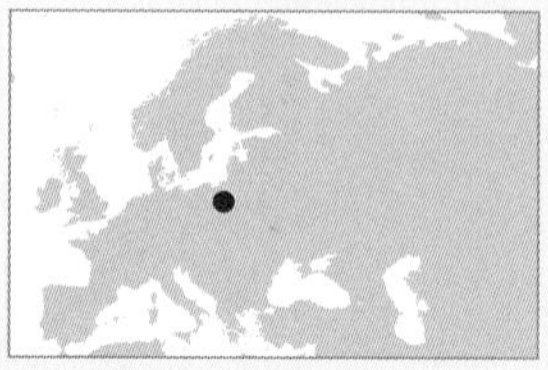

KEY

Towns

Chapel tent

TATAR FORCES: Cavalry; Camp

POLISH FORCES: Infantry; Cavalry; Camp

TEUTONIC FORCES: Infantry; Artillery; Cavalry; Camp; Reserve

LITHUANIAN AND ALLIED FORCES: Cavalry; Camp

TIMELINE

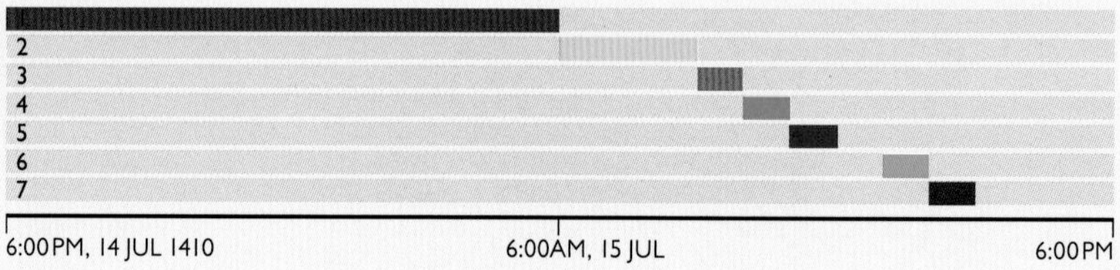

1
2
3
4
5
6
7
6:00PM, 14 JUL 1410
6:00AM, 15 JUL
6:00PM

GRUNWALD

The Teutonic Order, a crusader state, tried to halt a Polish–Lithuanian invasion of their territory in 1410 at Grunwald (also known as the Battle of Tannenberg). The Teutonic knights were enveloped and decimated, ending their dominance of the western Baltic.

In 1409, after years of tension, conflict erupted between the Teutonic Order and Poland–Lithuania when the Polish king, Wladyslaw Jagiello, supported a revolt against the Order in the formerly Polish region of Samogitia. After inconclusive fighting, the Kings of Bohemia and Hungary brokered an armistice, but the belligerents used the brief peace to recruit allies. Wladyslaw's cousin Vytautas, Grand Duke of Lithuania, won the support of Tatars, Russians, and Moldavians, while the Grand Master of the Teutonic Order, Ulrich von Jungingen, drew knights from Western Europe.

Jagiello sent feint attacks north into Samogitia and west into Pomerania, combining his and Vytautas's armies, to conceal a huge main assault aimed at Marienburg, the Order's headquarters. Jagiello's 40,000-strong force crossed the Vistula River on 2 July 1410, and von Jungingen – who made the mistake of dividing his army – rushed to the Drewenz River, the last obstacle in the way of Marienburg, so forcing his opponents east towards Grunwald.

The defeat at Grunwald was almost the end of the Order, with only a small part of the Teutonic force escaping back to Marienburg. However, as Jagiello did not follow them immediately, the new Grand Master, Heinrich von Plauen, had time to shore up the defences at Marienburg and gather reinforcements. Jagiello withdrew, and in February 1411 he signed the Peace of Torun, giving him only a part of the Order's territory. Nonetheless, the Teutonic Order was broken as a force and eventually slipped into political irrelevance.

6 THE TATARS AND LITHUANIANS RETURN
1:00–2:00 PM

With the Lithuanian retreat on the right flank and the Polish advances on the left, the opposing armies wheeled round clockwise, still locked in intense combat. Grand Master von Jungingen personally led his cavalry reserve banners in a last attempt to crush Jagiello. Vytautas, who had by now regrouped the remainder of his light cavalry, infiltrated behind the Order's lines, supported by the Tatars who had also returned to the battlefield.

7 THE KNIGHTS COLLAPSE
2:00–3:00 PM

The Order's left flank buckled under pressure from Jagiello at the front and the Lithuanians and Tatars at the rear, while Polish cavalry smashed through the centre, breaking von Jungingen's force in two. Many knights, including von Jungingen himself, were slaughtered by Polish infantry – some as they tried to surrender, others as they retreated to a wagon fort near their camp. Only about 1,500 of the Teutonic Orders' troops escaped the battlefield.

△ **Shield of the Teutonic Order**
The Teutonic Order was a military order founded in Acre in the Holy Land in 1192 to protect Christian pilgrims.

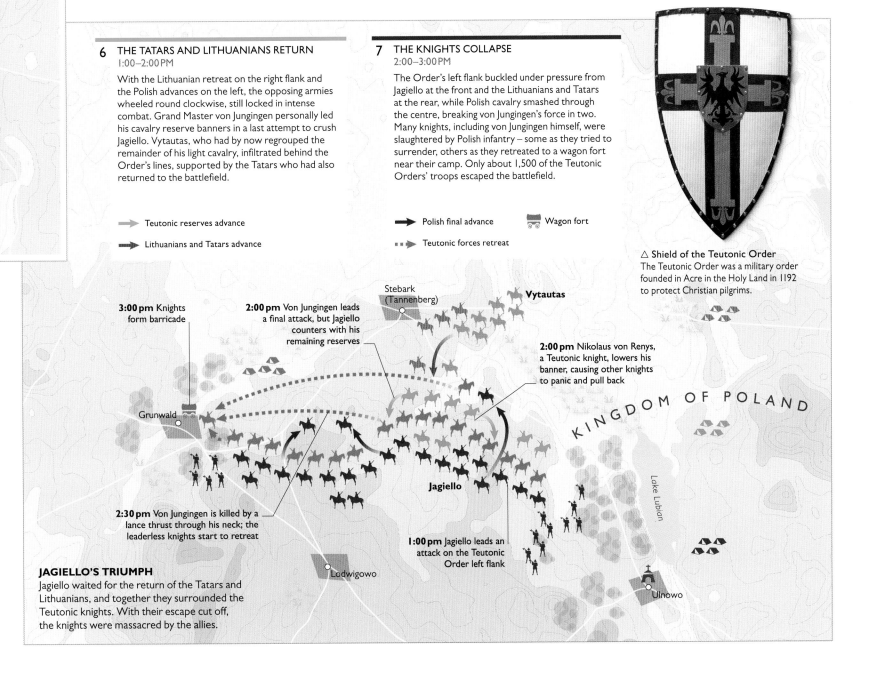

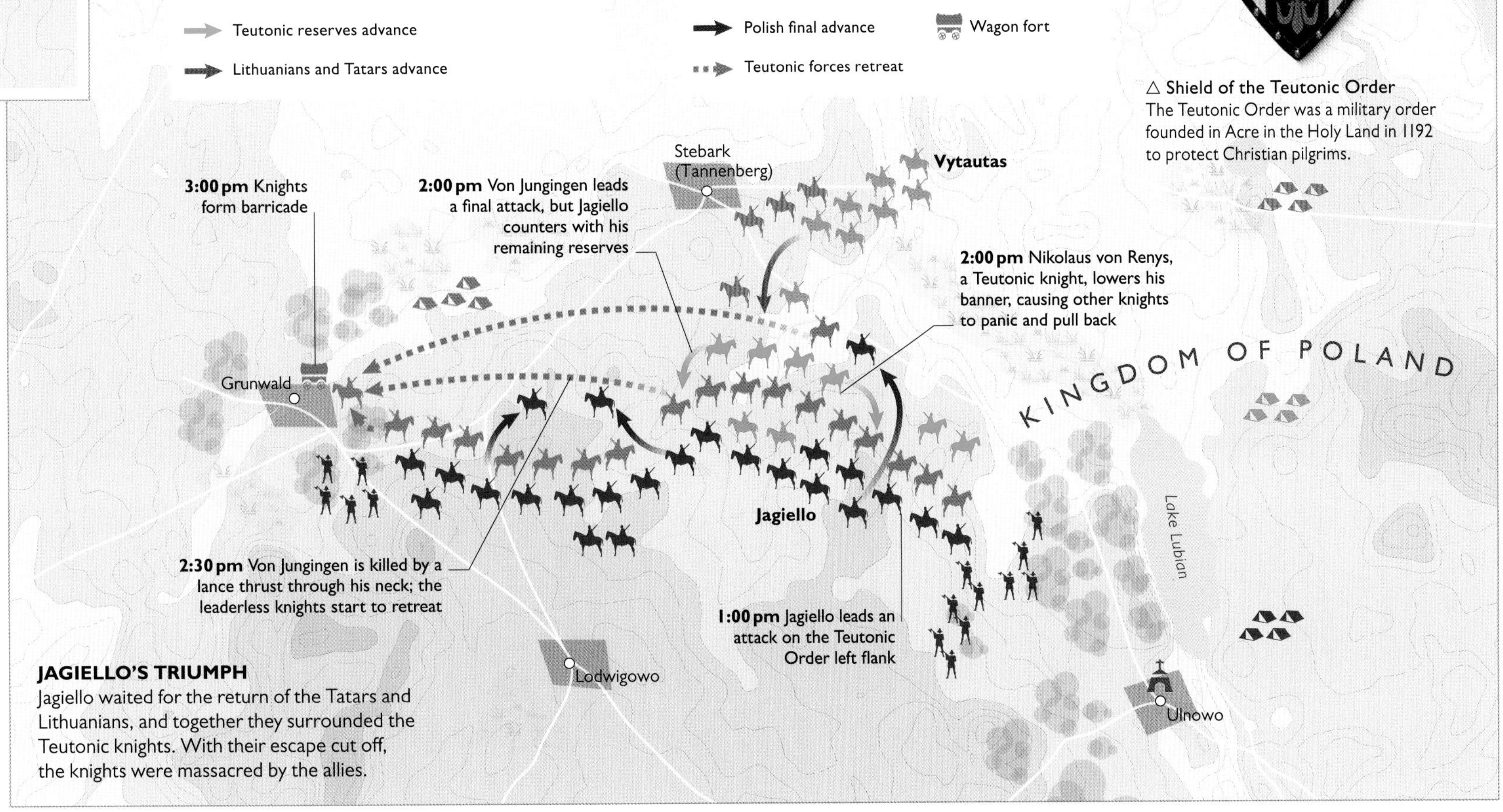
Teutonic reserves advance
Lithuanians and Tatars advance
Polish final advance
Wagon fort
Teutonic forces retreat
Stebark (Tannenberg)
Vytautas
3:00 pm Knights form barricade
2:00 pm Von Jungingen leads a final attack, but Jagiello counters with his remaining reserves
2:00 pm Nikolaus von Renys, a Teutonic knight, lowers his banner, causing other knights to panic and pull back
KINGDOM OF POLAND
Grunwald
Jagiello
Lake Lubian
2:30 pm Von Jungingen is killed by a lance thrust through his neck; the leaderless knights start to retreat
1:00 pm Jagiello leads an attack on the Teutonic Order left flank
Lodwigowo
Ulnowo

JAGIELLO'S TRIUMPH
Jagiello waited for the return of the Tatars and Lithuanians, and together they surrounded the Teutonic knights. With their escape cut off, the knights were massacred by the allies.

AGINCOURT

In the summer of 1415, King Henry V of England invaded France to pursue his claim to the French throne. Two months later, he inflicted a devastating defeat on the French. Hampered by heavy mud and a narrow field, thousands of French men-at-arms perished in a hail of arrows from the English longbowmen.

King Henry V of England had inherited his great-grandfather Edward III's claim to the French throne, which provoked the Hundred Year's War between England and France in 1337. In 1414, he interrupted a 25-year-long truce between the two countries by demanding French recognition of his permanent right to Aquitaine, Normandy, and other English possessions in France, and the hand in marriage of Catherine, daughter of King Charles VI of France.

When the French rejected this, Henry assembled an army of around 12,000 men, and landed at Harfleur in northern France in August 1415. The siege of the town proved protracted, and as winter approached, Henry decided that rather than return to England, he would turn towards English-held Calais. This delay allowed the French, led by Constable Charles d'Albret, to raise their own force, which blocked the English army from crossing the Somme, and forced them over 100 km (60 miles) south to find an unguarded ford. Despite the advantage that d'Albret's manoeuvring had secured (and his larger forces), the French army suffered a crushing defeat at Agincourt. The French leadership was decimated, and Charles VI was forced to consent to the Treaty of Troyes, which in 1420 agreed Henry V's marriage to Catherine and recognized him as heir to the French throne.

THE ENGLISH AND FRENCH ARMIES MEET

As Henry V's army made its way to the coast, the French assembled a large army. They finally intercepted the English forces near the village of Agincourt (Azincourt in French).

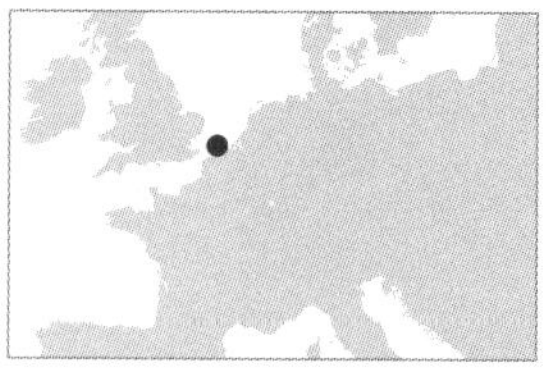

KEY

Towns

FRENCH FORCES: Mounted men-at-arms; Unmounted men-at-arms; Archers

ENGLISH FORCES: Army; Longbowmen

TIMELINE

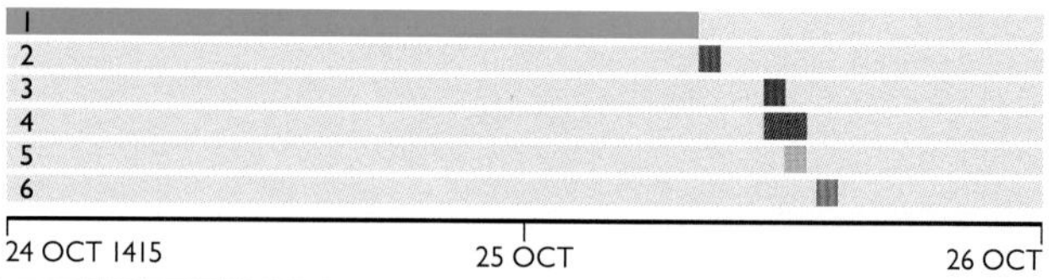
1
2
3
4
5
6
24 OCT 1415
25 OCT
26 OCT

△ **Pitched battle**
In this miniature from a 15th-century manuscript, the English army is shown attacking the defeated and fleeing French forces.

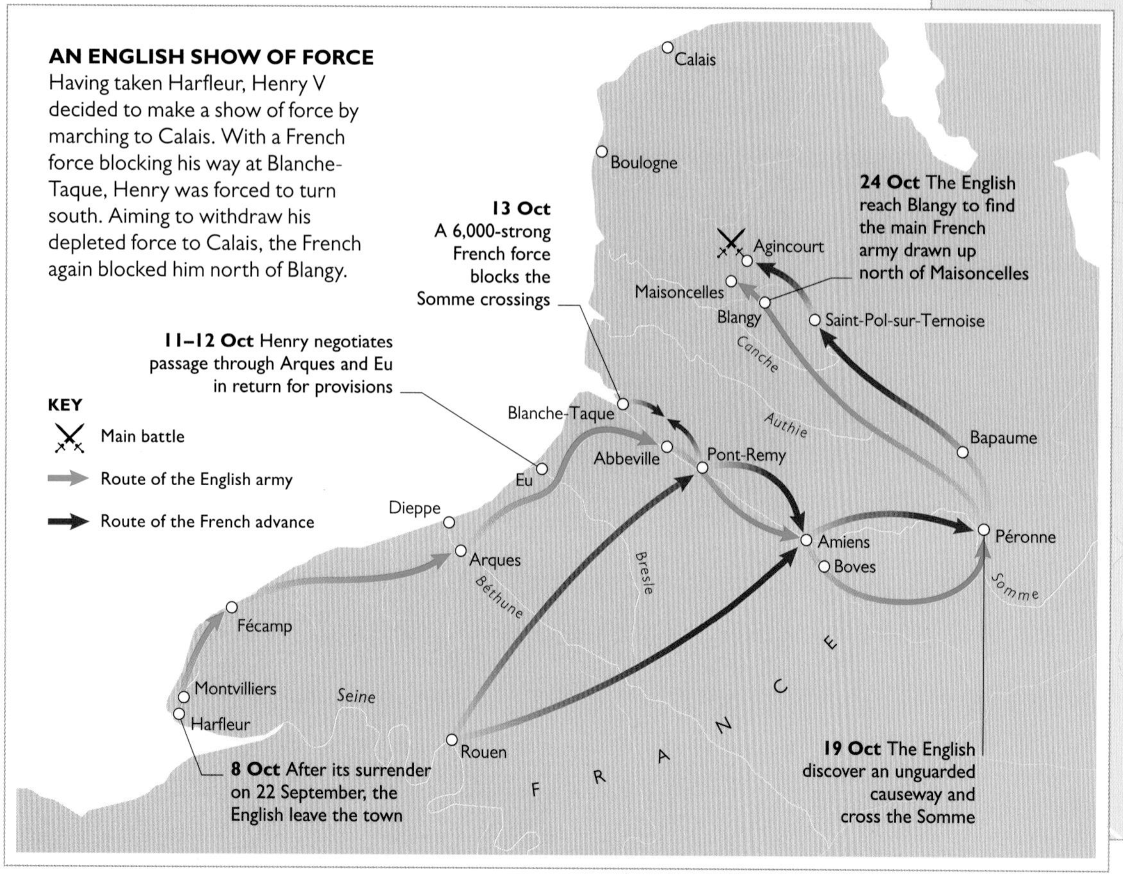
AN ENGLISH SHOW OF FORCE
Having taken Harfleur, Henry V decided to make a show of force by marching to Calais. With a French force blocking his way at Blanche-Taque, Henry was forced to turn south. Aiming to withdraw his depleted force to Calais, the French again blocked him north of Blangy.
KEY
Main battle
Route of the English army
Route of the French advance
Calais
Boulogne
Agincourt
Maisoncelles
Blangy
Saint-Pol-sur-Ternoise
Canche
Authie
Blanche-Taque
Abbeville
Pont-Remy
Bapaume
Eu
Dieppe
Arques
Béthune
Bresle
Amiens
Boves
Péronne
Somme
Fécamp
Montivilliers
Harfleur
Seine
Rouen
FRANCE
13 Oct A 6,000-strong French force blocks the Somme crossings
24 Oct The English reach Blangy to find the main French army drawn up north of Maisoncelles
11–12 Oct Henry negotiates passage through Arques and Eu in return for provisions
8 Oct After its surrender on 22 September, the English leave the town
19 Oct The English discover an unguarded causeway and cross the Somme

1 THE ARMIES DEPLOY
24 OCTOBER–8:00 AM, 25 OCTOBER

Both armies arrived near the village of Agincourt on 24 October. Early the next morning, the English deployed in a line, with Henry in the centre, his cousin Edward Duke of York on the right, and Baron Camoys on the left. The French arrayed their force in three "battles", with most of the nobles in the vanguard, and the archers and crossbowmen in the second line.

English advance

2 THE LONGBOWMEN PREPARE
8:00 AM

Henry deployed his longbowmen on either flank. They set sharpened stakes protruding at an angle in the ground. This prevented horsemen from approaching, and gave the bowmen shelter from which they could launch volleys of arrows with a range of up to 200 m (650 ft). With the archers in place, the armies waited.

//// Line of stakes

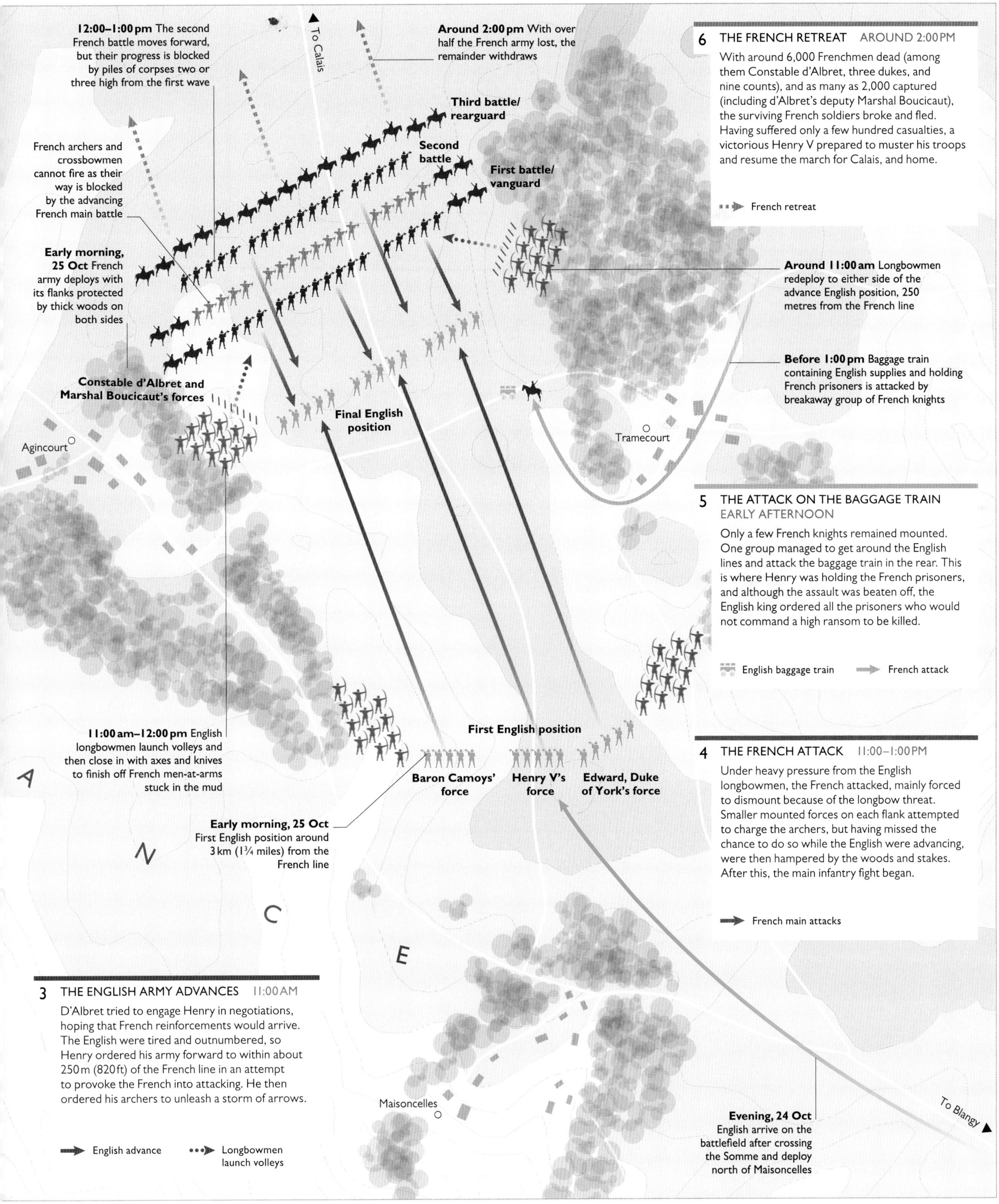

12:00–1:00 pm The second French battle moves forward, but their progress is blocked by piles of corpses two or three high from the first wave
To Calais
Around 2:00 pm With over half the French army lost, the remainder withdraws
Third battle/ rearguard
Second battle
First battle/ vanguard
French archers and crossbowmen cannot fire as their way is blocked by the advancing French main battle
Early morning, 25 Oct French army deploys with its flanks protected by thick woods on both sides
Around 11:00 am Longbowmen redeploy to either side of the advance English position, 250 metres from the French line
Before 1:00 pm Baggage train containing English supplies and holding French prisoners is attacked by breakaway group of French knights
Constable d'Albret and Marshal Boucicaut's forces
Final English position
Agincourt
Tramecourt
11:00 am–12:00 pm English longbowmen launch volleys and then close in with axes and knives to finish off French men-at-arms stuck in the mud
First English position
Baron Camoys' force
Henry V's force
Edward, Duke of York's force
Early morning, 25 Oct First English position around 3 km (1¾ miles) from the French line
F R A N C E
Maisoncelles
To Blangy
Evening, 24 Oct English arrive on the battlefield after crossing the Somme and deploy north of Maisoncelles

6 THE FRENCH RETREAT AROUND 2:00 PM

With around 6,000 Frenchmen dead (among them Constable d'Albret, three dukes, and nine counts), and as many as 2,000 captured (including d'Albret's deputy Marshal Boucicaut), the surviving French soldiers broke and fled. Having suffered only a few hundred casualties, a victorious Henry V prepared to muster his troops and resume the march for Calais, and home.

French retreat

5 THE ATTACK ON THE BAGGAGE TRAIN EARLY AFTERNOON

Only a few French knights remained mounted. One group managed to get around the English lines and attack the baggage train in the rear. This is where Henry was holding the French prisoners, and although the assault was beaten off, the English king ordered all the prisoners who would not command a high ransom to be killed.

English baggage train — French attack

4 THE FRENCH ATTACK 11:00–1:00 PM

Under heavy pressure from the English longbowmen, the French attacked, mainly forced to dismount because of the longbow threat. Smaller mounted forces on each flank attempted to charge the archers, but having missed the chance to do so while the English were advancing, were then hampered by the woods and stakes. After this, the main infantry fight began.

French main attacks

3 THE ENGLISH ARMY ADVANCES 11:00 AM

D'Albret tried to engage Henry in negotiations, hoping that French reinforcements would arrive. The English were tired and outnumbered, so Henry ordered his army forward to within about 250 m (820 ft) of the French line in an attempt to provoke the French into attacking. He then ordered his archers to unleash a storm of arrows.

English advance — Longbowmen launch volleys

SIEGE OF ORLÉANS

The successful defence of Orléans in 1428–29 was a turning point in the Hundred Years War between England and France, and came at a key moment at which the English seemed poised to win the war. The French victory resulted from the inspired intervention of Joan of Arc.

When the Treaty of Troyes was signed in 1420, the king of England was recognized as successor to the French throne, and the English and their allies controlled Paris and Reims. However, resistance continued, and in 1428 the Earl of Salisbury led an army to attack Orléans, a strategically important city on the River Loire.

On 12 October, the English planned to storm the city across the bridge over the Loire defended by a fortified gatehouse, Les Tourelles. However, by the time the English took Les Tourelles on 24 October, the defenders had rendered the bridge unusable. Two days later, Salisbury was fatally wounded and command devolved to the Earl of Suffolk, who abandoned the assault and built forts and earthworks for a long siege. Suffolk did not have enough troops for a total blockade, but by the new year the city's inhabitants were going hungry. In February, a 17-year-old peasant girl, Joan of Arc, began a journey to the Dauphin's court at Chinon.

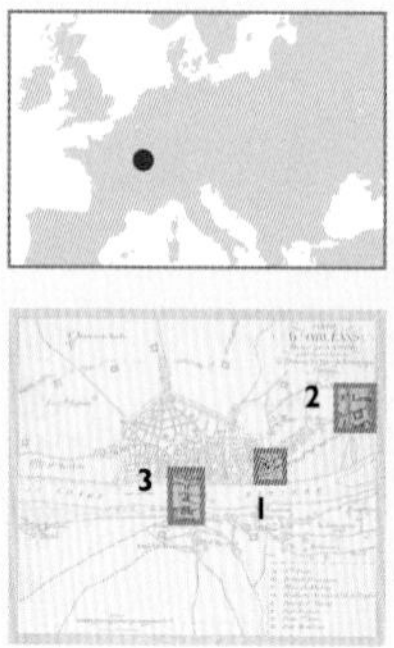

1
2
3

KEY

1 Joan of Arc and French forces entered the city with supplies on 29 April.

2 St Loup became the first English-held fort to fall to the French on 4 May.

3 French troops forced the English from Les Tourelles gatehouse on 7 May.

Claiming divine inspiration, she persuaded the leaders to let her attempt a relief of Orléans. Whether through her impact on morale or her tactical sense, she achieved the raising of the siege (see below), and set the stage for the expulsion of the English from France.

"Of the love or hatred God has for the English, I know nothing, but I do know that they will all be thrown out of France..."

ATTRIBUTED TO JOAN OF ARC, TRIAL RECORDS, 1431

THE RELIEF OF ORLÉANS

On 29 April 1429, Joan of Arc entered Orléans with vital supplies escorted by 500 soldiers, slipping through English lines from the east. Greeted rapturously by the people, she demanded action, but the French commander Jean de Dunois sought reinforcements before taking the English strongpoint at St Loup on 4 May. Two days later the French, with Joan in the forefront, crossed the river to attack the English fortified positions south of the city. After fierce fighting, the Augustines fell on 6 May and Les Tourelles the following day. The British abandoned the siege on 8 May.

KEY

- English fortifications
- French army advances
- French attacks

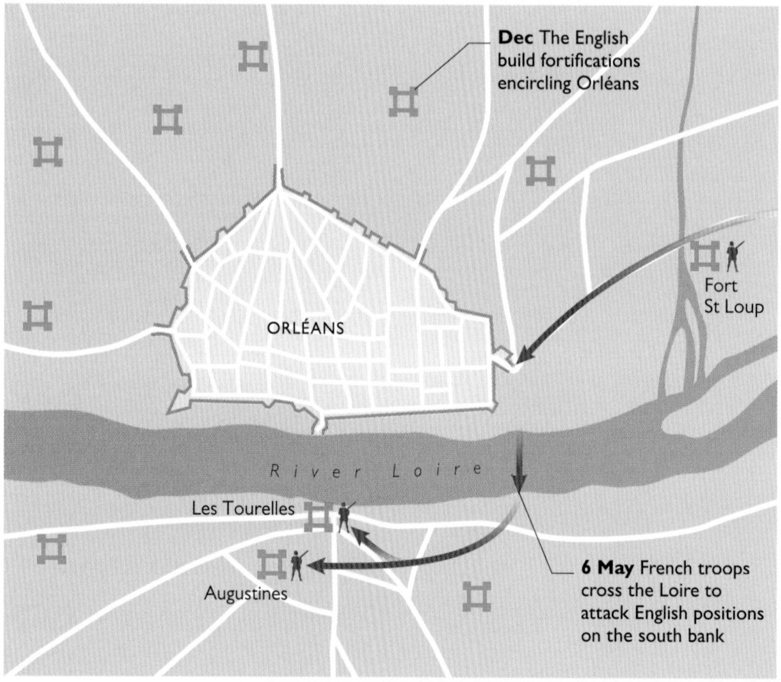

Dec The English build fortifications encircling Orléans
Fort St Loup
ORLÉANS
River Loire
Les Tourelles
Augustines
6 May French troops cross the Loire to attack English positions on the south bank

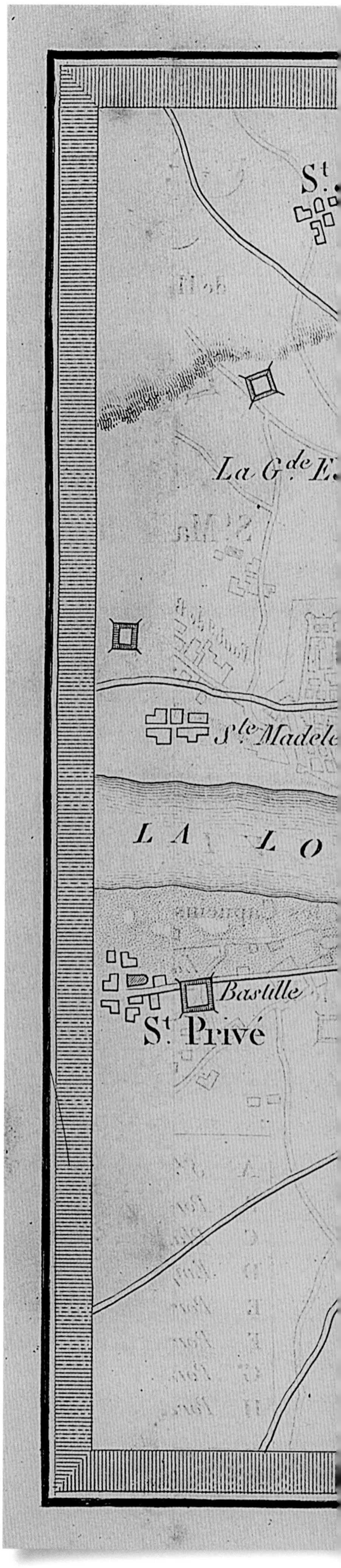

Bastille
St. Privé

▷ **A city under siege**
This plan of the siege of Orléans by French 19th-century cartographer Aristide Michel Perrot first appeared in a history of the Dukes of Bourgogne published in 1839. It shows the compact walled city surrounded by scattered English strongholds.

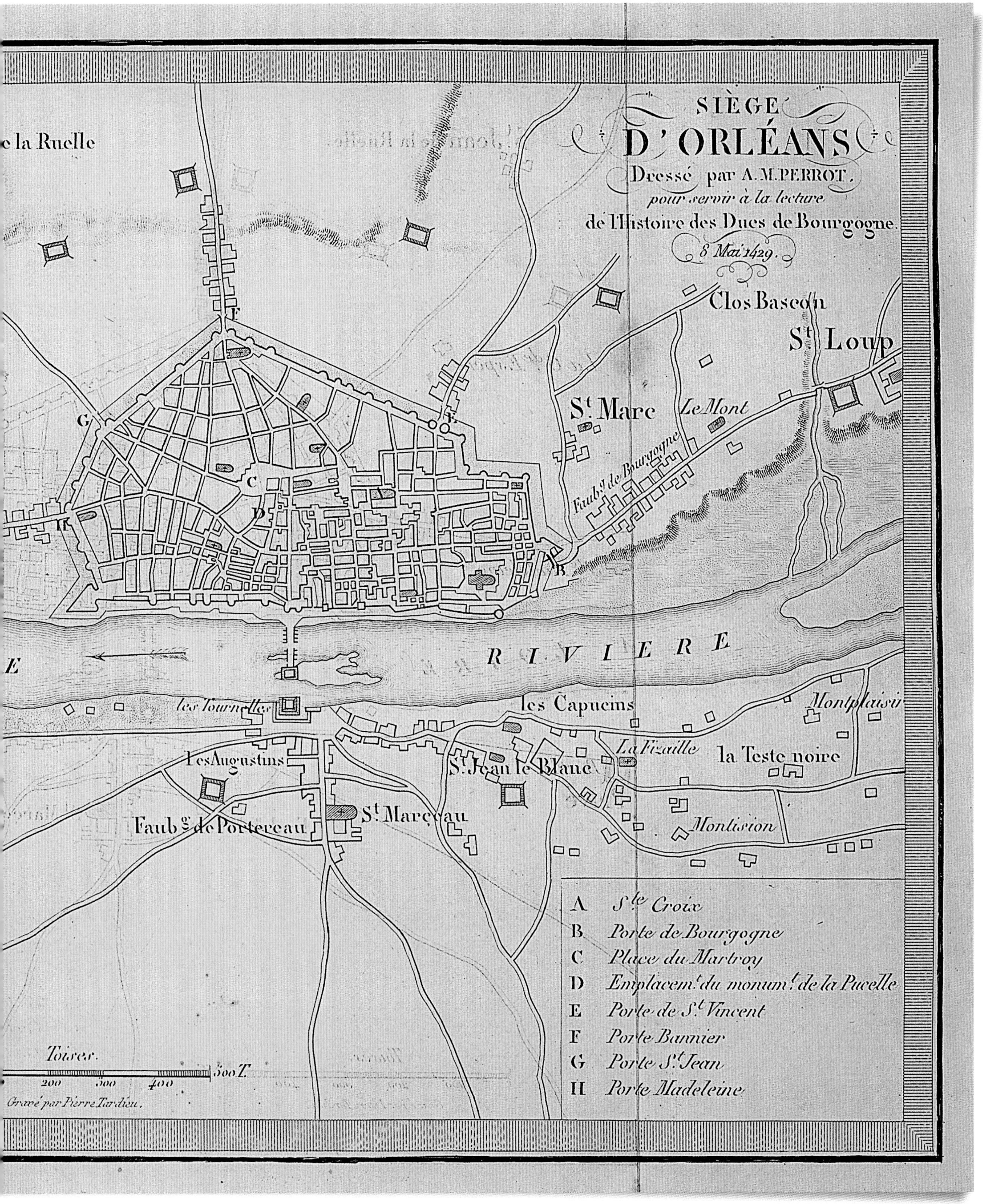
SIÈGE
D'ORLÉANS
Dressé par A. M. PERROT,
pour servir à la lecture
de l'Histoire des Ducs de Bourgogne.
8 Mai 1429.
la Ruelle
Clos Bascon
St. Loup
St. Marc
Le Mont
Faub.g de Bourgogne
RIVIERE
les Tournelles
les Capucins
Montplaisir
La Fizaille
la Teste noire
Les Augustins
St. Jean le Blanc
Faub.g de Portereau
St. Marçeau
Montlision
A St.e Croix
B Porte de Bourgogne
C Place du Martroy
D Emplacem.t du monum.t de la Pucelle
E Porte de St. Vincent
F Porte Bannier
G Porte St. Jean
H Porte Madeleine
Toises.
200 300 400 500 T.
Gravé par Pierre Tardieu.

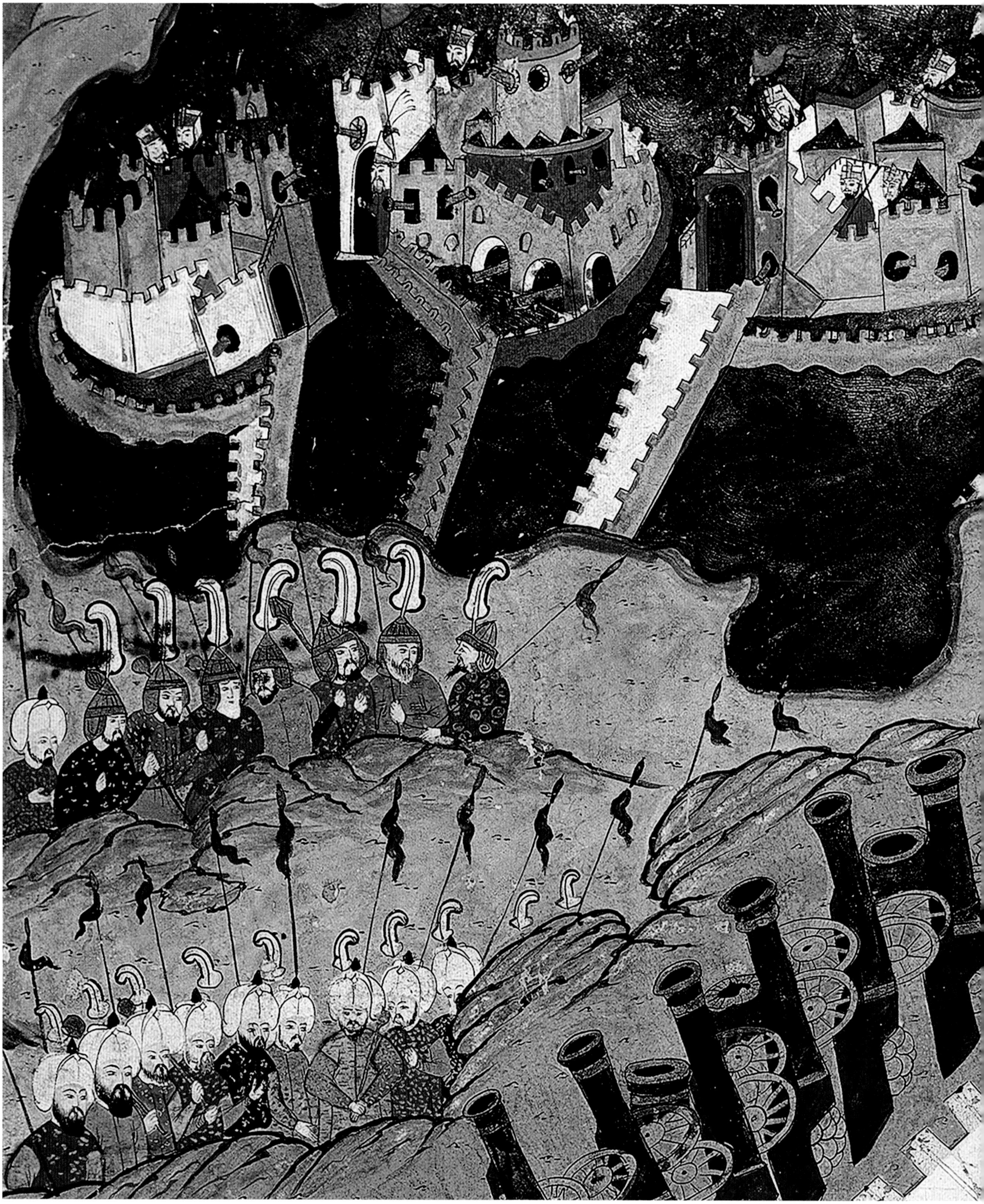

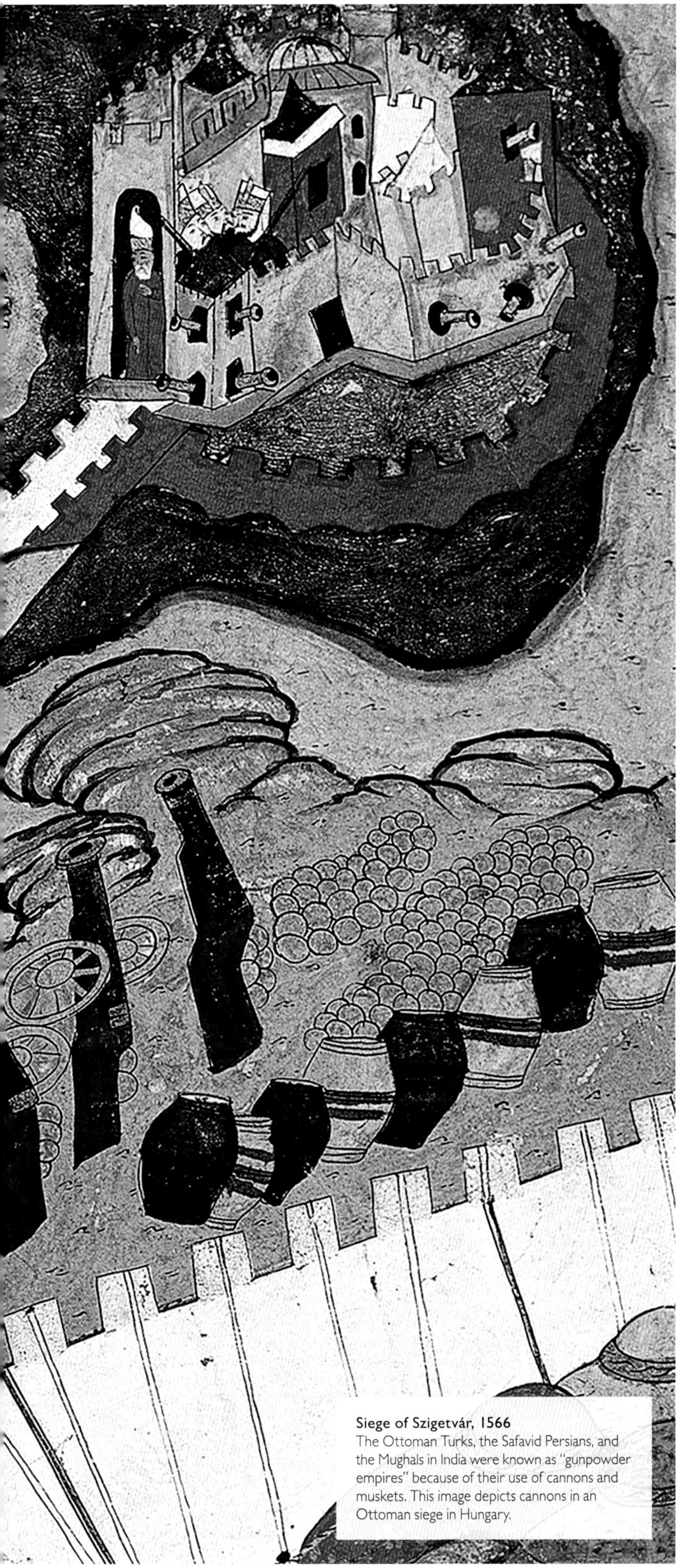

Siege of Szigetvár, 1566
The Ottoman Turks, the Safavid Persians, and the Mughals in India were known as "gunpowder empires" because of their use of cannons and muskets. This image depicts cannons in an Ottoman siege in Hungary.

GUNPOWDER WEAPONS

In use in China as early as the 10th century, gunpowder-based weapons developed gradually. By 1500, the impact of these weapons transformed the tactics used in battles and sieges throughout Asia and Europe.

△ **Swivel gun**
In the 15th century European ships began mounting cannons, which at first comprised small guns such as this rotating weapon.

By the 13th century, knowledge of various gunpowder weapons – bombs, rockets, and incendiary devices – had reached Europe, and by 1346 English armies began deploying small cannons on the battlefield. From the late 14th century, several European empires competed to produce powerful siege guns. Called bombards, these cumbersome artillery pieces were highly effective against the stone walls of medieval cities and castles. Adopted by the Turkish Ottoman army, these bombards were used to breach Constantinople's previously impregnable walls in 1453 (see p.96). Field cannons and handguns developed in parallel with siege artillery. At Castillon, also in 1453, French cannons decimated charging English knights. Hand-held firearms took longer to develop; although unreliable and inaccurate, arquebuses and later muskets had begun to supplant bows in the early 16th century.

Changing tactics

Vulnerable to cannon and musket fire, the knights evolved into a lightly armoured cavalryman wielding pistol and sword. In response to siege cannons, a new generation of low-lying, thick-walled, star-shaped forts was built across Europe with earth ramparts resistant to cannonballs and platforms for cannons to be used in defence.

△ **14th-century fire lance**
Invented in China, the fire lance was a gunpowder-filled tube attached to a spear, a one-shot fire weapon with a short range. This example is from Europe, although few were used in European warfare.

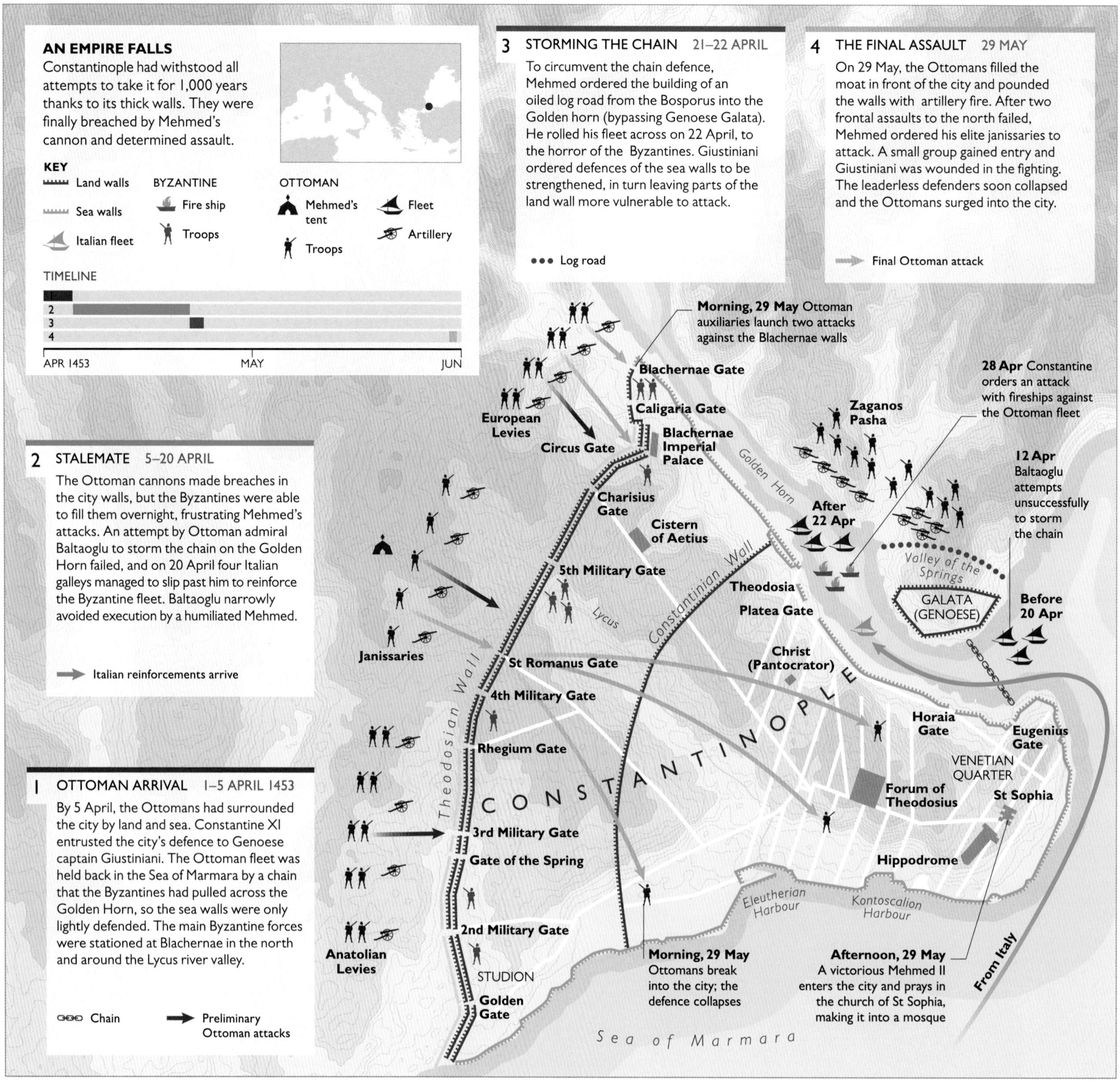
AN EMPIRE FALLS
Constantinople had withstood all attempts to take it for 1,000 years thanks to its thick walls. They were finally breached by Mehmed's cannon and determined assault.
KEY
Land walls
Sea walls
Italian fleet
BYZANTINE
Fire ship
Troops
OTTOMAN
Mehmed's tent
Troops
Fleet
Artillery
TIMELINE
1
2
3
4
APR 1453
MAY
JUN
3 STORMING THE CHAIN 21–22 APRIL
To circumvent the chain defence, Mehmed ordered the building of an oiled log road from the Bosporus into the Golden horn (bypassing Genoese Galata). He rolled his fleet across on 22 April, to the horror of the Byzantines. Giustiniani ordered defences of the sea walls to be strengthened, in turn leaving parts of the land wall more vulnerable to attack.
Log road
4 THE FINAL ASSAULT 29 MAY
On 29 May, the Ottomans filled the moat in front of the city and pounded the walls with artillery fire. After two frontal assaults to the north failed, Mehmed ordered his elite janissaries to attack. A small group gained entry and Giustiniani was wounded in the fighting. The leaderless defenders soon collapsed and the Ottomans surged into the city.
Final Ottoman attack
2 STALEMATE 5–20 APRIL
The Ottoman cannons made breaches in the city walls, but the Byzantines were able to fill them overnight, frustrating Mehmed's attacks. An attempt by Ottoman admiral Baltaoglu to storm the chain on the Golden Horn failed, and on 20 April four Italian galleys managed to slip past him to reinforce the Byzantine fleet. Baltaoglu narrowly avoided execution by a humiliated Mehmed.
Italian reinforcements arrive
1 OTTOMAN ARRIVAL 1–5 APRIL 1453
By 5 April, the Ottomans had surrounded the city by land and sea. Constantine XI entrusted the city's defence to Genoese captain Giustiniani. The Ottoman fleet was held back in the Sea of Marmara by a chain that the Byzantines had pulled across the Golden Horn, so the sea walls were only lightly defended. The main Byzantine forces were stationed at Blachernae in the north and around the Lycus river valley.
Chain
Preliminary Ottoman attacks
Morning, 29 May Ottoman auxiliaries launch two attacks against the Blachernae walls
Blachernae Gate
Caligaria Gate
European Levies
Circus Gate
Blachernae Imperial Palace
Golden Horn
Charisius Gate
Cistern of Aetius
5th Military Gate
Constantinian Wall
Theodosia
Platea Gate
Lycus
Janissaries
St Romanus Gate
Christ (Pantocrator)
4th Military Gate
Theodosian Wall
Rhegium Gate
CONSTANTINOPLE
3rd Military Gate
Gate of the Spring
2nd Military Gate
Anatolian Levies
STUDION
Golden Gate
Zaganos Pasha
28 Apr Constantine orders an attack with fireships against the Ottoman fleet
12 Apr Baltaoglu attempts unsuccessfully to storm the chain
After 22 Apr
Valley of the Springs
GALATA (GENOESE)
Before 20 Apr
Horaia Gate
Eugenius Gate
VENETIAN QUARTER
Forum of Theodosius
St Sophia
Hippodrome
Eleutherian Harbour
Kontoscalion Harbour
From Italy
Morning, 29 May Ottomans break into the city; the defence collapses
Afternoon, 29 May A victorious Mehmed II enters the city and prays in the church of St Sophia, making it into a mosque
Sea of Marmara

THE FALL OF CONSTANTINOPLE

In 1453, Ottoman Sultan Mehmed II moved to capture the Byzantine capital Constantinople. Its formidable walls resisted weeks of pummelling by Mehmed's artillery, but the city fell on 29 May, putting an end to the Byzantine empire.

In 1451, Sultan Mehmed II ascended the Ottoman throne. Setting his sights on the capture of Constantinople, he built a fortress on the Bosphorus to throttle the sea-entrance to the Byzantine capital and assembled a 100-strong fleet and an army of 80,000 men. Equipped with huge Hungarian cannons, he marched against the walled city.

The Byzantine emperor Constantine XI had appealed for military help from western Christians, but his pleas had largely been ignored and he could muster only around 8,000 native defenders. Only the city walls, which had withstood attacks for more than 1,000 years, offered hope, but even they could not resist Mehmed's assault on 29 May 1453. Constantinople became the capital of the Ottoman empire and Mehmed and his successors pursued the conquest of the Balkans, reaching the gates of Vienna by 1529.

THE CONQUEST OF GRANADA

The reconquest of Muslim-held territory in the Iberian Peninsula by Spanish kingdoms stalled in the 13th century with stubborn defence by the Muslim Emirate of Granada. A campaign by Ferdinand of Aragon and Isabella of Castile culminated in the capture of Granada in 1492 and the expulsion of its Muslim population.

The hopes of Spain's Christian rulers that the Reconquista might be complete after the defeat of the Almohad caliphate at Las Navas de Tolosa (see p.75) were premature. Although Córdoba and Seville were retaken in 1236 and 1248, the Christian advance south faltered, and Muslim resistance concentrated in to their sole remaining territory, the Nasrid emirate of Granada.

The balance of power shifted with the marriage of Isabella of Castile and Ferdinand II of Aragon in 1469. The combined might of their kingdoms gave them greater leverage over a Nasrid dynasty, which had become riven by a struggle for power between the sultan, Boabdil, his father, Abū al-Hasan Alī, and his uncle, al-Zaghal. In 1483, Boabdil was captured by the Castilians; he was released on the condition that he would help the Spanish subdue and occupy those parts of Granada under the control of al-Zaghal. Fatally divided, the Nasrids could not offer coordinated resistance to the campaigns that culminated in Granada's capture in 1492, after which Boabdil was allowed to leave with his supporters, and religious freedoms were guaranteed.

THE END OF THE RECONQUISTA
Divisions in the last Muslim-held Emirate in Spain allowed Castile and Aragon to take most of its towns in a decade-long campaign from 1482, culminating in the fall of its capital, Granada, in 1492.

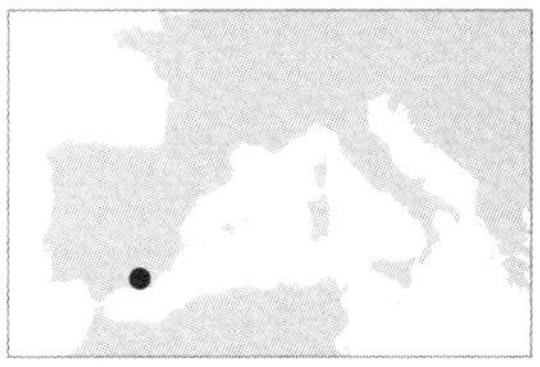

KEY

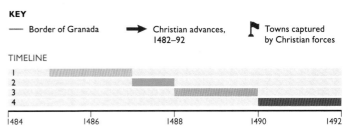

— Border of Granada
➔ Christian advances, 1482–92
Towns captured by Christian forces

TIMELINE

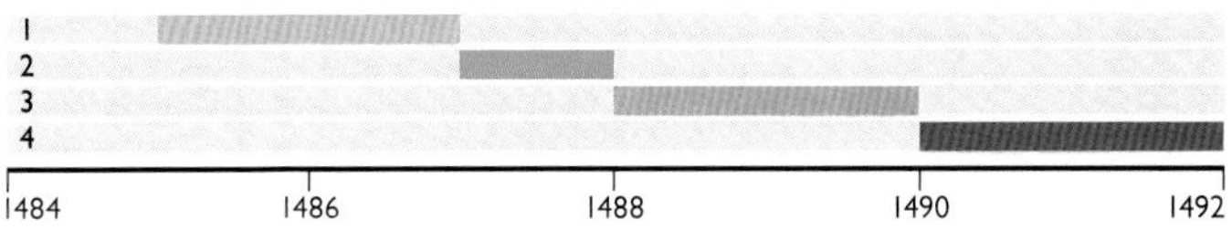
1
2
3
4
1484
1486
1488
1490
1492

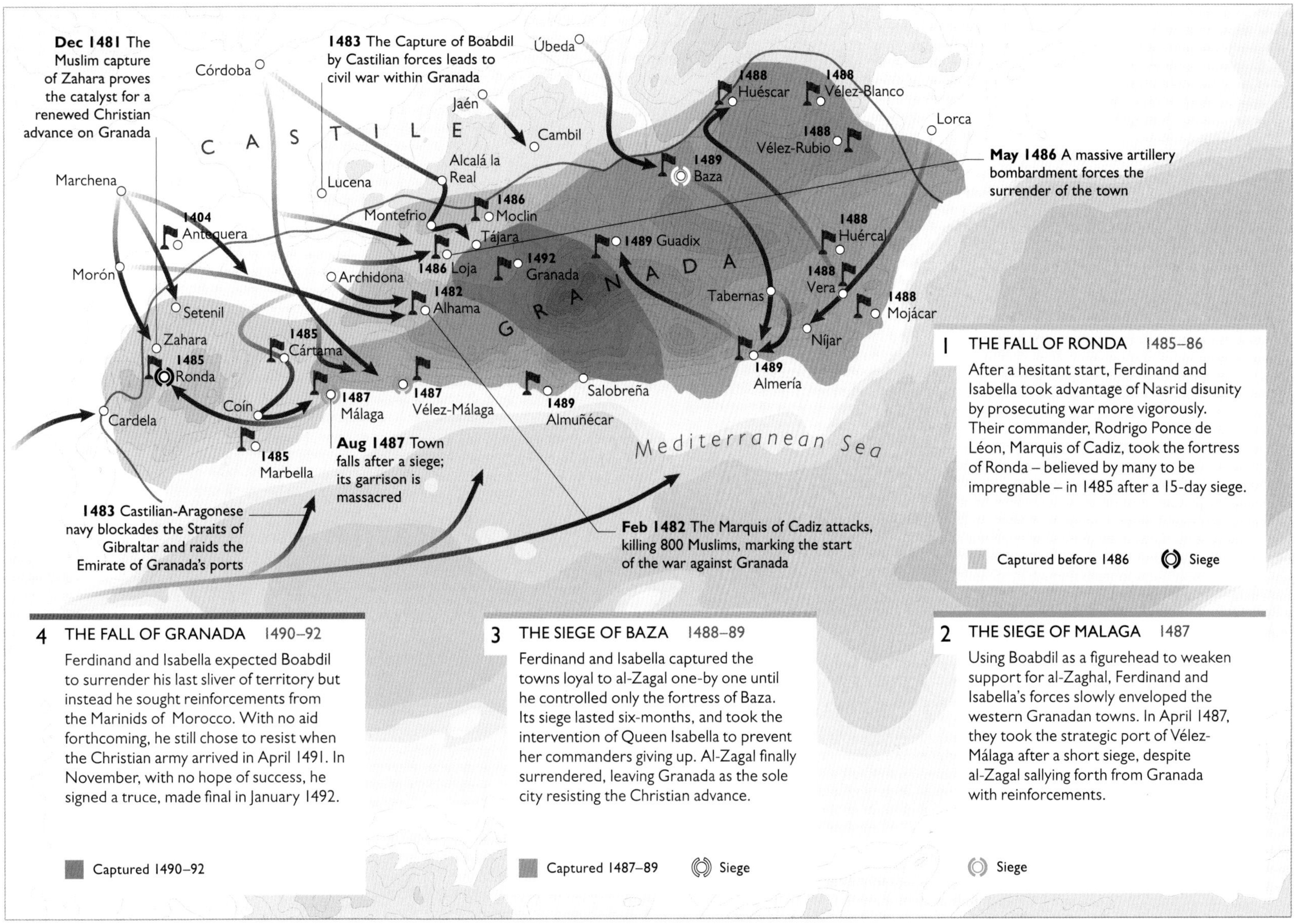
Dec 1481 The Muslim capture of Zahara proves the catalyst for a renewed Christian advance on Granada
1483 The Capture of Boabdil by Castilian forces leads to civil war within Granada
Córdoba
Úbeda
Jaén
Cambil
C A S T I L E
Marchena
Lucena
Alcalá la Real
1486 Moclin
Montefrio
Tájara
1404 Antequera
Morón
1486 Loja
Archidona
1482 Alhama
1492 Granada
1489 Guadix
G R A N A D A
Setenil
Zahara
1485 Ronda
1485 Cártama
Coín
Cardela
1485 Marbella
1487 Málaga
1487 Vélez-Málaga
1489 Almuñécar
Salobreña
Aug 1487 Town falls after a siege; its garrison is massacred
1483 Castilian-Aragonese navy blockades the Straits of Gibraltar and raids the Emirate of Granada's ports
Feb 1482 The Marquis of Cadiz attacks, killing 800 Muslims, marking the start of the war against Granada
Mediterranean Sea
1488 Huéscar
1488 Vélez-Blanco
1488 Vélez-Rubio
Lorca
1489 Baza
May 1486 A massive artillery bombardment forces the surrender of the town
1488 Huércal
1488 Vera
1488 Mojácar
Tabernas
Níjar
1489 Almería

1 THE FALL OF RONDA 1485–86

After a hesitant start, Ferdinand and Isabella took advantage of Nasrid disunity by prosecuting war more vigorously. Their commander, Rodrigo Ponce de Léon, Marquis of Cadiz, took the fortress of Ronda – believed by many to be impregnable – in 1485 after a 15-day siege.

Captured before 1486 | Siege

4 THE FALL OF GRANADA 1490–92

Ferdinand and Isabella expected Boabdil to surrender his last sliver of territory but instead he sought reinforcements from the Marinids of Morocco. With no aid forthcoming, he still chose to resist when the Christian army arrived in April 1491. In November, with no hope of success, he signed a truce, made final in January 1492.

Captured 1490–92

3 THE SIEGE OF BAZA 1488–89

Ferdinand and Isabella captured the towns loyal to al-Zagal one-by one until he controlled only the fortress of Baza. Its siege lasted six-months, and took the intervention of Queen Isabella to prevent her commanders giving up. Al-Zagal finally surrendered, leaving Granada as the sole city resisting the Christian advance.

Captured 1487–89 | Siege

2 THE SIEGE OF MALAGA 1487

Using Boabdil as a figurehead to weaken support for al-Zaghal, Ferdinand and Isabella's forces slowly enveloped the western Granadan towns. In April 1487, they took the strategic port of Vélez-Málaga after a short siege, despite al-Zagal sallying forth from Granada with reinforcements.

Siege

DIRECTORY: 1000–1500

AL-MANSURAH

8–11 FEBRUARY 1250

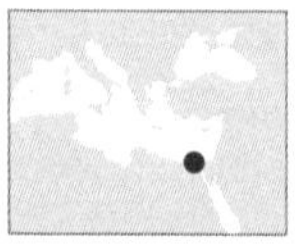

Al-Mansurah was a key battle of the Seventh Crusade (1248–54), the last major Christian attempt to wrest Palestine from Muslim control. Led by French king Louis IX, the crusaders launched a direct attack on Egypt, the seat of the Muslim Ayyubid dynasty that held Jerusalem. After capturing the Egyptian port of Damietta, the crusaders marched south towards Cairo. Their advance was blocked by the Ayyubid army encamped on the opposite side of a canal near the town of al-Mansurah.

The battle began when several hundred elite knights – the Knights Templar – led by Louis' brother Robert of Artois crossed the canal along with an English contingent headed by William of Salisbury, and launched a surprise attack on the Muslim camp. The Egyptians fled in disarray into the town. Instead of waiting for Louis to arrive with his crossbowmen and infantry, the knights impulsively pursued the enemy. Mamluk generals took command of the Egyptian forces and reorganized them to trap the enemy in the town's narrow streets. The crusaders were besieged from all sides and slaughtered. Both Robert of Artois and William of Salisbury were killed along with most of the Knights Templar.

What remained of Louis' main army repulsed repeated onslaughts, but unwisely disdained retreat. The Egyptians seized and destroyed several supply vessels of the crusaders. Short of food and decimated by disease, Louis' forces at last tried to retreat to Damietta in April, but were defeated and captured on the way. Many crusaders died, and Louis was ransomed for a huge sum.

▷ **This 15th-century manuscript painting shows Muslim forces killing the crusaders**

"I will assault your territory… my mind would not be changed."

LOUIS IX, IN A DECLARATION OF WAR TO THE EGYPTIAN SULTAN

XIANGYANG

1268–73

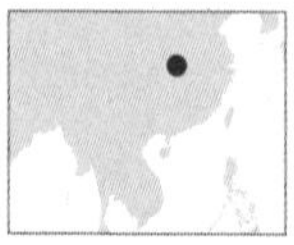

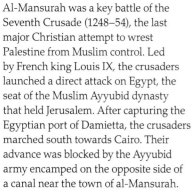

The five-year siege of Xiangyang, in present-day Hubei province in China, was a decisive event in the Mongol conquest of the country. By 1260, the Mongols had taken control of northern China, where their leader Kublai Khan had founded the Yuan dynasty, but the more populous and wealthy lands of southern China remained under the rule of the native Song dynasty. The geography of the region, with its large rivers and fortified cities, was unsuited to the traditional fighting techniques of Mongol steppe horsemen (see p.78). Identifying the fortified city of Xiangyang on the Han River as a key gateway to the south, Kublai placed it under siege in 1268. Despite the Mongols' complete inexperience in naval operations, Kublai assembled a fleet of 5,000 vessels to blockade the river. He brought in engineers from Persia to build siege equipment, including powerful stone-throwing counterweight trebuchets. Primitive incendiary and gunpowder devices added to the pressure on both sides' forces.

After many attempts to relieve the siege failed, the city surrendered in March 1273. The Song dynasty fell six years later, leaving Kublai Khan as the sole ruler of China.

COURTRAI

11 JULY 1302

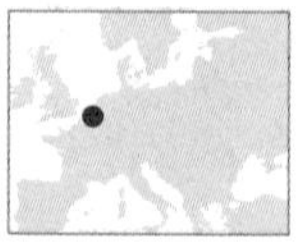

Also known as the Battle of the Golden Spurs, the medieval encounter fought outside the Flemish city of Courtrai, or Kortrijk, (in present-day Belgium) is famous as a victory of common Flemish foot soldiers against the French knights. The Flemings had risen in revolt against the occupation of their territory by the French king Philip IV. In the summer of 1302, a Flemish force besieged the French-held Courtrai castle. Philip sent an army under Count Robert II of Artois to suppress the revolt. The rival forces were roughly equal in number, with around 10,000 men, but the Flemings were mainly town militia and almost exclusively on foot, while the French included some 2,500 armoured horsemen. The Flemings took up position behind streams and ditches on marshy ground. When the French horsemen charged, their mounts floundered and fell in the ditches. The Flemish infantry rushed forward, wielding pikes and spiked clubs known as *goedendags*, to murderous effect. Robert was among a thousand French nobles and knights who lost their lives. The victorious Flemings retrieved about 500 pairs of spurs from the battlefield, giving the battle its popular name.

POITIERS

19 SEPTEMBER 1356

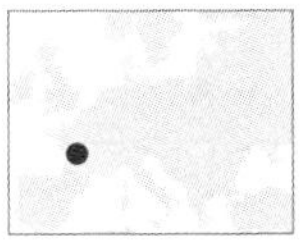

The Battle of Poitiers was a major defeat for France in the Hundred Years War (see p.57) against England. A force of several thousand men led by Edward, the Prince of Wales, also known as the Black Prince, raided central France from English-ruled Aquitaine. The French king Jean II intercepted the raiders outside the city of Poitiers with a much larger army. The English could not evade without abandoning their hard-won plunder, so they decided to accept battle and to exploit the local defensive terrain, in particular a thick hedge through which the road south ran.

On 19 September, Edward drew up his army for battle, his knights on foot and his longbowmen on the flanks. A first wave of French knights attacked on horseback, but their mounts were cut down by the arrows of Edward's longbowmen. A second wave led by the Dauphin – Jean II's heir – advanced on foot and engaged the English in savage close-quarter fighting. Finally, as King Jean himself stepped forward to enter the fray, Edward ordered his forces to charge. A reserve of 200 mounted English knights rode around and attacked the French from the rear. Amid complete carnage, the king and many French nobles were captured. King Jean remained a prisoner in England until 1360, when France agreed a ransom of three million gold crowns in exchange for his safe return.

ANKARA

20 JULY 1402

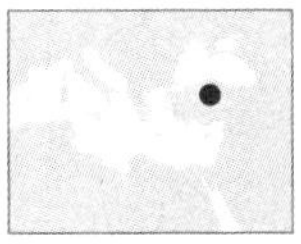

The Battle of Ankara was a contest between two outstanding military commanders: Ottoman sultan Bayezid I and the Turko-Mongol warrior Timur (Tamerlane). Based in Samarkand in Central Asia, Timur had conquered a vast swathe of Asia, from Delhi to Damascus, earning a reputation for massacre and devastation. In 1402, he invaded Ottoman territory in Anatolia (modern-day Turkey). Bayezid led his forces eastwards across the country to confront the intruder, but Timur outmanoeuvred him, swerving behind the Ottoman army and occupying its former camp.

Bayezid's soldiers became exhausted and ran out of water when Timur diverted the nearby stream. Timur's steppe horsemen, armed with composite bows, overwhelmed the slower-moving Turkish forces. Bayezid's Serbian vassals fought fiercely, but many of his other allies defected to Timur. Bayezid himself fled the battlefield with a cavalry escort but was captured. He died in captivity the following year, although legends of his imprisonment in a cage are dubious.

Timur died in 1405 while marching against China, and his short-lived empire quickly collapsed into civil war, but the Ottoman Empire was itself wracked by civil war until 1413, before reaching new heights under later sultans like Mehmed II (see p.96) and Suleiman I (see pp.112–17).

▽ A 16th-century painting depicting Bayezid I in Timur's captivity

NICOPOLIS

25 SEPTEMBER 1396

△ Mounted Ottoman Turks attack the Christian knights at the Battle of Nicopolis

The crushing defeat of a Christian army in 1396 at present-day Nikopol in northern Bulgaria set the Ottoman Turks on course to create one of the world's biggest empires. Encroaching on southeast Europe, the Ottoman sultan Bayezid I threatened to attack the Christian kingdom of Hungary.

In response, the Hungarian king Sigismund gathered a multinational crusader army including French and Hospitaller knights, and besieged the Ottoman stronghold at Nicopolis. Bayezid led his army north to relieve the siege, accompanied by Serbian knights who had become Ottoman vassals since the Battle of Kosovo in 1389 (see pp.86–87) His arrival surprised the crusaders, who hastily prepared for battle. Plagued by divided command and disputes over status, the Christian army attacked the Ottomans without knowing their strength or the disposition of their forces. Bayezid's disciplined army withstood the charge of the Christian knights before counter-attacking with devastating effect. Bayezid was merciless in victory, killing all enemy prisoners he took, except for those who could be profitably ransomed or enslaved.

BOSWORTH FIELD

22 AUGUST 1485

The defeat of King Richard III at Bosworth Field in the English Midlands brought the Tudor dynasty to the throne of England. For 30 years, the royal houses of York and Lancaster had competed for power in the Wars of the Roses. The Yorkists appeared to have triumphed after victory at Tewkesbury in 1471, but the unpopularity of King Richard III provided an opportunity for the exiled Lancastrian Henry Tudor to bid for the throne. Sailing from France, Henry landed at Milford Haven in Wales and marched into England, gathering support along the way. Richard intercepted him near the town of Market Bosworth in Leicestershire.

Both armies fielded several thousand men. The king had the larger force, but their loyalty was uncertain. At the height of the battle, Richard led his knights in a bold thrust towards Henry and his army. At that moment the powerful Stanley contingent switched sides and attacked Richard. He was surrounded and killed. Henry took power and became the first English monarch of the Tudor dynasty.

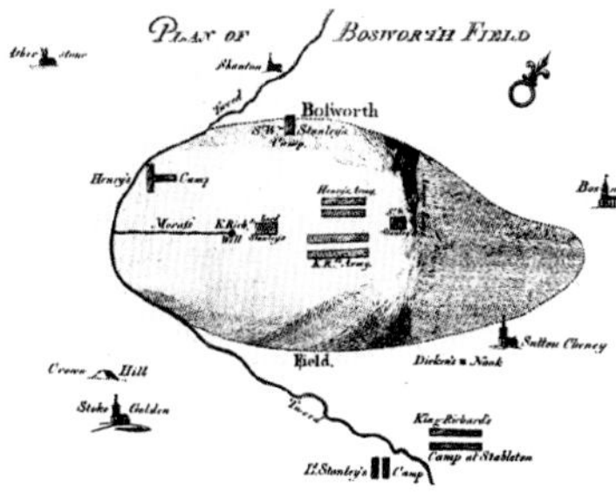
Plan of Bosworth Field
Bosworth

△ Plan showing the two armies positioned at Bosworth Field

1500–1700

EARLY GUNPOWDER WEAPONS UNDERWENT NUMEROUS IMPROVEMENTS, AND ARMIES BECAME MORE STRUCTURED AND PROFESSIONAL. WARS OF RELIGION AND SUCCESSION TOOK PLACE ACROSS THE WORLD, WHILE WARSHIPS DEVELOPED INTO LARGE SHIPS OF THE LINE DELIVERING ENORMOUSLY INCREASED FIREPOWER.

△ **Heavy protection**
This chainmail helmet was worn by Mughal cavalrymen in 16th-century India – a time in which mounted warriors were still a significant force on the battlefield.

1500–1700

The 16th and 17th centuries saw changes in war as gunpowder made the battlefield more lethal. In Asia, states fielded armies larger than ever in wars of territorial expansion, while increasingly professional armies fought religious and dynastic wars in Europe.

Before 1500, combat mainly involved small armies of feudal levies and knights, but 200 years later, professional armies of thousands of uniformed soldiers, trained in military manoeuvres, began to fight massive engagements. These armies were equipped with muskets and field artillery.

The introduction of gunpowder helped to provoke these changes. Hand-held arquebuses and muskets became increasingly widespread, playing a growing role in battles as seen in engagements of the Italian Wars such as Cerignola in 1503 and Bicocca in 1522. Firing mechanisms were gradually refined from matchlock to wheellock and then flintlock. Firing rates and range also gradually improved. Together, this made traditional armoured cavalry, armed with lances instead of firearms, redundant, and infantry began to dominate the battlefield alongside horsemen with little or no armour wielding swords and pistols. A parallel evolution occurred in artillery, which had struggled to damage city walls in the 15th century. By 1600, field guns had grown in calibre to threaten all but the most formidable defences. In response, engineers such as France's Sebastian le Prestre de Vauban and his Dutch counterpart, Menno van Coehoorn, improved the design of fortifications and advocated new techniques of siege warfare (see pp.148–49).

> *"War is not to be avoided, but is only put off to the advantage of others."*
>
> NICCOLÒ MACHIAVELLI, *THE PRINCE*, 1513

Combat turned back towards wars of manoeuvre – historically practised by smaller armies – and the new infantry-driven armies grew larger. These massive forces required increasingly complex organization and training, and insignia and uniforms became a feature of military life. Formal military drills were introduced in the 1590s by the Dutch commander Maurice of Nassau.

Changing ways of war

The increased expense of such armies caused changes in the way countries were governed, leading to more centralization of power. Nations better equipped to fight did so with more

◁ **Channel encounter**
In this painting from c.1620, the Spanish Armada clash with Elizabeth I's forces in the English Channel in 1588 (see pp.120–21). The battle was the largest 16th-century naval confrontation in northern Europe and sparked a naval arms race.

NEW DEVELOPMENTS

The increasing pace of technological development in gunpowder armaments drove a military revolution in Europe. As the cost of warfare rose, states developed a greater ability to raise taxation that, in turn, enhanced their ability to wage wars, leading to further conflicts. Non-European powers adopted gunpowder weaponry as well. It enabled them, in some cases, to resist European encroachment on their territory, and in others, aided territorial expansion or fuelled civil wars.

c.1500 The wheellock firing mechanism, using a rotating metal wheel to ignite gunpowder charge, is developed, allowing effective hand-held pistols

1511 Scotland launches the *Great Michael*, a cannon-armed warship with twice the displacement of England's *Mary Rose* two years earlier

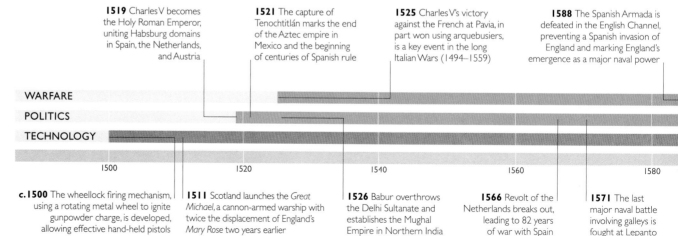

1519 Charles V becomes the Holy Roman Emperor, uniting Habsburg domains in Spain, the Netherlands, and Austria

1521 The capture of Tenochtitlán marks the end of the Aztec empire in Mexico and the beginning of centuries of Spanish rule

1525 Charles V's victory against the French at Pavia, in part won using arquebusiers, is a key event in the long Italian Wars (1494–1559)

1526 Babur overthrows the Delhi Sultanate and establishes the Mughal Empire in Northern India

1566 Revolt of the Netherlands breaks out, leading to 82 years of war with Spain

1571 The last major naval battle involving galleys is fought at Lepanto

1588 The Spanish Armada is defeated in the English Channel, preventing a Spanish invasion of England and marking England's emergence as a major naval power

▷ **First shots**
Musketeers and pistol-wielding cavalry dominated at the Battle of the White Mountain (see p.128) in 1620, the first major battle of the Thirty Years War.

◁ **Failed king**
England's Charles I's attempt to fund his wars by raising tax without consulting with the Parliament ended in a civil war and his execution in 1649.

frequency. Europe was torn apart in a series of religious wars between Catholic and Protestant factions, culminating in the Thirty Years War (1618–48), in which as many as eight million soldiers and civilians died. Subsequently, religious warfare waned, but Europe became the scene of large-scale dynastic conflicts as monarchs such as Louis XIV of France sought territorial gains against Habsburg Spain and the Netherlands. Non-European powers, too, fought larger wars. The Ottoman Empire in Turkey, the Safavid Empire in Iran, and the Mughal Empire in India moved away from a dependence on feudal cavalry to develop centrally recruited forces, which owed primary allegiance to the rulers. Japan developed a military culture all of its own, based on the *daimyo* (warlords) and their samurai retainers, who engaged in a series of civil wars until the country was reunited under the Tokugawa shoguns from 1603.

Warfare at sea experienced equally profound changes. Warships in both Europe and Asia had been carrying a few small cannon since the 14th century, primarily for anti-personnel use, but from around 1500 the increasing deployment by European navies of heavy cannons changed the way naval battles were fought. Galleys with ranks of oarsmen, which fought in battles such as at Lepanto (see pp.118–19) were gradually replaced by ships of the line that fired broadsides through hinged gunports. Seafaring nations such as England, the Netherlands, and France spent massive sums on their navies, extending their rivalry to seaborne conflicts across the Atlantic and in the Indian Ocean. Just as on land, only the richest and well-organized states could compete militarily in a world where the cost of warfare was ever rising.

c.1590 Paper cartridges become more widespread, making it easier to load muzzle-loading firearms, and increasing firing rates

1600 Tokugawa victory at Sekigahara marks a key stage in the re-establishment of Japanese unity

1603 Tokugawa Ieyasu unites Japan after 150 years of civil war, beginning the Tokugawa shogunate

c.1615 First "true" flintlock firing mechanism is developed, improving the efficiency and reliability of guns

1632 Swedish king Gustavus Adolphus dies in battle as his forces win the Battle of Lützen against an army of the Holy Roman Empire

1643 Accession of Louis XIV of France, whose 72-year reign marks an apogee in French power

1645 The defeat of King Charles I's royalist forces against the Parliamentarian forces at Naseby leads to the end of the first phase of the English Civil War

1655–1703 Vauban builds a series of fortresses in France, adapted to the new era of long-range firearms and heavy artillery

1660 English monarchy is restored after 18 years of civil war and republican rule

1683 The defeat of the Ottomans at the Siege of Vienna marks the limit of their expansion out of the Balkans

1600 · 1620 · 1640 · 1660 · 1680 · 1700

3 FAILED ATTACKS
10 JUNE–23 JUNE 1521

The Spanish made a series of attacks up the causeways, but were fought back by the Aztecs. On 15 June, Cortés ordered the burning of the suburbs that his soldiers entered to reduce resistance. In fierce back and forth assaults in late June, several dozen Spanish soldiers (nearly including Cortés himself) were captured and sacrificed in the main temple (Templo Mayor).

2 BATTLES ON THE LAKE
1 JUNE–10 JUNE

Having built 13 brigantines (light ships) in Tlaxcala, Cortés had them carried to the lake, where they began intercepting Aztec supply canoes. A battle with 1,000 Aztec canoes broke out, in which the Spanish were victorious. The Spanish took Iztapalapa and a defensive position on Tepeleco. The Aztecs used defensive stakes to impale the brigantines, and captured two ships.

1 BEGINNING THE SIEGE
LATE APRIL–22 JUNE 1521

Accompanied by tens of thousands of warriors from Texcoco, Chalco, and Tlaxcala, Cortés arrived at Coyoacán in late April. He split his forces into three to cover all the causeways leading into Tenochtitlán, with Alvarado going to Tacuba, de Olid staying at Coyoacán, and de Sandoval marching on Iztapalapa. They took up position and stopped supplies entering the city.

4 RAZING TENOCHTITLÁN
30 JUNE–31 JULY 1521

Cortés paused operations to persuade former allies back into his camp. From mid-July, he conducted assaults into Tenochtitlán and its northern sister-city of Tlatelolco. The main marketplace and temple of Tlatelolco were burnt by Alvarado. To the south, the Spanish made steady gains, winning control of most of the island.

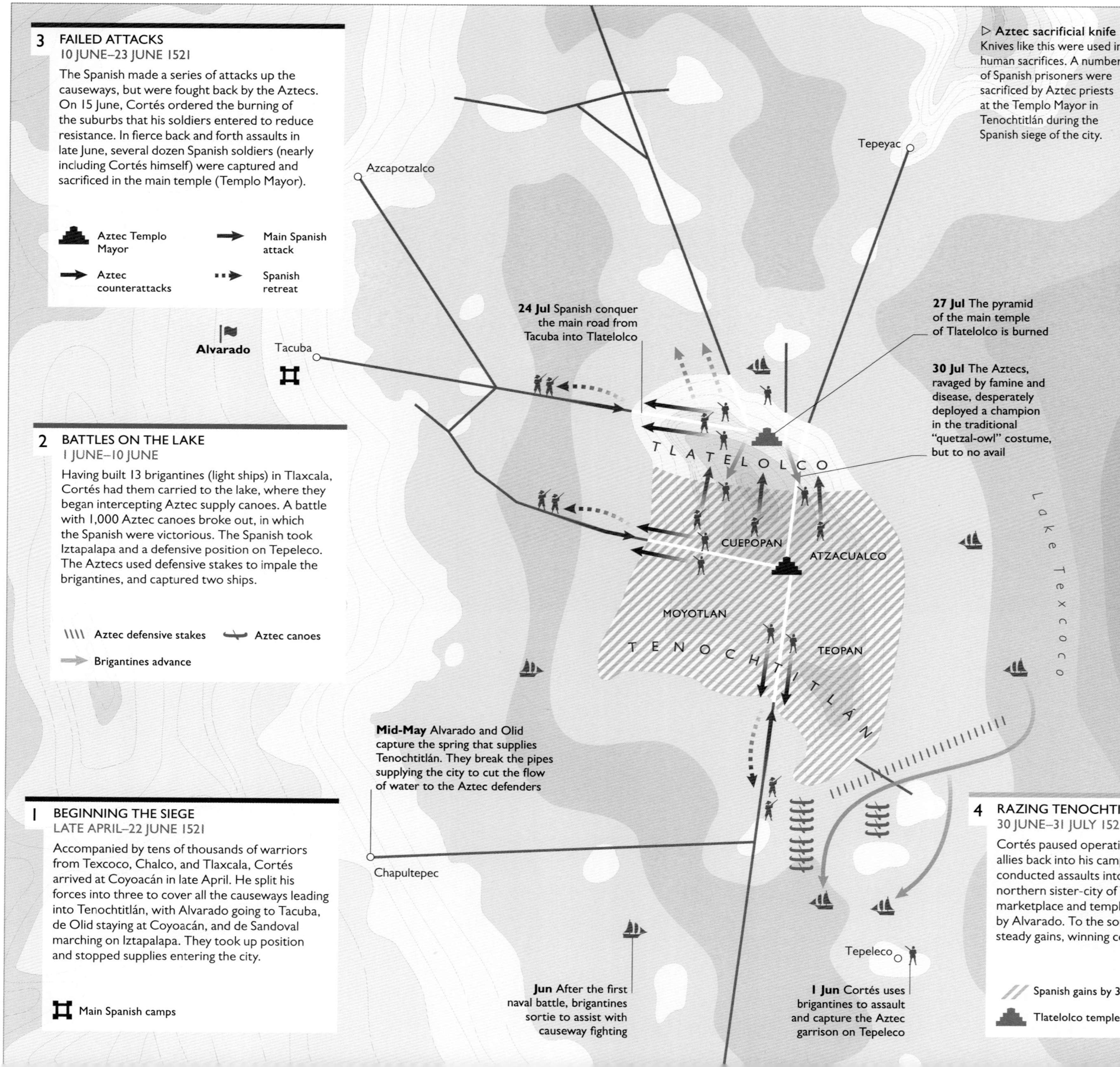
Aztec Templo Mayor
Main Spanish attack
Aztec counterattacks
Spanish retreat
Aztec defensive stakes
Aztec canoes
Brigantines advance
Main Spanish camps
Spanish gains by 31 Jul
Tlatelolco temple compound
Alvarado
Tacuba
Azcapotzalco
Tepeyac
Chapultepec
Tepeleco
Lake Texcoco
TLATELOLCO
TENOCHTITLÁN
CUEPOPAN
ATZACUALCO
MOYOTLAN
TEOPAN
24 Jul Spanish conquer the main road from Tacuba into Tlatelolco
27 Jul The pyramid of the main temple of Tlatelolco is burned
30 Jul The Aztecs, ravaged by famine and disease, desperately deployed a champion in the traditional "quetzal-owl" costume, but to no avail
Mid-May Alvarado and Olid capture the spring that supplies Tenochtitlán. They break the pipes supplying the city to cut the flow of water to the Aztec defenders
Jun After the first naval battle, brigantines sortie to assist with causeway fighting
1 Jun Cortés uses brigantines to assault and capture the Aztec garrison on Tepeleco

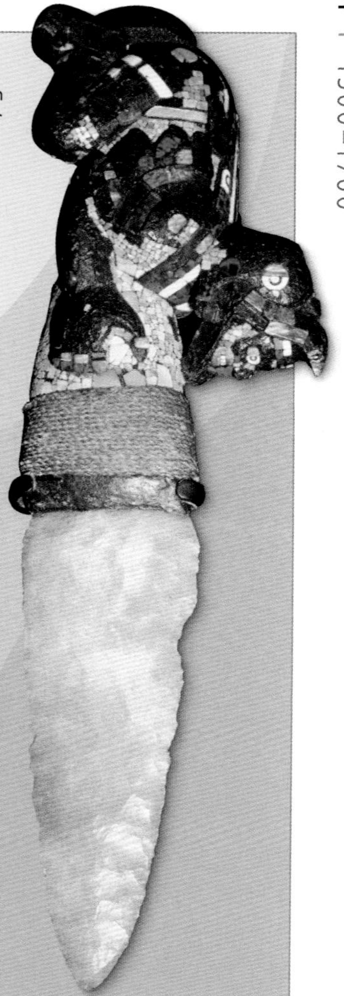

▷ **Aztec sacrificial knife**
Knives like this were used in human sacrifices. A number of Spanish prisoners were sacrificed by Aztec priests at the Templo Mayor in Tenochtitlán during the Spanish siege of the city.

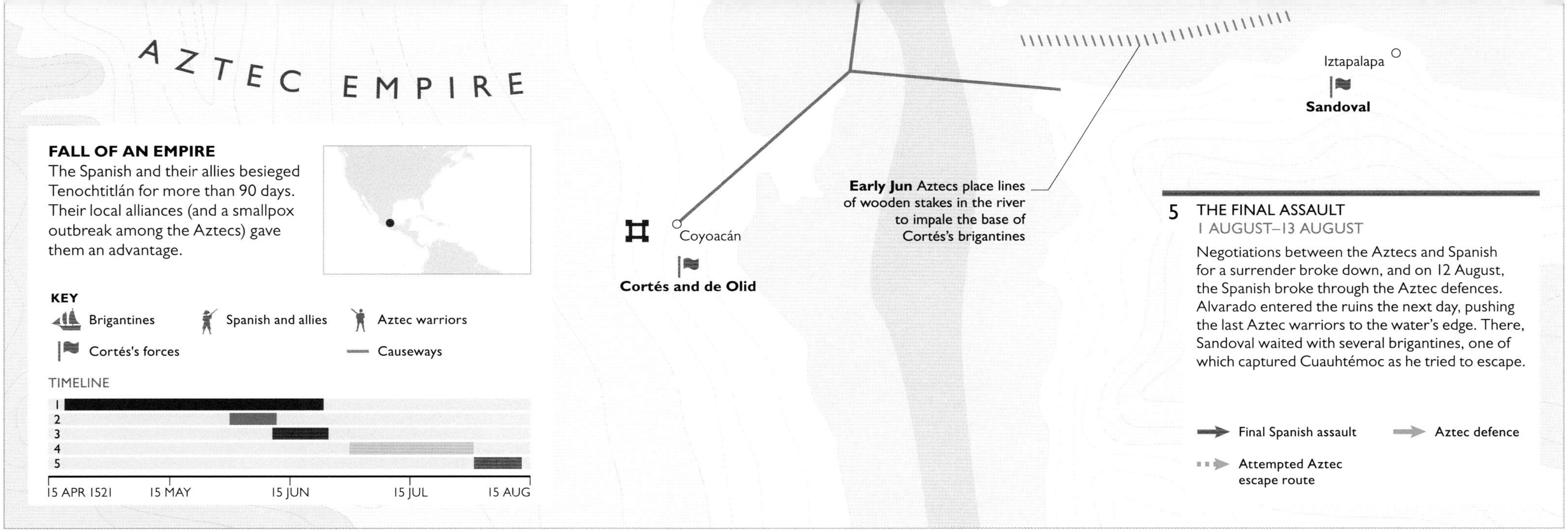
AZTEC EMPIRE
Coyoacán
Cortés and de Olid
Early Jun Aztecs place lines of wooden stakes in the river to impale the base of Cortés's brigantines
Iztapalapa
Sandoval
KEY
Brigantines
Spanish and allies
Aztec warriors
Cortés's forces
Causeways
TIMELINE
1
2
3
4
5
15 APR 1521
15 MAY
15 JUN
15 JUL
15 AUG
Final Spanish assault
Aztec defence
Attempted Aztec escape route

FALL OF AN EMPIRE
The Spanish and their allies besieged Tenochtitlán for more than 90 days. Their local alliances (and a smallpox outbreak among the Aztecs) gave them an advantage.

5 THE FINAL ASSAULT
1 AUGUST–13 AUGUST

Negotiations between the Aztecs and Spanish for a surrender broke down, and on 12 August, the Spanish broke through the Aztec defences. Alvarado entered the ruins the next day, pushing the last Aztec warriors to the water's edge. There, Sandoval waited with several brigantines, one of which captured Cuauhtémoc as he tried to escape.

THE SIEGE OF TENOCHTITLÁN

Hernán Cortés's invasion of Mexico in 1519 culminated in a three-month siege of the Aztec capital, Tenochtitlán. Despite ferocious resistance, the Spanish and their native allies seized the last redoubt in August 1521, leading to the collapse of the Aztec empire.

The landing of conquistador Hernán Cortés (see pp.106–107) near present-day San Juan de Ulúa in April 1519 prompted a wary but peaceful response from the Aztec emperor Moctezuma II. Although his force numbered little more than 600, Cortés swiftly recruited allies from the local peoples who resented Aztec rule, and marched to the Aztec capital Tenochtitlán, entering it on 8 November. Although relations were initially cordial, they soon soured, and Cortés placed Moctezuma under house arrest, seeking to take direct control of the empire. The tactic failed and an anti-Spanish uprising broke out, during which Moctezuma was killed. On 30 June 1520, Cortés was driven from Tenochtitlán with huge losses. The Spanish army escaped to Tlaxcala, and it took almost 10 months to rebuild native alliances and return to Tenochtitlán, where the Aztecs had endured a smallpox epidemic.

The siege was protracted, lasting from May until August 1521, and the city's position on an island made direct attack difficult. But its near-destruction, the capture of the new emperor Cuauhtémoc, and the death or execution of much of the Aztec nobility shattered opposition to the Spanish. The fall of the city left them in control of the former Aztec empire and its rich resources for the next 300 years.

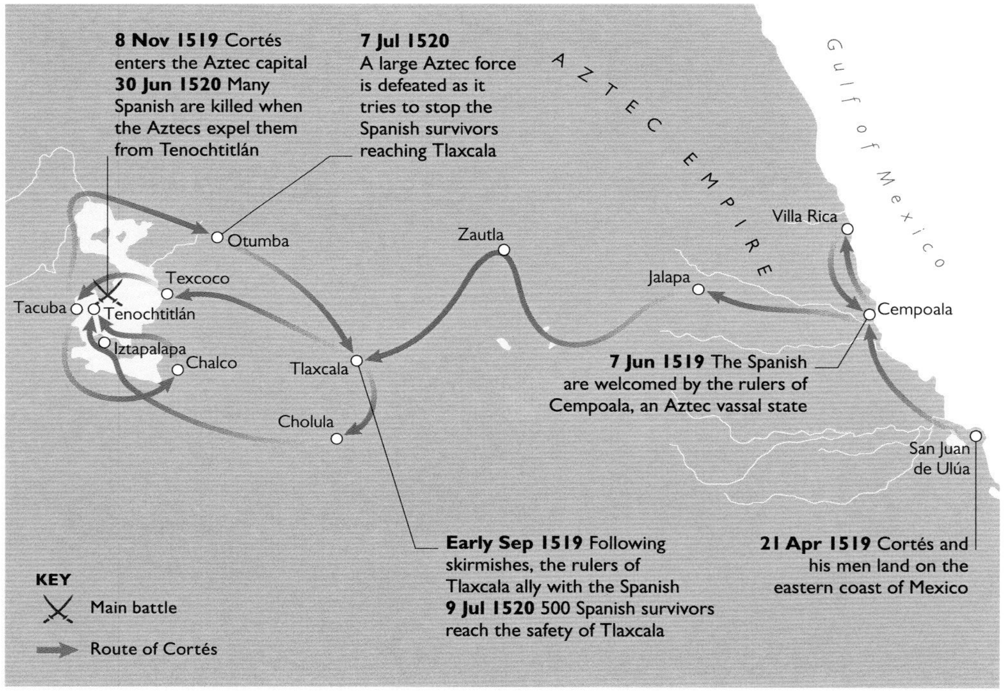
8 Nov 1519 Cortés enters the Aztec capital
30 Jun 1520 Many Spanish are killed when the Aztecs expel them from Tenochtitlán
7 Jul 1520 A large Aztec force is defeated as it tries to stop the Spanish survivors reaching Tlaxcala
AZTEC EMPIRE
Gulf of Mexico
Villa Rica
Otumba
Zautla
Jalapa
Texcoco
Tacuba
Tenochtitlán
Iztapalapa
Chalco
Tlaxcala
Cempoala
7 Jun 1519 The Spanish are welcomed by the rulers of Cempoala, an Aztec vassal state
Cholula
San Juan de Ulúa
Early Sep 1519 Following skirmishes, the rulers of Tlaxcala ally with the Spanish
9 Jul 1520 500 Spanish survivors reach the safety of Tlaxcala
21 Apr 1519 Cortés and his men land on the eastern coast of Mexico
KEY
Main battle
Route of Cortés

THE MARCH ON TENOCHTITLÁN
After Cortés landed in April 1519, he proved adept at building alliances with the Aztecs' subject peoples. The addition of the Tlaxcalans (long-standing rivals to the Aztecs) to the alliance made the Spanish a potent threat and aided their entry into Tenochtitlán in November. They were expelled eight months later, barely escaping across the city's causeways, and Cortés's forces were only saved from destruction in an ambush at Otumba by the inexperience of Aztecs in facing the Spanish cavalry in the open.

Load bearers
In this 16th-century illustration by artist Theodore de Bry, Spanish conquistadors can be seen exploiting the indigenous people by making them carry baggage and equipment.

THE SPANISH CONQUISTADORS

During the 16th century, small bands of Spanish nobles, soldiers, and assorted explorers launched countless expeditions in the New World, resulting in the Spanish conquest of large parts of the Americas.

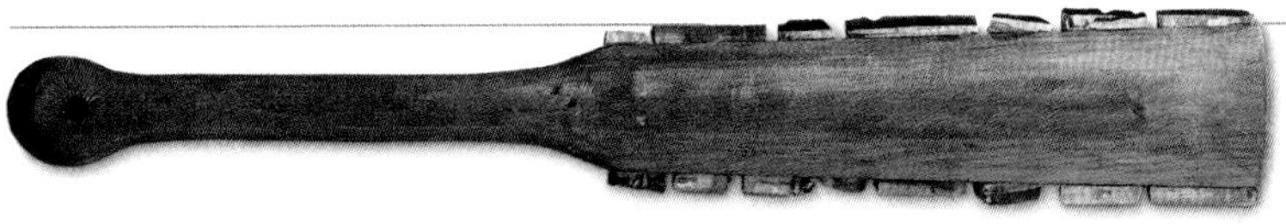

△ **Effective weapon**
The *macuahuitl*, a wooden club edged with obsidian blades, was one of the primary weapons of the Aztecs.

For a long time, the retelling of Spain's conquest of the Americas was dominated by the myth of invading soldiers with superior weapons toppling large but primitive indigenous empires. These conquerors, known as conquistadors, came with horses, steel swords, armour, pikes, and crossbows, and some arquebuses and light cannons – all unheard of in the Americas. In reality, while some of the armies they faced were equipped with basic stone weaponry, others were large, well trained, and part of sophisticated civilizations.

Cunning invaders

The conquest of Mexico in 1519–21 by Spanish soldier Hernán Cortés succeeded mainly due to his use of local allies and cunning diplomacy rather than advanced weapons (see pp.104–105). Cortés was fighting against an Aztec empire that had both a long list of enemies, and restless subjects. He also unwittingly took advantage of a smallpox epidemic that the Spaniards had brought with them. In some instances, however, such as Francisco Pizarro's conquest of the Inca empire in 1532–33 with only a tiny force, Spanish technology and organization played a more clear role in ensuring victory.

Technological superiority, however, did not protect conquistadors from weather, illness, hunger, and thirst, elements that saw many expeditions fail. Often, the ability of conquistadors to exploit existing divisions earned them lasting victories that reshaped the continent.

△ **Aztecs greet Cortés**
This 16th-century illustration by Dominican missionary Diego Durán shows Aztec ruler Moctezuma II welcoming Hernán Cortés and his army. The Aztecs can be seen wearing simple cotton cloaks, while the armour-clad Spanish wield weapons.

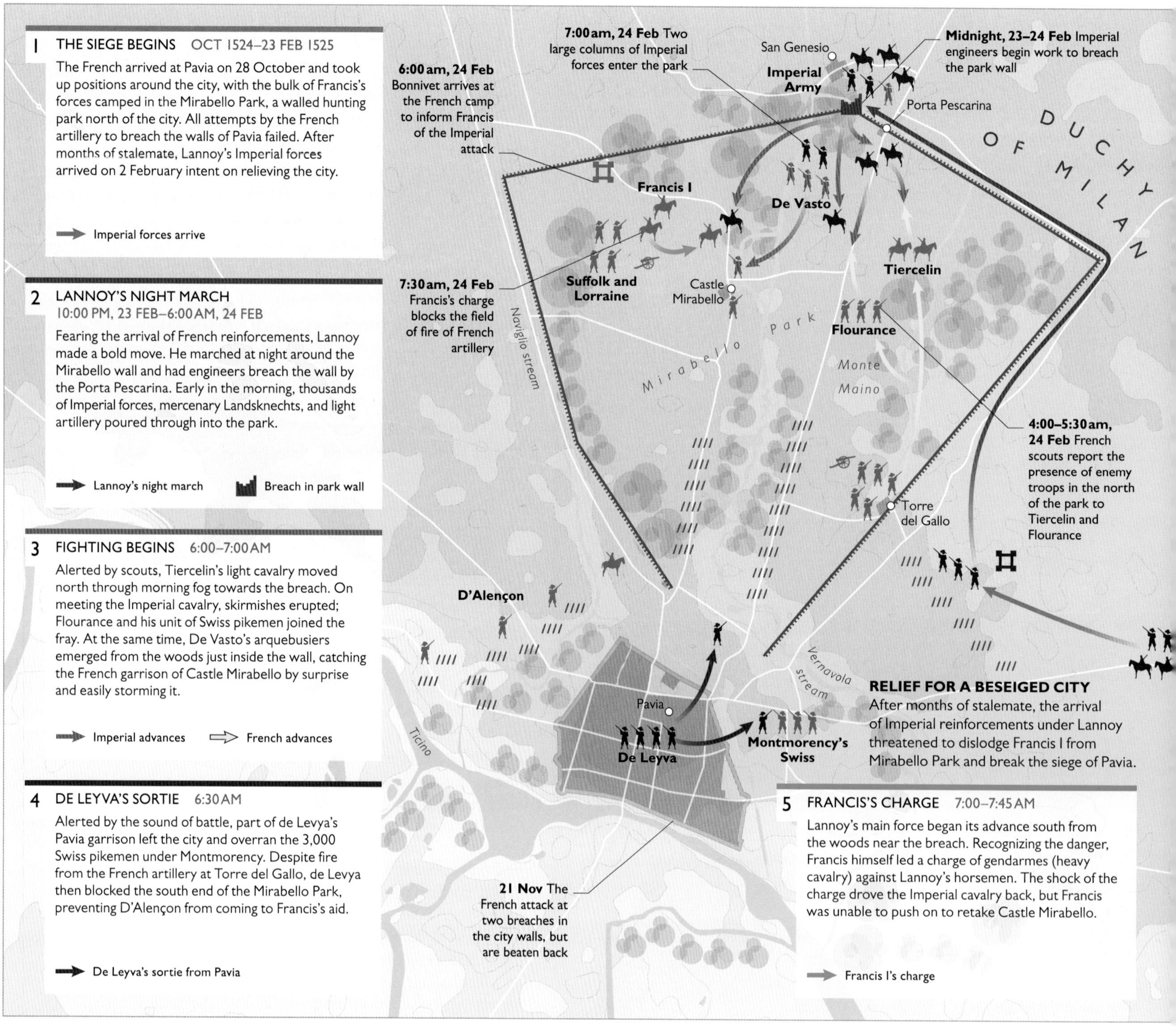
1 THE SIEGE BEGINS OCT 1524–23 FEB 1525
The French arrived at Pavia on 28 October and took up positions around the city, with the bulk of Francis's forces camped in the Mirabello Park, a walled hunting park north of the city. All attempts by the French artillery to breach the walls of Pavia failed. After months of stalemate, Lannoy's Imperial forces arrived on 2 February intent on relieving the city.
Imperial forces arrive
2 LANNOY'S NIGHT MARCH 10:00 PM, 23 FEB–6:00 AM, 24 FEB
Fearing the arrival of French reinforcements, Lannoy made a bold move. He marched at night around the Mirabello wall and had engineers breach the wall by the Porta Pescarina. Early in the morning, thousands of Imperial forces, mercenary Landsknechts, and light artillery poured through into the park.
Lannoy's night march
Breach in park wall
3 FIGHTING BEGINS 6:00–7:00 AM
Alerted by scouts, Tiercelin's light cavalry moved north through morning fog towards the breach. On meeting the Imperial cavalry, skirmishes erupted; Flourance and his unit of Swiss pikemen joined the fray. At the same time, De Vasto's arquebusiers emerged from the woods just inside the wall, catching the French garrison of Castle Mirabello by surprise and easily storming it.
Imperial advances
French advances
4 DE LEYVA'S SORTIE 6:30 AM
Alerted by the sound of battle, part of de Levya's Pavia garrison left the city and overran the 3,000 Swiss pikemen under Montmorency. Despite fire from the French artillery at Torre del Gallo, de Levya then blocked the south end of the Mirabello Park, preventing D'Alençon from coming to Francis's aid.
De Leyva's sortie from Pavia
6:00 am, 24 Feb Bonnivet arrives at the French camp to inform Francis of the Imperial attack
7:00 am, 24 Feb Two large columns of Imperial forces enter the park
San Genesio
Imperial Army
Midnight, 23–24 Feb Imperial engineers begin work to breach the park wall
Porta Pescarina
DUCHY OF MILAN
Francis I
De Vasto
Suffolk and Lorraine
Castle Mirabello
Tiercelin
7:30 am, 24 Feb Francis's charge blocks the field of fire of French artillery
Naviglio stream
Mirabello Park
Flourance
Monte Maino
4:00–5:30 am, 24 Feb French scouts report the presence of enemy troops in the north of the park to Tiercelin and Flourance
Torre del Gallo
D'Alençon
Vernavola stream
Ticino
Pavia
De Leyva
Montmorency's Swiss
RELIEF FOR A BESEIGED CITY
After months of stalemate, the arrival of Imperial reinforcements under Lannoy threatened to dislodge Francis I from Mirabello Park and break the siege of Pavia.
21 Nov The French attack at two breaches in the city walls, but are beaten back
5 FRANCIS'S CHARGE 7:00–7:45 AM
Lannoy's main force began its advance south from the woods near the breach. Recognizing the danger, Francis himself led a charge of gendarmes (heavy cavalry) against Lannoy's horsemen. The shock of the charge drove the Imperial cavalry back, but Francis was unable to push on to retake Castle Mirabello.
Francis I's charge

PAVIA

Francis I of France's attempt to wrest control of northern Italy from the Habsburgs foundered at Pavia in 1525 when a night march by Imperial troops caught him unawares. In a battle dominated for the first time by gunpowder weapons, his army was cut to pieces.

The Italian Wars of 1494–1559 were sparked by France's ambition to dominate northern Italy. In September 1524, Imperial Habsburg troops had been forced to retreat back into Italy after their failed siege of Marseilles; then in October 1524, Francis I began an offensive, first taking Milan with his 40,000-strong army, then pursuing the main Imperial force under Charles de Lannoy. He stopped to besiege the strategic town of Pavia, which was garrisoned by mercenaries under Antonio de Leyva. However, the siege became deadlocked, allowing Lannoy to regroup, reinforce, and eventually outflank him when the Imperial forces arrived in early February. Francis was captured, imprisoned, and forced to sign a treaty waiving all French claims in Italy. He repudiated the treaty as soon as he was released, and forged a new anti-Habsburg alliance that included Henry VIII of England. The Italian Wars dragged on intermittently until 1559.

FRANCIS I DEFEATED

Francis I's invasion of northern Italy stalled at Pavia. The length of the siege allowed imperial reinforcements to reach the city and relieve its garrison. After a surprise night-march, they broke into the walled park where the main French force was stationed, taking advantage of the confusion to achieve the defeat of Francis's army.

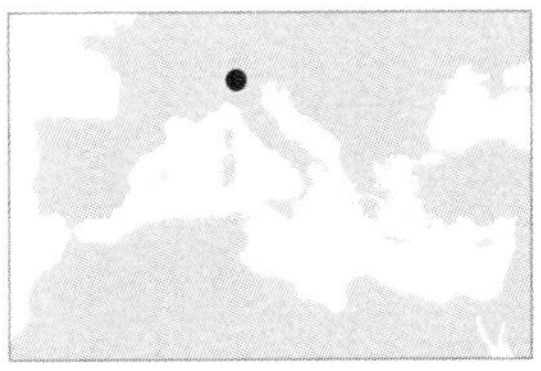

KEY

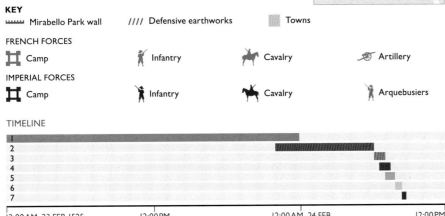

Mirabello Park wall | Defensive earthworks | Towns

FRENCH FORCES: Camp | Infantry | Cavalry | Artillery

IMPERIAL FORCES: Camp | Infantry | Cavalry | Arquebusiers

TIMELINE

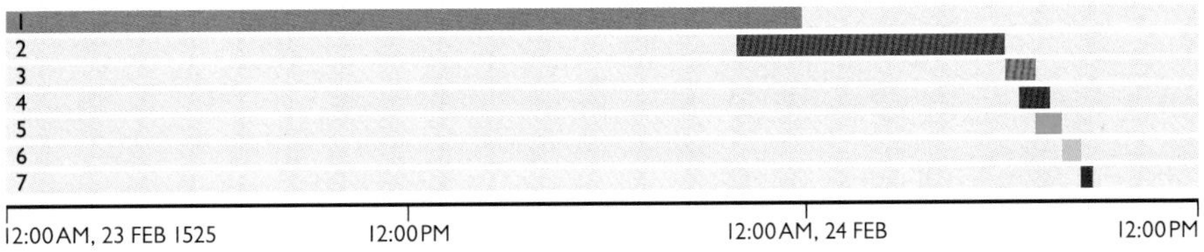
1
2
3
4
5
6
7
12:00AM, 23 FEB 1525
12:00PM
12:00AM, 24 FEB
12:00PM

THE ARQUEBUS

The arquebus appeared in Europe and the Ottoman Empire during the 15th century. It was a matchlock gun: a lit match was lowered by a trigger into a powder pan to spark the explosion. Its muzzle-loading mechanism was cumbersome, and damp made the powder too wet to ignite. The gun's weight meant it had to be fired resting on external support. However, these were the first guns to make a difference on the battlefield: they could inflict disruption and losses on cavalry and infantry, especially when volley fire was developed by the Ottomans, Ming Chinese, and Dutch.

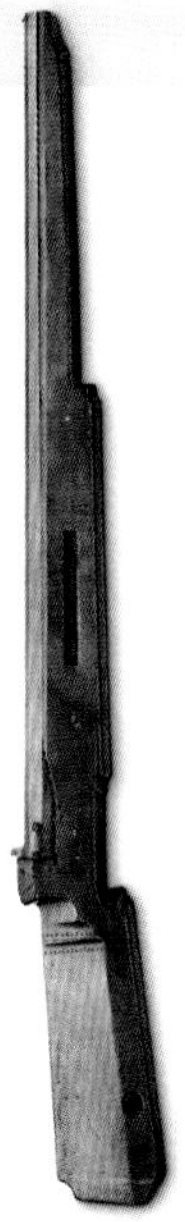

An early arquebus

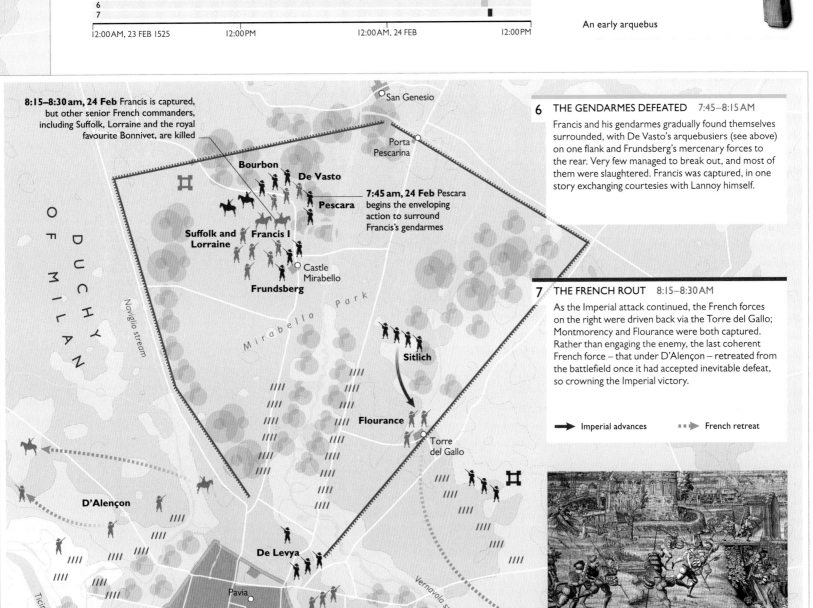

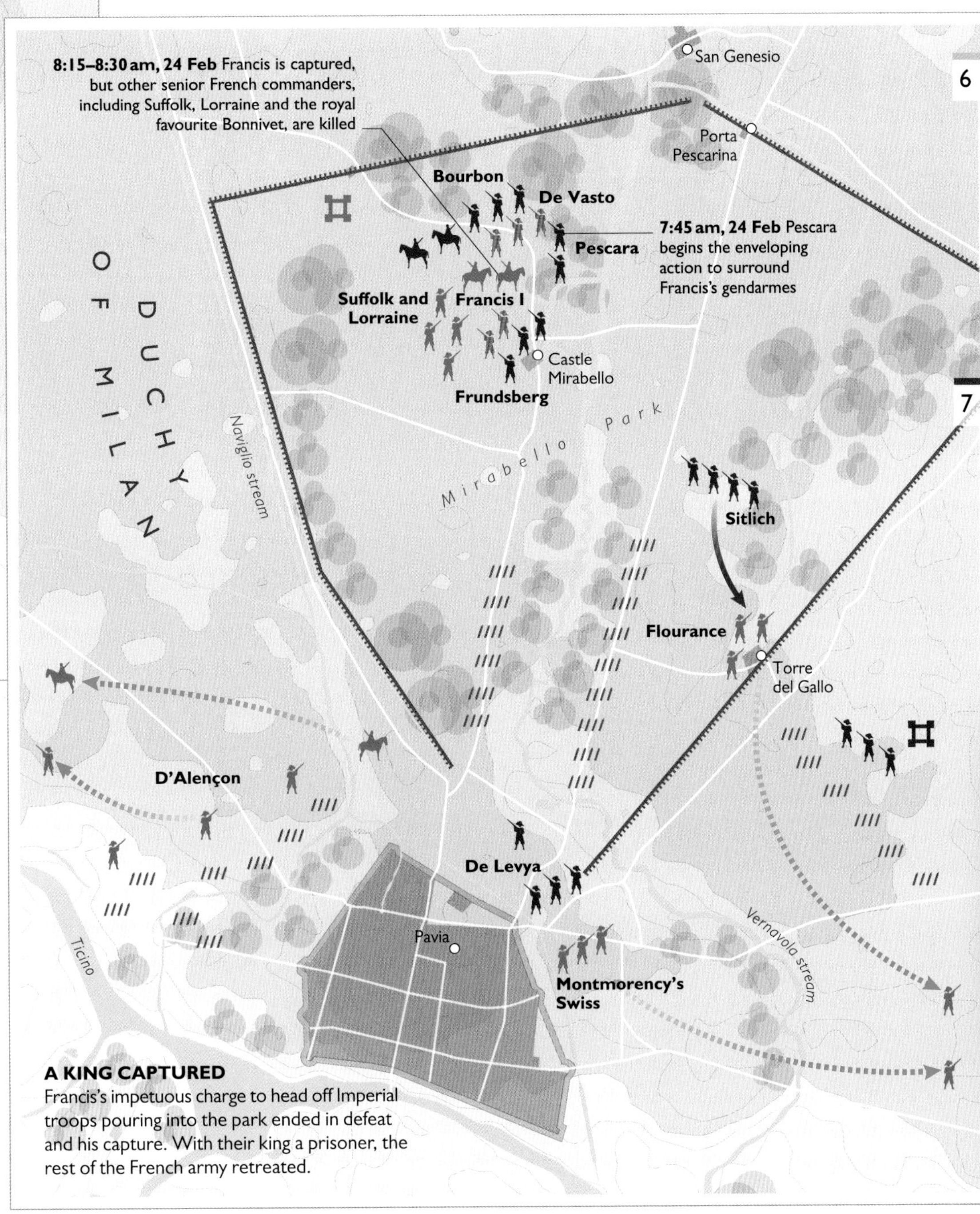
8:15–8:30 am, 24 Feb Francis is captured, but other senior French commanders, including Suffolk, Lorraine and the royal favourite Bonnivet, are killed
San Genesio
Porta Pescarina
Bourbon
De Vasto
Pescara
7:45 am, 24 Feb Pescara begins the enveloping action to surround Francis's gendarmes
Suffolk and Lorraine
Francis I
Castle Mirabello
Frundsberg
DUCHY OF MILAN
Naviglio stream
Mirabello Park
Sitlich
Flourance
Torre del Gallo
D'Alençon
De Levya
Pavia
Ticino
Vernavola stream
Montmorency's Swiss

6 THE GENDARMES DEFEATED 7:45–8:15AM

Francis and his gendarmes gradually found themselves surrounded, with De Vasto's arquebusiers (see above) on one flank and Frundsberg's mercenary forces to the rear. Very few managed to break out, and most of them were slaughtered. Francis was captured, in one story exchanging courtesies with Lannoy himself.

7 THE FRENCH ROUT 8:15–8:30AM

As the Imperial attack continued, the French forces on the right were driven back via the Torre del Gallo; Montmorency and Flourance were both captured. Rather than engaging the enemy, the last coherent French force – that under D'Alençon – retreated from the battlefield once it had accepted inevitable defeat, so crowning the Imperial victory.

Imperial advances | French retreat

A KING CAPTURED

Francis's impetuous charge to head off Imperial troops pouring into the park ended in defeat and his capture. With their king a prisoner, the rest of the French army retreated.

△ **The French camp under attack**
This depiction of fighting in Mirabello Park is a detail from one of seven tapestries showing scenes from the battle, produced a few years afterwards by Flemish artist Bernard van Orley.

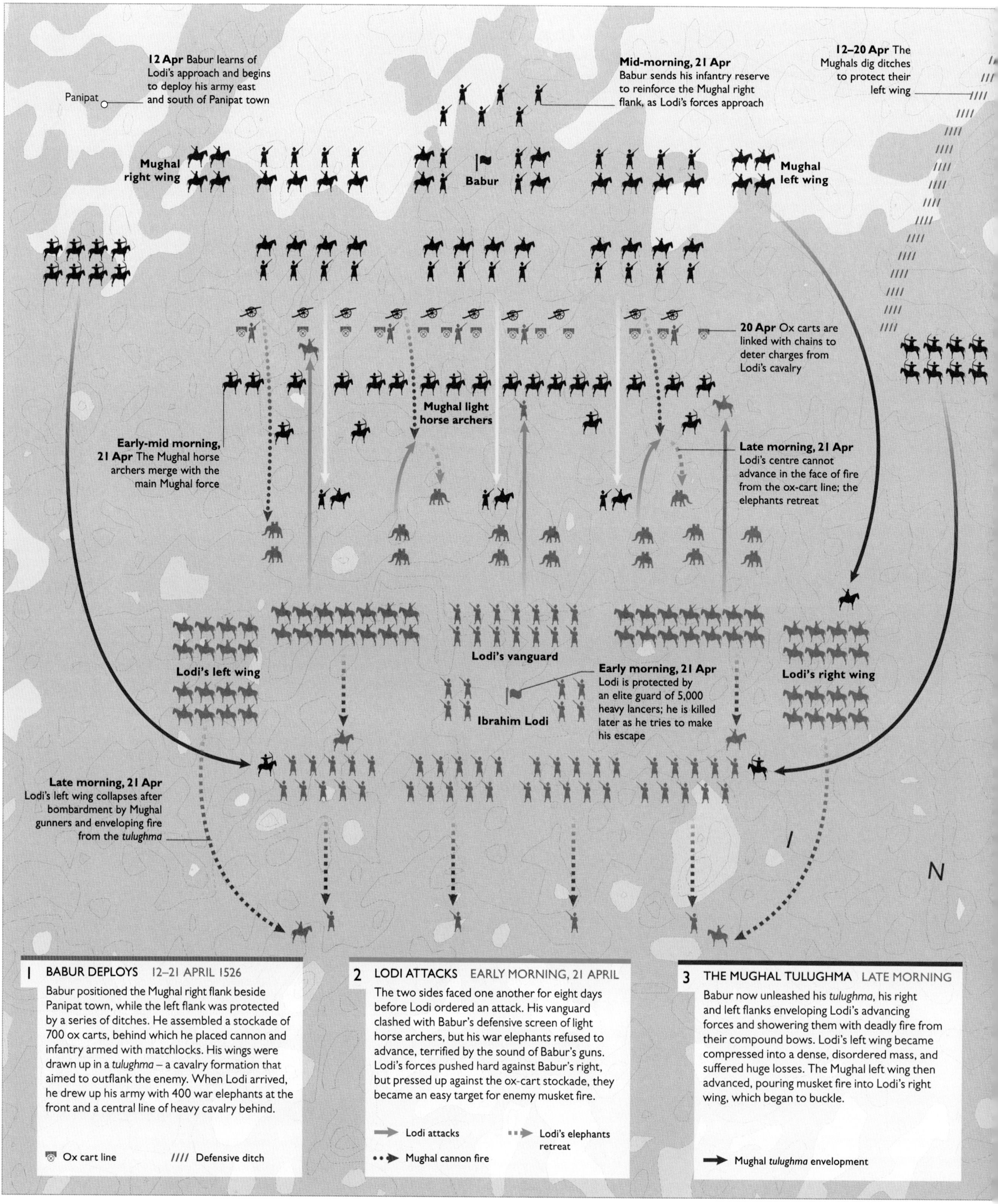

Panipat
12 Apr Babur learns of Lodi's approach and begins to deploy his army east and south of Panipat town
Mid-morning, 21 Apr Babur sends his infantry reserve to reinforce the Mughal right flank, as Lodi's forces approach
12–20 Apr The Mughals dig ditches to protect their left wing
Mughal right wing
Babur
Mughal left wing
20 Apr Ox carts are linked with chains to deter charges from Lodi's cavalry
Mughal light horse archers
Early-mid morning, 21 Apr The Mughal horse archers merge with the main Mughal force
Late morning, 21 Apr Lodi's centre cannot advance in the face of fire from the ox-cart line; the elephants retreat
Lodi's vanguard
Lodi's left wing
Lodi's right wing
Early morning, 21 Apr Lodi is protected by an elite guard of 5,000 heavy lancers; he is killed later as he tries to make his escape
Ibrahim Lodi
Late morning, 21 Apr Lodi's left wing collapses after bombardment by Mughal gunners and enveloping fire from the *tulughma*
N

1 BABUR DEPLOYS 12–21 APRIL 1526

Babur positioned the Mughal right flank beside Panipat town, while the left flank was protected by a series of ditches. He assembled a stockade of 700 ox carts, behind which he placed cannon and infantry armed with matchlocks. His wings were drawn up in a *tulughma* – a cavalry formation that aimed to outflank the enemy. When Lodi arrived, he drew up his army with 400 war elephants at the front and a central line of heavy cavalry behind.

Ox cart line | //// Defensive ditch

2 LODI ATTACKS EARLY MORNING, 21 APRIL

The two sides faced one another for eight days before Lodi ordered an attack. His vanguard clashed with Babur's defensive screen of light horse archers, but his war elephants refused to advance, terrified by the sound of Babur's guns. Lodi's forces pushed hard against Babur's right, but pressed up against the ox-cart stockade, they became an easy target for enemy musket fire.

Lodi attacks | Lodi's elephants retreat | Mughal cannon fire

3 THE MUGHAL TULUGHMA LATE MORNING

Babur now unleashed his *tulughma*, his right and left flanks enveloping Lodi's advancing forces and showering them with deadly fire from their compound bows. Lodi's left wing became compressed into a dense, disordered mass, and suffered huge losses. The Mughal left wing then advanced, pouring musket fire into Lodi's right wing, which began to buckle.

Mughal *tulughma* envelopment

BABUR'S BRILLIANCE
Ibrahim Lodi's army boasted several hundred war elephants. They were no match, though, for Babur's Mughal army, which was armed with cannons and musketeers.

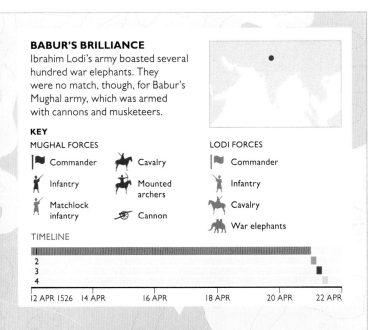

KEY

MUGHAL FORCES
- Commander
- Cavalry
- Infantry
- Mounted archers
- Matchlock infantry
- Cannon

LODI FORCES
- Commander
- Infantry
- Cavalry
- War elephants

TIMELINE

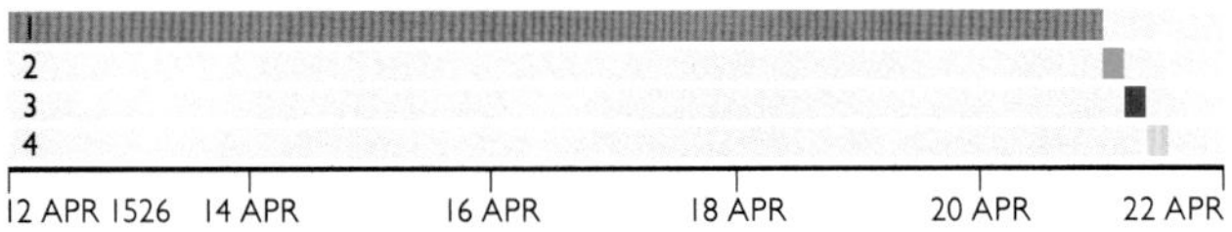

2
3
4
12 APR 1526
14 APR
16 APR
18 APR
20 APR
22 APR

△ **Gunpowder against elephants**
Lodi's delay in launching his attack allowed Babur time to build his defences and position his cannons and musketeers. Lodi's elephants were no match for Babur's firepower and battlefield fortifications.

D I A

4 LODI ROUTED MIDDAY
The Mughal centre now advanced against the disorganized enemy force. Lodi attempted a cavalry charge in a bid to escape but was cut down as he fought his way through the Mughal lines. Leaderless, Lodi's army collapsed, and the reserve line – which had not yet been enveloped – disintegrated and fled. Lodi had suffered 15,000 casualties, four times the Mughal losses.

- Secondary Mughal advance
- Lodi's army retreats

PANIPAT

Through tactical brilliance and the use of gunpowder weapons, the Central Asian warlord Babur won a stunning victory against the Sultan of Delhi, Ibrahim Lodi, at Panipat in April 1526. He went on to conquer much of Northern India, founding the Mughal empire, which would last for the following three centuries.

Descended from the Mongol leaders Genghis Khan (see p.78) and Timur, Babur became ruler of Fergana (in present-day Uzbekistan) in 1494. He began to carve out a kingdom for himself, seizing Kabul in 1504. His ambitions, however, extended further, and from 1519 he sent several exploratory raids into the Punjab, which was ruled by Ibrahim Lodi, the Sultan of Delhi. Lodi's authority over his own nobles was weak, and some of them plotted his overthrow with Babur.

Seeing an opportunity, Babur raised an army of 10,000 men trained in the use of gunpowder weapons acquired from the Ottoman Turks. In November 1525, the army swept into Punjab, capturing Sialkot and Ambala, moving ever closer to Lodi's capital. Babur repelled a counterattack by Lodi's forces near the Yamuna river on 2 April 1526, but then heard that the Sultan's main force of 100,000 was approaching. He drew up at Panipat, 85 km (50 miles) north of Delhi, to face them.

Babur's tactical brilliance in combining nomad manoeuvrability with modern weaponry shattered his enemy's far larger army, and Lodi's death on the battlefield led to the rapid collapse of the Delhi sultanate. Within five years, Babur was master of Northern India. Although his son Humayun was deposed in 1540, the rule of his grandson Akbar (r. 1556–1605) saw the Mughal empire that Babur had founded reach its apogee and extend into central India.

THE MUGHAL EMPIRE
Babur had planned to annex only the Punjab to his Kabul-based kingdom, but his unexpectedly decisive victory at Panipat allowed him to expand his control far to the south. Although Babur's son Humayun lost the empire, his grandson Akbar conducted a long series of campaigns that regained its core domains and expanded Mughal control as far south as Berar. His successors made further conquests, and by the death of Aurangzeb, the sixth Mughal emperor in 1707, only the tip of the subcontinent and a few European enclaves eluded Mughal rule.

KEY
- Babur's Afghan kingdom
- Babur's conquests to 1539
- Mughal empire under Akbar, 1556
- Conquered by 1605
- Conquered by 1707
- Regions acquired, with date

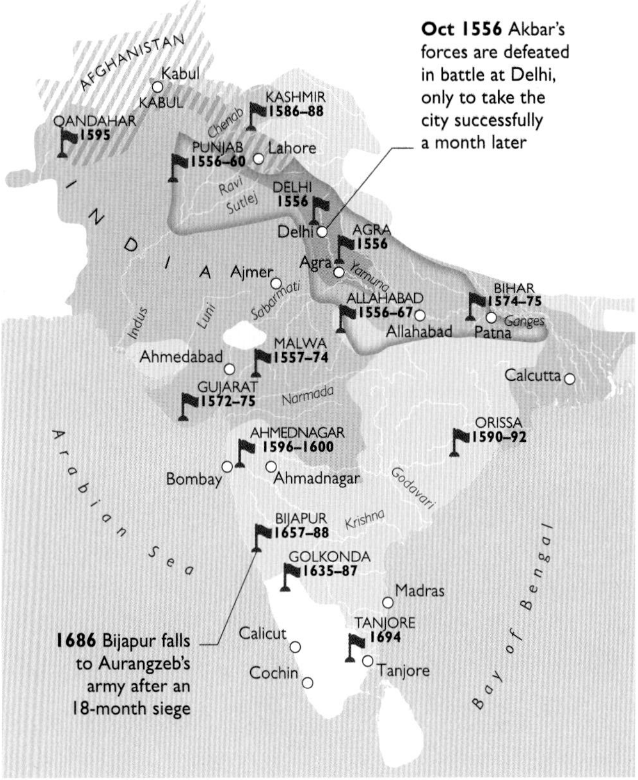

Oct 1556 Akbar's forces are defeated in battle at Delhi, only to take the city successfully a month later
AFGHANISTAN
Kabul
KABUL
KASHMIR 1586–88
QANDAHAR 1595
Chenab
PUNJAB 1556–60
Lahore
Ravi
Sutlej
DELHI 1556
Delhi
AGRA 1556
Agra
Yamuna
I N D I A
Ajmer
Sabarmati
Luni
Indus
ALLAHABAD 1556–67
Allahabad
BIHAR 1574–75
Patna
Ganges
MALWA 1557–74
Ahmedabad
GUJARAT 1572–75
Narmada
Calcutta
ORISSA 1590–92
AHMEDNAGAR 1596–1600
Bombay
Ahmadnagar
Godavari
Arabian Sea
BIJAPUR 1657–88
Krishna
GOLKONDA 1635–87
Madras
Bay of Bengal
1686 Bijapur falls to Aurangzeb's army after an 18-month siege
Calicut
TANJORE 1694
Tanjore
Cochin

OTTOMAN GAINS
The Ottoman capture of Constantinople in 1453 was followed by advances in the Balkans. Only the Kingdom of Hungary stood between the Ottomans and the territory of the Austrian Habsburgs. After Mohács, Suleiman besieged Vienna in 1529 and annexed a broad swathe of Hungary in 1541. This was the high tide of Ottoman expansion in the Balkans.

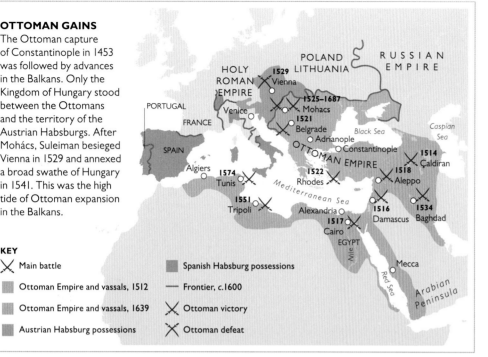

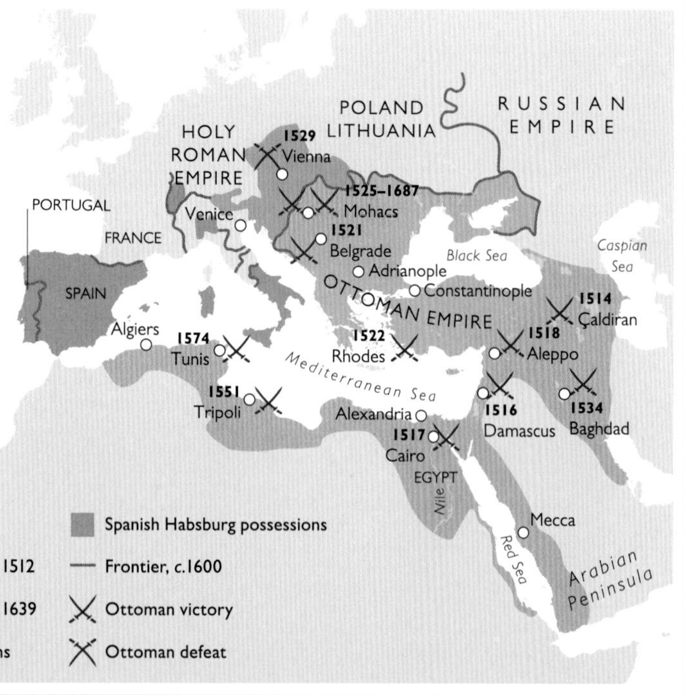
POLAND LITHUANIA
RUSSIAN EMPIRE
HOLY ROMAN EMPIRE
1529 Vienna
1525–1687 Mohacs
PORTUGAL
FRANCE
Venice
1521 Belgrade
Black Sea
Caspian Sea
SPAIN
Adrianople
Constantinople
OTTOMAN EMPIRE
1514 Çaldiran
Algiers
1574 Tunis
1522 Rhodes
1518 Aleppo
Mediterranean Sea
1551 Tripoli
Alexandria
1516 Damascus
1534 Baghdad
1517 Cairo
EGYPT
Nile
Mecca
Red Sea
Arabian Peninsula
KEY
Main battle
Ottoman Empire and vassals, 1512
Ottoman Empire and vassals, 1639
Austrian Habsburg possessions
Spanish Habsburg possessions
Frontier, c.1600
Ottoman victory
Ottoman defeat

THE JANISSARIES

The Janissaries, shown here being inspected by the Sultan, were the elite infantry of the Ottoman army. Born Christian, they were raised as Muslims and trained as warriors from a young age; their ability with firearms made them formidable. The expense of their salaries and their rebellious tendencies eventually led to their disbandment in 1807.

1 THE ARMIES ARRIVE
1:00PM, 29 AUGUST 1526

The Hungarians arrived first at the north of the battlefield, their left flank protected by marshes. The Ottomans marched in battle formation for seven hours to face their enemy. The Hungarian troops under Pál Tomori charged the Rumelian contingent, which had arrived first; composed mostly of irregulars, the Rumelians fell back.

Initial Hungarian attack — Rumelian retreat

2 THE OTTOMANS REINFORCED
1:00–2:00PM

The Rumelian retreat allowed Tomori almost to overrun Suleiman's position; Suleiman himself was struck by a bullet. However, more Ottoman units – including the elite janissaries – soon arrived to provide support. Turkish artillery positioned on a ridge overlooking the battlefield began to fire on Louis's frontline troops and his smaller artillery contingent.

Janissaries advance

3 THE HUNGARIAN ADVANCE AND REPULSE
2:00–3:00PM

Tomori tried to exploit his success by charging the Ottoman guns, and Louis ordered the rest of his cavalry into action. However, the arrival of further Anatolian contingents soon gave the Ottomans overwhelming numerical superiority. The bloody close-quarters combat that ensued ended in the near destruction of the Hungarian infantry.

Hungarian advance — Arrival of Ottoman reinforcements

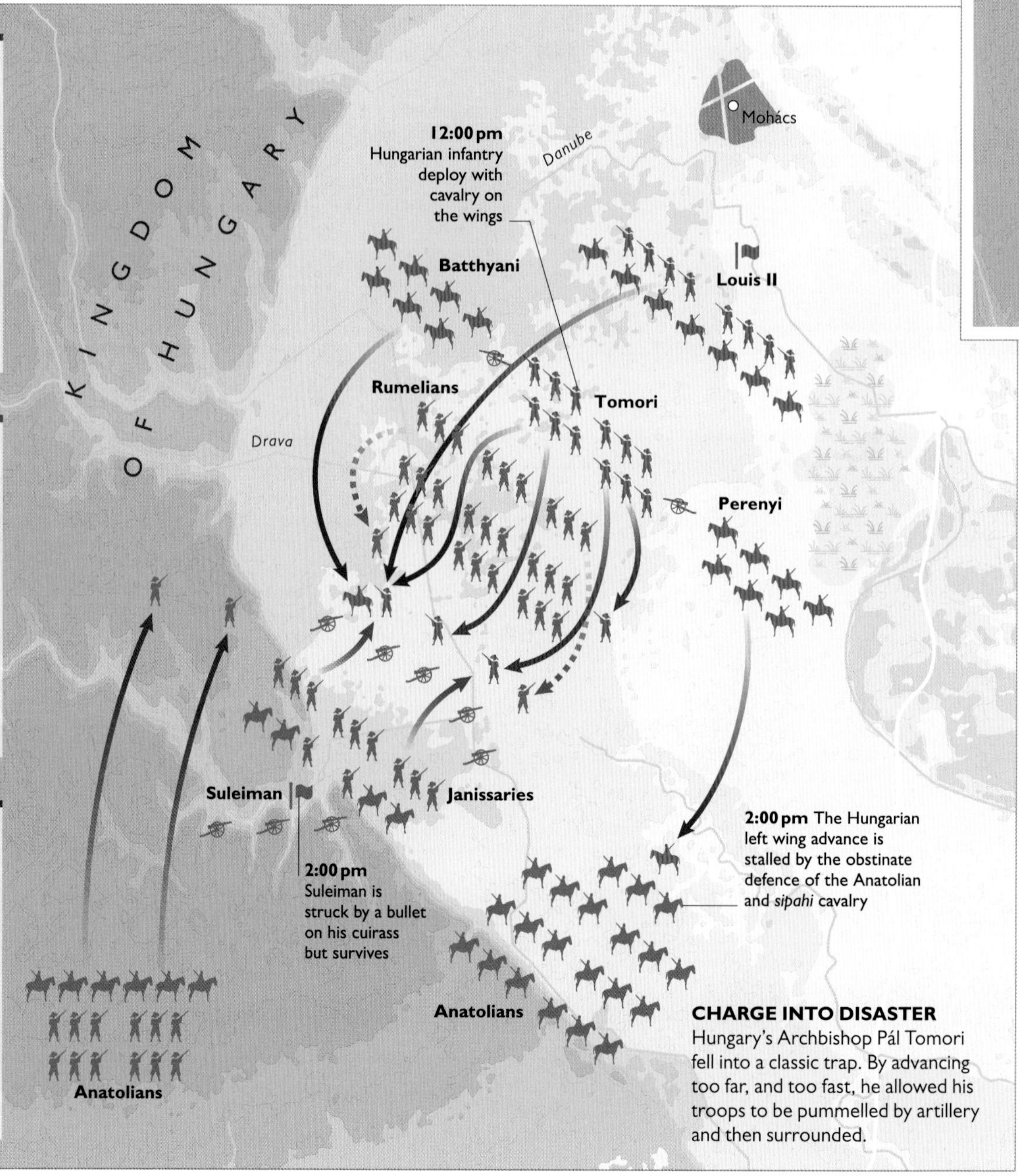
KINGDOM OF HUNGARY
Mohács
Danube
12:00 pm
Hungarian infantry deploy with cavalry on the wings
Batthyani
Louis II
Rumelians
Tomori
Drava
Perenyi
Suleiman
Janissaries
2:00 pm
Suleiman is struck by a bullet on his cuirass but survives
2:00 pm The Hungarian left wing advance is stalled by the obstinate defence of the Anatolian and *sipahi* cavalry
Anatolians
Anatolians

CHARGE INTO DISASTER
Hungary's Archbishop Pál Tomori fell into a classic trap. By advancing too far, and too fast, he allowed his troops to be pummelled by artillery and then surrounded.

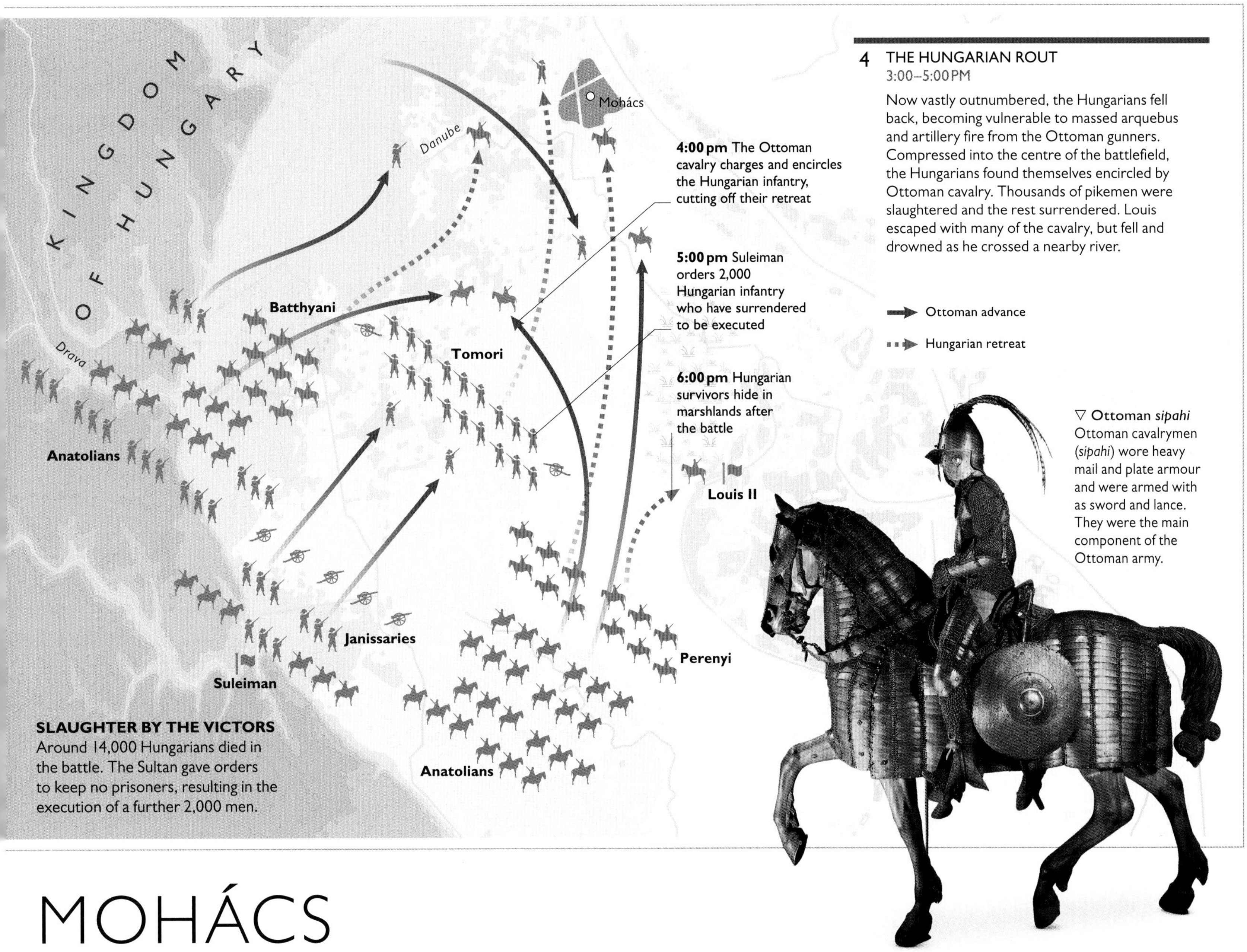
KINGDOM OF HUNGARY
Danube
Drava
Mohács
Batthyani
Tomori
Anatolians
Janissaries
Suleiman
Anatolians
Perenyi
Louis II
4:00 pm The Ottoman cavalry charges and encircles the Hungarian infantry, cutting off their retreat
5:00 pm Suleiman orders 2,000 Hungarian infantry who have surrendered to be executed
6:00 pm Hungarian survivors hide in marshlands after the battle
Ottoman advance
Hungarian retreat

4 THE HUNGARIAN ROUT
3:00–5:00 PM

Now vastly outnumbered, the Hungarians fell back, becoming vulnerable to massed arquebus and artillery fire from the Ottoman gunners. Compressed into the centre of the battlefield, the Hungarians found themselves encircled by Ottoman cavalry. Thousands of pikemen were slaughtered and the rest surrendered. Louis escaped with many of the cavalry, but fell and drowned as he crossed a nearby river.

SLAUGHTER BY THE VICTORS
Around 14,000 Hungarians died in the battle. The Sultan gave orders to keep no prisoners, resulting in the execution of a further 2,000 men.

▽ Ottoman *sipahi*
Ottoman cavalrymen (*sipahi*) wore heavy mail and plate armour and were armed with as sword and lance. They were the main component of the Ottoman army.

MOHÁCS

The defeat of Louis II's Hungarian army by Ottoman Sultan Suleiman the Magnificent at Mohács in 1526 was a disaster for his kingdom. With Louis dead and his force cut apart, Hungary was rapidly overrun by the Ottomans and ceased to exist as an independent nation.

By the 1520s, steady Ottoman expansion in the Balkans, which had begun with the capture of Gallipoli in 1354, was encroaching on the borders of Hungary. Weakened by a huge peasant revolt in 1514, and internal power struggles between its king Vladislaus II and powerful magnates, Hungary was in a vulnerable position when Louis II took the throne in 1516.

In 1521, Suleiman captured the strategically important city of Belgrade, a staging post to Hungary. Four years later he made an alliance with Francis I of France which effectively neutralized Hungary's possible allies in the West. In April the following year he set out from Constantinople with a 50,000-strong force, while Louis tried to raise an army from a reluctant Hungarian nobility. Unsure of where Suleiman would strike, Louis held back at Buda, his capital, before advancing to meet defeat and his death at Mohács.

Suleiman failed to capitalize on his victory, delaying an advance to Buda. Instead, Hungary fell apart into rival kingdoms – the eastern part under Jan Zapolya, a Hungarian noble, and the west and Croatia ruled by Ferdinand I, the Holy Roman Emperor. Part of Zapolya's kingdom fell to the Ottomans in 1541, and Hungary would not emerge as an independent nation until 1918.

HUNGARY CRUSHED
The unexpectedly decisive nature of Suleiman's victory led to the rapid fall of the Hungarian monarchy and set the scene for Turkish and Habsburg supremacy in Hungary.

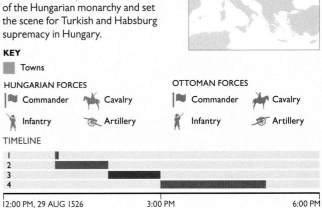

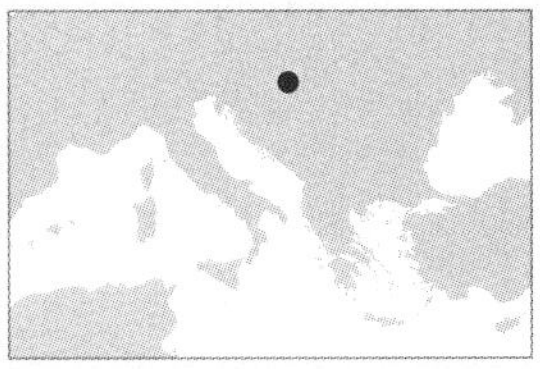

KEY

Towns

HUNGARIAN FORCES: Commander, Cavalry, Infantry, Artillery

OTTOMAN FORCES: Commander, Cavalry, Infantry, Artillery

TIMELINE

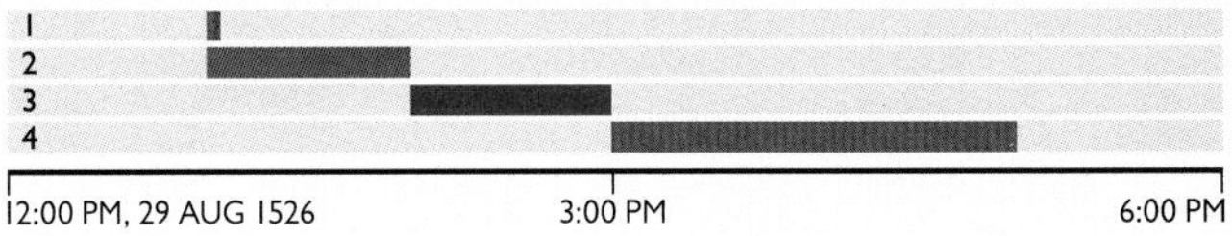
1
2
3
4
12:00 PM, 29 AUG 1526
3:00 PM
6:00 PM

Armed and equipped
This late 16th-century painting shows Ottoman sultan Selim II's (1524–74) army. On the left are the janissaries carrying muskets, while the cavalry, wielding shields and lances, can be seen on the right.

THE OTTOMAN ARMY

A key player in Europe and the Mediterranean basin for centuries, the Ottoman army was a terrifying professional force that displayed formidable military tactics from the 14th to the 18th centuries.

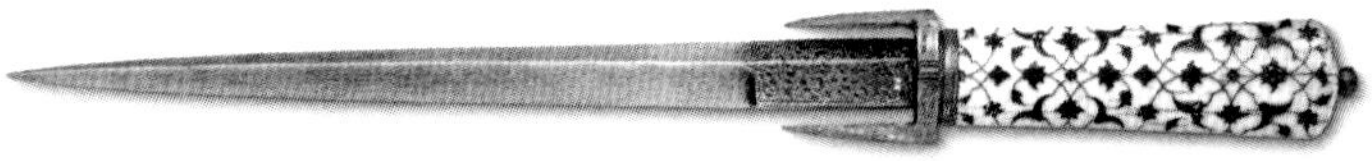

△ **Skill and craftsmanship**
This 17th-century *hancer* (dagger) with a straight blade and an ornate ivory handle shows the superior craftsmanship of the Ottomans.

The Ottoman army was a large force with three distinct components. At its core was the central force, controlled, paid, and trained by the state. In the 17th century, the force consisted of tens of thousands of troops, mainly infantry, including the sultan's elite infantry bodyguard, the janissaries. These troops were usually long-term professionals, initially conscripted as slave-soldiers in the Turkish medieval tradition, but who were later recruited as volunteers. Supporting the central army was a larger feudal and provincial levy. The levies were mainly light cavalry, but included infantry as well. They were often poorly trained, ill-equipped, and unmotivated. The rest of the army was formed by auxiliary contingents from vassal states, either of Islamic or Christian faith, who participated in specific expeditions. They varied not only in quality, but also in the nature of their composition. While Tatars, Mamluks, and other Eastern forces often accompanied the army, other vassals were not uncommon. Serbian knights fought with the Ottomans at the Battle of Nicopolis (see p.97) in 1396, while Emeric Thököly's 20,000 catholic Hungarians fought with the Ottoman army in the second siege of Vienna in 1683.

A skilled force

The Ottoman central force was mostly well-trained and equipped. The cavalry favoured traditional weapons that were lighter than those of their European counterparts. Ottoman artillery was excellent and often employed in higher numbers than in European armies.

SULEIMAN I 1494–1566

Better known as Suleiman the Magnificent (r.1520–66), Suleiman I led the Ottoman Empire to its zenith. He led various battles during his reign, most notably the ones at Belgrade (1521), Rhodes (1522), and Mohács in Hungary (1526, see pp.112–13). However, his army lost at Vienna in 1529, followed by the Great Siege of Malta (see pp.116–17), which limited the Ottomans' reach into Western Europe. By the time he died, large parts of southeast Europe, the North African coast, and the Middle East were under Ottoman control.

THE SIEGE OF MALTA

The attempt by the Ottoman Sultan, Suleiman the Magnificent, to take the island of Malta from the Knights Hospitaller in 1565 was met with fierce resistance. Grand Master de Valette and his knights defended a line of fortresses for almost four months until a relieving fleet forced the Ottoman besiegers to withdraw.

By the mid-16th century, the Ottoman empire was threatening to penetrate the western Mediterranean. One bulwark against this was the Mediterranean island of Malta. Since 1530, the island had been a stronghold of the Knights Hospitaller, a Christian military order that lost its last base at Rhodes in 1522, and who countered attacks by Ottoman-backed corsairs (privateers) on Christian shipping. In 1551, the corsair Dragut responded by pillaging Gozo but failed to take the main island of Malta. After a Christian expedition against the corsair base at Tripoli was defeated at Djerba in 1560, it was only a matter of time before Suleiman ordered an attack on Malta to crush the Knights' resistance.

Jean de Valette, the Hospitaller Grand Master, prepared well, reinforcing the defences of the island. When the assault finally came in May 1565, he was able to hold out long enough for a relief fleet to drive off the Ottoman expeditionary force. This revived Christian morale enough that a new alliance assembled and was able to defeat the Ottoman navy at Lepanto in 1571 (see pp.118–19).

"What men call sovereignty is worldly strife and constant war."

FROM A POEM BY SULEIMAN THE MAGNIFICENT, *C.*16TH CENTURY

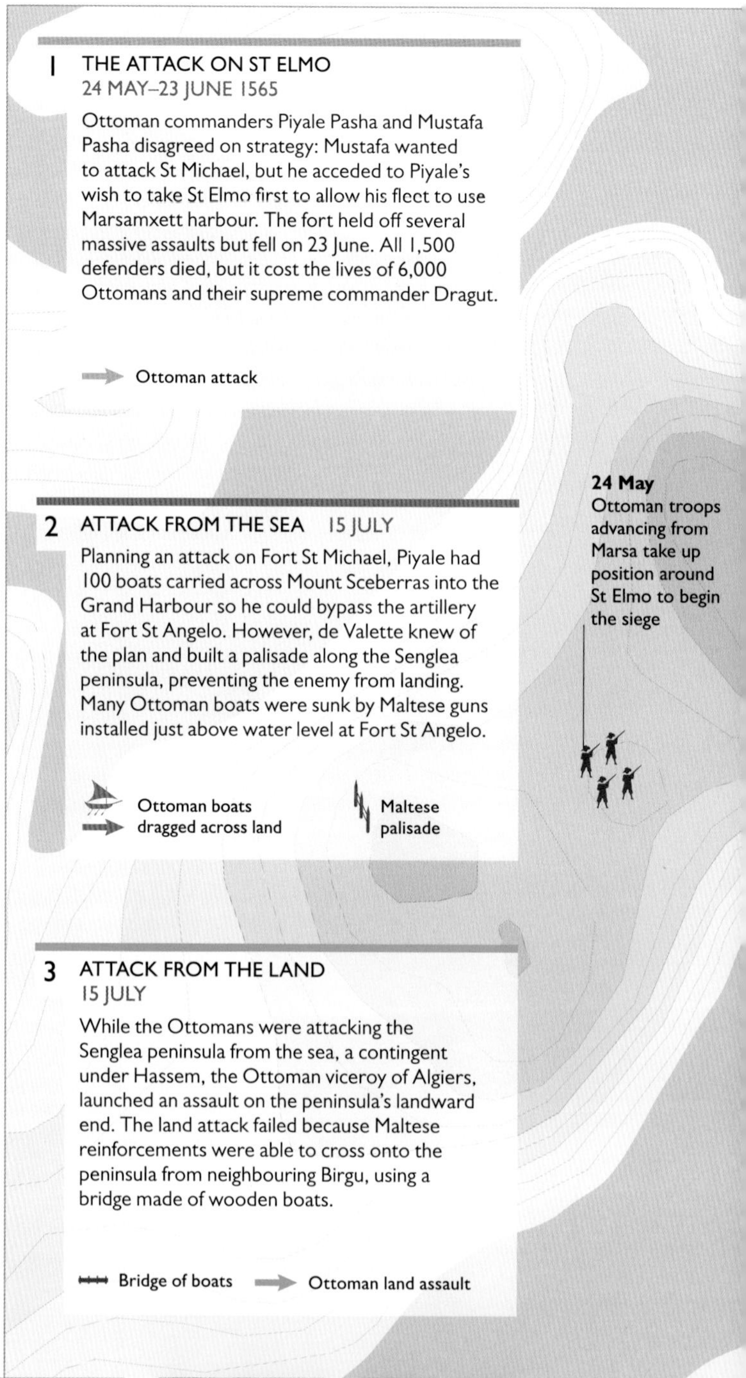

24 May
Ottoman troops advancing from Marsa take up position around St Elmo to begin the siege
Corradino Heights

1 THE ATTACK ON ST ELMO
24 MAY–23 JUNE 1565

Ottoman commanders Piyale Pasha and Mustafa Pasha disagreed on strategy: Mustafa wanted to attack St Michael, but he acceded to Piyale's wish to take St Elmo first to allow his fleet to use Marsamxett harbour. The fort held off several massive assaults but fell on 23 June. All 1,500 defenders died, but it cost the lives of 6,000 Ottomans and their supreme commander Dragut.

Ottoman attack

2 ATTACK FROM THE SEA 15 JULY

Planning an attack on Fort St Michael, Piyale had 100 boats carried across Mount Sceberras into the Grand Harbour so he could bypass the artillery at Fort St Angelo. However, de Valette knew of the plan and built a palisade along the Senglea peninsula, preventing the enemy from landing. Many Ottoman boats were sunk by Maltese guns installed just above water level at Fort St Angelo.

Ottoman boats dragged across land
Maltese palisade

3 ATTACK FROM THE LAND
15 JULY

While the Ottomans were attacking the Senglea peninsula from the sea, a contingent under Hassem, the Ottoman viceroy of Algiers, launched an assault on the peninsula's landward end. The land attack failed because Maltese reinforcements were able to cross onto the peninsula from neighbouring Birgu, using a bridge made of wooden boats.

Bridge of boats
Ottoman land assault

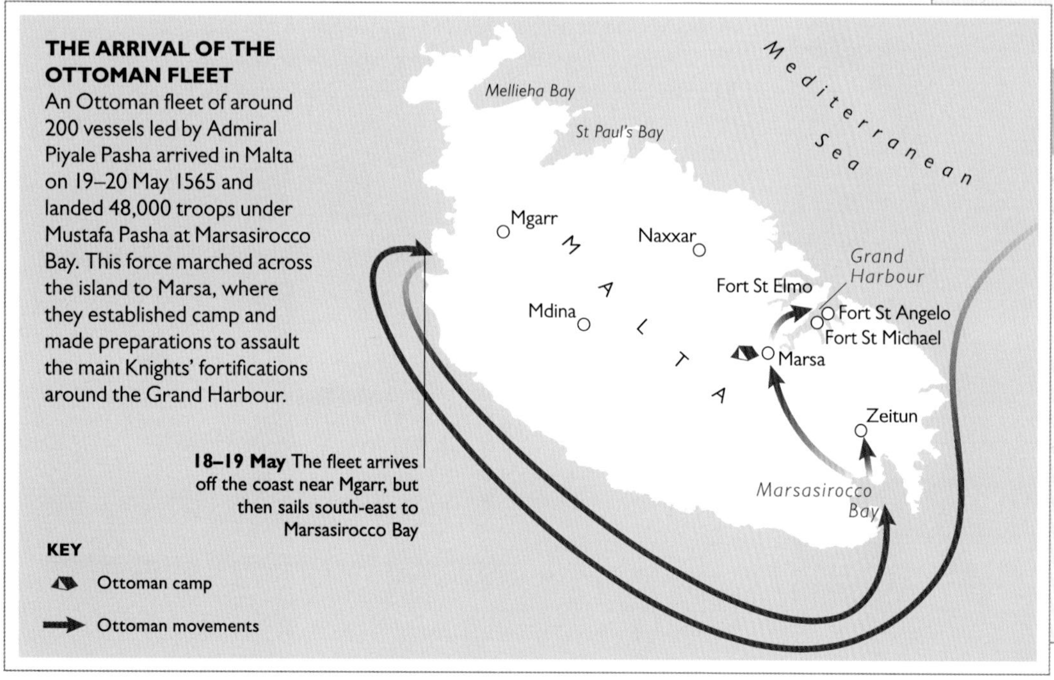

THE ARRIVAL OF THE OTTOMAN FLEET
An Ottoman fleet of around 200 vessels led by Admiral Piyale Pasha arrived in Malta on 19–20 May 1565 and landed 48,000 troops under Mustafa Pasha at Marsasirocco Bay. This force marched across the island to Marsa, where they established camp and made preparations to assault the main Knights' fortifications around the Grand Harbour.
Mediterranean Sea
Mellieha Bay
St Paul's Bay
Mgarr
Naxxar
MALTA
Mdina
Fort St Elmo
Grand Harbour
Fort St Angelo
Fort St Michael
Marsa
Zeitun
Marsasirocco Bay
18–19 May The fleet arrives off the coast near Mgarr, but then sails south-east to Marsasirocco Bay
KEY
Ottoman camp
Ottoman movements

△ **The Ottoman fleet arrives**
This 17th-century miniature from Istanbul shows the Ottoman fleet at Malta. Its arrival prompted many of Malta's islanders to take refuge in the island's walled cities.

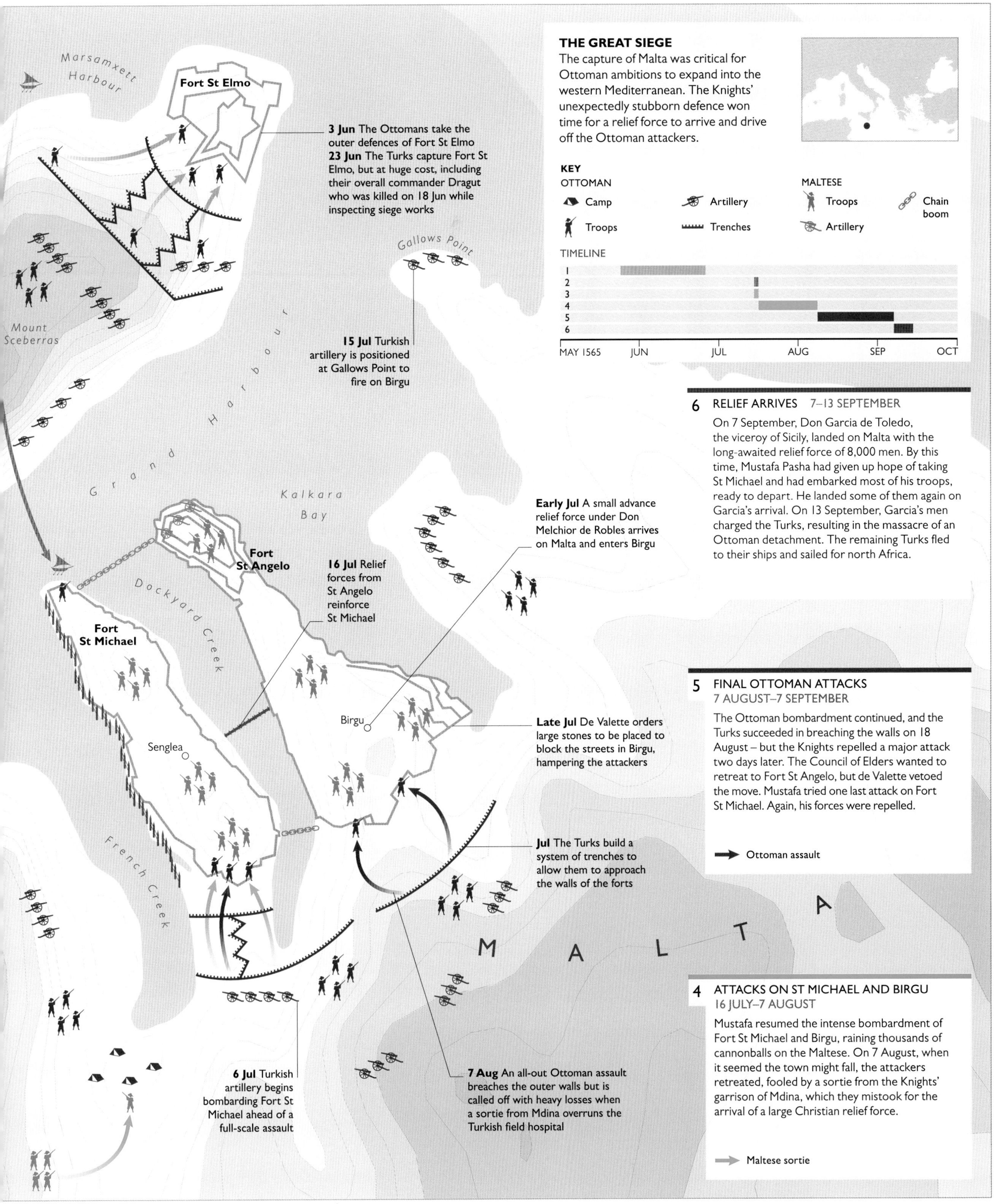

Marsamxett Harbour
Fort St Elmo
3 Jun The Ottomans take the outer defences of Fort St Elmo
23 Jun The Turks capture Fort St Elmo, but at huge cost, including their overall commander Dragut who was killed on 18 Jun while inspecting siege works
Gallows Point
Mount Sceberras
15 Jul Turkish artillery is positioned at Gallows Point to fire on Birgu
Grand Harbour
Kalkara Bay
Early Jul A small advance relief force under Don Melchior de Robles arrives on Malta and enters Birgu
Fort St Angelo
16 Jul Relief forces from St Angelo reinforce St Michael
Dockyard Creek
Fort St Michael
Birgu
Senglea
Late Jul De Valette orders large stones to be placed to block the streets in Birgu, hampering the attackers
French Creek
Jul The Turks build a system of trenches to allow them to approach the walls of the forts
MALTA
6 Jul Turkish artillery begins bombarding Fort St Michael ahead of a full-scale assault
7 Aug An all-out Ottoman assault breaches the outer walls but is called off with heavy losses when a sortie from Mdina overruns the Turkish field hospital

THE GREAT SIEGE

The capture of Malta was critical for Ottoman ambitions to expand into the western Mediterranean. The Knights' unexpectedly stubborn defence won time for a relief force to arrive and drive off the Ottoman attackers.

KEY

OTTOMAN
- Camp
- Troops
- Artillery
- Trenches

MALTESE
- Troops
- Artillery
- Chain boom

TIMELINE

1, 2, 3, 4, 5, 6

MAY 1565 · JUN · JUL · AUG · SEP · OCT

6 RELIEF ARRIVES 7–13 SEPTEMBER

On 7 September, Don Garcia de Toledo, the viceroy of Sicily, landed on Malta with the long-awaited relief force of 8,000 men. By this time, Mustafa Pasha had given up hope of taking St Michael and had embarked most of his troops, ready to depart. He landed some of them again on Garcia's arrival. On 13 September, Garcia's men charged the Turks, resulting in the massacre of an Ottoman detachment. The remaining Turks fled to their ships and sailed for north Africa.

5 FINAL OTTOMAN ATTACKS 7 AUGUST–7 SEPTEMBER

The Ottoman bombardment continued, and the Turks succeeded in breaching the walls on 18 August – but the Knights repelled a major attack two days later. The Council of Elders wanted to retreat to Fort St Angelo, but de Valette vetoed the move. Mustafa tried one last attack on Fort St Michael. Again, his forces were repelled.

Ottoman assault

4 ATTACKS ON ST MICHAEL AND BIRGU 16 JULY–7 AUGUST

Mustafa resumed the intense bombardment of Fort St Michael and Birgu, raining thousands of cannonballs on the Maltese. On 7 August, when it seemed the town might fall, the attackers retreated, fooled by a sortie from the Knights' garrison of Mdina, which they mistook for the arrival of a large Christian relief force.

Maltese sortie

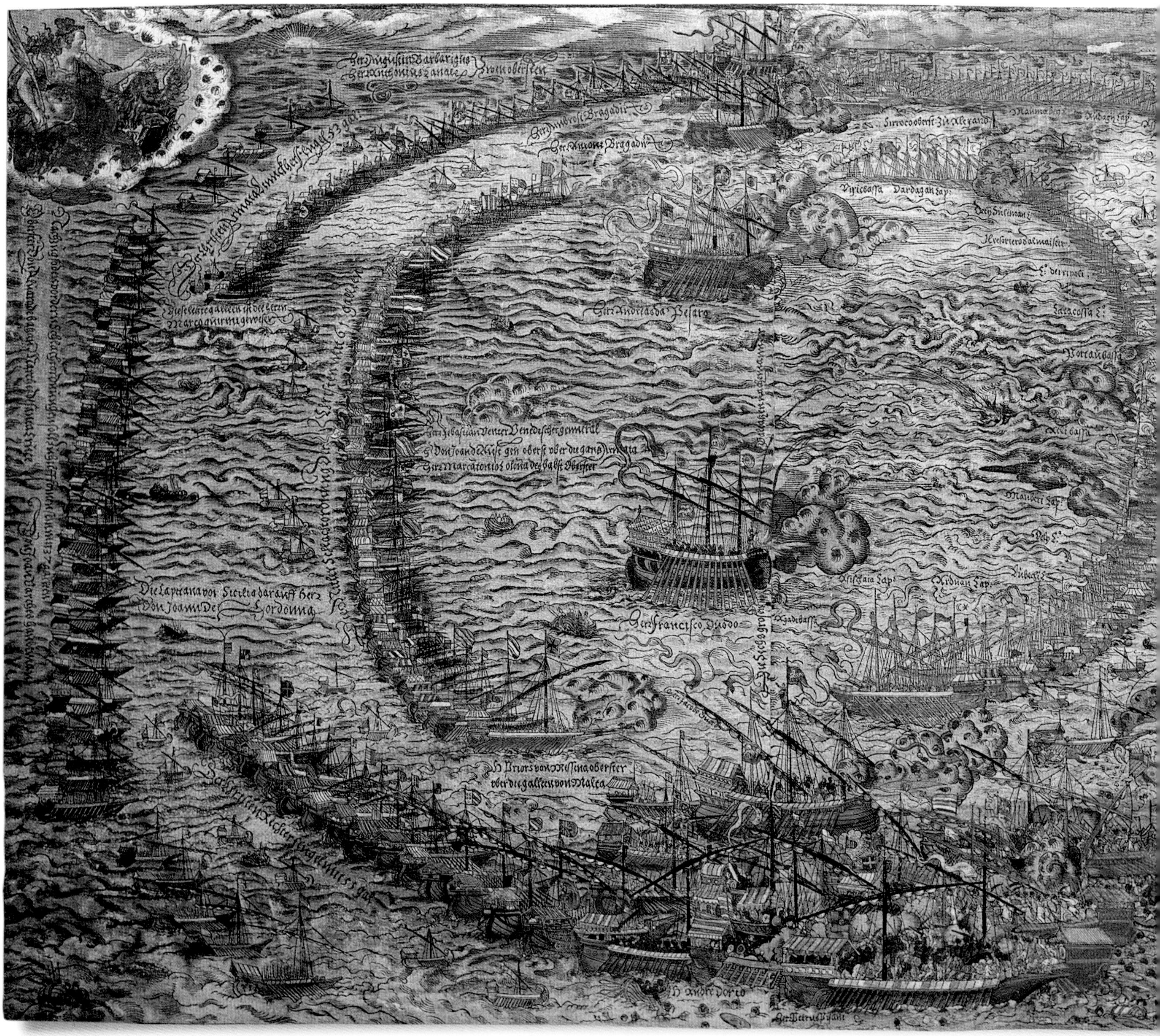

△ **Ships in formation**
This 16th-century coloured, gold-embossed woodcut by Jacopo Amman von Jost depicts the beginning of the Battle of Lepanto, showing clearly the crescent formations of the Christian and Ottoman fleets, the huge galleases billowing gun-smoke, and the flanks engaged in close quarters combat.

▷ **The power of a city-state**
In the corner of the illustration, the symbols of Venice and Victory look out over the battle. The Republic of Venice used a winged lion as its symbol, while Victory is depicted as a female figure.

1

2

◁ **Heavy firepower**
The Venetian galleasses were large, heavily armed galleys powered by both sails and oars. Deployed across the front of the Christian fleet, these cumbersome ships were intended to fire on the enemy at close quarters.

▷ **Santa Cruz's reserves**
Commanded by the Spanish Marquess of Santa Cruz, the reserve squadron was vital to the Christian victory after they closed the dangerous gap which opened between the centre and Doria's squadrons on the right.

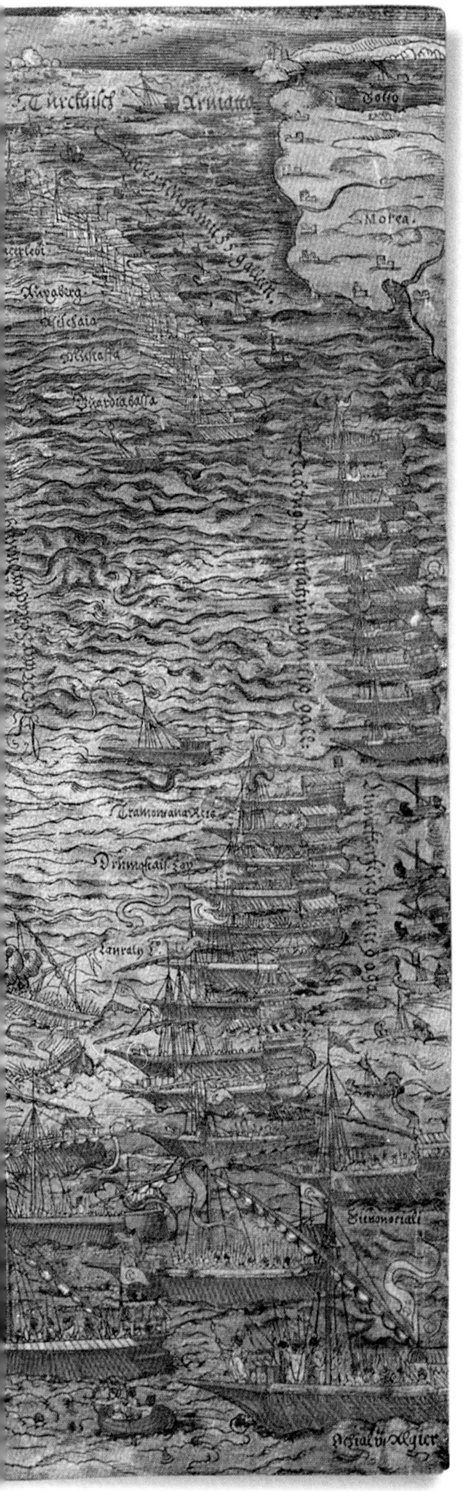

3

LEPANTO

At Lepanto, Don John of Austria led the Christian fleet against the Ottoman Turkish fleet of Ali Pasha. The last major battle in the West fought with rowing vessels, it shattered the myth of Ottoman invincibility. Although their fleet was rebuilt, it was soon overshadowed by new European naval technology.

In 1570, the Fourth Ottoman–Venetian War, or the War of Cyprus, broke out between the Ottoman Empire and the Republic of Venice. The Ottoman Turks invaded the Venetian-held Cyprus. By 1571, the pope had organised Christian states into a coalition – the Holy League. On 16 September that year, a large Holy League fleet led by Don John sailed from Sicily to relieve Cyprus (which fell before it could intervene).

Don John met the Turkish fleet under Ali Pasha near Lepanto on 7 October. Both sides drew up in crescent formation. The Turkish fleet was larger, with over 220 galleys and 56 galliots, but the Christian fleet was better armed and disciplined. Don John had 60,000 soldiers and oarsmen on over 200 galleys, each with a heavy cannon in its bow, as well as smaller guns. He also had six Venetian 44-gun galleasses. The fleets engaged; as the ships locked together, the sea turned into a battlefield. Barbarigo and Suluk were killed; Ali Pasha's flagship *Sultana* was captured and Ali Pasha slain. Two hours later, the Christians had taken 117 galleys and 20 galliots, destroyed 50 other ships, and taken 10,000 prisoners. They also freed thousands of Christian galley slaves. Of the Turkish commanders, only Uluch Ali escaped, taking around a sixth of the original force to Constantinople. The battle stalled Ottoman expansion in the region and dented their fearsome naval reputation.

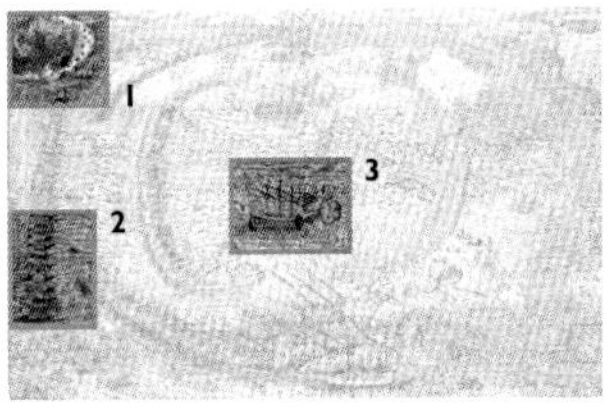
1
2
3

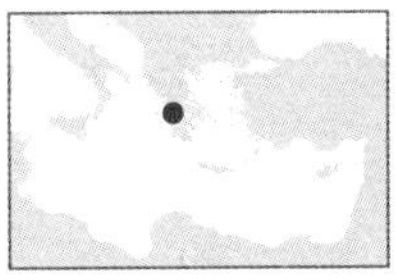

LOCATOR

"... the heavy ordnance of the galleasses was more destructive than ever yet had been witnessed in naval gunnery..."

EDWARD SHEPHERD CREASY ON LEPANTO, *HISTORY OF THE OTTOMAN TURKS*, 1878

MELÉE IN THE SEA

On the Turkish right, Suluc's galleys rowed beyond the end of the Christian line. Barbarigo turned his bows to the shore, and engaged in close fighting until, with the help of Santa Cruz's reserves, Suluc retreated. In the centre, Pasha Ali's galleys engaged Don John's ships. On the Turkish left, Uluch Ali drew Doria's squadron south, and attacked the gap in the Christian line. There was fierce fighting, but when Santa Cruz's reserves joined, the Turkish centre collapsed.

KEY

- Allied Christian fleet
- Turkish fleet
- Galleasses
- Turkish attack and retreat
- Allied Christian advance
- Shoals

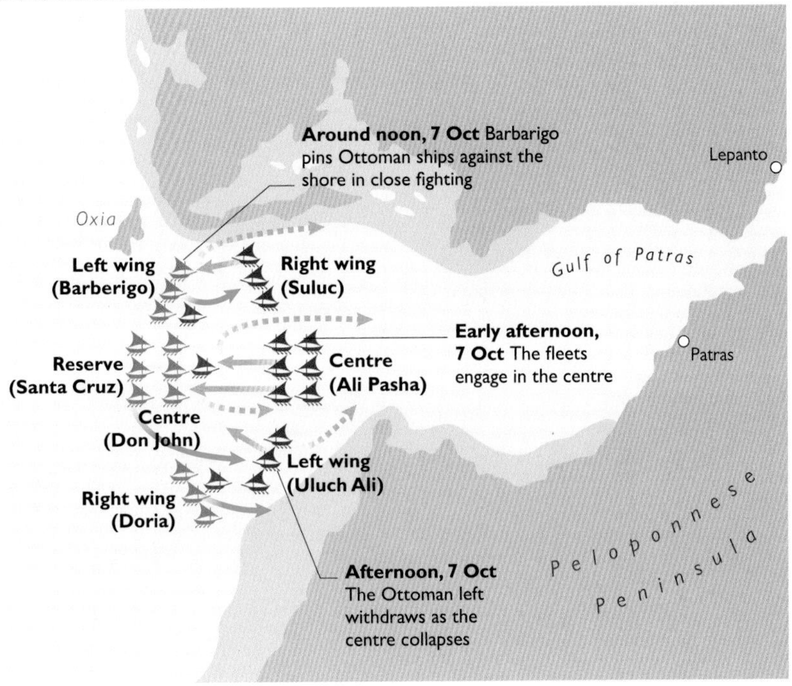
Around noon, 7 Oct Barbarigo pins Ottoman ships against the shore in close fighting
Lepanto
Oxia
Gulf of Patras
Left wing (Barberigo)
Right wing (Suluc)
Early afternoon, 7 Oct The fleets engage in the centre
Patras
Reserve (Santa Cruz)
Centre (Ali Pasha)
Centre (Don John)
Left wing (Uluch Ali)
Right wing (Doria)
Afternoon, 7 Oct The Ottoman left withdraws as the centre collapses
Peloponnese Peninsula

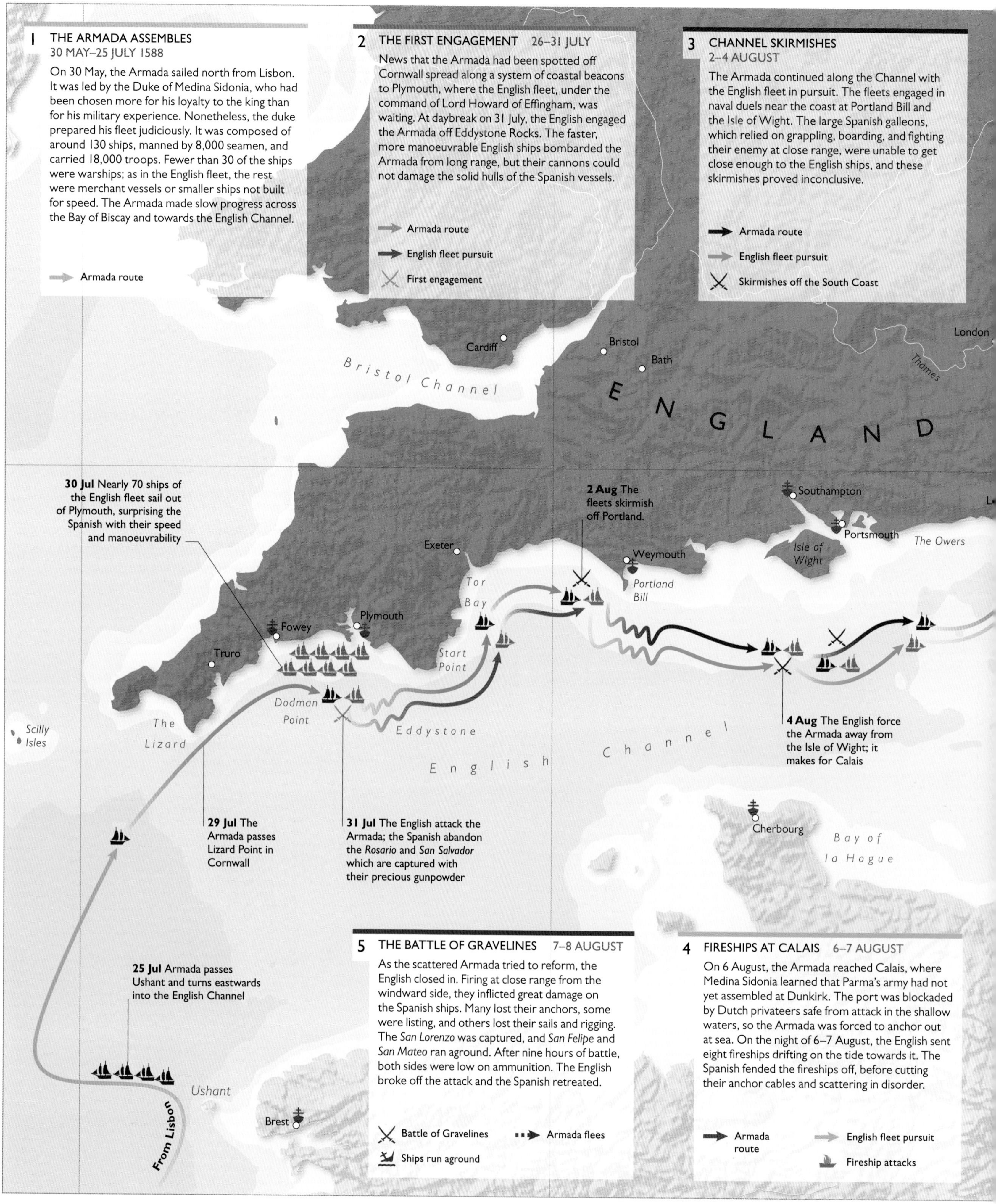
Armada route
Armada route
English fleet pursuit
First engagement
Armada route
English fleet pursuit
Skirmishes off the South Coast
London
Bristol
Cardiff
Bath
Thames
Bristol Channel
ENGLAND
30 Jul Nearly 70 ships of the English fleet sail out of Plymouth, surprising the Spanish with their speed and manoeuvrability
2 Aug The fleets skirmish off Portland.
Southampton
Portsmouth
Isle of Wight
The Owers
Exeter
Weymouth
Portland Bill
Tor Bay
Plymouth
Fowey
Truro
Start Point
Dodman Point
Scilly Isles
The Lizard
Eddystone
English Channel
4 Aug The English force the Armada away from the Isle of Wight; it makes for Calais
29 Jul The Armada passes Lizard Point in Cornwall
31 Jul The English attack the Armada; the Spanish abandon the Rosario and San Salvador which are captured with their precious gunpowder
Cherbourg
Bay of la Hogue
25 Jul Armada passes Ushant and turns eastwards into the English Channel
Ushant
Brest
From Lisbon
Battle of Gravelines
Armada flees
Ships run aground
Armada route
English fleet pursuit
Fireship attacks

1 THE ARMADA ASSEMBLES
30 MAY–25 JULY 1588

On 30 May, the Armada sailed north from Lisbon. It was led by the Duke of Medina Sidonia, who had been chosen more for his loyalty to the king than for his military experience. Nonetheless, the duke prepared his fleet judiciously. It was composed of around 130 ships, manned by 8,000 seamen, and carried 18,000 troops. Fewer than 30 of the ships were warships; as in the English fleet, the rest were merchant vessels or smaller ships not built for speed. The Armada made slow progress across the Bay of Biscay and towards the English Channel.

2 THE FIRST ENGAGEMENT 26–31 JULY

News that the Armada had been spotted off Cornwall spread along a system of coastal beacons to Plymouth, where the English fleet, under the command of Lord Howard of Effingham, was waiting. At daybreak on 31 July, the English engaged the Armada off Eddystone Rocks. The faster, more manoeuvrable English ships bombarded the Armada from long range, but their cannons could not damage the solid hulls of the Spanish vessels.

3 CHANNEL SKIRMISHES
2–4 AUGUST

The Armada continued along the Channel with the English fleet in pursuit. The fleets engaged in naval duels near the coast at Portland Bill and the Isle of Wight. The large Spanish galleons, which relied on grappling, boarding, and fighting their enemy at close range, were unable to get close enough to the English ships, and these skirmishes proved inconclusive.

5 THE BATTLE OF GRAVELINES 7–8 AUGUST

As the scattered Armada tried to reform, the English closed in. Firing at close range from the windward side, they inflicted great damage on the Spanish ships. Many lost their anchors, some were listing, and others lost their sails and rigging. The *San Lorenzo* was captured, and *San Felipe* and *San Mateo* ran aground. After nine hours of battle, both sides were low on ammunition. The English broke off the attack and the Spanish retreated.

4 FIRESHIPS AT CALAIS 6–7 AUGUST

On 6 August, the Armada reached Calais, where Medina Sidonia learned that Parma's army had not yet assembled at Dunkirk. The port was blockaded by Dutch privateers safe from attack in the shallow waters, so the Armada was forced to anchor out at sea. On the night of 6–7 August, the English sent eight fireships drifting on the tide towards it. The Spanish fended the fireships off, before cutting their anchor cables and scattering in disorder.

THE SPANISH ARMADA

In 1588, King Philip II of Spain dispatched a vast fleet, the Armada, to invade England and remove Queen Elizabeth I from the throne. Harried through the Channel by English warships, the Armada was devastated by storms after fleeing the Battle of Gravelines.

In 1585, rivalry between the Catholic king of Spain, Philip II, and the Protestant queen of England, Elizabeth I, became an undeclared war. Philip had earlier been co-monarch of England through his marriage to Elizabeth's half-sister, Queen Mary I, who had died childless. Moreover, Philip was angry that Elizabeth was aiding Protestant rebels in the Spanish Netherlands, and that English privateers were raiding Spanish ships.

In spring 1587, Philip began assembling the "Great and Most Fortunate Navy" with which to depose Elizabeth. It was delayed by an English raid on Cadiz, and finally set sail from Lisbon with around 130 ships at the end of May 1588. The plan was for the Armada to journey east through the English Channel to rendezvous with 30,000 soldiers gathered by the Duke of Parma in the Spanish Netherlands, before going on to invade England. However, after facing the English fleet in the Channel, and failing to rendezvous with the Duke, the Armada was scattered at the Battle of Gravelines. Regrouping, it fled north to the Atlantic, where it was devastated by storms.

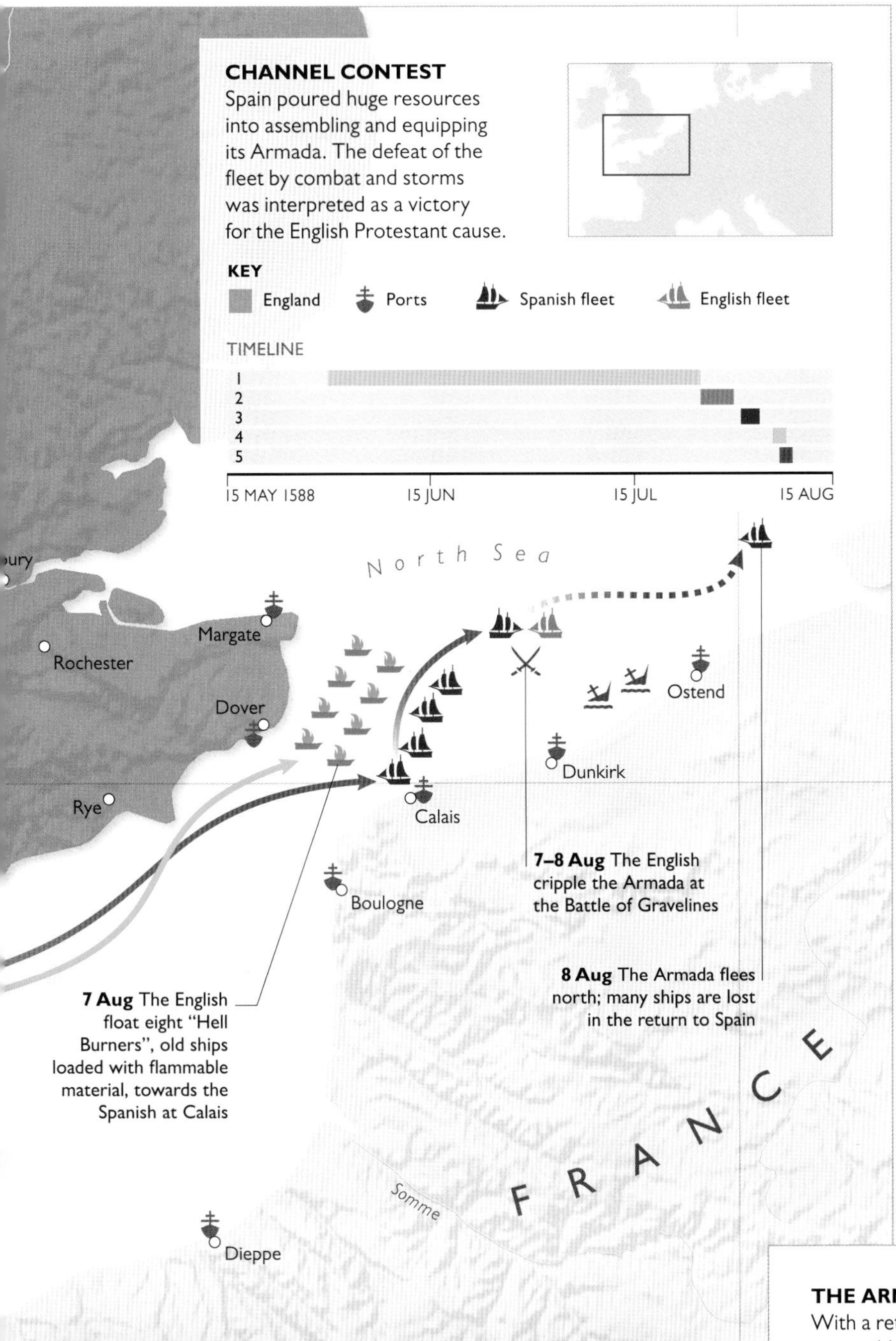
KEY
England
Ports
Spanish fleet
English fleet
TIMELINE
1
2
3
4
5
15 MAY 1588
15 JUN
15 JUL
15 AUG
North Sea
Margate
Rochester
Dover
Rye
Calais
Dunkirk
Ostend
Boulogne
Dieppe
Somme
FRANCE
7–8 Aug The English cripple the Armada at the Battle of Gravelines
8 Aug The Armada flees north; many ships are lost in the return to Spain
7 Aug The English float eight "Hell Burners", old ships loaded with flammable material, towards the Spanish at Calais

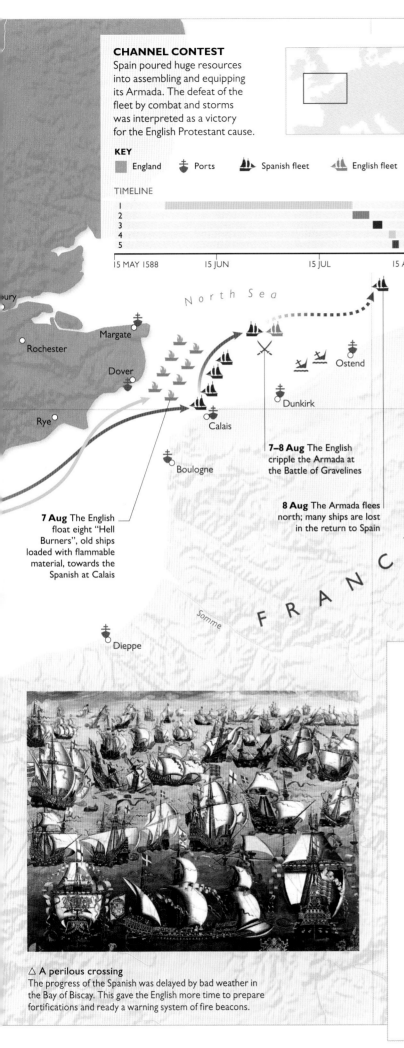

CHANNEL CONTEST
Spain poured huge resources into assembling and equipping its Armada. The defeat of the fleet by combat and storms was interpreted as a victory for the English Protestant cause.

△ **A perilous crossing**
The progress of the Spanish was delayed by bad weather in the Bay of Biscay. This gave the English more time to prepare fortifications and ready a warning system of fire beacons.

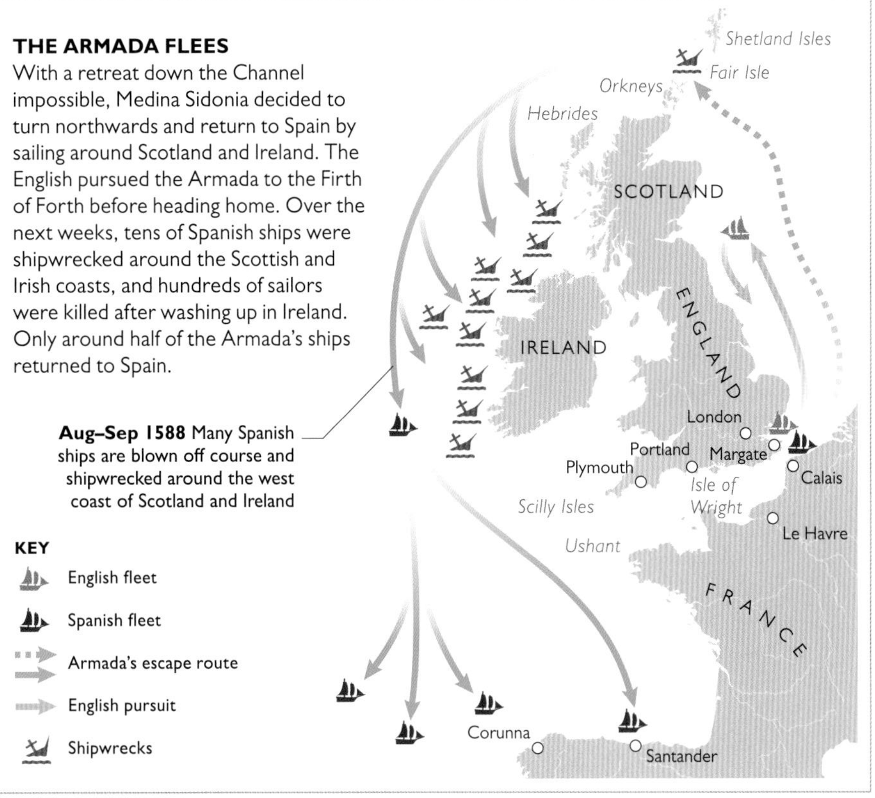
Shetland Isles
Fair Isle
Orkneys
Hebrides
SCOTLAND
IRELAND
ENGLAND
London
Portland
Margate
Calais
Plymouth
Isle of Wright
Scilly Isles
Le Havre
Ushant
FRANCE
Corunna
Santander
Aug–Sep 1588 Many Spanish ships are blown off course and shipwrecked around the west coast of Scotland and Ireland
KEY
English fleet
Spanish fleet
Armada's escape route
English pursuit
Shipwrecks

THE ARMADA FLEES
With a retreat down the Channel impossible, Medina Sidonia decided to turn northwards and return to Spain by sailing around Scotland and Ireland. The English pursued the Armada to the Firth of Forth before heading home. Over the next weeks, tens of Spanish ships were shipwrecked around the Scottish and Irish coasts, and hundreds of sailors were killed after washing up in Ireland. Only around half of the Armada's ships returned to Spain.

Battle of Scheveningen (1653)
This 17th-century painting shows English and Dutch fleets using full-rigged galleons mounted with large broadside guns. *Brederode* (left), the Dutch flagship seen firing on the English ship, was armed with more than 50 guns.

GALLEYS AND GALLEONS

Between the 15th and 17th centuries, naval warfare saw not just a constant evolution in tactics, technology, and objectives, but also a growing expansion in the reach of European navies across the globe.

△ **Bar shot**
This projectile was designed to damage sails and their rigging. The two halves extended and tumbled in flight.

At the start of the 16th century, the sail-and-oar powered, sleek-hulled galley was the primary warship, supported by a smaller number of converted merchant vessels. This was the height of galley warfare, especially in the Mediterranean, where Christian nations warred between themselves and against the Ottoman Empire. Fleets, at times mustering hundreds of ships, clashed repeatedly during battle. The battle at Lepanto in 1571 (see pp.118–19) epitomized this, with hundreds of galleys lined up abreast and fighting mainly at close quarters.

The emergence of galleons

At the same time, especially outside the Mediterranean, converted sea-going merchant ships evolved into purpose-built warships. Known as galleons, these large vessels were powered by sail and carried numerous cannons; they were also better suited for longer voyages and rougher seas. Where galley warfare involved ramming, and boarding, the heavily armed galleons used cannon fire from a distance, relying less heavily on boarding actions. By the end of the 17th century, they had become the dominant form of warship.

Galleys remained in use for some time in sheltered coastal waters, and were a part of Russian and Swedish navies in the Baltic Sea until the early 19th century. The superior firepower and endurance of galleons, however, made them increasingly dominant on the open sea, as seen in their leading role during the Spanish Armada campaign of 1588 (see pp.120–21), just 17 years after the Battle of Lepanto.

△ **Oar to sail**
Spanish artist Rafael Monleón's painting depicts a galleon (left) and a galley (right) from the 16th century. Galleys, propelled mainly by oars, had a long, slender hull. Galleons, on the other hand, were powered by sails and carried rows of guns on their decks.

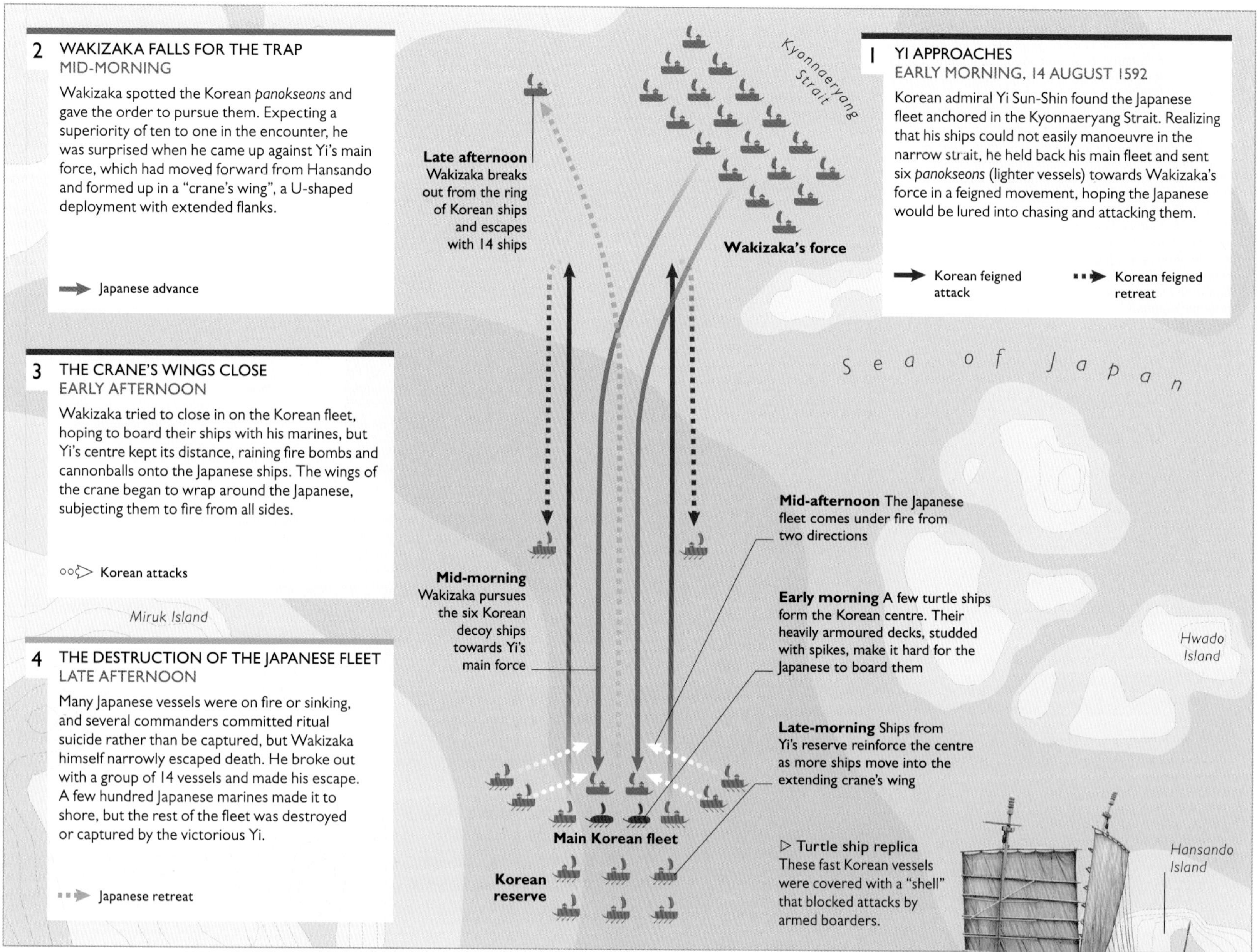
Kyonnaeryang Strait
Wakizaka's force
Late afternoon Wakizaka breaks out from the ring of Korean ships and escapes with 14 ships
Sea of Japan
Mid-afternoon The Japanese fleet comes under fire from two directions
Mid-morning Wakizaka pursues the six Korean decoy ships towards Yi's main force
Early morning A few turtle ships form the Korean centre. Their heavily armoured decks, studded with spikes, make it hard for the Japanese to board them
Late-morning Ships from Yi's reserve reinforce the centre as more ships move into the extending crane's wing
Main Korean fleet
Korean reserve
Miruk Island
Hwado Island
Hansando Island

1 YI APPROACHES
EARLY MORNING, 14 AUGUST 1592

Korean admiral Yi Sun-Shin found the Japanese fleet anchored in the Kyonnaeryang Strait. Realizing that his ships could not easily manoeuvre in the narrow strait, he held back his main fleet and sent six *panokseons* (lighter vessels) towards Wakizaka's force in a feigned movement, hoping the Japanese would be lured into chasing and attacking them.

Korean feigned attack
Korean feigned retreat

2 WAKIZAKA FALLS FOR THE TRAP
MID-MORNING

Wakizaka spotted the Korean *panokseons* and gave the order to pursue them. Expecting a superiority of ten to one in the encounter, he was surprised when he came up against Yi's main force, which had moved forward from Hansando and formed up in a "crane's wing", a U-shaped deployment with extended flanks.

Japanese advance

3 THE CRANE'S WINGS CLOSE
EARLY AFTERNOON

Wakizaka tried to close in on the Korean fleet, hoping to board their ships with his marines, but Yi's centre kept its distance, raining fire bombs and cannonballs onto the Japanese ships. The wings of the crane began to wrap around the Japanese, subjecting them to fire from all sides.

Korean attacks

4 THE DESTRUCTION OF THE JAPANESE FLEET
LATE AFTERNOON

Many Japanese vessels were on fire or sinking, and several commanders committed ritual suicide rather than be captured, but Wakizaka himself narrowly escaped death. He broke out with a group of 14 vessels and made his escape. A few hundred Japanese marines made it to shore, but the rest of the fleet was destroyed or captured by the victorious Yi.

Japanese retreat

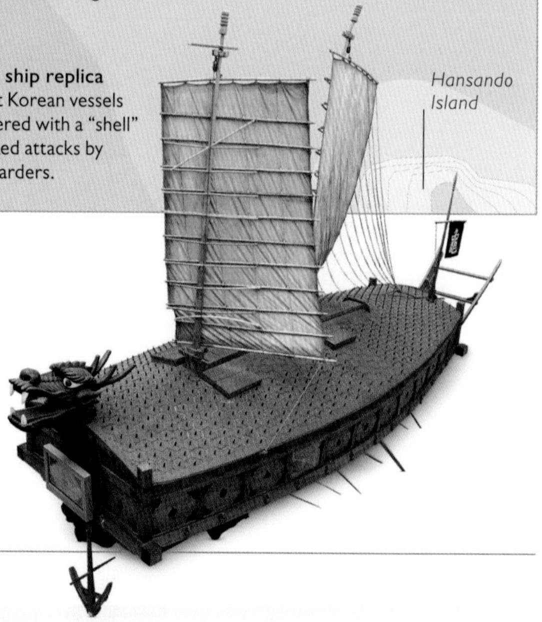

▷ **Turtle ship replica**
These fast Korean vessels were covered with a "shell" that blocked attacks by armed boarders.

HANSANDO

In the waters off Hansando Island, Korean admiral Yi Sun-Shin helped to resist the occupation of Korea launched by Japanese warlord Toyotomi Hideyoshi. He lured the Japanese into a trap, where his armoured ships destroyed the enemy fleet.

By 1592, warlord Toyotomi Hideyoshi had almost completed the reunification of Japan. As the country's de facto leader, he developed an aggressive foreign policy by which he hoped to subjugate Ming China. This prompted the occupation of most of Korea as a conduit for his armies.

The Korean fleet, however, remained intact, and its heavy cannons and armoured "turtle ships" were a particular threat to the lighter Japanese vessels. Hideyoshi called on warlord Wakizaka Yasuharu to deal with Korean admiral Yi Sun-Shin and his fleet. Wakizaka set sail with around 75 ships, without waiting for the reinforcements that would have given him a clear advantage.

The Korean fleet encountered the Japanese near Hansando Island on 14 August 1592, and roundly defeated them. Although the Japanese continued to advance in the aftermath of the battle, support for Korea from Ming China prompted Hideyoshi to agree a ceasefire and mutual withdrawal from most of Korea in May 1954.

NAVAL STRATEGY

Yi Sun-Shin skilfully lured the Japanese fleet into open water off Hansando Island where his ships could surround it and exploit the Japanese lack of cannon by firing from a distance while evading boarding attempts.

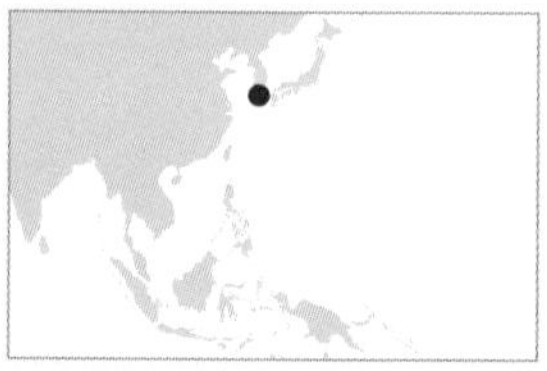

KEY

Japanese fleet

KOREAN FLEET

Light vessels (*panokseon*)

Turtle ships (*kobukson*)

TIMELINE

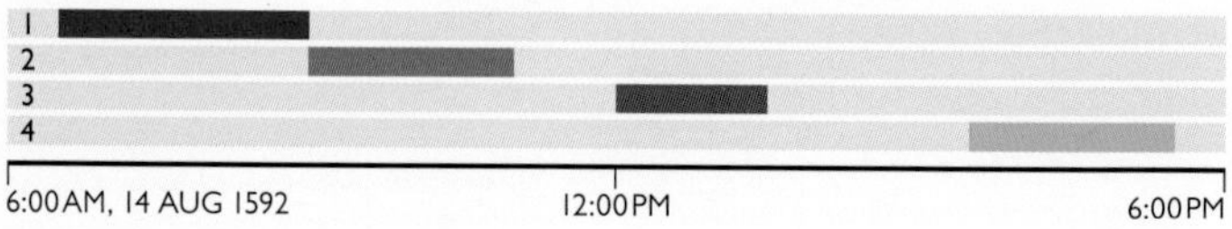
1
2
3
4
6:00AM, 14 AUG 1592
12:00PM
6:00PM

SEKIGAHARA

The bid by the feudal lord Tokugawa Ieyasu to achieve supremacy in Japan was opposed by a coalition led by Ishida Mitsunari, whose Western Army clashed with Tokugawa's Eastern Army at Sekigahara in October 1600. The defection of key parts of Mitsunari's force handed Ieyasu's forces a crushing victory and allowed him to establish a Tokugawa shogunate.

The death of Toyotomi Hideyoshi (see p.124) in 1598 meant that his lieutenant Tokugawa Ieyasu was now Japan's most important warlord. Brushing aside the regency of Hideyoshi's son Hideyori, Ieyasu began to cement his rule. He faced opposition, however, that coalesced around Ishida Mitsunari, a loyalist to Hideyori's cause. In preparation for conflict, both sides hurried to take strategic positions around the imperial capital Kyoto. Mitsunari's Western Army captured Fushimi Castle and Ogaki Castle, but the Eastern Army, meanwhile, took Gifu Castle. This prompted Mitsunari to redeploy to a defensive position near the village of Sekigahara, where the Eastern force confronted him on 21 October. Ieyasu's decisive victory there shattered the Western alliance.

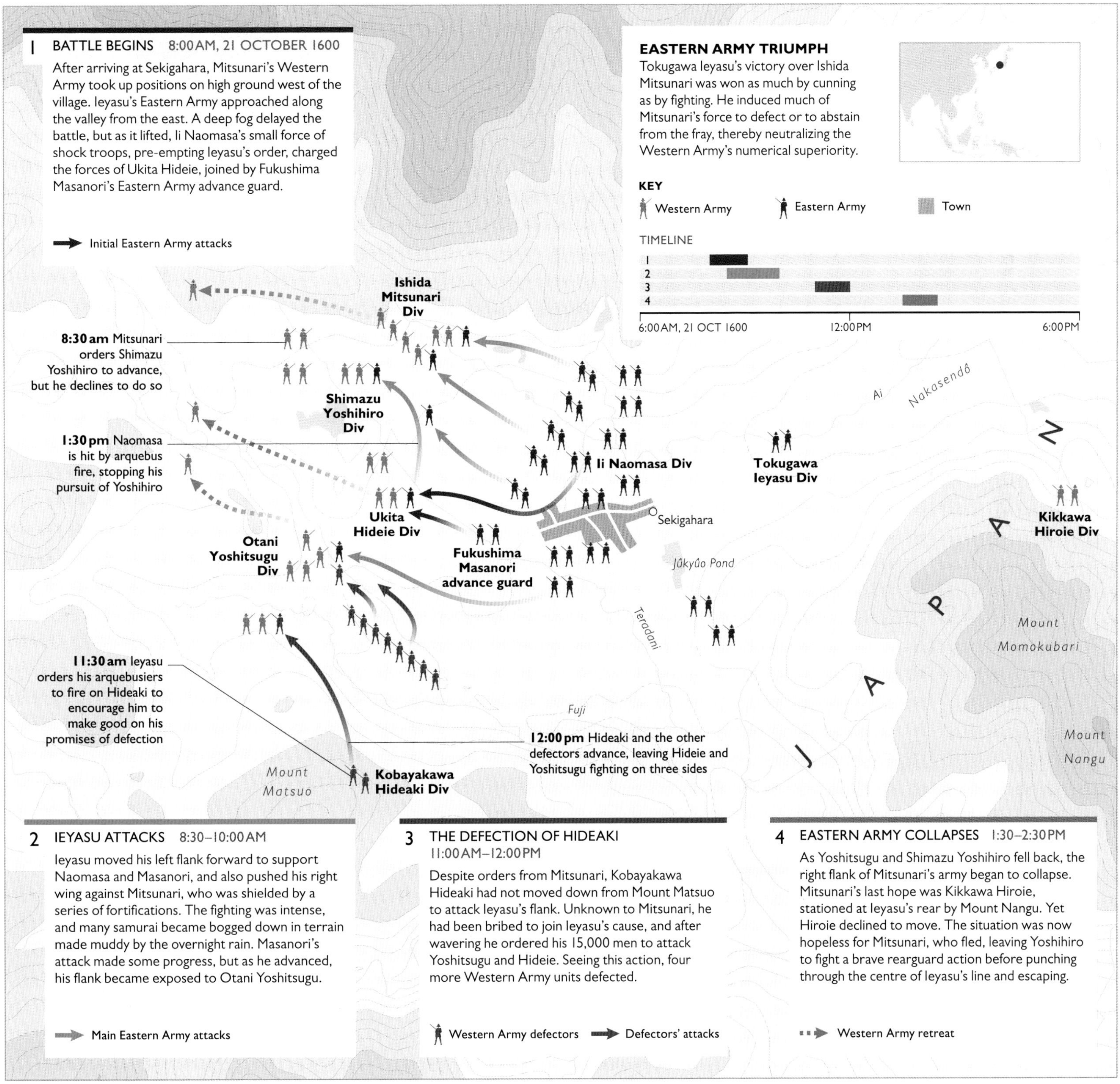
1 BATTLE BEGINS 8:00AM, 21 OCTOBER 1600
After arriving at Sekigahara, Mitsunari's Western Army took up positions on high ground west of the village. Ieyasu's Eastern Army approached along the valley from the east. A deep fog delayed the battle, but as it lifted, Ii Naomasa's small force of shock troops, pre-empting Ieyasu's order, charged the forces of Ukita Hideie, joined by Fukushima Masanori's Eastern Army advance guard.
Initial Eastern Army attacks
EASTERN ARMY TRIUMPH
Tokugawa Ieyasu's victory over Ishida Mitsunari was won as much by cunning as by fighting. He induced much of Mitsunari's force to defect or to abstain from the fray, thereby neutralizing the Western Army's numerical superiority.
KEY
Western Army
Eastern Army
Town
TIMELINE
1
2
3
4
6:00AM, 21 OCT 1600
12:00PM
6:00PM
Ishida Mitsunari Div
8:30am Mitsunari orders Shimazu Yoshihiro to advance, but he declines to do so
Shimazu Yoshihiro Div
1:30pm Naomasa is hit by arquebus fire, stopping his pursuit of Yoshihiro
Ii Naomasa Div
Tokugawa Ieyasu Div
Ai
Nakasendô
JAPAN
Kikkawa Hiroie Div
Sekigahara
Ukita Hideie Div
Fukushima Masanori advance guard
Otani Yoshitsugu Div
Jûkyûo Pond
Teradani
Mount Momokubari
11:30am Ieyasu orders his arquebusiers to fire on Hideaki to encourage him to make good on his promises of defection
Fuji
12:00pm Hideaki and the other defectors advance, leaving Hideie and Yoshitsugu fighting on three sides
Mount Nangu
Mount Matsuo
Kobayakawa Hideaki Div
2 IEYASU ATTACKS 8:30–10:00AM
Ieyasu moved his left flank forward to support Naomasa and Masanori, and also pushed his right wing against Mitsunari, who was shielded by a series of fortifications. The fighting was intense, and many samurai became bogged down in terrain made muddy by the overnight rain. Masanori's attack made some progress, but as he advanced, his flank became exposed to Otani Yoshitsugu.
Main Eastern Army attacks
3 THE DEFECTION OF HIDEAKI 11:00AM–12:00PM
Despite orders from Mitsunari, Kobayakawa Hideaki had not moved down from Mount Matsuo to attack Ieyasu's flank. Unknown to Mitsunari, he had been bribed to join Ieyasu's cause, and after wavering he ordered his 15,000 men to attack Yoshitsugu and Hideie. Seeing this action, four more Western Army units defected.
Western Army defectors
Defectors' attacks
4 EASTERN ARMY COLLAPSES 1:30–2:30PM
As Yoshitsugu and Shimazu Yoshihiro fell back, the right flank of Mitsunari's army began to collapse. Mitsunari's last hope was Kikkawa Hiroie, stationed at Ieyasu's rear by Mount Nangu. Yet Hiroie declined to move. The situation was now hopeless for Mitsunari, who fled, leaving Yoshihiro to fight a brave rearguard action before punching through the centre of Ieyasu's line and escaping.
Western Army retreat

Samurai legend
This 19th-century wooden plaque depicts Minamoto no Yoshitsune (left) being welcomed to Hokkaido by his subjects. Yoshitsune is considered one of Japan's greatest samurai warriors due to his heroics in the Genpei War.

SAMURAI AND SHOGUNS

As medieval Japan's power changed hands, a new warrior caste evolved as a hybrid military and police force – the samurai. They had become a staple of Japanese warfare and politics by the 12th century.

△ **Weapon of choice**
This long sword, or *katana*, was worn by samurai during the Edo period (1603–1868).

In the late 8th century CE, after fears of an impending invasion from Tang China had receded, the elaborate military forces of the Japanese imperial court stood down. They were replaced by a new group of private military professionals called samurai, largely employed to deal with internal disturbances and police duties. Armed with bows and swords, samurai fought on horseback and rented their services to the court and the state when needed. In turn, they were remunerated in money and land deeds. This system prevailed during the Genpei War (see p.68), the two Mongol invasions of the 13th century, and the period of the two rival courts – the Nanbokucho period – from 1336 to 1392.

Changes in power

With the Onin War (1467–77) and the decline of centralized bureaucracy, the Sengoku era (1467–1615) saw the rise of a new power structure in Japan. The shogunate was a powerful national office for which the samurai duelled. Clan lords called *daimyo* had private retinues, which grew alongside their direct control over the farming estates, and they began to fight each other for possession of land rather than being mobilized by a central authority. This trend accelerated with the introduction of the Portuguese arquebus (see p.95) in 1543. This made it easy for warlords to field large armies with less training than archers. Shoguns and the dominant samurai warrior caste continued to rule Japan until the mid-19th century.

THE FEUDAL SYSTEM IN JAPAN

For most of the medieval period, the imperial court retained full control over lands and titles, and samurai could receive land deeds in exchange for services; however, these were not hereditary. As a result, the first few shoguns were agents of the court rather than autonomous lords. It was only in the 15th–16th centuries that samurai lords such as Uesugi Kenshin (1530–78, right) came to independently control specific provinces, and administered as well as defended them.

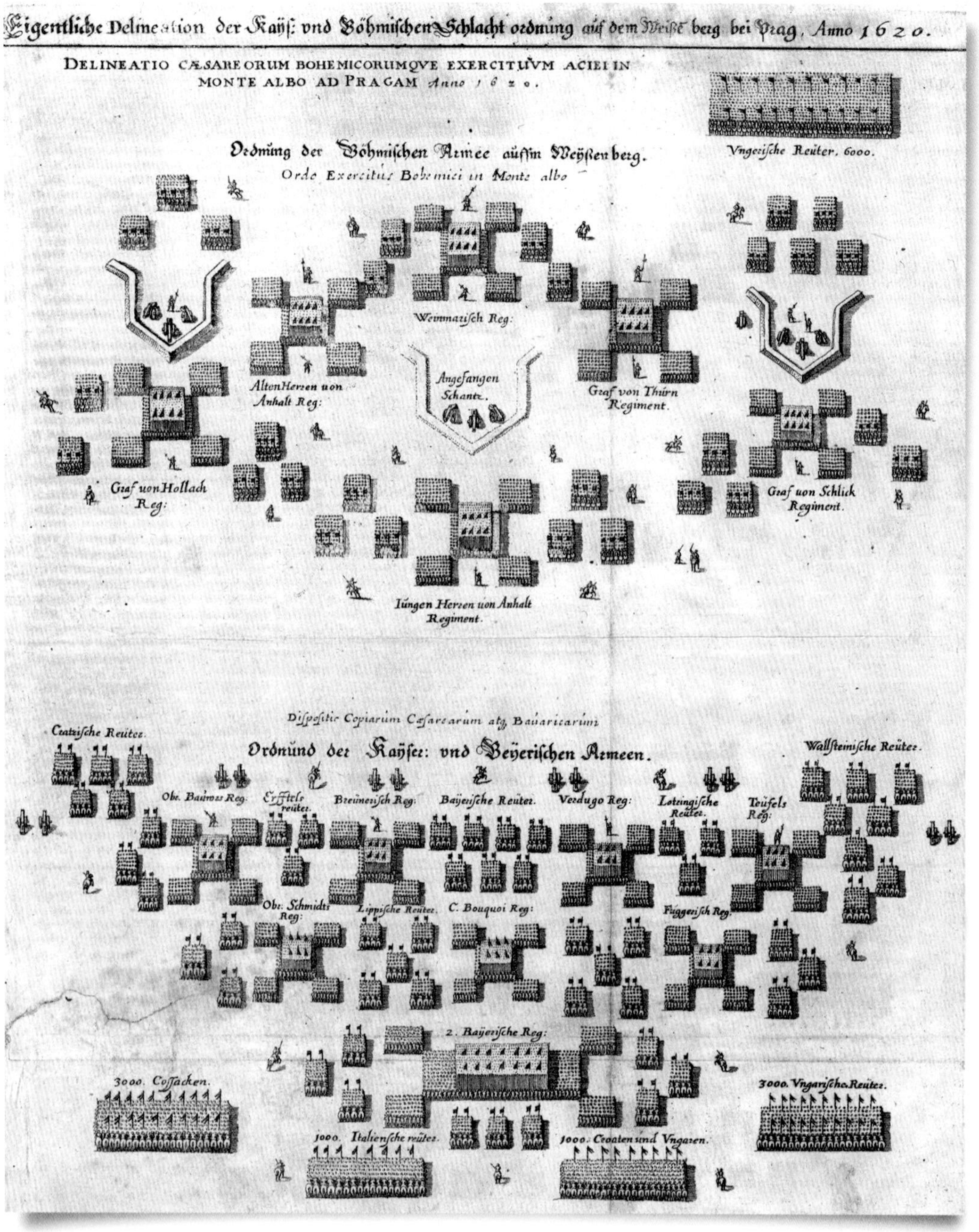
Eigentliche Delineation der Käys: vnd Böhmischen Schlacht ordnung auf dem Weiße berg bei Prag, Anno 1620.
DELINEATIO CÆSAREORUM BOHEMICORUMQVE EXERCITUUM ACIEI IN MONTE ALBO AD PRAGAM Anno 1620.
Ordnung der Böhmischen Armee aufm Weißenberg.
Orde Exercitus Bohemici in Monte albo
Vngerische Reüter. 6000.
Wemmarisch Reg:
Alten Herren von Anhalt Reg:
Angefangen Schantz.
Graf von Thürn Regiment.
Graf von Hollach Reg:
Graf von Schlick Regiment.
Jungen Herren von Anhalt Regiment.
Ordnung der Kayser: vnd Beyerischen Armeen.
Croatische Reuter.
Wallsteinische Reüter.
Bayerische Reuter.
Verdugo Reg:
Teüfels Reg:
Obr: Schmidts Reg:
C. Bouquoi Reg:
Fuggerisch Reg:
2. Bayerische Reg:
3000. Cossacken.
3000. Vngarische Reüter.
1000. Italienische reüter.
1000. Croaten und Vngaren.

1

Ordnund der Kays
Erfftels reüter.
Breünerisch Reg:

2

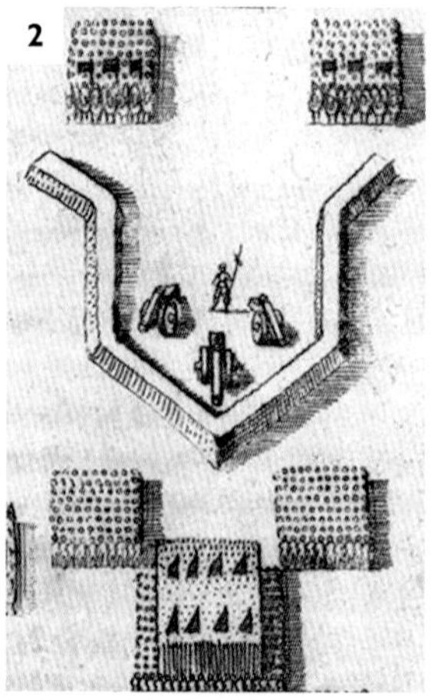

△ **The "Apostles"**
The Catholic League had a dozen heavy guns they nicknamed the "12 Apostles". They fired at around 12:15pm to signal the advance.

◁ **Redoubt**
The Bohemians dug in on the hillside above the plateau, and were partially protected by the walls of Prague's Star Palace.

▽ **Tercio**
The Catholic infantry formed up in *tercios* – a formation of up to 3,000 infantry with pikes in the centre and muskets concentrated in the sleeves on each of its four corners.

3

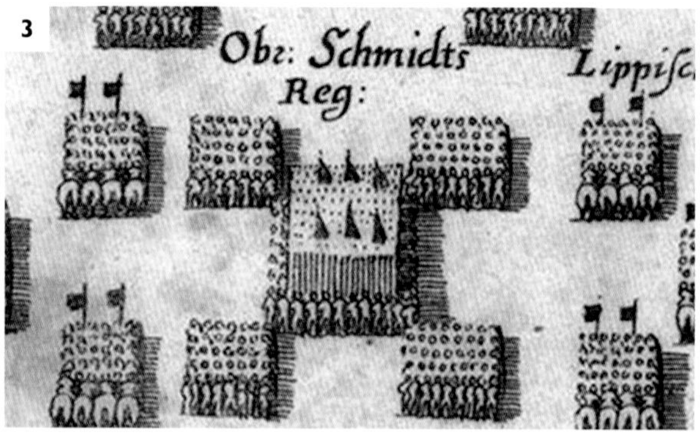
Obr: Schmidts Reg:

◁ **Initial positions**
This 1662 plan of the battle is from *Theatrum Europaeum*, a 21-volume history of German-speaking lands. It shows the positions of the Bohemian forces (above) and Imperial forces (below) at the start of the battle.

WHITE MOUNTAIN

On 8 November 1620, the Habsburg Holy Roman Empire won its first major victory over the Protestant Union in the Thirty Years War (1618–48) at White Mountain, near Prague in Bohemia. There the Bohemian army was routed and the Bohemian Revolt crushed.

In 1617, the Habsburg Ferdinand of Austria was crowned King of Bohemia and immediately began removing the religious freedoms of his Protestant subjects, which led to the Bohemian Revolt (1618–20). By 1620, Ferdinand, by then Holy Roman Emperor, was determined to end the revolt, and by November his Imperial forces had pushed the Bohemian army back to the outskirts of Prague.

On the morning of 8 November, the dwindling Bohemian army assembled at White Mountain, a low plateau on the road to Prague, to face around 25,000 Imperial soldiers. On the right, the Catholic soldiers advanced, sweeping away the Protestant cavalry and charging the disintegrating enemy left. As the Bohemian flank crumbled, its cavalry charged the Imperial infantry. The cavalry was soon forced to retire, however, and the Bohemian infantry managed only one volley before it too fled towards Prague. The battle was over in less than two hours.

The Bohemian revolt ended after the rout at White Mountain; Prague fell and Bohemia was reabsorbed into the Holy Roman Empire. The Protestants would have to wait until the Battle of Breitenfeld (see pp.130–31) for their first major victory in the Thirty Years War.

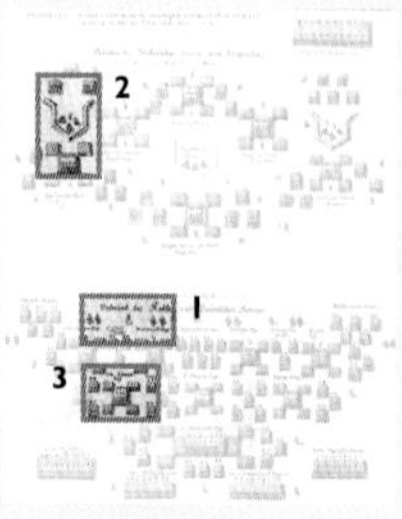
2
1
3

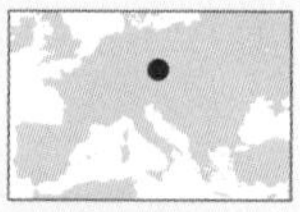

LOCATOR

THE SIEGE OF BREDA

The nine-month siege of Breda was one of Spain's greatest victories in the Eighty Years War (1568–1648) fought over Dutch independence from Spanish rule. Spain's vast siege works were a marvel of military engineering, attracting visitors from across Europe.

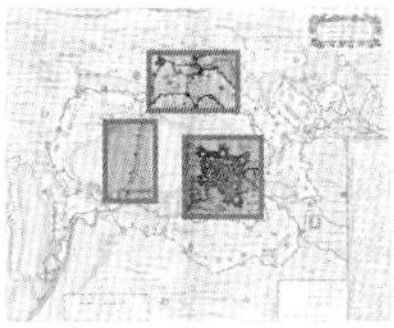

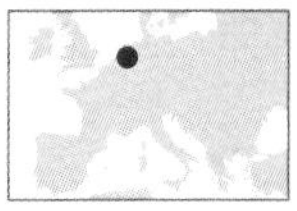

KEY

1 The bastion fortress of Breda had six major hornworks – smaller fortifications designed to slow the enemy's attack.

2 Spinola's lines of circumvallation consisted of the trenches, forts, and redoubts encircling Breda.

3 The Black Dyke was a causeway built by the Spanish to cross the flooded low-lying land.

In 1566, the Low Countries revolted against their Habsburg ruler, King Philip II of Spain, beginning the Dutch Revolt that would become the Eighty Years War. In 1624, Spanish forces besieged Breda – a crucial fortress on the southern frontier of the United Provinces of the Netherlands, who had claimed independence from Spanish rule in 1581.

The Spanish general Ambrogio Spinola encircled Breda with a large army, aiming to starve it into submission. In less than a month, his men had built a complex network of siege works around the city. Both sides used the rivers and drains to flood fields or dry up navigable channels for tactical advantage. Spinola drove off two attempts to lift the siege before Breda's governor, Justin of Nassau, finally surrendered on 5 June 1625. Over half of the Dutch garrison of several thousand had died. Although the siege helped restore the Spanish army's reputation, Spanish resources were overstretched. Breda was retaken in 1637, and Spain was forced to recognise Dutch independence in 1648.

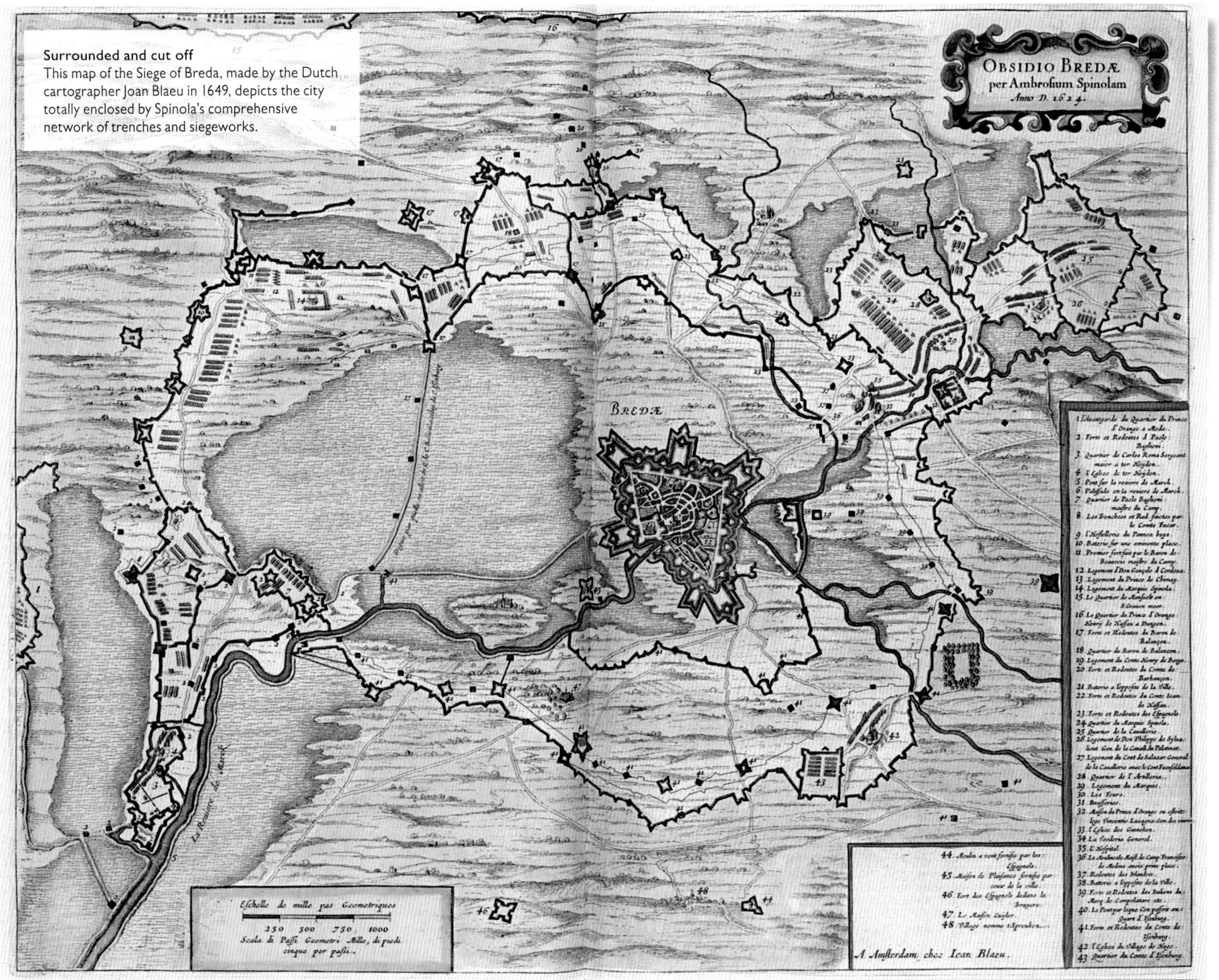
Obsidio Bredæ
per Ambrosium Spinolam
Anno D. 1624.
Bredæ
Eschelle de mille pas Geometriques
250 500 750 1000
Scala di Passi Geometri Mille, di piedi cinque per passi.
A Amsterdam, chez Iean Blaeu.

Surrounded and cut off
This map of the Siege of Breda, made by the Dutch cartographer Joan Blaeu in 1649, depicts the city totally enclosed by Spinola's comprehensive network of trenches and siegeworks.

BREITENFELD

The Swedish king Gustavus Adolphus established his reputation as a tactical genius in 1631 against Imperial Catholic forces at Breitenfeld. He shattered his foe's more traditional formations and revived the Protestant cause in the Thirty Years War.

The Thirty Years War began in Bohemia in 1618 as a Protestant revolt against attempts by Holy Roman Emperors Matthias (r. 1612–19) and then Ferdinand II (r. 1619–37) to reimpose Catholicism. It spread to involve Spain, France, and opposing coalitions of German princes. By 1630, the Protestant cause was under pressure as the Imperial Catholic commander Tilly campaigned to mop up the last German princes still supporting it. However, the intervention of the Swedish ruler Gustavus Adolphus changed the balance of power. Gustavus enticed Johann Georg, elector of Saxony, into an alliance, and used the brutal sack of Magdeburg by Imperial troops in May 1631 to attract further allies. Sensing the danger, Tilly invaded Saxony, but before he had a chance to rendezvous with reinforcements at Jena, his 35,000-strong army encountered Gustavus at Breitenfeld, northwest of Leipzig. Gustavus's adaptability and his army's discipline won him a resounding victory. Further successes followed, leading to an upsurge in Protestant fortunes. However, Gustavus himself was killed at Lützen in 1632 and the war dragged on until 1648.

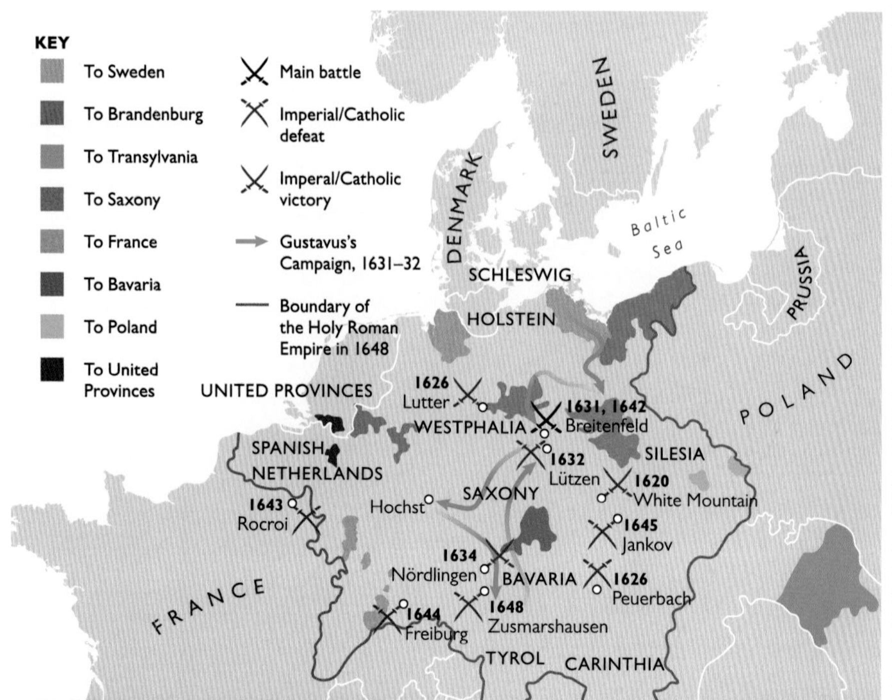
KEY
To Sweden
To Brandenburg
To Transylvania
To Saxony
To France
To Bavaria
To Poland
To United Provinces
Main battle
Imperial/Catholic defeat
Imperial/Catholic victory
Gustavus's Campaign, 1631–32
Boundary of the Holy Roman Empire in 1648
SWEDEN
DENMARK
Baltic Sea
PRUSSIA
SCHLESWIG
HOLSTEIN
POLAND
UNITED PROVINCES
1626 Lutter
WESTPHALIA
1631, 1642 Breitenfeld
SPANISH NETHERLANDS
1632 Lützen
SILESIA
1620 White Mountain
1643 Rocroi
Hochst
SAXONY
1645 Jankov
1634 Nördlingen
BAVARIA
1626 Peuerbach
FRANCE
1644 Freiburg
1648 Zusmarshausen
TYROL
CARINTHIA
OTTOMAN EMPIRE

THE END OF THE THIRTY YEARS WAR
Treaties known as the Peace of Westphalia signed in 1648 ended the Thirty Years War – a conflict in the Holy Roman Empire that pitted Habsburg Austria and Spain and their Catholic allies against Protestant powers. The Peace awarded Imperial territory to Sweden, France, and their allies.

1 THE DEPLOYMENT 9:00AM–12:00PM, 17 SEPTEMBER 1631
Gustavus deployed his 42,000-strong force just south of the Loberbach River and around the village of Podelwitz. Johann Georg's Saxons were on the left; the main Swedish cavalry on the right. Gustavus deployed his infantry in thin six-deep ranks. In contrast, Tilly drew up 17 *tercios* – unwieldy phalanx-like infantry units – at his centre, with the cavalry under Pappenheim and Furstenberg at the wings.

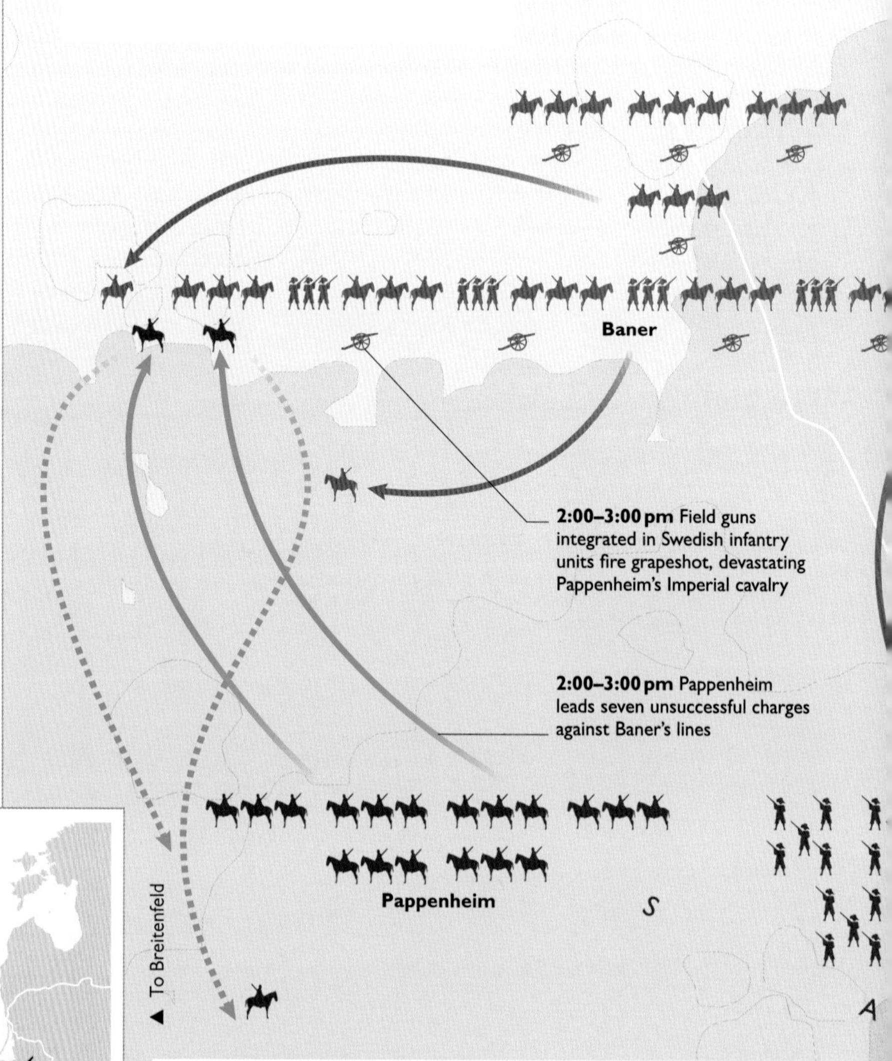
Loberbach
Baner
2:00–3:00 pm Field guns integrated in Swedish infantry units fire grapeshot, devastating Pappenheim's Imperial cavalry
2:00–3:00 pm Pappenheim leads seven unsuccessful charges against Baner's lines
Pappenheim
To Breitenfeld

FLEXIBLE TACTICS
Gustavus Adolphus victory at Breitenfeld resulted from the greater mobility of his ranks and his ability to adapt tactics rapidly on the battlefield. The victory saved the Protestant cause in the Thirty Years War.

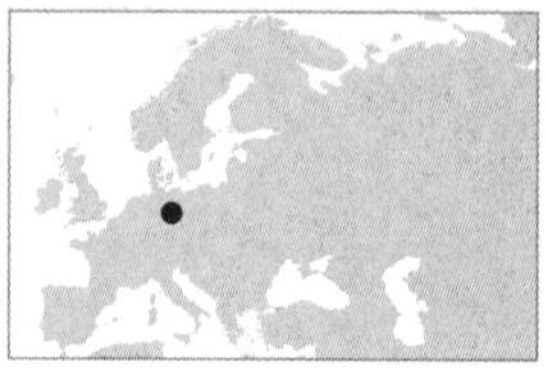

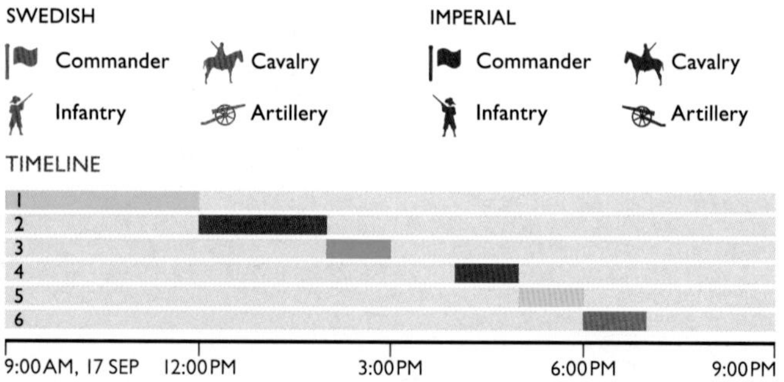
KEY
SWEDISH
Commander
Cavalry
Infantry
Artillery
IMPERIAL
Commander
Cavalry
Infantry
Artillery
TIMELINE
1
2
3
4
5
6
9:00AM, 17 SEP
12:00PM
3:00PM
6:00PM
9:00PM

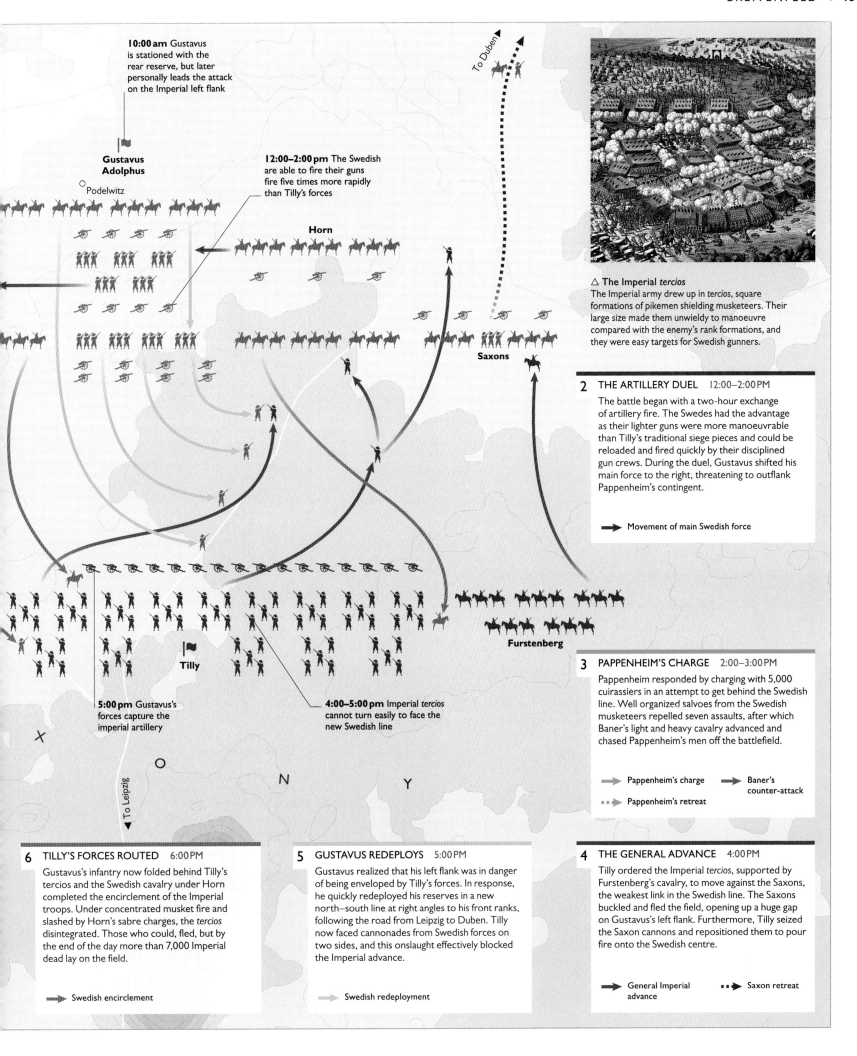

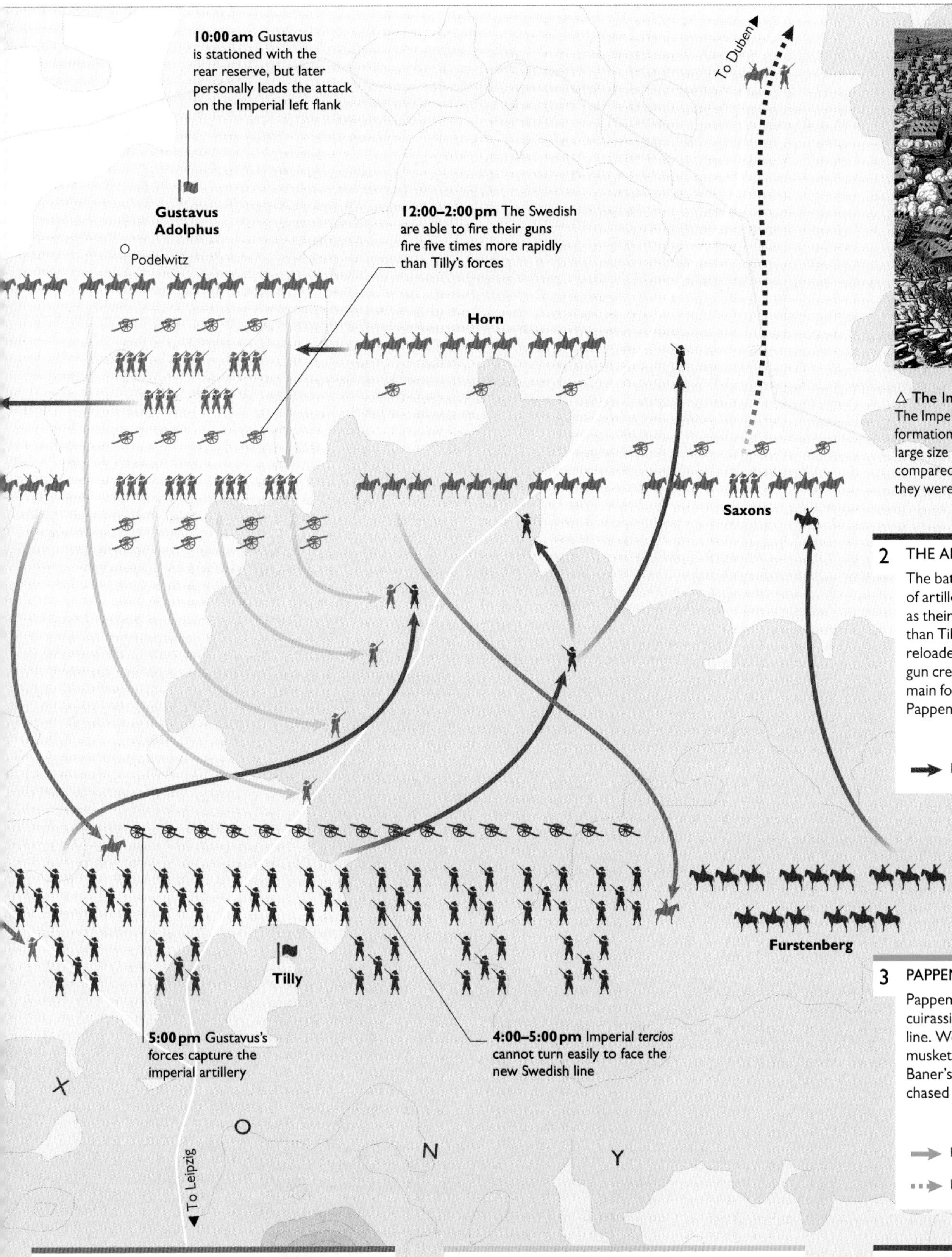
10:00 am Gustavus is stationed with the rear reserve, but later personally leads the attack on the Imperial left flank
To Duben
Gustavus Adolphus
Podelwitz
12:00–2:00 pm The Swedish are able to fire their guns fire five times more rapidly than Tilly's forces
Horn
Saxons
Tilly
Furstenberg
5:00 pm Gustavus's forces capture the imperial artillery
4:00–5:00 pm Imperial *tercios* cannot turn easily to face the new Swedish line
X
O
N
Y
To Leipzig

△ **The Imperial *tercios***
The Imperial army drew up in *tercios*, square formations of pikemen shielding musketeers. Their large size made them unwieldy to manoeuvre compared with the enemy's rank formations, and they were easy targets for Swedish gunners.

2 THE ARTILLERY DUEL 12:00–2:00 PM

The battle began with a two-hour exchange of artillery fire. The Swedes had the advantage as their lighter guns were more manoeuvrable than Tilly's traditional siege pieces and could be reloaded and fired quickly by their disciplined gun crews. During the duel, Gustavus shifted his main force to the right, threatening to outflank Pappenheim's contingent.

Movement of main Swedish force

3 PAPPENHEIM'S CHARGE 2:00–3:00 PM

Pappenheim responded by charging with 5,000 cuirassiers in an attempt to get behind the Swedish line. Well organized salvoes from the Swedish musketeers repelled seven assaults, after which Baner's light and heavy cavalry advanced and chased Pappenheim's men off the battlefield.

Pappenheim's charge
Baner's counter-attack
Pappenheim's retreat

6 TILLY'S FORCES ROUTED 6:00 PM

Gustavus's infantry now folded behind Tilly's tercios and the Swedish cavalry under Horn completed the encirclement of the Imperial troops. Under concentrated musket fire and slashed by Horn's sabre charges, the *tercios* disintegrated. Those who could, fled, but by the end of the day more than 7,000 Imperial dead lay on the field.

Swedish encirclement

5 GUSTAVUS REDEPLOYS 5:00 PM

Gustavus realized that his left flank was in danger of being enveloped by Tilly's forces. In response, he quickly redeployed his reserves in a new north–south line at right angles to his front ranks, following the road from Leipzig to Duben. Tilly now faced cannonades from Swedish forces on two sides, and this onslaught effectively blocked the Imperial advance.

Swedish redeployment

4 THE GENERAL ADVANCE 4:00 PM

Tilly ordered the Imperial *tercios*, supported by Furstenberg's cavalry, to move against the Saxons, the weakest link in the Swedish line. The Saxons buckled and fled the field, opening up a huge gap on Gustavus's left flank. Furthermore, Tilly seized the Saxon cannons and repositioned them to pour fire onto the Swedish centre.

General Imperial advance
Saxon retreat

PIKE AND MUSKET WARFARE

Bodies of pikemen and musketeers were the most characteristic feature of European battles from the 1500s to the late 17th century. Military tacticians were faced with the challenge of how best to combine the two.

Despite the unreliability of early gunpowder weapons, the idea of arming massed infantry with the arquebus and matchlock musket marked a bold step forwards. Pikes, in contrast, were primitive arms that nevertheless retained their effectiveness against cavalry. From the 1470s, the Swiss had demonstrated the effectiveness of dense bodies of pikemen in battle not only for defence but also in attack (often described as "push of pike"), and adding musketeers to these ranks created the dominant fighting formations of the 16th century, such as the Spanish *tercios*. Cavalry, traditionally the elite arm of many forces, found itself no longer the dominant force on the battlefield.

Initially, musketeers were deployed in relatively small numbers to aid the pikemen, but by the 17th century commanders came to appreciate the potential of massed musketeers firing disciplined volleys. By the time of the English Civil Wars (1642–51), muskets regularly outnumbered pikes by two to one, and the firearm troops were organized in their own formations on the flanks of the pikemen. The cavalry charge, by horsemen armed with pistols and swords, also regained its potency. The introduction of flintlock muskets fitted with socket bayonets had made the pike obsolete by around 1700.

△ **Matchlock musket**
An inaccurate and unreliable firearm, the matchlock was most effective when fired in disciplined volleys. This German musket dates from around 1580.

THE *LANDSKNECHT*

First raised in 1486–87, the *Landsknecht* were bands of mercenaries originally recruited to serve the Holy Roman Empire. Chiefly consisting of pikemen, their ranks also included firearm troops and elite soldiers wielding double-handed swords and halberds. The *Landsknecht* earned a fearsome reputation on and off the battlefield, their swaggering unruliness reflected in their colourful, ripped clothing. They played a prominent role in the Italian Wars (1494–1559) and, as *lansquenets*, in the French Wars of Religion (1562–98).

Fighting in formation
A battle scene painted by Pieter Snayers from the Eighty Years War, fought between the Dutch and the Spanish from 1568 to 1648, shows dense pike squares with borders of musketeers defying squadrons of pistol-armed cavalry.

NASEBY

The English Civil Wars (1642–51) were fought between Parliamentarians (supporters of Parliamentary rule) and Royalists (supporters of the absolutist king, Charles I). On 14 June 1645, the Parliamentarian New Model Army won a victory over Royalist forces at Naseby that proved to be a turning point in the conflict.

In 1642, relations between England's king, Charles I, and the country's parliament erupted into civil war. War had ravaged England for three years, when Sir Thomas Fairfax, commander-in-chief of Parliament's New Model Army (a recently formed army made up of professional soldiers) launched a siege of the Royalist city of Oxford in May 1645. The Royalist commander, Prince Rupert of the Rhine, responded by taking Leicester, a Parliamentarian stronghold 99 km (61 miles) to the north. Marching from Oxford with around 14,000 soldiers, Fairfax located the Royalists 42 km (26 miles) south of Leicester on 12 June. With around 9,000 men, the Royalists withdrew, before deciding to make a stand near the village of Naseby on 14 June.

Despite the disparity in their numbers, Parliament's victory was not inevitable. Prince Rupert was a seasoned soldier, and the New Model Army was relatively inexperienced. However, Rupert made two serious errors. First, he gave up an excellent defensive position in his eagerness to engage the enemy, thus ceding the choice of battleground to Fairfax and his second-in-command, Oliver Cromwell. Second, soon after the battle began, he led his cavalry in pursuit of the enemy cavalry, leaving the infantry unsupported at a crucial moment. Parliament's ensuing victory was devastating: 5,000 Royalists were taken prisoner, and the King lost many experienced officers. Parliament had won a decisive advantage in the war.

> *"The Earl of Carnwath took the King's Horse by the Bridle [...] saying, Will you go upon your Death?"*
>
> SIR EDWARD WALKER, THE KING'S SECRETARY, C.17TH CENTURY

OLIVER CROMWELL
1599–1658

English military and political leader Oliver Cromwell is best known for making England a republic and leading the Commonwealth of England. In 1628, he became an MP and supported Parliament in its struggles against the King. When war broke out, he helped to build a strong professional army to fight on the Parliamentarian side. Cromwell was a self-taught soldier, and helped establish the New Model Army from scratch. From 1653 until his death five years later, he was Lord Protector, the head of state of the Commonwealth of England. After his death, the monarchy was restored, and Charles II became king.

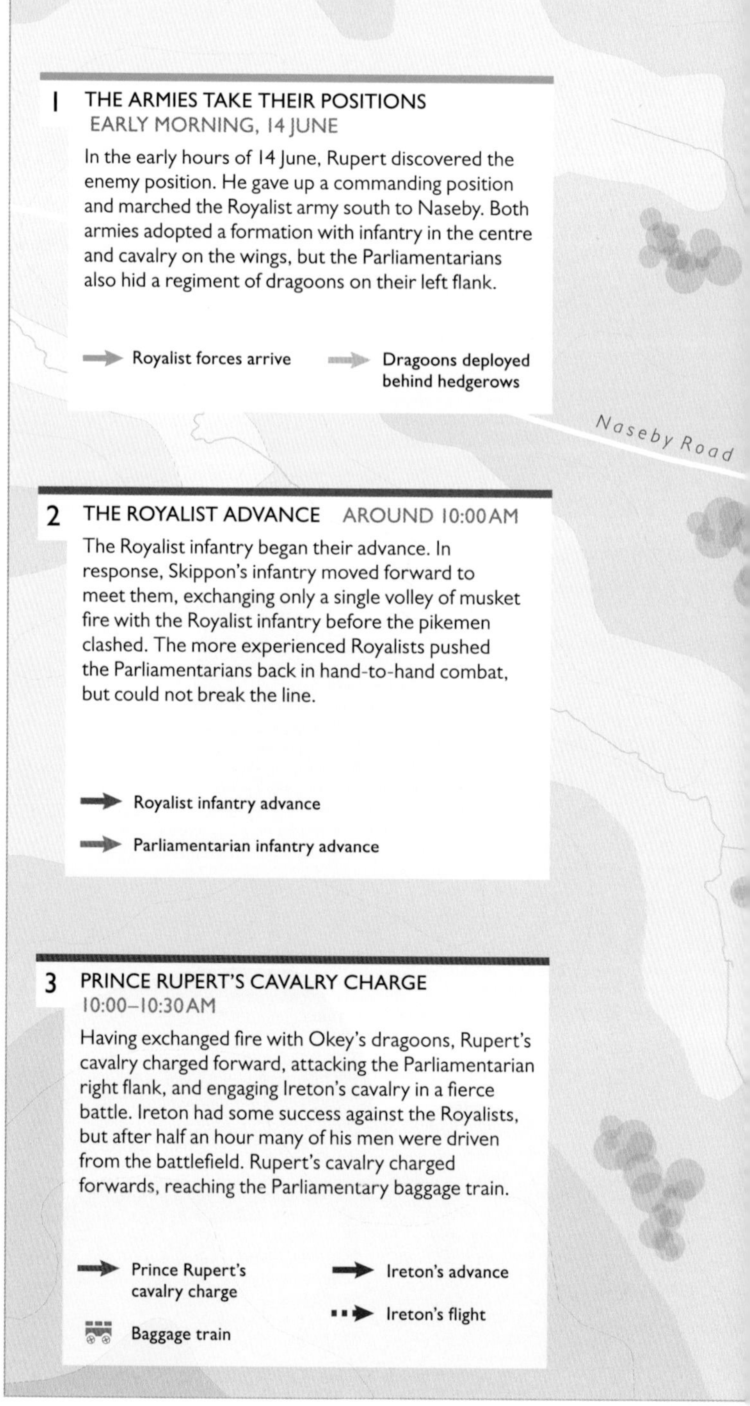
Naseby Road

THE ROYALISTS ATTACK

Prince Rupert's Royalist forces chose to engage the Parliamentarian forces in battle. They took up position outside the village of Naseby, in the English East Midlands.

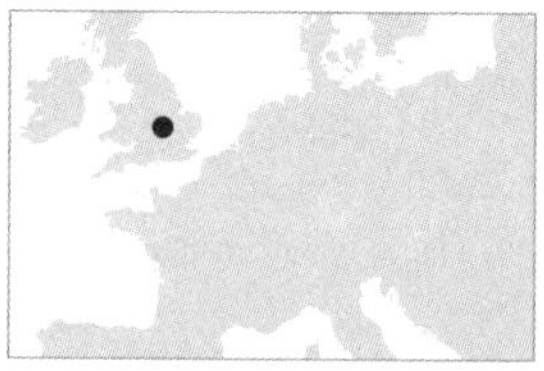

KEY

Town

PARLIAMENTARIAN FORCES: Infantry; Musketeers; Cavalry; Commander

ROYALIST FORCES: Infantry; Commander; Cavalry

TIMELINE

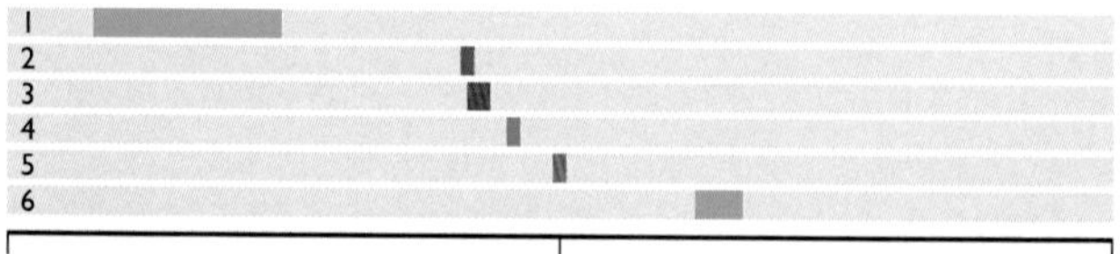
1
2
3
4
5
6
14 JUN 1645
12PM
15 JUN

1 THE ARMIES TAKE THEIR POSITIONS
EARLY MORNING, 14 JUNE

In the early hours of 14 June, Rupert discovered the enemy position. He gave up a commanding position and marched the Royalist army south to Naseby. Both armies adopted a formation with infantry in the centre and cavalry on the wings, but the Parliamentarians also hid a regiment of dragoons on their left flank.

→ Royalist forces arrive
→ Dragoons deployed behind hedgerows

2 THE ROYALIST ADVANCE AROUND 10:00 AM

The Royalist infantry began their advance. In response, Skippon's infantry moved forward to meet them, exchanging only a single volley of musket fire with the Royalist infantry before the pikemen clashed. The more experienced Royalists pushed the Parliamentarians back in hand-to-hand combat, but could not break the line.

→ Royalist infantry advance
→ Parliamentarian infantry advance

3 PRINCE RUPERT'S CAVALRY CHARGE
10:00–10:30 AM

Having exchanged fire with Okey's dragoons, Rupert's cavalry charged forward, attacking the Parliamentarian right flank, and engaging Ireton's cavalry in a fierce battle. Ireton had some success against the Royalists, but after half an hour many of his men were driven from the battlefield. Rupert's cavalry charged forwards, reaching the Parliamentary baggage train.

→ Prince Rupert's cavalry charge
→ Ireton's advance
→ Ireton's flight
Baggage train

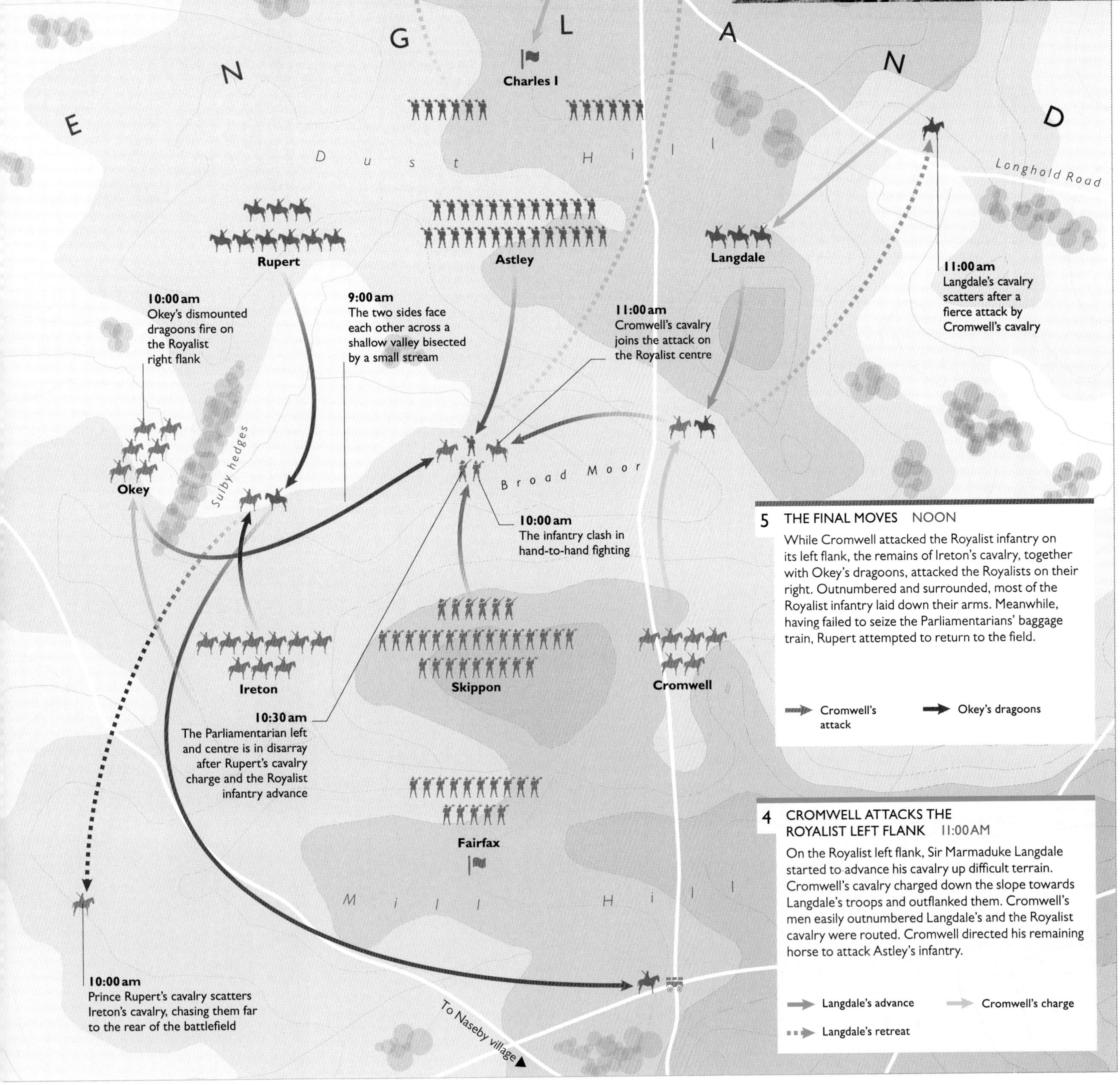
Sibbertoft
Mid-afternoon
King Charles retreats as his few remaining troops flee the battlefield in disorder
Charles I
E N G L A N D
Dust Hill
Longhold Road
Rupert
Astley
Langdale
11:00 am
Langdale's cavalry scatters after a fierce attack by Cromwell's cavalry
10:00 am
Okey's dismounted dragoons fire on the Royalist right flank
9:00 am
The two sides face each other across a shallow valley bisected by a small stream
11:00 am
Cromwell's cavalry joins the attack on the Royalist centre
Okey
Sulby hedges
Broad Moor
10:00 am
The infantry clash in hand-to-hand fighting
Ireton
Skippon
Cromwell
10:30 am
The Parliamentarian left and centre is in disarray after Rupert's cavalry charge and the Royalist infantry advance
Fairfax
Mill Hill
10:00 am
Prince Rupert's cavalry scatters Ireton's cavalry, chasing them far to the rear of the battlefield
To Naseby village

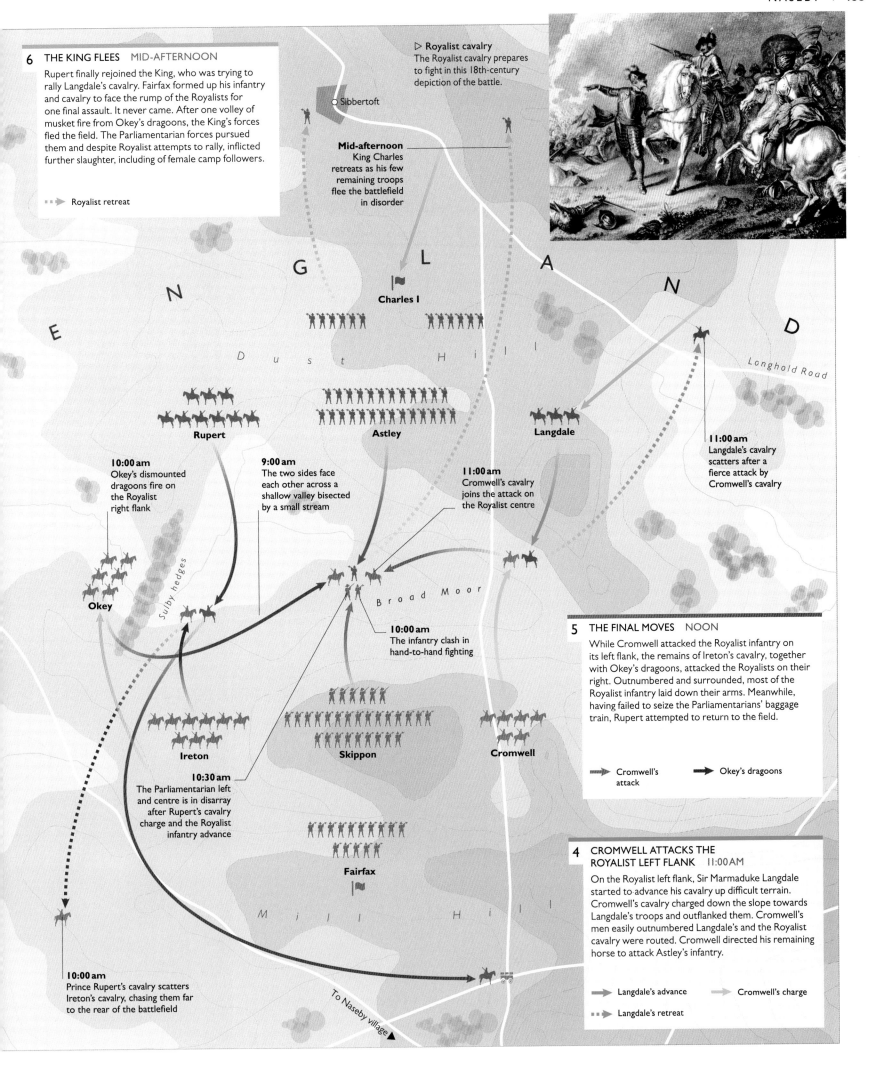

6 THE KING FLEES MID-AFTERNOON

Rupert finally rejoined the King, who was trying to rally Langdale's cavalry. Fairfax formed up his infantry and cavalry to face the rump of the Royalists for one final assault. It never came. After one volley of musket fire from Okey's dragoons, the King's forces fled the field. The Parliamentarian forces pursued them and despite Royalist attempts to rally, inflicted further slaughter, including of female camp followers.

Royalist retreat

▷ **Royalist cavalry**
The Royalist cavalry prepares to fight in this 18th-century depiction of the battle.

5 THE FINAL MOVES NOON

While Cromwell attacked the Royalist infantry on its left flank, the remains of Ireton's cavalry, together with Okey's dragoons, attacked the Royalists on their right. Outnumbered and surrounded, most of the Royalist infantry laid down their arms. Meanwhile, having failed to seize the Parliamentarians' baggage train, Rupert attempted to return to the field.

Cromwell's attack
Okey's dragoons

4 CROMWELL ATTACKS THE ROYALIST LEFT FLANK 11:00AM

On the Royalist left flank, Sir Marmaduke Langdale started to advance his cavalry up difficult terrain. Cromwell's cavalry charged down the slope towards Langdale's troops and outflanked them. Cromwell's men easily outnumbered Langdale's and the Royalist cavalry were routed. Cromwell directed his remaining horse to attack Astley's infantry.

Langdale's advance
Cromwell's charge
Langdale's retreat

THE SIEGE OF VIENNA

On 12 September 1683, John III Sobieski led an army to relieve the Ottoman Turkish siege of Vienna. Decided by reputedly the largest cavalry charge in history, Sobieski's victory heralded the end of Ottoman dominance in Eastern Europe.

▷ **Relief of the siege**
In this contemporary Dutch engraving of the siege and battle of Vienna, the encampments of the Ottoman Turks can be seen ringing the star-shaped fortifications protecting Vienna. In the foreground are some of the many baggage camels used by the Turks.

Since 1664, the Habsburg-Ottoman borders in Hungary had enjoyed peace. When Hungarian Protestants and others led by Imre Thokoly rebelled against the Roman Catholic Habsburgs from 1681, they appealed to Ottoman Grand Vizier Kara Mustafa Pasha, who came to their aid with over 100,000 men. On 14 July 1683, he besieged the Habsburg capital, Vienna. The city was well prepared, with strengthened walls, a bolstered garrison, and its suburbs razed so they could not provide cover. Turkish artillery had little impact on the city walls, but in time food supplies in Vienna ran low; disease afflicted both armies.

On 11 September, Sobieski and Charles of Lorraine arrived with around 80,000 German and Polish soldiers. Under Sobieski, they assembled north and northwest of Vienna. On the morning of 12 September, the army swept down on the Turkish encampments. Kara Mustafa diverted part of his forces from the siege while trying to take the city, but the Turkish resistance crumbled after Sobieski charged with around 18,000 horsemen. Under attack from all sides, including from the Vienna garrison, the Turks fled. Sobieski's victory set the stage for the reconquest of Hungary and marked the end of Ottoman expansion into Europe.

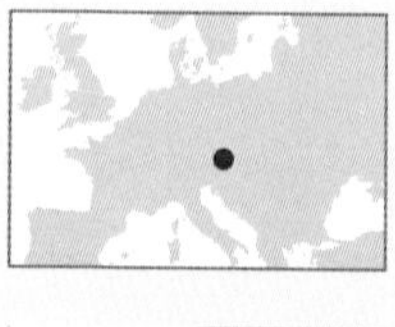

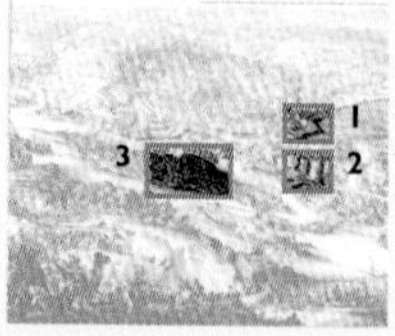

3
1
2

KEY

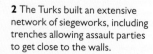

1 The star-shaped defences held out just long enough against the Turks bombarding and mining them.

2 The Turks built an extensive network of siegeworks, including trenches allowing assault parties to get close to the walls.

3 Leopoldstadt island was taken by the Turks, but its bridges were destroyed and the river was too fast and deep to attack the main city.

"We have to save to-day, not a single city, but the whole of Christendom."

KING JOHN III SOBIESKI, QUOTED IN *THE SIEGES OF VIENNA BY THE TURKS*, 1879

ORDER OF BATTLE

During the morning of 12 September, Charles of Lorraine's men on the allied left slowly but steadily advanced down the rough terrain on the east end of the Kahlenberg ridge, pushing the Turks back. Meanwhile the Ottoman Janissary and *Sipahi* units fiercely attacked the city. By late afternoon, Sobieski's men were formed up on the open ground on the allied right. Charles was pressing forward on the left, when Sobieski launched a large-scale cavalry attack and smashed through the Turkish lines.

KEY

- Towns
- Ottoman forces
- Ottoman attacks
- Ottoman retreats
- Polish forces
- Sobieski's advance
- Charles of Lorraine's advance

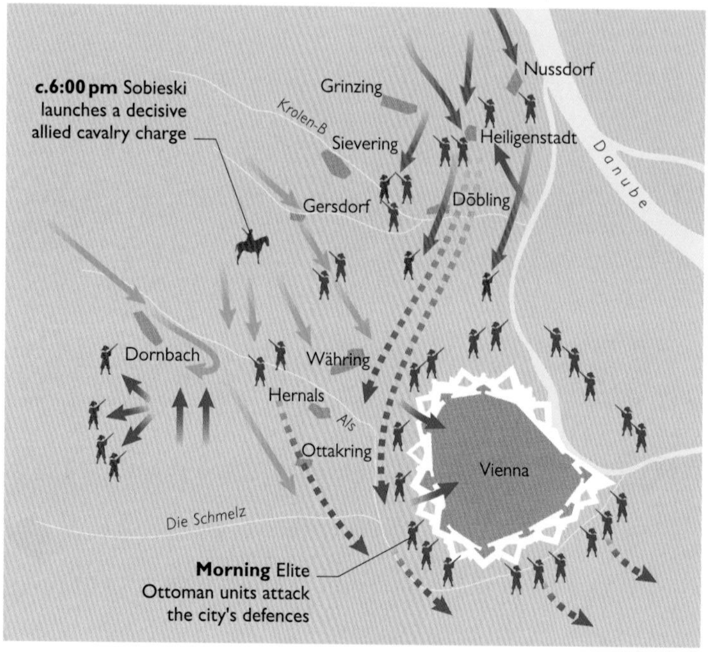

c.6:00 pm Sobieski launches a decisive allied cavalry charge
Grinzing
Nussdorf
Krolen-B
Sievering
Heiligenstadt
Danube
Gersdorf
Döbling
Dornbach
Währing
Hernals
Als
Ottakring
Vienna
Die Schmelz
Morning Elite Ottoman units attack the city's defences

Amstelodami apud Nicolaum Visscher
cum Privil. Ordin. General.

DIRECTORY: 1500–1700

MARIGNANO
13–14 SEPTEMBER 1515

Between 1494 and 1559, France, Spain, and the Italian states fought for the control of Italy in a series of wars that involved much of Europe. In 1515, the conflict centred on the Duchy of Milan, then in the hands of the Old Swiss Confederacy (a loose federation of small independent states within the Holy Roman Empire). The French army, led by King Francis I, crossed the Alps with 72 cannons to retake Milan. The two armies met on 13 September at the village of Marignano (present-day Melegnano), southeast of Milan. The French, numbering around 30,000, outnumbered the Swiss who had little more than 20,000 soldiers, but they could not secure a victory. The following day, the French cannons continued to batter the advancing Swiss infantry, regarded as the best in Europe. It was only after the arrival of a Venetian force to reinforce the French that the Swiss finally withdrew. The French victory returned the Duchy of Milan to Francis I, and the Perpetual Peace Treaty, signed at Fribourg on 29 November 1516, ushered in several hundred years of close cooperation between the Swiss and the French.

△ 16th-century pen-and-ink illustration of Marignano

RIDANIYA
22 JANUARY 1517

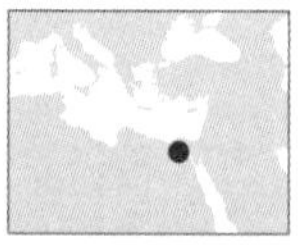

The period following the conquest of Constantinople (see p.96) was marked by an Ottoman bid for expansion. Sultan Selim I pushed south to attack the Mamluk Sultanate, which ruled over Egypt as well as the holy cities of Mecca, Medina, and Jerusalem. After defeating the Mamluk forces at Marj Dabik, Syria, in 1516, Selim's army marched towards Cairo, Egypt.

The Mamluk sultan Tuman bay II and his army were entrenched at Ridaniya outside the city, and on 22 January the two sides clashed. The main body of the Ottoman force attacked the Mamluk troops and a cavalry force attacked their flank. Tuman reached Selim's tent with a group of men, and the Grand Vizier of the Ottoman Empire, Hadım Sinan Pasha, was killed in the ensuing action. However, Tuman's forces were eventually routed. While Tuman fled up the Nile, Selim took Cairo and captured Caliph Al-Mutawakkil II, the 17th and last caliph of the Mamluk Sultanate. Tuman continued guerrilla activities against the Ottomans until he was captured and hanged in April 1517. Selim went on to annex the entire Mamluk Sultanate to the Ottoman Empire.

ALCAZARQUIVIR
4 AUGUST 1578

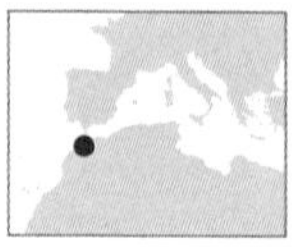

In 1578, Sebastian I of Portugal invaded Morocco to help Abu Abdallah Mohammed II regain power after he was deposed as sultan by his uncle, Abd Al-Malik I. On 24 June, Sebastian sailed from the Algarve, carrying nearly 20,000 soldiers and considerable artillery to Portuguese Morocco. After landing south of Tangiers, he was joined by Abu Abdallah and 6,000 Moorish troops.

They marched into the interior, where they met Abd Al-Malik and his much larger army on 4 August, at the Wadi al-Makhāzin near Ksar el-Kebir (Alcazarquivir). Abd Al-Malik drew up his forces on a broad front, with 10,000 cavalry on the wings and the Moors in the centre. After exchanging several volleys of musket and artillery fire, the two sides advanced. The Portuguese flanks gave way as the Sultan's cavalry encircled them. After four hours of fighting, Sebastian and Abu Adbdallah's army was defeated – about 8,000 died, including King Sebastian and most of the Portuguese nobles, and almost all the rest were captured. The battle soon brought an end to the Aviz dynasty (1385–1580) in Portugal, and the kingdom was integrated into the Iberian Union under the Spanish Philippine dynasty for 60 years.

COUTRAS
20 OCTOBER 1587

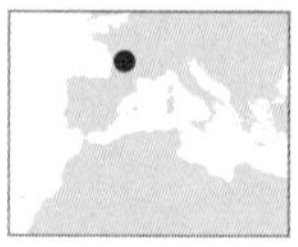

Between 1562 and 1598, France was wracked by war between the Roman Catholics and the Reformist Protestant Huguenots. On 18 July 1585, the French king Henry III reluctantly issued an edict banishing all Protestants from the kingdom, effectively declaring war against the Protestants and their figurehead, the Huguenot heir presumptive to the French throne, Henry of Navarre. Philip II of Spain fomented this tangled conflict by supporting the Catholic League under Henry of Lorraine, creating the "War of the Three Henrys". On 20 October 1587, Henry of Navarre met the royalist commander, the Duke of Joyeuse, in a battle at Coutras in the Aquitaine region in southwest France. Joyeuse mispositioned his artillery and squandered his first cavalry charge. Meanwhile, Navarre made excellent use of his artillery and drew up his troops with platoons of musketeers nestled within the cavalry squadrons as support. The royalist army was broken by a charge from the Protestant light cavalry, and Joyeuse was captured and executed. The battle was the first major Protestant victory in battle. Navarre took the throne in 1589 after Henry III died, but had to convert to Catholicism in 1593 to keep it.

MYONGYANG

16 SEPTEMBER 1597

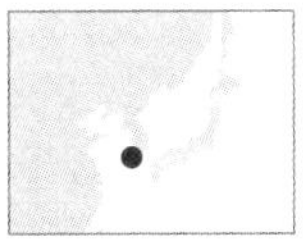

In a battle later known as the "Miracle of Myongyang", Admiral Yi Sunsin led the Korean Joseon Kingdom's navy to victory against the Japanese navy as it sought to take control of the Yellow Sea. The Korean fleet had been decimated by the Japanese at Chilchonryang earlier that year, and Yi is said to have had only 13 *panokseons* (cannon-armed vessels propelled by sails and oars) to face ten times as many Japanese warships.

The tactically brilliant Yi used his knowledge of the local conditions to change the odds. After holding off the Japanese at Oranpo, Yi withdrew to the Myongyang Strait, where the strong currents changed direction every three hours. When the Japanese fleet entered the Strait, it was carried towards the Yellow Sea, straight to where Yi's ships were waiting in the narrow passage to unleash a barrage of cannon fire and fire arrows. By the time the currents changed, the Japanese fleet was already in chaos. Japan lost around 30 ships and many of its officers in the battle, and the fleet commander Todo Takatora was wounded.

LÜTZEN

16 NOVEMBER 1632

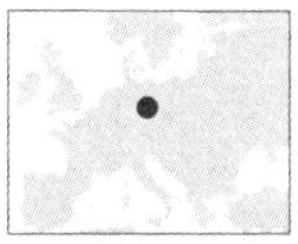

After victory at Breitenfeld (see pp.130–31), the Swedish king Gustavus Adolphus led the Allied forces of the Protestant Union and Sweden south to Bavaria (in southern Germany), where they were eventually pushed back by the Imperial Roman Catholic Army under commander Albrecht von Wallenstein. In September 1632, Wallenstein's forces invaded Saxony, and the two sides clashed at Lützen on 16 November. Both forces were relatively evenly matched as they advanced through fog towards each other – each army had around 20,000 troops. The Swedes began well, driving forward on the right. Count Pappenheim arrived with Imperial reinforcements but was fatally wounded by a cannonball. In the early afternoon, as Gustavus Adolphus led a cavalry charge on the heavily engaged flank, he was separated from his men. He was shot several times, stabbed, and was found fallen from his horse. The rest of the Swedish line was repulsed by the Imperial centre and right; determined to avenge their king, they returned to the fray and eventually captured the Imperial guns after bitter fighting. Wallenstein retreated under cover of night. The battle was one of the most important of the Thirty Years War (1618–48) and ended the Catholic threat to Saxony. However, with the death of Gustavus Adolphus, the "Lion of the North", the Protestant cause lost one of its most able leaders and Sweden lost the king who had overseen its rise as one of Europe's great powers.

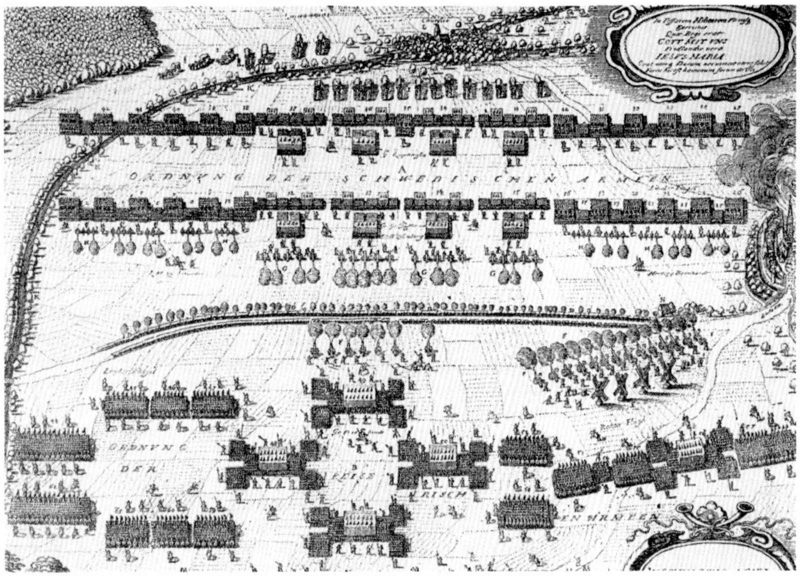

◁ Plan showing the Protestant Swedish Army arrayed against the Roman Catholic Imperial Army at Lützen

SOLEBAY

7 JUNE 1672

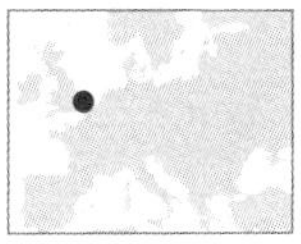

In April 1672, the English king Charles II declared war on the Dutch Republic. By early June 1672, the allied English and French fleets were anchored in Southwold Bay (also called Solebay) on the Suffolk coast in East England, under the command of the Duke of York. The Dutch fleet surprised them at dawn on 7 June with the wind in its sails. The allied ships hastily prepared for battle and struggled out to sea.

Whether a deliberate decision or due to a misunderstanding, the Comte d'Estrées, commanding the French fleet, steered the 30 French ships south and engaged only at long range, while most of the Dutch fleet focused its attacks on the 60 English ships. The *Royal James*, the flagship of the Earl of Sandwich, was raked with broadsides at point blank range and then struck by a fire ship. The fighting ended at sunset with both fleets losing many men and having many ships damaged. Although inconclusive, the Battle of Solebay still ended Anglo-French plans to blockade the Dutch.

△ The burning of HMS *Royal James* in the battle

THE BOYNE

1 JULY 1690

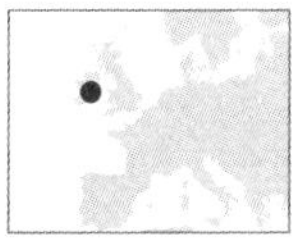

In the Glorious Revolution of 1688, the Catholic King of England and Ireland, James II, was deposed by his nephew and son-in-law, the Protestant William III, known as William of Orange. Determined to regain his crown, James landed in Ireland in 1689 with an under-equipped force of French troops and English, Scottish, and Irish volunteers. He quickly gained control of most of Ireland and moved to Dublin. In June 1690, William landed in Ulster and headed south with around 36,000 men, including professional soldiers from Holland and Denmark armed with modern flintlocks.

APPARUIT ET DISSIPAVIT
LIBERATA HIBERNIA
MDCLXXXX

△ Medal commemorating the battle

The two armies met on 1 July 1690 on the banks of the River Boyne, 48km (30 miles) north of Dublin. William sent a third of his men to cross the river at Roughgrange in a flanking manoeuvre, and James sent half his army to meet them. The two forces never engaged – they were kept apart by a swampy ravine throughout the battle. Meanwhile, William's elite Dutch Blue Guards drove back the Jacobite infantry at the Oldbridge ford. The Jacobite cavalry held them there until William's cavalry crossed the river, forcing the Jacobites to retreat. James fled to France, leaving his still largely intact army to fight a desperate rearguard action. After the battle, Dublin and Waterford soon capitulated and by the end of 1691, all of southern Ireland had been subdued. The battle marked the start of Ireland's social, political, and economic domination by the Protestant minority.

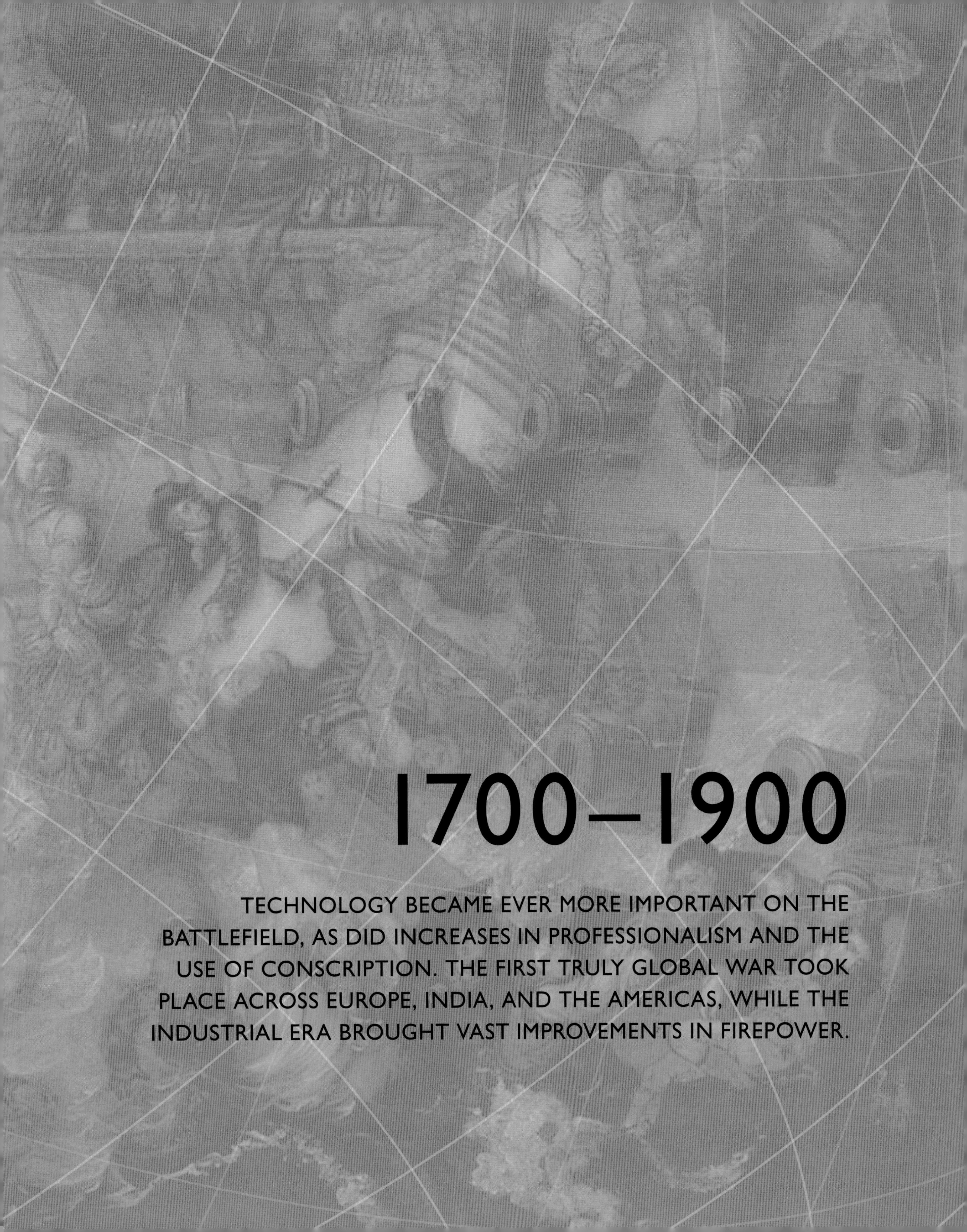

1700–1900

TECHNOLOGY BECAME EVER MORE IMPORTANT ON THE BATTLEFIELD, AS DID INCREASES IN PROFESSIONALISM AND THE USE OF CONSCRIPTION. THE FIRST TRULY GLOBAL WAR TOOK PLACE ACROSS EUROPE, INDIA, AND THE AMERICAS, WHILE THE INDUSTRIAL ERA BROUGHT VAST IMPROVEMENTS IN FIREPOWER.

△ **Imperial crest**
This silver-plated grenadier's cap plate shows the crest of Tsar Peter III, whose grandfather Peter the Great made Russia a reputable military power around 1700.

▽ **Doomed charge**
British painter Elizabeth Thompson depicts the charge of the Royal Scots Greys at Waterloo in her 19th-century painting *Scotland Forever*. The Scots overran a French infantry formation but were decimated by the reserve cavalry.

1700–1900

Warfare changed radically in the 18th and 19th centuries. Professional armies and navies fought wars on a global scale, while massed conscripts clashed in their hundreds of thousands. The exploitation of new technologies and resources became just as important as fighting spirit.

By 1700, European powers were still embroiled in the dynastic conflicts they had conducted for centuries. Although the Duke of Marlborough's Anglo-Austrian army that beat the French in 1714 during the War of the Spanish Succession was large compared to its predecessors, and the Duke himself was a military genius, the technology and tactics he deployed were generally similar to those used earlier.

The Seven Years War (1756–63) signalled a change. Beginning as a territorial dispute between Austria and Prussia over Silesia (in present-day central Europe), it spiralled into the first truly global conflict, involving not only France and Britain but also their colonial possessions in North America and India. Frederick the Great of Prussia honed his growing army into a formidable fighting force. His heavy infantry, drilled in rapid battlefield manoeuvres, outfought their less well-drilled opponents. Aided by the king's tactical brilliance, they won stunning victories such as at Leuthen (see p.151) in 1757.

> *"Now, more than ever, the artillery is the indispensable companion of the infantry."*
>
> GENERAL COLMAR VON DER GOLTZ, 1883

Large armies trained to perform traditional manoeuvres proved to be of less use in North America, where the American colonies rose up against Britain over political rights and unjust taxation. With local knowledge and adept use of skirmishing tactics and long rifles, the Americans won a War of Independence in 1783. They also laid the framework for a new style of army, composed of citizen-soldiers, which the French took up and refined after their own revolution in 1789. Within five years, the French army had become a million-strong force, and increasingly began to employ professional leaders to replace old aristocratic officers. Such a massive force required new tactics and organization. Napoleon Bonaparte, whose exceptional leadership was clear from his first commands in Italy where he won victories such as at Marengo (see pp.160–61), came up with these tactics and streamlined military logistics.

CHANGING TIMES

The scope, cost, and casualties of war rose between 1700 and 1900. The size of armies, their professionalism, and the advent of new firearms made warfare a more lethal and expensive proposition. Access to greater manpower resources, money, and technology, and the ability to build global alliances became the prerequisites of military success. As a result of this shift, non-European states struggling against the colonial domination of Europe were left at a distinct disadvantage.

WARFARE
POLITICS
TECHNOLOGY

1700 · 1720 · 1740 · 1760 · 1780

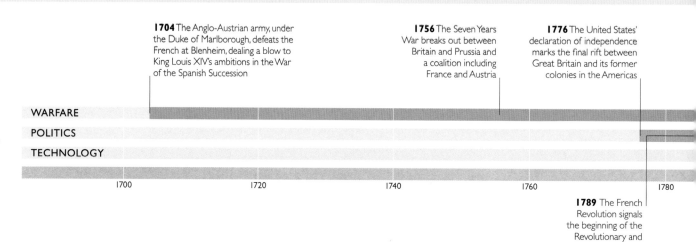

1704 The Anglo-Austrian army, under the Duke of Marlborough, defeats the French at Blenheim, dealing a blow to King Louis XIV's ambitions in the War of the Spanish Succession

1756 The Seven Years War breaks out between Britain and Prussia and a coalition including France and Austria

1776 The United States' declaration of independence marks the final rift between Great Britain and its former colonies in the Americas

1789 The French Revolution signals the beginning of the Revolutionary and Napoleonic Wars

◁ **Crucial invention**
American-born British inventor Hiram Maxim operates the Maxim gun, an early type of machine gun that he invented in 1884. Its rapid rate of fire allowed small numbers of troops massive killing power.

Napoleon developed the corps as independent smaller formations within his army, and aggressively used outflanking manoeuvres to destroy his opponents from the rear. He insisted that his troops live off the land by foraging to reduce dependence on traditional supply lines. These organizational and strategic innovations won Napoleon some stunning successes until the opposing coalitions matched them and turned the tables, leading to his downfall in 1814 and final defeat at Waterloo (see pp.178–79).

The industrialization of war

By the mid-19th century, mass recruitment in combination with growing industrialization led to the first truly modern armies. The Union and Confederate armies, which fought in the American Civil War (1861–65) over the issue of slavery, adopted technologies such as the railway and the telegraph. They also took up new types of firearms, such as groove-barrelled rifles firing minié balls (bullets for rifled muskets) that provided greater range and lethality. This made infantry charges, such as the Confederates' final throw at the Battle of Gettysburg (see pp.186–87), potentially suicidal. In this new environment, non-European armies struggled to compete with the advancing technology of European interlopers, winning only occasional victories, such as the Zulu triumph against the British at Isandlwana (see p.193) in 1879, in the face of tactically inept opponents. Mostly, though, their fate was that of the Sudanese Mahdists at Omdurman (see p.195) – cut down by Maxim guns as they tried to charge against the British forces. In warfare, the future would belong to those who combined this superior technology with effective tactics and strategic leadership.

△ **Final push**
Union troops resist as General George Pickett's Confederate infantry struggles to reach the crest of Cemetery Ridge during the Battle of Gettysburg (see pp.186–87). The charge cost the Confederacy several thousand casualties, and marked the clear defeat of Lee's invasion of the north.

1800 · 1820 · 1840 · 1860 · 1880 · 1900

1805 Admiral Horatio Nelson's victory at Trafalgar begins a century of British naval dominance

1815 An Anglo-Prussian army defeats Napoleon Bonaparte, leading to his renewed deposition and exile

1815 The Congress of Vienna establishes a new political order after the turmoil of the Napoleonic Wars

1830 The opening of the first intercity railway ushers in a period where troops can be moved by rail

1833 The electric telegraph is developed, helping news move rapidly between capitals and the battle front

1849 The French army adopts Claude-Etienne Minié's minié ball – a bullet that expands in the grooved barrels of rifles making them easier to load and increasing the range of firearms

1861–65 The American Civil War is fought between the Union and the Confederate states

1862 American inventor Richard Gatling develops the Gatling gun, the first reliable machine gun to be capable of rapid bursts of fire

1863 General Robert E. Lee's defeat at Gettysburg derails the Confederacy's attempt to cut off Union railway supply lines in Harrisburg, Pennsylvania, and forces the Union into a political solution to end the war

1871 The defeat of France and capture of Napoleon III is followed by German unification into the German Empire, as well as similar unification in Italy when Italian forces take Rome

1876 American general George Custer is defeated by a Native American coalition led by Lakota-Sioux at Little Bighorn

BLENHEIM

In the War of the Spanish Succession (1701–14) between France and the Grand Alliance, Blenheim was key in checking initial French gains. The Duke of Marlborough marched from the Netherlands to the Danube, before leading the Grand Alliance to victory on 13 August 1704 through a bloody but decisive succession of attacks.

In 1700, the Habsburg king of Spain, Charles II, died and left his throne to Philip, the grandson of the Bourbon French king Louis XIV. This succession fuelled a rivalry between the two great houses of Europe that broke out into war in 1701. On one side was France and its allies, including Bavaria; on the other side was the Grand Alliance, comprising the Holy Roman Empire, Britain, and the United Provinces of the Netherlands.

In 1704, a Franco-Bavarian force advanced on Vienna, threatening to destroy the Austrian Habsburgs and break the Grand Alliance. To relieve the pressure on Austria, the British commander, the Duke of Marlborough, marched an army from the Low Countries in just five weeks. He was joined by allied forces on the way. The Grand Alliance forces surprised the enemy army when they took up their positions near the town of Blindheim (Blenheim) on the banks of the Danube. Across a wide plain were the Franco-Bavarian forces commanded by the Elector of Bavaria, Marshal Marsin, and Marshal Tallard. They occupied a long rise between the heavily defended villages of Lutzingen, Oberglau, and Blenheim. After heavy fighting on 13 August, Marlborough pinned down the enemy forces in the three villages. He then launched the main body of his attack, driving through Tallard's forces in the centre to secure a spectacular victory for the Grand Alliance.

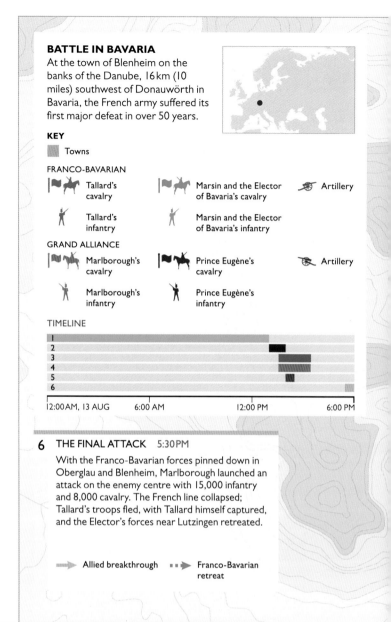

BATTLE IN BAVARIA

At the town of Blenheim on the banks of the Danube, 16 km (10 miles) southwest of Donauwörth in Bavaria, the French army suffered its first major defeat in over 50 years.

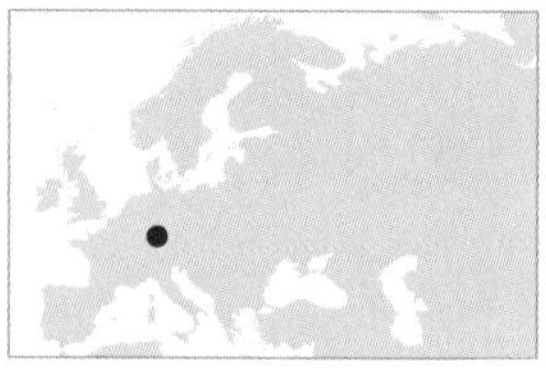

KEY

Towns

FRANCO-BAVARIAN

- Tallard's cavalry
- Marsin and the Elector of Bavaria's cavalry
- Artillery
- Tallard's infantry
- Marsin and the Elector of Bavaria's infantry

GRAND ALLIANCE

- Marlborough's cavalry
- Prince Eugène's cavalry
- Artillery
- Marlborough's infantry
- Prince Eugène's infantry

TIMELINE

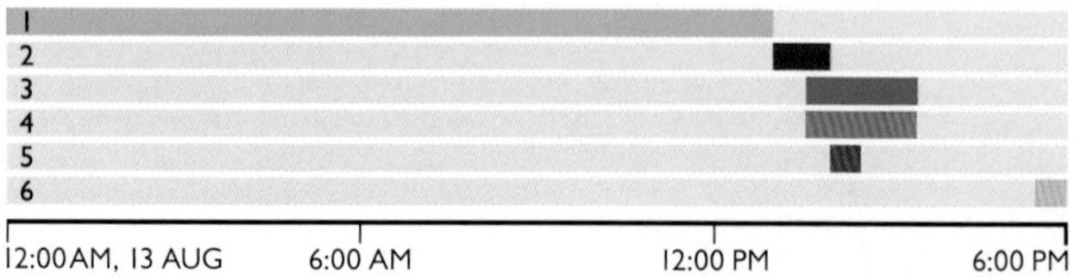

1
2
3
4
5
6
12:00AM, 13 AUG
6:00 AM
12:00 PM
6:00 PM

6 THE FINAL ATTACK 5:30PM

With the Franco-Bavarian forces pinned down in Oberglau and Blenheim, Marlborough launched an attack on the enemy centre with 15,000 infantry and 8,000 cavalry. The French line collapsed; Tallard's troops fled, with Tallard himself captured, and the Elector's forces near Lutzingen retreated.

Allied breakthrough — Franco-Bavarian retreat

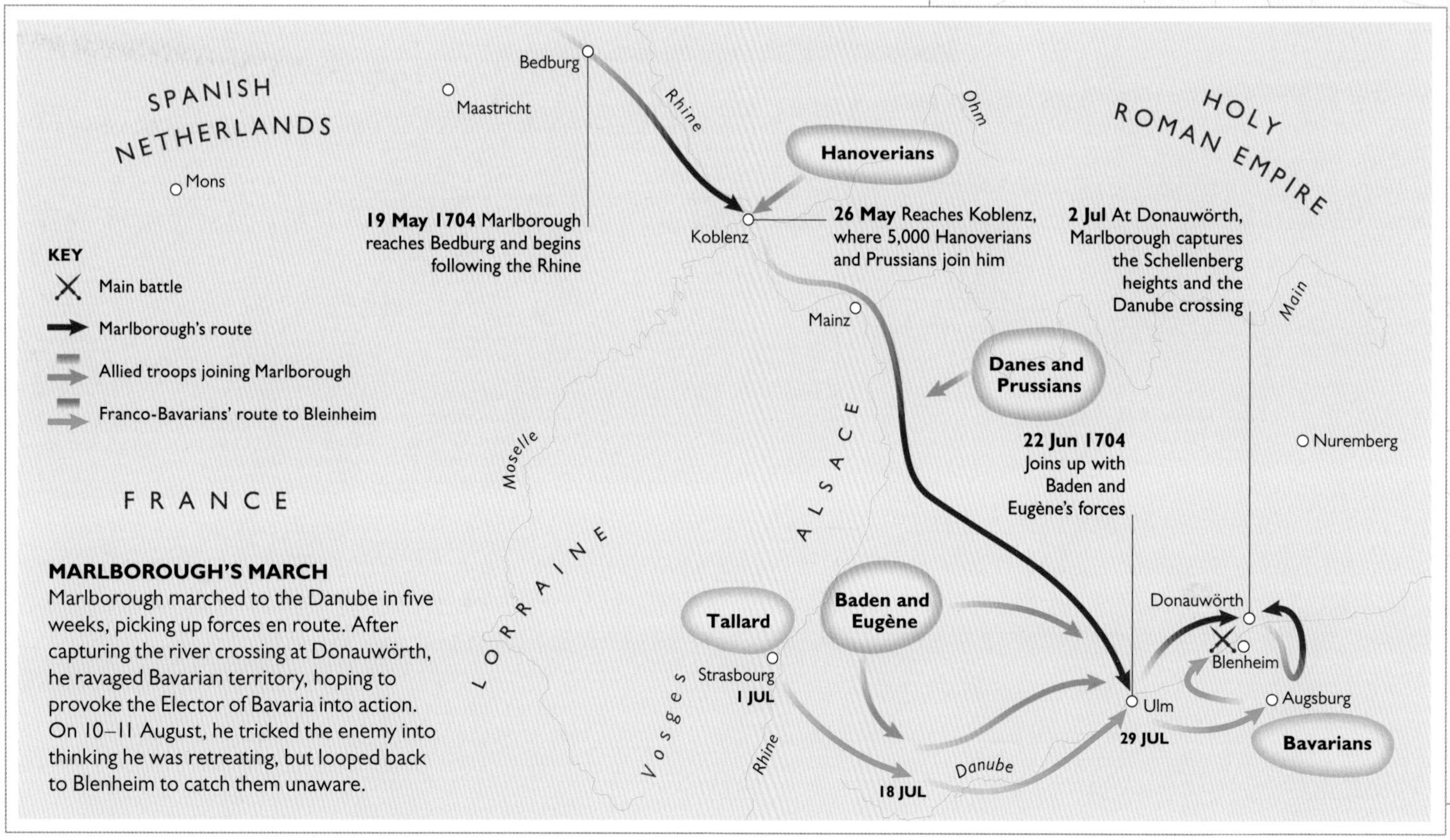

SPANISH NETHERLANDS
Maastricht
Mons
Bedburg
Rhine
Ohm
HOLY ROMAN EMPIRE
Hanoverians
19 May 1704 Marlborough reaches Bedburg and begins following the Rhine
Koblenz
26 May Reaches Koblenz, where 5,000 Hanoverians and Prussians join him
2 Jul At Donauwörth, Marlborough captures the Schellenberg heights and the Danube crossing
Main
Mainz
KEY
Main battle
Marlborough's route
Allied troops joining Marlborough
Franco-Bavarians' route to Bleinheim
Danes and Prussians
Nuremberg
22 Jun 1704 Joins up with Baden and Eugène's forces
Moselle
FRANCE
ALSACE
LORRAINE
Tallard
Baden and Eugène
Donauwörth
Blenheim
Strasbourg
1 JUL
Vosges
Rhine
Ulm
29 JUL
Augsburg
Bavarians
Danube
18 JUL

MARLBOROUGH'S MARCH

Marlborough marched to the Danube in five weeks, picking up forces en route. After capturing the river crossing at Donauwörth, he ravaged Bavarian territory, hoping to provoke the Elector of Bavaria into action. On 10–11 August, he tricked the enemy into thinking he was retreating, but looped back to Blenheim to catch them unaware.

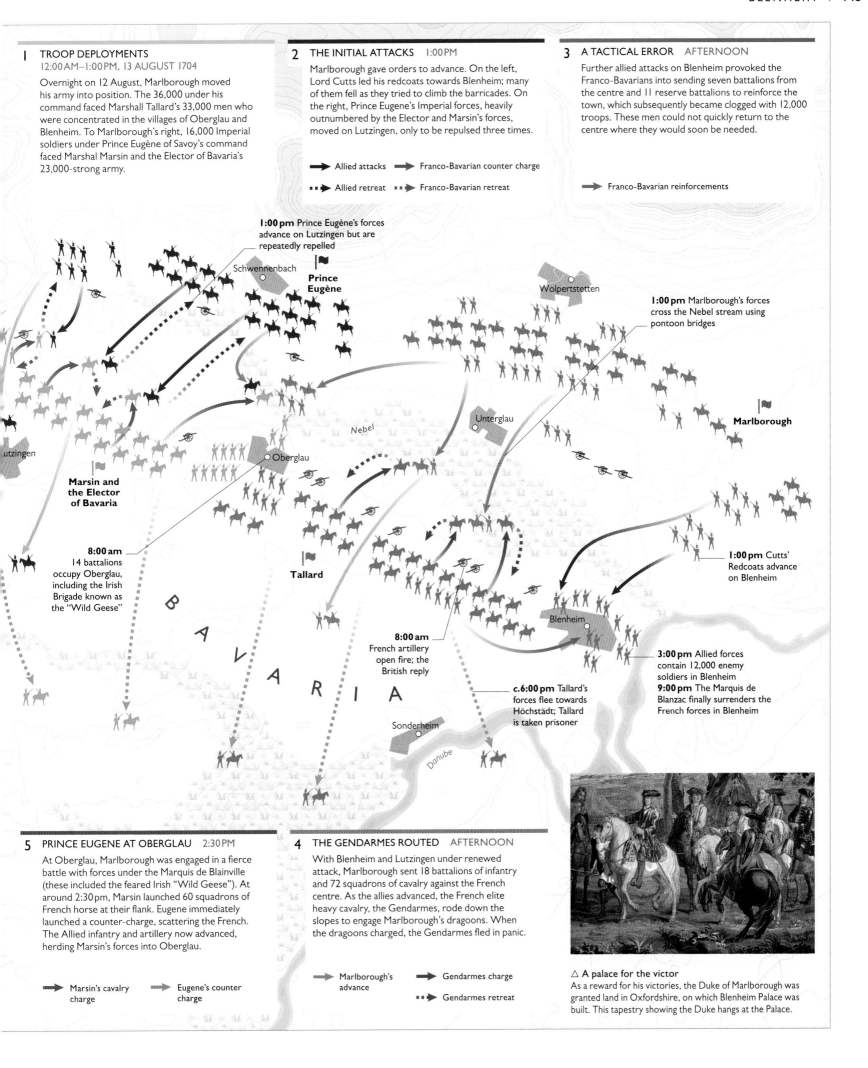

1 TROOP DEPLOYMENTS 12:00AM–1:00PM, 13 AUGUST 1704

Overnight on 12 August, Marlborough moved his army into position. The 36,000 under his command faced Marshall Tallard's 33,000 men who were concentrated in the villages of Oberglau and Blenheim. To Marlborough's right, 16,000 Imperial soldiers under Prince Eugène of Savoy's command faced Marshal Marsin and the Elector of Bavaria's 23,000-strong army.

2 THE INITIAL ATTACKS 1:00PM

Marlborough gave orders to advance. On the left, Lord Cutts led his redcoats towards Blenheim; many of them fell as they tried to climb the barricades. On the right, Prince Eugene's Imperial forces, heavily outnumbered by the Elector and Marsin's forces, moved on Lutzingen, only to be repulsed three times.

Allied attacks
Franco-Bavarian counter charge
Allied retreat
Franco-Bavarian retreat

3 A TACTICAL ERROR AFTERNOON

Further allied attacks on Blenheim provoked the Franco-Bavarians into sending seven battalions from the centre and 11 reserve battalions to reinforce the town, which subsequently became clogged with 12,000 troops. These men could not quickly return to the centre where they would soon be needed.

Franco-Bavarian reinforcements

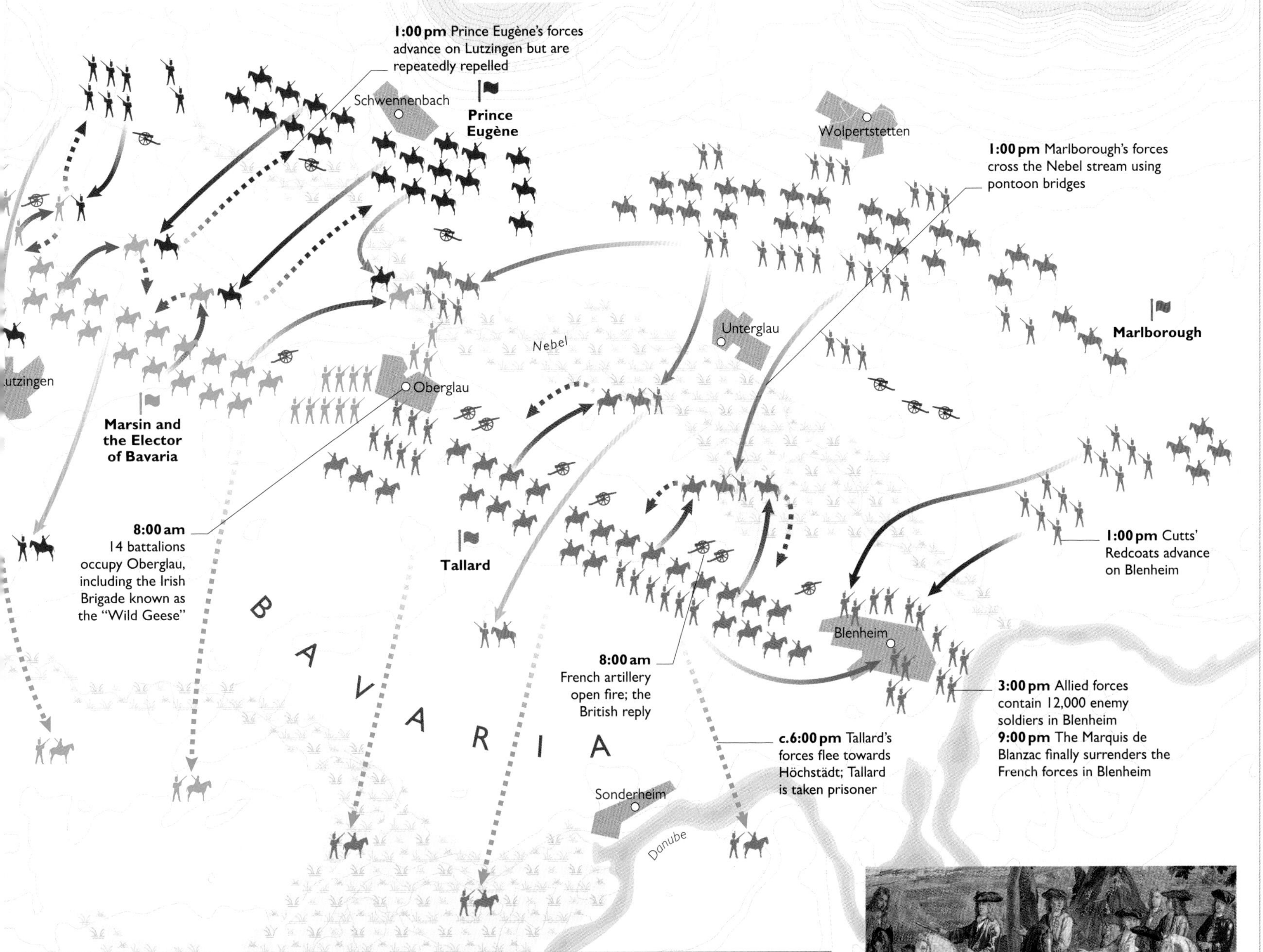
1:00 pm Prince Eugène's forces advance on Lutzingen but are repeatedly repelled
Schwennenbach
Prince Eugène
Wolpertstetten
1:00 pm Marlborough's forces cross the Nebel stream using pontoon bridges
Unterglau
Nebel
Marlborough
Lutzingen
Oberglau
Marsin and the Elector of Bavaria
8:00 am 14 battalions occupy Oberglau, including the Irish Brigade known as the "Wild Geese"
Tallard
1:00 pm Cutts' Redcoats advance on Blenheim
BAVARIA
Blenheim
8:00 am French artillery open fire; the British reply
3:00 pm Allied forces contain 12,000 enemy soldiers in Blenheim
9:00 pm The Marquis de Blanzac finally surrenders the French forces in Blenheim
c.6:00 pm Tallard's forces flee towards Höchstädt; Tallard is taken prisoner
Sonderheim
Danube

5 PRINCE EUGENE AT OBERGLAU 2:30PM

At Oberglau, Marlborough was engaged in a fierce battle with forces under the Marquis de Blainville (these included the feared Irish "Wild Geese"). At around 2:30pm, Marsin launched 60 squadrons of French horse at their flank. Eugene immediately launched a counter-charge, scattering the French. The Allied infantry and artillery now advanced, herding Marsin's forces into Oberglau.

Marsin's cavalry charge
Eugene's counter charge

4 THE GENDARMES ROUTED AFTERNOON

With Blenheim and Lutzingen under renewed attack, Marlborough sent 18 battalions of infantry and 72 squadrons of cavalry against the French centre. As the allies advanced, the French elite heavy cavalry, the Gendarmes, rode down the slopes to engage Marlborough's dragoons. When the dragoons charged, the Gendarmes fled in panic.

Marlborough's advance
Gendarmes charge
Gendarmes retreat

△ **A palace for the victor**
As a reward for his victories, the Duke of Marlborough was granted land in Oxfordshire, on which Blenheim Palace was built. This tapestry showing the Duke hangs at the Palace.

THE RISE OF RUSSIA

Charles XII attacked Russia from Grodno, his base in Poland. After their defeat at Poltava, the Swedes lost control of their empire as Peter the Great's Russia came to dominate the Polish and Baltic lands.

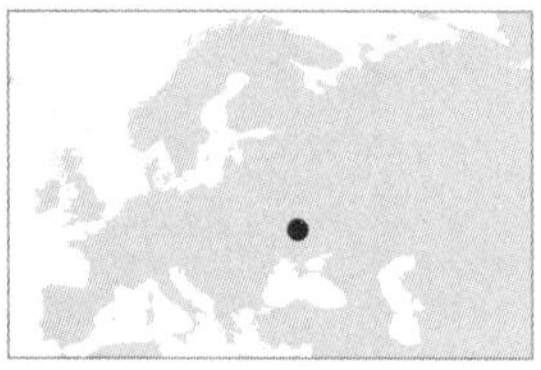

KEY

- Towns
- SWEDISH FORCES: Commander, Infantry, Cavalry
- RUSSIAN FORCES: Infantry, Cavalry, Artillery
- Redoubts
- Fortifications

TIMELINE

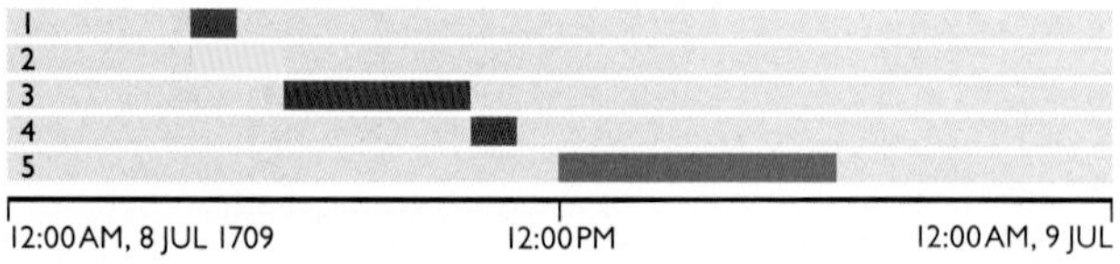
1
2
3
4
5
12:00 AM, 8 JUL 1709
12:00 PM
12:00 AM, 9 JUL

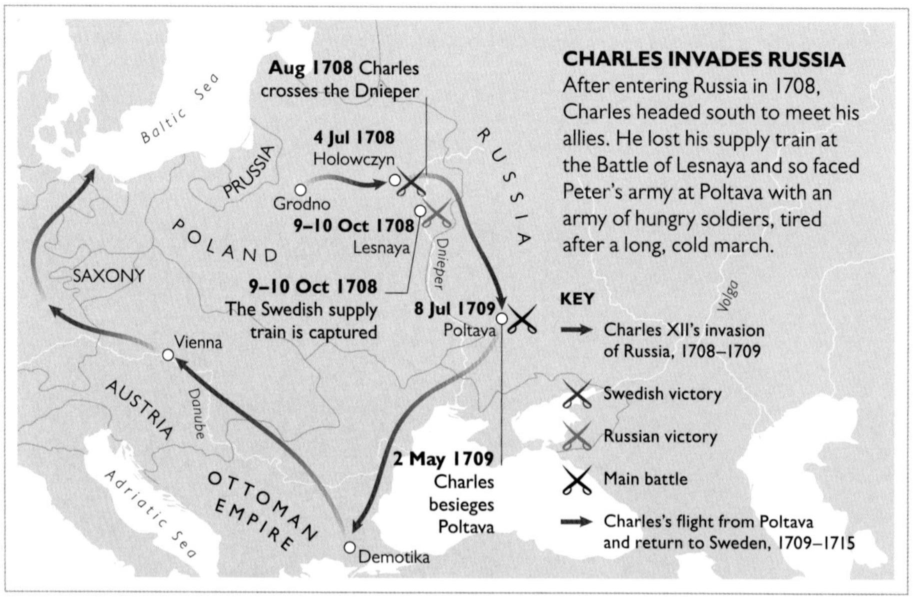
Baltic Sea
PRUSSIA
POLAND
SAXONY
AUSTRIA
RUSSIA
OTTOMAN EMPIRE
Adriatic Sea
Danube
Dnieper
Volga
Vienna
Grodno
Demotika
Aug 1708 Charles crosses the Dnieper
4 Jul 1708 Holowczyn
9–10 Oct 1708 Lesnaya
9–10 Oct 1708 The Swedish supply train is captured
8 Jul 1709 Poltava
2 May 1709 Charles besieges Poltava

CHARLES INVADES RUSSIA

After entering Russia in 1708, Charles headed south to meet his allies. He lost his supply train at the Battle of Lesnaya and so faced Peter's army at Poltava with an army of hungry soldiers, tired after a long, cold march.

KEY

- Charles XII's invasion of Russia, 1708–1709
- Swedish victory
- Russian victory
- Main battle
- Charles's flight from Poltava and return to Sweden, 1709–1715

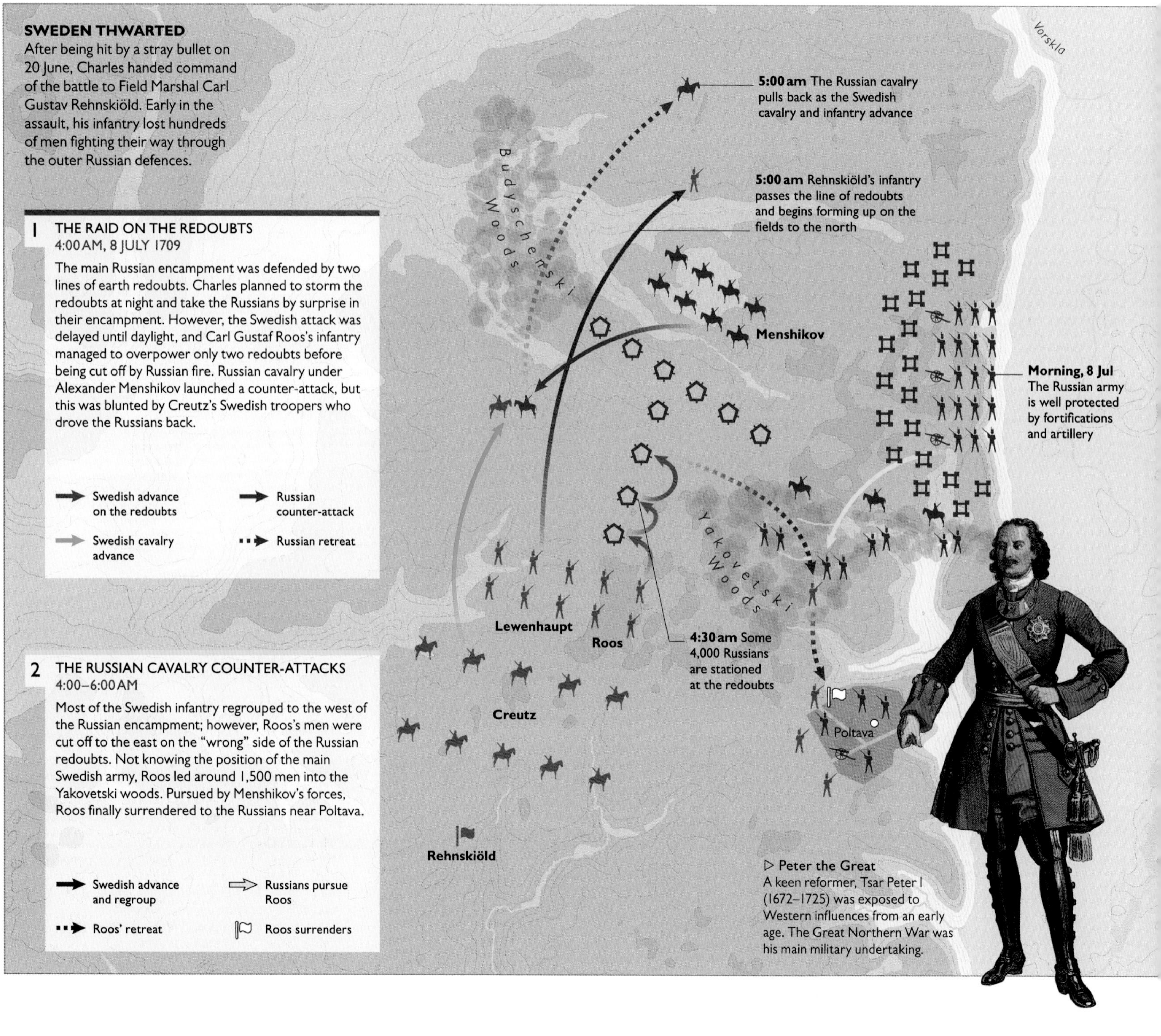
Vorskla
Budyschenski Woods
Yakovetski Woods
5:00 am The Russian cavalry pulls back as the Swedish cavalry and infantry advance
5:00 am Rehnskiöld's infantry passes the line of redoubts and begins forming up on the fields to the north
Menshikov
Morning, 8 Jul The Russian army is well protected by fortifications and artillery
Lewenhaupt
Roos
Creutz
Rehnskiöld
4:30 am Some 4,000 Russians are stationed at the redoubts
Poltava

SWEDEN THWARTED

After being hit by a stray bullet on 20 June, Charles handed command of the battle to Field Marshal Carl Gustav Rehnskiöld. Early in the assault, his infantry lost hundreds of men fighting their way through the outer Russian defences.

1 THE RAID ON THE REDOUBTS
4:00 AM, 8 JULY 1709

The main Russian encampment was defended by two lines of earth redoubts. Charles planned to storm the redoubts at night and take the Russians by surprise in their encampment. However, the Swedish attack was delayed until daylight, and Carl Gustaf Roos's infantry managed to overpower only two redoubts before being cut off by Russian fire. Russian cavalry under Alexander Menshikov launched a counter-attack, but this was blunted by Creutz's Swedish troopers who drove the Russians back.

- Swedish advance on the redoubts
- Russian counter-attack
- Swedish cavalry advance
- Russian retreat

2 THE RUSSIAN CAVALRY COUNTER-ATTACKS
4:00–6:00 AM

Most of the Swedish infantry regrouped to the west of the Russian encampment; however, Roos's men were cut off to the east on the "wrong" side of the Russian redoubts. Not knowing the position of the main Swedish army, Roos led around 1,500 men into the Yakovetski woods. Pursued by Menshikov's forces, Roos finally surrendered to the Russians near Poltava.

- Swedish advance and regroup
- Russians pursue Roos
- Roos' retreat
- Roos surrenders

▷ Peter the Great
A keen reformer, Tsar Peter I (1672–1725) was exposed to Western influences from an early age. The Great Northern War was his main military undertaking.

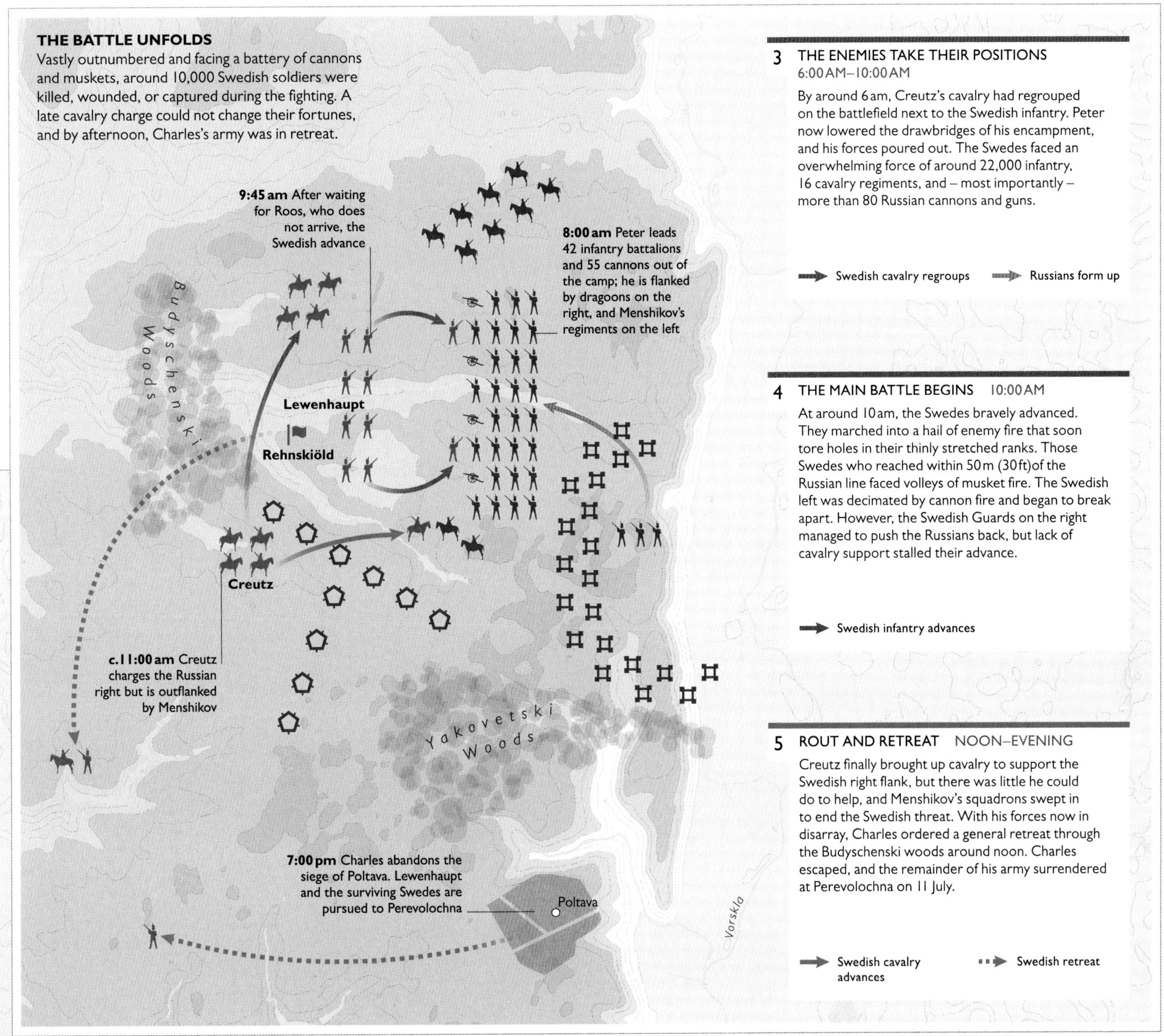
THE BATTLE UNFOLDS
Vastly outnumbered and facing a battery of cannons and muskets, around 10,000 Swedish soldiers were killed, wounded, or captured during the fighting. A late cavalry charge could not change their fortunes, and by afternoon, Charles's army was in retreat.
9:45 am After waiting for Roos, who does not arrive, the Swedish advance
8:00 am Peter leads 42 infantry battalions and 55 cannons out of the camp; he is flanked by dragoons on the right, and Menshikov's regiments on the left
Budyschenski Woods
Lewenhaupt
Rehnskiöld
Creutz
c.11:00 am Creutz charges the Russian right but is outflanked by Menshikov
Yakovetski Woods
7:00 pm Charles abandons the siege of Poltava. Lewenhaupt and the surviving Swedes are pursued to Perevolochna
Poltava
Vorskla
3 THE ENEMIES TAKE THEIR POSITIONS
6:00 AM–10:00 AM
By around 6 am, Creutz's cavalry had regrouped on the battlefield next to the Swedish infantry. Peter now lowered the drawbridges of his encampment, and his forces poured out. The Swedes faced an overwhelming force of around 22,000 infantry, 16 cavalry regiments, and – most importantly – more than 80 Russian cannons and guns.
Swedish cavalry regroups
Russians form up
4 THE MAIN BATTLE BEGINS 10:00 AM
At around 10 am, the Swedes bravely advanced. They marched into a hail of enemy fire that soon tore holes in their thinly stretched ranks. Those Swedes who reached within 50 m (30 ft)of the Russian line faced volleys of musket fire. The Swedish left was decimated by cannon fire and began to break apart. However, the Swedish Guards on the right managed to push the Russians back, but lack of cavalry support stalled their advance.
Swedish infantry advances
5 ROUT AND RETREAT NOON–EVENING
Creutz finally brought up cavalry to support the Swedish right flank, but there was little he could do to help, and Menshikov's squadrons swept in to end the Swedish threat. With his forces now in disarray, Charles ordered a general retreat through the Budyschenski woods around noon. Charles escaped, and the remainder of his army surrendered at Perevolochna on 11 July.
Swedish cavalry advances
Swedish retreat

POLTAVA

In July 1709, Tsar Peter the Great and the Russian army defeated the Swedish forces of King Charles XII at Poltava, in present-day Ukraine. Peter's victory signalled the beginning of Russian supremacy in northeast Europe and decline of the Swedish Empire as a great power.

The Great Northern War (1700–21) began by Poland-Saxony, Russia, and Denmark attempting to dismantle the Swedish Empire, which had dominated the Baltic region for a century. By 1709, however, it had become a contest between two ambitious rulers: the gifted general Charles XII of Sweden, and Peter I, who was transforming Russia into a powerful modern state. Charles's army invaded Russia in 1708, and after a cold, crippling march, arrived at the fortified town of Poltava (in the territory of the Cossack Hetmanate), which it besieged. Eager to break the siege and crush the Swedes, Peter deployed his army of around 40,000 (against more than 25,000) in a encampment protected by ten redoubts. The Swedes planned an audacious, surprise night advance, which failed: a third of the attacking infantry was caught in the redoubts, and the rest were overwhelmed by the full weight of the Russian army.

ADVANCES IN SIEGE WARFARE

Across Europe, the design of fortifications and the conduct of sieges entered a new era in the late 17th century as innovative engineers made significant developments in construction and tactics.

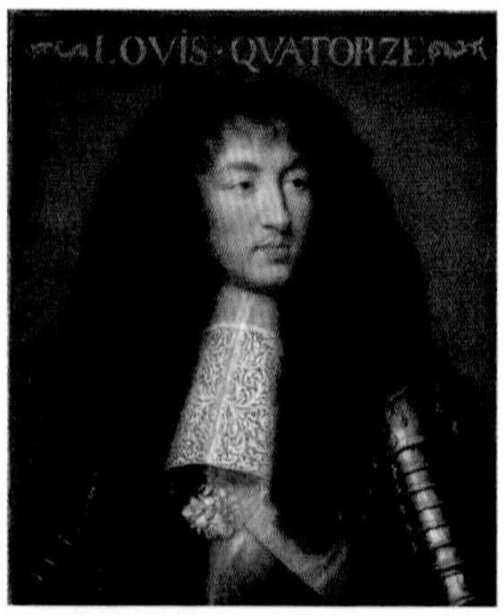
LOVIS·QVATORZE

△ **Reign of sieges**
The French king Louis XIV oversaw the construction of several fortifications along France's frontiers, and was present at half of Vauban's 40 sieges.

Siege warfare had been a prominent feature of European warfare since the 11th century, when castles became widespread and sieges began to outnumber pitched battles. The introduction of cannons in the 15th century revolutionized castle design, resulting in the development of "star forts" – polygonal fortresses with bastions protruding at each angle – designed to withstand cannon fire.

By the start of the 17th century, fortifications had become more complex and added outworks such as ravelins to the star-fort design (see below). Structures were built lower and used earth to better withstand cannon fire. By Louis XIV's reign (1643–1715) in France, sieges had become the focal point of conflicts. The influence of the king's chief engineer, Sébastien le Prestre de Vauban (later Marquis), on the design of fortifications and siege warfare was huge. A scientific approach allowed him to adapt siege warfare to incorporate increasingly powerful guns. Vauban also constructed fortresses and fortified cities, and built two lines of forts along France's northeastern frontier.

Weaponry evolved for siege warfare, including mortars that launched explosive shells over walls or into siege trenches, and grenades hurled by grenadiers, a new type of elite soldier.

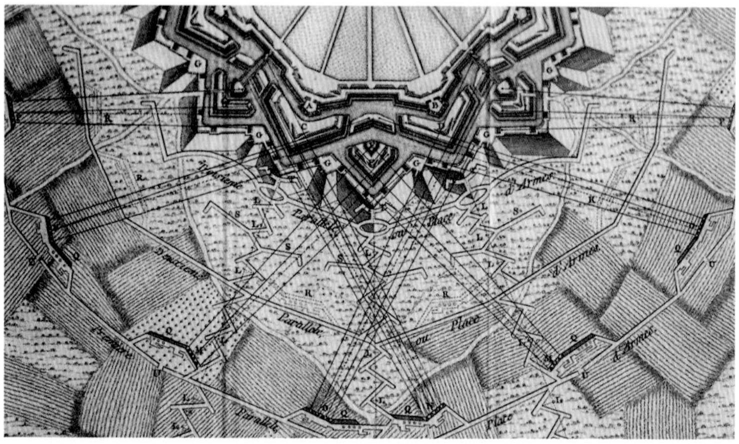

△ **Enhanced Spanish defenses**
This plan of a mid-17th century fortification in Badajoz shows improvements made to the star-fort design. Wedge-shaped bastions, or outworks, called "ravelins" or "demi-lunes", provided tactical advantage for artillery fire.

Louis XIV's assault, 1673
The king's army besieges the fortress city of Maastricht in this 17th-century painting by Flemish painter Adam Frans van der Meulen. The French army overcame the Dutch defenses within a month, and this siege saw the introduction of the siege parallel by Vauban.

PLASSEY

Treachery and luck helped secure the British East India Company a victory over the Nawab of Bengal supported by a few French guns at Plassey, Bengal, on 23 June 1757. The battle helped secure British domination in India.

In the 1750s, French, Dutch, and British companies competed for trade in Bengal. The Nawab (ruler) of Bengal, Siraj-ud-Daula, resented the trade practices and colonial ambitions of the British East India Company (EIC), so in June 1756 he marched with a large army and captured the British trading post of Calcutta (Kolkata). EIC reinforcements under Colonel Robert Clive retook the city in January 1757. By this time, Britain and France were fighting in what became the Seven Years War (see p.142), so Clive decided to capture the French trading base at Chandernagore (Chandannager). This prompted the Nawab to ally with the French in a bid to oust the British. At a battle fought near Plassey (Palashi) on 23 June, the British were outnumbered. Some Bengali commanders, however, including their chief Mir Jafar, had secretly agreed not to fight. This, together with the enemy's lack of usable powder, helped Clive win the battle.

△ **Nawab's artillery**
The Bengali artillery pieces, complete with gunners, cannonballs, and powder, were carried on giant platforms. These were pulled by teams of 50 oxen, sometimes assisted by elephants.

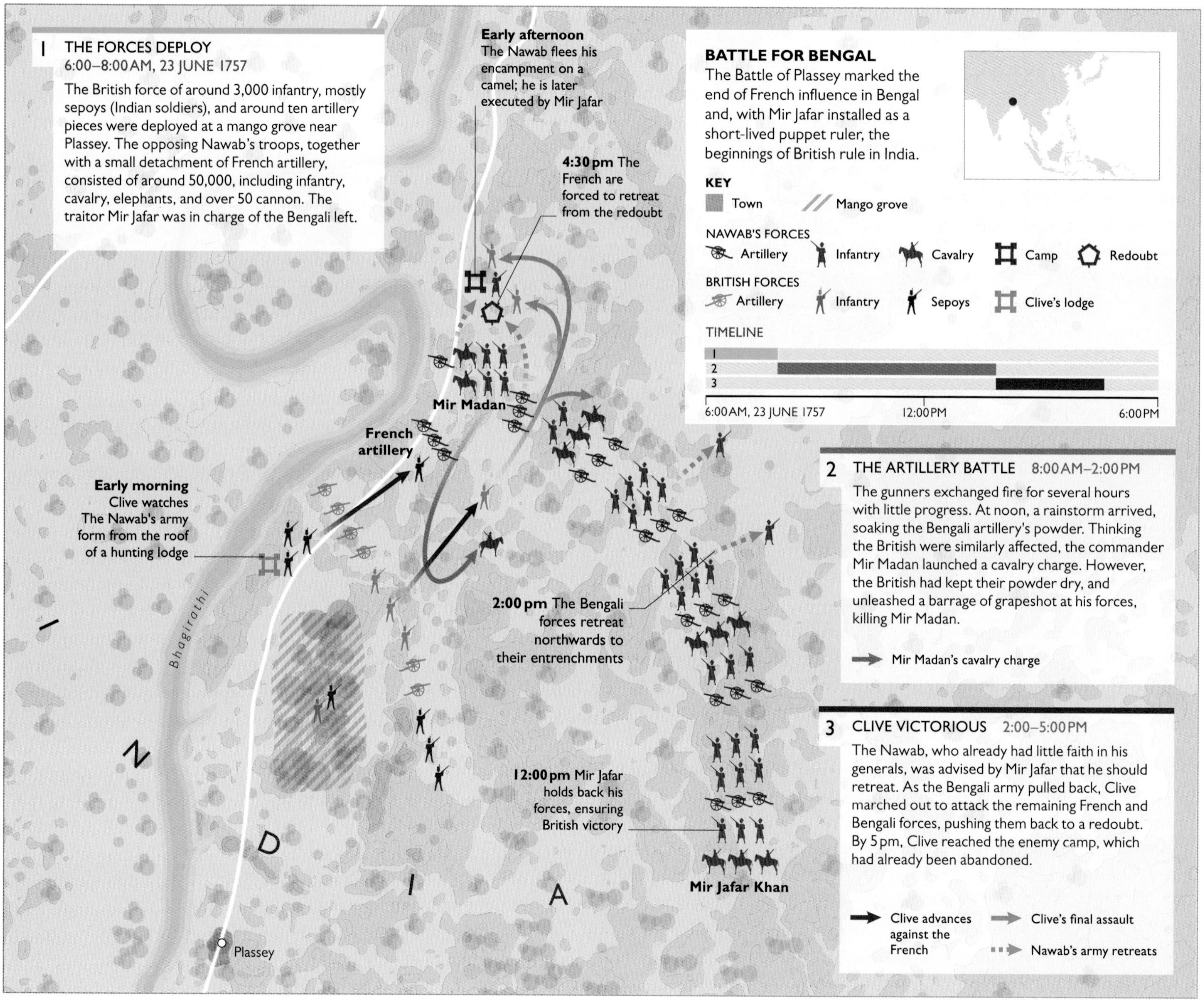
1 THE FORCES DEPLOY
6:00–8:00 AM, 23 JUNE 1757
The British force of around 3,000 infantry, mostly sepoys (Indian soldiers), and around ten artillery pieces were deployed at a mango grove near Plassey. The opposing Nawab's troops, together with a small detachment of French artillery, consisted of around 50,000, including infantry, cavalry, elephants, and over 50 cannon. The traitor Mir Jafar was in charge of the Bengali left.
Early afternoon
The Nawab flees his encampment on a camel; he is later executed by Mir Jafar
4:30 pm The French are forced to retreat from the redoubt
BATTLE FOR BENGAL
The Battle of Plassey marked the end of French influence in Bengal and, with Mir Jafar installed as a short-lived puppet ruler, the beginnings of British rule in India.
KEY
Town
Mango grove
NAWAB'S FORCES
Artillery
Infantry
Cavalry
Camp
Redoubt
BRITISH FORCES
Artillery
Infantry
Sepoys
Clive's lodge
TIMELINE
1
2
3
6:00 AM, 23 JUNE 1757
12:00 PM
6:00 PM
Mir Madan
French artillery
Early morning
Clive watches
The Nawab's army
form from the roof
of a hunting lodge
Bhagirathi
2:00 pm The Bengali forces retreat northwards to their entrenchments
2 THE ARTILLERY BATTLE 8:00 AM–2:00 PM
The gunners exchanged fire for several hours with little progress. At noon, a rainstorm arrived, soaking the Bengali artillery's powder. Thinking the British were similarly affected, the commander Mir Madan launched a cavalry charge. However, the British had kept their powder dry, and unleashed a barrage of grapeshot at his forces, killing Mir Madan.
Mir Madan's cavalry charge
3 CLIVE VICTORIOUS 2:00–5:00 PM
The Nawab, who already had little faith in his generals, was advised by Mir Jafar that he should retreat. As the Bengali army pulled back, Clive marched out to attack the remaining French and Bengali forces, pushing them back to a redoubt. By 5 pm, Clive reached the enemy camp, which had already been abandoned.
12:00 pm Mir Jafar holds back his forces, ensuring British victory
Mir Jafar Khan
I N D I A
Plassey
Clive advances against the French
Clive's final assault
Nawab's army retreats

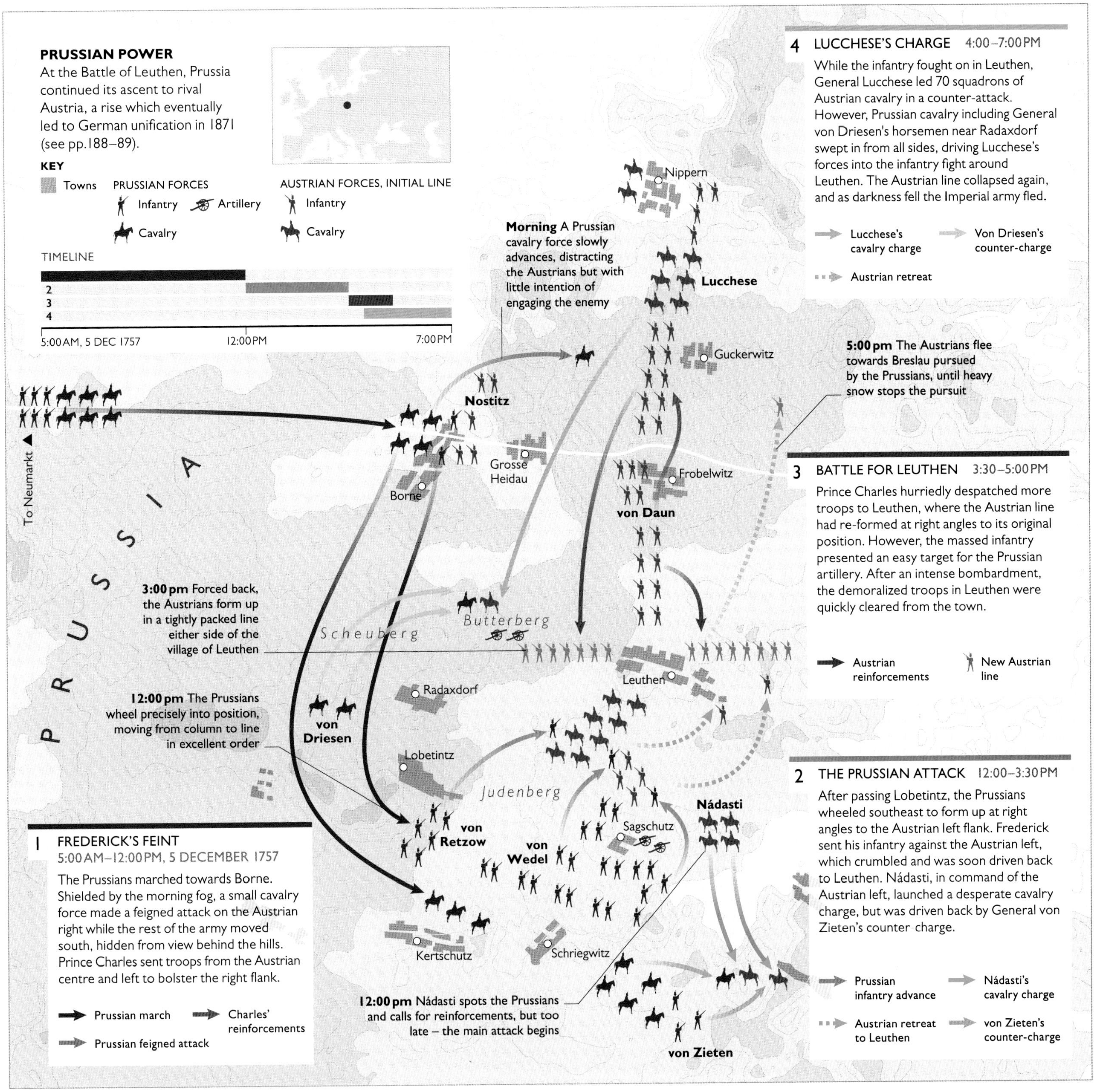
PRUSSIAN POWER
At the Battle of Leuthen, Prussia continued its ascent to rival Austria, a rise which eventually led to German unification in 1871 (see pp.188–89).
KEY
Towns
PRUSSIAN FORCES
Infantry
Artillery
Cavalry
AUSTRIAN FORCES, INITIAL LINE
Infantry
Cavalry
TIMELINE
1
2
3
4
5:00AM, 5 DEC 1757
12:00PM
7:00PM
4 LUCCHESE'S CHARGE 4:00–7:00PM
While the infantry fought on in Leuthen, General Lucchese led 70 squadrons of Austrian cavalry in a counter-attack. However, Prussian cavalry including General von Driesen's horsemen near Radaxdorf swept in from all sides, driving Lucchese's forces into the infantry fight around Leuthen. The Austrian line collapsed again, and as darkness fell the Imperial army fled.
Lucchese's cavalry charge
Von Driesen's counter-charge
Austrian retreat
Morning A Prussian cavalry force slowly advances, distracting the Austrians but with little intention of engaging the enemy
Nippern
Lucchese
Guckerwitz
5:00 pm The Austrians flee towards Breslau pursued by the Prussians, until heavy snow stops the pursuit
Nostitz
Grosse Heidau
Borne
Frobelwitz
von Daun
To Neumarkt
PRUSSIA
3 BATTLE FOR LEUTHEN 3:30–5:00PM
Prince Charles hurriedly despatched more troops to Leuthen, where the Austrian line had re-formed at right angles to its original position. However, the massed infantry presented an easy target for the Prussian artillery. After an intense bombardment, the demoralized troops in Leuthen were quickly cleared from the town.
Austrian reinforcements
New Austrian line
3:00 pm Forced back, the Austrians form up in a tightly packed line either side of the village of Leuthen
Scheuberg
Butterberg
Leuthen
Radaxdorf
12:00 pm The Prussians wheel precisely into position, moving from column to line in excellent order
von Driesen
Lobetintz
Judenberg
Nádasti
2 THE PRUSSIAN ATTACK 12:00–3:30PM
After passing Lobetintz, the Prussians wheeled southeast to form up at right angles to the Austrian left flank. Frederick sent his infantry against the Austrian left, which crumbled and was soon driven back to Leuthen. Nádasti, in command of the Austrian left, launched a desperate cavalry charge, but was driven back by General von Zieten's counter charge.
Sagschutz
von Retzow
von Wedel
1 FREDERICK'S FEINT
5:00AM–12:00PM, 5 DECEMBER 1757
The Prussians marched towards Borne. Shielded by the morning fog, a small cavalry force made a feigned attack on the Austrian right while the rest of the army moved south, hidden from view behind the hills. Prince Charles sent troops from the Austrian centre and left to bolster the right flank.
Prussian march
Charles' reinforcements
Prussian feigned attack
Kertschutz
Schriegwitz
12:00 pm Nádasti spots the Prussians and calls for reinforcements, but too late – the main attack begins
von Zieten
Prussian infantry advance
Nádasti's cavalry charge
Austrian retreat to Leuthen
von Zieten's counter-charge

LEUTHEN

The 1757 Battle of Leuthen was one of the key battles in the Seven Years War. Frederick II of Prussia achieved victory against a much larger Austrian army, and his audacious flanking manoeuvre confirmed his reputation as Europe's foremost military commander.

In Europe, the main conflict of the Seven Years War (see p.142) centred on attempts by France and the Austrian Habsburg Empire to constrain an expansionist Prussia led by Frederick II. In late 1757, Frederick returned from facing the French to confront the Austrians, who had retaken Silesia. On 5 December, an Imperial force of over 60,000 under Prince Charles of Lorraine and Count von Daun gathered at Leuthen (Lutynia, in modern-day Poland) to tackle Frederick. The vast Austrian army, stretching 8km (5 miles) across, faced Frederick's force of around 35,000 men, situated on a low line of hills. After feinting towards the Austrian right, Frederick moved his troops, hidden by the hills, across the enemy front to attack the Austrian left – a bold move that required great discipline from his troops. Losses were heavy on both sides, but Frederick's tactic paid off and the Austrians were routed.

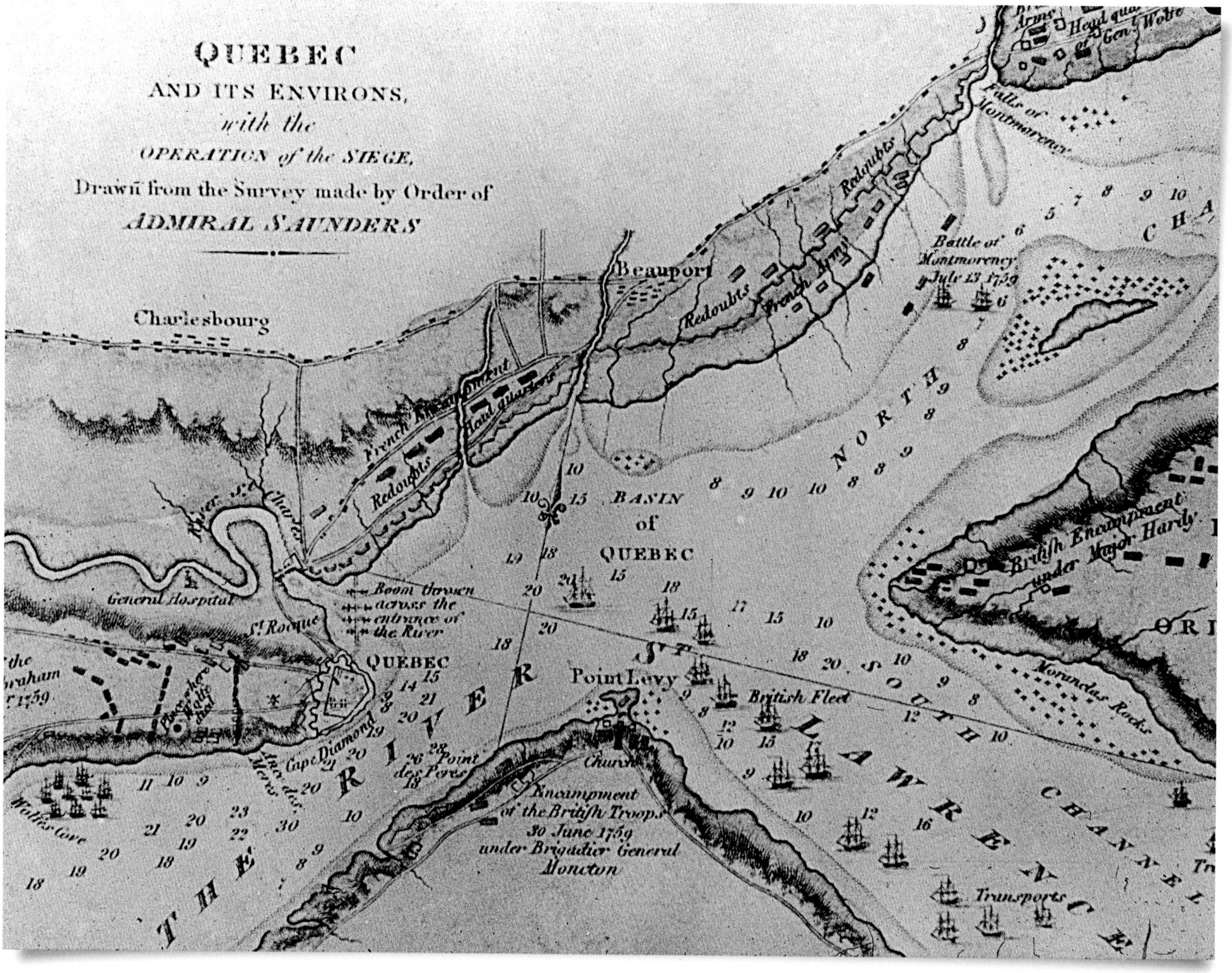
QUEBEC
AND ITS ENVIRONS,
with the
OPERATION of the SIEGE,
Drawn from the Survey made by Order of
ADMIRAL SAUNDERS
Charlesbourg
Beauport
Redoubts
French Army
Falls of Montmorency
Battle of Montmorency
French Encampment
Head Quarters
BASIN of QUEBEC
NORTH
General Hospital
St Roque
Boom thrown across the entrance of the River
QUEBEC
Point Levy
British Fleet
British Encampment under Major Hardy
Church
Encampment of the British Troops 30 June 1759 under Brigadier General Monckton
Wolfes Cove
Cape Diamond
Point des Peres
THE RIVER ST LAWRENCE
SOUTH CHANNEL
Transports

△ Siege of Quebec
Based on a survey ordered by the British fleet commander, this map shows the French defences during the siege of Quebec, including the boom blocking the St Charles River and the coastal redoubts.

PLAINS OF ABRAHAM

In this pivotal battle in the French and Indian War (1754–63), a British force under Major General James Wolfe surprised the French at Quebec, capturing the town after a three-month siege. The battle paved the way for British control of Canada.

In June 1759, five years after Britain and France started fighting for control of North America, a British force under General James Wolfe travelled up the St Lawrence River to attack Quebec, the capital city of the colony of New France, which had been claimed by the French in 1534. Wolfe established a base opposite Quebec on the Île d'Orléans and besieged the city. His attempt to land at Beauport on 31 July was repelled, and illness swept through the British camp. By September, Wolfe was running out of time before the winter, when ice would inevitably force him to withdraw. Wolfe gambled on landing upstream west of Quebec at L'Anse-au-Foulon, a cove at the bottom of the 54-m (177-ft) high promontory of Quebec. On 12 September, under cover of dark, Colonel William Howe and 24 volunteers scaled the cliff, overpowered the French garrison, and secured the area. By morning, more than 4,000 British soldiers had assembled on the Plains of Abraham. The French, led by the Marquis de Montcalm, marched out from Quebec to repel the British threat to their supply line from Montreal. Both Montcalm and Wolfe were fatally wounded, but the French were driven back by close range musketry, and Quebec surrendered on 18 September.

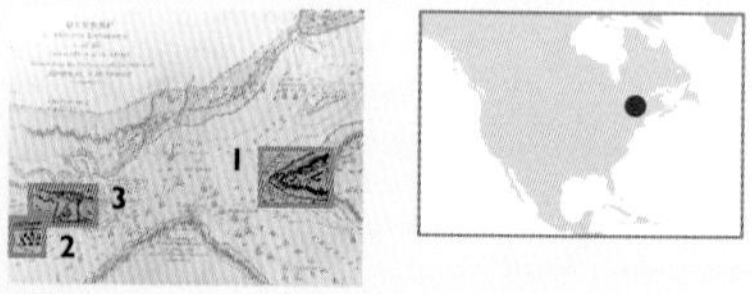
1
2
3

KEY

1 Wolfe besieged Quebec from the Île d'Orléans (28 June–18 September 1759).

2 A small British force climbed the cliffs at L'Anse-au-Foulon and secured the road.

3 The British lay down to avoid cannon fire, before firing two point blank musket volleys.

BUNKER HILL

In the first major battle of the American Revolutionary War (1775–83), the British suffered heavy losses while dislodging a group of patriots from two hills in Charlestown, near Boston. The action only strengthened the patriots' determination to secure independence for Britain's American colonies.

Increasing tension between Britain and its American colonies over taxation, self-rule, trade, territorial expansion, and more led to the American Revolutionary War in April 1775. After skirmishes between patriots (who wanted independence) and loyalists (supporters of the British regime) at Lexington and Concord, Massachusetts, rebel militias besieged Boston. By 17 June 1775, around 6,000 British troops were hemmed in by 15,000 American patriots, who had also just occupied the Charlestown peninsula overlooking the British positions in Boston. The British commander-in-chief, General Thomas Gage, ordered General William Howe – who had scaled the cliffs at Quebec in 1759 – to lead the British forces into their first major battle of the war. After an artillery bombardment, British troops landed on the peninsula, but it took three attempts before the patriots were pushed back, and over 1,000 British forces were killed or injured, while the patriots had only 450 casualties. A hollow victory for the British, it served only to give heart to the patriots, who saw how well they could fare against Britain's famously disciplined redcoats.

WAR OF INDEPENDENCE
New England was at the heart of the American Revolution and was the scene of the first skirmishes of the war, at Lexington and Concord, near Boston (19 April 1775).

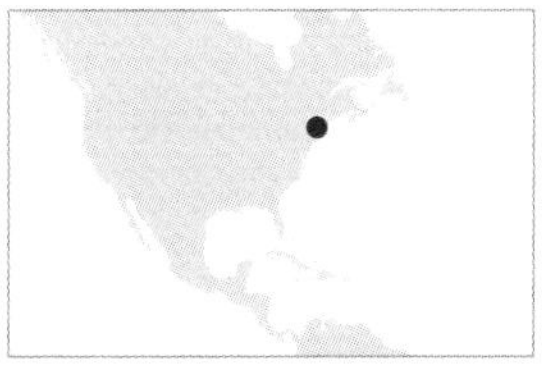

KEY

AMERICAN FORCES: Troops, Artillery

BRITISH FORCES: Troops, Fleet, Artillery

TIMELINE

1, 2, 3

16 JUN 1775 | 17 JUN | 18 JUN

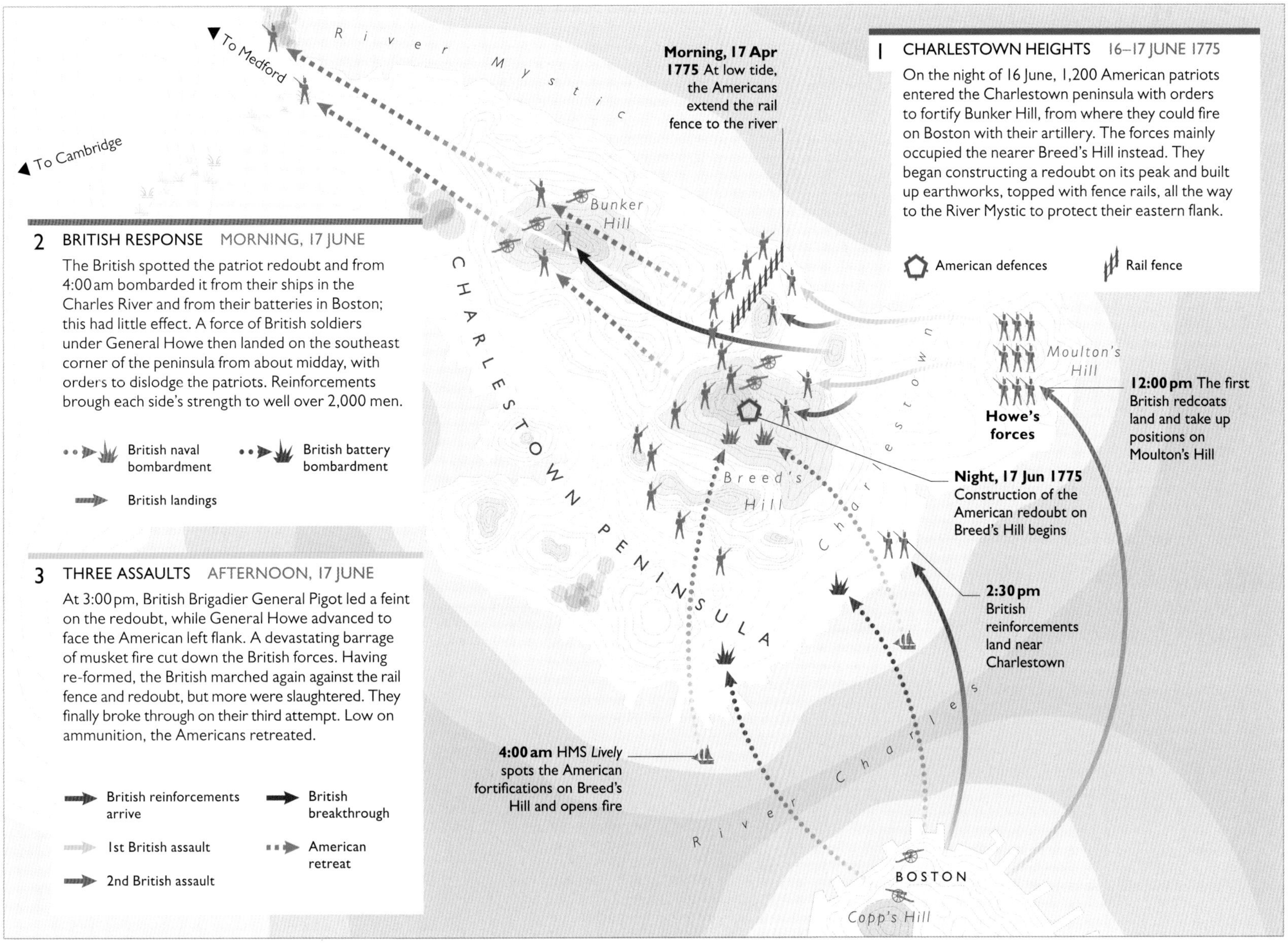

River Mystic
To Medford
To Cambridge
Bunker Hill
CHARLESTOWN PENINSULA
Breed's Hill
Moulton's Hill
Charlestown
River Charles
BOSTON
Copp's Hill
Howe's forces
Morning, 17 Apr 1775 At low tide, the Americans extend the rail fence to the river
12:00 pm The first British redcoats land and take up positions on Moulton's Hill
Night, 17 Jun 1775 Construction of the American redoubt on Breed's Hill begins
2:30 pm British reinforcements land near Charlestown
4:00 am HMS *Lively* spots the American fortifications on Breed's Hill and opens fire

1 CHARLESTOWN HEIGHTS 16–17 JUNE 1775

On the night of 16 June, 1,200 American patriots entered the Charlestown peninsula with orders to fortify Bunker Hill, from where they could fire on Boston with their artillery. The forces mainly occupied the nearer Breed's Hill instead. They began constructing a redoubt on its peak and built up earthworks, topped with fence rails, all the way to the River Mystic to protect their eastern flank.

American defences · Rail fence

2 BRITISH RESPONSE MORNING, 17 JUNE

The British spotted the patriot redoubt and from 4:00 am bombarded it from their ships in the Charles River and from their batteries in Boston; this had little effect. A force of British soldiers under General Howe then landed on the southeast corner of the peninsula from about midday, with orders to dislodge the patriots. Reinforcements brough each side's strength to well over 2,000 men.

British naval bombardment · British battery bombardment · British landings

3 THREE ASSAULTS AFTERNOON, 17 JUNE

At 3:00 pm, British Brigadier General Pigot led a feint on the redoubt, while General Howe advanced to face the American left flank. A devastating barrage of musket fire cut down the British forces. Having re-formed, the British marched again against the rail fence and redoubt, but more were slaughtered. They finally broke through on their third attempt. Low on ammunition, the Americans retreated.

British reinforcements arrive · British breakthrough · 1st British assault · American retreat · 2nd British assault

THE MARCH OF BURGOYNE'S ARMY

Burgoyne's army endured a punishing march towards Albany. Desperate for supplies, he ordered a raid on Bennington that cost him 1,000 men. The Americans sent a force to relieve Fort Stanwix, which was besieged by the British under Colonel St Leger. With St Leger held up, Burgoyne was left with just 6,000 men to face the revolutionary forces at Saratoga.

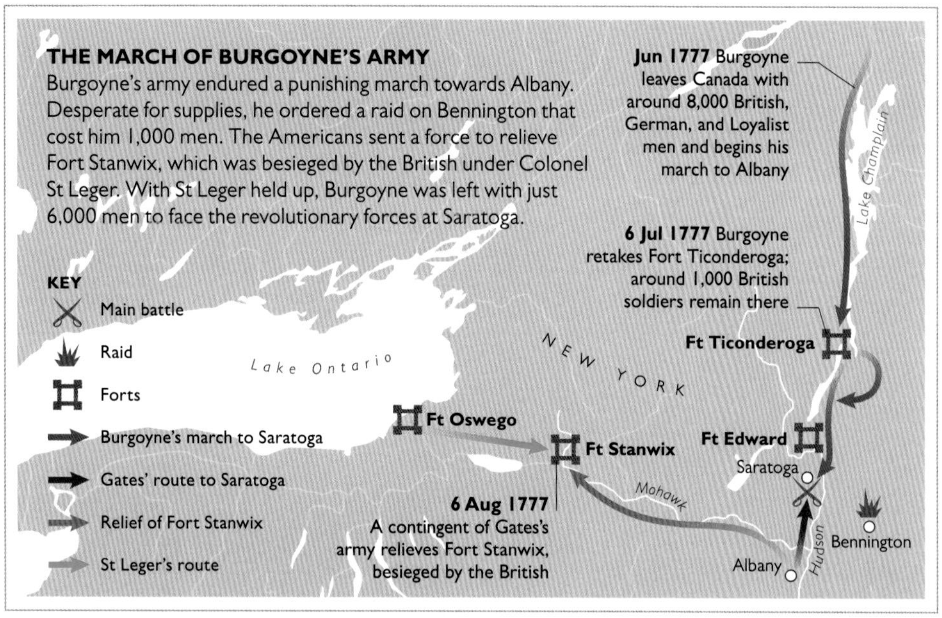
KEY
Main battle
Raid
Forts
Burgoyne's march to Saratoga
Gates' route to Saratoga
Relief of Fort Stanwix
St Leger's route
Jun 1777 Burgoyne leaves Canada with around 8,000 British, German, and Loyalist men and begins his march to Albany
6 Jul 1777 Burgoyne retakes Fort Ticonderoga; around 1,000 British soldiers remain there
6 Aug 1777 A contingent of Gates's army relieves Fort Stanwix, besieged by the British
Lake Ontario
Lake Champlain
NEW YORK
Ft Ticonderoga
Ft Oswego
Ft Stanwix
Ft Edward
Saratoga
Mohawk
Hudson
Bennington
Albany

SARATOGA CAMPAIGN

The battles at Saratoga marked the end of Britain's 1777 campaign to gain control of the strategically important Hudson River valley, running north of New York on America's east coast.

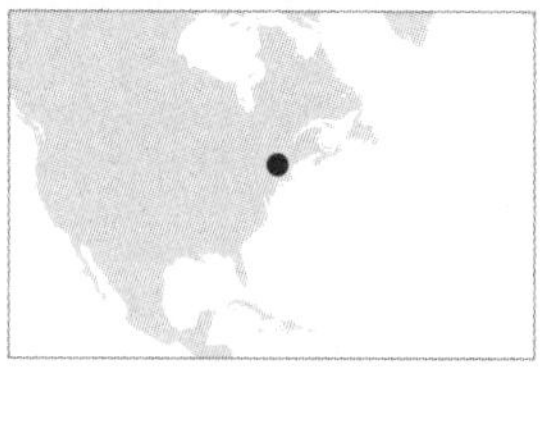

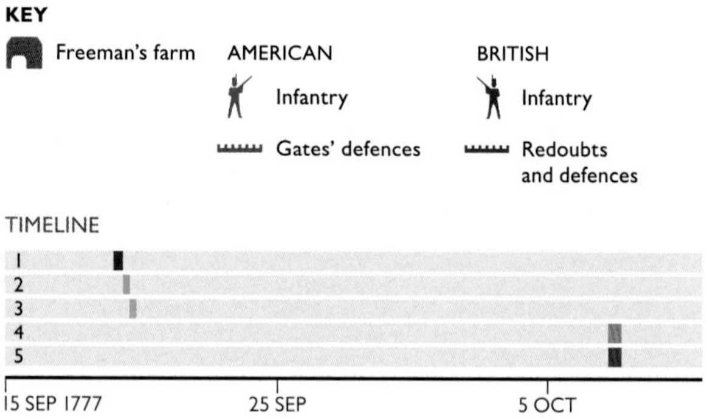
KEY
Freeman's farm
AMERICAN
Infantry
Gates' defences
BRITISH
Infantry
Redoubts and defences
TIMELINE
1
2
3
4
5
15 SEP 1777
25 SEP
5 OCT

1 BURGOYNE PREPARES
MORNING, 19 SEPTEMBER 1777

The British advanced in three columns: Baron Riedesel led the left column in a feint on the American position at Bemis Heights; Brigadier Simon Fraser led the right to Freeman's Farm, with the ultimate goal of capturing the high ground northwest of Bemis Heights; and Burgoyne and General James Hamilton took a central position.

Burgoyne's forces' advance

2 FIRST SKIRMISHES EARLY AFTERNOON

Benedict Arnold, Gates's subordinate, guessed the British plan and pressed a reluctant Gates (who wished to remain within his fortified position) to advance to cut off the enemy's progress. When Fraser's skirmishers appeared at the edge of Freeman's Farm, American sharpshooters led by Daniel Morgan cut them down and picked off most of the British officers. Morgan's men gave chase but quickly ran into the main body of Fraser's troops.

Morgan's probe

3 RIEDESEL COMES TO THE RESCUE
AFTERNOON

Burgoyne brought up his forces to support Fraser, and Gates sent several militia regiments into the growing fray. Around 3pm, Burgoyne gave instructions to Riedesel to send reinforcements. Riedesel advanced and began firing on the Americans' right flank and Gates' men withdrew to Bemis Heights. Burgoyne claimed victory, but he had lost 600 men.

Gates' main attack
Gates' retreat
Riedesel's reinforcements

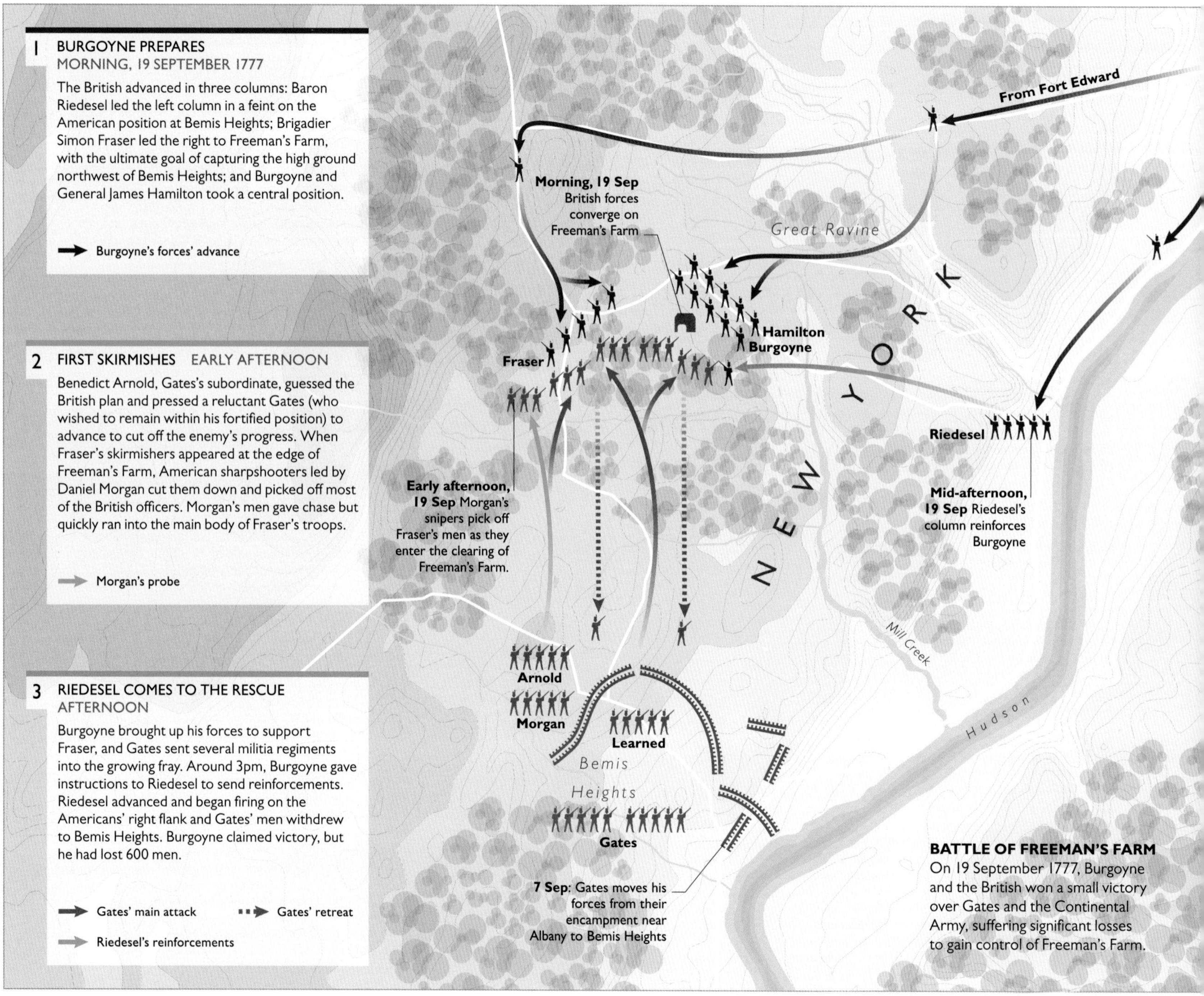
From Fort Edward
Morning, 19 Sep British forces converge on Freeman's Farm
Great Ravine
Hamilton
Burgoyne
Fraser
NEW YORK
Riedesel
Early afternoon, 19 Sep Morgan's snipers pick off Fraser's men as they enter the clearing of Freeman's Farm.
Mid-afternoon, 19 Sep Riedesel's column reinforces Burgoyne
Mill Creek
Arnold
Morgan
Learned
Bemis Heights
Gates
Hudson
7 Sep: Gates moves his forces from their encampment near Albany to Bemis Heights

BATTLE OF FREEMAN'S FARM

On 19 September 1777, Burgoyne and the British won a small victory over Gates and the Continental Army, suffering significant losses to gain control of Freeman's Farm.

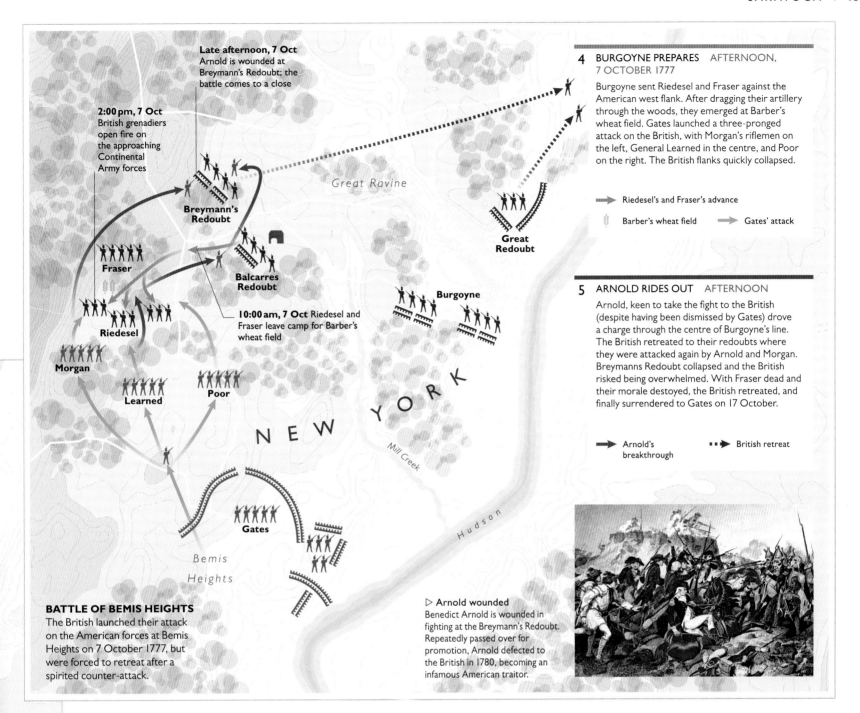

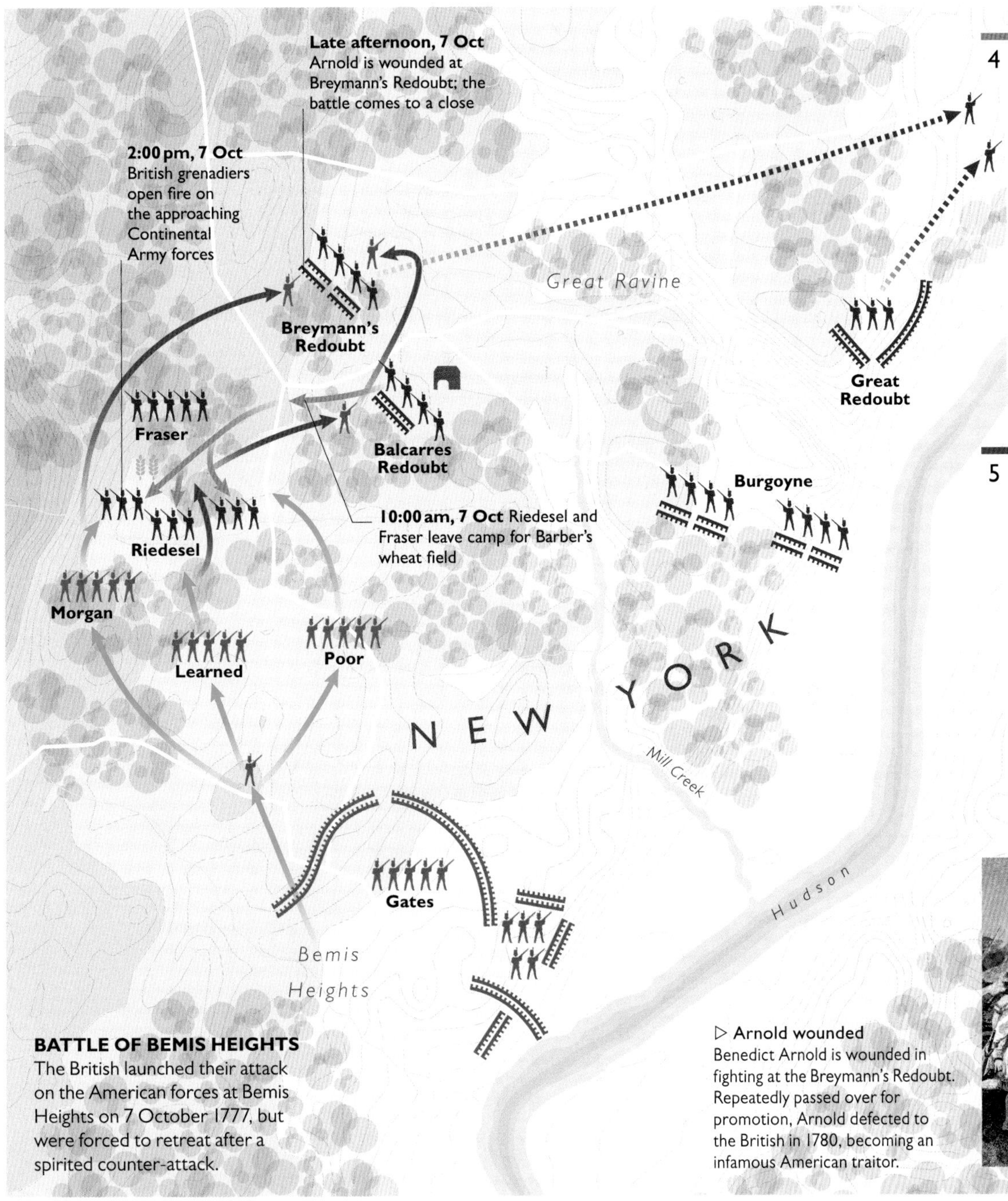
Late afternoon, 7 Oct
Arnold is wounded at Breymann's Redoubt; the battle comes to a close
2:00 pm, 7 Oct
British grenadiers open fire on the approaching Continental Army forces
Breymann's Redoubt
Great Ravine
Great Redoubt
Fraser
Balcarres Redoubt
10:00 am, 7 Oct Riedesel and Fraser leave camp for Barber's wheat field
Riedesel
Burgoyne
Morgan
Learned
Poor
NEW YORK
Mill Creek
Gates
Hudson
Bemis Heights

BATTLE OF BEMIS HEIGHTS
The British launched their attack on the American forces at Bemis Heights on 7 October 1777, but were forced to retreat after a spirited counter-attack.

4 BURGOYNE PREPARES AFTERNOON, 7 OCTOBER 1777

Burgoyne sent Riedesel and Fraser against the American west flank. After dragging their artillery through the woods, they emerged at Barber's wheat field. Gates launched a three-pronged attack on the British, with Morgan's riflemen on the left, General Learned in the centre, and Poor on the right. The British flanks quickly collapsed.

Riedesel's and Fraser's advance
Barber's wheat field
Gates' attack

5 ARNOLD RIDES OUT AFTERNOON

Arnold, keen to take the fight to the British (despite having been dismissed by Gates) drove a charge through the centre of Burgoyne's line. The British retreated to their redoubts where they were attacked again by Arnold and Morgan. Breymanns Redoubt collapsed and the British risked being overwhelmed. With Fraser dead and their morale destoyed, the British retreated, and finally surrendered to Gates on 17 October.

Arnold's breakthrough
British retreat

▷ **Arnold wounded**
Benedict Arnold is wounded in fighting at the Breymann's Redoubt. Repeatedly passed over for promotion, Arnold defected to the British in 1780, becoming an infamous American traitor.

SARATOGA

Two battles fought near Saratoga in 1777 marked a turning point in the American Revolutionary War. Around 6,000 British soldiers and Allied were captured, boosting the American Continental Army's morale and bringing France into the war with Britain.

In 1777, after two years of the American Revolutionary War (1775–83), the British formulated a plan to break the rebellion for good. Three armies were to converge on the port city of Albany and separate the New England colonies – which the British saw as the heart of the rebellion – from the more Loyalist middle and southern colonies. General John Burgoyne's army was to march south from Canada and rendezvous with a smaller British force under Colonel Barry St Leger, arriving from the west; a third army, under General William Howe, would push north from New York City, pressing the American defenders from three sides.

However, St Leger's progress towards Albany was delayed by heavy American resistance at Fort Stanwix, and Howe's army diverted to attack Philadelphia. Burgoyne was left alone to face General Horatio Gates's larger and growing force of Continental Army soldiers, which had occupied Bemis Heights – high ground on the road to Albany. Their first battle lasted several hours; the Americans fell back, but Burgoyne lost several hundred men. On 7 October, Burgoyne attempted to attack the American position at Bemis Heights, but his forces were quickly overrun. He withdrew having lost hundreds more men, and finally surrendered on 17 October.

F
D
E

The Siege of Yorktown, 1781
This print depicts the the decisive concluding victory of the American War of Independence – the British surrender at Yorktown. The Franco–American army and navy trapped the British Army under General Charles Cornwallis.

AMERICA'S ARMY

In April 1775, conflict broke out between rebels and British troops in North America. On 14 June, the Second Continental Congress authorized the creation of the Continental Army to fight against the British.

LIBERTY

△ **Knapsack with insignia**
Regimental and company designations were often embroidered on the knapsacks of the Continental Army's soldiers, as shown on this reproduction.

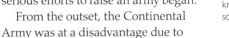

The Continental Army was created in the belief that a trained army, rather than a citizens' militia, would give the colonies a fighting chance against the British. The first troops to become a part of the army were the militiamen already deployed in the Siege of Boston (April 1775–March 1776). Soon, volunteers began enlisting. However, it was only in 1777 that serious efforts to raise an army began.

From the outset, the Continental Army was at a disadvantage due to inadequate training and a lack of equipment, money, and uniforms. The army's initial battlefield performance yielded mixed results, with defeat at New York and victory at the Siege of Boston in 1776. It won small victories at Trenton and Princeton also in 1776, but was defeated again the following year at Brandywine and Germantown. Its first clear victory was at Saratoga (see pp.154–55), and won the upper hand at the battle at Monmouth Court House in 1778. However, the troops were beaten again at Camden in 1780.

Although beset by problems, the army nevertheless received praise from some foreign observers. Training, leadership, and equipment improved over time, but not at a constant rate, and Congress funding was never steady due to political disagreements or lack of resources. In the end, the army's success in overthrowing the British owed more to the intervention of France and Spain than its own performance. In 1783, after the independence for the 13 colonies, the first act of the Congress was to disband most of the Continental Army.

GEORGE WASHINGTON 1732–99

Washington was a subordinate commander during the French and Indian War (1754–63), before resigning his commision and becoming active in politics. After the creation of the Continental Army, Congress appointed him as its commander-in-chief. He was an able administrator and trainer, and he played a key role in securing American victory in the War of Independence. He went on to become the first President of the newly created United States in 1789.

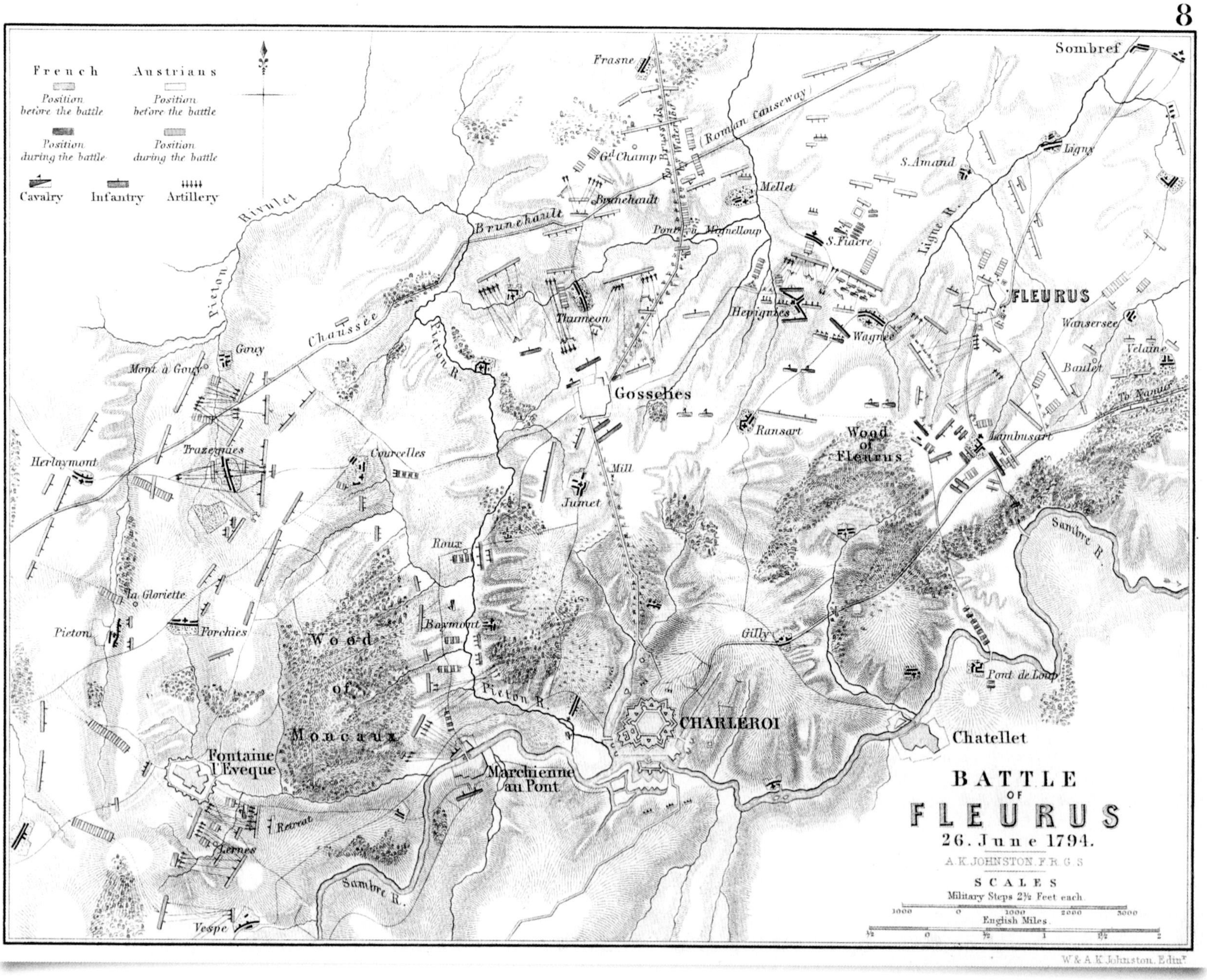
8
French
Austrians
Position before the battle
Position before the battle
Position during the battle
Position during the battle
Cavalry
Infantry
Artillery
Frasne
Sombref
Roman Causeway
Ligny
S. Amand
Gd Champ
Mellet
Bruneehault
Brunehault
Pont à Migneloup
S. Fiacre
Ligne R.
FLEURUS
Wanseree
Velaine
Baulet
To Namur
Heppignies
Wagnée
Rivulet
Pieton
Chaussée
Gouy
Mont à Gouy
Gosselies
Ransart
Wood of Fleurus
Lambusart
Herlaymont
Trazegnies
Courcelles
Mill
Jumet
Sambre R.
Roux
La Gloriette
Pieton
Forchies
Wood of Moncaux
Baymont
Pieton R.
Gilly
Pont de Loup
CHARLEROI
Chatellet
Fontaine l'Eveque
Marchienne au Pont
Retreat
Lernes
Sambre R.
Vespe
BATTLE OF FLEURUS
26. June 1794.
A.K. JOHNSTON. F.R.G.S.
SCALES
Military Steps 2½ Feet each.
English Miles
W. & A. K. Johnston, Edinr.

△ **Fleurus battle map from 1848**
The battle took place in 1794 on the outskirts of Charleroi, north of the River Sambre in modern-day Belgium. It was the key battle in the First Coalition period of the French Revolutionary Wars.

FLEURUS

Notable for the first use of an observation balloon in battle, the Battle of Fleurus gave the army of revolutionary France its most significant victory against the First Coalition (1792–97), allowing it to seize Belgium and the Dutch Republic.

After the French Revolution in 1789, France's republican government came under attack from Europe's monarchies, who feared the spread of its ideals, and from 1793 the French used mass conscription to raise a large army. On 12 June 1794, France's General Jourdan and around 70,000 soldiers laid siege to the town of Charleroi, and on 25 June Prince Josias of Saxe-Coburg and around 50,000 Austrian and Dutch soldiers arrived, seeking to lift the siege. Too late to save Charleroi, Saxe-Coburg deployed five columns on 26 June to attack the French line, which was drawn up in an arc around the city with its advance guard at Fleurus to the northeast. Reports from the observation balloon *L'Entreprenant* kept Jourdan informed of Austrian movements. The French left and right wings were initially driven back, but they and the centre held as Jourdan redeployed his troops. Saxe-Coburg lost his nerve and the Austrians retreated after 15 hours of desperate fighting. The battle was a strategic victory for the French that allowed them to go on the offensive and annexe the Austrian Netherlands.

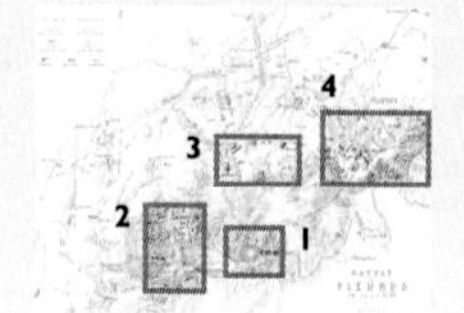
1
2
3
4

KEY

1 Charleroi surrendered to General Jourdan on 25 June, as an Austrian relief force arrived to lift the siege.

2 The French left flank controlled the French escape route across the River Sambre.

3 French reserves at Junet and Ransart bolstered the left and right wings.

4 The Austrians captured Lambusart, but French reinforcements recaptured it.

BATTLE OF THE PYRAMIDS

At Embabeh near the pyramids, Egypt, on 21 July 1798, General Napoleon Bonaparte led the French to victory against the Egyptian Mamluk forces through the innovative use of massive divisional infantry squares.

In May 1798, Napoleon, one of the revolutionary government's most trusted generals, set sail to invade Egypt with around 30 warships and several divisions of troops on 400 transport vessels. His aim was to gain a new source of revenue while blocking the English trade route to India via the Red Sea. Landing in Egypt on 1 July, he took Alexandria the next day, then headed south along the west bank of the Nile to meet the army of the Mamluk chieftain Murad Bey at Embabeh on 21 July. That afternoon, 6,000 Mamluk cavalry charged the 25,000-strong French army. The French formed five large divisional squares with cannons on the outer edges and infantry in ranks six deep protecting the cavalry and transport in the centre. The squares repulsed numerous charges, before the Bon division stormed Embabeh and routed the Mamluk garrison. Many Egyptian soldiers drowned trying to escape across the Nile. The Mamluks abandoned Cairo to Napoleon, but within a fortnight the British destroyed the French fleet at the Battle of the Nile.

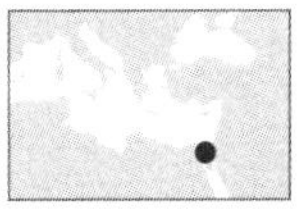

LOCATOR

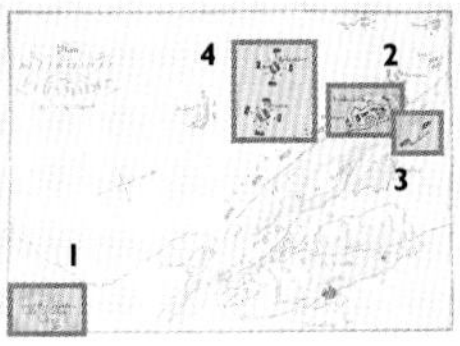
4
2
3
1

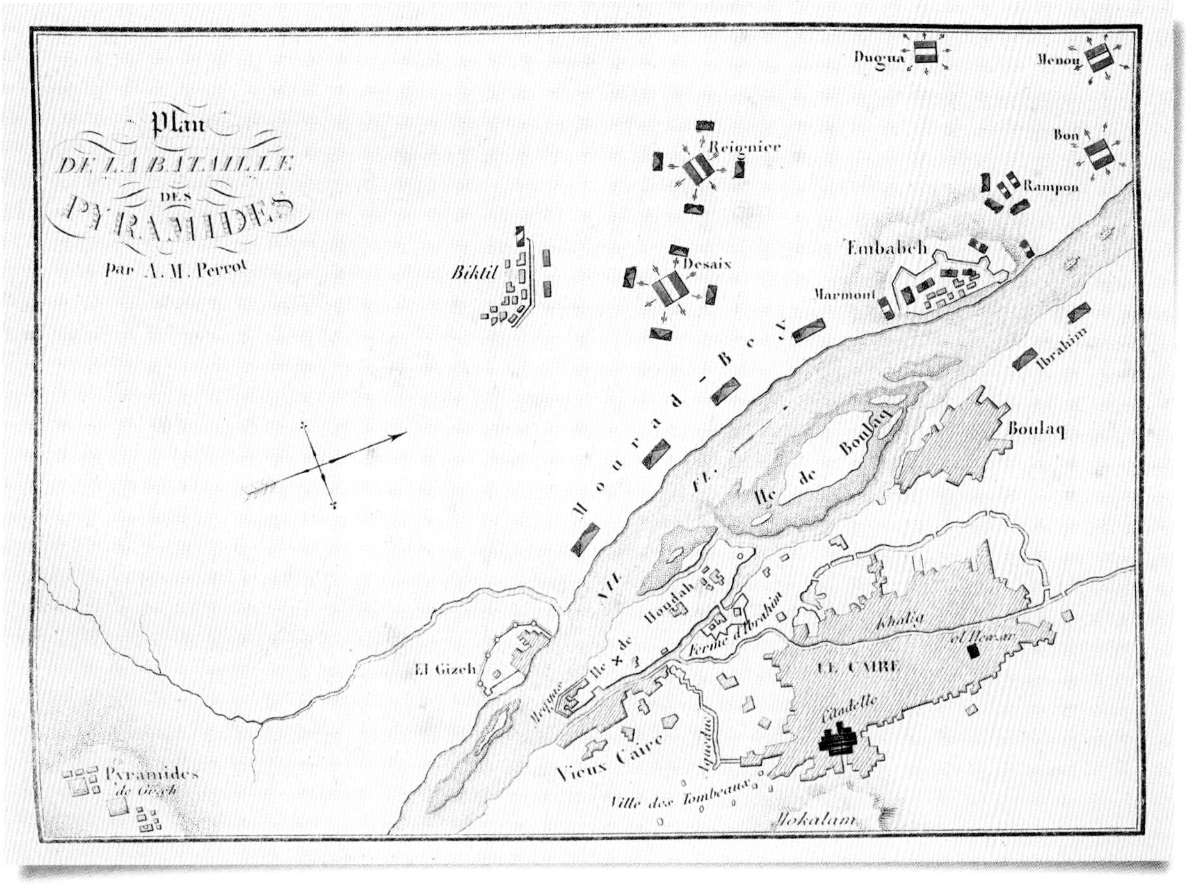
Plan
DE LA BATAILLE
DES
PYRAMIDES
par A. M. Perrot
Dugua
Menou
Reignier
Bon
Rampon
Desaix
Biktil
Embabeh
Marmont
Ibrahim
Mourad - Bey
Boulaq
Ile de Boulaq
Fl. Nil
Ile de Roudah
Ferme d'Ibrahim
El Gizeh
Khalig
LE CAIRE
Citadelle
Vieux Caire
Ville des Tombeaux
Mokatam
Pyramides de Gizeh

◁ **French battle map from 1828**
The Battle of the Pyramids took place at Embabeh, on the west bank of the Nile, 6 km (4 miles) from Cairo and 15 km (9 miles) from the pyramids at Giza.

4

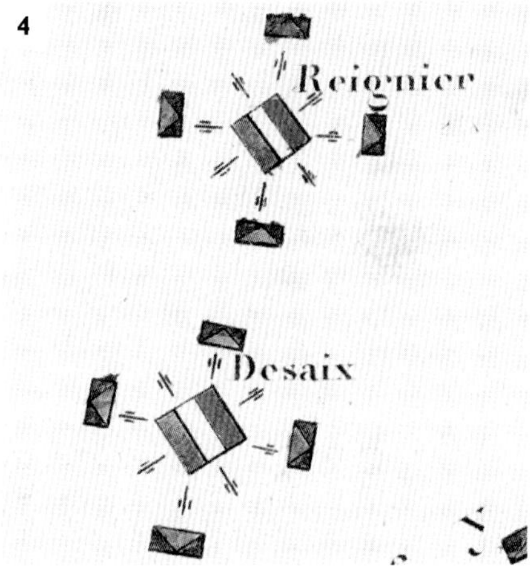
Reignier
Desaix

△ **Massed infantry and cannons**
Napoleon's large infantry squares proved highly effective against the Mamluk cavalry. This was to be Napoleon's only significant tactical innovation.

▽ **Egyptian reserves**
A second Egyptian force, under Murad's co-ruler, Ibrahim Bey, remained on the east bank and took no part in the battle.

1

Pyramides
de Gizeh

△ **Landmark battle**
The pyramids are used to name the battle, although the action took place some distance away. Paintings of the campaign often feature famous landmarks.

2

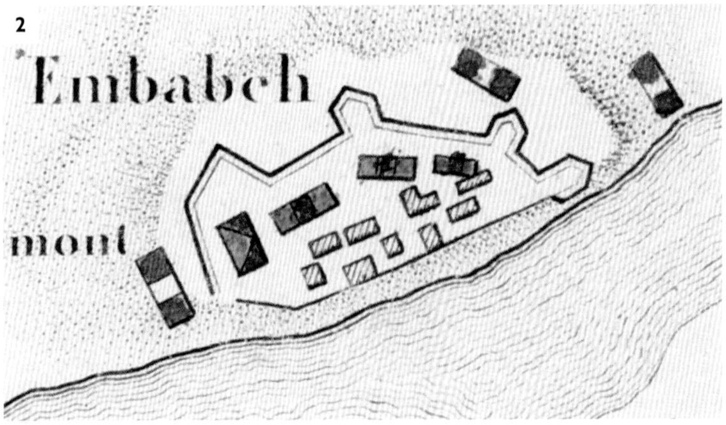
Embabeh
mont

3

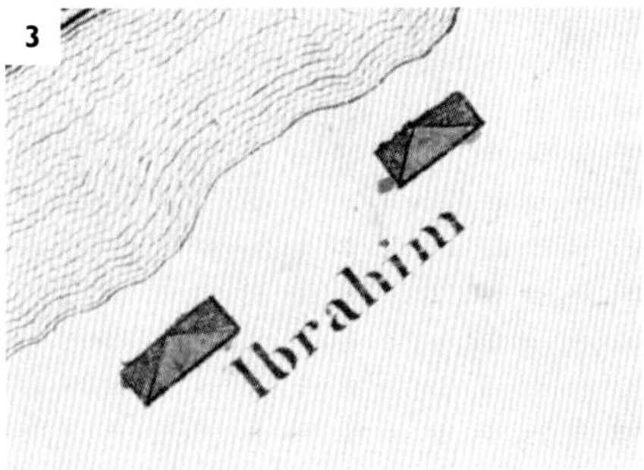
Ibrahim

◁ **Strategic objective**
Stormed by French troops during the battle, Embabeh (now Imbaba) was an important market town on the upper Nile delta.

THE ROUTE TO MARENGO

In mid-May 1800, Napoleon secretly crossed the Great St. Bernard pass into Italy, while further French forces crossed the Alps further north. The French moved south, seizing Milan, Pavia, Piacenza, and Stradella, and cutting off the main Austrian supply route east along the Po River. After Austrian general Ott took Genoa by siege on 4 June, however, many more Austrian troops were freed to address the threat from Napoleon, and Ott ordered them to march to Alessandria.

KEY

Main battle

FRENCH FORCES
- Commander
- French advance

AUSTRIAN FORCES
- Commander
- Austrian movements

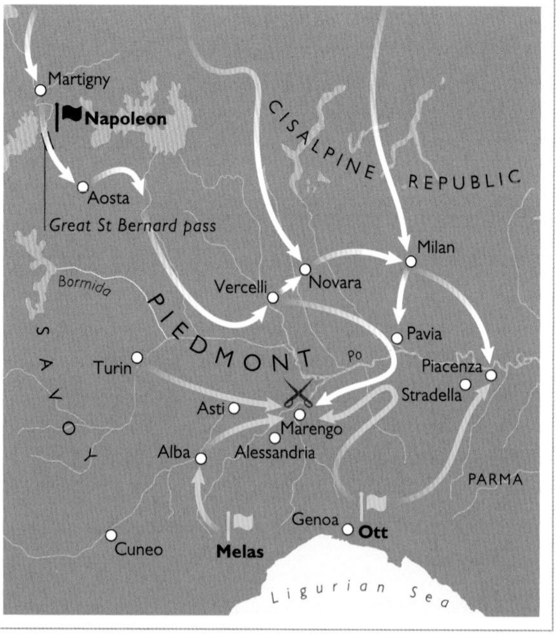

Martigny
Napoleon
Aosta
Great St Bernard pass
CISALPINE REPUBLIC
Milan
Novara
Vercelli
Bormida
PIEDMONT
SAVOY
Turin
Po
Pavia
Piacenza
Stradella
Asti
Marengo
Alessandria
Alba
PARMA
Cuneo
Genoa
Ott
Melas
Ligurian Sea

ITALIAN CONFLICT

Within a day of Napoleon's victory on the Marengo plain outside Alessandria, the Austrians agreed to evacuate northwest Italy and suspend military operations in Italy.

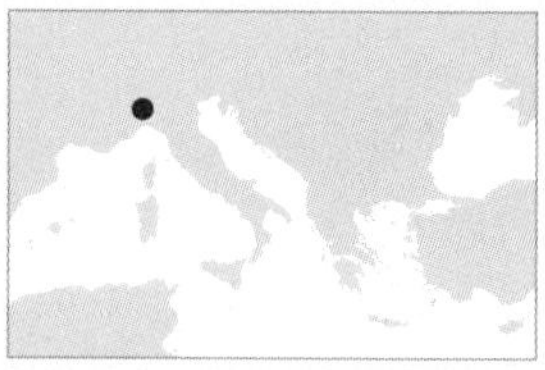

KEY

Towns

AUSTRIAN FORCES
- Commander
- Cavalry
- Infantry

FRENCH FORCES
- Commander
- Cavalry
- Infantry
- Artillery

TIMELINE

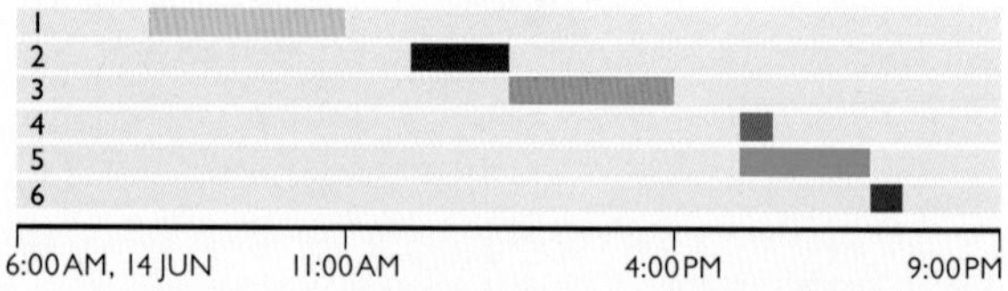

1
2
3
4
5
6
6:00AM, 14 JUN
11:00AM
4:00PM
9:00PM

AUSTRIAN DOMINANCE

After hours of inconclusive fighting, the Austrians finally broke the French line and forced the French to withdraw back toward San Juliano by late afternoon.

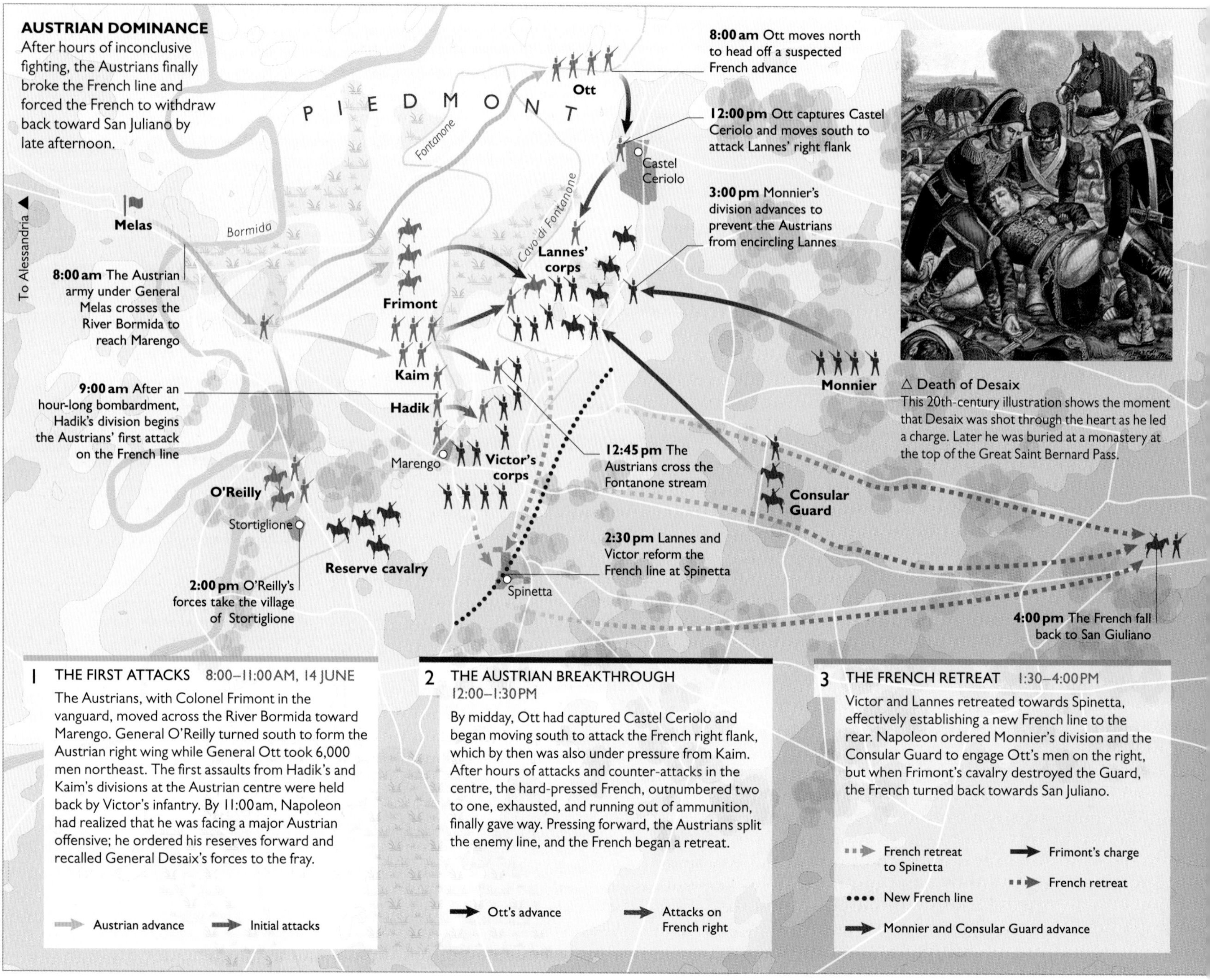

PIEDMONT
Ott
8:00 am Ott moves north to head off a suspected French advance
12:00 pm Ott captures Castel Ceriolo and moves south to attack Lannes' right flank
Castel Ceriolo
3:00 pm Monnier's division advances to prevent the Austrians from encircling Lannes
Fontanone
Cavo di Fontanone
To Alessandria
Melas
Bormida
8:00 am The Austrian army under General Melas crosses the River Bormida to reach Marengo
Lannes' corps
Frimont
Kaim
Hadik
9:00 am After an hour-long bombardment, Hadik's division begins the Austrians' first attack on the French line
Monnier
Marengo
Victor's corps
12:45 pm The Austrians cross the Fontanone stream
O'Reilly
Consular Guard
Stortiglione
Reserve cavalry
2:30 pm Lannes and Victor reform the French line at Spinetta
Spinetta
2:00 pm O'Reilly's forces take the village of Stortiglione
4:00 pm The French fall back to San Giuliano

△ Death of Desaix
This 20th-century illustration shows the moment that Desaix was shot through the heart as he led a charge. Later he was buried at a monastery at the top of the Great Saint Bernard Pass.

1 THE FIRST ATTACKS 8:00–11:00AM, 14 JUNE

The Austrians, with Colonel Frimont in the vanguard, moved across the River Bormida toward Marengo. General O'Reilly turned south to form the Austrian right wing while General Ott took 6,000 men northeast. The first assaults from Hadik's and Kaim's divisions at the Austrian centre were held back by Victor's infantry. By 11:00am, Napoleon had realized that he was facing a major Austrian offensive; he ordered his reserves forward and recalled General Desaix's forces to the fray.

- Austrian advance
- Initial attacks

2 THE AUSTRIAN BREAKTHROUGH 12:00–1:30PM

By midday, Ott had captured Castel Ceriolo and began moving south to attack the French right flank, which by then was also under pressure from Kaim. After hours of attacks and counter-attacks in the centre, the hard-pressed French, outnumbered two to one, exhausted, and running out of ammunition, finally gave way. Pressing forward, the Austrians split the enemy line, and the French began a retreat.

- Ott's advance
- Attacks on French right

3 THE FRENCH RETREAT 1:30–4:00PM

Victor and Lannes retreated towards Spinetta, effectively establishing a new French line to the rear. Napoleon ordered Monnier's division and the Consular Guard to engage Ott's men on the right, but when Frimont's cavalry destroyed the Guard, the French turned back towards San Juliano.

- French retreat to Spinetta
- Frimont's charge
- French retreat
- New French line
- Monnier and Consular Guard advance

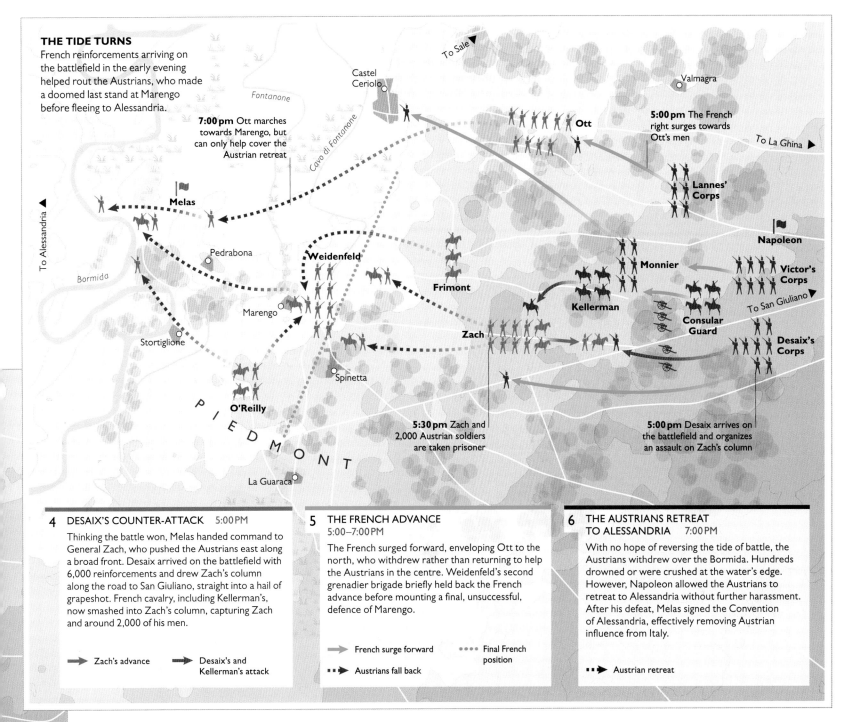

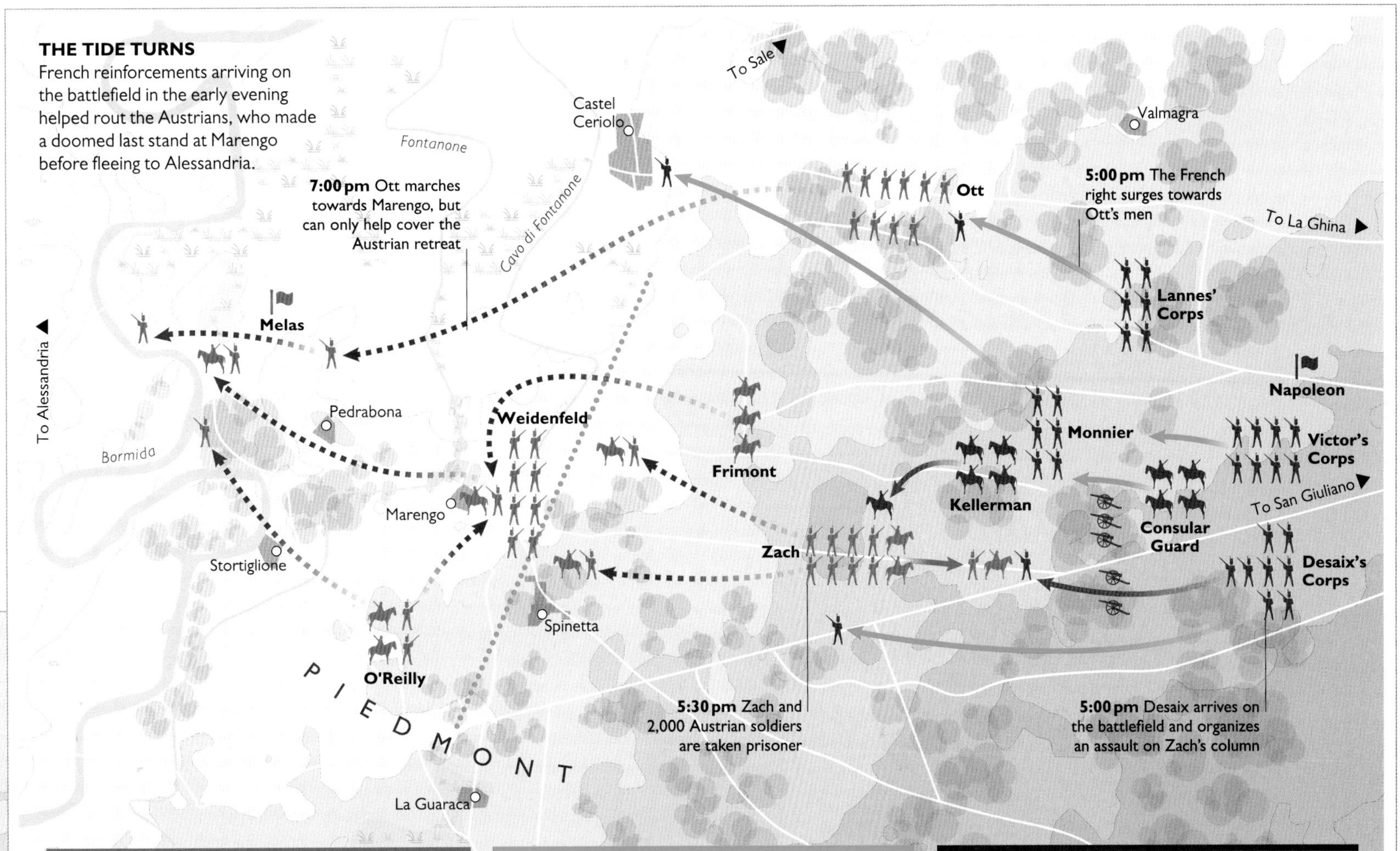
THE TIDE TURNS
French reinforcements arriving on the battlefield in the early evening helped rout the Austrians, who made a doomed last stand at Marengo before fleeing to Alessandria.
7:00 pm Ott marches towards Marengo, but can only help cover the Austrian retreat
5:00 pm The French right surges towards Ott's men
5:30 pm Zach and 2,000 Austrian soldiers are taken prisoner
5:00 pm Desaix arrives on the battlefield and organizes an assault on Zach's column
To Sale
Castel Ceriolo
Valmagra
Fontanone
Cavo di Fontanone
Ott
To La Ghina
Lannes' Corps
Melas
To Alessandria
Napoleon
Pedrabona
Bormida
Weidenfeld
Frimont
Monnier
Victor's Corps
Kellerman
To San Giuliano
Consular Guard
Marengo
Stortiglione
Zach
Desaix's Corps
Spinetta
O'Reilly
PIEDMONT
La Guaraca

4 DESAIX'S COUNTER-ATTACK 5:00 PM

Thinking the battle won, Melas handed command to General Zach, who pushed the Austrians east along a broad front. Desaix arrived on the battlefield with 6,000 reinforcements and drew Zach's column along the road to San Giuliano, straight into a hail of grapeshot. French cavalry, including Kellerman's, now smashed into Zach's column, capturing Zach and around 2,000 of his men.

Zach's advance — Desaix's and Kellerman's attack

5 THE FRENCH ADVANCE 5:00–7:00 PM

The French surged forward, enveloping Ott to the north, who withdrew rather than returning to help the Austrians in the centre. Weidenfeld's second grenadier brigade briefly held back the French advance before mounting a final, unsuccessful, defence of Marengo.

French surge forward — Final French position — Austrians fall back

6 THE AUSTRIANS RETREAT TO ALESSANDRIA 7:00 PM

With no hope of reversing the tide of battle, the Austrians withdrew over the Bormida. Hundreds drowned or were crushed at the water's edge. However, Napoleon allowed the Austrians to retreat to Alessandria without further harassment. After his defeat, Melas signed the Convention of Alessandria, effectively removing Austrian influence from Italy.

Austrian retreat

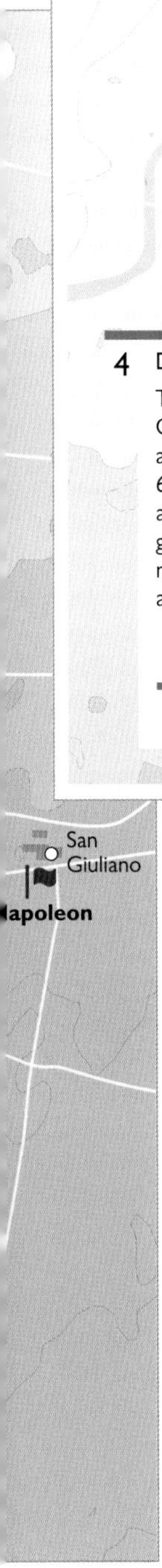
San Giuliano

MARENGO

On 14 June 1800, after crossing the Alps into Italy, Napoleon won a narrow victory against the Austrians at Marengo. The battle helped to destroy the Second European Coalition that threatened Revolutionary France and solidified Napoleon's reputation as France's saviour.

By 1800, France had endured over a decade of revolutionary turmoil and years of war against European powers. It now faced a Second Coalition of countries (including Austria, Russia, Britain, and Turkey), which had already pushed back French forces in Germany, Holland, and Italy. In October 1799, Napoleon returned to France after campaigning in Egypt against the British. He dismissed the unpopular Directory government and replaced it with a new constitution, the Consulate, positioning himself as one of three Consuls. Intending to lift morale and to cement his political position, he turned to Italy, hoping to secure a victory against the Austrian armies there that would force a peace settlement. Taking direct command of the Reserve Army, Napoleon marched over the 2,500 m (8,100 feet) high Great St. Bernard Pass into northwest Italy to support the French armies already fighting there. Closing in on the Austrian armies at Alessandia, he wrongly assumed that the enemy would flee rather than fight, so despatched Generals Desaix and La Poype to block their escape. It was a miscalculation: he was taken by surprise and almost routed when the Austrians attacked at Marengo.

NELSON'S APPROACH
The British fleet had the wind behind it off the port (left) quarter, putting Collingwood's column in the lee (downwind) position. The wind during the battle was light and variable, so all ships moved slowly.

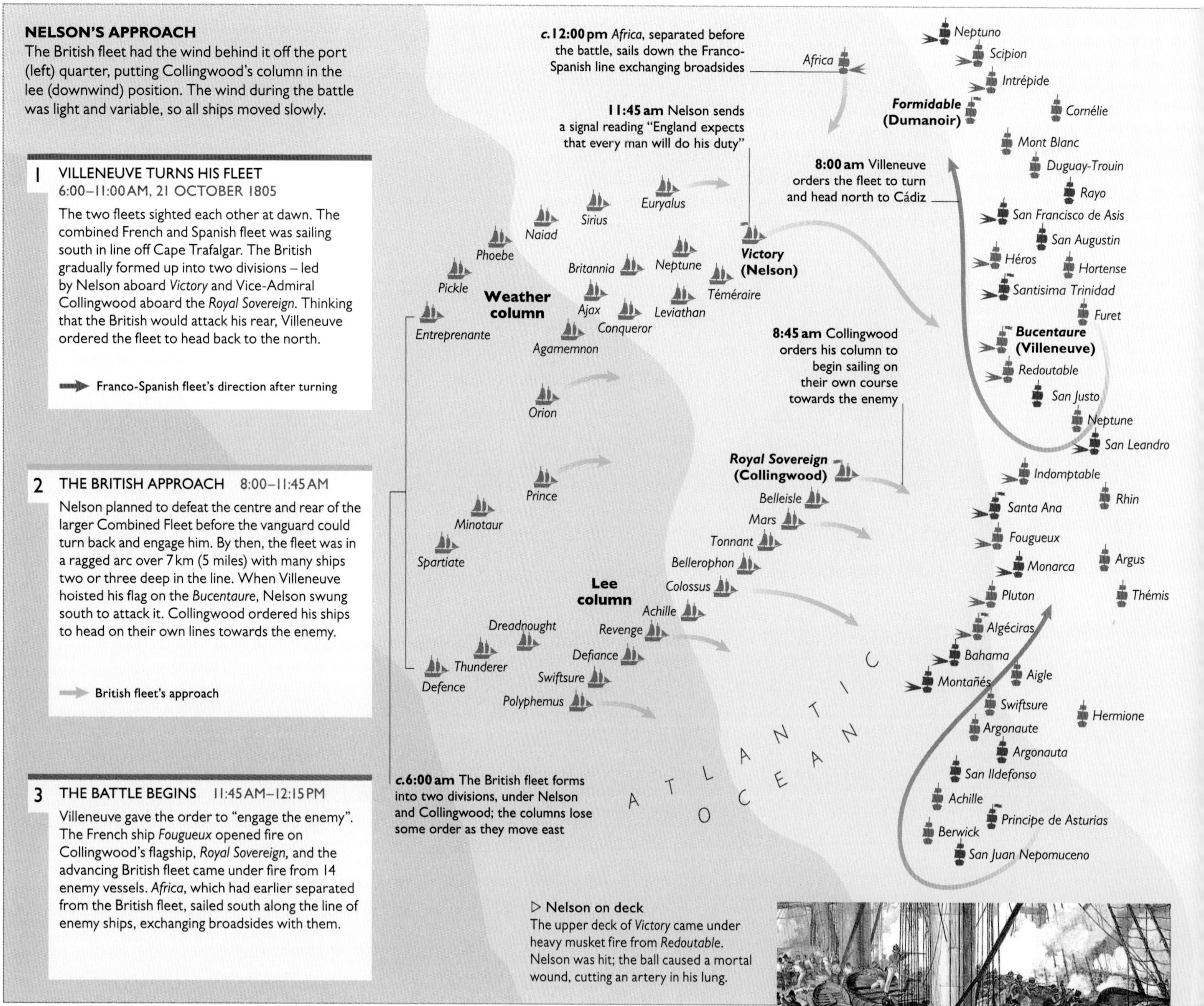

c.12:00 pm *Africa*, separated before the battle, sails down the Franco-Spanish line exchanging broadsides
11:45 am Nelson sends a signal reading "England expects that every man will do his duty"
8:00 am Villeneuve orders the fleet to turn and head north to Cádiz
8:45 am Collingwood orders his column to begin sailing on their own course towards the enemy
c.6:00 am The British fleet forms into two divisions, under Nelson and Collingwood; the columns lose some order as they move east
Weather column
Lee column
ATLANTIC OCEAN
Africa
Euryalus
Sirius
Naiad
Phoebe
Pickle
Entreprenante
Britannia
Neptune
Victory (Nelson)
Téméraire
Ajax
Leviathan
Conqueror
Agamemnon
Orion
Prince
Minotaur
Spartiate
Royal Sovereign (Collingwood)
Belleisle
Mars
Tonnant
Bellerophon
Colossus
Achille
Revenge
Dreadnought
Defiance
Thunderer
Swiftsure
Defence
Polyphemus
Neptuno
Scipion
Intrépide
Formidable (Dumanoir)
Cornélie
Mont Blanc
Duguay-Trouin
Rayo
San Francisco de Asis
San Augustin
Héros
Hortense
Santisima Trinidad
Furet
Bucentaure (Villeneuve)
Redoutable
San Justo
Neptune
San Leandro
Indomptable
Rhin
Santa Ana
Fougueux
Monarca
Argus
Pluton
Thémis
Algéciras
Bahama
Montañés
Aigle
Swiftsure
Hermione
Argonaute
Argonauta
San Ildefonso
Achille
Principe de Asturias
Berwick
San Juan Nepomuceno

1 VILLENEUVE TURNS HIS FLEET
6:00–11:00AM, 21 OCTOBER 1805

The two fleets sighted each other at dawn. The combined French and Spanish fleet was sailing south in line off Cape Trafalgar. The British gradually formed up into two divisions – led by Nelson aboard *Victory* and Vice-Admiral Collingwood aboard the *Royal Sovereign*. Thinking that the British would attack his rear, Villeneuve ordered the fleet to head back to the north.

Franco-Spanish fleet's direction after turning

2 THE BRITISH APPROACH 8:00–11:45AM

Nelson planned to defeat the centre and rear of the larger Combined Fleet before the vanguard could turn back and engage him. By then, the fleet was in a ragged arc over 7km (5 miles) with many ships two or three deep in the line. When Villeneuve hoisted his flag on the *Bucentaure*, Nelson swung south to attack it. Collingwood ordered his ships to head on their own lines towards the enemy.

British fleet's approach

3 THE BATTLE BEGINS 11:45AM–12:15PM

Villeneuve gave the order to "engage the enemy". The French ship *Fougueux* opened fire on Collingwood's flagship, *Royal Sovereign*, and the advancing British fleet came under fire from 14 enemy vessels. *Africa*, which had earlier separated from the British fleet, sailed south along the line of enemy ships, exchanging broadsides with them.

▷ **Nelson on deck**
The upper deck of *Victory* came under heavy musket fire from *Redoutable*. Nelson was hit; the ball caused a mortal wound, cutting an artery in his lung.

TRAFALGAR

The largest sea battle of the Napoleonic Wars, Trafalgar was a hard-fought contest that confirmed Britain as the world's supreme naval power and Admiral Horatio Nelson as the foremost naval commander of the era.

In 1804, a British attack pushed Spain into the War of the Third Coalition (1803–1806) as an ally of France, providing Napoleon with the ships he needed to challenge Britain directly. In September 1805, the 33 ships of the line of the Franco-Spanish fleet under Vice-Admiral Villeneuve were anchored in Cádiz, southwest Spain, watched carefully by 27 British ships of the line under Nelson. On 19 October, Villeneuve sailed out of Cádiz to support Napoleon's campaign in Italy. Nelson gave chase and caught up with him off the Cape of Trafalgar on 21 October. Outnumbered and outgunned, Nelson launched a daring attack that could have ended in disaster. Rather than lining up in parallel with the enemy to exchange broadsides, he sailed his ships directly at them in two columns. The leading ships were exposed to enemy fire, but drove straight through the Franco-Spanish line, prompting what Nelson called a "pell-mell" battle that favoured the superior British gunnery and seamanship. It paid off: the British lost no ships while over 20 French and Spanish ships were captured. Napoleon's ambition to invade England was shattered, and Britain's naval supremacy assured.

INVASION FLEET

Napoleon brought the French and Spanish fleets together for a planned invasion of England. Nelson pursued the new Combined Fleet across the Atlantic and back, finally catching up off the Spanish coast near Cádiz.

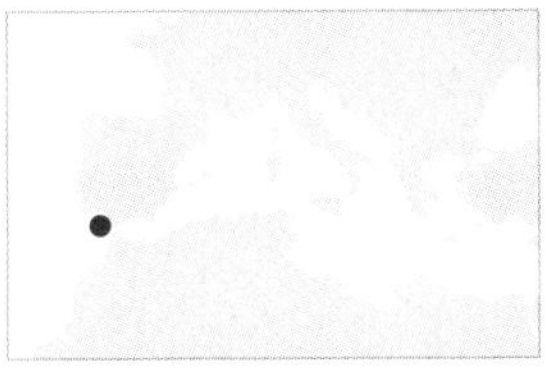

KEY

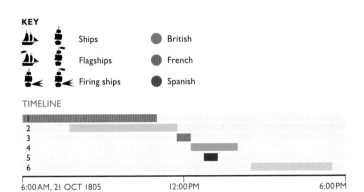

Ships — British
Flagships — French
Firing ships — Spanish

TIMELINE

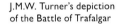

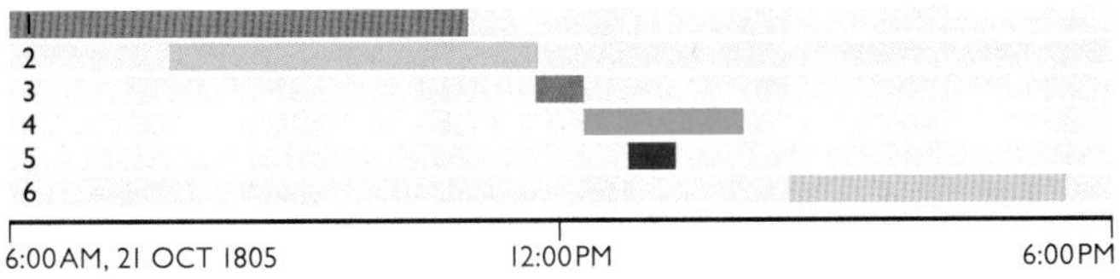
1
2
3
4
5
6
6:00AM, 21 OCT 1805
12:00PM
6:00PM

NELSON AND *VICTORY*

Nelson's flagship HMS *Victory* was heavily fired upon as she led one attack column, but she broke the enemy line, and Villeneuve's flagship *Bucentaure* received a devastating point blank stern rake from *Victory*'s broadside guns. *Victory*'s tiller ropes were shot through, so her rudder had to be moved from below deck to bring her alongside *Redoubtable*. Nelson was fatally wounded as French marines fired on *Victory*. At 4:30 pm, after hearing that the British had won, Nelson died.

J.M.W. Turner's depiction of the Battle of Trafalgar

PELL-MELL BATTLE

Once among the Combined Fleet, the experienced Royal Navy gunners wrought havoc. The French and Spanish ships were unable to inflict the same level of damage.

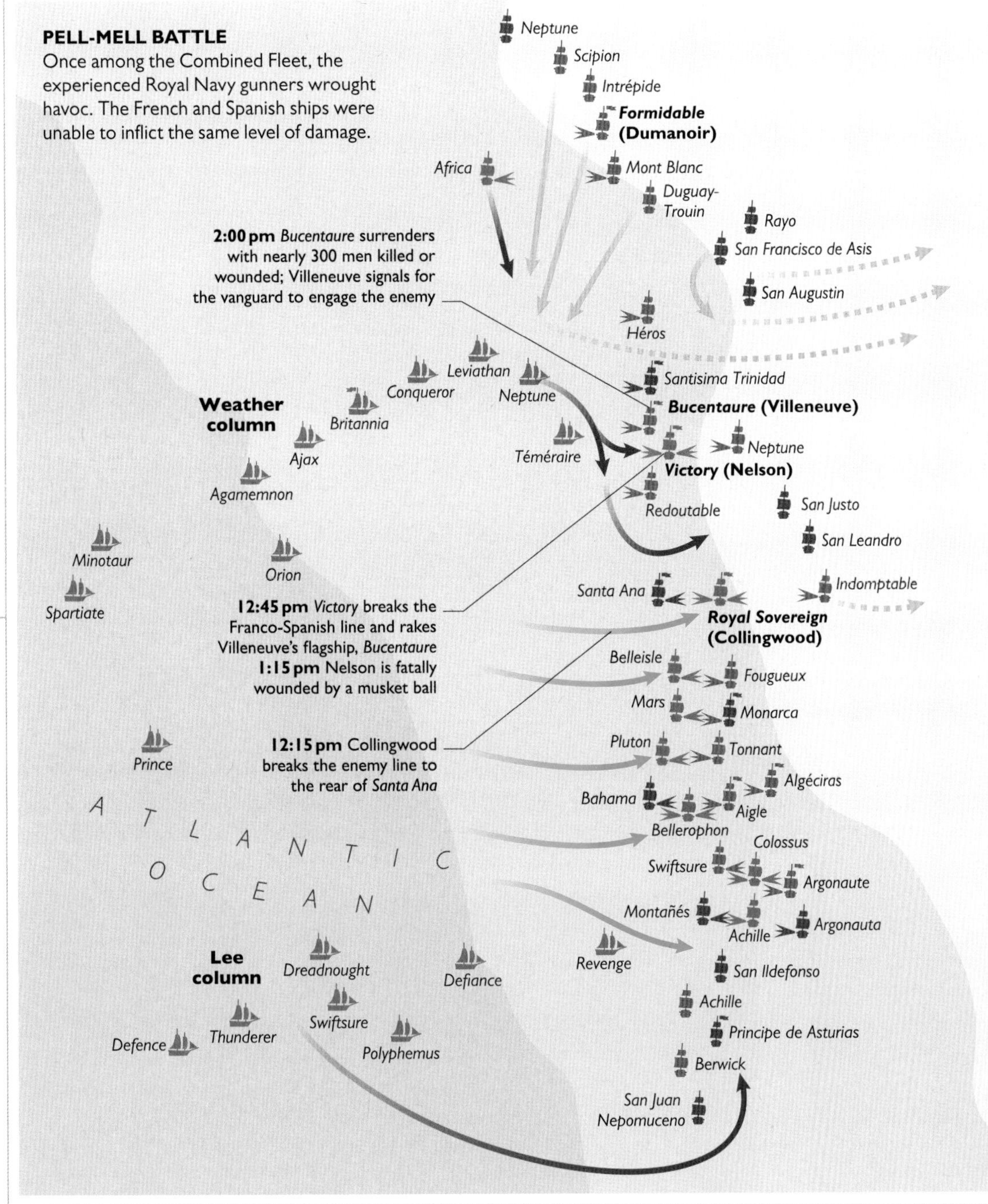
Neptune
Scipion
Intrépide
Formidable (Dumanoir)
Africa
Mont Blanc
Duguay-Trouin
Rayo
San Francisco de Asis
San Augustin
Héros
2:00 pm Bucentaure surrenders with nearly 300 men killed or wounded; Villeneuve signals for the vanguard to engage the enemy
Leviathan
Conqueror
Neptune
Weather column
Britannia
Ajax
Agamemnon
Téméraire
Santisima Trinidad
Bucentaure (Villeneuve)
Neptune
Victory (Nelson)
Redoutable
San Justo
San Leandro
Minotaur
Spartiate
Orion
12:45 pm Victory breaks the Franco-Spanish line and rakes Villeneuve's flagship, Bucentaure
1:15 pm Nelson is fatally wounded by a musket ball
Santa Ana
Royal Sovereign (Collingwood)
Indomptable
Belleisle
Fougueux
Mars
Monarca
Prince
12:15 pm Collingwood breaks the enemy line to the rear of Santa Ana
Pluton
Tonnant
Algéciras
Bahama
Aigle
Bellerophon
Colossus
ATLANTIC OCEAN
Swiftsure
Argonaute
Montañés
Achille
Argonauta
Revenge
Lee column
Dreadnought
Defiance
San Ildefonso
Achille
Thunderer
Swiftsure
Defence
Polyphemus
Principe de Asturias
Berwick
San Juan Nepomuceno
Franco–Spanish vanguard advances
Flight of French and Spanish Ships
Nelson's column engages the enemy
Collingwood's first group
Collingwood's second group

6 FRANCO-SPANISH VANGUARD ENGAGES AND THE BATTLE ENDS 2:30–5:30 PM

With the centre and rear of the Franco-Spanish line heavily engaged, Rear-Admiral Dumanoir of the *Formidable* turned and led several ships of the vanguard to engage the stragglers of Nelson's division. However, as the rear of his fleet was overwhelmed, Dumanoir called off the engagement and headed away from the fighting towards the Straits of Gibraltar.

5 NELSON JOINS THE MELEE 12:45–1:15 PM

At 12:45 pm, Nelson's flagship, *Victory*, crossed the Franco-Spanish line and unleashed a broadside down the length of *Bucentaure*. *Temeraire*, *Conqueror*, and *Neptune* joined battle, and *Victory* locked masts with *Redoubtable*. Nelson was hit in the shoulder by a French musket and carried below decks. *Temeraire* fired on *Redoubtable*, preventing her crew from boarding *Victory*.

4 COLLINGWOOD'S COLUMN BREAKS THE LINE 12:15–2:00 PM

Just after midday, Collingwood's *Royal Sovereign* ran the gauntlet of broadsides from *Fougueux*, *Indomptable*, *San Justo*, and *San Leandro*, before breaking the enemy line to the rear of *Santa Ana*. Collingwood was then isolated until the rest of his first group engaged the enemy. At around 1:30 pm, a second group enveloped the rear of the Combined Fleet and joined the general mêlée.

NELSON'S NAVY

A string of naval victories from 1793–1815, many involving or commanded by Horatio Nelson, saw Britain's Royal Navy emerge as master of the world's oceans. Its success was built on gunnery, leadership, and attacking spirit.

△ **Small and powerful**
Naval guns were mounted on wheeled carriages that rolled backwards with the recoil from firing their solid iron shot. This 6-pounder cannon was the smallest calibre found on board.

The Royal Navy's warships were not notably superior to the warships of the other European navies it repeatedly defeated. Its mix of two- or three-deck ships of the line, mounting 74–120 guns each, and single-deck frigates were typical of its time. Under Nelson, Britain's most famous naval commander, the Royal Navy – unlike its enemies – practised gunnery on a daily basis. Nelson's tactic of breaking up the formal lines in which naval battles were traditionally fought gave his gunners the maximum chance to batter the enemy with their well-rehearsed broadsides – simultaneous volleys of gunfire from one side of a ship. The Royal Navy's "Articles of War" – provisions governing the naval code of conduct – required all commanders to engage the enemy aggressively at every opportunity. This offensive spirit was reinforced by the award of prize money for enemy ships taken.

Diverse band

Nevertheless, Nelson's Royal Navy was not a perfect military machine. In times of war, most of its sailors were "impressed" (forcibly recruited) from civilian seafarers. As demand outran supply, the ranks were filled with non-sailors and even convicts. The motley crew was kept in line through harsh punishments, including flogging. Although there were some mutinies, morale on the whole held surprisingly well. Nepotism ran high, but many officers also achieved high positions by showing outstanding courage and individual initiative, fulfilling Nelson's ideal of a "band of brothers" bonded in battle.

ADMIRAL HORATIO NELSON 1758–1805

Born in 1758, Horatio Nelson joined the Royal Navy in 1771 as a midshipman at the age of 12. Always in the thick of the fighting, he lost the sight of an eye in 1794 and his right arm in 1797. Unorthodox and often insubordinate, Nelson's bold destruction of a French fleet at the battle of the Nile in 1798 made him a national hero. He was killed by a sniper in the course of his greatest victory over the French and Spanish at Trafalgar (see pp.162–63) in 1805.

Fiery end
The Battle of the Nile, 1798, depicted here by American artist Mather Brown, reaches its violent climax as the French flagship *L'Orient*, met with a heavy bombardment of shots fired by Nelson's strategically positioned British ships, catches fire and explodes.

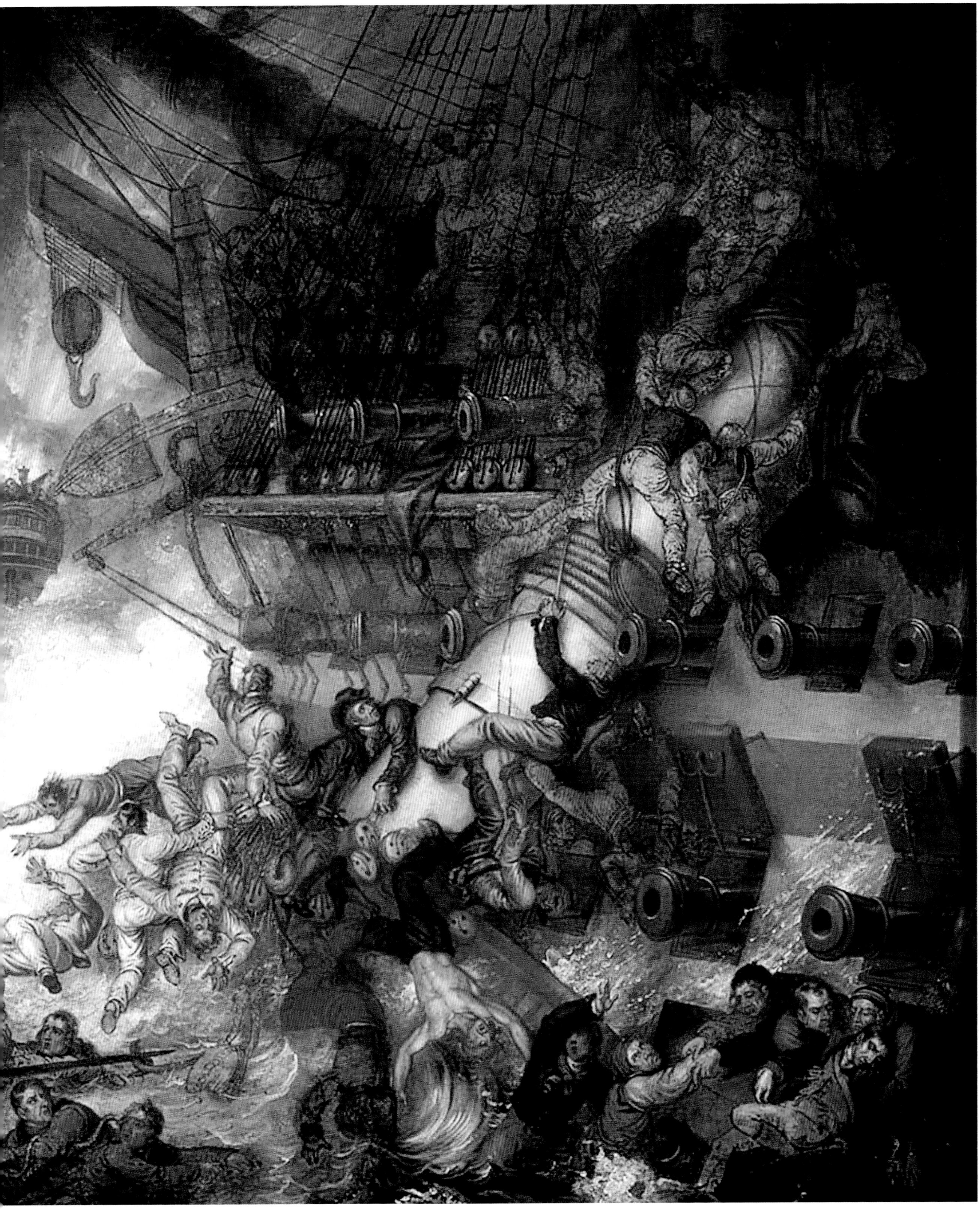

1 NAPOLEON BAITS THE TRAP
23 NOV–1 DEC 1805

Napoleon wished to trick the Allies into thinking he was unwilling to fight. To do this, he abandoned the strong position he had taken on the Pratzen Heights and scattered his troops in a line to the right, along the Goldbach stream. He kept his main force, under Marshal Soult, hidden from view, concealing his true strength and intentions.

2 THE RUSSO-AUSTRIAN ARMY TAKES ITS POSITIONS 1–2 DECEMBER

On 1 December the Allies occupied the Pratzen Heights. The bulk of the Allied army, organized into five columns, prepared for an attack on Napoleon's understrength right flank. On the right, Bagration's forces were positioned to engage the enemy's left flank, while Prince Constantine held the Imperial Guard in reserve.

3 THE ATTACK ON THE FRENCH RIGHT
8:00AM, 2 DECEMBER

The battle began when Austrian units attacked the French at Telnitz. They were repulsed at first, but, reinforced by Langeron and Prebyshevsky's columns, they had great superiority of numbers. The timely arrival of Marshal Davout's troops, who had marched for two days from Vienna, bolstered the French. Their right flank held strong.

Allied advance on the French right

Davout's arrival

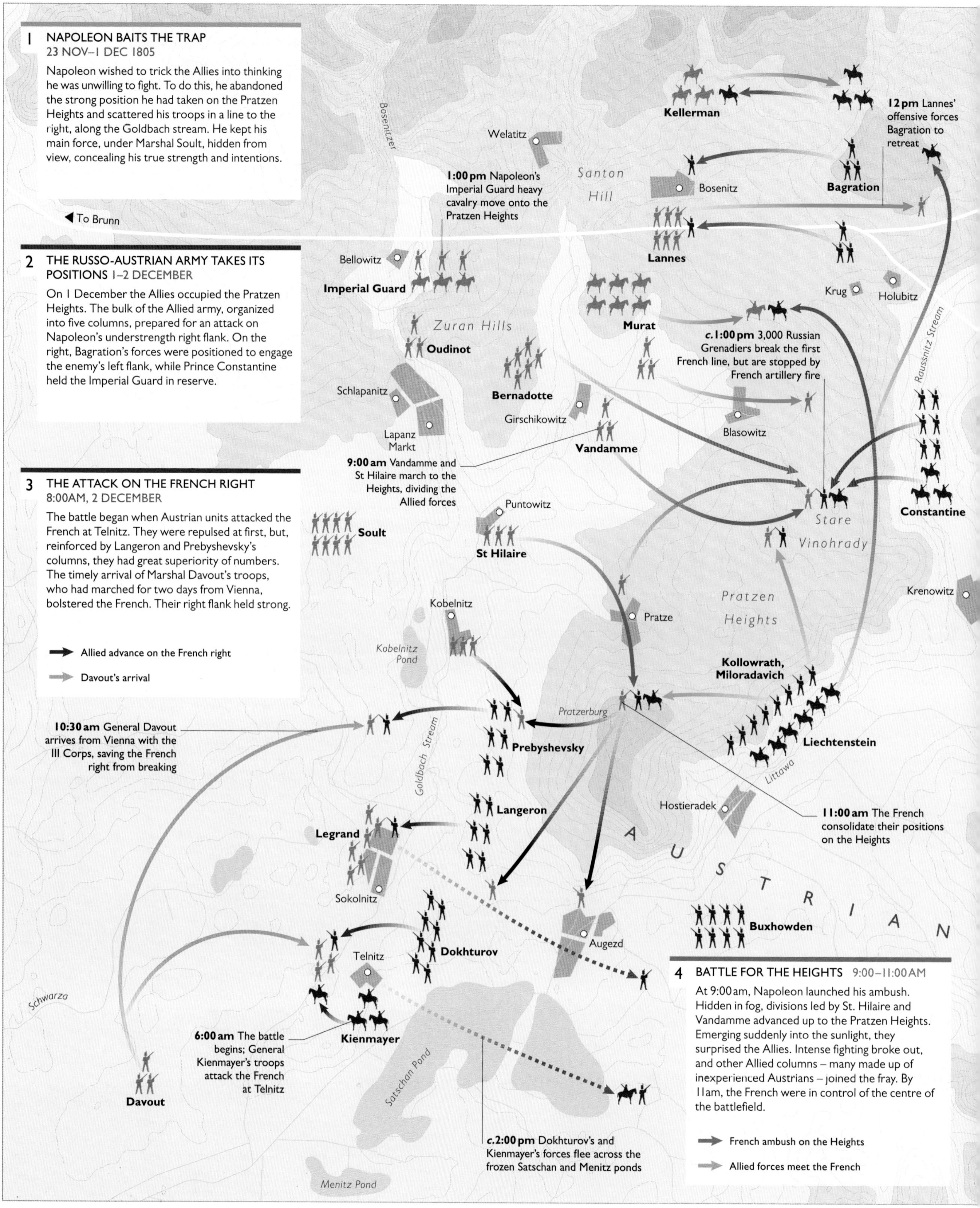

To Brunn
Bosenitzer
Welatitz
Santon Hill
Kellerman
12 pm Lannes' offensive forces Bagration to retreat
Bosenitz
Bagration
1:00 pm Napoleon's Imperial Guard heavy cavalry move onto the Pratzen Heights
Lannes
Bellowitz
Imperial Guard
Krug
Holubitz
Zuran Hills
Murat
Oudinot
c.1:00 pm 3,000 Russian Grenadiers break the first French line, but are stopped by French artillery fire
Raussnitz Stream
Bernadotte
Schlapanitz
Girschikowitz
Blasowitz
Lapanz Markt
Vandamme
9:00 am Vandamme and St Hilaire march to the Heights, dividing the Allied forces
Puntowitz
Stare Vinohrady
Constantine
Soult
St Hilaire
Kobelnitz
Pratze
Pratzen Heights
Krenowitz
Kobelnitz Pond
Kollowrath, Miloradavich
Pratzerburg
10:30 am General Davout arrives from Vienna with the III Corps, saving the French right from breaking
Goldbach Stream
Prebyshevsky
Liechtenstein
Littawa
Langeron
Hostieradek
11:00 am The French consolidate their positions on the Heights
Legrand
AUSTRIAN
Sokolnitz
Buxhowden
Augezd
Telnitz
Dokhturov
Schwarza
6:00 am The battle begins; General Kienmayer's troops attack the French at Telnitz
Kienmayer
Satschan Pond
Davout
c.2:00 pm Dokhturov's and Kienmayer's forces flee across the frozen Satschan and Menitz ponds
Menitz Pond

4 BATTLE FOR THE HEIGHTS 9:00–11:00AM

At 9:00am, Napoleon launched his ambush. Hidden in fog, divisions led by St. Hilaire and Vandamme advanced up to the Pratzen Heights. Emerging suddenly into the sunlight, they surprised the Allies. Intense fighting broke out, and other Allied columns – many made up of inexperienced Austrians – joined the fray. By 11am, the French were in control of the centre of the battlefield.

French ambush on the Heights

Allied forces meet the French

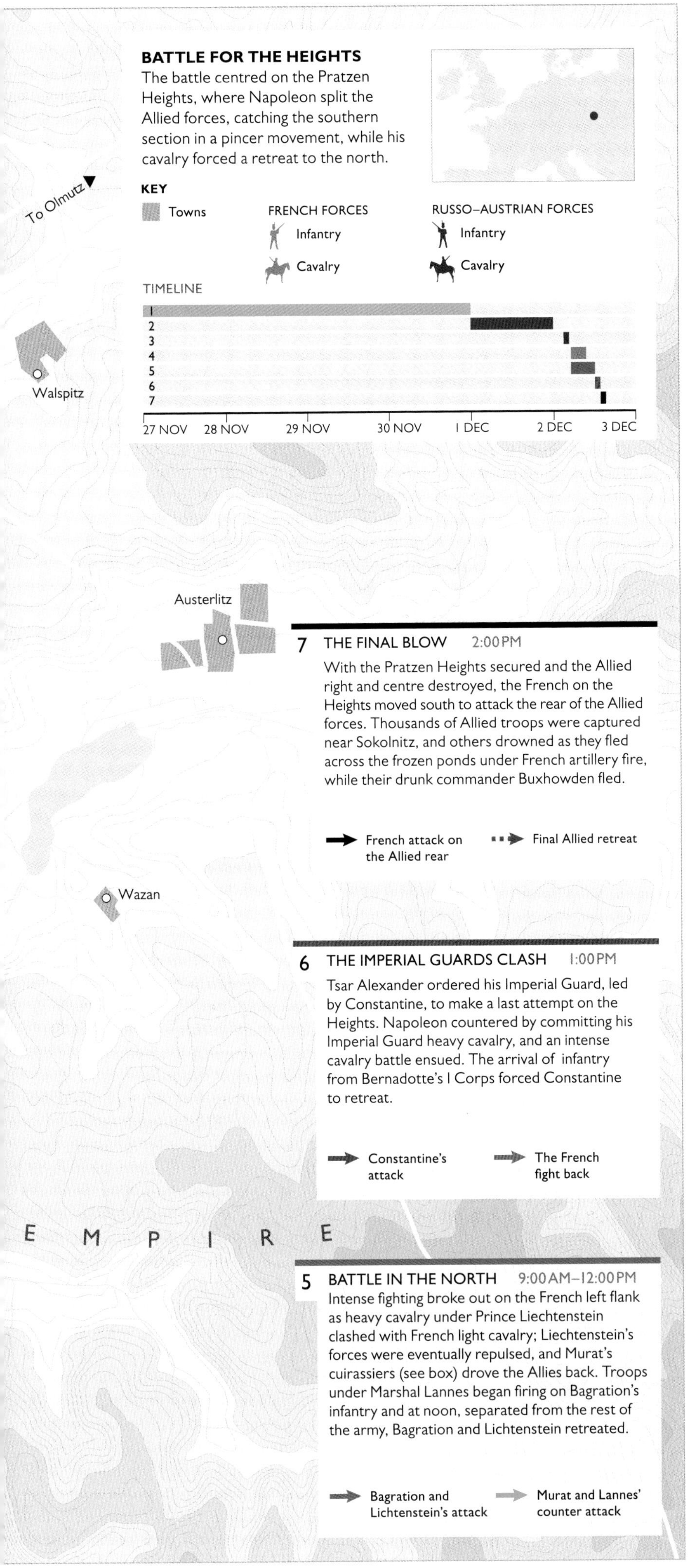
To Olmutz
Walspitz
Austerlitz
Wazan
E M P I R E

BATTLE FOR THE HEIGHTS

The battle centred on the Pratzen Heights, where Napoleon split the Allied forces, catching the southern section in a pincer movement, while his cavalry forced a retreat to the north.

KEY

Towns

FRENCH FORCES: Infantry, Cavalry

RUSSO–AUSTRIAN FORCES: Infantry, Cavalry

TIMELINE

1 2 3 4 5 6 7

27 NOV · 28 NOV · 29 NOV · 30 NOV · 1 DEC · 2 DEC · 3 DEC

7 THE FINAL BLOW 2:00PM

With the Pratzen Heights secured and the Allied right and centre destroyed, the French on the Heights moved south to attack the rear of the Allied forces. Thousands of Allied troops were captured near Sokolnitz, and others drowned as they fled across the frozen ponds under French artillery fire, while their drunk commander Buxhowden fled.

French attack on the Allied rear — Final Allied retreat

6 THE IMPERIAL GUARDS CLASH 1:00PM

Tsar Alexander ordered his Imperial Guard, led by Constantine, to make a last attempt on the Heights. Napoleon countered by committing his Imperial Guard heavy cavalry, and an intense cavalry battle ensued. The arrival of infantry from Bernadotte's I Corps forced Constantine to retreat.

Constantine's attack — The French fight back

5 BATTLE IN THE NORTH 9:00AM–12:00PM

Intense fighting broke out on the French left flank as heavy cavalry under Prince Liechtenstein clashed with French light cavalry; Liechtenstein's forces were eventually repulsed, and Murat's cuirassiers (see box) drove the Allies back. Troops under Marshal Lannes began firing on Bagration's infantry and at noon, separated from the rest of the army, Bagration and Lichtenstein retreated.

Bagration and Lichtenstein's attack — Murat and Lannes' counter attack

AUSTERLITZ

On 2 December 1805, Napoleon outwitted a larger Russo-Austrian force to secure one of his most brilliant victories. The result of exceptional tactical skill and hard fighting, his victory forced Austria to make peace, and weakened the anti-French Third Coalition.

By November 1805, Napoleon and his imperial army – the Grande Armée – had pushed deep into central Europe, defeating an Austrian army numbering more than 70,000 at Ulm, and occupying Vienna on 13 November. Now far from France and at the end of overstretched supply lines, Napoleon faced a large Allied Russo-Austrian army, led by Tsar Alexander I, which was advancing from the east, and the prospect of Prussia joining the Third Coalition (Britain, Russia, and Austria) of forces ranged against him. Ignoring advice to withdraw, Napoleon resolved to confront his enemy.

Napoleon chose to do battle near the village of Austerlitz in Moravia (in modern-day Czech Republic). To the north were two hills – Santon and Zuran – and in front was a field suitable for cavalry action. The centrepiece was a long, low hill – The Pratzen Heights – of which Napoleon said to his generals: "Gentlemen, examine this ground carefully; it is going to be a battlefield." He formulated a plan to convince the Allied army that he was weak, spurring it into an attack on his right flank. Once they were committed, he planned to drive through the enemy's centre and launch a cavalry attack on its right. The Allies played into his hands, and in the ensuing battle only 9,000 of Napoleon's 73,000 men were killed or wounded. Allied casualties and prisoners totalled at least a third of their larger army, and Austria was forced to withdraw from the Third Coalition war.

> *"This victory will finish our campaign, and we shall be able to go into winter quarters."*
>
> NAPOLEON'S SPEECH TO HIS ARMY ON THE EVE OF BATTLE

CUIRASSIERS

The cuirassiers were the heaviest and most elite cavalry units deployed in the Napoleonic Wars by the French, but also by Russian and Austrian armies. Armed with pistols, carbines, and long straight sabres, and distinguished by their body armour (the cuirass), cuirassiers rode huge horses and formed a powerful strike force which could change the course of a battle. Napoleon was well aware of the impact these forces could have, and increased the number of French cuirassier regiments from one to fourteen.

French cuirassiers' helmet

TALAVERA

In May 1808, a popular revolt had broken out in Spain against Napoleon's rule over the country. The following year, a British force marched into Spain, where it joined up with the Spanish army to take on the French army of Joseph Bonaparte (Napoleon's brother) in a fierce set-piece battle at Talavera, near Madrid.

In July 1809, a British army, led by General Sir Arthur Wellesley (later the Duke of Wellington), advanced into Spain to link up with the Spanish army under General de la Cuesta. The combined force encountered the French outside Talavera, 120 km (75 miles) southwest of Madrid; around 20,000 British and around 35,000 Spanish troops faced over 45,000 French soldiers under Joseph Bonaparte. The allies took up positions along the Portiña, a stream running north from Talavera.

Late on 27 July, the French mounted a surprise attack on the allies but were driven off after frantic fighting. The British repulsed a second attack at dawn the next day. Knowing that a second Spanish army had reached Madrid, Joseph had no choice but to try to defeat Wellesley's forces outright. That afternoon, the French attacked the British lines at three points. The French almost broke through in the centre, but Wellesley reinforced the British line so that it held. The French withdrew that night, though both sides had suffered heavily, with over 7,000 casualties each. Following his victory, Wellesley was given the title Viscount Wellington, but he soon withdrew to Portgual to avoid encirclement, and successive Spanish efforts to liberate Madrid were defeated.

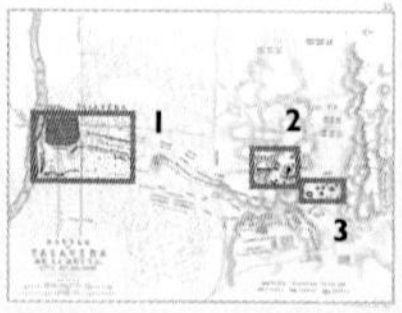

1
2
3

KEY

1 The Spanish positions in and around Talavera were protected by stone-walled olive groves and anchored on the River Tagus.

2 The Cerro de Medellín – a key strongpoint for the British. French attacks on this location on the 27 and 28 July failed.

3 French infantry squares formed to face the British cavalry's charge, which came to grief in a hidden ravine.

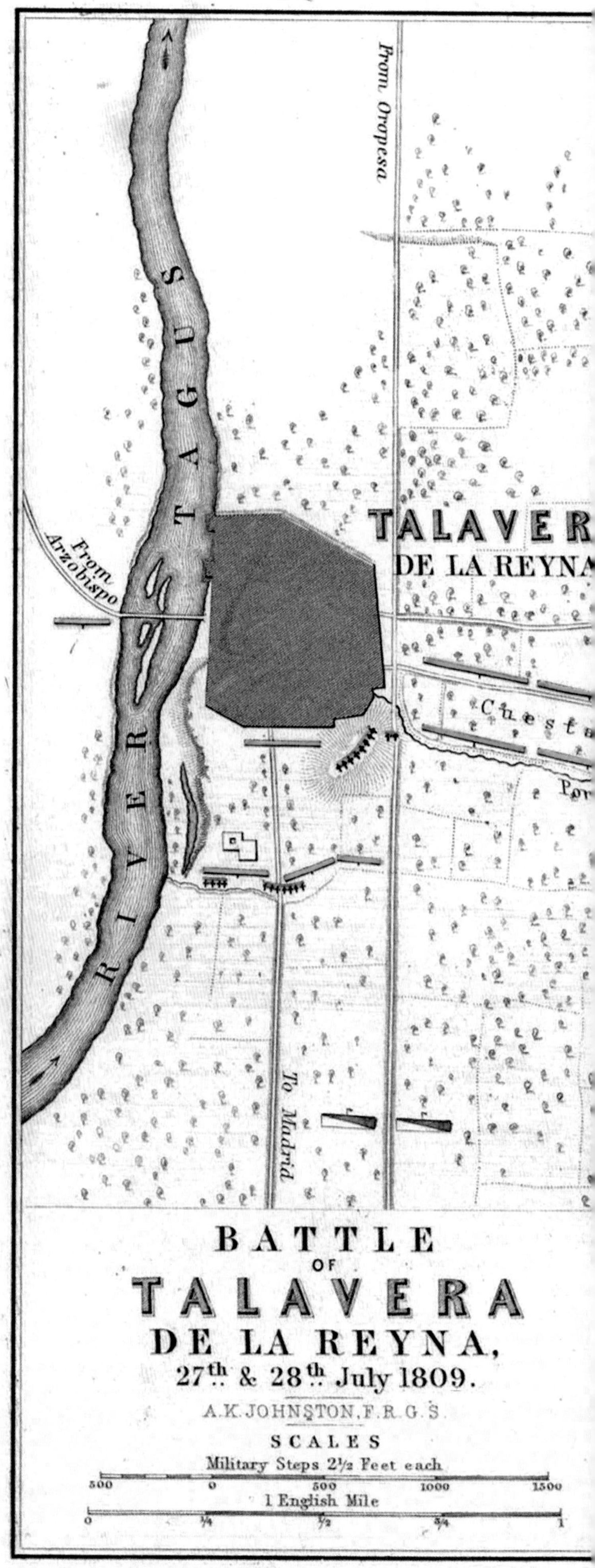

From Oropesa
RIVER TAGUS
From Arzobispo
TALAVER
DE LA REYNA
Cuesta
To Madrid
BATTLE
OF
TALAVERA
DE LA REYNA,
27th & 28th July 1809.
A.K. JOHNSTON, F.R.G.S.
SCALES
Military Steps 2½ Feet each
500 0 500 1000 1500
1 English Mile
0 ¼ ½ ¾ 1

▷ **The field of battle**
This hand-coloured engraved map from the atlas to Alison's History of Europe (1848) shows the Anglo-Spanish and French positions during the main action.

THE MAIN ATTACK
On 28 July, the French attacked at three points. Leval's attack was driven back by Campbell's 4th Division. In the centre, Sherbrooke's men pursued Sebastiani and Lapisse's line too far, creating a gap in the allied line. As the French attacked again, Wellesley had to shore up the line. Finally, Ruffin and Villatte attempted to outflank the allies. A chaotic British cavalry charge failed, but lacking support, the French disengaged.

KEY
- English
- Spanish
- French
- Artillery
- Ruffin and Villatte's attack
- Sebastiani and Lapisse's attack
- Leval's attack
- British counter-attacks

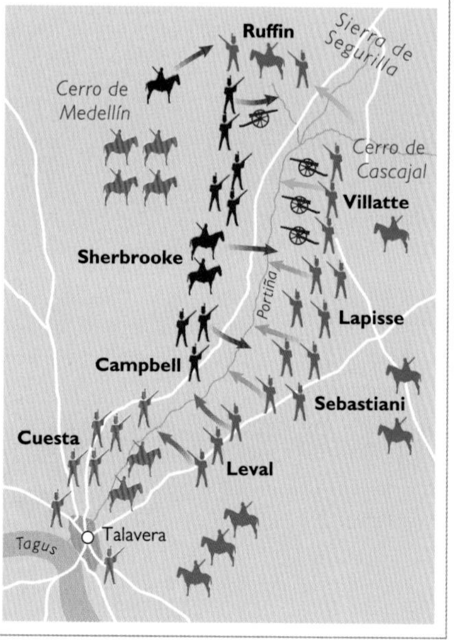

Ruffin
Sierra de Segurilla
Cerro de Medellín
Cerro de Cascajal
Villatte
Sherbrooke
Portiña
Lapisse
Campbell
Sebastiani
Cuesta
Leval
Tagus
Talavera

53

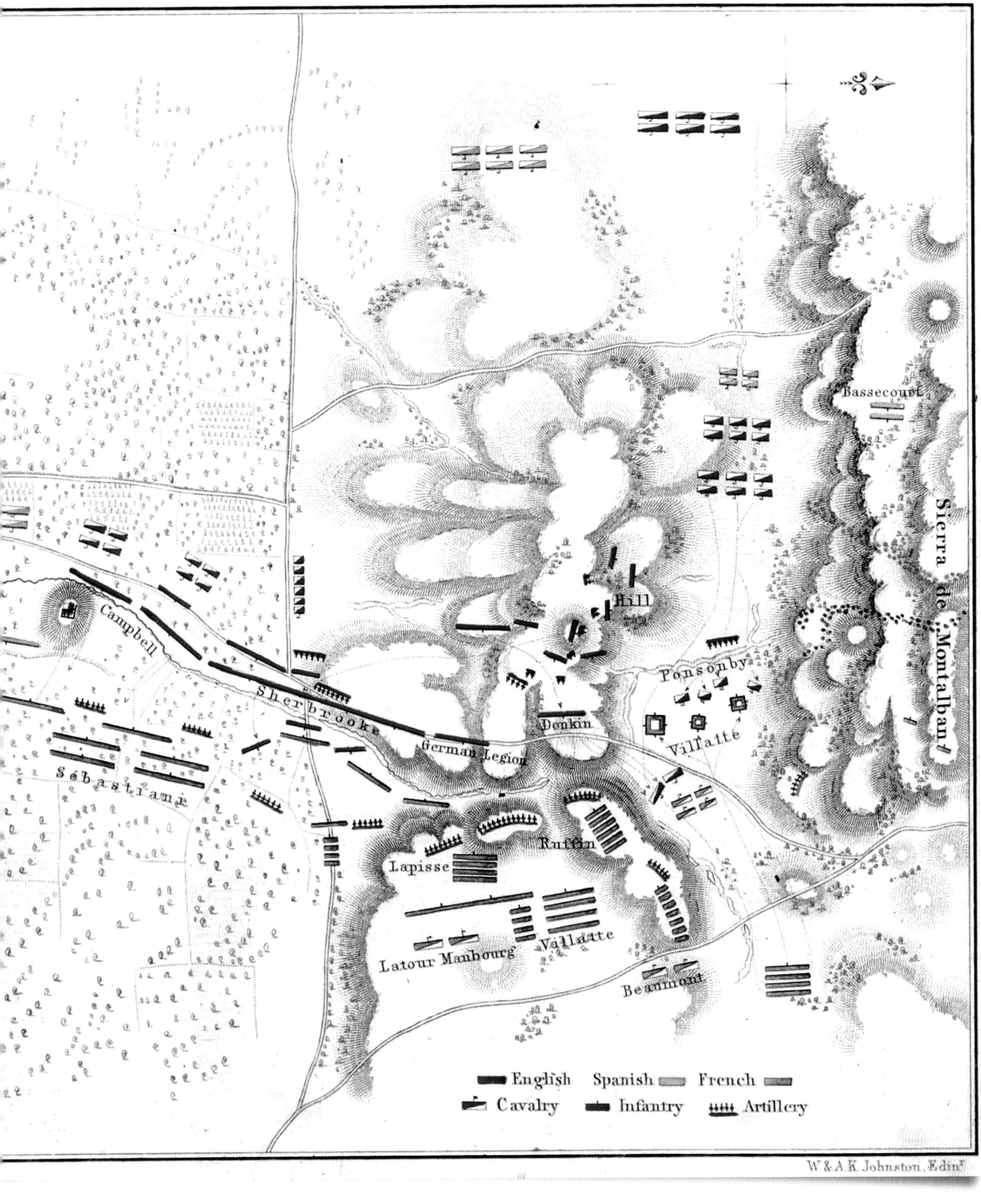
Bassecourt
Sierra de Montalban
Hill
Campbell
Ponsonby
Sherbrooke
Donkin
German Legion
Villatte
Sébastiani
Ruffin
Lapisse
Villatte
Latour Maubourg
Beaumont
English Spanish French
Cavalry Infantry Artillery

W & A K. Johnston, Edin.

Königsberg
Tilsit
Danzig
PRUSSIA
RUSSIAN EMPIRE
Kovno
Vilna
Borodino
Smorgon'
Studyanka
Krasnoy
Smolensk
Moscow
Maloyaroslavets
Vistula
GRAND DUCHY OF WARSAW
Warsaw
Hecoum
Cracow
AUSTRIAN EMPIRE
KEY
Main battle
Russian victories
French victories
French forces
French retreat
RUSSIAN CAMPAIGN
Napoleon's invasion of Russia came at a huge cost. The Russian army frustrated the French by retreating to Moscow and then deserting the city. Exhausted, the French had to march home with winter setting in.

△ **The bloodiest battle**
Fighting was brutal as both sides struggled to control the Raevsky Redoubt. Of the over 250,000 soldiers who fought at Borodino, around 70,000 were killed or injured – making it the bloodiest single day of the war.

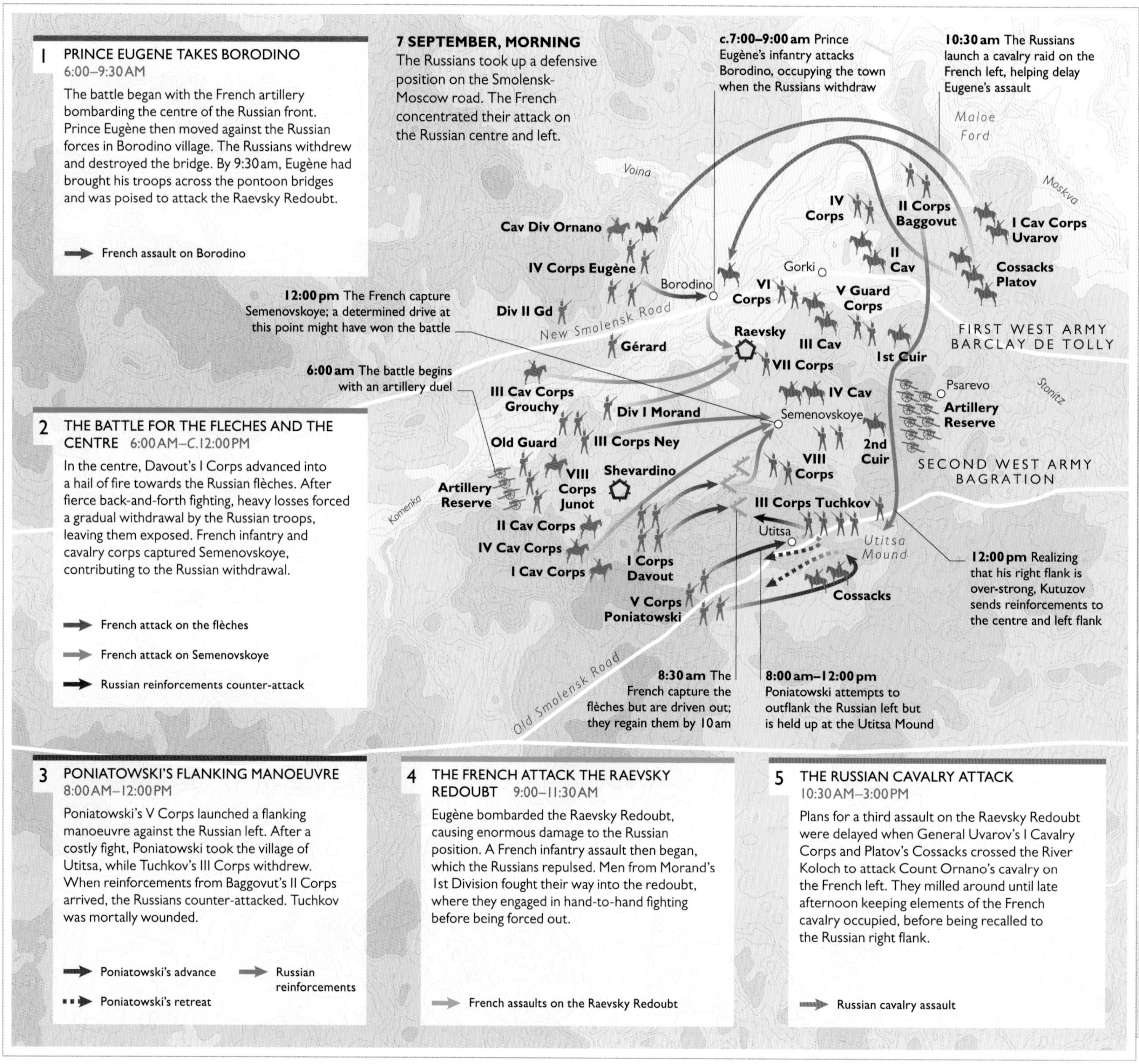
7 SEPTEMBER, MORNING
The Russians took up a defensive position on the Smolensk-Moscow road. The French concentrated their attack on the Russian centre and left.
c.7:00–9:00 am Prince Eugène's infantry attacks Borodino, occupying the town when the Russians withdraw
10:30 am The Russians launch a cavalry raid on the French left, helping delay Eugène's assault
Maloe Ford
Voina
Moskva
IV Corps
II Corps Baggovut
I Cav Corps Uvarov
Cav Div Ornano
II Cav
Cossacks Platov
IV Corps Eugène
Gorki
Borodino
VI Corps
V Guard Corps
12:00 pm The French capture Semenovskoye; a determined drive at this point might have won the battle
Div II Gd
New Smolensk Road
Raevsky
III Cav
FIRST WEST ARMY BARCLAY DE TOLLY
Gérard
1st Cuir
VII Corps
6:00 am The battle begins with an artillery duel
Psarevo
Stonitz
III Cav Corps Grouchy
Div I Morand
IV Cav
Artillery Reserve
Semenovskoye
Old Guard
III Corps Ney
2nd Cuir
VIII Corps
SECOND WEST ARMY BAGRATION
Shevardino
VIII Corps Junot
Artillery Reserve
Kamenka
III Corps Tuchkov
II Cav Corps
Utitsa
IV Cav Corps
Utitsa Mound
I Corps Davout
I Cav Corps
12:00 pm Realizing that his right flank is over-strong, Kutuzov sends reinforcements to the centre and left flank
Cossacks
V Corps Poniatowski
Old Smolensk Road
8:30 am The French capture the flèches but are driven out; they regain them by 10 am
8:00 am–12:00 pm Poniatowski attempts to outflank the Russian left but is held up at the Utitsa Mound

1 PRINCE EUGENE TAKES BORODINO
6:00–9:30 AM

The battle began with the French artillery bombarding the centre of the Russian front. Prince Eugène then moved against the Russian forces in Borodino village. The Russians withdrew and destroyed the bridge. By 9:30 am, Eugène had brought his troops across the pontoon bridges and was poised to attack the Raevsky Redoubt.

French assault on Borodino

2 THE BATTLE FOR THE FLECHES AND THE CENTRE 6:00 AM–C.12:00 PM

In the centre, Davout's I Corps advanced into a hail of fire towards the Russian flèches. After fierce back-and-forth fighting, heavy losses forced a gradual withdrawal by the Russian troops, leaving them exposed. French infantry and cavalry corps captured Semenovskoye, contributing to the Russian withdrawal.

French attack on the flèches
French attack on Semenovskoye
Russian reinforcements counter-attack

3 PONIATOWSKI'S FLANKING MANOEUVRE
8:00 AM–12:00 PM

Poniatowski's V Corps launched a flanking manoeuvre against the Russian left. After a costly fight, Poniatowski took the village of Utitsa, while Tuchkov's III Corps withdrew. When reinforcements from Baggovut's II Corps arrived, the Russians counter-attacked. Tuchkov was mortally wounded.

Poniatowski's advance
Poniatowski's retreat
Russian reinforcements

4 THE FRENCH ATTACK THE RAEVSKY REDOUBT 9:00–11:30 AM

Eugène bombarded the Raevsky Redoubt, causing enormous damage to the Russian position. A French infantry assault then began, which the Russians repulsed. Men from Morand's 1st Division fought their way into the redoubt, where they engaged in hand-to-hand fighting before being forced out.

French assaults on the Raevsky Redoubt

5 THE RUSSIAN CAVALRY ATTACK
10:30 AM–3:00 PM

Plans for a third assault on the Raevsky Redoubt were delayed when General Uvarov's I Cavalry Corps and Platov's Cossacks crossed the River Koloch to attack Count Ornano's cavalry on the French left. They milled around until late afternoon keeping elements of the French cavalry occupied, before being recalled to the Russian right flank.

Russian cavalry assault

BORODINO

As Napoleon's Grande Armée marched into Russia, the Russians retreated, drawing the French deep into Russian territory. Exhausted by the brutal march, the French finally faced the Tsar's army at Borodino. Thousands would die in the bloodiest battle of the Napoleonic wars.

In June 1812, Napoleon marched an army of several hundred thousand men into Russia. Unlike many of his earlier campaigns, however, this invasion was soon beset with problems: the Russians avoided large-scale battle and instead drew Napoleon's Grande Armée deep into Russian territory. There, hunger, disease, exhaustion, and bad weather took a costly toll on the French forces.

Finally, in early September, the Russian commander Field Marshal Kutuzov took up position at Borodino, only 110km (70 miles) west of Moscow, the spiritual capital of Russia. The Russians hastily built a series of fortifications, although they worried about the vulnerability of their left.

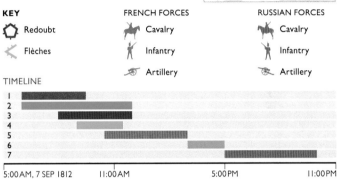

Napoleon, however, displayed little of his usual strategic genius. On 7 September, he opted for a frontal assault on the Russian fortifications that, over the course of the day, resulted in at least 70,000 casualties in total. By 5pm, the French had captured the Russian fortifications, and the Russians had no reserves left. However, Napoleon refused to commit his Guard to win a decisive victory, and the Russian forces were able to retreat in an orderly manner.

Seven days later, Napoleon occupied Moscow in what proved to be a hollow victory. Within weeks, the French were forced to set out on a catastrophic retreat through the Russian winter.

THE RUSSIANS TAKE POSITION

Field Marshal Kutuzov took up position on the Smolensk-Moscow road. The Russian side constructed a series of fortifications that would become the main focus of the French attack throughout the 15 September.

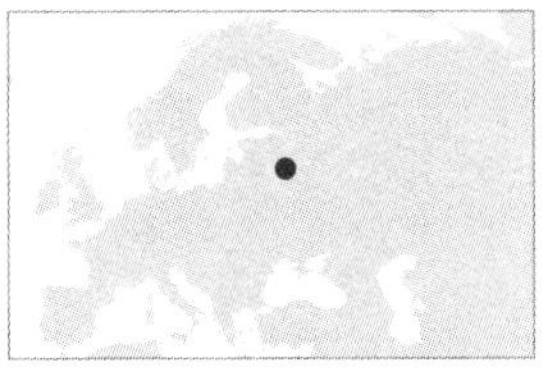

KEY
- Redoubt
- Flèches

FRENCH FORCES
- Cavalry
- Infantry
- Artillery

RUSSIAN FORCES
- Cavalry
- Infantry
- Artillery

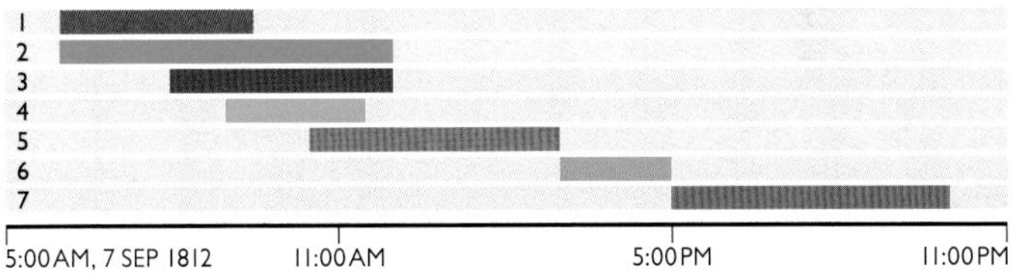

TIMELINE
1
2
3
4
5
6
7
5:00AM, 7 SEP 1812
11:00AM
5:00PM
11:00PM

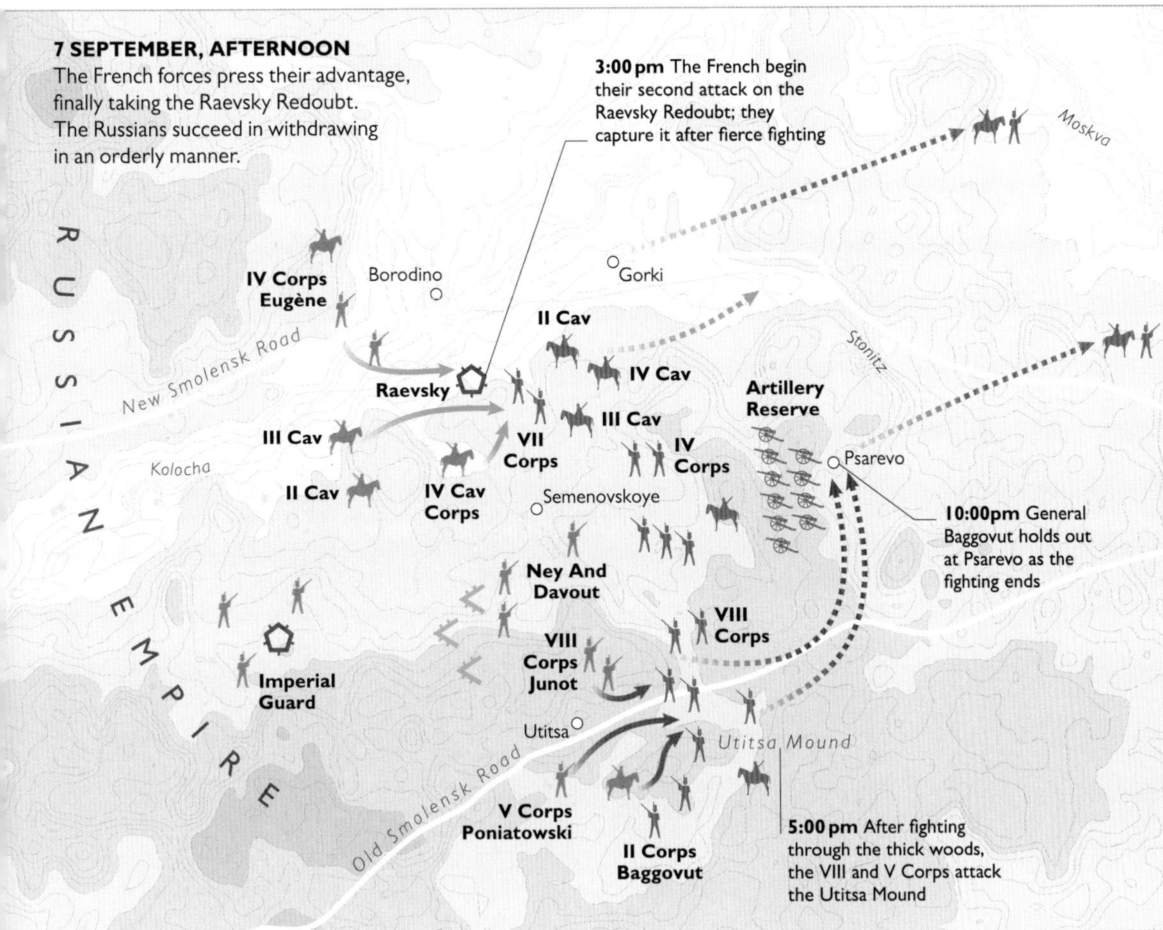

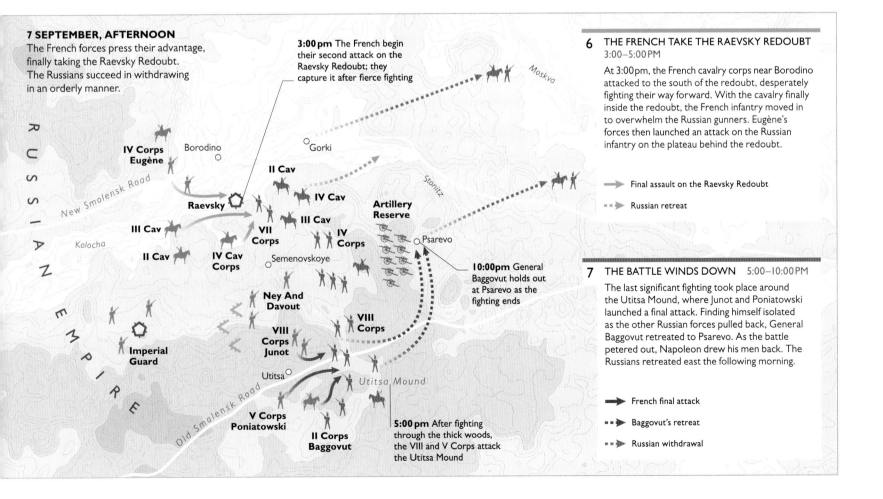

7 SEPTEMBER, AFTERNOON
The French forces press their advantage, finally taking the Raevsky Redoubt. The Russians succeed in withdrawing in an orderly manner.
3:00 pm The French begin their second attack on the Raevsky Redoubt; they capture it after fierce fighting
Moskva
RUSSIAN EMPIRE
IV Corps Eugène
Borodino
Gorki
New Smolensk Road
Raevsky
II Cav
IV Cav
III Cav
Stonitz
Artillery Reserve
III Cav
VII Corps
IV Corps
Psarevo
Kolocha
II Cav
IV Cav Corps
Semenovskoye
10:00pm General Baggovut holds out at Psarevo as the fighting ends
Ney And Davout
VIII Corps
VIII Corps Junot
Imperial Guard
Utitsa
Utitsa Mound
Old Smolensk Road
V Corps Poniatowski
II Corps Baggovut
5:00 pm After fighting through the thick woods, the VIII and V Corps attack the Utitsa Mound

6 THE FRENCH TAKE THE RAEVSKY REDOUBT
3:00–5:00PM

At 3:00pm, the French cavalry corps near Borodino attacked to the south of the redoubt, desperately fighting their way forward. With the cavalry finally inside the redoubt, the French infantry moved in to overwhelm the Russian gunners. Eugène's forces then launched an attack on the Russian infantry on the plateau behind the redoubt.

- Final assault on the Raevsky Redoubt
- Russian retreat

7 THE BATTLE WINDS DOWN 5:00–10:00PM

The last significant fighting took place around the Utitsa Mound, where Junot and Poniatowski launched a final attack. Finding himself isolated as the other Russian forces pulled back, General Baggovut retreated to Psarevo. As the battle petered out, Napoleon drew his men back. The Russians retreated east the following morning.

- French final attack
- Baggovut's retreat
- Russian withdrawal

NAPOLEON AND HIS ARMY

Starting his military career at the age of 16 as an artillery officer, Napoleon crowned himself the Emperor of the French in 1804. By 1807, his Grand Armée had decisively defeated all major continental European armies.

△ **The shako**
Under Napoleon, the cylindrical shako, made of leather and felt, replaced the bicorne as the headgear of the infantry.

Under Napoleon, the French army enjoyed important organizational and tactical advantages over other European armies of the time. The army was a product of the former monarchy and of the new regime that had formed after the French Revolution (1789). It had benefited from reforms under the old regime, which included improvements in light infantry tactics and the standardization of field artillery; they also paved the way for the autonomous divisional and corps structure which Napoleon used to such effect.

Napoleon's innovations

From the new regime, Napoleon inherited mass conscription, an economy geared towards war, and an offensive outlook that kept the war away from France as much as possible. Napoleon made increasing use of large artillery formations to breach enemy lines. He also organized the Grand Armée into corps, which were, in essence, highly mobile miniature armies, capable of fighting independently. The Battle of Ulm (1805) was the first field test where the corps successfully demonstrated their effectiveness and agility. To all this, Napoleon added operational brilliance, strategic intuition, and the ability to bond with his soldiers, be it marshals or lowly grenadiers.

△ **Army of the Ocean Coasts**
In this early 19th-century painting, Napoleon inspects his troops at a training camp in Boulogne in August 1804. The newly formed army, known as the *Armée des côtes de l'Océan* (Army of the Ocean Coasts), later became the Grande Armée.

Napoleon in action
This 1808 painting by Louis-Francois, Baron Lejeune, shows Napoleon (centre) directing the French infantry squares at the Battle of the Pyramids (see p.159). Such infantry formations were used to repulse massed cavalry charges.

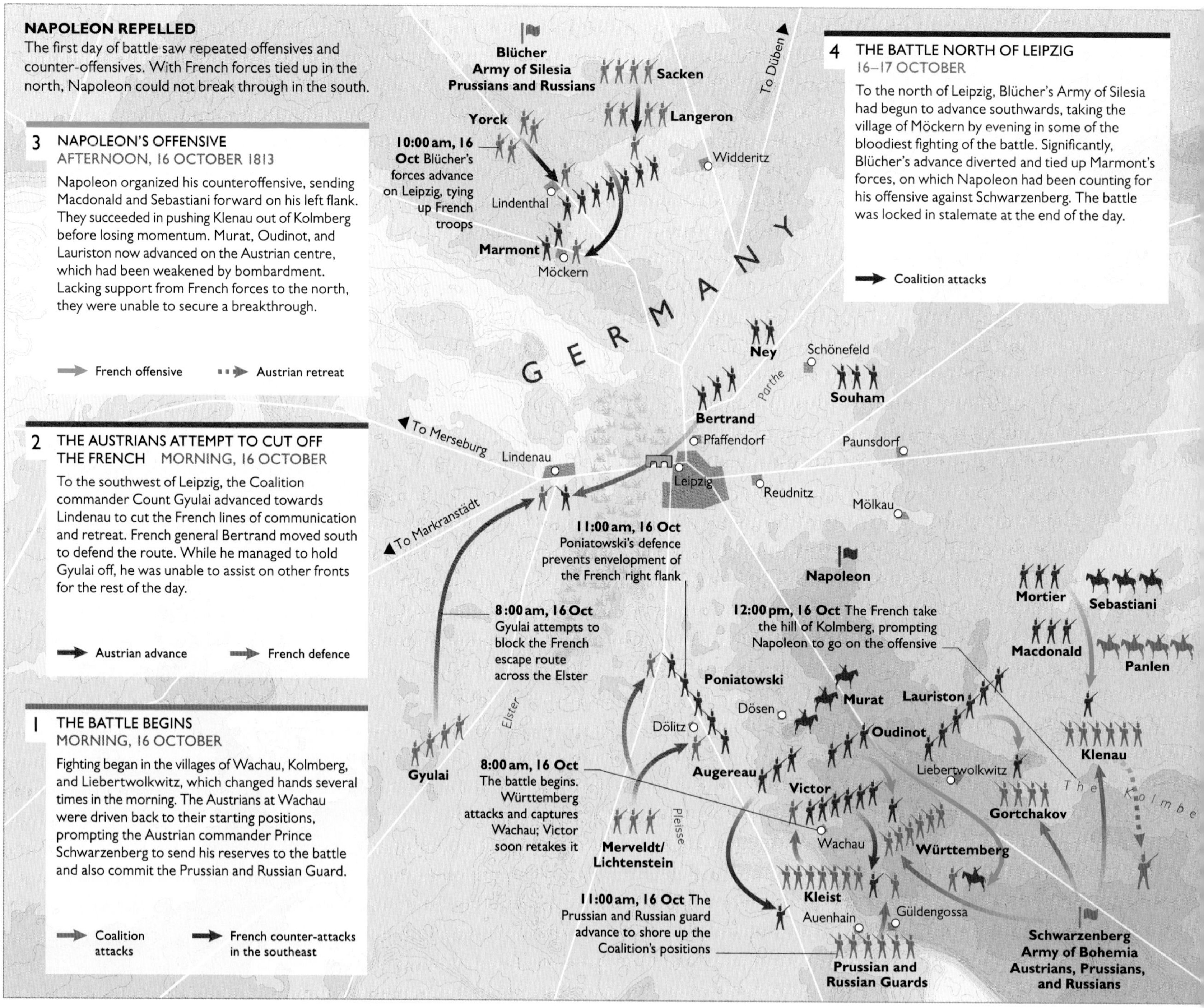
NAPOLEON REPELLED
The first day of battle saw repeated offensives and counter-offensives. With French forces tied up in the north, Napoleon could not break through in the south.
3 NAPOLEON'S OFFENSIVE
AFTERNOON, 16 OCTOBER 1813
Napoleon organized his counteroffensive, sending Macdonald and Sebastiani forward on his left flank. They succeeded in pushing Klenau out of Kolmberg before losing momentum. Murat, Oudinot, and Lauriston now advanced on the Austrian centre, which had been weakened by bombardment. Lacking support from French forces to the north, they were unable to secure a breakthrough.
French offensive
Austrian retreat
2 THE AUSTRIANS ATTEMPT TO CUT OFF THE FRENCH MORNING, 16 OCTOBER
To the southwest of Leipzig, the Coalition commander Count Gyulai advanced towards Lindenau to cut the French lines of communication and retreat. French general Bertrand moved south to defend the route. While he managed to hold Gyulai off, he was unable to assist on other fronts for the rest of the day.
Austrian advance
French defence
1 THE BATTLE BEGINS
MORNING, 16 OCTOBER
Fighting began in the villages of Wachau, Kolmberg, and Liebertwolkwitz, which changed hands several times in the morning. The Austrians at Wachau were driven back to their starting positions, prompting the Austrian commander Prince Schwarzenberg to send his reserves to the battle and also commit the Prussian and Russian Guard.
Coalition attacks
French counter-attacks in the southeast
4 THE BATTLE NORTH OF LEIPZIG
16–17 OCTOBER
To the north of Leipzig, Blücher's Army of Silesia had begun to advance southwards, taking the village of Möckern by evening in some of the bloodiest fighting of the battle. Significantly, Blücher's advance diverted and tied up Marmont's forces, on which Napoleon had been counting for his offensive against Schwarzenberg. The battle was locked in stalemate at the end of the day.
Coalition attacks
Blücher
Army of Silesia
Prussians and Russians
Sacken
To Düben
Yorck
Langeron
10:00 am, 16 Oct Blücher's forces advance on Leipzig, tying up French troops
Widderitz
Lindenthal
Marmont
Möckern
GERMANY
Ney
Schönefeld
Souham
Parthe
Bertrand
To Merseburg
Pfaffendorf
Paunsdorf
Lindenau
Leipzig
Reudnitz
Mölkau
To Markranstädt
11:00 am, 16 Oct Poniatowski's defence prevents envelopment of the French right flank
Napoleon
Mortier
Sebastiani
12:00 pm, 16 Oct The French take the hill of Kolmberg, prompting Napoleon to go on the offensive
Macdonald
Panlen
8:00 am, 16 Oct Gyulai attempts to block the French escape route across the Elster
Poniatowski
Dösen
Murat
Lauriston
Elster
Dölitz
Oudinot
Klenau
Gyulai
8:00 am, 16 Oct The battle begins. Württemberg attacks and captures Wachau; Victor soon retakes it
Augereau
Liebertwolkwitz
Victor
The Kolmbe
Gortchakov
Pleisse
Merveldt/ Lichtenstein
Wachau
Württemberg
11:00 am, 16 Oct The Prussian and Russian guard advance to shore up the Coalition's positions
Kleist
Auenhain
Güldengossa
Prussian and Russian Guards
Schwarzenberg
Army of Bohemia
Austrians, Prussians, and Russians

LEIPZIG

At Leipzig in Saxony on 16–18 October 1813, the combined armies of the Sixth Coalition decisively defeated Napoleon in the largest land battle in Europe before World War I. It involved around 500,000 men, of whom almost 100,000 were killed or wounded.

After his disastrous invasion of Russia in 1812, Napoleon began a campaign in Germany in May 1813. He hoped to force Prussia to reverse its decision to join Russia and Sweden in the Sixth Coalition (March 1813–May 1814). Initial French successes prompted an armistice in June, but the Coalition held firm and was joined by Austria when hostilities resumed in August, eventually forcing Napoleon to retreat. He concentrated over 175,000 men and over 600 guns at Leipzig. Four coalition armies converged on the city, eventually totalling over 300,000 troops with twice as many cannons as the French. The battle began on 16 October with brutal hand-to-hand fighting between Napoleon's forces and the Armies of Bohemia and Silesia in the villages to the north and southeast of the city. By dawn on 18 October, Napoleon was surrounded and at the end of the day, the French had been pushed into Leipzig's suburbs. In the early hours of 19 October, the Grande Armée withdrew over the only bridge across the Elster River. When a French corporal blew up the bridge, leaving around 50,000 Frenchmen trapped in Leipzig, he turned a tactical Coalition victory into a decisive one.

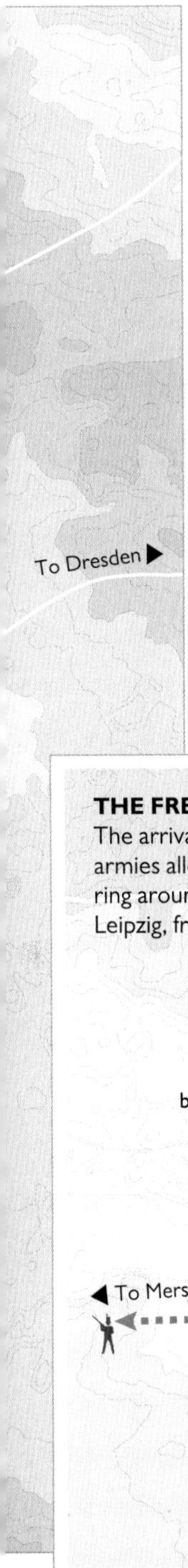
To Dresden

THE BATTLE OF THE NATIONS

At Leipzig in Saxony, eastern Germany, Napoleon's domination east of the Rhine was brutally quashed by the forces of the Sixth Coalition The battle marked the beginning of the end of the First French Empire.

KEY

Bridge over Elster
Towns/Cities

COALITION FORCES
Commander
Cavalry
Infantry
Reinforcements

FRENCH FORCES
Commander
Cavalry
Infantry

TIMELINE

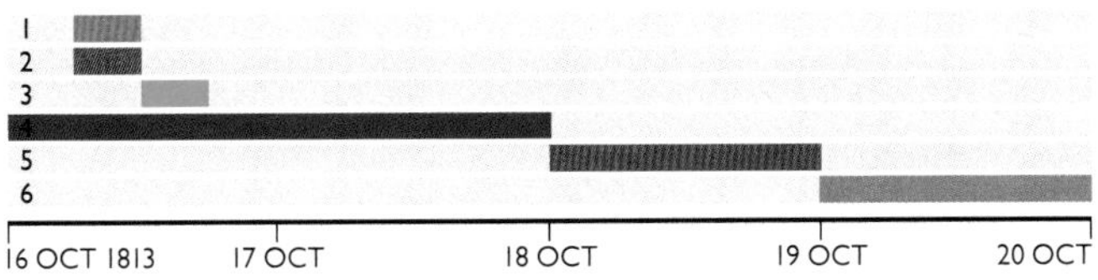
1
2
3
4
5
6
16 OCT 1813
17 OCT
18 OCT
19 OCT
20 OCT

△ **Schwarzenberg delivers news of victory**
This 1835 lithograph by Franz Wolf shows the Austrian commander, Field Marshal Schwarzenberg, delivering news of victory at Leipzig to sovereigns of the Coalition.

THE FRENCH ESCAPE

The arrival of Bennigsen's and Bernadotte's armies allowed the coalition to tighten the ring around the French, who were forced into Leipzig, from which they escaped to the west.

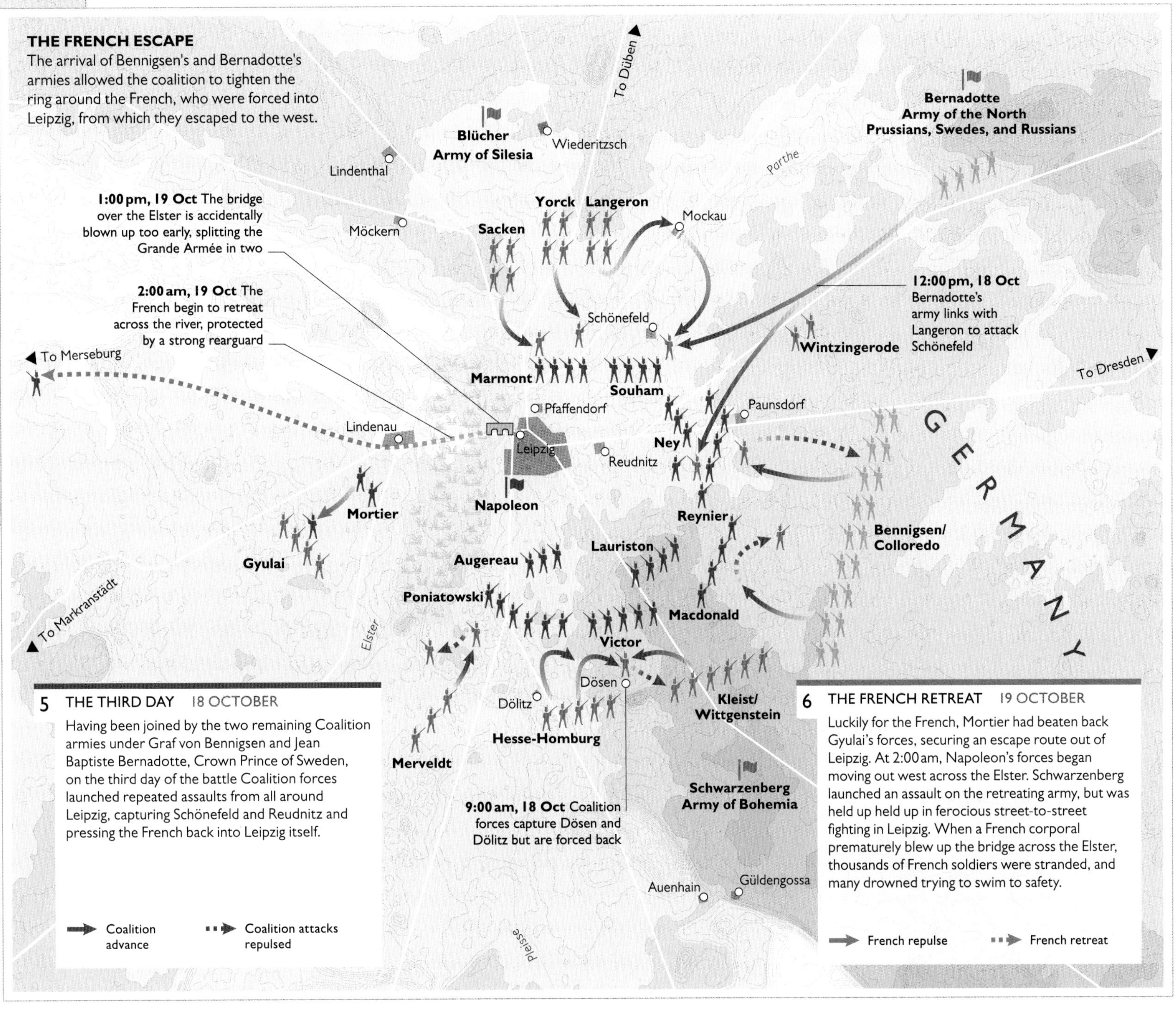
To Düben
Bernadotte
Army of the North
Prussians, Swedes, and Russians
Blücher
Army of Silesia
Wiederitzsch
Lindenthal
Parthe
1:00 pm, 19 Oct The bridge over the Elster is accidentally blown up too early, splitting the Grande Armée in two
Yorck
Langeron
Mockau
Möckern
Sacken
12:00 pm, 18 Oct Bernadotte's army links with Langeron to attack Schönefeld
2:00 am, 19 Oct The French begin to retreat across the river, protected by a strong rearguard
Schönefeld
Wintzingerode
To Merseburg
Marmont
Souham
To Dresden
Pfaffendorf
Paunsdorf
Lindenau
Ney
Leipzig
Reudnitz
GERMANY
Napoleon
Mortier
Reynier
Bennigsen/
Colloredo
Gyulai
Lauriston
Augereau
To Markranstädt
Poniatowski
Macdonald
Elster
Victor
Dösen
Dölitz
Kleist/
Wittgenstein
Hesse-Homburg
Merveldt
Schwarzenberg
Army of Bohemia
9:00 am, 18 Oct Coalition forces capture Dösen and Dölitz but are forced back
Auenhain
Güldengossa
Pleisse

5 THE THIRD DAY 18 OCTOBER

Having been joined by the two remaining Coalition armies under Graf von Bennigsen and Jean Baptiste Bernadotte, Crown Prince of Sweden, on the third day of the battle Coalition forces launched repeated assaults from all around Leipzig, capturing Schönefeld and Reudnitz and pressing the French back into Leipzig itself.

Coalition advance
Coalition attacks repulsed

6 THE FRENCH RETREAT 19 OCTOBER

Luckily for the French, Mortier had beaten back Gyulai's forces, securing an escape route out of Leipzig. At 2:00 am, Napoleon's forces began moving out west across the Elster. Schwarzenberg launched an assault on the retreating army, but was held up held up in ferocious street-to-street fighting in Leipzig. When a French corporal prematurely blew up the bridge across the Elster, thousands of French soldiers were stranded, and many drowned trying to swim to safety.

French repulse
French retreat

NEW ORLEANS

On 8 January 1815, Major General Andrew Jackson (the future US president) and a disparate group of militia fighters, freed slaves, Choctaw people, and pirates withstood an assault by a larger British force. It was to be the final battle of the War of 1812 between the US and Great Britain.

In June 1812, the US declared war on Britain over British attempts to blockade US trade, impress US seamen into the Royal Navy, and stop the US from expanding its territory. Hostilities officially ended with the Treaty of Ghent, signed on 24 December 1814, but it was weeks before news of the peace reached the US. Meanwhile, the British in the US pressed ahead with plans to capture the strategically important city of New Orleans.

With British forces sighted, the US Major General Andrew Jackson declared martial law in New Orleans. Over 5,000 men, including the pirate Jean Lafitte, responded to the call to defend the city. The action began when Jackson launched a night raid on the British camp. He then built defences, known as Line Jackson, along the Rodriguez Canal, and sent 1,000 troops and 16 cannon to take up positions on the west bank of the Mississippi River. After several skirmishes the British, commanded by Sir Edward Pakenham, launched a disastrous attack on the Line Jackson on 8 January. Over 2,000 of the 8,000-strong British force were cut down by Jackson's guns in a battle that lasted under two hours. The British withdrew on 18 January, when news of the peace treaty finally reached the US.

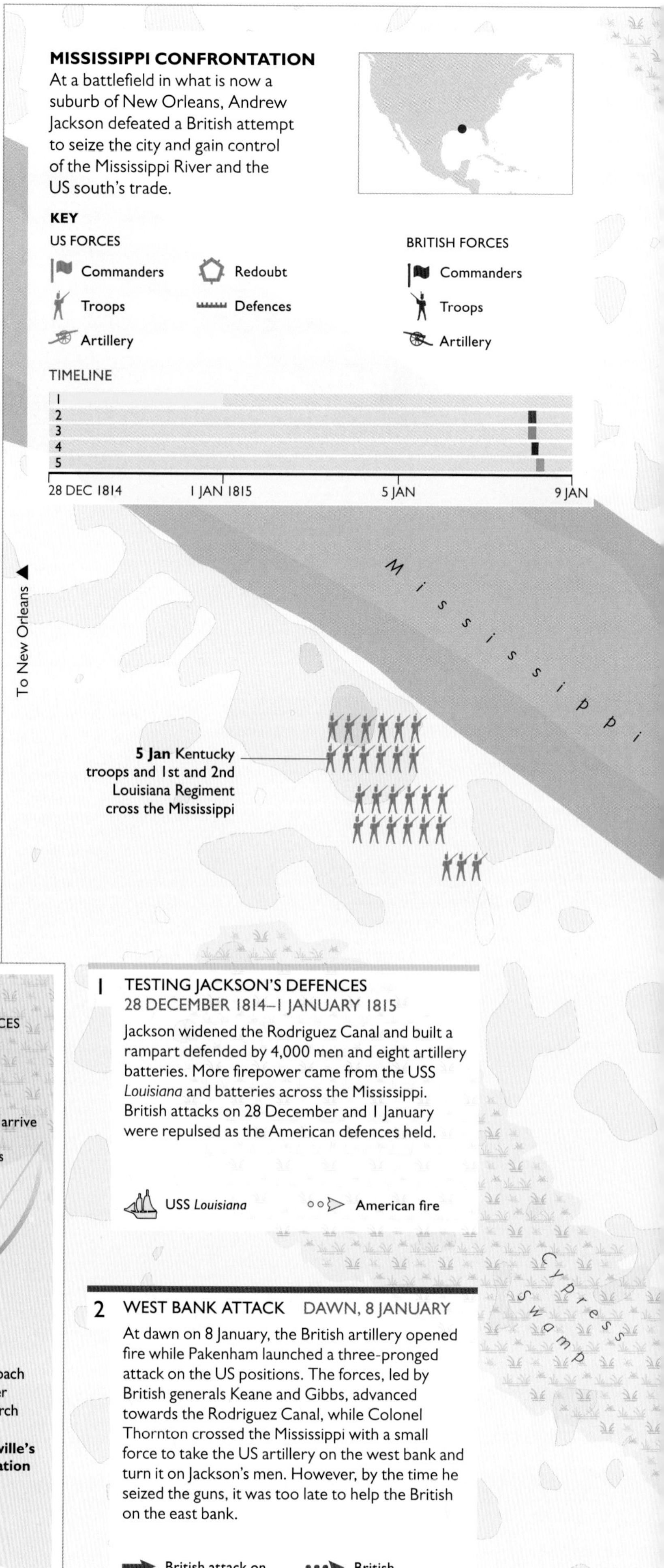
MISSISSIPPI CONFRONTATION
At a battlefield in what is now a suburb of New Orleans, Andrew Jackson defeated a British attempt to seize the city and gain control of the Mississippi River and the US south's trade.
KEY
US FORCES
Commanders
Redoubt
Troops
Defences
Artillery
BRITISH FORCES
Commanders
Troops
Artillery
TIMELINE
1
2
3
4
5
28 DEC 1814
1 JAN 1815
5 JAN
9 JAN
To New Orleans
Mississippi
5 Jan Kentucky troops and 1st and 2nd Louisiana Regiment cross the Mississippi
1 TESTING JACKSON'S DEFENCES
28 DECEMBER 1814–1 JANUARY 1815
Jackson widened the Rodriguez Canal and built a rampart defended by 4,000 men and eight artillery batteries. More firepower came from the USS Louisiana and batteries across the Mississippi. British attacks on 28 December and 1 January were repulsed as the American defences held.
USS Louisiana
American fire
Cypress Swamp
2 WEST BANK ATTACK DAWN, 8 JANUARY
At dawn on 8 January, the British artillery opened fire while Pakenham launched a three-pronged attack on the US positions. The forces, led by British generals Keane and Gibbs, advanced towards the Rodriguez Canal, while Colonel Thornton crossed the Mississippi with a small force to take the US artillery on the west bank and turn it on Jackson's men. However, by the time he seized the guns, it was too late to help the British on the east bank.
British attack on the west bank
British artillery fire

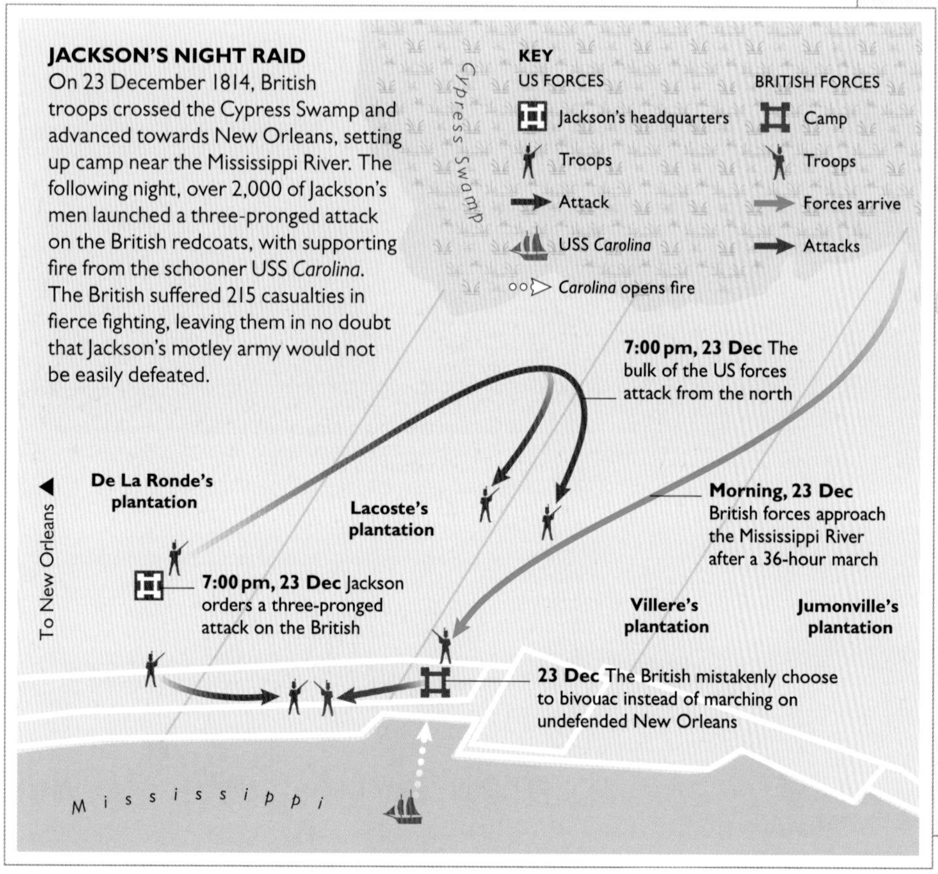
JACKSON'S NIGHT RAID
On 23 December 1814, British troops crossed the Cypress Swamp and advanced towards New Orleans, setting up camp near the Mississippi River. The following night, over 2,000 of Jackson's men launched a three-pronged attack on the British redcoats, with supporting fire from the schooner USS Carolina. The British suffered 215 casualties in fierce fighting, leaving them in no doubt that Jackson's motley army would not be easily defeated.
KEY
US FORCES
Jackson's headquarters
Troops
Attack
USS Carolina
Carolina opens fire
BRITISH FORCES
Camp
Troops
Forces arrive
Attacks
Cypress Swamp
7:00 pm, 23 Dec The bulk of the US forces attack from the north
De La Ronde's plantation
Lacoste's plantation
Morning, 23 Dec British forces approach the Mississippi River after a 36-hour march
To New Orleans
7:00 pm, 23 Dec Jackson orders a three-pronged attack on the British
Villere's plantation
Jumonville's plantation
23 Dec The British mistakenly choose to bivouac instead of marching on undefended New Orleans
Mississippi

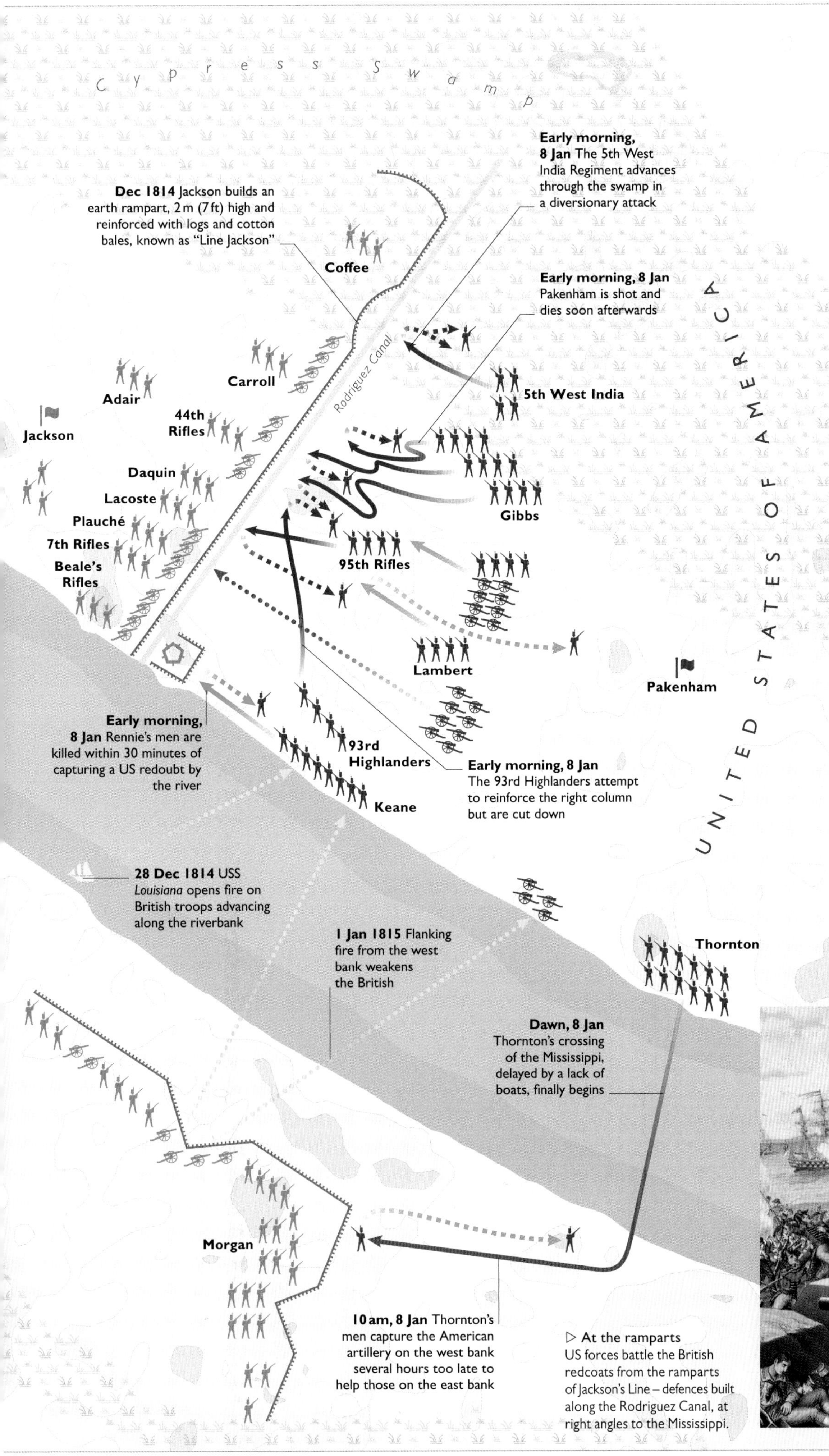

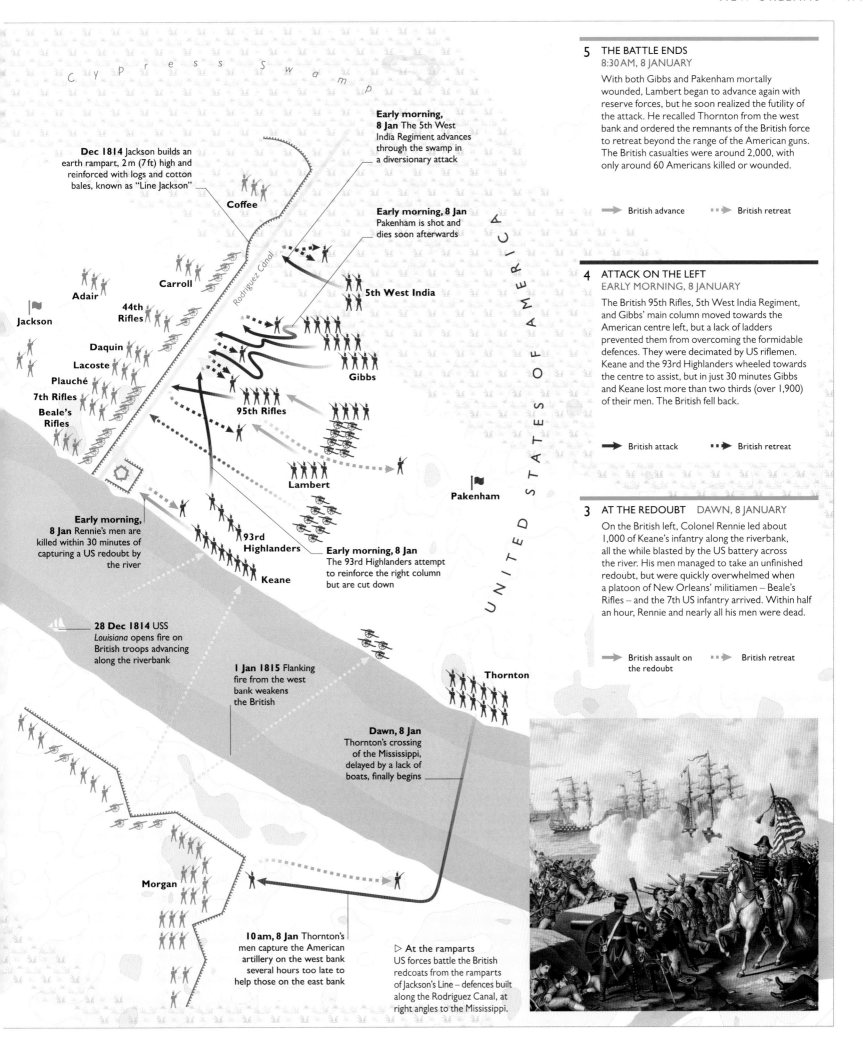

Cypress Swamp
Dec 1814 Jackson builds an earth rampart, 2 m (7 ft) high and reinforced with logs and cotton bales, known as "Line Jackson"
Early morning, 8 Jan The 5th West India Regiment advances through the swamp in a diversionary attack
Early morning, 8 Jan Pakenham is shot and dies soon afterwards
Coffee
Carroll
Adair
Jackson
44th Rifles
Rodriguez Canal
5th West India
Daquin
Lacoste
Plauché
7th Rifles
Beale's Rifles
Gibbs
95th Rifles
Lambert
Pakenham
UNITED STATES OF AMERICA
Early morning, 8 Jan Rennie's men are killed within 30 minutes of capturing a US redoubt by the river
93rd Highlanders
Keane
Early morning, 8 Jan The 93rd Highlanders attempt to reinforce the right column but are cut down
28 Dec 1814 USS Louisiana opens fire on British troops advancing along the riverbank
1 Jan 1815 Flanking fire from the west bank weakens the British
Thornton
Dawn, 8 Jan Thornton's crossing of the Mississippi, delayed by a lack of boats, finally begins
Morgan
10 am, 8 Jan Thornton's men capture the American artillery on the west bank several hours too late to help those on the east bank

5 THE BATTLE ENDS
8:30 AM, 8 JANUARY

With both Gibbs and Pakenham mortally wounded, Lambert began to advance again with reserve forces, but he soon realized the futility of the attack. He recalled Thornton from the west bank and ordered the remnants of the British force to retreat beyond the range of the American guns. The British casualties were around 2,000, with only around 60 Americans killed or wounded.

British advance | British retreat

4 ATTACK ON THE LEFT
EARLY MORNING, 8 JANUARY

The British 95th Rifles, 5th West India Regiment, and Gibbs' main column moved towards the American centre left, but a lack of ladders prevented them from overcoming the formidable defences. They were decimated by US riflemen. Keane and the 93rd Highlanders wheeled towards the centre to assist, but in just 30 minutes Gibbs and Keane lost more than two thirds (over 1,900) of their men. The British fell back.

British attack | British retreat

3 AT THE REDOUBT DAWN, 8 JANUARY

On the British left, Colonel Rennie led about 1,000 of Keane's infantry along the riverbank, all the while blasted by the US battery across the river. His men managed to take an unfinished redoubt, but were quickly overwhelmed when a platoon of New Orleans' militiamen – Beale's Rifles – and the 7th US infantry arrived. Within half an hour, Rennie and nearly all his men were dead.

British assault on the redoubt | British retreat

▷ **At the ramparts**
US forces battle the British redcoats from the ramparts of Jackson's Line – defences built along the Rodriguez Canal, at right angles to the Mississippi.

2 ATTACK ON THE CENTRE 1:30–2:30PM

After an ineffective bombardment of Wellington's centre, Napoleon ordered General D'Erlon's infantry to advance. Hundreds of them were gunned down, and those that reached the ridge were met by Major General Picton's redcoats and the cavalry of Major General Ponsonby and General Somerset. Ponsonby's brigade then rashly charged the French artillery, losing over 1,000 men.

3 MARSHAL NEY'S ATTACK 3:00–5:00PM

As Wellington reformed his line on the ridge, Marshal Ney misread his movements as a retreat and launched a mass cavalry assault on Wellington's centre. It was a huge mistake. Ney rode into more than 10,000 Anglo-Allied troops formed into impenetrable squares bristling with guns and bayonets (see box). For two hours, Ney's squadrons charged the squares, but without infantry to engage the Allied soldiers at close quarters, they could not break a single one.

4 BATTLE FOR LA HAYE SAINTE 4:00–6:00PM

An assault by Marshal Ney captured the garrison at La Haye Sainte which had exhausted its ammunition. Ney loosed his artillery on the Anglo-Allied infantry, giving French forces a chance to break through Wellington's centre. However, Napoleon's reserves were tied up in a desperate fight around Plancenoit with Bulow's Prussian corps which was threatening the French rear.

1 ATTACK ON HOUGOUMONT
11:00AM–7:00PM, 18 JUNE 1815

Wellington's position at Waterloo was protected by two garrisoned farms. At 11:00am, the French attacked Hougoumont farm, trying to tempt Wellington to send reinforcements and weaken his centre in the process. Instead, the French battered Hougoumont for hours, tying up an entire corps against far fewer Anglo-Allies.

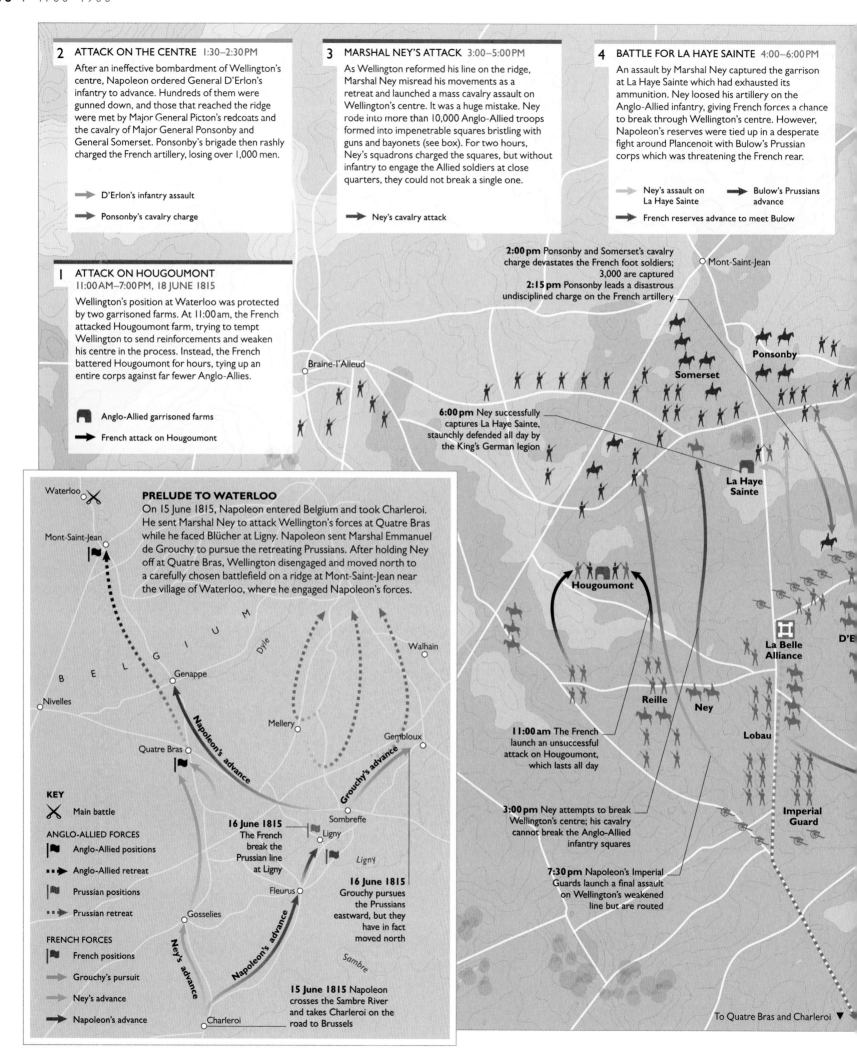

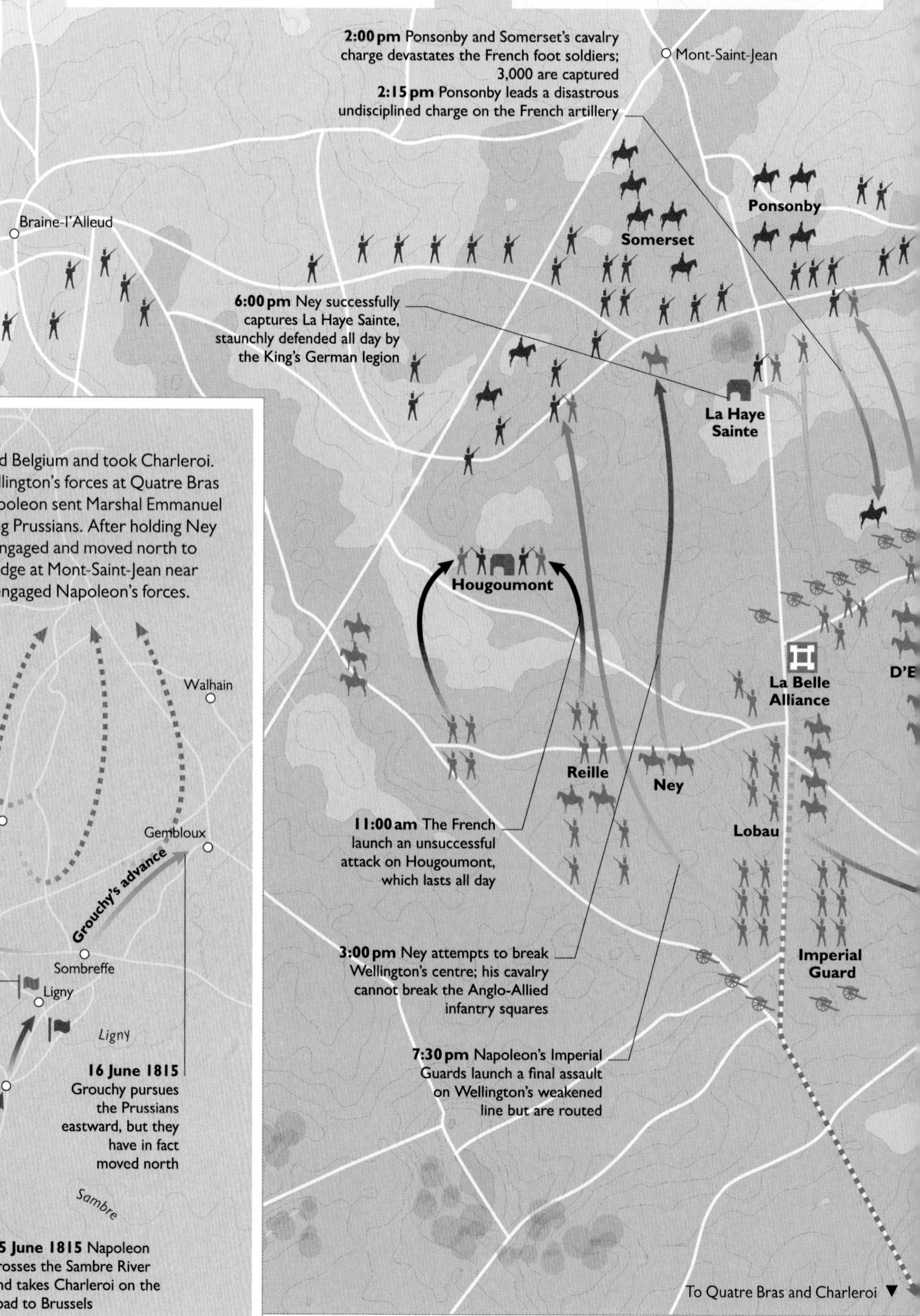
D'Erlon's infantry assault
Ponsonby's cavalry charge
Ney's cavalry attack
Ney's assault on La Haye Sainte
Bulow's Prussians advance
French reserves advance to meet Bulow
Anglo-Allied garrisoned farms
French attack on Hougoumont
2:00 pm Ponsonby and Somerset's cavalry charge devastates the French foot soldiers; 3,000 are captured
2:15 pm Ponsonby leads a disastrous undisciplined charge on the French artillery
Mont-Saint-Jean
Braine-l'Alleud
Ponsonby
Somerset
6:00 pm Ney successfully captures La Haye Sainte, staunchly defended all day by the King's German legion
La Haye Sainte
Hougoumont
La Belle Alliance
D'E
Reille
Ney
Lobau
11:00 am The French launch an unsuccessful attack on Hougoumont, which lasts all day
Imperial Guard
3:00 pm Ney attempts to break Wellington's centre; his cavalry cannot break the Anglo-Allied infantry squares
7:30 pm Napoleon's Imperial Guards launch a final assault on Wellington's weakened line but are routed
To Quatre Bras and Charleroi ▼

PRELUDE TO WATERLOO

On 15 June 1815, Napoleon entered Belgium and took Charleroi. He sent Marshal Ney to attack Wellington's forces at Quatre Bras while he faced Blücher at Ligny. Napoleon sent Marshal Emmanuel de Grouchy to pursue the retreating Prussians. After holding Ney off at Quatre Bras, Wellington disengaged and moved north to a carefully chosen battlefield on a ridge at Mont-Saint-Jean near the village of Waterloo, where he engaged Napoleon's forces.

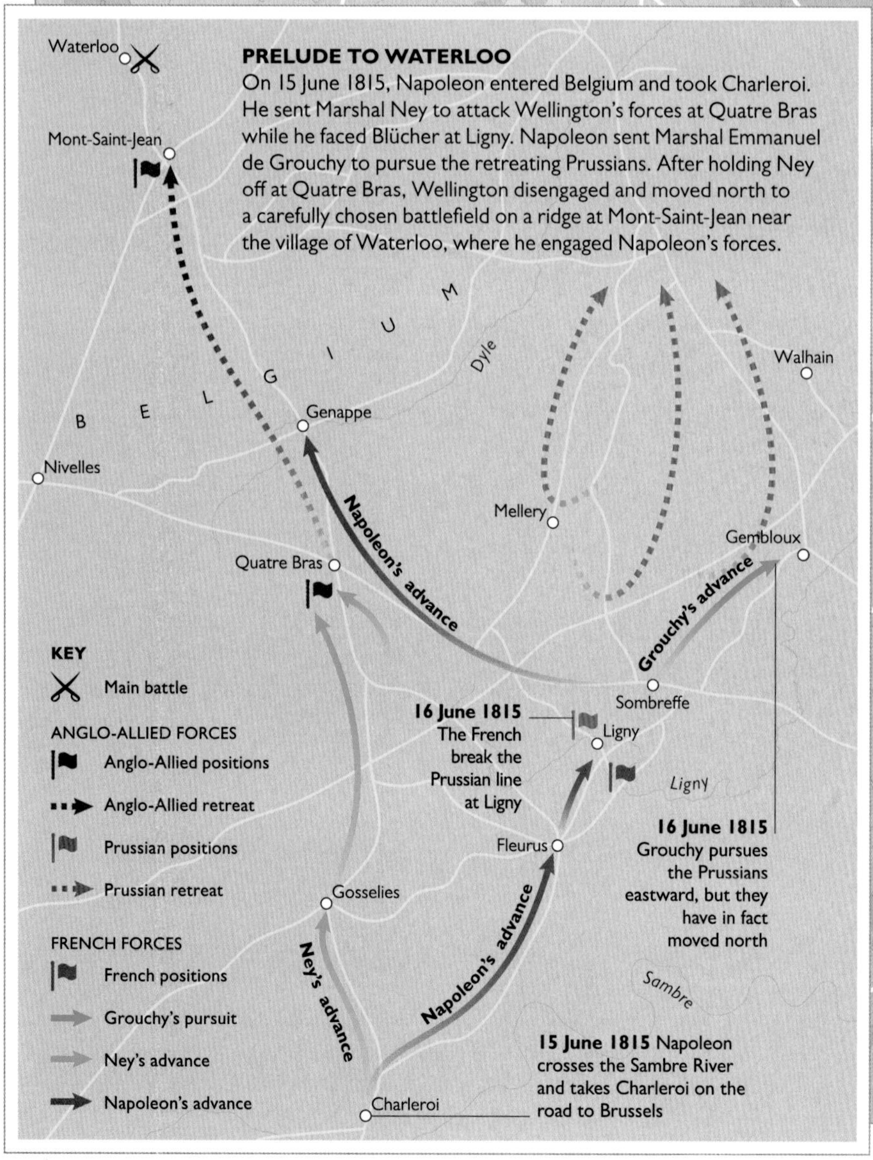
Waterloo
Mont-Saint-Jean
B E L G I U M
Dyle
Walhain
Genappe
Nivelles
Mellery
Gembloux
Quatre Bras
Napoleon's advance
Grouchy's advance
Sombreffe
16 June 1815 The French break the Prussian line at Ligny
Ligny
Fleurus
16 June 1815 Grouchy pursues the Prussians eastward, but they have in fact moved north
Gosselies
Ney's advance
Sambre
15 June 1815 Napoleon crosses the Sambre River and takes Charleroi on the road to Brussels
Charleroi
KEY
Main battle
ANGLO-ALLIED FORCES
Anglo-Allied positions
Anglo-Allied retreat
Prussian positions
Prussian retreat
FRENCH FORCES
French positions
Grouchy's pursuit
Ney's advance
Napoleon's advance

▷ **Wellington's cavalry**
The British cavalry was known for its bravery, but also for its tendency to get carried away in the heat of battle, as shown by Ponsonby's ill-fated charge on the French artillery.

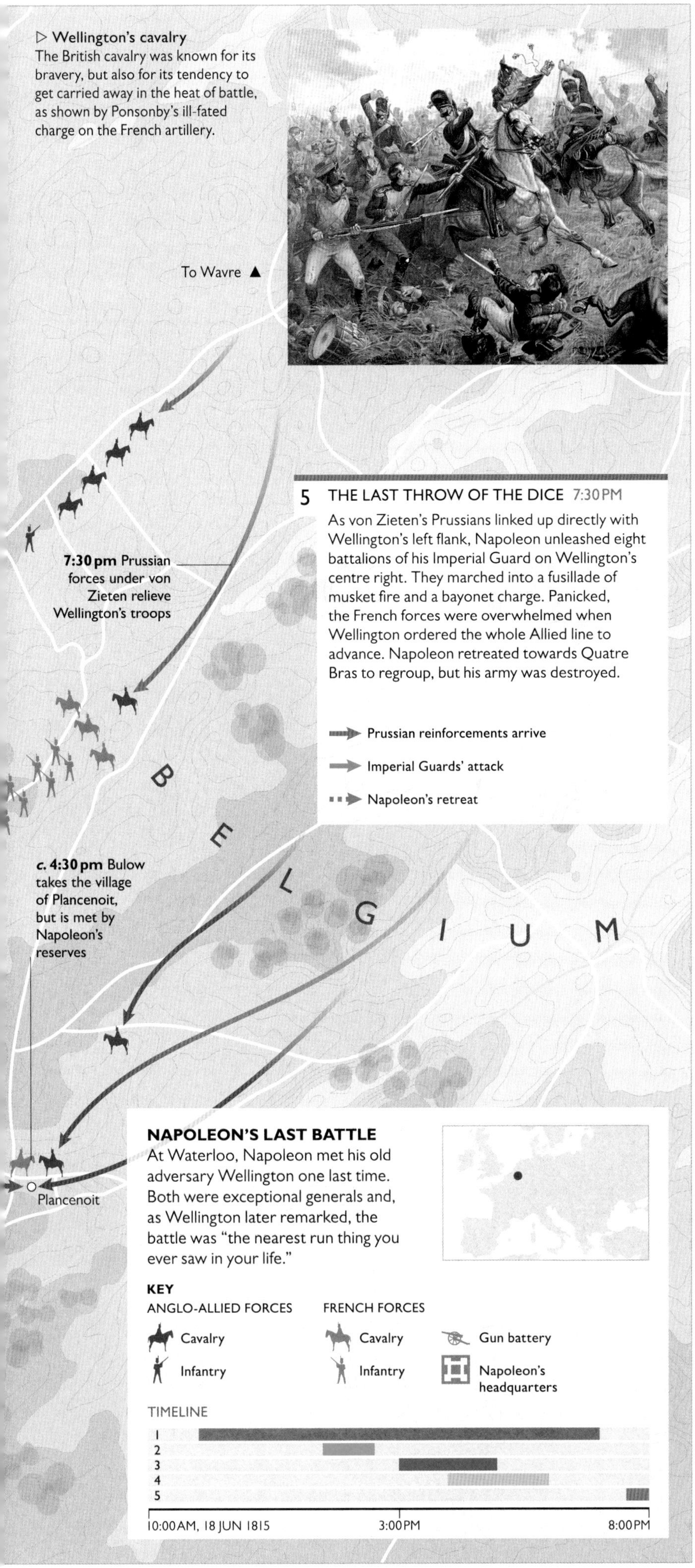

To Wavre ▲
7:30 pm Prussian forces under von Zieten relieve Wellington's troops
B E L G I U M
c. 4:30 pm Bulow takes the village of Plancenoit, but is met by Napoleon's reserves
Plancenoit
Prussian reinforcements arrive
Imperial Guards' attack
Napoleon's retreat

5 **THE LAST THROW OF THE DICE** 7:30PM

As von Zieten's Prussians linked up directly with Wellington's left flank, Napoleon unleashed eight battalions of his Imperial Guard on Wellington's centre right. They marched into a fusillade of musket fire and a bayonet charge. Panicked, the French forces were overwhelmed when Wellington ordered the whole Allied line to advance. Napoleon retreated towards Quatre Bras to regroup, but his army was destroyed.

NAPOLEON'S LAST BATTLE

At Waterloo, Napoleon met his old adversary Wellington one last time. Both were exceptional generals and, as Wellington later remarked, the battle was "the nearest run thing you ever saw in your life."

KEY

ANGLO-ALLIED FORCES: Cavalry; Infantry

FRENCH FORCES: Cavalry; Infantry; Gun battery; Napoleon's headquarters

TIMELINE

1
2
3
4
5
10:00AM, 18 JUN 1815
3:00PM
8:00PM

WATERLOO

On 18 June 1815, the Anglo-Allied and Prussian armies under the Duke of Wellington and General Blücher finally ended the Napoleonic Wars (1803–15) with a victory over Napoleon. The decisive battle took place near the village of Waterloo in Belgium.

In March 1815, news reached Europe's leaders that Napoleon had escaped from the Mediterranean island of Elba, where he had been exiled after the Battle of Paris (1814). Napoleon had landed in France on 1 March and returned to Paris, where he quickly rebuilt support and reclaimed his imperial title, Napoleon I, in a period known as the Hundred Days. By 20 March, he had raised a large army.

Great Britain, Prussia, Austria, and Russia formed a coalition to defeat Napoleon. By June, the Duke of Wellington, one of England's great military commanders, was in charge of an Anglo-Allied army of more than 100,000 troops in Brussels, while in Namur, Prussian Field Marshal Gebhard Leberecht von Blücher was camped with a similarly sized force; Russian and Austrian armies totalling more than 200,000 men each were also on their way to battle France.

On 15 June, Napoleon marched into Belgium. He clashed with Wellington and Blücher on the following day at Quatre Bras and Ligny. After heavy fighting, Blücher fell back to Wavre while Wellington moved to Mont-Saint-Jean near the village of Waterloo, where he would face Napoleon one last time. At breakfast on 18 June, Napoleon told his commanders that the coming battle would be "l'affaire d'un déjeuner" (a picnic); it proved to be anything but. Wellington's Anglo-Allied forces withstood repeated French attacks, despite heavy pressure on their positions at La Haye Sainte and Hougoumont. The arrival of Blücher's Prussians freed Wellington to launch a final offensive that drove the French from the field. Napoleon fled; he was blocked from sailing to America on 15 July and was exiled once more.

THE BRITISH INFANTRY SQUARE

Infantry squares (pictured below) were composed of around 500 soldiers, arranged in two or more tightly packed ranks on each side, with reserves in the middle. The infantry would fire volleys at any approaching cavalry, causing the fallen horses to obstruct further attacks. The squares were almost impervious to cavalry but were vulnerable to musket fire and especially susceptible to artillery fire.

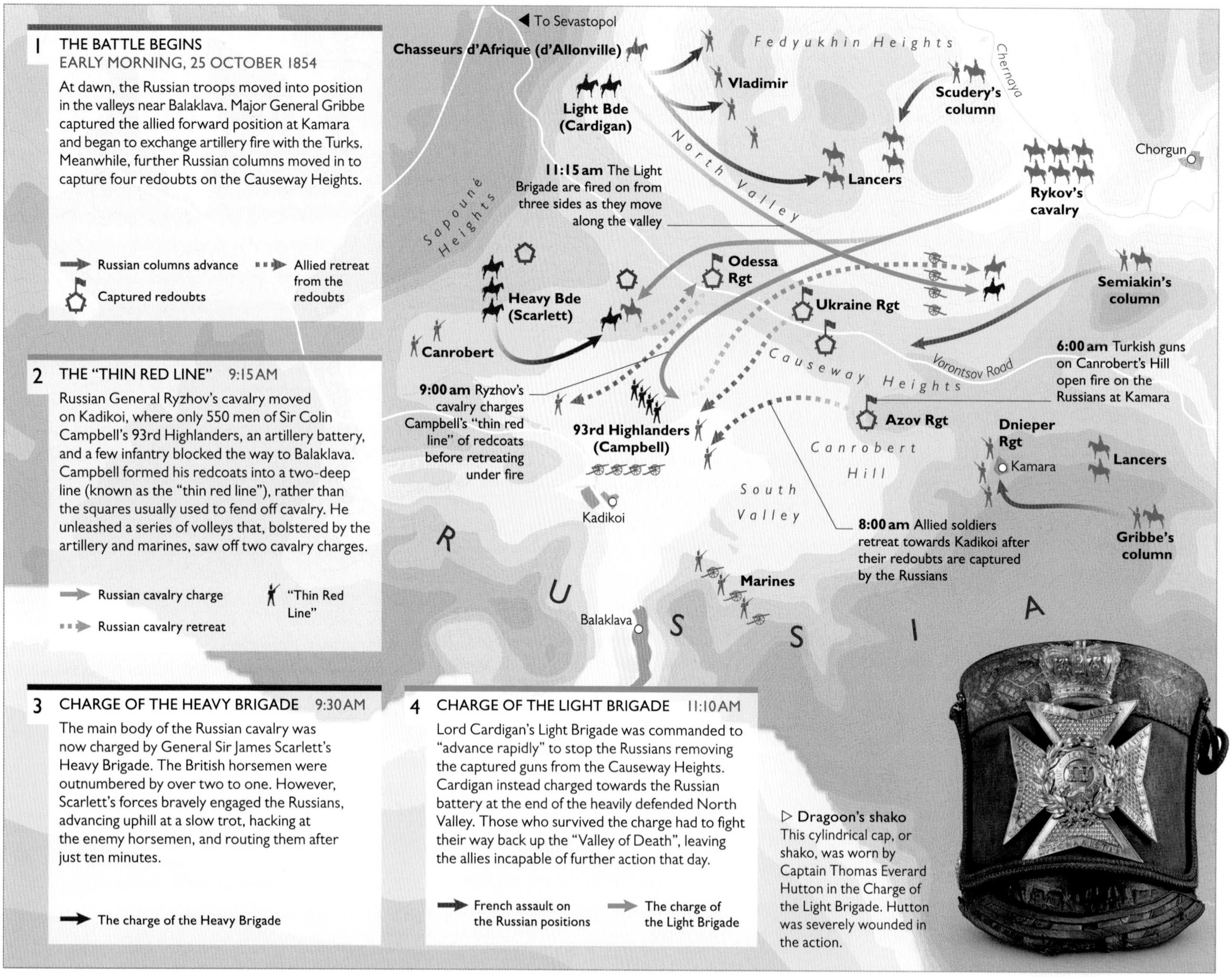

To Sevastopol
Fedyukhin Heights
Chernaya
Chasseurs d'Afrique (d'Allonville)
Vladimir
Scudery's column
Light Bde (Cardigan)
North Valley
Lancers
Chorgun
Rykov's cavalry
11:15 am The Light Brigade are fired on from three sides as they move along the valley
Sapoune Heights
Odessa Rgt
Heavy Bde (Scarlett)
Ukraine Rgt
Semiakin's column
Canrobert
Causeway Heights
Vorontsov Road
6:00 am Turkish guns on Canrobert's Hill open fire on the Russians at Kamara
9:00 am Ryzhov's cavalry charges Campbell's "thin red line" of redcoats before retreating under fire
93rd Highlanders (Campbell)
Azov Rgt
Dnieper Rgt
Canrobert Hill
Kamara
Lancers
South Valley
Kadikoi
8:00 am Allied soldiers retreat towards Kadikoi after their redoubts are captured by the Russians
Gribbe's column
Marines
Balaklava
RUSSIA

1 THE BATTLE BEGINS
EARLY MORNING, 25 OCTOBER 1854

At dawn, the Russian troops moved into position in the valleys near Balaklava. Major General Gribbe captured the allied forward position at Kamara and began to exchange artillery fire with the Turks. Meanwhile, further Russian columns moved in to capture four redoubts on the Causeway Heights.

Russian columns advance · Allied retreat from the redoubts · Captured redoubts

2 THE "THIN RED LINE" 9:15AM

Russian General Ryzhov's cavalry moved on Kadikoi, where only 550 men of Sir Colin Campbell's 93rd Highlanders, an artillery battery, and a few infantry blocked the way to Balaklava. Campbell formed his redcoats into a two-deep line (known as the "thin red line"), rather than the squares usually used to fend off cavalry. He unleashed a series of volleys that, bolstered by the artillery and marines, saw off two cavalry charges.

Russian cavalry charge · "Thin Red Line" · Russian cavalry retreat

3 CHARGE OF THE HEAVY BRIGADE 9:30AM

The main body of the Russian cavalry was now charged by General Sir James Scarlett's Heavy Brigade. The British horsemen were outnumbered by over two to one. However, Scarlett's forces bravely engaged the Russians, advancing uphill at a slow trot, hacking at the enemy horsemen, and routing them after just ten minutes.

The charge of the Heavy Brigade

4 CHARGE OF THE LIGHT BRIGADE 11:10AM

Lord Cardigan's Light Brigade was commanded to "advance rapidly" to stop the Russians removing the captured guns from the Causeway Heights. Cardigan instead charged towards the Russian battery at the end of the heavily defended North Valley. Those who survived the charge had to fight their way back up the "Valley of Death", leaving the allies incapable of further action that day.

French assault on the Russian positions · The charge of the Light Brigade

▷ **Dragoon's shako**
This cylindrical cap, or shako, was worn by Captain Thomas Everard Hutton in the Charge of the Light Brigade. Hutton was severely wounded in the action.

BALAKLAVA

An indecisive battle in the Crimean War (1853–56) between Russian and allied forces, Balaklava is famed for the stand made by the "thin red line" and for the disastrous charge of the Light Brigade.

In 1854, Britain, France, and Turkey invaded the Crimea in response to a Russian attack in the Balkans the previous year. The allied expedition achieved a victory at the Battle of the Alma on 20 September. This left open the path to the Russian naval base of Sevastopol, which the allies besieged on 25 October. The Russians tried to drive a wedge between the siege line at Sevastopol and the British base at Balaklava. The battle ended in stalemate: the British retained control of Balaklava, but the Russians took control of the main road from there to Sevastopol. The battle's place in history was secured by the stand of Sir Colin Campbell's 93rd Highlanders, known as the "thin red line", the successful charge of the Heavy Brigade, and the infamous mistake that led to the disastrous charge of the Light Brigade through a valley lined with enemy guns.

CRIMEAN CONFLICT
The Battle of Balaklava was prompted by the long siege of Sevastapol, home to Russia's Black Sea Fleet. The siege finally ended in September 1855 when the Russians blew up the forts and evacuated the city.

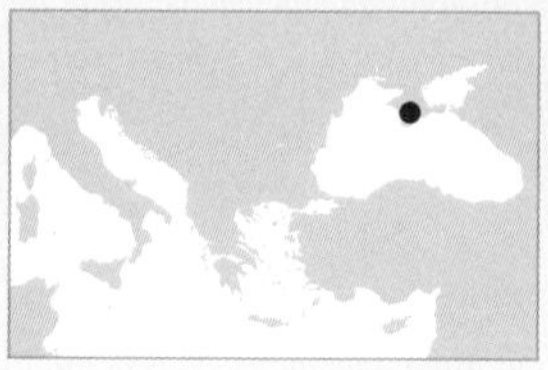

KEY

Redoubts · Towns

BRITISH FORCES: Cavalry

ALLIED FORCES: Cavalry · Infantry · Batteries

RUSSIAN FORCES: Cavalry · Infantry · Batteries

TIMELINE

1, 2, 3, 4

6:00AM, 25 OCT 1854 · 9:00AM · 12:00PM

SOLFERINO

The last battle in the Second War of Italian Independence (April–July 1859) took place in Solferino, northern Italy, where a French-Piedmontese army defeated the Austrians.

In 1859, the French Emperor Napoleon III allied with King Victor Emmanuel II of Piedmont–Sardinia to drive the Austrian army out of northern Italy. Napoleon led his army to victories at Montebello, Palestro, and Magenta before meeting the Austrians again on the Medole plain. Here, the Austrian Emperor Franz Josef I had gathered around 120,000 infantry, 10,000 cavalry, and 430 guns. The battle was broken into three main actions. The French infantry and cavalry fought at Solferino as well as further south, at Guidizzolo. To the north, the Piedmontese held off the enemy at San Martino, until the Austrians retreated back across the River Mincio, fearing encirclement.

BIRTH OF A NATION

The clash at Solferino advanced the cause of Italian unification, completed when Rome became the capital of the new Kingdom of Italy in 1871. The carnage at Solferino prompted Henry Dunant to found the Red Cross in 1863.

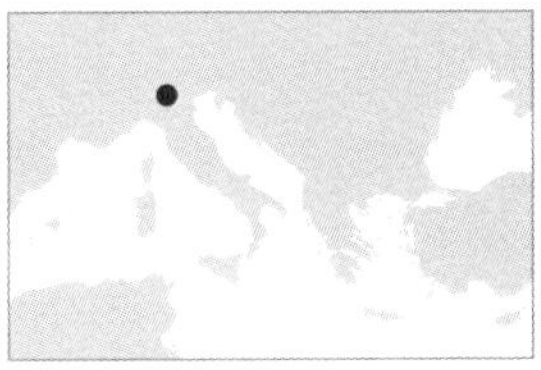

KEY

Railway

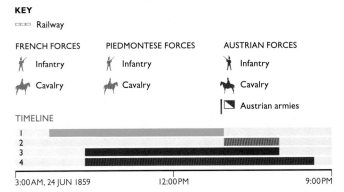

FRENCH FORCES	PIEDMONTESE FORCES	AUSTRIAN FORCES
Infantry	Infantry	Infantry
Cavalry	Cavalry	Cavalry
		Austrian armies

TIMELINE

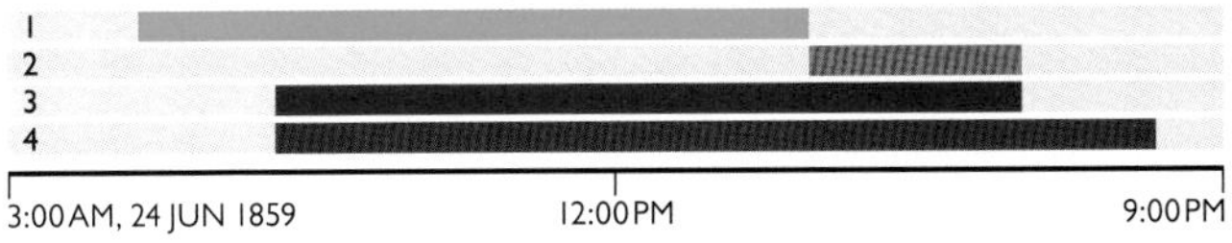

1
2
3
4
3:00AM, 24 JUN 1859
12:00PM
9:00PM

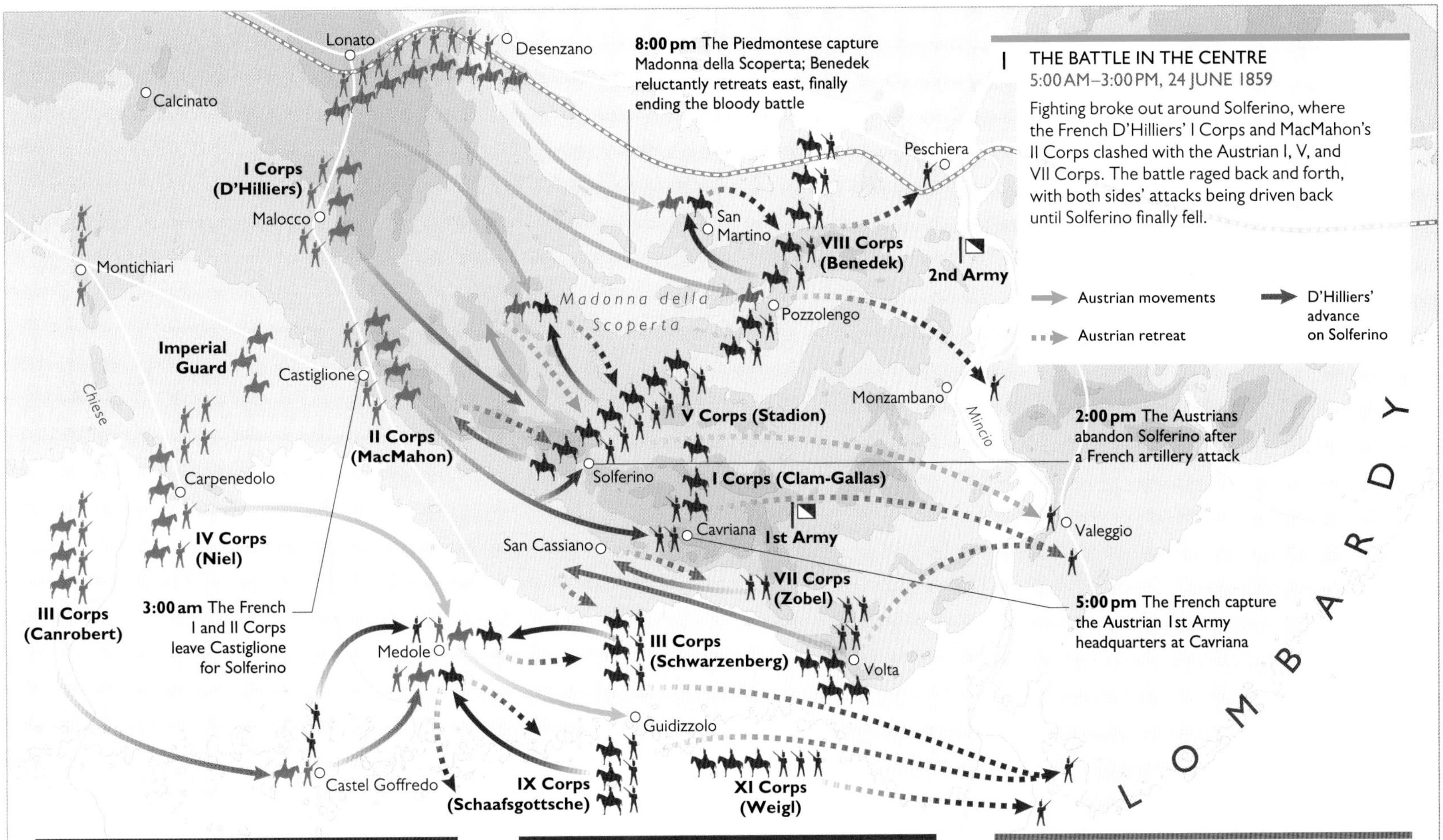

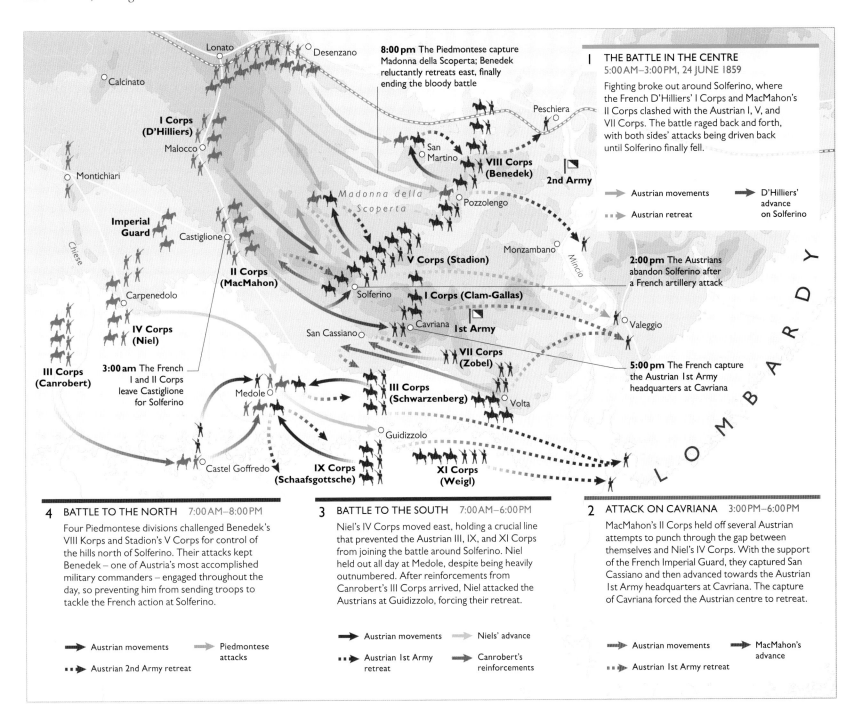

Lonato
Desenzano
Calcinato
8:00 pm The Piedmontese capture Madonna della Scoperta; Benedek reluctantly retreats east, finally ending the bloody battle
1 THE BATTLE IN THE CENTRE
5:00AM–3:00PM, 24 JUNE 1859
Fighting broke out around Solferino, where the French D'Hilliers' I Corps and MacMahon's II Corps clashed with the Austrian I, V, and VII Corps. The battle raged back and forth, with both sides' attacks being driven back until Solferino finally fell.
Austrian movements
D'Hilliers' advance on Solferino
Austrian retreat
Peschiera
I Corps (D'Hilliers)
Malocco
San Martino
VIII Corps (Benedek)
2nd Army
Montichiari
Madonna della Scoperta
Pozzolengo
Imperial Guard
Castiglione
Chiese
Monzambano
Mincio
V Corps (Stadion)
II Corps (MacMahon)
2:00 pm The Austrians abandon Solferino after a French artillery attack
Carpenedolo
Solferino
I Corps (Clam-Gallas)
Valeggio
IV Corps (Niel)
San Cassiano
Cavriana
1st Army
VII Corps (Zobel)
5:00 pm The French capture the Austrian 1st Army headquarters at Cavriana
III Corps (Canrobert)
3:00 am The French I and II Corps leave Castiglione for Solferino
Medole
III Corps (Schwarzenberg)
Volta
Guidizzolo
LOMBARDY
Castel Goffredo
IX Corps (Schaafsgottsche)
XI Corps (Weigl)

4 BATTLE TO THE NORTH 7:00AM–8:00PM

Four Piedmontese divisions challenged Benedek's VIII Korps and Stadion's V Corps for control of the hills north of Solferino. Their attacks kept Benedek – one of Austria's most accomplished military commanders – engaged throughout the day, so preventing him from sending troops to tackle the French action at Solferino.

Austrian movements
Piedmontese attacks
Austrian 2nd Army retreat

3 BATTLE TO THE SOUTH 7:00AM–6:00PM

Niel's IV Corps moved east, holding a crucial line that prevented the Austrian III, IX, and XI Corps from joining the battle around Solferino. Niel held out all day at Medole, despite being heavily outnumbered. After reinforcements from Canrobert's III Corps arrived, Niel attacked the Austrians at Guidizzolo, forcing their retreat.

Austrian movements
Niels' advance
Austrian 1st Army retreat
Canrobert's reinforcements

2 ATTACK ON CAVRIANA 3:00PM–6:00PM

MacMahon's II Corps held off several Austrian attempts to punch through the gap between themselves and Niel's IV Corps. With the support of the French Imperial Guard, they captured San Cassiano and then advanced towards the Austrian 1st Army headquarters at Cavriana. The capture of Cavriana forced the Austrian centre to retreat.

Austrian movements
MacMahon's advance
Austrian 1st Army retreat

ANTIETAM

The bloodiest day of battle in US history took place at Antietam Creek during the American Civil War (1861–65). A large Union army, led by General George McClellan, paid a heavy price to cut short the invasion of Maryland by the Confederate Army of Northern Virginia, under the command of Robert E. Lee.

In 1861, civil war broke out in the US between the Union and the rebel states of the Confederacy. By the following year, the Confederate general Robert E. Lee had won victories at the Seven Days' Battles and the Second Battle of Bull Run (Manassas). In September 1862, Lee invaded Maryland with the Army of Northern Virginia, hoping that success there would garner European support for the Confederacy and damage President Lincoln's standing in the upcoming Congressional elections.

As Lee moved west he split his army in two, but the Union's General George McClellan missed this chance to engage the divided forces. By the time McClellan finally caught up with Lee at Antietam Creek, near Sharpsburg, Maryland, on 17 September, the Confederates had regrouped. Even so, Lee was vastly outnumbered by around two to one. Believing that Lee had reserves, McClellan refused to commit his full force, again missing the chance to destroy Lee's army. After a brutal day's fighting, the battle ended in stalemate. McClellan let Lee slip back into Virginia, and the Union claimed a strategic victory. The Confederacy's hopes of European support were dashed and, emboldened by having seen off a major Confederate offensive, on 22 September 1862 Lincoln issued the Emancipation Proclamation, freeing all slaves in the Confederate states.

SWING STATE

Maryland straddled the south and north and was a key battleground in the fight between secessionists and Unionists. The state was invaded three times by Confederates during the American Civil War.

KEY

CONFEDERATE ARMY	UNION ARMY	
Infantry	Infantry	Miller's cornfield
Force	Force	Dunker Church
Artillery	Artillery	Philip Pry House
		Lower bridge

TIMELINE

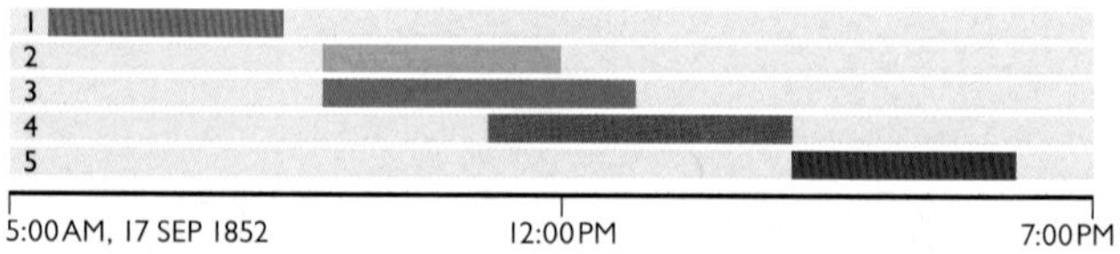

1
2
3
4
5
5:00AM, 17 SEP 1852
12:00PM
7:00PM

△ **Absolution at "Bloody Lane"**
This painting by Don Troiani shows Union troops of the Irish Brigade advancing towards "Bloody Lane". The "fighting chaplain" Father William Corby is shown giving absolution.

LEE'S CAMPAIGN

Lee crossed into Maryland on 4 September 1862. He then split his forces, sending Jackson, McLaws, and Walker to attack the Union garrisons at Martinsburg and Harpers Ferry, and D.H. Hill to protect the mountain passes. Hill and McLaws held the passes long enough for Harpers Ferry to be taken, allowing Lee to concentrate his army at Antietam Creek to face McClellan's slowly pursuing Union forces.

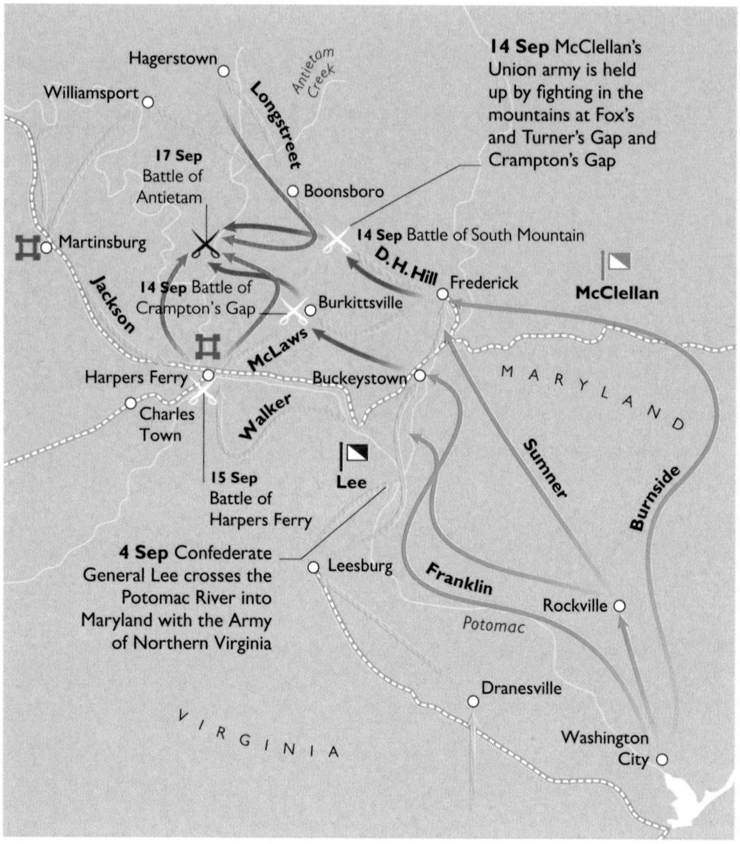

Hagerstown
Williamsport
Antietam Creek
Longstreet
17 Sep Battle of Antietam
Boonsboro
14 Sep McClellan's Union army is held up by fighting in the mountains at Fox's and Turner's Gap and Crampton's Gap
14 Sep Battle of South Mountain
Martinsburg
D.H. Hill
Frederick
McClellan
Jackson
14 Sep Battle of Crampton's Gap
Burkittsville
McLaws
Harpers Ferry
Buckeystown
MARYLAND
Charles Town
Walker
Sumner
Burnside
Lee
15 Sep Battle of Harpers Ferry
4 Sep Confederate General Lee crosses the Potomac River into Maryland with the Army of Northern Virginia
Leesburg
Franklin
Rockville
Potomac
Dranesville
VIRGINIA
Washington City

KEY

- Main battle
- Battle
- Union garrisons
- Union movements, 3–13 Sep
- Union movements, 14–17 Sep
- Confederate movements, 3–13 Sep
- Confederate movements, 14–17 Sep
- Railways

5 THE FINAL ASSAULT 3:00PM–NIGHTFALL

Burnside advanced against the Confederate line southeast of Sharpsburg, but was met by General A.P. Hill's Light Division, which had arrived after a 17-mile (27-km) march from Harpers Ferry. Again, the battle might have been won if McClellan had released his reserves, but Burnside was left to fight with his exhausted and inexperienced troops until nightfall ended the battle.

- Union assault
- Union retreat
- Confederate advance and attack

4 LOWER BRIDGE 11:00–3:00PM

The fighting in the north had nearly ceased by the time the Union's Major General Burnside began to advance against the Confederate right further south. His men captured the sole bridge across Antietam Creek, hoping to outflank their enemy, but the bridge was so narrow that his force could not easily cross and was held there for several hours by just 500 Confederate soldiers.

- Union advance

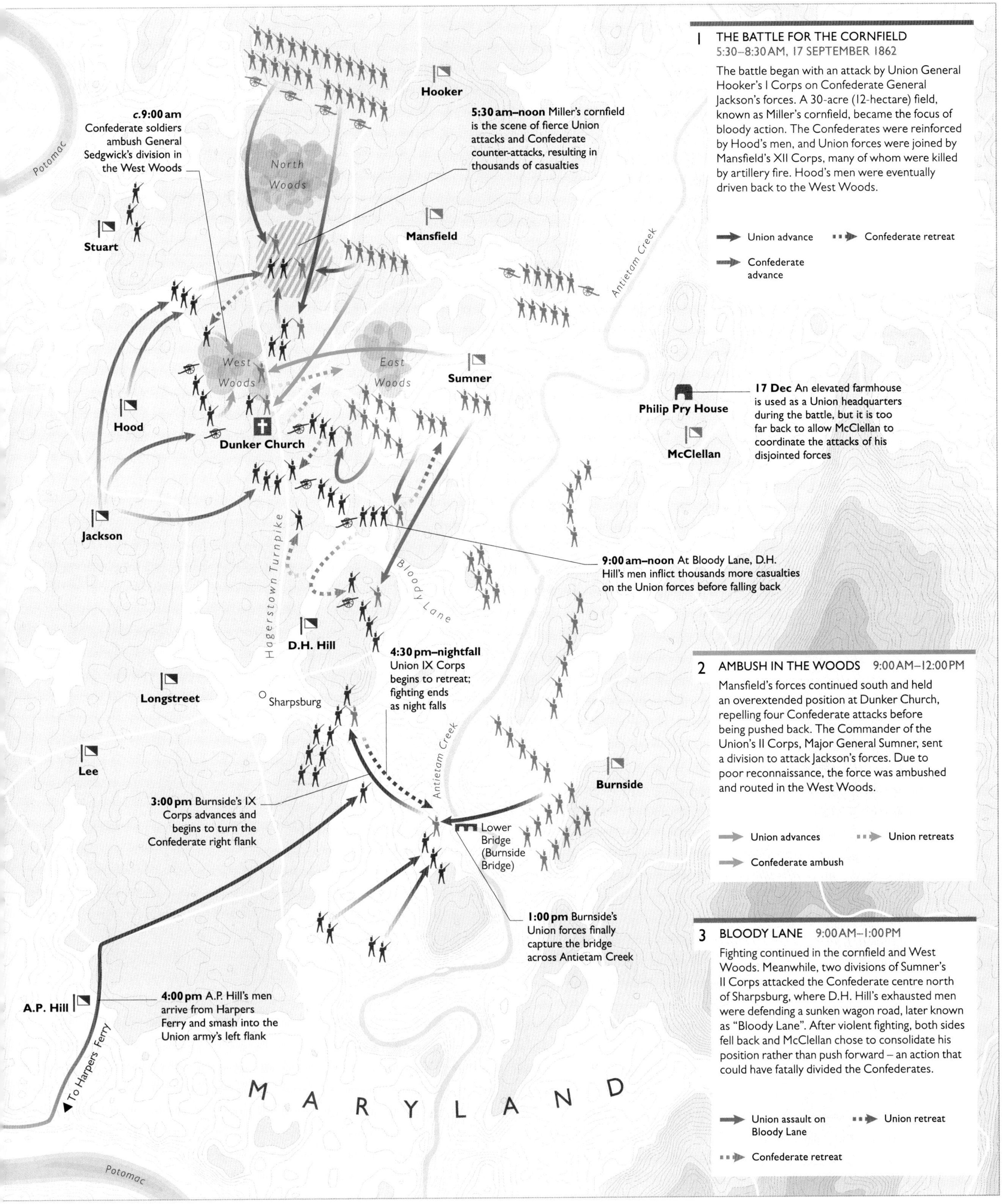
Hooker
c.9:00 am Confederate soldiers ambush General Sedgwick's division in the West Woods
5:30 am–noon Miller's cornfield is the scene of fierce Union attacks and Confederate counter-attacks, resulting in thousands of casualties
Potomac
North Woods
Stuart
Mansfield
Antietam Creek
West Woods
East Woods
Sumner
Hood
Dunker Church
Philip Pry House
17 Dec An elevated farmhouse is used as a Union headquarters during the battle, but it is too far back to allow McClellan to coordinate the attacks of his disjointed forces
McClellan
Jackson
Hagerstown Turnpike
Bloody Lane
9:00 am–noon At Bloody Lane, D.H. Hill's men inflict thousands more casualties on the Union forces before falling back
D.H. Hill
4:30 pm–nightfall Union IX Corps begins to retreat; fighting ends as night falls
Longstreet
Sharpsburg
Antietam Creek
Lee
Burnside
3:00 pm Burnside's IX Corps advances and begins to turn the Confederate right flank
Lower Bridge (Burnside Bridge)
1:00 pm Burnside's Union forces finally capture the bridge across Antietam Creek
A.P. Hill
4:00 pm A.P. Hill's men arrive from Harpers Ferry and smash into the Union army's left flank
To Harpers Ferry
MARYLAND
Potomac

1 THE BATTLE FOR THE CORNFIELD

5:30–8:30 AM, 17 SEPTEMBER 1862

The battle began with an attack by Union General Hooker's I Corps on Confederate General Jackson's forces. A 30-acre (12-hectare) field, known as Miller's cornfield, became the focus of bloody action. The Confederates were reinforced by Hood's men, and Union forces were joined by Mansfield's XII Corps, many of whom were killed by artillery fire. Hood's men were eventually driven back to the West Woods.

Union advance
Confederate retreat
Confederate advance

2 AMBUSH IN THE WOODS 9:00 AM–12:00 PM

Mansfield's forces continued south and held an overextended position at Dunker Church, repelling four Confederate attacks before being pushed back. The Commander of the Union's II Corps, Major General Sumner, sent a division to attack Jackson's forces. Due to poor reconnaissance, the force was ambushed and routed in the West Woods.

Union advances
Union retreats
Confederate ambush

3 BLOODY LANE 9:00 AM–1:00 PM

Fighting continued in the cornfield and West Woods. Meanwhile, two divisions of Sumner's II Corps attacked the Confederate centre north of Sharpsburg, where D.H. Hill's exhausted men were defending a sunken wagon road, later known as "Bloody Lane". After violent fighting, both sides fell back and McClellan chose to consolidate his position rather than push forward – an action that could have fatally divided the Confederates.

Union assault on Bloody Lane
Union retreat
Confederate retreat

ARMS OF THE CIVIL WAR

The American Civil War of 1861–65 was the first modern war. Advances in communication and technology expanded the scope of the war – more troops were deployed, weapons became more lethal, and battlelines grew.

△ **Confederacy flag**
The stars represent seceded states, with more added later. From May 1863, the Confederacy shifted to the "Stainless Banner" with a cross-shaped motif on a white rectangular field.

The civil war was fought between the Northern states, loyal to the Union, and the slave-owning Southern states that seceded to form the Confederacy. While both sides began equal in strength, with around 200,000 troops each, by 1863 there were twice as many Union troops serving as there were Confederate.

On the battlefield, artillery was murderous at short range due to improved canister shots and shrapnel shells, but it was still mostly ineffective at long range. Offensive bombardments were less useful since guns were somewhat inaccurate, and explosive shells were still in their infancy at this time. Infantry firepower had improved thanks to rifled muskets and advances in ammunition, but massed formations were still needed for infantry to be accurate at any but the shortest ranges. Firepower had made mounted charges suicidal, but cavalry remained indispensable for scouting, screening, and raiding. The introduction of repeating carbines – quick-loading guns – made cavalry an excellent mobile force.

Field entrenchments became commonplace for soldiers facing an enormous amount of firepower. By 1864, attacks had become so costly in terms of casualties that only the Union had the manpower needed to maintain offensives, culminating in its victory in 1865.

△ **Underwater threat**
The Confederates used naval mines, then called "torpedoes", to defend their waterways. At the Battle of Mobile Bay (1864), the Union fleet (right), despite the loss of one of its ships, continued to charge through a channel seeded with contact mines to attack the Confederate navy.

Union artillery battery
This image is from the Battle of Seven Pines, Virginia (31 May–1 June 1862), also known as Fair Oaks. Artillery was widely used throughout the civil war, with projectiles ranging in weight from 10lbs to 300lbs.

GETTYSBURG

A turning point in the American Civil War, the Battle of Gettysburg in 1863 saw the Union army halt the Confederate invasion of Pennsylvania. Instead of the decisive victory they needed to offset their resource inferiority, the Confederates suffered a major defeat.

Riding high on his victory over the Union at Chancellorsville, Virginia, in May 1863, Confederate general Robert E. Lee believed that another decisive win could end northern support for the Civil War. In June, he marched into Pennsylvania with soldiers of the Army of Northern Virginia. General George G. Meade, commander of the Union Army of the Potomac, shadowed Lee's movements, and the two sides met at Gettysburg. The battle had a confused start: Lieutenant General A.P. Hill, commander of the Confederate III Corps, sent men into Gettysburg to investigate a sighting of Union forces there the day before. Two Union brigades opened fire on Hill's men, and more units arrived from both sides to join a battle that went on to span three days, involved around 75,000 Confederate and 100,000 Union soldiers, and ended in Lee's retreat to Virginia. It was the bloodiest battle to take place on American soil, with an estimated 50,000 casualties. Abraham Lincoln famously used the opening of the National Cemetery at Gettysburg in November 1863 to reaffirm the North's commitment to ending slavery and winning the war.

> *"Government of the people, by the people, for the people, shall not perish from the earth."*
>
> ABRAHAM LINCOLN, 19 NOVEMBER 1863

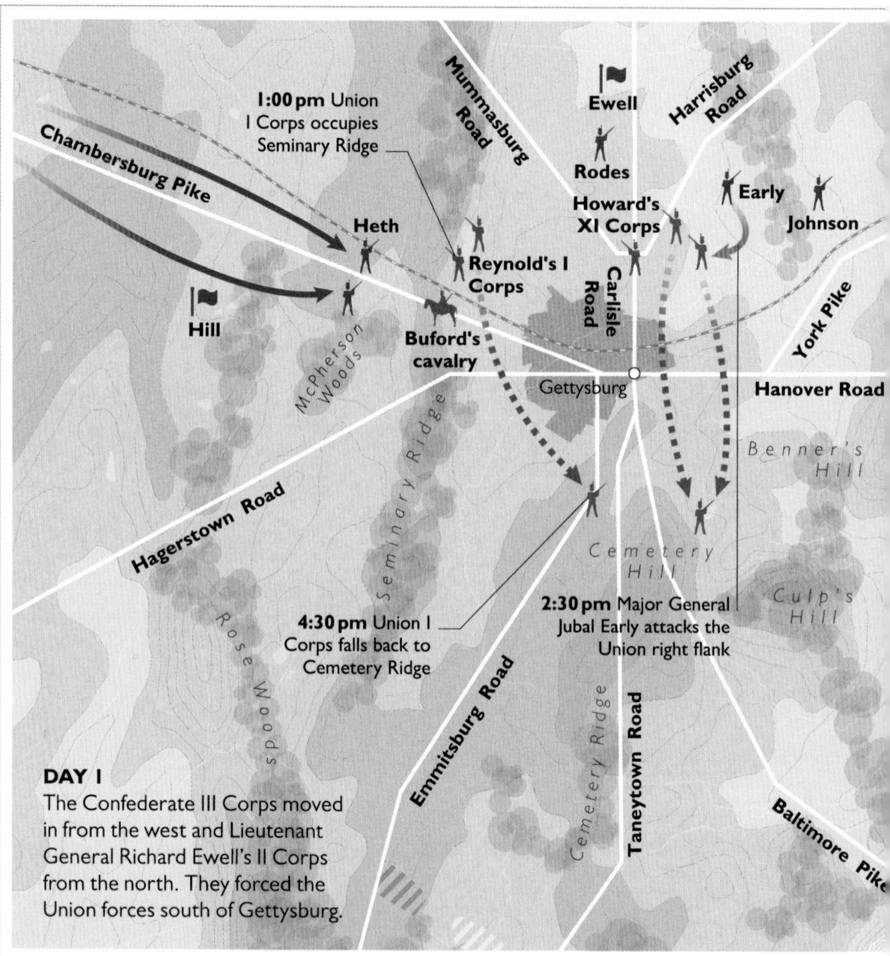
1:00 pm Union I Corps occupies Seminary Ridge
Mummasburg Road
Ewell
Harrisburg Road
Chambersburg Pike
Rodes
Howard's XI Corps
Early
Johnson
Heth
Reynold's I Corps
Carlisle Road
Hill
Buford's cavalry
McPherson Woods
York Pike
Gettysburg
Hanover Road
Benner's Hill
Seminary Ridge
Hagerstown Road
Cemetery Hill
Culp's Hill
4:30 pm Union I Corps falls back to Cemetery Ridge
2:30 pm Major General Jubal Early attacks the Union right flank
Rose Woods
Emmitsburg Road
Cemetery Ridge
Taneytown Road
Baltimore Pike

DAY 1
The Confederate III Corps moved in from the west and Lieutenant General Richard Ewell's II Corps from the north. They forced the Union forces south of Gettysburg.

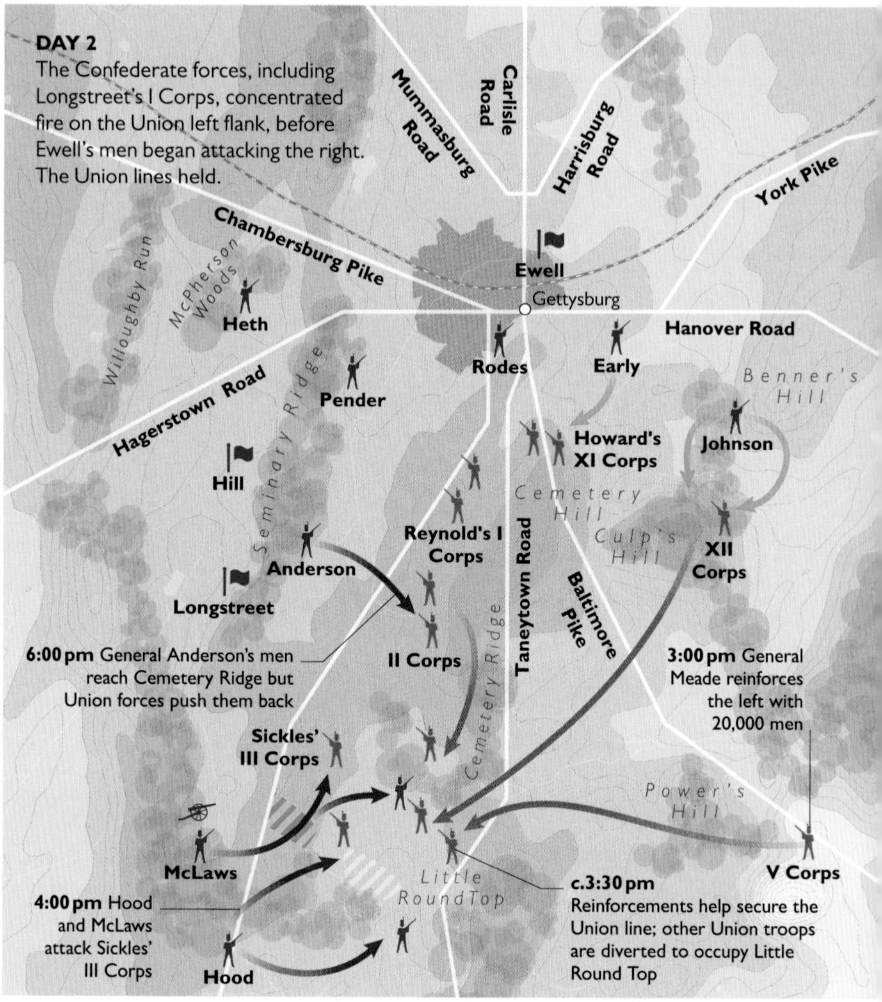
Mummasburg Road
Carlisle Road
Harrisburg Road
York Pike
Chambersburg Pike
Ewell
Gettysburg
Willoughby Run
McPherson Woods
Heth
Hanover Road
Rodes
Early
Benner's Hill
Hagerstown Road
Pender
Seminary Ridge
Howard's XI Corps
Johnson
Hill
Cemetery Hill
Culp's Hill
Reynold's I Corps
XII Corps
Anderson
Longstreet
Taneytown Road
Baltimore Pike
II Corps
6:00 pm General Anderson's men reach Cemetery Ridge but Union forces push them back
3:00 pm General Meade reinforces the left with 20,000 men
Cemetery Ridge
Sickles' III Corps
Power's Hill
McLaws
V Corps
Little Round Top
4:00 pm Hood and McLaws attack Sickles' III Corps
c.3:30 pm Reinforcements help secure the Union line; other Union troops are diverted to occupy Little Round Top
Hood

DAY 2
The Confederate forces, including Longstreet's I Corps, concentrated fire on the Union left flank, before Ewell's men began attacking the right. The Union lines held.

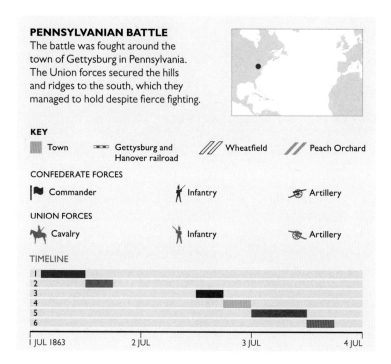

PENNSYLVANIAN BATTLE
The battle was fought around the town of Gettysburg in Pennsylvania. The Union forces secured the hills and ridges to the south, which they managed to hold despite fierce fighting.

KEY
Town — Gettysburg and Hanover railroad — Wheatfield — Peach Orchard

CONFEDERATE FORCES
Commander — Infantry — Artillery

UNION FORCES
Cavalry — Infantry — Artillery

TIMELINE

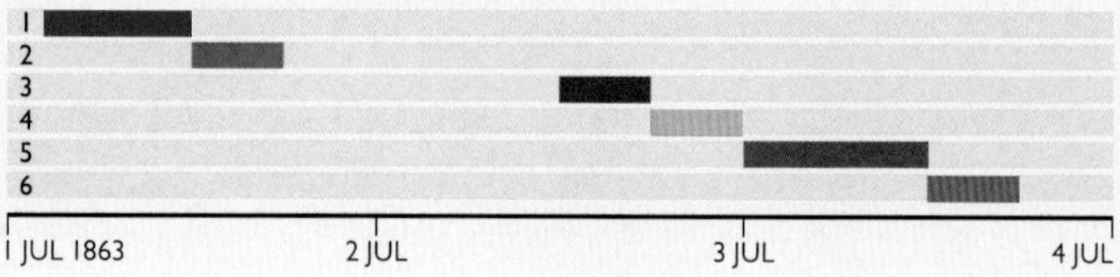
1
2
3
4
5
6
1 JUL 1863
2 JUL
3 JUL
4 JUL

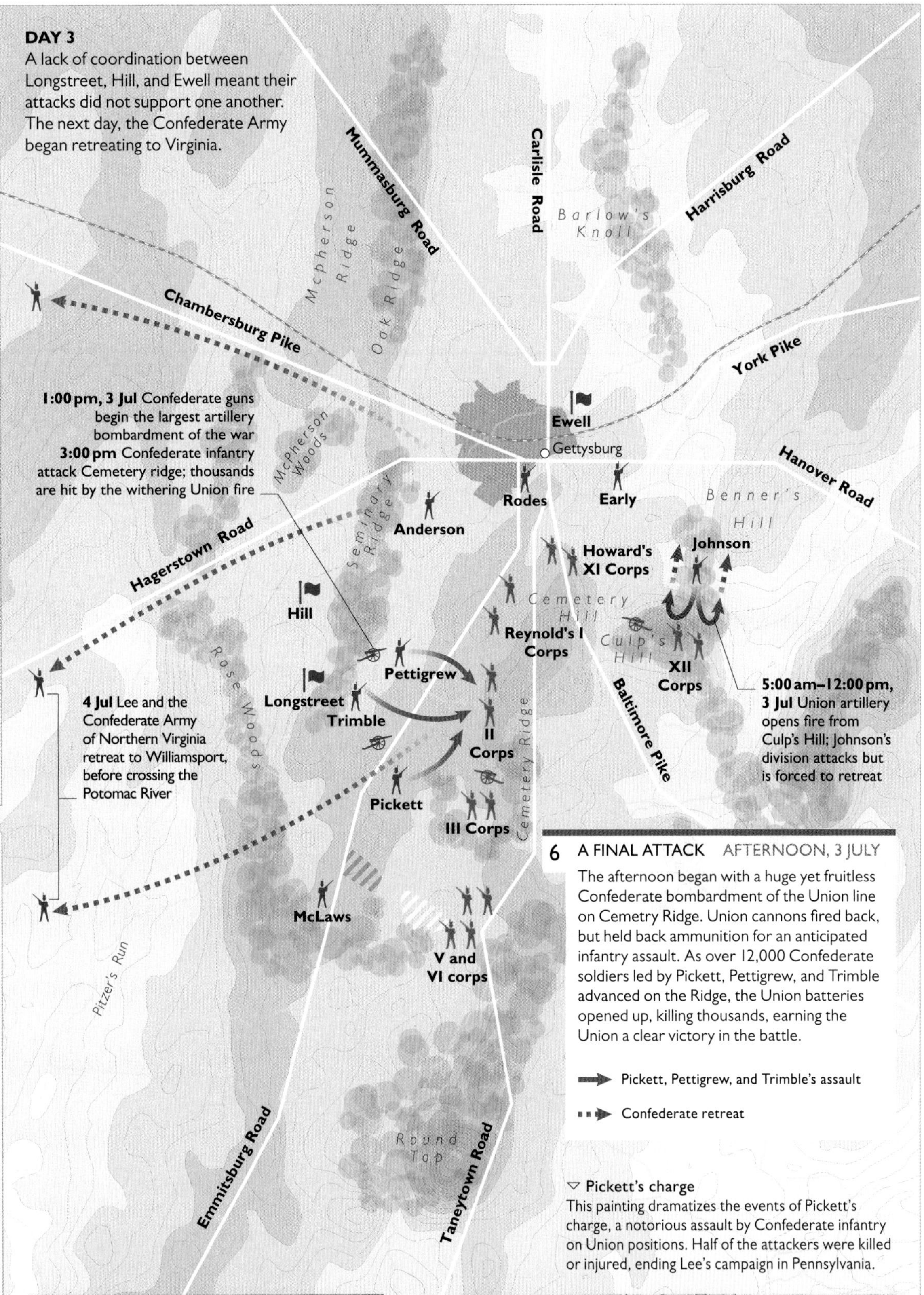

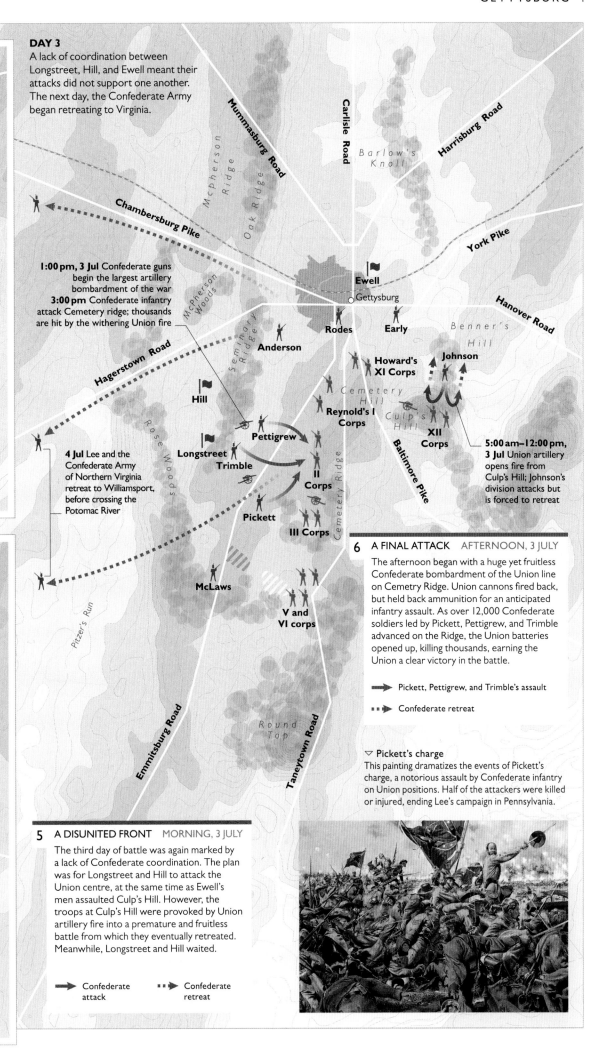

DAY 3
A lack of coordination between Longstreet, Hill, and Ewell meant their attacks did not support one another. The next day, the Confederate Army began retreating to Virginia.
Mummasburg Road
Carlisle Road
Harrisburg Road
Barlow's Knoll
McPherson Ridge
Oak Ridge
Chambersburg Pike
York Pike
Ewell
Gettysburg
Hanover Road
McPherson Woods
1:00 pm, 3 Jul Confederate guns begin the largest artillery bombardment of the war
3:00 pm Confederate infantry attack Cemetery ridge; thousands are hit by the withering Union fire
Rodes
Early
Benner's Hill
Hagerstown Road
Seminary Ridge
Anderson
Howard's XI Corps
Johnson
Hill
Cemetery Hill
Reynold's I Corps
Culp's Hill
XII Corps
Pettigrew
Longstreet
Trimble
Rose Woods
Baltimore Pike
5:00 am–12:00 pm, 3 Jul Union artillery opens fire from Culp's Hill; Johnson's division attacks but is forced to retreat
4 Jul Lee and the Confederate Army of Northern Virginia retreat to Williamsport, before crossing the Potomac River
II Corps
Cemetery Ridge
Pickett
III Corps
McLaws
V and VI corps
Pitzer's Run
Emmitsburg Road
Round Top
Taneytown Road

1 BATTLE BEGINS MORNING, 1 JULY 1863

A division of A.P. Hill's Confederate force moved along the Chambersburg Pike towards Gettysburg, where they met and engaged two Union cavalry brigades led by John Buford. The Union cavalry fell back a short distance to the ridges northwest of Gettysburg, where John Reynolds' I Corps was forming up. More units from both sides soon arrived, and chaotic fighting broke out around McPherson Woods and the nearby railway cutting. By early afternoon, the battle lines were drawn.

First Confederate attacks

2 THE UNION RIGHT FLANK COLLAPSES AFTERNOON, 1 JULY 1863

Confederate Lieutenant General Ewell's troops faced the Union forces deployed in an arc north of Gettysburg. General Jubal Early's division launched a fierce attack on the Union right flank, forcing the XI Corps to retreat to Cemetery Hill. Exposed and under fire, the Union I Corps also fell back. Ewell, however, halted his attack, deeming it too risky to attempt a rushed dusk assault on the hill.

Early's attack — Union retreat

3 ATTACK ON THE UNION LEFT AFTERNOON, 2 JULY

The next day, Confederate artillery opened fire on the Union left flank, where Sickles' III Corps occupied an exposed salient. General Meade rushed reinforcements to the Union left; elsewhere Union troops secured the strategically vital Little Round Top hill just in time. Sickles' men suffered heavy losses in intense fighting with McLaws' and Hood's Confederate divisions in the Wheatfield and Peach Orchard, but the Union line held.

Confederate attack on Union left

Union reinforcements

4 EWELL ATTACKS EVENING, 2 JULY

After firing fruitlessly on the Union lines for two hours, Ewell finally ordered two attacks. General Edward Johnson's Division moved on Culp's Hill, only to be held off by remnants of the Union XII Corps, sustaining heavy casualties. Jubal Early's men were sent to take East Cemetery Hill, where they became bogged down in a fierce fight with Union soldiers. Support from Rodes' Division arrived too late to help the Confederates.

Confederate attack on Union right

5 A DISUNITED FRONT MORNING, 3 JULY

The third day of battle was again marked by a lack of Confederate coordination. The plan was for Longstreet and Hill to attack the Union centre, at the same time as Ewell's men assaulted Culp's Hill. However, the troops at Culp's Hill were provoked by Union artillery fire into a premature and fruitless battle from which they eventually retreated. Meanwhile, Longstreet and Hill waited.

Confederate attack — Confederate retreat

6 A FINAL ATTACK AFTERNOON, 3 JULY

The afternoon began with a huge yet fruitless Confederate bombardment of the Union line on Cemetry Ridge. Union cannons fired back, but held back ammunition for an anticipated infantry assault. As over 12,000 Confederate soldiers led by Pickett, Pettigrew, and Trimble advanced on the Ridge, the Union batteries opened up, killing thousands, earning the Union a clear victory in the battle.

Pickett, Pettigrew, and Trimble's assault

Confederate retreat

▽ **Pickett's charge**
This painting dramatizes the events of Pickett's charge, a notorious assault by Confederate infantry on Union positions. Half of the attackers were killed or injured, ending Lee's campaign in Pennsylvania.

KÖNIGGRÄTZ

Superior tactics and modern, breech-loading rifles helped Prussia beat a large and well positioned Austrian force at Königgrätz. The battle decided the Austro-Prussian Seven Weeks War (14 June–22 July 1866) and ended Austrian political dominance among German states.

1
Sendrazitz
IV. Corps
Ober-
Lodhenitz
II. Corps

In the mid-19th century, Austria and Prussia vied for control of the states of the German Confederation. In a bid to unite them, and curb Austro-Hungarian power, Prussian Minister President Otto von Bismarck and Graf Helmuth von Moltke, Chief of Prussian General Staff, planned a war against Austria. In June 1866, Bismarck provoked a clash over Schleswig-Holstein (then joint territory of Austria and Prussia), and war began.

The Prussian armies rapidly invaded Saxony and Bohemia, and after several indecisive skirmishes, Austrian general Benedek pulled back northwest of the fortified town of Königgrätz. Prussia's First and Elbe Armies attacked the Austrian left and centre in the early morning of 3 July. The Austrian army and its allies had strong cavalry and long range artillery, but the wooded terrain and Benedek's caution offset these advantages. The Austrian infantry's muzzle-loading rifles proved no match for the Prussians' breech-loading "needle-guns". When the Prussian Second Army attacked the Austrian right, Benedek fell back.

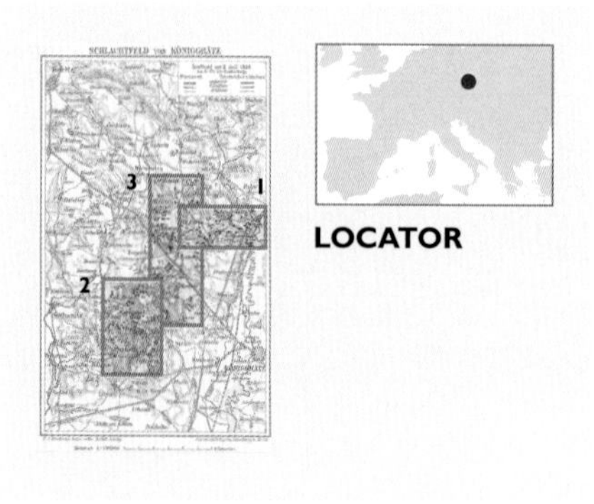
1
2
3
LOCATOR

2
Probluz
Nied. Prim
Ober Prim
Neu Prim
Radikowitz
Techlowitz

△ **A wasted opportunity**
Benedek felt that the damp weather made a cavalry charge too risky, but his cavalry fought a rearguard action with the Prussians that involved over 10,000 horsemen.

◁ **The fight on the Prussian right**
The Army of the Elbe faced the Austrian's Saxon allies; it captured Problus and Nieder Prim at around 3 pm, but the Prussian commander Herwarth von Bittenfeld did not press on with the encirclement.

ENGAGEMENT BY THE ELBE
Prussia's First and Elbe Armies attacked the Austrians and their Saxon allies on the left from 7:00 am on 3 July. The Austrians pulled back to their defensive positions around Maslowed, Lipa, and Langenhof, and pinned down the Prussians for hours with heavy artillery fire. An Austrian counter-attack at 11:00 am nearly unhinged the Prussian left flank at the Swiepwald. The arriving Prussian Second Army then steadily crushed the Austrian right. At around 3:00 pm, Field Marshal Ramming staged a last counter-attack before retreating with the rest of the Austrian army across the Elbe. Over 40,000 of his troops had been killed, wounded, or captured.

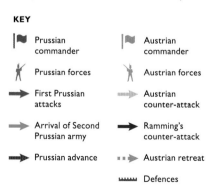

KEY
- Prussian commander
- Prussian forces
- First Prussian attacks
- Arrival of Second Prussian army
- Prussian advance
- Austrian commander
- Austrian forces
- Austrian counter-attack
- Ramming's counter-attack
- Austrian retreat
- Defences

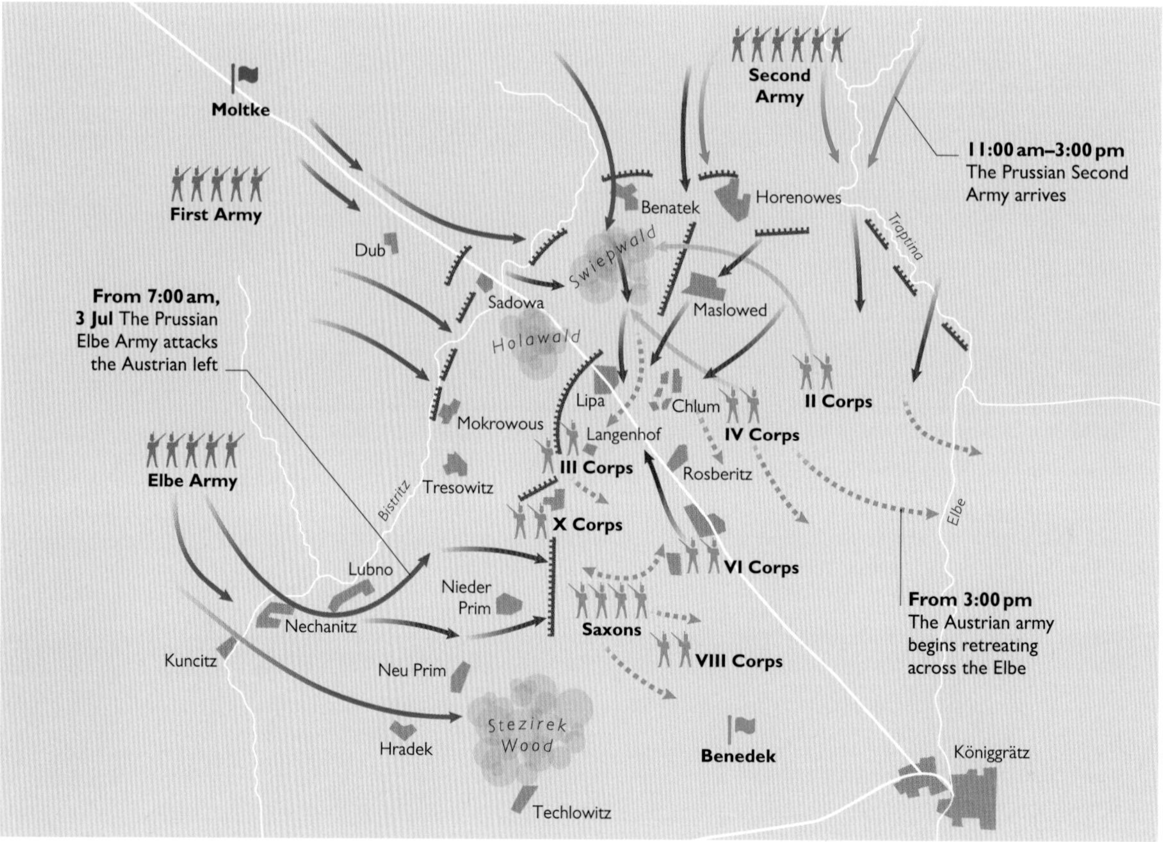
Moltke
First Army
Second Army
11:00 am–3:00 pm
The Prussian Second Army arrives
Benatek
Horenowes
Trotina
Dub
Swiepwald
Sadowa
Maslowed
Holawald
From 7:00 am, 3 Jul The Prussian Elbe Army attacks the Austrian left
Lipa
Chlum
II Corps
Mokrowous
Langenhof
IV Corps
III Corps
Rosberitz
Elbe Army
Tresowitz
Bistritz
X Corps
VI Corps
Lubno
Nieder Prim
Nechanitz
Saxons
VIII Corps
Elbe
From 3:00 pm
The Austrian army begins retreating across the Elbe
Kuncitz
Neu Prim
Stezirek Wood
Hradek
Benedek
Königgrätz
Techlowitz

3

Mastow
IV. Corps
III. Corps
Chlum
Rozberitz
VI.
Wschestar
Rositz
Briza
Brizer W.
Ziegel
Klacow
Charbuzitz

△ Austria's last attack
Chlum and Roseberitz were the scenes of the last Austrian counter-attack; the Austrian Field-Marshal Ramming retook the villages before being forced to retreat.

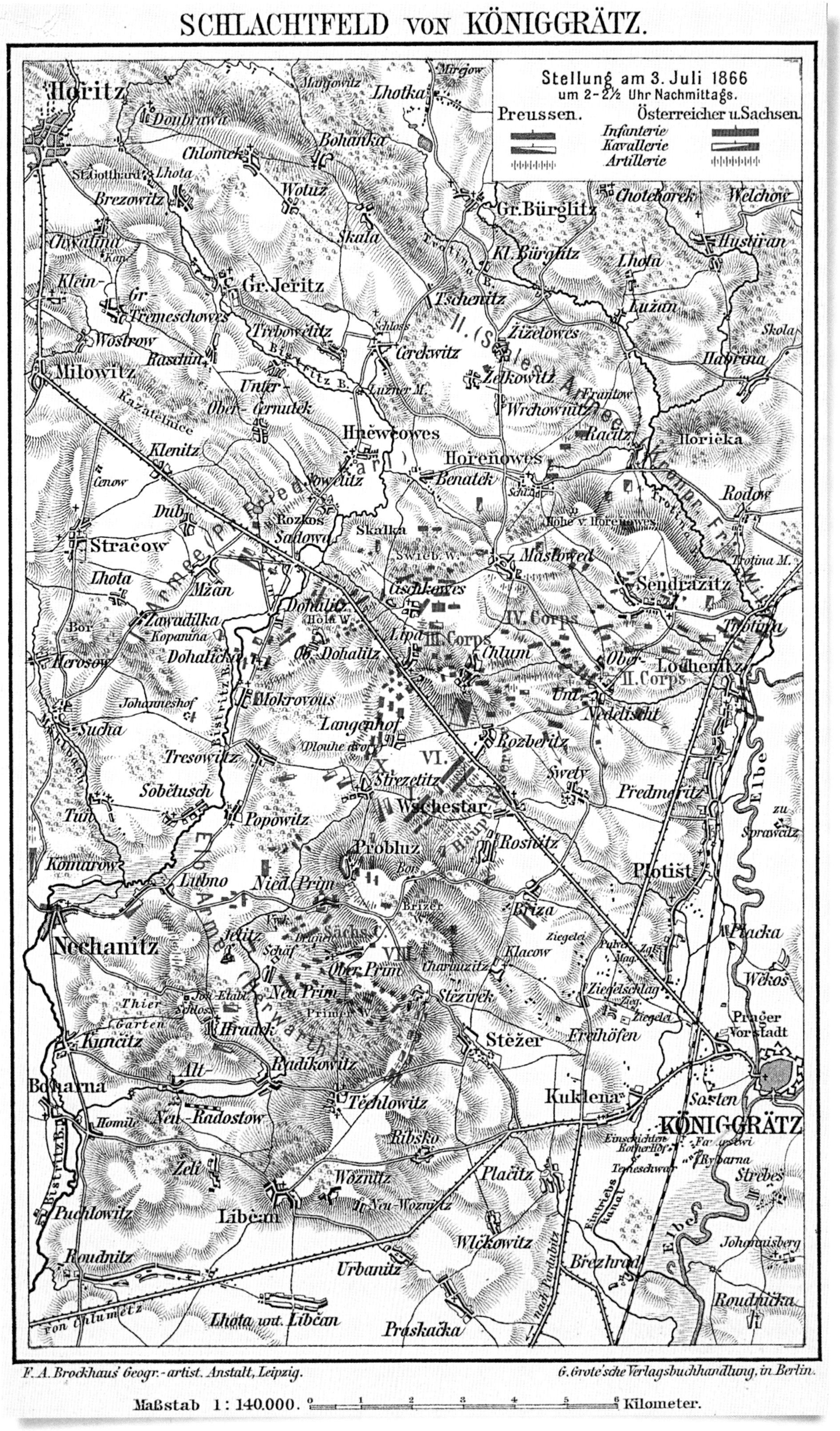
SCHLACHTFELD VON KÖNIGGRÄTZ.
Stellung am 3. Juli 1866
um 2-2½ Uhr Nachmittags.
Preussen.
Österreicher u. Sachsen.
Infanterie
Kavallerie
Artillerie
Horitz
Lhotka
Chlum
Gr. Bürglitz
Gr. Jeritz
Milowitz
Horeňowes
Benatek
Maslowed
Sendrazitz
Stracow
Dub
Sadowa
Lipa
IV. Corps
III. Corps
II. Corps
Rozberitz
Wschestar
Probluz
Nechanitz
Stežer
Kuklena
KÖNIGGRÄTZ
Libčan
Urbanitz
Praskačka
Elbe
F. A. Brockhaus' Geogr.-artist. Anstalt, Leipzig.
G. Grote'sche Verlagsbuchhandlung, in Berlin.
Maßstab 1 : 140.000.
Kilometer.

▷ Sadova, near Königgrätz
This map shows the battlefield at Sadova in the afternoon of 3 July, shortly before the Austrians retreated to avoid encirclement by the Prussian armies.

SEDAN

In a pivotal battle of the Franco-Prussian War (1870–71), the Germans, led by the brilliant General Helmuth von Moltke, trapped the French Army of Châlons at Sedan on 1 September 1870. Napoleon III's surrender prompted the collapse of the French Empire.

The Franco–Prussian War was rooted in a contest for European dominance between Otto von Bismarck, the Prussian Chancellor of the North German Confederation, and the French emperor, Napoleon III. The French declared war on 19 July 1870, the emperor eager to match the military achievements of his uncle, Napoleon Bonaparte. However, the Germans had the finest artillery in the world, and a sublime strategist in General Helmuth von Moltke.

In August, Moltke trapped the 180,000-strong French Army of the Rhine at Metz. The French Army of Châlons, under Patrice de MacMahon, tried to relieve the Army of the Rhine but in doing so became hemmed in at the town of Sedan, which sat in a low valley on a bend in the River Meuse.

On 1 September, the Germans closed in, encircling Sedan and bombarding the French with artillery fire from around 400 guns. After attempts to break out failed, the French surrendered. Napoleon III and 100,000 of his men were taken into Prussian captivity, and the Second Napoleonic Empire collapsed. The new French Third Republic continued the war, but was defeated in 1871. The humiliating terms of the peace treaty, signed in May of the same year, fuelled French resentment that contributed to World War I.

> *"War is a necessary part of God's arrangement of the world."*
>
> HELMUTH VON MOLTKE, 1880

ADVANCES IN ARTILLERY

In the 19th century, the German steel manufacturer Alfred Krupp, nicknamed "The Cannon King", mastered the difficult process of casting steel and began machining rifled steel guns of exceptional quality. Equipped with hundreds of Krupp guns, including the 6-pounder breech loading cannon capable of firing a shell containing zinc balls and explosives over 4.5 km (2¾ miles) with great accuracy, the Prussians had a major advantage at Sedan.

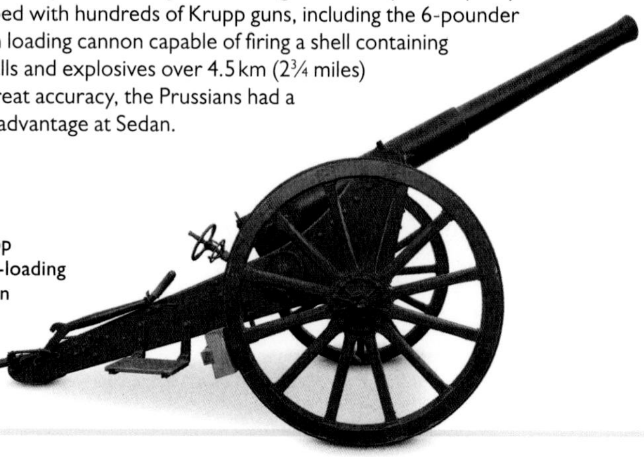

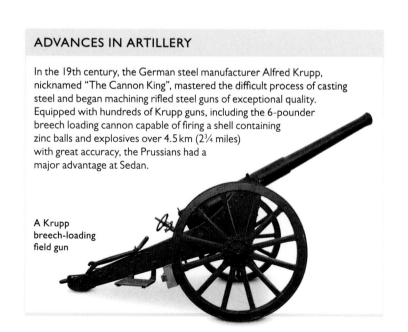

A Krupp breech-loading field gun

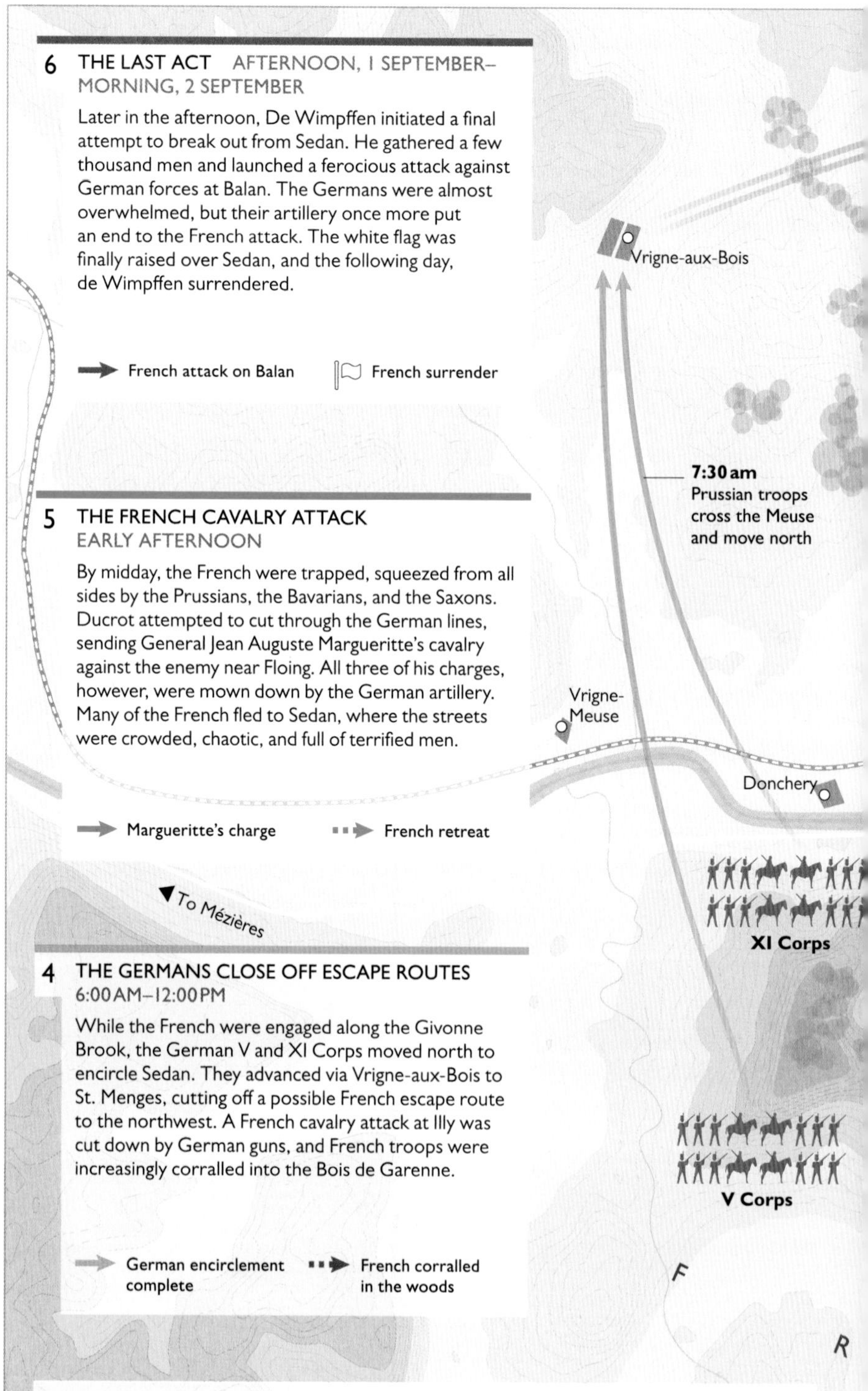

Vrigne-aux-Bois
7:30 am
Prussian troops cross the Meuse and move north
Vrigne-Meuse
Donchery
To Mézières
XI Corps
V Corps
F
R

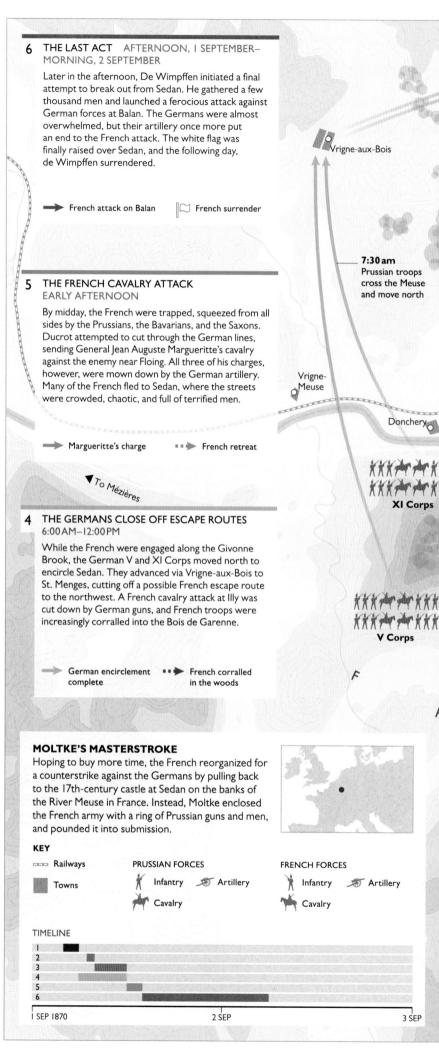

6 THE LAST ACT AFTERNOON, 1 SEPTEMBER–MORNING, 2 SEPTEMBER

Later in the afternoon, De Wimpffen initiated a final attempt to break out from Sedan. He gathered a few thousand men and launched a ferocious attack against German forces at Balan. The Germans were almost overwhelmed, but their artillery once more put an end to the French attack. The white flag was finally raised over Sedan, and the following day, de Wimpffen surrendered.

French attack on Balan — French surrender

5 THE FRENCH CAVALRY ATTACK EARLY AFTERNOON

By midday, the French were trapped, squeezed from all sides by the Prussians, the Bavarians, and the Saxons. Ducrot attempted to cut through the German lines, sending General Jean Auguste Margueritte's cavalry against the enemy near Floing. All three of his charges, however, were mown down by the German artillery. Many of the French fled to Sedan, where the streets were crowded, chaotic, and full of terrified men.

Margueritte's charge — French retreat

4 THE GERMANS CLOSE OFF ESCAPE ROUTES 6:00AM–12:00PM

While the French were engaged along the Givonne Brook, the German V and XI Corps moved north to encircle Sedan. They advanced via Vrigne-aux-Bois to St. Menges, cutting off a possible French escape route to the northwest. A French cavalry attack at Illy was cut down by German guns, and French troops were increasingly corralled into the Bois de Garenne.

German encirclement complete — French corralled in the woods

MOLTKE'S MASTERSTROKE

Hoping to buy more time, the French reorganized for a counterstrike against the Germans by pulling back to the 17th-century castle at Sedan on the banks of the River Meuse in France. Instead, Moltke enclosed the French army with a ring of Prussian guns and men, and pounded it into submission.

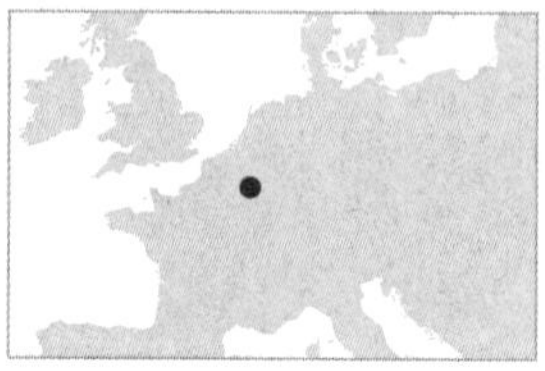

KEY

Railways

Towns

PRUSSIAN FORCES: Infantry, Artillery, Cavalry

FRENCH FORCES: Infantry, Artillery, Cavalry

TIMELINE

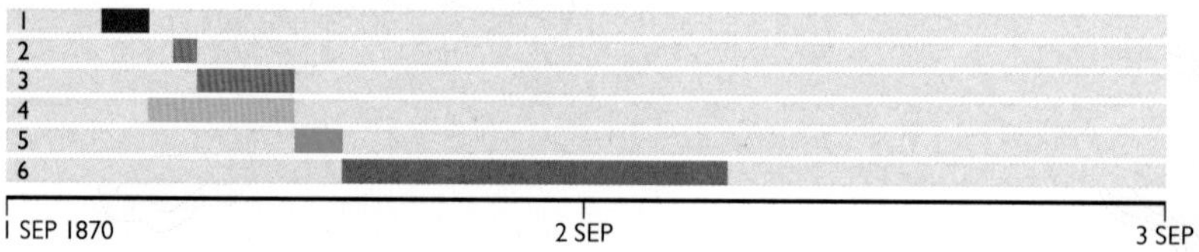

1
2
3
4
5
6
1 SEP 1870
2 SEP
3 SEP

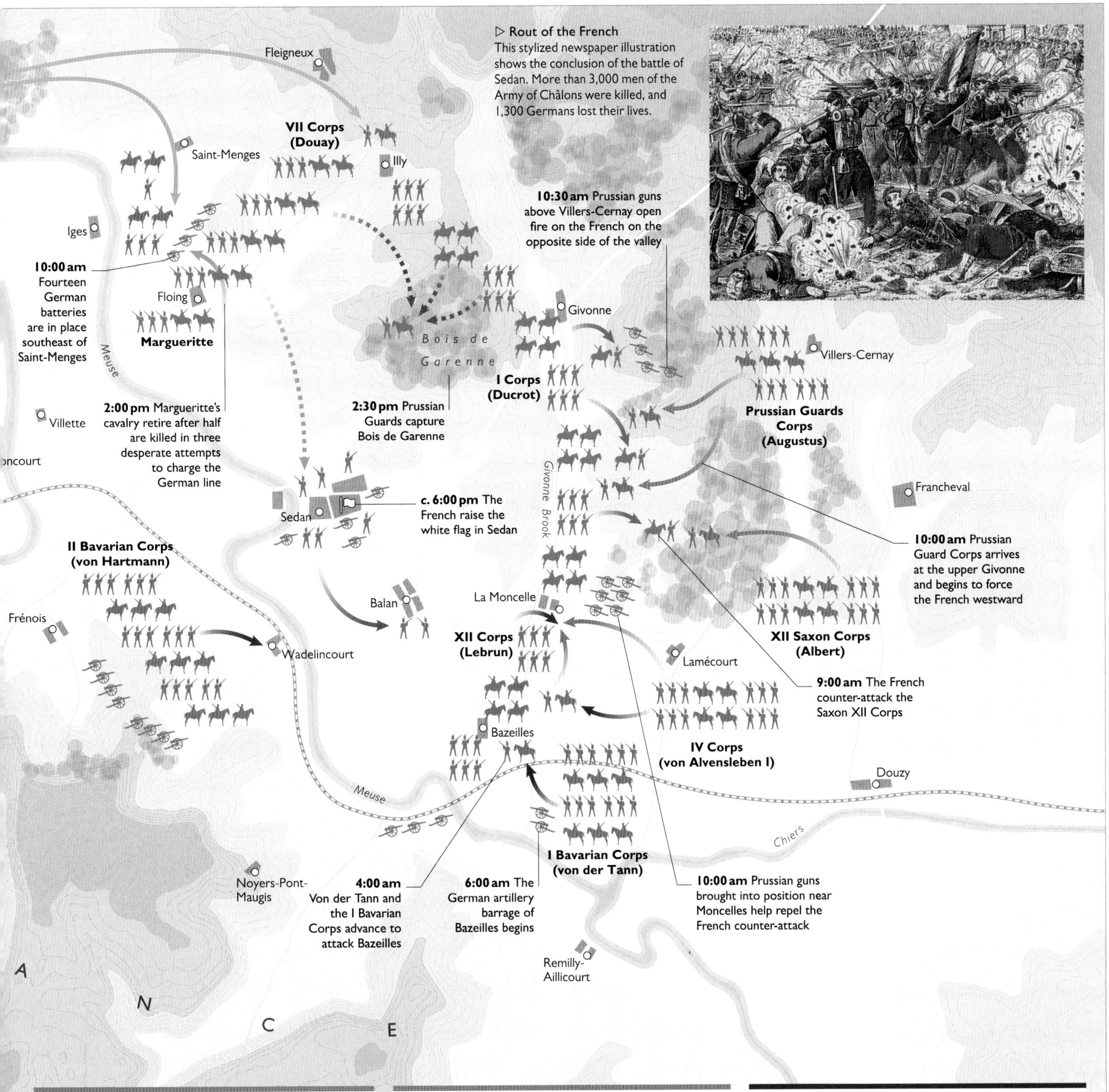
Fleigneux
VII Corps (Douay)
Saint-Menges
Illy
Iges
10:00 am Fourteen German batteries are in place southeast of Saint-Menges
Floing
Marguerite
Meuse
Givonne
Bois de Garenne
10:30 am Prussian guns above Villers-Cernay open fire on the French on the opposite side of the valley
Villers-Cernay
I Corps (Ducrot)
Villette
2:00 pm Margueritte's cavalry retire after half are killed in three desperate attempts to charge the German line
2:30 pm Prussian Guards capture Bois de Garenne
Prussian Guards Corps (Augustus)
Givonne Brook
Francheval
Sedan
c. 6:00 pm The French raise the white flag in Sedan
10:00 am Prussian Guard Corps arrives at the upper Givonne and begins to force the French westward
II Bavarian Corps (von Hartmann)
Balan
La Moncelle
Frénois
Wadelincourt
XII Corps (Lebrun)
Lamécourt
XII Saxon Corps (Albert)
9:00 am The French counter-attack the Saxon XII Corps
Bazeilles
IV Corps (von Alvensleben I)
Douzy
Meuse
Chiers
I Bavarian Corps (von der Tann)
Noyers-Pont-Maugis
4:00 am Von der Tann and the I Bavarian Corps advance to attack Bazeilles
6:00 am The German artillery barrage of Bazeilles begins
10:00 am Prussian guns brought into position near Moncelles help repel the French counter-attack
Remilly-Aillicourt
A
N
C
E

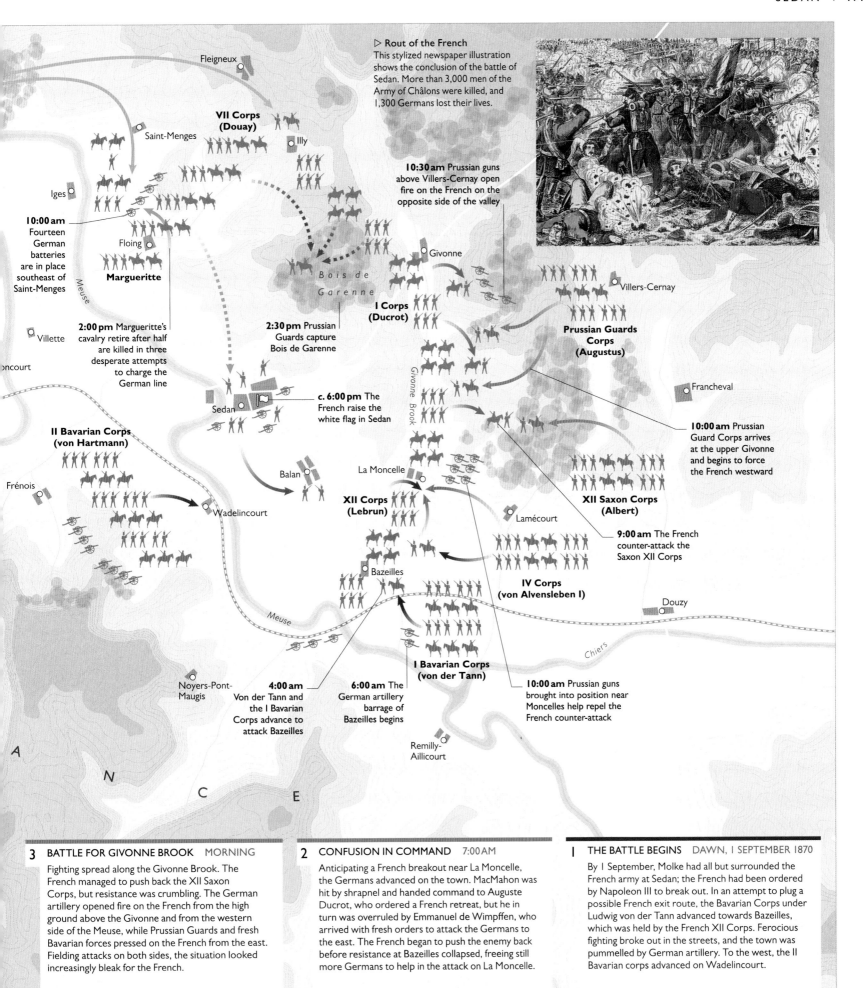

▷ **Rout of the French**
This stylized newspaper illustration shows the conclusion of the battle of Sedan. More than 3,000 men of the Army of Châlons were killed, and 1,300 Germans lost their lives.

1 THE BATTLE BEGINS DAWN, 1 SEPTEMBER 1870

By 1 September, Molke had all but surrounded the French army at Sedan; the French had been ordered by Napoleon III to break out. In an attempt to plug a possible French exit route, the Bavarian Corps under Ludwig von der Tann advanced towards Bazeilles, which was held by the French XII Corps. Ferocious fighting broke out in the streets, and the town was pummelled by German artillery. To the west, the II Bavarian corps advanced on Wadelincourt.

➡ German assault

2 CONFUSION IN COMMAND 7:00 AM

Anticipating a French breakout near La Moncelle, the Germans advanced on the town. MacMahon was hit by shrapnel and handed command to Auguste Ducrot, who ordered a French retreat, but he in turn was overruled by Emmanuel de Wimpffen, who arrived with fresh orders to attack the Germans to the east. The French began to push the enemy back before resistance at Bazeilles collapsed, freeing still more Germans to help in the attack on La Moncelle.

➡ German advance ➡ French counter-attack

3 BATTLE FOR GIVONNE BROOK MORNING

Fighting spread along the Givonne Brook. The French managed to push back the XII Saxon Corps, but resistance was crumbling. The German artillery opened fire on the French from the high ground above the Givonne and from the western side of the Meuse, while Prussian Guards and fresh Bavarian forces pressed on the French from the east. Fielding attacks on both sides, the situation looked increasingly bleak for the French.

➡ German advance ➡ French counter-attack

LITTLE BIGHORN

Near the Little Bighorn River, in present-day Montana, Sitting Bull and around 2,000 warriors from the Native Peoples of the Northern Plains outmanoeuvred and massacred nearly half of the over 600 horsemen of the US Seventh Cavalry.

In 1875, tensions flared up between the US Government and the Lakota, Dakota Sioux, and Arapaho peoples when American gold miners began settling in territory west of the Missouri River, given exclusively to the Native Americans in a treaty in 1868. War became inevitable when the government refused to remove the settlers and ordered the Native American tribes to return to their reservations.

In spring 1876, around 2,000 warriors joined Sitting Bull – a charismatic Lakota leader – at his camp on the Little Bighorn River. Lieutenant Colonel George A. Custer and the Seventh Cavalry were sent to track down Sitting Bull, and reached the camp on 25 June. Rather than wait for reinforcements, Custer attacked, but was overwhelmed in what was a resounding victory for the Native Peoples of the Northern Plains.

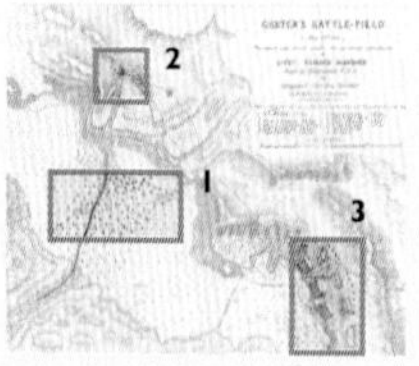
2
1
3

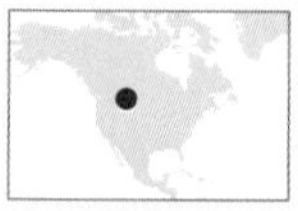

LOCATOR

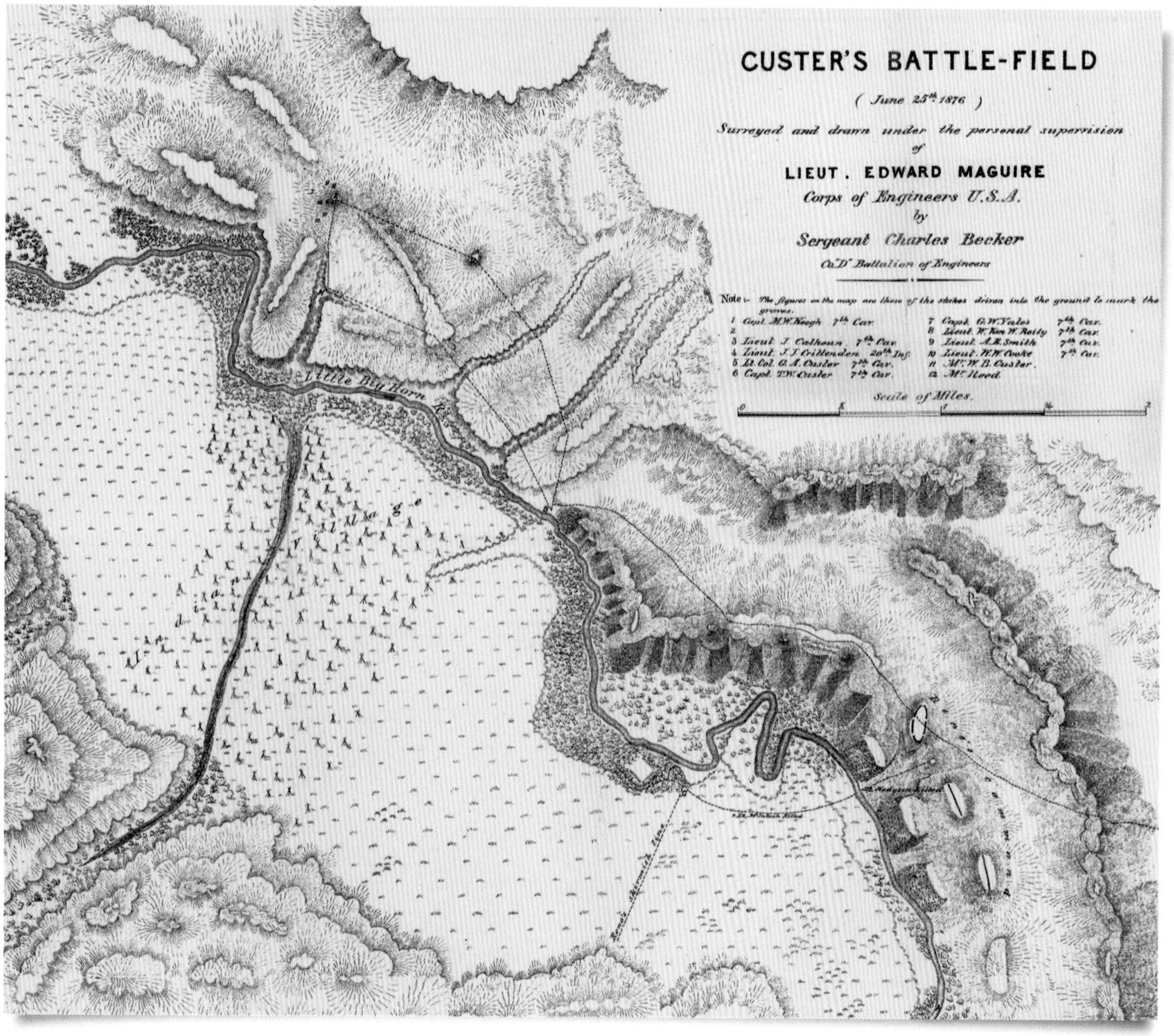
CUSTER'S BATTLE-FIELD
(June 25th 1876)
Surveyed and drawn under the personal supervision of
LIEUT. EDWARD MAGUIRE
Corps of Engineers U.S.A.
by
Sergeant Charles Becker
Co. "D" Battalion of Engineers
Note:- The figures on the map are those of the stakes driven into the ground to mark the graves.
1 Capt. M.W. Keogh 7th Cav.
2
3 Lieut. J. Calhoun 7th Cav.
4 Lieut. J.J. Crittenden 20th Inf.
5 Lt. Col. G.A. Custer 7th Cav.
6 Capt. T.W. Custer 7th Cav.
7 Capt. G.W. Yates 7th Cav.
8 Lieut. W. Van W. Reily 7th Cav.
9 Lieut. A.E. Smith 7th Cav.
10 Lieut. W.W. Cooke 7th Cav.
11 Mr. W.B. Custer.
12 Mr. Reed
Scale of Miles.
Little Big Horn R.
Village

△ **The battlefield**
This map shows the site of the battle as drawn by a member of the US Corps of Engineers. It also records the grave-markers left for Custer and his commanding officers, although their last movements remain open to debate.

▷ **Sitting Bull's village**
Sitting Bull and Crazy Horse gathered 2,000 warriors and their families in this village. It was the largest Native American settlement that the US forces had ever encountered.

1
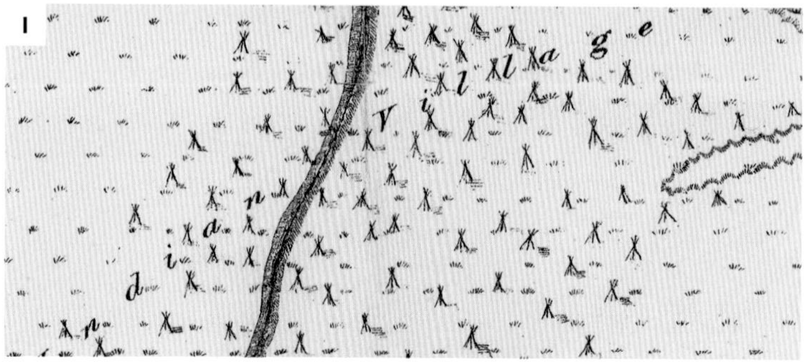
Village
Indian

3
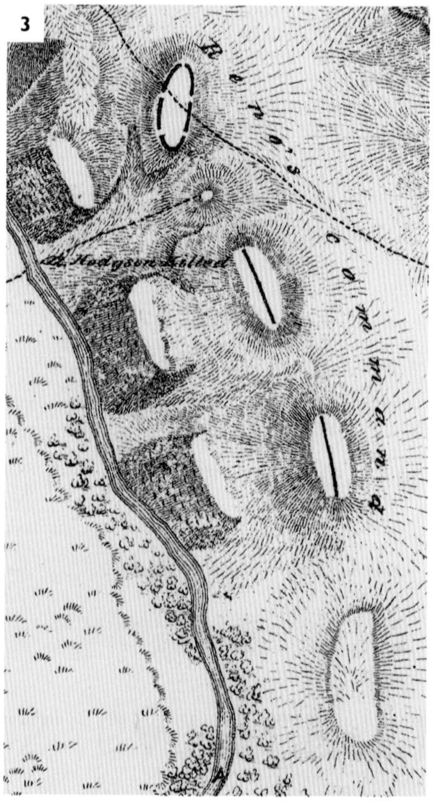

△ **Defensive position**
Companies under Major Marcus Reno and Captain Frederick Benteen held out in these hills until relieved by General Terry's column on 27 June.

▽ **Custer's "last stand"**
Custer fought to the last at this site. In truth he was fatally outnumbered and isolated, and his "stand" was perhaps more myth than reality.

2
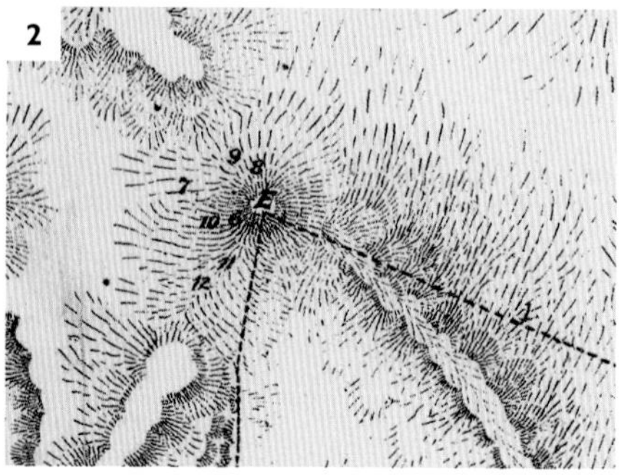

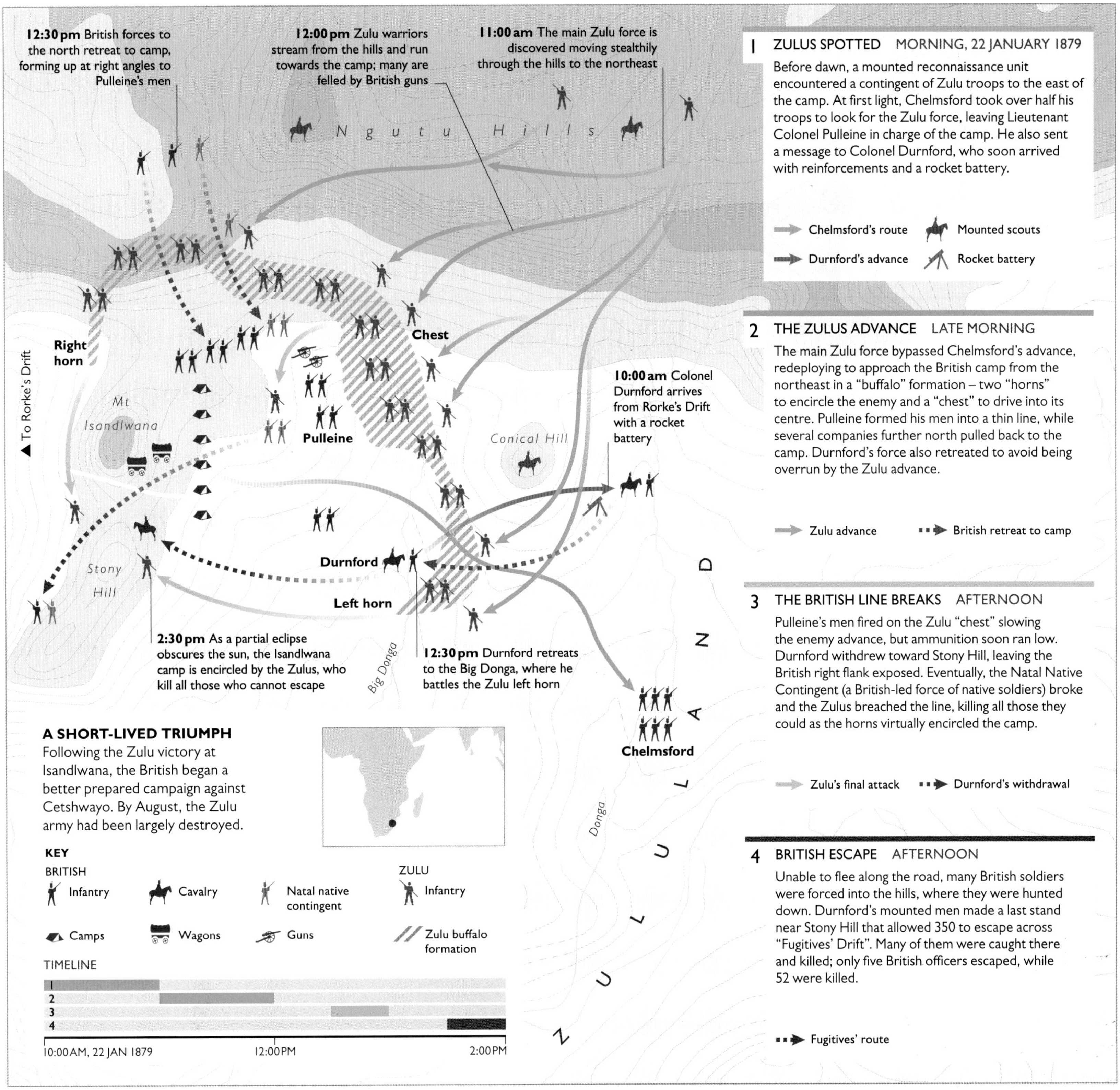
12:30 pm British forces to the north retreat to camp, forming up at right angles to Pulleine's men
12:00 pm Zulu warriors stream from the hills and run towards the camp; many are felled by British guns
11:00 am The main Zulu force is discovered moving stealthily through the hills to the northeast
N g u t u H i l l s
Right horn
Chest
Mt Isandlwana
Pulleine
Conical Hill
10:00 am Colonel Durnford arrives from Rorke's Drift with a rocket battery
To Rorke's Drift
Stony Hill
Durnford
Left horn
2:30 pm As a partial eclipse obscures the sun, the Isandlwana camp is encircled by the Zulus, who kill all those who cannot escape
Big Donga
12:30 pm Durnford retreats to the Big Donga, where he battles the Zulu left horn
Chelmsford
Donga
Z U L U L A N D
1 ZULUS SPOTTED MORNING, 22 JANUARY 1879
Before dawn, a mounted reconnaissance unit encountered a contingent of Zulu troops to the east of the camp. At first light, Chelmsford took over half his troops to look for the Zulu force, leaving Lieutenant Colonel Pulleine in charge of the camp. He also sent a message to Colonel Durnford, who soon arrived with reinforcements and a rocket battery.
Chelmsford's route
Mounted scouts
Durnford's advance
Rocket battery
2 THE ZULUS ADVANCE LATE MORNING
The main Zulu force bypassed Chelmsford's advance, redeploying to approach the British camp from the northeast in a "buffalo" formation – two "horns" to encircle the enemy and a "chest" to drive into its centre. Pulleine formed his men into a thin line, while several companies further north pulled back to the camp. Durnford's force also retreated to avoid being overrun by the Zulu advance.
Zulu advance
British retreat to camp
3 THE BRITISH LINE BREAKS AFTERNOON
Pulleine's men fired on the Zulu "chest" slowing the enemy advance, but ammunition soon ran low. Durnford withdrew toward Stony Hill, leaving the British right flank exposed. Eventually, the Natal Native Contingent (a British-led force of native soldiers) broke and the Zulus breached the line, killing all those they could as the horns virtually encircled the camp.
Zulu's final attack
Durnford's withdrawal
4 BRITISH ESCAPE AFTERNOON
Unable to flee along the road, many British soldiers were forced into the hills, where they were hunted down. Durnford's mounted men made a last stand near Stony Hill that allowed 350 to escape across "Fugitives' Drift". Many of them were caught there and killed; only five British officers escaped, while 52 were killed.
Fugitives' route
A SHORT-LIVED TRIUMPH
Following the Zulu victory at Isandlwana, the British began a better prepared campaign against Cetshwayo. By August, the Zulu army had been largely destroyed.
KEY
BRITISH
Infantry
Cavalry
Natal native contingent
Camps
Wagons
Guns
ZULU
Infantry
Zulu buffalo formation
TIMELINE
1
2
3
4
10:00AM, 22 JAN 1879
12:00PM
2:00PM

ISANDLWANA

Seeking to expand their territories in South Africa, British colonial authorities demanded that the Zulu king Cetshwayo disband his army. He refused, and conflict resulted. On 22 January 1879, 20,000 Zulu warriors armed with spears, shields, and old muskets surprised and overwhelmed 1,800 British, colonial, and native troops at the British camp at Isandlwana.

In January 1879, Lord Chelmsford, commander of British forces in South Africa, invaded Zululand with three columns totalling around 16,000 British and African troops. After sending one column to the north and one south, Chelmsford accompanied the central column, entering Zululand on 11 January. He crossed the Buffalo River at Rorke's Drift mission, where one battalion established a base camp. Chelmsford pushed on with his wagon train, setting up camp at Isandlwana Hill on 20 January. Meanwhile, the Zulus had raised a huge army of around 20,000 men. Part went to meet the British column to the south, and most headed for Chelmsford's camp at Isandlwana. The discipline, speed, and skill of the Zulus prevailed, and the soldiers in the camp were overrun; 1,300 of them were killed. The Zulus then attacked Rorke's Drift, where the 150 British soldiers guarding the camp made a resolute stand behind walls made of mealie ration sacks.

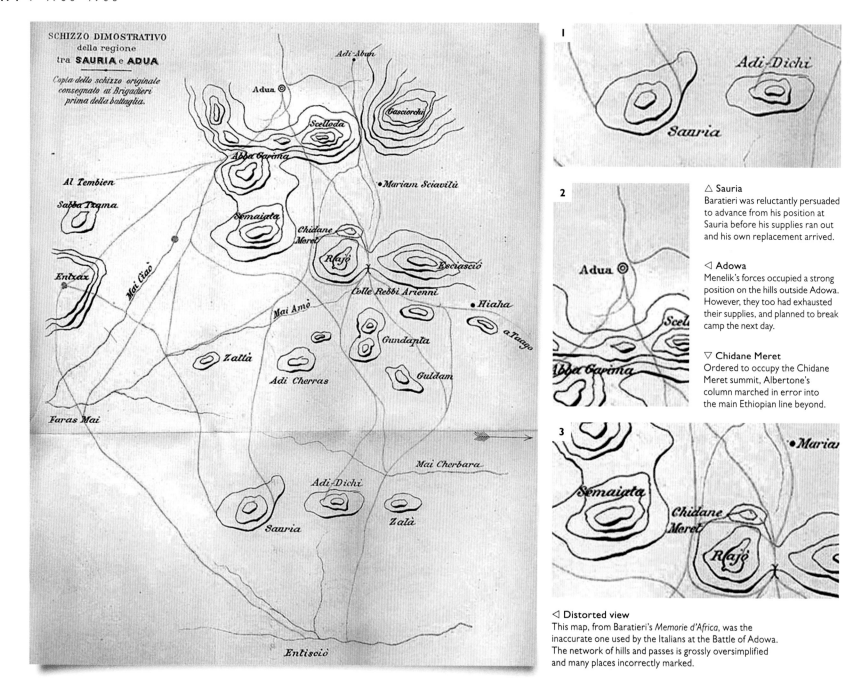

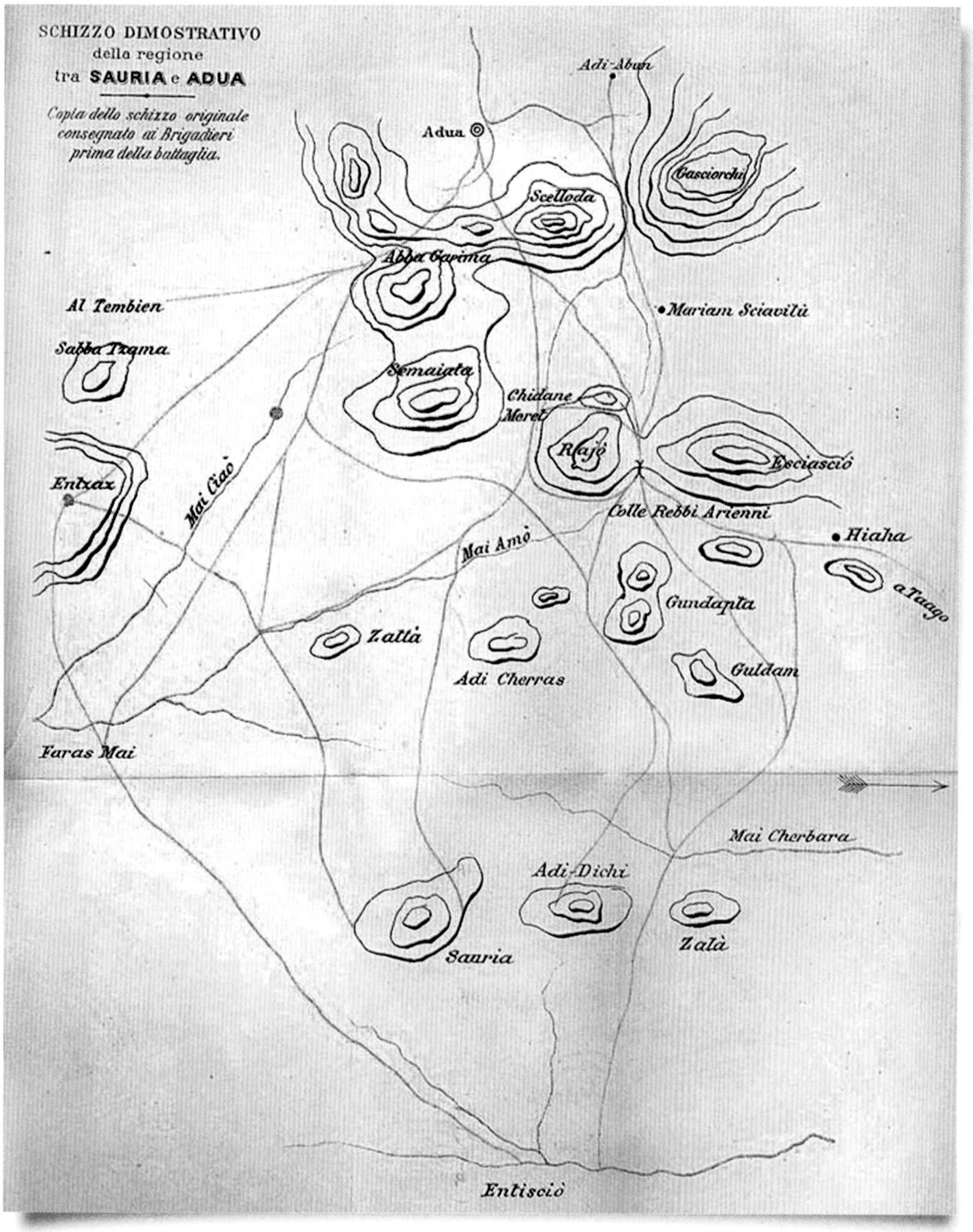
SCHIZZO DIMOSTRATIVO
della regione
tra SAURIA e ADUA
Copia dello schizzo originale consegnato ai Brigadieri prima della battaglia.
Adua
Adi-Abun
Scelloda
Gasciorchi
Abba Garima
Al Tembien
Sabba Tzama
•Mariam Sciavitù
Semaiata
Chidane Meret
Rajò
Esciasciò
Mai Ciao
Colle Rebbi Arienni
•Hiaha
Mai Amò
a Tzago
Gundapta
Zalla
Adi Cherras
Guldam
Faras Mai
Mai Cherbara
Adi-Dichi
Sauria
Zalà
Entisciò

1

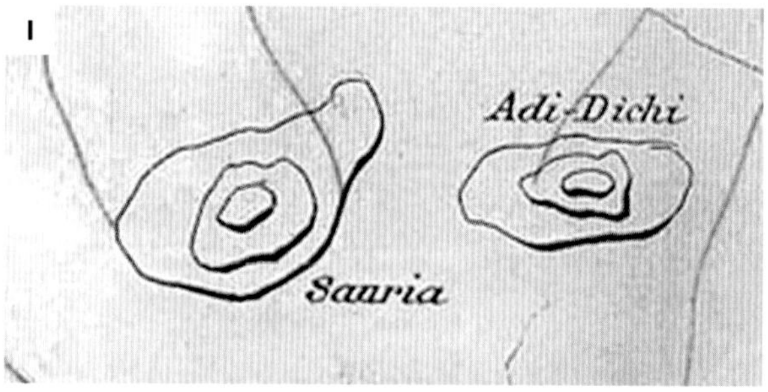
Adi-Dichi
Sauria

2

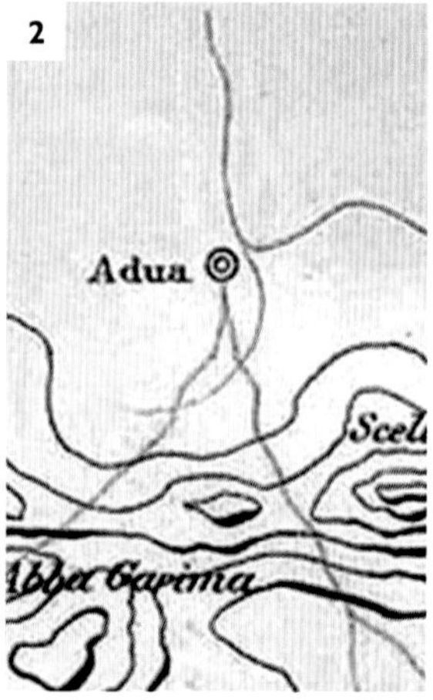
Adua
Abba Garima

△ **Sauria**
Baratieri was reluctantly persuaded to advance from his position at Sauria before his supplies ran out and his own replacement arrived.

◁ **Adowa**
Menelik's forces occupied a strong position on the hills outside Adowa. However, they too had exhausted their supplies, and planned to break camp the next day.

▽ **Chidane Meret**
Ordered to occupy the Chidane Meret summit, Albertone's column marched in error into the main Ethiopian line beyond.

3

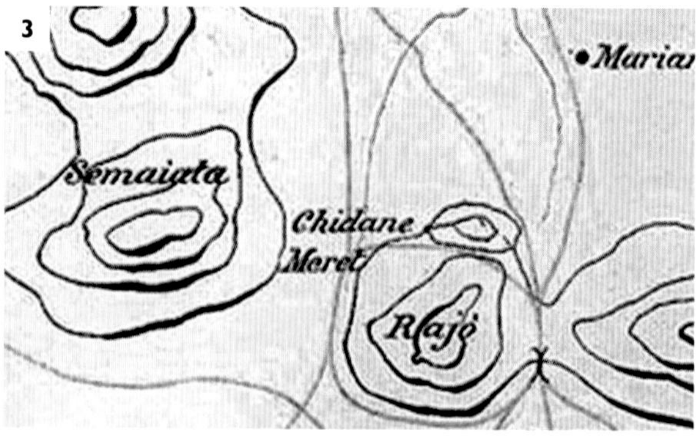
Semaiata
Chidane
Meret
Rajò

◁ **Distorted view**
This map, from Baratieri's *Memorie d'Africa*, was the inaccurate one used by the Italians at the Battle of Adowa. The network of hills and passes is grossly oversimplified and many places incorrectly marked.

ADOWA

On 1 March 1896, Ethiopian Emperor Menelik II led his army to defeat an invading Italian force at Adowa that fatally underestimated their opponents' strengh. The battle ensured that Ethiopia was never colonized by a European power.

Italy began establishing its first African colony, Eritrea, in 1882. Tensions between Italy and the Ethiopian Empire led to full-scale war in 1895. Menelik overran an Italian outpost in his first battle at Amba Alagi on 7 December 1895. In February 1896, the Italian governor of Eritrea, General Oreste Baratieri, led around 10,000 poorly trained Italian conscripts and several thousand Eritrean *Askari* towards Adowa to face the Emperor's well-equipped and experienced forces.

Early on 1 March, four Italian brigades advanced towards Adowa. On the left, Albertone was to secure the high ground at Chidane Meret, while on the right and centre Elena, Dabormida, and Arimondi's brigades were to head to the passes around Rebbi Aryaeni. However, the Italian maps proved to be wildly inaccurate. Albertone found himself kilometres from the rest of the army and encircled by tens of thousands of Ethiopians; a massacre ensued. The other Italian columns were shattered piecemeal as Menelik released his horsemen and Shewan reserve.

Over half of Baratieri's men had been killed, wounded or captured, with at least as many Ethiopian losses. Ethiopia's victory ensured that it would remain the only African country uncolonized by Europeans.

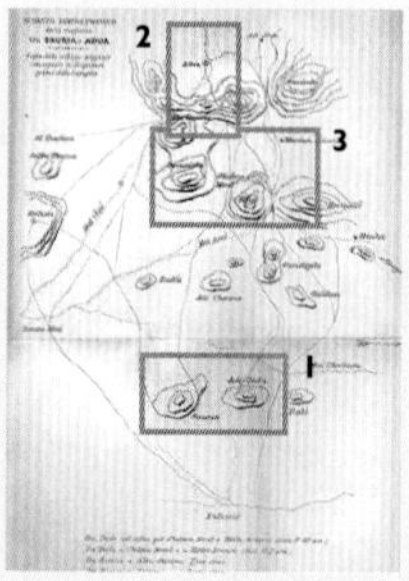
2
3
1

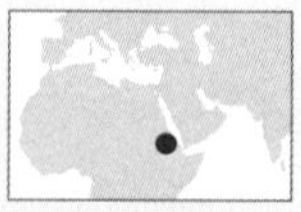

LOCATOR

OMDURMAN

At Omdurman, modern weapons, including the Maxim gun and rapid-fire rifles and artillery, helped Anglo-Egyptian forces under Major General Sir Herbert Kitchener defeat the Mahdist army of Abdullah al-Taashi in a battle that saw the British army's last major cavalry charge.

In 1898, charged with regaining British control of the Sudan, General Kitchener led 8,000 British regulars and 17,000 Sudanese and Egyptian troops on an expedition down the Nile. They camped at El Egeiga on the banks of the Nile on 1 September.

Soon after sunrise on 2 September, tens of thousands of the enemy advanced from a wide arc around the British camp. They were swiftly cut down by the British artillery, Maxim guns, and rapid-fire rifles. At 9 am, Kitchener's troops began to advance on Omdurman. The 21st Lancers (including Lieutenant Winston Churchill) charged a few hundred dervishes but found themselves fighting a few thousand, prompting a fierce battle. Meanwhile, Kitchener's rearguard, a Sudanese brigade, were attacked by over 15,000 warriors from the Khalifa's reserve. Aided by reinforcements, the rearguard drove off the Mahdists.

That afternoon, Kitchener entered Omdurman unopposed. Less than 50 British had been killed; the Mahdist dead, however, numbered over 10,000.

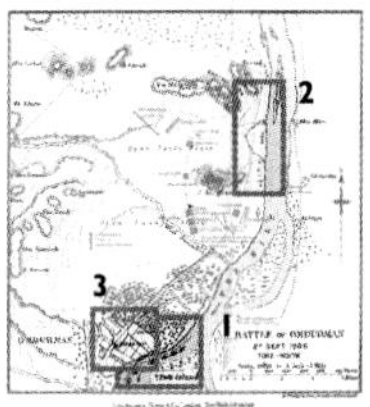
2
3
1

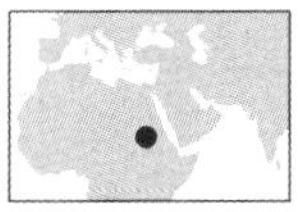

LOCATOR

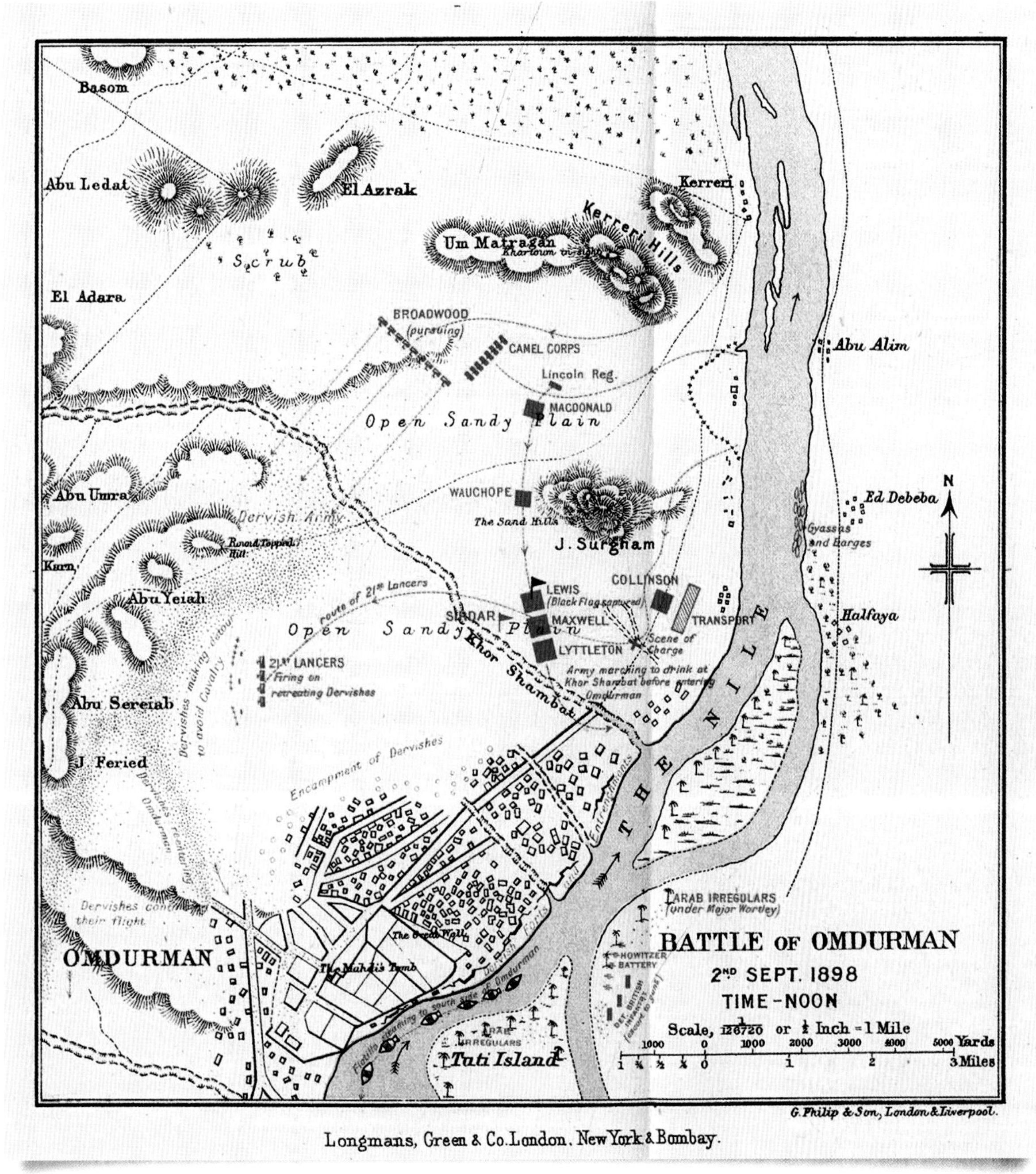
Basom
Abu Ledat
El Azrak
Kerreri
Kerreri Hills
Um Mairagan
Scrub
El Adara
BROADWOOD (pursuing)
CAMEL CORPS
Lincoln Reg.
MACDONALD
Open Sandy Plain
Abu Alim
Abu Umra
WAUCHOPE
The Sand Hills
J. Surgham
Dervish Army
Round Topped Hill
Ed Debeba
Gyassas and Barges
N
Kurn
Abu Yeiah
route of 21st Lancers
LEWIS (Black Flag captured)
COLLINSON
SIRDAR
MAXWELL
TRANSPORT
LYTTLETON
Scene of Charge
Halfaya
21st LANCERS Firing on retreating Dervishes
Khor Shambat
Army marching to drink at Khor Shambat before entering Omdurman
THE NILE
Abu Sereiah
J. Feried
Encampment of Dervishes
Dervishes making detour to avoid Cavalry
Dervishes retreating to Omdurman
Dervishes continue their flight
ARAB IRREGULARS (under Major Wortley)
OMDURMAN
The Great Wall
The Mahdi's Tomb
HOWITZER BATTERY
BATTLE OF OMDURMAN
2ND SEPT. 1898
TIME-NOON
Scale, 1/126720 or 1/2 Inch = 1 Mile
1000 0 1000 2000 3000 4000 5000 Yards
1 0 1 2 3 Miles
ARAB IRREGULARS
Tuti Island
G. Philip & Son, London & Liverpool.
Longmans, Green & Co. London, New York & Bombay.

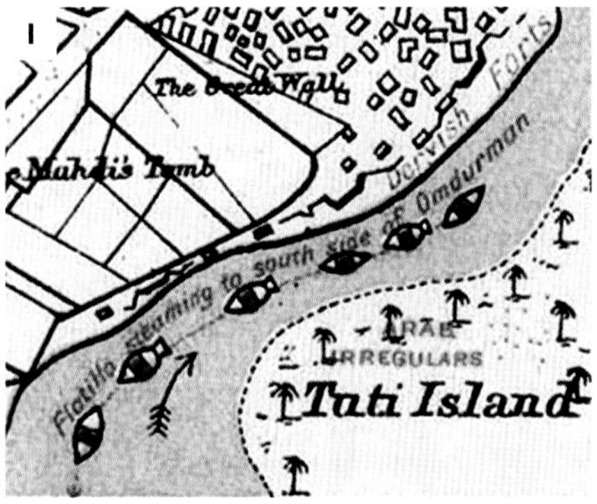
1
The Great Wall
Mahdi's Tomb
Dervish Forts
Omdurman
Flotilla steaming to south side of Omdurman
ARAB IRREGULARS
Tati Island

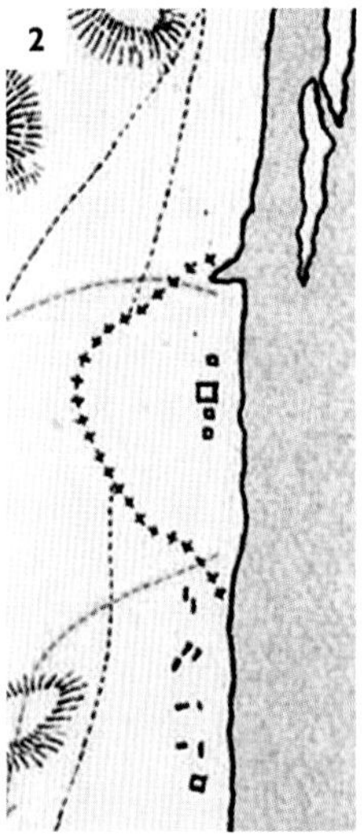
2

△ **The Nile**
Kitchener's gunboats bombarded Omdurman, damaging the city walls and the tomb of the Mahdi.

◁ **El Egeiga**
Kitchener's camp was protected by trenches and a *zariba* (a fence made from thorn bushes).

▽ **Mahdi's Tomb**
The Mahdi's great tomb in Omdurman was destroyed by the British after the battle. Only the top brass ornament has survived.

3
The Great Wall
The Mahdi's Tomb
steaming to south side

◁ **War on the Nile**
This map is taken from Winston Churchill's 1899 account of the Sudan campaign, *The River War*, and depicts the British marching on Omduran while pursuing the defeated Mahdists.

THE FIREPOWER REVOLUTION

During the 19th century a series of technological innovations multiplied the rate of fire, range, and power of military armaments, leading to the greatest change in warfare since the introduction of gunpowder.

△ **Gatling gun**
An early rapid-fire weapon, the Gatling gun had multiple barrels. Rotated by hand, each barrel fired a shot in turn.

Until the 1830s, soldiers used muzzle-loading, smooth-barrelled muskets and cannons, and gunpowder was the only explosive. The revolution in infantry firepower began in the 1840s with the Prussian Dreyse needle gun. A bolt-action, breech-loaded rifle, it fired a cartridge with propellant, primer, and ball in one package, and could fire six rounds per minute. By the 1880s, bolt-operated rifles were limited only by aiming time. These were used alongside automatic machine guns, which had evolved from manually operated precursors such as the Gatling gun of the 1860s. Artillery developed hand-in-hand with the rifle. By 1898, the French had a breech-loading, 75mm field gun that fired 15 rounds per minute. New nitrate-based explosives gave artillery greater power from the late 1800s. At sea, battleships carried breech-loaded guns firing high-explosive shells effective up to around 9km (5miles).

Deadly impact

In use by 1900, these new weapons made old tactics obsolete on land and sea. Soldiers advancing over open ground – on foot or on horseback – could now be mowed down by entrenched infantry. While the growing lethality of weapons was offset to an extent by greater troop dispersion and increased combat ranges, larger armies and longer battles meant that overall casualties increased to unprecedented levels, as is evident from World War I (see pp.208-24).

SIR HIRAM STEVENS MAXIM 1840–1916

Born in the US, Sir Hiram Stevens Maxim (far left) emigrated to Britain in 1881. He is best known for inventing the Maxim machine gun in 1884. The first self-powered machine gun, it was capable of firing 600 rounds per minute. During the colonial wars (see p.195), the British Army used this gun to deadly effect. Maxim later became deaf, as his hearing was damaged by years of exposure to the noise of his guns.

Naval artillery
In the Russo–Japanese War of 1904–1905, the Imperial Japanese Navy used torpedoes and high-explosive shells to achieve decisive victories. This painting shows Japanese sailors deploying torpedoes in the naval battle of Port Arthur, Manchuria.

DIRECTORY: 1700–1900

CULLODEN

16 APRIL 1746

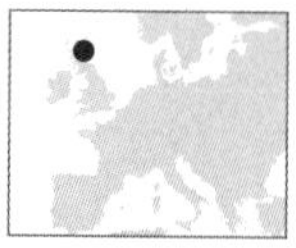

In 1745, Jacobite rebels made their last attempt to restore the Stuarts to the British throne. They were led by Charles Edward Stuart (known as Bonnie Prince Charlie), the grandson of the exiled Stuart king, James II. After a failed invasion of England, the rebels retreated to Inverness, Scotland, in 1746. On the night of 15 April, the Jacobites marched to surprise the government army under the Duke of Cumberland. Realizing midway that they would arrive too late, they began to retrace their steps, leading to much confusion. They were caught at dawn by the duke's forces at Drumossie Moor, near the village of Culloden. Charles decided to face the duke head on in battle. The exhausted rebel soldiers held their positions while the government artillery bombarded them. Charles finally unleashed the famous "Highland charge". The Scottish Highlanders ran across the sodden and smoke-shrouded moor into a barrage of gunfire and grapeshot. Many never reached the enemy line, and those who did were met with bayonets. The battle was over in less than an hour and the Jacobites fled. Many more were hunted down and butchered in the weeks after, while Charles escaped to France, his dreams of a Stuart restoration shattered.

QUIBERON BAY

20 NOVEMBER 1759

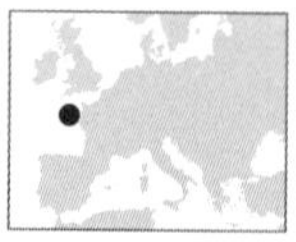

In 1759, France planned to reverse its failing fortunes in the Seven Years War (see pp.150–51) by invading Britain. About 20,000 troops were assembled in Brittany, waiting for the French fleet to escort them to Scotland. However, the fleet was blockaded in Brest by Admiral Edward Hawke. When a gale forced Hawke to withdraw, Comte de Conflans, commander of the French fleet, set sail for Quiberon Bay; but the British fleet soon reappeared. Outnumbered and struggling in the high winds, Conflan's fleet entered the narrow mouth of the bay, followed by Hawke. After a chaotic mêlée, the British lost only two ships, while the French lost seven (with the rest forced to scatter). As one of the Royal Navy's greatest victories, the battle secured Britain's dominance of the seas.

△ Allied commanders at Yorktown give orders for the final attack

YORKTOWN

28 SEPTEMBER–19 OCTOBER 1781

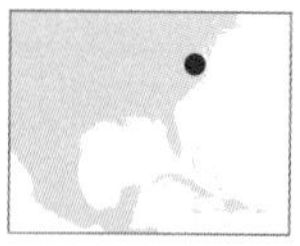

After failing to take control of North Carolina during the American War of Independence (1775–83), Lieutenant General Charles Cornwallis and the British army regrouped in August 1781 at Yorktown on Chesapeake Bay, Virginia. Cornwallis fortified both Yorktown and the nearby Gloucester. He was confident that he would be supplied by sea.

However, on 5 September, Admiral François de Grasse defeated the British fleet off Chesapeake Bay, and Yorktown was cut off. On 29 September, General George Washington and the French commander, the Count of Rochambeau, surrounded Yorktown with 19,000 men. Under constant bombardment by the British, Rochambeau orgnanized a system of trenches, bunkers, and batteries around the town. By 9 October, all the guns were in place and opened fire. The siege lines were moved closer to the British line. After the allies captured two British redoubts on 14 October, Cornwallis ordered his men to evacuate Yorktown and make for Gloucester. However, bad weather and a shortage of ammunition led him to surrender on 19 October. The siege of Yorktown, the last major action in the war, prompted negotiations that led to America's independence in 1783.

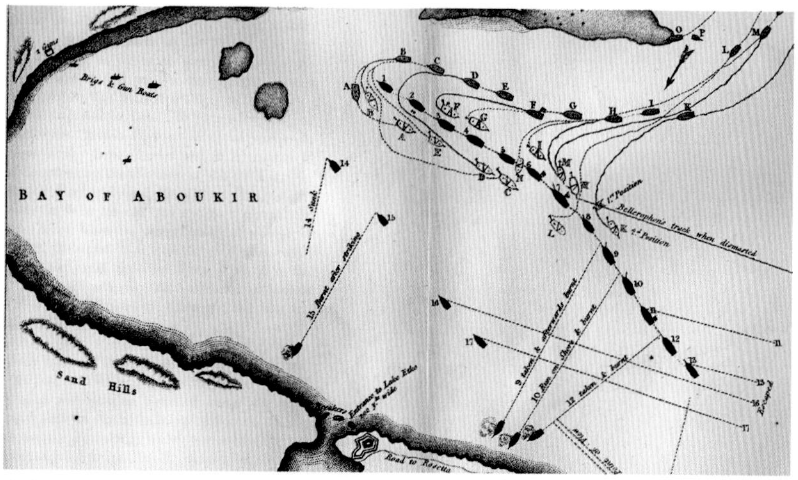
BAY OF ABOUKIR
Sand Hills

△ Contemporary chart of the battle at Aboukir Bay

ABOUKIR BAY

1 AUGUST 1798

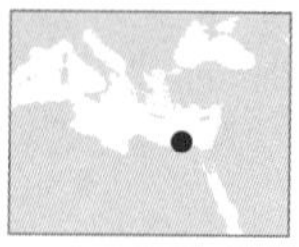

In May 1798, Napoleon Bonaparte sailed from France for Egypt, with an invasion force escorted by 13 ships of the line and 4 frigates led by Admiral Francois-Paul Brueys. Evading the Royal Navy in the Mediterranean, they reached Aboukir Bay by July. British Admiral Nelson, in command of 13 ships of the line and one 50-gun ship, discovered the French fleet in August. He ordered an attack on the French vanguard and centre, knowing the wind would not allow the French rear to fight. In a surprising move, one of his captains manoeuvred his ships between the anchored French fleet and the shore. As night fell, the French ships were battered from both sides. Brueys was killed and at 10:00pm his flagship *L'Orient* exploded, killing several hundred sailors. Admiral Villeneuve, in the rear of the French line, slipped away at dawn, saving just two ships of the line and two frigates from the British. Nelson was hailed as a hero for his victory.

WAGRAM

5–6 JULY 1809

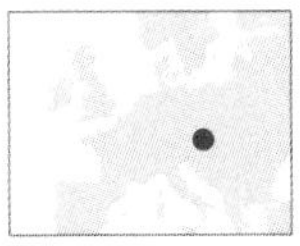

In 1809, Austrian forces marched through Bavaria in an attempt to reclaim the German territories lost to France after the Battle of Austerlitz (see pp.166–67). In response, Napoleon took command of the Grand Army of Germany and captured Vienna but suffered a humiliating defeat in May at Aspern-Essling at the hand of Austrian troops. By July, he desperately needed a victory to restore his reputation.

On the night of 4–5 July, the French army crossed to the left bank of the River Danube to attack the Austrians. The Austrian army was thinly spread in an arc running along the Russbach Heights and centred on the village of Wagram. The main battle commenced at dawn on 6 July. The Austrians, led by Archduke Charles, launched a series of attacks and nearly enveloped the French left flank. Napoleon reinforced his left and pounded the Austrian lines with the concentrated firepower of a battery of around 100 guns. While Marshal André Masséna counter-attacked the Austrian right and MacDonald's V Corps threatened to break the Austrian centre, Marshal Louis-Nicolas Davout drove back the Austrian left. With no reserves to bolster his increasingly battered line, Charles retreated and, his men's morale shattered, sought an armistice. The unprecedented amount of artillery used – around 1,000 pieces and 180,000 rounds of ammunition – made the battle particularly bloody: up to 80,000 of the 300,000 involved were killed or wounded.

BOYACÁ

7 AUGUST 1819

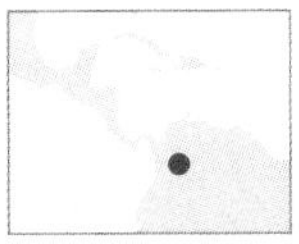

From 1809, Spain's South American colonies began fighting for their independence. Central to the struggle was Venezuelan military and political leader Simón Bolívar. In 1819, Bolívar and General Francisco de Paula Santander led an army on a gruelling mountain crossing from Venezuela into New Granada (present-day Colombia), hoping to capture its capital, Bogotá. The army was made up of around 3,000 local guerrillas, including *llaneros* (cowboys), and British and Irish veterans of the Napoleonic Wars (1803–15).

After clashing with the Spanish forces, under Colonel José María Barreiro at Gameza (12 July) and Pantano de Vargas (25 July), Bolívar waited for Barreiro's army at the River Teatinos. On 7 August, Santander ambushed the Spanish vanguard after it crossed over the Boyacá Bridge, cutting it off from the rear. Meanwhile, Bolívar attacked the main body of the Spanish to the rear. The Royalists were swiftly overcome, and Bolívar's men took over 1,600 prisoners, some of whom (including Barreiro) were executed after Bolivar took Bogota due to his 1813 decree of "War to the Death". The battle at Boyacá Bridge was a turning point for the independence movement. Bolívar went on to liberate Venezuela, Ecuador, and Peru.

◁ Simón Bolívar rides his rearing horse in this 19th-century statue by Adamo Tadolini, of which there are casts in Caracas, Lima, and San Francisco.

NAVARINO

20 OCTOBER 1827

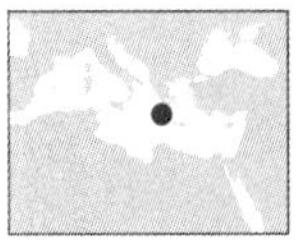

The Greek struggle for independence from Ottoman rule began in 1821. Ottoman forces, assisted by an Egyptian army under Ibrahim Pasha, fought to suppress the revolt. By 1827, the nationalists controlled only a few areas. Britain, France, and Russia, however, demanded that the Ottomans accept an armistice. The allies assembled a fleet of 27 ships under Admiral Sir Edward Codrington in the Mediterranean. The Ottomans gathered a larger force of Turkish and Egyptian ships under Tahir Pasha in Navarino Bay on the west coast of Greece. On 20 October, Codrington's fleet sailed into the bay and anchored among the Egyptian-Turkish ships. Tensions were high and fighting soon broke out. The ships fired on each other from close range, trying to inflict as much damage as possible while trying to escape the enemy's broadsides. The allies, though outnumbered, had far better guns and, after three hours, the Egyptian-Turkish fleet abandoned the fight. The Ottomans lost almost all of their ships, while the allies lost none. Greece finally secured its independence in 1830, after the Ottomans' defeat in the Russo-Turkish war of 1828–29.

△ Russian painter Ivan Aivazovsky's 1846 depiction of the Battle of Navarino

VICKSBURG

18 MAY–4 JULY 1863

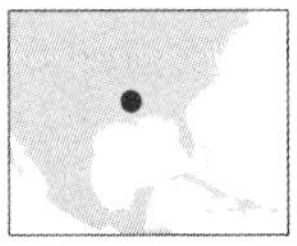

One of the most successful Union campaigns of the American Civil War (1861–65), the Siege of Vicksburg sealed the reputation of Major-General Ulysses Grant. Union forces had previously made several unsuccessful attempts to capture the strategically vital town on the east bank of the Mississippi. Grant and the Army of the Tennessee converged again on the town in May 1863.

Vicksburg was held by 29,000 Confederate soldiers under Lieutenant General John C. Pemberton and protected by a 13-km (8-mile) arc of fortifications and artillery on the cliff. By 18 May, Grant had surrounded the town, but his attempts to storm it on 19 and 22 May failed and he lost more than 4,000 men. Grant then turned to besieging the town by constructing trenches that trapped Pemberton's army. The attempts of Confederate forces to relieve Pemberton failed, and conditions in the town, cut off and under constant bombardment by the Union artillery, quickly deteriorated. After nearly seven weeks, running short on food and supplies, Pemberton surrendered to the Union. The capture of Vicksburg, swiftly followed by another victory at Port Hudson, gave the Union control of the Mississippi, cutting off a crucial Confederate supply line and splitting the Confederacy in two.

1900–PRESENT

THE MODERN ERA SAW NEW AND INCREASINGLY DEADLY FORMS OF MECHANIZATION IN BATTLE, AND TOOK WARFARE TO THE SKIES. GLOBAL CONFLICTS RAGED ON A SCALE NEVER SEEN BEFORE, PUSHING MILITARY TECHNOLOGY TO NEW HEIGHTS; FROM THESE WARS CAME THE DAWNING OF THE NUCLEAR AGE.

1900–PRESENT

The 20th century was an age of mechanized global warfare in which industry, mass conscription, and nationalist ideology combined to create conflicts on a vast scale. Rapid advances in technology have resulted in computerized battlefields with precision weapons, unrecognizable to previous generations of soldiers.

The fragmentation of the Balkans in the 19th century created a tinderbox that erupted into war in 1914 when a Serbian nationalist assassinated Austro-Hungarian Archduke Franz Ferdinand. World War I pitted Germany, Austria-Hungary, and the Ottoman Empire against Russia, Britain, France, and their allies. As the war progressed, mobile warfare morphed into an attritional confrontation along trench lines on the Western Front. Along this 700-km (400-mile) stretch of land, battles such as Verdun (see pp.214–15) and the Somme (see pp.220–21) cost hundreds of thousands of lives for little territorial gain. New technology, such as poison gas, early tanks, and aircraft was used in a bid to unlock the stalemate. However, it was the exhaustion of the blockaded Central Powers and the entry of the US that ended the war in 1918.

From *Blitzkrieg* to the atom bomb

The hope that World War I would be "the war to end all wars" proved false. The damage it had caused shaped the politics of Europe and facilitated the rise of Adolf Hitler in Germany, who envisioned a Greater German Reich for the Germanic people. Nazi expansionism led to the inevitable – Britain and France declared war on Germany after its forces invaded Poland in 1939. Germany's use of *Blitzkrieg*

> *"Fighting in the air is not sport, it is scientific murder."*
>
> US PILOT EDDIE RICKENBACKER, 1919

△ **Over the top**
British troops scramble out of their trenches during the Battle of the Somme in 1916. More than 19,000 soldiers died during the first day of the offensive as they struggled to reach the German lines. They were scythed down by machine-guns which the preliminary British artillery bombardment had failed to destroy.

THE WORLD WARS

In the 20th century, the two World Wars cost around 80 million lives. After World War II, the nuclear stand-off between the US and the USSR during the Cold War precluded direct wars. However, they fought wars to defend their influence, such as in Vietnam and Afghanistan, or sponsored wars between their allies. In the Cold War's wake, regional wars erupted and nuclear weapons proliferated. The Soviet Union was dissolved, but Russia and China continue to challenge US global dominance.

WARFARE | POLITICS | TECHNOLOGY

1910 | 1920 | 1930 | 1940 | 1950

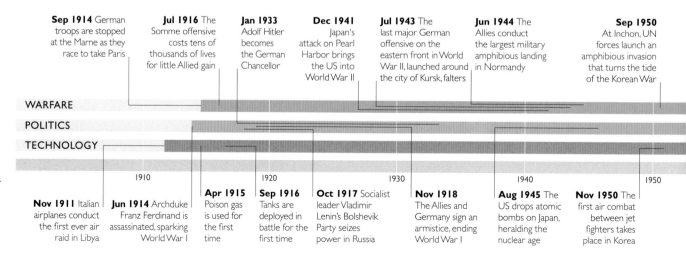

- **Nov 1911** Italian airplanes conduct the first ever air raid in Libya
- **Jun 1914** Archduke Franz Ferdinand is assassinated, sparking World War I
- **Sep 1914** German troops are stopped at the Marne as they race to take Paris
- **Apr 1915** Poison gas is used for the first time
- **Jul 1916** The Somme offensive costs tens of thousands of lives for little Allied gain
- **Sep 1916** Tanks are deployed in battle for the first time
- **Oct 1917** Socialist leader Vladimir Lenin's Bolshevik Party seizes power in Russia
- **Nov 1918** The Allies and Germany sign an armistice, ending World War I
- **Jan 1933** Adolf Hitler becomes the German Chancellor
- **Dec 1941** Japan's attack on Pearl Harbor brings the US into World War II
- **Jul 1943** The last major German offensive on the eastern front in World War II, launched around the city of Kursk, falters
- **Jun 1944** The Allies conduct the largest military amphibious landing in Normandy
- **Aug 1945** The US drops atomic bombs on Japan, heralding the nuclear age
- **Sep 1950** At Inchon, UN forces launch an amphibious invasion that turns the tide of the Korean War
- **Nov 1950** The first air combat between jet fighters takes place in Korea

△ **Guerrilla gun**
The Soviet-designed RPD machine gun was introduced in 1944. Its reliability and durability made it a staple of guerrilla forces such as the Viet Cong.

Sieg um jeden Preis!

◁ **Total War**
This German poster shows civilian workers and a grenade-throwing soldier with the slogan "Victory at any Price". World War II was a "total war", in which the whole of society played a role.

("lightning war") tactics, spearheaded by its highly mobile panzer tank force, won a string of rapid victories. Britain's superior air organization and development of radar, however, allowed it to defeat the German air force in the Battle of Britain in 1940 (see pp.232–33) and avoid invasion.

Air power became vital in World War II. Aircraft carriers combined naval and air warfare in confrontations such as the Battle of Midway (see pp.238–39). Germany's submarine blockade of Britain failed due to Allied countermeasures, and when Hitler's invasion of the USSR in 1941 failed to inflict a knock-out blow, Germany faced an increasingly unwinnable war on two fronts. US entry was again decisive, especially after the Allies made a massive amphibious landing in Normandy in 1944 (see pp.248–49).

Nuclear weapons dropped by the US on the Japanese cities of Hiroshima and Nagasaki ended the Pacific phase of the war in 1945. They also heralded the Cold War – a new ideological conflict between the USSR and the US, and their supporters. "Hot wars" erupted when local disputes became proxy wars sponsored by these two superpowers, such as in Vietnam, where the USSR and the US backed North and South Vietnam respectively. This proxy rivalry fuelled conflicts across the world, from Korea and Afghanistan to Angola and Nicaragua, and successive Arab-Israeli wars.

Technology fails to triumph

The collapse of the USSR in 1991 did not end large-scale warfare. The Middle East in particular has seen a chaotic series of conflicts starting with the US-led expulsion of invading Iraqi forces from Kuwait in 1991 (see pp.270–71). A war on the same scale as any World War now seems unlikely. While wars are now fought with precision-guided missiles, computer-operated drones, and stealth bombers that integrate electronics and computer technology, guns and knives are still commonly used in persistent civil wars.

▽ **Operation Iraqi Freedom**
US-led coalition forces, including Britain's 7th Armoured Brigade, gathered in the Kuwaiti Desert in March 2003. The land offensive against Iraq followed next, ending in the overthrow of Saddam Hussein.

Mar 1957 Ghana becomes the first African colony to achieve independence

Oct–Nov 1962 In the Sino-Indian War, China and India clash over border disputes in harsh mountain conditions

Jun 1967 In the Six-Day War, Israeli forces defeat an Arab coalition and take territories in the West Bank, Golan, and Sinai

Jan 1968 In the Tet Offensive, the Viet Cong launch a series of attacks throughout South Vietnam

Feb 1979 Exiled Islamic leader Ayatollah Khomeini returns to Iran, marking the victory of Islamist forces in the Iranian Revolution

Sep 1980 Iraqi forces invade western Iran, triggering the Iran-Iraq war, which rages on for eight years

Jan–Feb 1991 In an operation codenamed Desert Storm, a US-led coalition army expels Iraqi President Saddam Hussein's forces from Kuwait

Dec 1991 The Soviet Union is dissolved and breaks up into 15 independent countries

Oct 2001 The first armed drone strike is conducted by the US in Afghanistan

2007–2008 A global financial crisis destabilizes the world economy and plunges many countries into recession

2011 The Arab Spring, a series of anti-government uprisings in the Arab world, overthrows dictatorial regimes in Tunisia and Egypt

1960 1970 1980 1990 2000 2010 2020

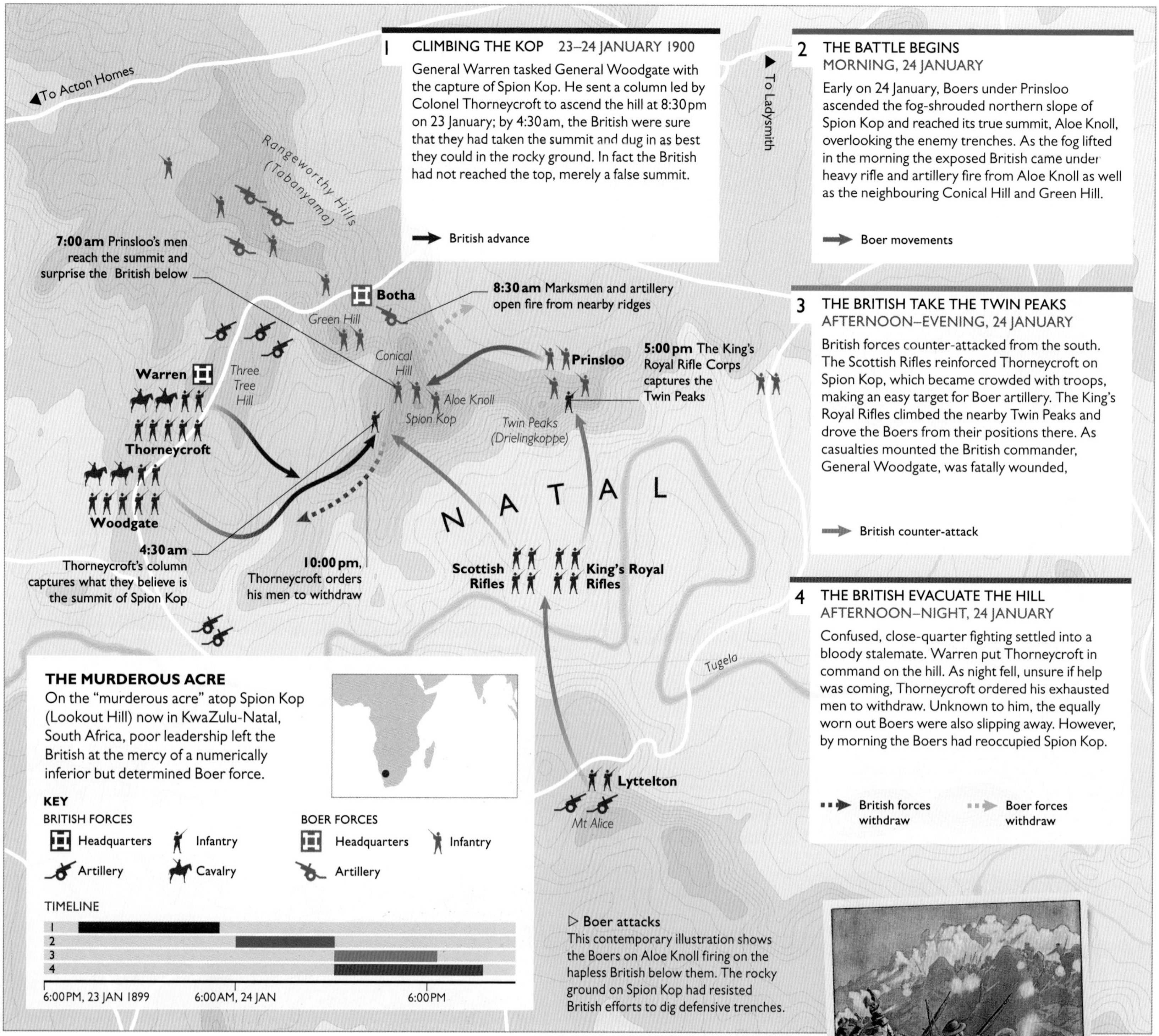

1 CLIMBING THE KOP 23–24 JANUARY 1900
General Warren tasked General Woodgate with the capture of Spion Kop. He sent a column led by Colonel Thorneycroft to ascend the hill at 8:30pm on 23 January; by 4:30am, the British were sure that they had taken the summit and dug in as best they could in the rocky ground. In fact the British had not reached the top, merely a false summit.
British advance
2 THE BATTLE BEGINS
MORNING, 24 JANUARY
Early on 24 January, Boers under Prinsloo ascended the fog-shrouded northern slope of Spion Kop and reached its true summit, Aloe Knoll, overlooking the enemy trenches. As the fog lifted in the morning the exposed British came under heavy rifle and artillery fire from Aloe Knoll as well as the neighbouring Conical Hill and Green Hill.
Boer movements
3 THE BRITISH TAKE THE TWIN PEAKS
AFTERNOON–EVENING, 24 JANUARY
British forces counter-attacked from the south. The Scottish Rifles reinforced Thorneycroft on Spion Kop, which became crowded with troops, making an easy target for Boer artillery. The King's Royal Rifles climbed the nearby Twin Peaks and drove the Boers from their positions there. As casualties mounted the British commander, General Woodgate, was fatally wounded,
British counter-attack
4 THE BRITISH EVACUATE THE HILL
AFTERNOON–NIGHT, 24 JANUARY
Confused, close-quarter fighting settled into a bloody stalemate. Warren put Thorneycroft in command on the hill. As night fell, unsure if help was coming, Thorneycroft ordered his exhausted men to withdraw. Unknown to him, the equally worn out Boers were also slipping away. However, by morning the Boers had reoccupied Spion Kop.
British forces withdraw
Boer forces withdraw
To Acton Homes
To Ladysmith
Rangeworthy Hills (Tabanyama)
7:00 am Prinsloo's men reach the summit and surprise the British below
Botha
8:30 am Marksmen and artillery open fire from nearby ridges
Green Hill
Conical Hill
Prinsloo
5:00 pm The King's Royal Rifle Corps captures the Twin Peaks
Warren
Three Tree Hill
Aloe Knoll
Spion Kop
Twin Peaks (Drielingkoppe)
Thorneycroft
Woodgate
NATAL
4:30 am Thorneycroft's column captures what they believe is the summit of Spion Kop
10:00 pm, Thorneycroft orders his men to withdraw
Scottish Rifles
King's Royal Rifles
Tugela
Lyttelton
Mt Alice
THE MURDEROUS ACRE
On the "murderous acre" atop Spion Kop (Lookout Hill) now in KwaZulu-Natal, South Africa, poor leadership left the British at the mercy of a numerically inferior but determined Boer force.
KEY
BRITISH FORCES
Headquarters
Infantry
Artillery
Cavalry
BOER FORCES
Headquarters
Infantry
Artillery
TIMELINE
1
2
3
4
6:00PM, 23 JAN 1899
6:00AM, 24 JAN
6:00PM

▷ **Boer attacks**
This contemporary illustration shows the Boers on Aloe Knoll firing on the hapless British below them. The rocky ground on Spion Kop had resisted British efforts to dig defensive trenches.

REPRISE DE SPION-KOP PAR LES BOERS

SPION KOP

In an attempt to lift the siege of Ladysmith in the Second Boer War (1899–1902), a British force tried to capture Spion Kop (hill). A tactical error saw them endure a day under heavy fire before they withdrew, leaving the Kop in Boer hands.

Between 1899 and 1902, Britain was engaged in a long, drawn-out war with the two Boer (Afrikaner) states – the South African Republic and Orange Free State. The causes of the war involved the of British imperialism and Boer independence, but were brought into immediate focus by conflict over the rights to exploit newly discovered gold mines in South Africa. The small Boer states were poorly armed compared to the British but in late 1899, their forces besieged Ladysmith in British-run Natal. As part of their effort to relieve the siege, the British sent General Warren to take control of Spion Kop, the highest point in a group of rocky hills overlooking the approaches to Ladysmith, defended by Botha's Boers. The British found themselves fatally exposed to enemy fire and suffered 250 dead and over 1,000 wounded before retreating. Ladysmith was finally relieved on 28 February 1900.

TSUSHIMA

In 1904, Russia and Japan went to war over influence in the disputed Chinese province of Manchuria. A climactic sea battle in the Straits of Tsushima the following spring gave Japan a decisive victory, marking its emergence as a new force on the world stage.

Hostilities between the two powers began when Japan launched a surprise attack on Russia's Far Eastern fleet stationed in Port Arthur on Manchuria's southern tip. Success in the raid allowed the Japanese to ship in troops to confront Russian forces in Manchuria.

In response, Tsar Nicholas sent the bulk of Russia's Baltic fleet to relieve the port. During its long voyage, news came that Port Arthur itself had fallen to the Japanese after a five-month siege. Japan's High Command had plenty of time to prepare their navy – already one of the most modern in the world – for the arrival of the Russian fleet.

When they finally met in the Straits of Tsushima, the Japanese established their superiority in just a few hours. Remnants of the Russian fleet fled to Vladivostok. Three months later, Russia was forced to sign a humiliating peace by which they agreed to abandon their Manchurian claims.

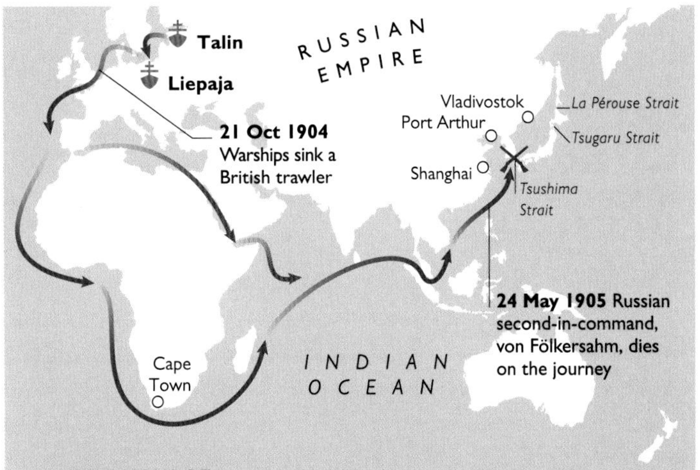
Talin
Liepaja
RUSSIAN EMPIRE
21 Oct 1904 Warships sink a British trawler
Vladivostok
Port Arthur
La Pérouse Strait
Tsugaru Strait
Shanghai
Tsushima Strait
24 May 1905 Russian second-in-command, von Fölkersahm, dies on the journey
Cape Town
INDIAN OCEAN
KEY
Main battle
Main fleet
Splinter group
Ports of embarkation

AN EPIC VOYAGE
Russia sent 42 ships, under Admiral Zinovy Rozhestvensky, halfway around the world to the Sea of Japan. En route, a night alarm led to shots being fired at British trawlers in the North Sea, almost leading to conflict with Britain. After a seven-month journey the fleet finally approached the Tsushima Strait.

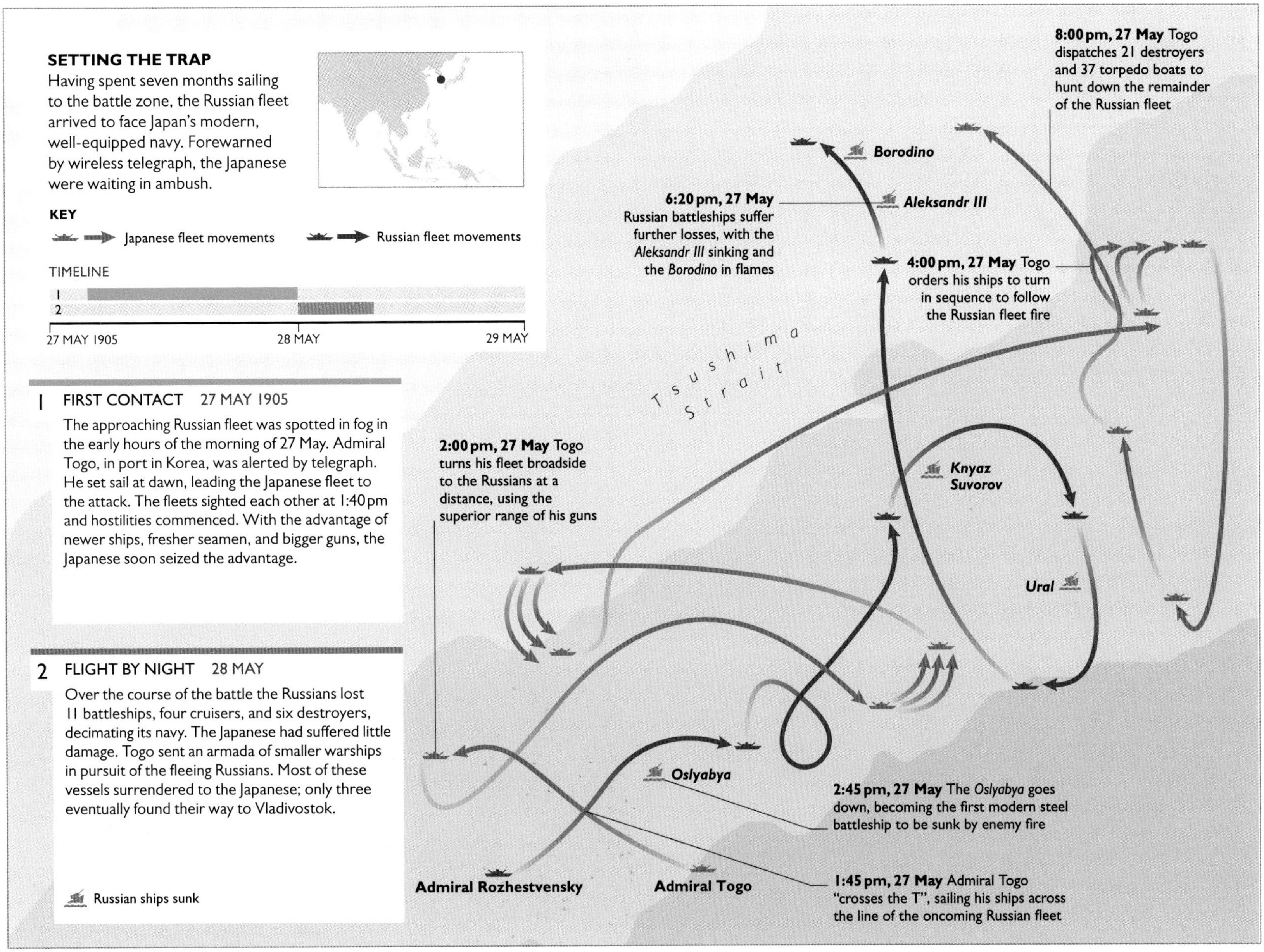
KEY
Japanese fleet movements
Russian fleet movements
TIMELINE
1
2
27 MAY 1905
28 MAY
29 MAY
Tsushima Strait
8:00 pm, 27 May Togo dispatches 21 destroyers and 37 torpedo boats to hunt down the remainder of the Russian fleet
Borodino
Aleksandr III
6:20 pm, 27 May Russian battleships suffer further losses, with the Aleksandr III sinking and the Borodino in flames
4:00 pm, 27 May Togo orders his ships to turn in sequence to follow the Russian fleet fire
2:00 pm, 27 May Togo turns his fleet broadside to the Russians at a distance, using the superior range of his guns
Knyaz Suvorov
Ural
Oslyabya
2:45 pm, 27 May The Oslyabya goes down, becoming the first modern steel battleship to be sunk by enemy fire
Admiral Rozhestvensky
Admiral Togo
1:45 pm, 27 May Admiral Togo "crosses the T", sailing his ships across the line of the oncoming Russian fleet
Russian ships sunk

SETTING THE TRAP
Having spent seven months sailing to the battle zone, the Russian fleet arrived to face Japan's modern, well-equipped navy. Forewarned by wireless telegraph, the Japanese were waiting in ambush.

1 FIRST CONTACT 27 MAY 1905
The approaching Russian fleet was spotted in fog in the early hours of the morning of 27 May. Admiral Togo, in port in Korea, was alerted by telegraph. He set sail at dawn, leading the Japanese fleet to the attack. The fleets sighted each other at 1:40 pm and hostilities commenced. With the advantage of newer ships, fresher seamen, and bigger guns, the Japanese soon seized the advantage.

2 FLIGHT BY NIGHT 28 MAY
Over the course of the battle the Russians lost 11 battleships, four cruisers, and six destroyers, decimating its navy. The Japanese had suffered little damage. Togo sent an armada of smaller warships in pursuit of the fleeing Russians. Most of these vessels surrendered to the Japanese; only three eventually found their way to Vladivostok.

THE AGE OF DREADNOUGHTS

In a bid to maintain its naval supremacy over other nations, Britain's Royal Navy launched the HMS *Dreadnought* in 1906. Taking firepower and speed to an unprecedented level, it marked the dawn of a new era of battleships.

Metal-hulled steamships had been in use since the 19th century. However, on its launch the *Dreadnought* made all other battleships of its time obsolete, and gave its name to a new class of ship. The first all-big-gun battleship, it carried ten 12-inch guns for long-range attacks, and it was also the first to use steam turbines, reaching speeds of up to 21 knots. It represented a good compromise in the holy trinity of naval design: speed, protection, and firepower. As the Royal Navy pushed forward an ambitious programme of naval construction, other nations including the US, Germany, Italy, and Japan followed suit and built their own dreadnoughts.

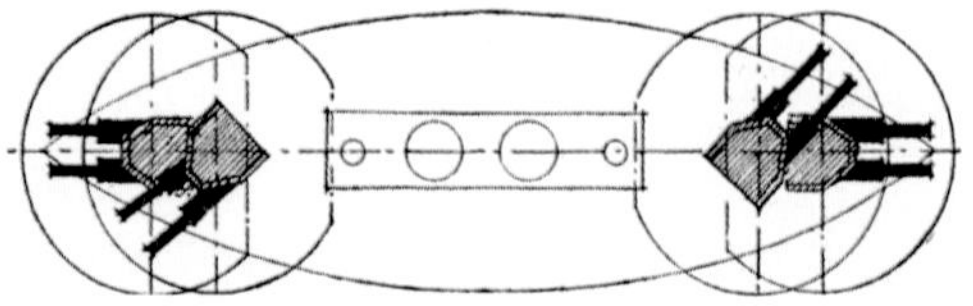

◁ **Super-firing turrets**
This sketch shows the positions of super-firing turrets. Each pair consists of one turret on deck level with the second mounted above and behind it.

New and improved

Competition was fierce, and soon the *Dreadnought* was itself rendered obsolete by more powerful battleships called super-dreadnoughts. The first of these, HMS *Orion,* launched in 1910 armed with 13.5-inch guns. Pairs of superimposed gun turrets, called super-firing turrets, were mounted on the centreline of its hull to improve firing arcs. Oil slowly replaced coal to fire the boilers that fed steam to the turbines. Super-dreadnoughts were supplanted by "fast battleships", which emphasized speed. The last of these retired from active service in 1991.

△ ***R*-class battleships**
These super-dreadnought battleships – the HMS *Royal Oak, Ramillies, Revenge,* and *Resolution* – belonged to the *Revenge* class. Their main armament comprised eight 15-inch guns in four turrets.

Last of the line
The HMS *Hood* was the final battlecruiser built by the Royal Navy. Battlecruisers were similar to fast battleships but lightly armoured to increase speed and firepower. The HMS *Hood* carried 15-inch guns in four twin-gun turrets, on the fore and aft of the ship, and was capable of 32 knots.

TANNENBERG

Within days of the outbreak of World War I, Russia fulfilled its treaty promises to its ally France by sending two armies to invade Prussia. While the 1st Army drove back the opposing German forces, the 2nd, to the south, was encircled and suffered a crushing defeat.

When war broke out in August 1914, Germany faced the prospect of conflict on two fronts – with France in the west, and Russia in the east. Russia was expected to take months to mobilize, so the German offensive prioritized a swift victory over France. While seven of Germany's eight armies concentrated on the Western front, Russia launched a surprise invasion of East Prussia, even before its own troops were properly prepared.

Attacking in the north, Russia's 1st Army had early successes, winning an indecisive victory at Gumbinnen that forced a German retreat. But instead of abandoning the province, the German forces redeployed to the south, where the Russian 2nd Army was advancing through the difficult terrain of the Masurian lakes. Hampered by poor communications, the 1st Army slowly advanced west rather than going south to help their compatriots. Outrunning its supply lines, the 2nd Army was cut off as a lethal cordon tightened around it. With no food and no escape route, the bulk of the Russian force had no option but to surrender. This was a massive propaganda boost for the German commanders Ludendorff and von Hindenburg, who portrayed the victory as revenge for the Teutonic Knights' defeat at nearby Grunwald five centuries earlier (see pp.88–89).

> *"The more ruthlessly war is conducted, the more merciful is it…"*
>
> PAUL VON HINDENBURG, 1914

PAUL VON HINDENBURG

Born into an aristocratic Prussian family, von Hindenburg (1847–1934) had retired from the army before being recalled to serve in 1914. Thanks to a productive partnership with strategist Erich Ludendorff he became Supreme Commander of the Central Powers from 1916. After Germany lost the war, von Hindenburg's war record led to his election as president of Germany in 1925. However, his presidency was marked by political turmoil, depression, and the rise of the Nazi Party.

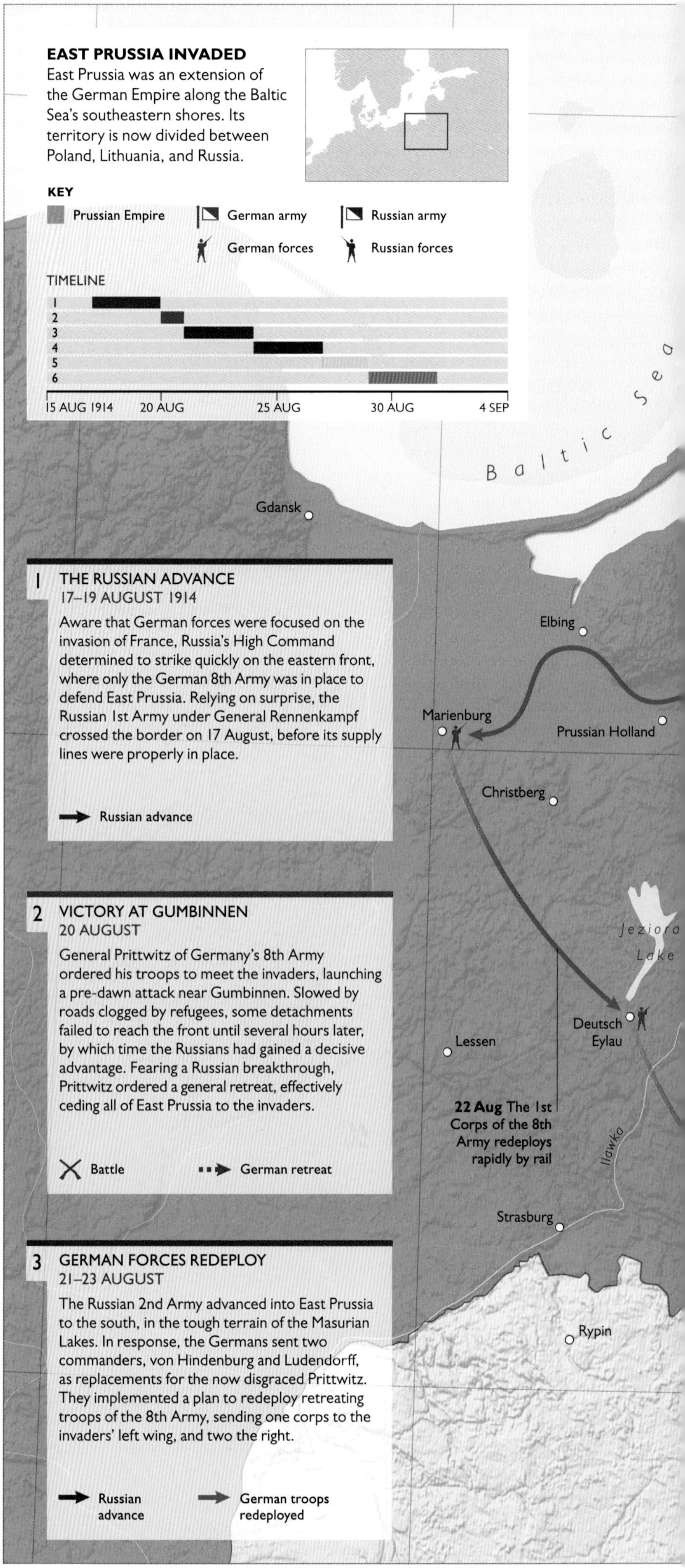
KEY
Prussian Empire
German army
Russian army
German forces
Russian forces
TIMELINE
1
2
3
4
5
6
15 AUG 1914
20 AUG
25 AUG
30 AUG
4 SEP
Baltic Sea
Gdansk
Elbing
Marienburg
Prussian Holland
Christberg
Jeziora Lake
Deutsch Eylau
Lessen
22 Aug The 1st Corps of the 8th Army redeploys rapidly by rail
Ilawka
Strasburg
Rypin
Russian advance
Battle
German retreat
Russian advance
German troops redeployed

EAST PRUSSIA INVADED

East Prussia was an extension of the German Empire along the Baltic Sea's southeastern shores. Its territory is now divided between Poland, Lithuania, and Russia.

1 THE RUSSIAN ADVANCE
17–19 AUGUST 1914

Aware that German forces were focused on the invasion of France, Russia's High Command determined to strike quickly on the eastern front, where only the German 8th Army was in place to defend East Prussia. Relying on surprise, the Russian 1st Army under General Rennenkampf crossed the border on 17 August, before its supply lines were properly in place.

2 VICTORY AT GUMBINNEN
20 AUGUST

General Prittwitz of Germany's 8th Army ordered his troops to meet the invaders, launching a pre-dawn attack near Gumbinnen. Slowed by roads clogged by refugees, some detachments failed to reach the front until several hours later, by which time the Russians had gained a decisive advantage. Fearing a Russian breakthrough, Prittwitz ordered a general retreat, effectively ceding all of East Prussia to the invaders.

3 GERMAN FORCES REDEPLOY
21–23 AUGUST

The Russian 2nd Army advanced into East Prussia to the south, in the tough terrain of the Masurian Lakes. In response, the Germans sent two commanders, von Hindenburg and Ludendorff, as replacements for the now disgraced Prittwitz. They implemented a plan to redeploy retreating troops of the 8th Army, sending one corps to the invaders' left wing, and two the right.

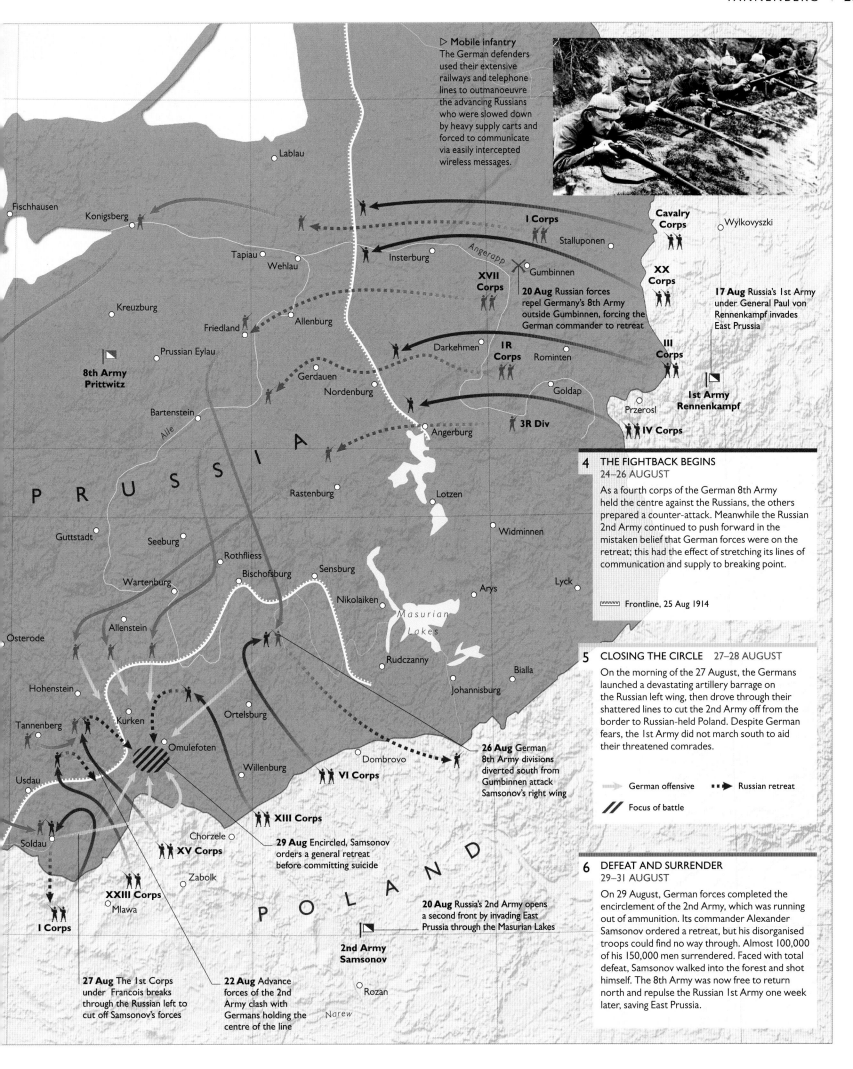

▷ **Mobile infantry**
The German defenders used their extensive railways and telephone lines to outmanoeuvre the advancing Russians who were slowed down by heavy supply carts and forced to communicate via easily intercepted wireless messages.

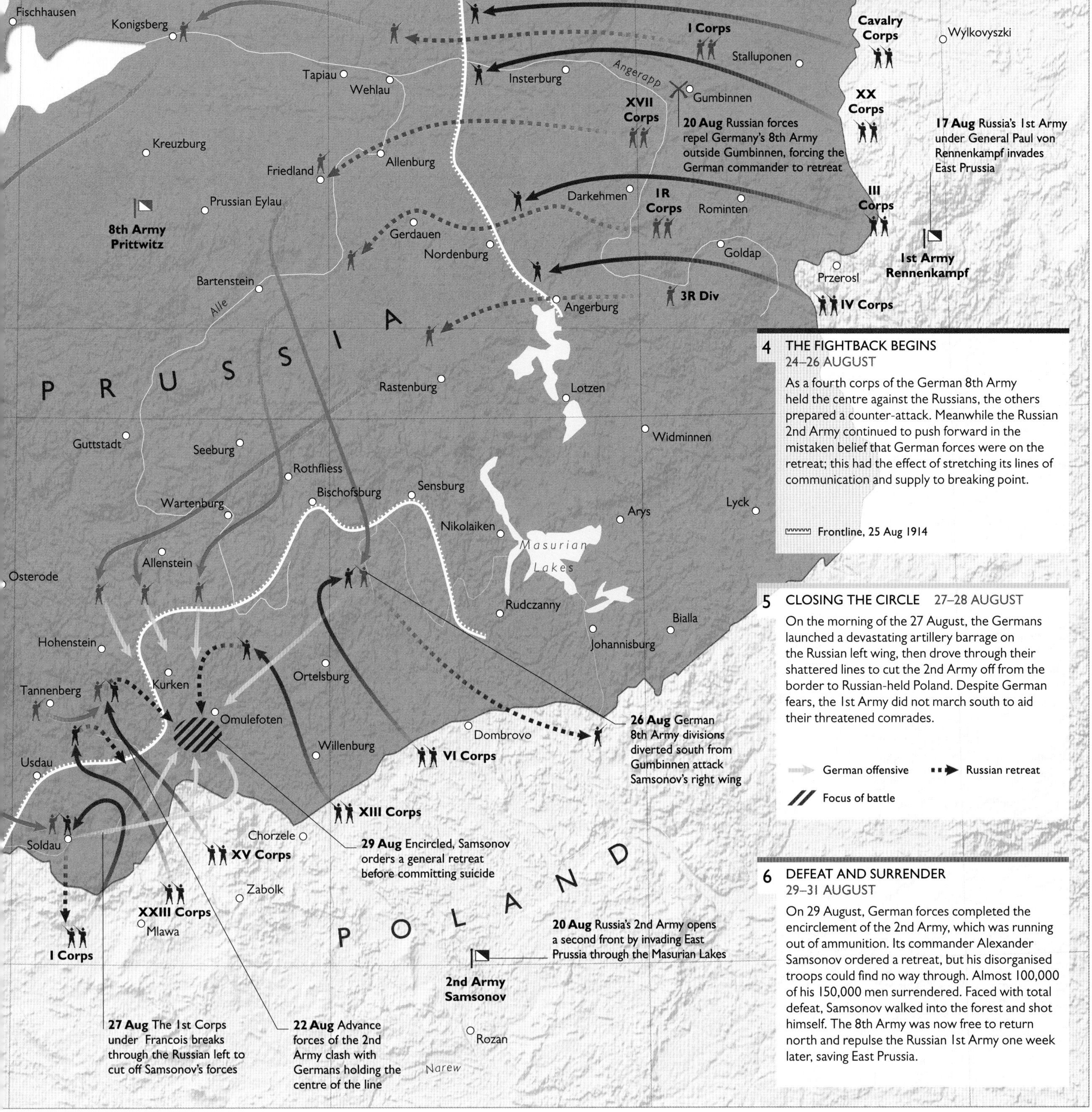
Lablau
Fischhausen
Konigsberg
I Corps
Cavalry Corps
Wylkovyszki
Stalluponen
Tapiau
Wehlau
Insterburg
Angerapp
Gumbinnen
XX Corps
XVII Corps
20 Aug Russian forces repel Germany's 8th Army outside Gumbinnen, forcing the German commander to retreat
17 Aug Russia's 1st Army under General Paul von Rennenkampf invades East Prussia
Kreuzburg
Allenburg
Friedland
Prussian Eylau
Darkehmen
IR Corps
Rominten
III Corps
8th Army Prittwitz
Gerdauen
Nordenburg
Goldap
1st Army Rennenkampf
Przerosl
Bartenstein
Alle
3R Div
IV Corps
Angerburg
PRUSSIA
Rastenburg
Lotzen
Guttstadt
Seeburg
Widminnen
Rothfliess
Bischofsburg
Sensburg
Wartenburg
Arys
Lyck
Nikolaiken
Allenstein
Masurian Lakes
Osterode
Rudczanny
Bialla
Hohenstein
Johannisburg
Kurken
Ortelsburg
Tannenberg
Omulefoten
26 Aug German 8th Army divisions diverted south from Gumbinnen attack Samsonov's right wing
Dombrovo
Willenburg
VI Corps
Usdau
XIII Corps
Soldau
Chorzele
XV Corps
29 Aug Encircled, Samsonov orders a general retreat before committing suicide
POLAND
Zabolk
XXIII Corps
Mlawa
20 Aug Russia's 2nd Army opens a second front by invading East Prussia through the Masurian Lakes
I Corps
2nd Army Samsonov
27 Aug The 1st Corps under Francois breaks through the Russian left to cut off Samsonov's forces
22 Aug Advance forces of the 2nd Army clash with Germans holding the centre of the line
Rozan
Narew

4 THE FIGHTBACK BEGINS
24–26 AUGUST

As a fourth corps of the German 8th Army held the centre against the Russians, the others prepared a counter-attack. Meanwhile the Russian 2nd Army continued to push forward in the mistaken belief that German forces were on the retreat; this had the effect of stretching its lines of communication and supply to breaking point.

Frontline, 25 Aug 1914

5 CLOSING THE CIRCLE 27–28 AUGUST

On the morning of the 27 August, the Germans launched a devastating artillery barrage on the Russian left wing, then drove through their shattered lines to cut the 2nd Army off from the border to Russian-held Poland. Despite German fears, the 1st Army did not march south to aid their threatened comrades.

German offensive — Russian retreat — Focus of battle

6 DEFEAT AND SURRENDER
29–31 AUGUST

On 29 August, German forces completed the encirclement of the 2nd Army, which was running out of ammunition. Its commander Alexander Samsonov ordered a retreat, but his disorganised troops could find no way through. Almost 100,000 of his 150,000 men surrendered. Faced with total defeat, Samsonov walked into the forest and shot himself. The 8th Army was now free to return north and repulse the Russian 1st Army one week later, saving East Prussia.

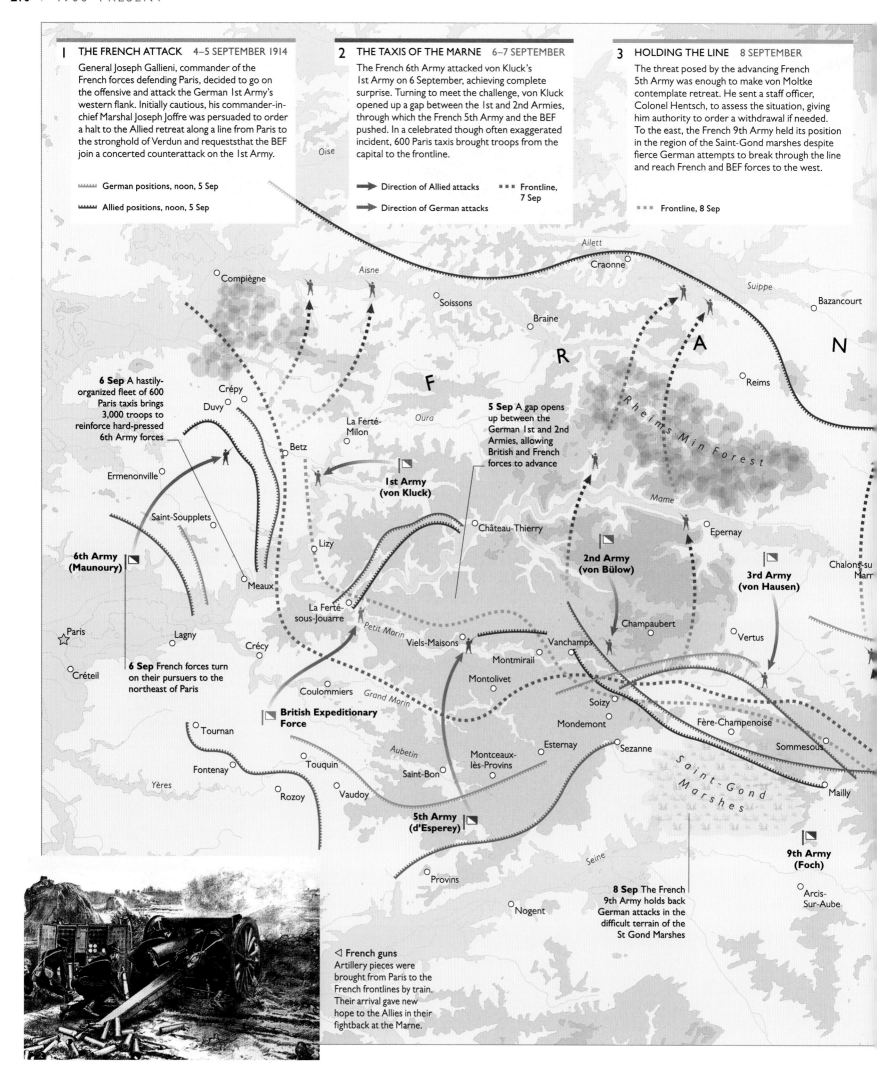

1 THE FRENCH ATTACK 4–5 SEPTEMBER 1914

General Joseph Gallieni, commander of the French forces defending Paris, decided to go on the offensive and attack the German 1st Army's western flank. Initially cautious, his commander-in-chief Marshal Joseph Joffre was persuaded to order a halt to the Allied retreat along a line from Paris to the stronghold of Verdun and requeststhat the BEF join a concerted counterattack on the 1st Army.

- German positions, noon, 5 Sep
- Allied positions, noon, 5 Sep

2 THE TAXIS OF THE MARNE 6–7 SEPTEMBER

The French 6th Army attacked von Kluck's 1st Army on 6 September, achieving complete surprise. Turning to meet the challenge, von Kluck opened up a gap between the 1st and 2nd Armies, through which the French 5th Army and the BEF pushed. In a celebrated though often exaggerated incident, 600 Paris taxis brought troops from the capital to the frontline.

- Direction of Allied attacks
- Direction of German attacks
- Frontline, 7 Sep

3 HOLDING THE LINE 8 SEPTEMBER

The threat posed by the advancing French 5th Army was enough to make von Moltke contemplate retreat. He sent a staff officer, Colonel Hentsch, to assess the situation, giving him authority to order a withdrawal if needed. To the east, the French 9th Army held its position in the region of the Saint-Gond marshes despite fierce German attempts to break through the line and reach French and BEF forces to the west.

- Frontline, 8 Sep

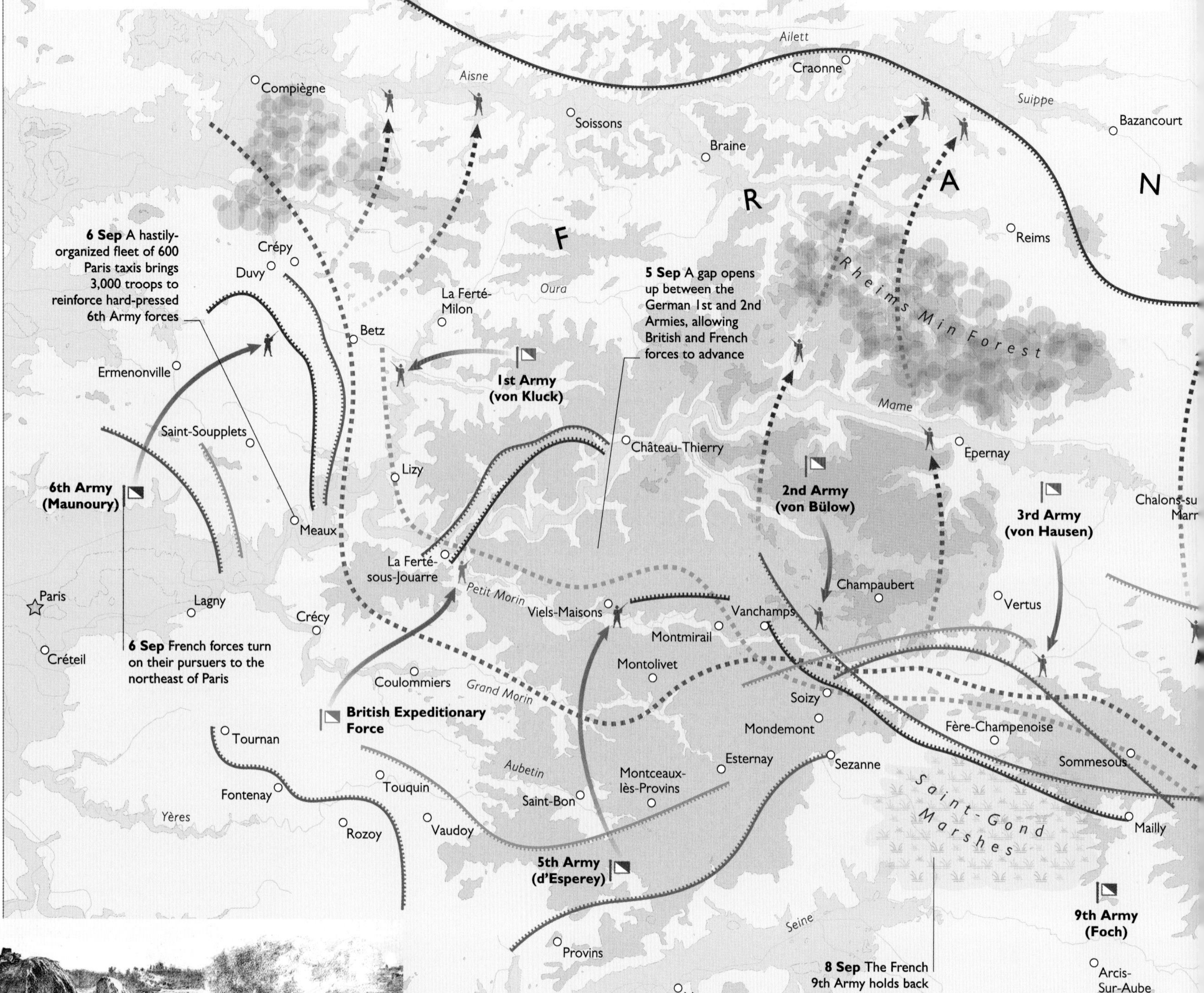

Oise
Ailett
Aisne
Craonne
Compiègne
Soissons
Suippe
Bazancourt
Braine
F
R
A
N
Reims
6 Sep A hastily-organized fleet of 600 Paris taxis brings 3,000 troops to reinforce hard-pressed 6th Army forces
Crépy
Duvy
Oura
La Ferté-Milon
5 Sep A gap opens up between the German 1st and 2nd Armies, allowing British and French forces to advance
Rheims Min Forest
Betz
Ermenonville
1st Army (von Kluck)
Marne
Saint-Soupplets
Château-Thierry
Epernay
Lizy
6th Army (Maunoury)
2nd Army (von Bülow)
3rd Army (von Hausen)
Chalons-su Marr
Meaux
La Ferté-sous-Jouarre
Champaubert
Petit Morin
Paris
Lagny
Viels-Maisons
Vanchamps
Vertus
Crécy
Montmirail
Créteil
6 Sep French forces turn on their pursuers to the northeast of Paris
Montolivet
Coulommiers
Grand Morin
Soizy
British Expeditionary Force
Mondemont
Fère-Champenoise
Tournan
Esternay
Sezanne
Sommesous
Aubetin
Montceaux-lès-Provins
Fontenay
Touquin
Saint-Bon
Saint-Gond Marshes
Yères
Rozoy
Vaudoy
Mailly
5th Army (d'Esperey)
9th Army (Foch)
Seine
Provins
8 Sep The French 9th Army holds back German attacks in the difficult terrain of the St Gond Marshes
Arcis-Sur-Aube
Nogent

◁ **French guns**
Artillery pieces were brought from Paris to the French frontlines by train. Their arrival gave new hope to the Allies in their fightback at the Marne.

FIRST MARNE

On 6 September 1914, French and British forces launched a counter-offensive against the seemingly unstoppable German advance on Paris. A turning point of World War I, the battle dashed German hopes of a quick victory over the Allied powers.

The war on the Western front opened with a remarkable series of victories for Germany as its armies marched into France through neutral Belgium. Within a month the Germans were threatening Paris, and French forces, supported by the six divisions of the British Expeditionary Force (BEF), had undertaken a demoralizing retreat.

The German plan for the invasion of France (the "Schlieffen Plan") called for German forces to push west, then south, and surround the French capital. However, on 2 September, Helmuth von Moltke, their commander-in-chief, decided instead to turn south at once and try to envelop the retreating Allies. Instead of protecting the vulnerable flank of this manoeuvre, General Alexander von Kluck's 1st Army continued to advance. This opened up his flank to an attack by the French 6th Army, which was protecting Paris. Seeing an opportunity, French commanders ordered the Allies to turn and confront the foe.

What followed was a series of engagements over a front extending for 150 km (90 miles), with heavy losses on both sides. The Germans, however, were at the end of overstretched supply lines. After three days, Helmuth von Moltke agreed to withdraw to a defensive line north of the River Aisne. The plans for a lightning campaign had failed; the scene was set for four years of attrition in the trenches.

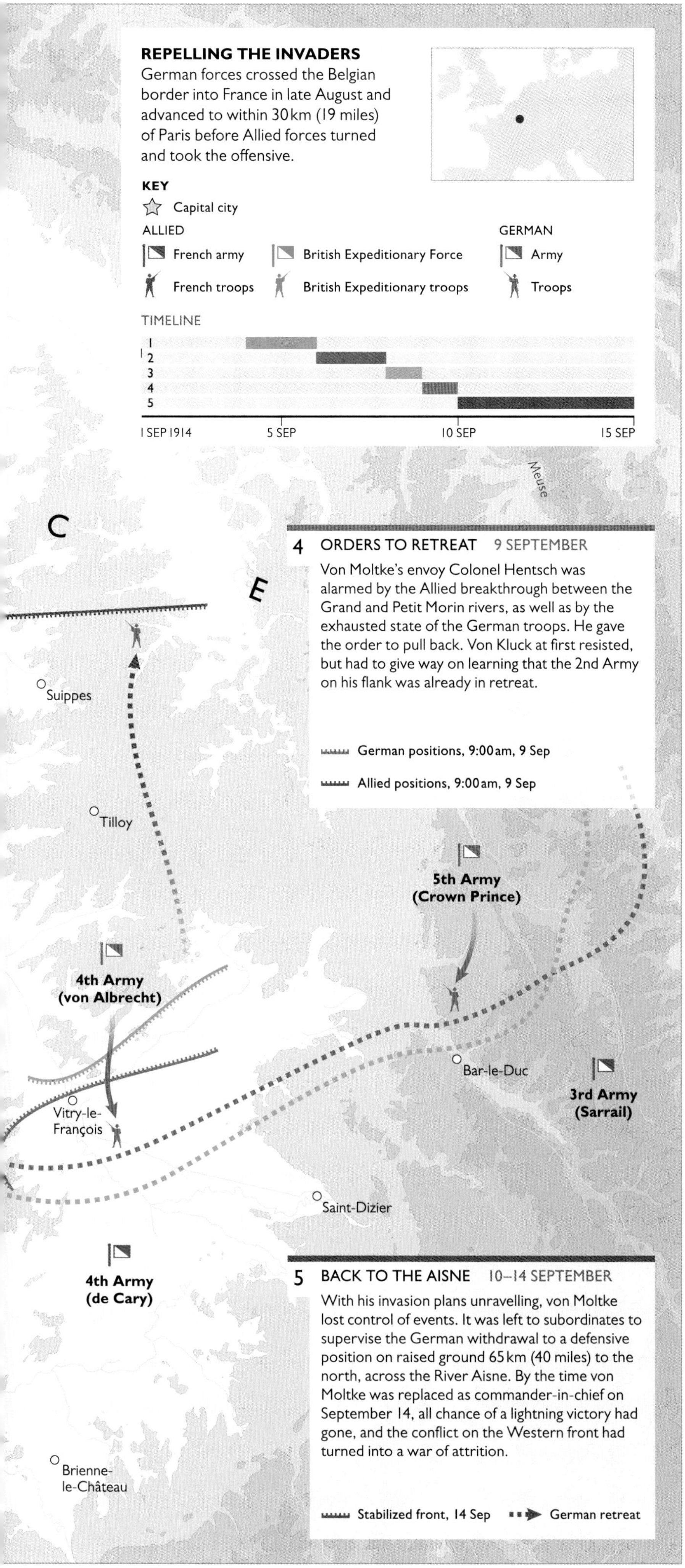
REPELLING THE INVADERS
German forces crossed the Belgian border into France in late August and advanced to within 30 km (19 miles) of Paris before Allied forces turned and took the offensive.
KEY
Capital city
ALLIED
French army
British Expeditionary Force
French troops
British Expeditionary troops
GERMAN
Army
Troops
TIMELINE
1
2
3
4
5
1 SEP 1914
5 SEP
10 SEP
15 SEP
Meuse
C
E
4 ORDERS TO RETREAT 9 SEPTEMBER
Von Moltke's envoy Colonel Hentsch was alarmed by the Allied breakthrough between the Grand and Petit Morin rivers, as well as by the exhausted state of the German troops. He gave the order to pull back. Von Kluck at first resisted, but had to give way on learning that the 2nd Army on his flank was already in retreat.
German positions, 9:00 am, 9 Sep
Allied positions, 9:00 am, 9 Sep
Suippes
Tilloy
5th Army
(Crown Prince)
4th Army
(von Albrecht)
Bar-le-Duc
3rd Army
(Sarrail)
Vitry-le-François
Saint-Dizier
4th Army
(de Cary)
5 BACK TO THE AISNE 10–14 SEPTEMBER
With his invasion plans unravelling, von Moltke lost control of events. It was left to subordinates to supervise the German withdrawal to a defensive position on raised ground 65 km (40 miles) to the north, across the River Aisne. By the time von Moltke was replaced as commander-in-chief on September 14, all chance of a lightning victory had gone, and the conflict on the Western front had turned into a war of attrition.
Brienne-le-Château
Stabilized front, 14 Sep
German retreat

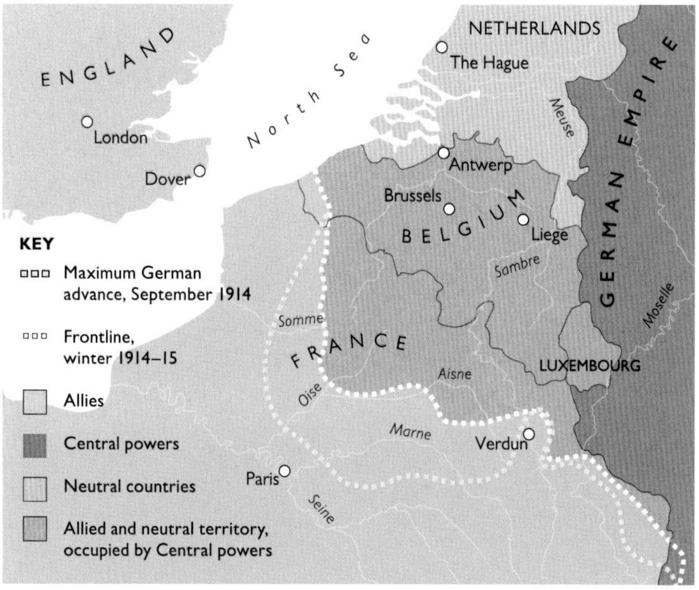
ENGLAND
London
Dover
North Sea
NETHERLANDS
The Hague
Meuse
Antwerp
Brussels
BELGIUM
Liege
Sambre
GERMAN EMPIRE
Moselle
LUXEMBOURG
FRANCE
Somme
Aisne
Oise
Marne
Verdun
Paris
Seine
KEY
Maximum German advance, September 1914
Frontline, winter 1914–15
Allies
Central powers
Neutral countries
Allied and neutral territory, occupied by Central powers

THE SCHLIEFFEN PLAN
German strategy at the start of World War I depended on delivering a knockout blow to France, allowing its forces to then concentrate on countering the threat from Russia in the east. The plan involved outflanking the French armies through neutral Belgium in contravention of treaty obligations, thereby bringing Britain into the war.

GALLIPOLI

The Gallipoli campaign was one of the most frustrating and controversial struggles of World War I, and became one of its defining moments. It came about as Allied leaders sought to bypass the stalemate on the Western front by attacking Germany's ally, Turkey.

By late 1914, the Western Front – the principal theatre of World War I – was bogged down in trench warfare, and Allied military leaders, including Britain's First Lord of the Admiralty Winston Churchill, looked for a breakthrough elsewhere. The most practical supply route from Britain and France to their ally Russia was through the Dardanelles strait into the Black Sea, but that was cut off in late October when Ottoman Turkey joined the war on the Central Powers' side. To aid Russia, Allied commanders determined to confront Turkey, and if possible force it out of the war. At first, they tried a naval assault through the Dardanelles strait to attack Istanbul; when that failed, troops were sent to seize the Gallipoli peninsula on its western shore. They established beachheads on the peninsula's southern tip and also 15km (10 miles) to the north, where Australian and New Zealand (ANZAC) forces dug into a tiny enclave dubbed Anzac Cove. However, Turkish resistance proved fiercer than expected, and drove back Allied attempts to break out of the redoubts. A second major offensive four months later at Suvla Bay failed to break the deadlock, and by the end of the year Allied commanders decided they had no option but to order an evacuation.

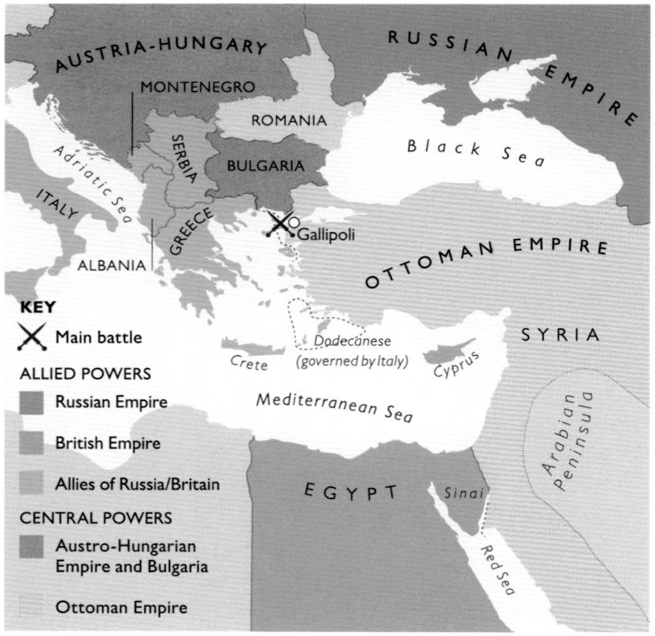
AUSTRIA-HUNGARY
RUSSIAN EMPIRE
MONTENEGRO
ROMANIA
SERBIA
BULGARIA
Black Sea
Adriatic Sea
ITALY
GREECE
ALBANIA
Gallipoli
OTTOMAN EMPIRE
SYRIA
Crete
Dodecanese (governed by Italy)
Cyprus
Mediterranean Sea
Arabian Peninsula
EGYPT
Sinai
Red Sea
KEY
Main battle
ALLIED POWERS
Russian Empire
British Empire
Allies of Russia/Britain
CENTRAL POWERS
Austro-Hungarian Empire and Bulgaria
Ottoman Empire

A CORRIDOR TO RUSSIA
Lying on the Ottoman Empire's western fringe, the Gallipoli peninsula controlled the Dardanelles strait that connects the Mediterranean to the Black Sea and so to Russia.

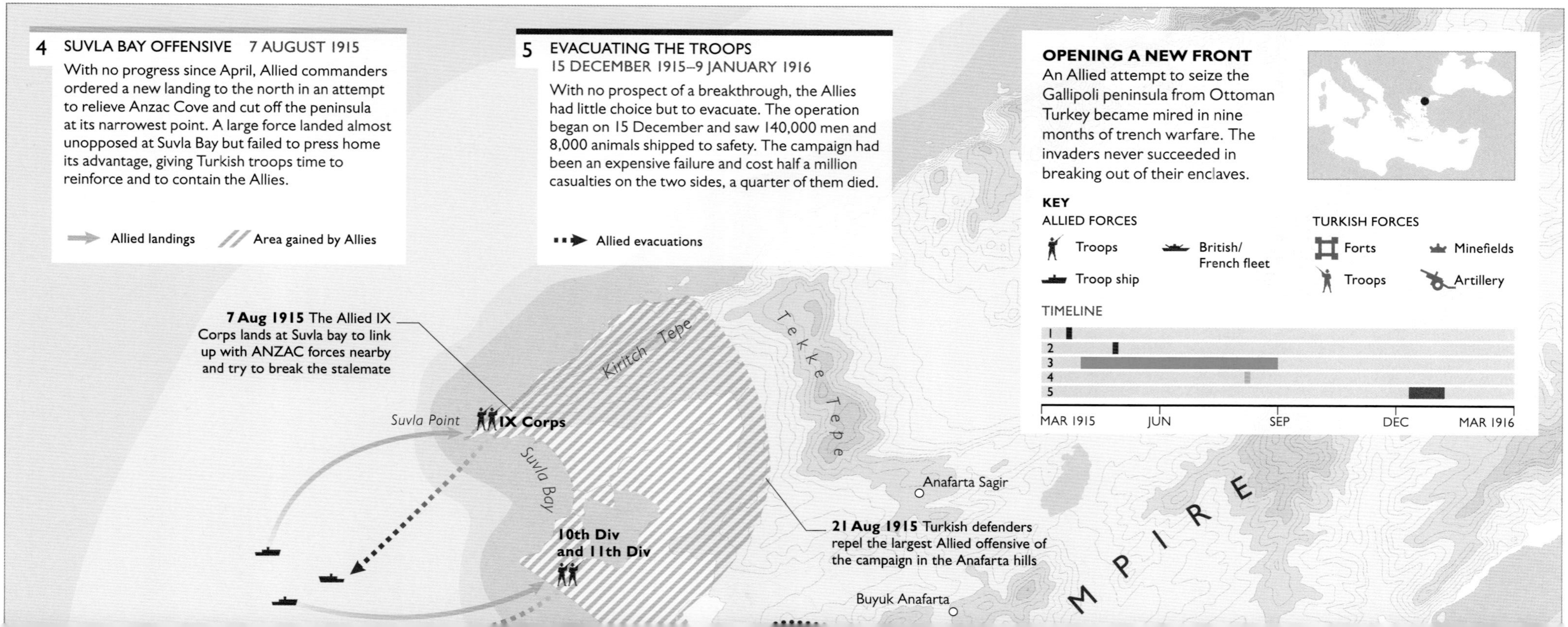
7 Aug 1915 The Allied IX Corps lands at Suvla bay to link up with ANZAC forces nearby and try to break the stalemate
Suvla Point
IX Corps
Kiritch Tepe
Tekke Tepe
Suvla Bay
10th Div and 11th Div
Anafarta Sagir
21 Aug 1915 Turkish defenders repel the largest Allied offensive of the campaign in the Anafarta hills
Buyuk Anafarta
EMPIRE
KEY
ALLIED FORCES
Troops
British/French fleet
Troop ship
TURKISH FORCES
Forts
Minefields
Troops
Artillery
TIMELINE
1
2
3
4
5
MAR 1915
JUN
SEP
DEC
MAR 1916

4 SUVLA BAY OFFENSIVE 7 AUGUST 1915
With no progress since April, Allied commanders ordered a new landing to the north in an attempt to relieve Anzac Cove and cut off the peninsula at its narrowest point. A large force landed almost unopposed at Suvla Bay but failed to press home its advantage, giving Turkish troops time to reinforce and to contain the Allies.

Allied landings — Area gained by Allies

5 EVACUATING THE TROOPS
15 DECEMBER 1915–9 JANUARY 1916
With no prospect of a breakthrough, the Allies had little choice but to evacuate. The operation began on 15 December and saw 140,000 men and 8,000 animals shipped to safety. The campaign had been an expensive failure and cost half a million casualties on the two sides, a quarter of them died.

Allied evacuations

OPENING A NEW FRONT
An Allied attempt to seize the Gallipoli peninsula from Ottoman Turkey became mired in nine months of trench warfare. The invaders never succeeded in breaking out of their enclaves.

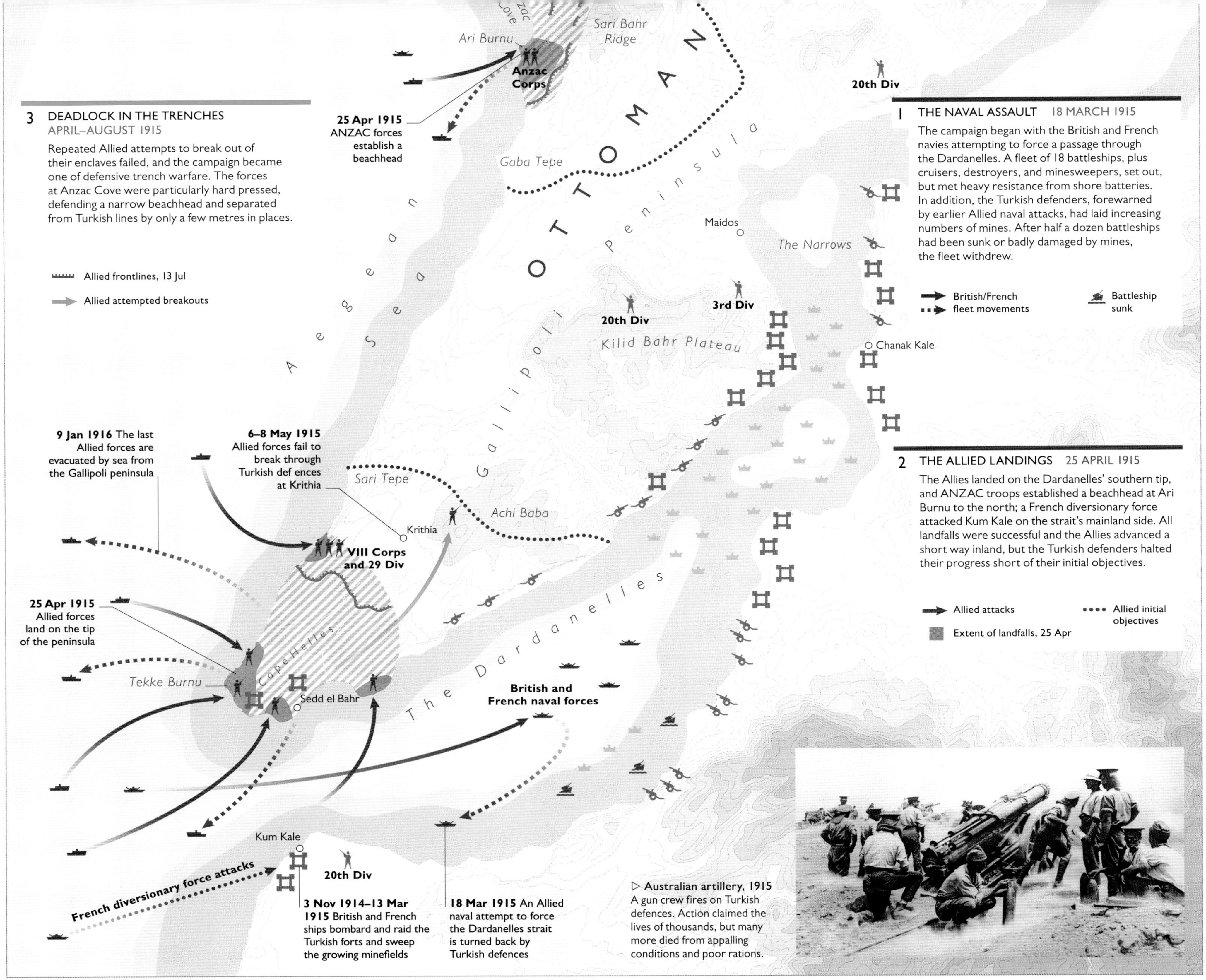
Ari Burnu
Anzac Cove
Anzac Corps
Sari Bahr Ridge
OTTOMAN
25 Apr 1915 ANZAC forces establish a beachhead
Gaba Tepe
Gallipoli Peninsula
Aegean Sea
Maidos
The Narrows
20th Div
3rd Div
20th Div
Kilid Bahr Plateau
Chanak Kale
9 Jan 1916 The last Allied forces are evacuated by sea from the Gallipoli peninsula
6–8 May 1915 Allied forces fail to break through Turkish def ences at Krithia
Sari Tepe
Krithia
Achi Baba
VIII Corps and 29 Div
25 Apr 1915 Allied forces land on the tip of the peninsula
Cape Helles
Tekke Burnu
Sedd el Bahr
The Dardanelles
British and French naval forces
Kum Kale
20th Div
French diversionary force attacks
3 Nov 1914–13 Mar 1915 British and French ships bombard and raid the Turkish forts and sweep the growing minefields
18 Mar 1915 An Allied naval attempt to force the Dardanelles strait is turned back by Turkish defences

1 THE NAVAL ASSAULT 18 MARCH 1915

The campaign began with the British and French navies attempting to force a passage through the Dardanelles. A fleet of 18 battleships, plus cruisers, destroyers, and minesweepers, set out, but met heavy resistance from shore batteries. In addition, the Turkish defenders, forewarned by earlier Allied naval attacks, had laid increasing numbers of mines. After half a dozen battleships had been sunk or badly damaged by mines, the fleet withdrew.

British/French fleet movements

Battleship sunk

2 THE ALLIED LANDINGS 25 APRIL 1915

The Allies landed on the Dardanelles' southern tip, and ANZAC troops established a beachhead at Ari Burnu to the north; a French diversionary force attacked Kum Kale on the strait's mainland side. All landfalls were successful and the Allies advanced a short way inland, but the Turkish defenders halted their progress short of their initial objectives.

Allied attacks

Allied initial objectives

Extent of landfalls, 25 Apr

3 DEADLOCK IN THE TRENCHES APRIL–AUGUST 1915

Repeated Allied attempts to break out of their enclaves failed, and the campaign became one of defensive trench warfare. The forces at Anzac Cove were particularly hard pressed, defending a narrow beachhead and separated from Turkish lines by only a few metres in places.

Allied frontlines, 13 Jul

Allied attempted breakouts

▷ **Australian artillery, 1915**
A gun crew fires on Turkish defences. Action claimed the lives of thousands, but many more died from appalling conditions and poor rations.

VERDUN

With the Western front deadlocked by the end of 1915, German military strategists sought a battleground where they might inflict so many casualties that the French would have to sue for peace. In early 1916, they launched an attack on their target, the fortress city of Verdun.

Verdun was the longest battle of World War I, and also one of the most costly in terms of casualties. Erich von Falkenhayn, Germany's Chief of the General Staff, chose the site partly because it lay in an exposed salient, served only by a single road and a narrow-gauge railway. Equally important, though, was its significance as France's chief military bastion to the east, with a historic role stretching back over more than a millennium.

The city itself was formidably defended, surrounded by a double ring of 28 smaller forts. German strategists were less concerned with taking it than with drawing French troops to its defence, where they could be picked off by heavy artillery, especially when counter-attacking to retake lost positions. As Falkenhayn predicted, the French did indeed decide to hold the site at any cost, pouring manpower into the trenches that protected it from the enemy forces to the north. However, the defenders proved unexpectedly tenacious, refusing to give ground except under extreme duress, and were surprisingly successful in launching counter-attacks. The result was a lethal stalemate that lasted through much of 1916. It ended in December 1916 with little territory gained on either side, and with each side having suffered around 350,000 casualties.

> *"Anyone who has not seen these fields of carnage will never be able to imagine it."*
>
> LETTER FROM A FRENCH SOLDIER, JULY 1916

ANIMALS IN WORLD WAR I

More than 16 million animals took part in World War I in cavalry, transport, and communications, and also as mascots to improve morale. Horses, donkeys, mules, and camels carried supplies and ammunition to the front, while dogs and pigeons delivered messages. Carrier pigeons played an important role at Verdun, where they were the only means of calling for relief for French troops trapped at Fort Vaux in June 1916.

German soldier and donkey wearing gas masks

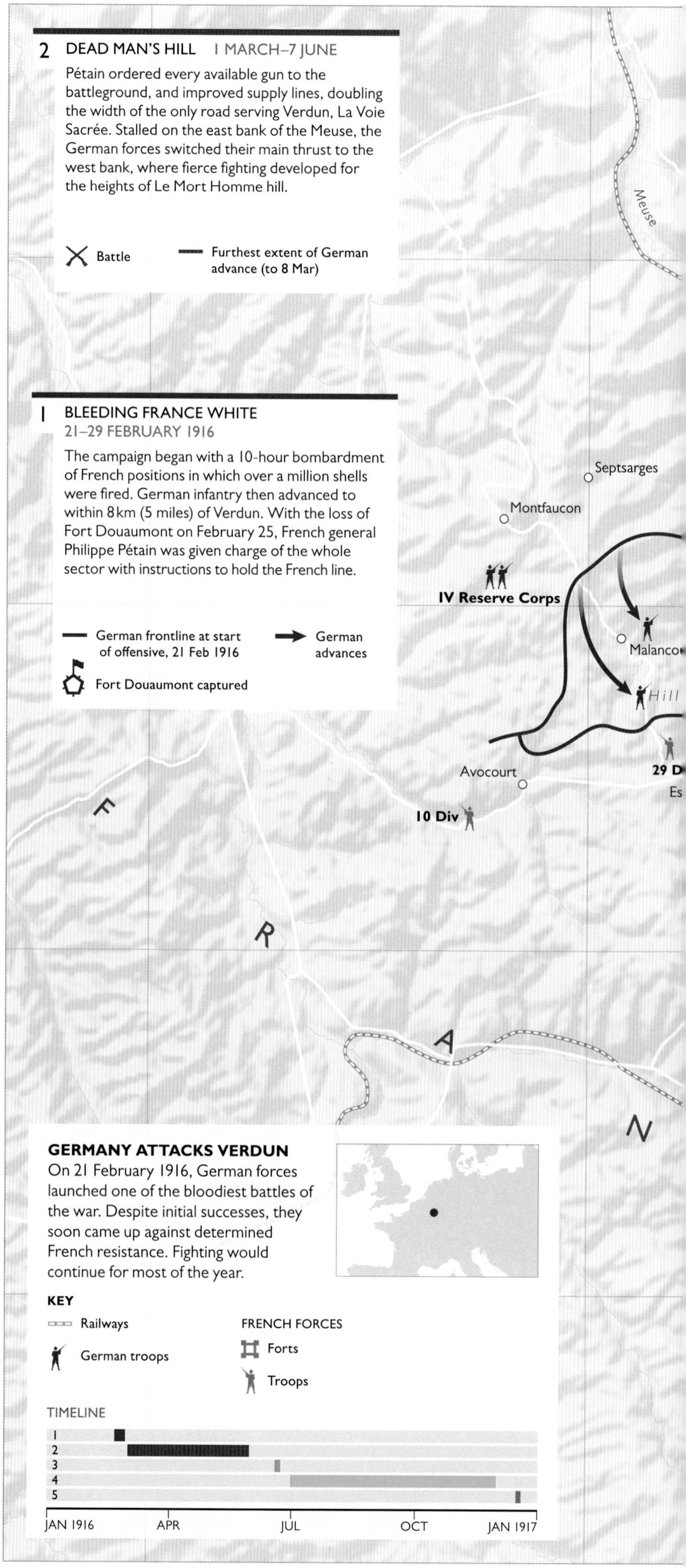
Meuse
Septsarges
Montfaucon
IV Reserve Corps
Malanco
Hill
29 D
Es
Avocourt
10 Div
F
R
A
N

2 DEAD MAN'S HILL 1 MARCH–7 JUNE

Pétain ordered every available gun to the battleground, and improved supply lines, doubling the width of the only road serving Verdun, La Voie Sacrée. Stalled on the east bank of the Meuse, the German forces switched their main thrust to the west bank, where fierce fighting developed for the heights of Le Mort Homme hill.

Battle — Furthest extent of German advance (to 8 Mar)

1 BLEEDING FRANCE WHITE
21–29 FEBRUARY 1916

The campaign began with a 10-hour bombardment of French positions in which over a million shells were fired. German infantry then advanced to within 8 km (5 miles) of Verdun. With the loss of Fort Douaumont on February 25, French general Philippe Pétain was given charge of the whole sector with instructions to hold the French line.

German frontline at start of offensive, 21 Feb 1916 — German advances — Fort Douaumont captured

GERMANY ATTACKS VERDUN

On 21 February 1916, German forces launched one of the bloodiest battles of the war. Despite initial successes, they soon came up against determined French resistance. Fighting would continue for most of the year.

KEY

Railways
German troops
FRENCH FORCES
Forts
Troops

TIMELINE

1
2
3
4
5

JAN 1916 APR JUL OCT JAN 1917

3 "THEY SHALL NOT PASS" 23 JUNE

German forces attempted a decisive breakthrough on 23 June, preparing the way with a preliminary barrage of phosgene gas shells. The French held their ground under the inspirational leadership of General Robert Nivelle, whose watchword was "They Shall Not Pass". Having reached the furthest point in the campaign, the German army had been brought to a halt.

4 COUNTER-ATTACK JULY–NOVEMBER

Combat continued at a lower level through the late summer as troops from each side were diverted to the Somme. The French launched a counter-offensive on 21 October. Over the next two weeks, their troops succeeded in retaking the lost forts of Douaumont and Vaux before ammunition shortages brought the advance to an end.

5 THE END OF THE CAMPAIGN 15–17 DECEMBER

The following month, the French launched a fresh attack northwest of the forts, retaking ground lost earlier, and pushing the German lines back a further 2 km (1¼ miles). The Battle of Louvemont, as it became known, marked the end of the campaign. In all, the German army had gained very little territory, having exhausted the French at the expense of suffering equally massive losses.

Attempted German advance
Phosgene gas attack
French advance
French gains, 24 Oct
Battle
French gains, 15 Dec

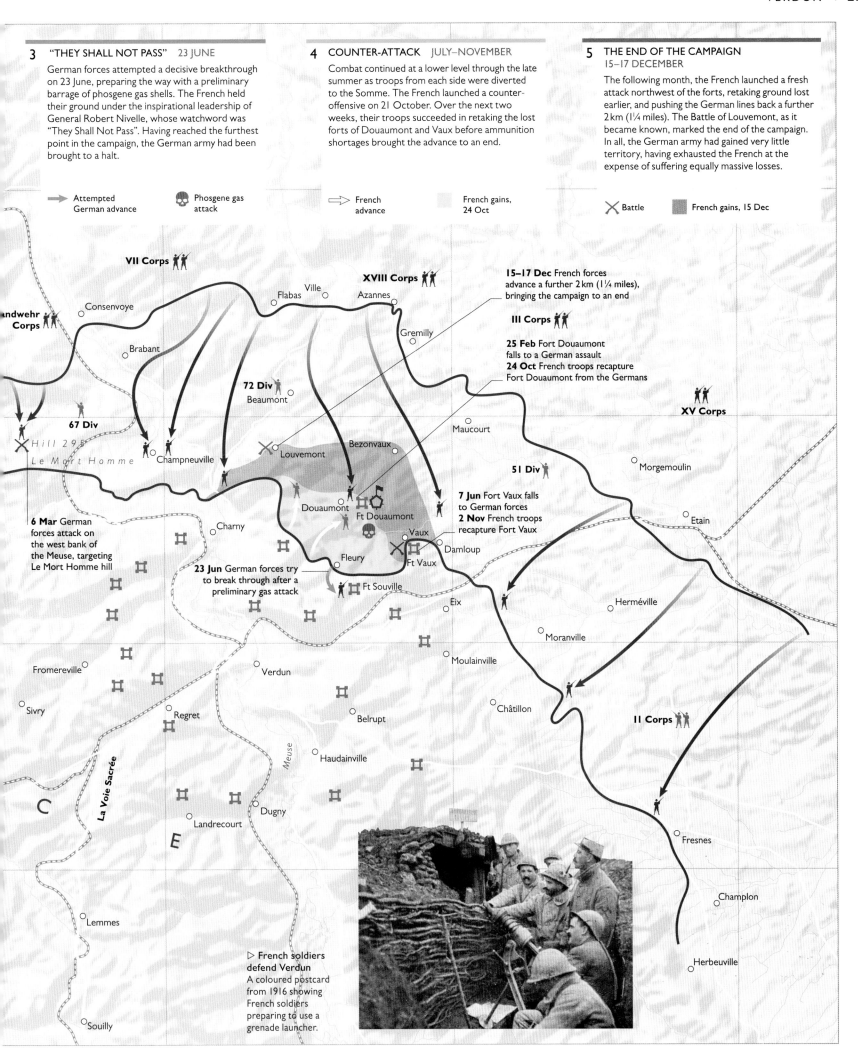

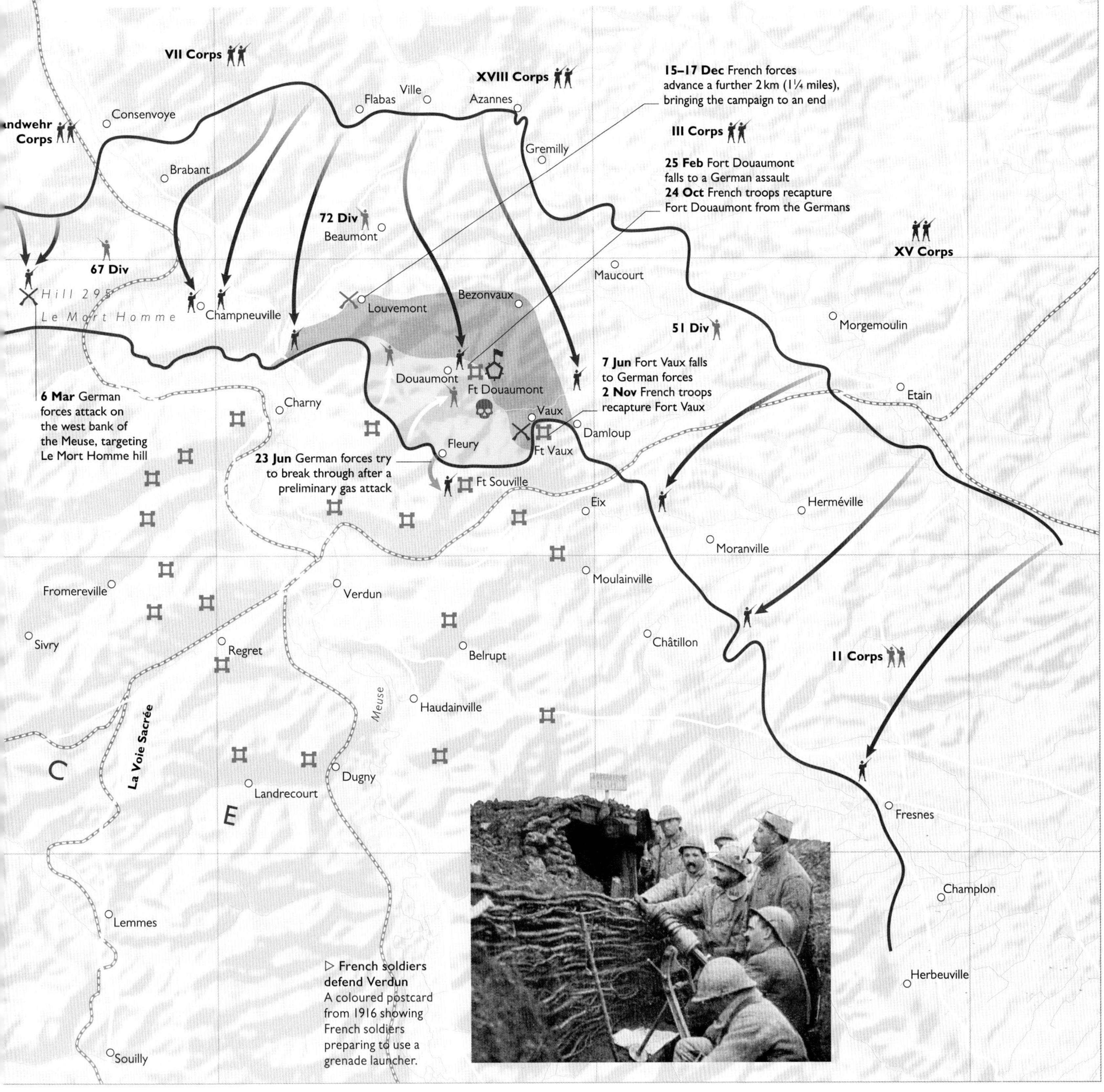
VII Corps
XVIII Corps
ndwehr Corps
III Corps
XV Corps
72 Div
67 Div
51 Div
II Corps
15–17 Dec French forces advance a further 2 km (1¼ miles), bringing the campaign to an end
25 Feb Fort Douaumont falls to a German assault
24 Oct French troops recapture Fort Douaumont from the Germans
7 Jun Fort Vaux falls to German forces
2 Nov French troops recapture Fort Vaux
6 Mar German forces attack on the west bank of the Meuse, targeting Le Mort Homme hill
23 Jun German forces try to break through after a preliminary gas attack
Consenvoye
Flabas
Ville
Azannes
Gremilly
Brabant
Beaumont
Hill 295
Le Mort Homme
Champneuville
Louvemont
Bezonvaux
Maucourt
Morgemoulin
Douaumont
Ft Douaumont
Charny
Vaux
Damloup
Ft Vaux
Fleury
Ft Souville
Etain
Eix
Herméville
Moranville
Moulainville
Fromereville
Verdun
Sivry
Regret
Belrupt
Châtillon
Haudainville
Meuse
La Voie Sacrée
Dugny
Landrecourt
Fresnes
Champlon
Lemmes
Herbeuville
Souilly
C
E

▷ **French soldiers defend Verdun**
A coloured postcard from 1916 showing French soldiers preparing to use a grenade launcher.

CHEMICAL WARFARE

On 22 April 1915, at Ypres, Belgium, the German army first discharged chlorine gas over the Allied trenches. It triggered panic, and later attacks killed and incapacitated hundreds of soldiers.

Although the Germans did not gain a decisive advantage at Ypres, other countries began developing chemical weapons in the hope that this would break the deadlock of trench warfare. The new gas weapons included choking agents such as chlorine and phosgene. At first these were released from cylinders, which required favourable wind conditions, and later as gas shells fired by artillery guns. Mortars and projectors were also used. From 1917, the persistent blistering agent dichlorodiethyl sulfide ("mustard gas") added to the horror, remaining toxic to exposed skin for several days.

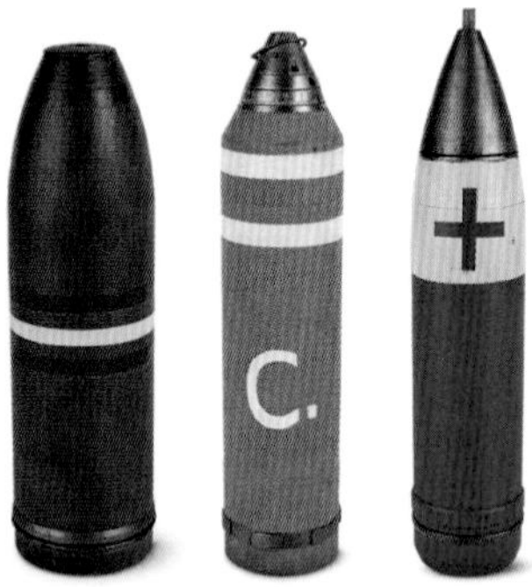
C.

△ **Colour-coded gas shells**
The Germans used blue-cross shells containing vomiting agents to prompt soldiers to remove their masks and so expose themselves to the green-cross lung agents.

Gas attacks in World War I did not bring about the anticipated breakthrough. Gas masks and protective clothing were introduced, and although they slowed down troops, they were effective – chemical weapons worked best against unprotected troops. However, gas remained a powerful psychological weapon, and could cause death and long-term injury where it did affect its targets.

Chemical warfare did not end in 1918, and France, Italy, and possibly Britain and Spain used it in their colonial wars. Despite a ban in 1925, chemical weapons, including new, more toxic nerve agents, were used in Ethiopia and China in the 1930s, and more recently in the 1980s Iran-Iraq war and the ongoing Syrian civil war.

△ **Mustard gas victims in World War I**
Here US artist John Singer Sargent depicts Allied soldiers temporarily blinded by mustard gas, which was rarely lethal but caused more casualties than all other chemical agents combined.

Gas attack in the trenches
This image taken during World War I shows Russian soldiers wearing an early type of gas mask. At the first sign of a gas attack, alarms would be sounded and soldiers would hurry to put on their masks.

JUTLAND

Jutland was the chief naval encounter of World War I and the most significant clash ever between dreadnought-class battleships. Although the British fleet suffered greater losses than the Germans, Britain came out of the conflict in control of the North Sea shipping lanes.

Britain and Germany had engaged in a high-profile naval arms race in the lead-up to World War I, so a clash between their dreadnoughts (steam-powered battleships with heavy calibre guns – see pp.206–207) was widely anticipated. In fact, it proved slow in coming, as neither side wished to put their deterrent force at risk from mines and submarines. When the fleets finally met in 1916 at Jutland, off the coast of Denmark, the encounter proved indecisive.

Although battleships played a key role in the conflict, much of the fighting was carried out by forces of smaller ships, including cruisers and destroyers, led by Britain's Admiral Beatty and Germany's Franz von Hipper. The main fleets, commanded by Admiral Jellicoe and Reinhard Scheer for Britain and Germany respectively, met in only two brief clashes, with battleship fire lasting barely 15 minutes.

The battle showed up weaknesses in the construction and armament of the British ships, which suffered greater losses – in all, 14 vessels against 11 vessels for the Germans. Similarly, the British Grand Fleet lost 6,094 seamen to the German High Seas Fleet's 2,551. These figures enabled the German military to claim a victory at the time. However, thanks to the size of its dreadnought fleet, Britain retained the upper hand strategically, and the German fleet never again risked a major sortie.

> *"There seems to be something wrong with our bloody ships today."*
>
> ADMIRAL DAVID BEATTY ON LOSING HMS *QUEEN MARY*

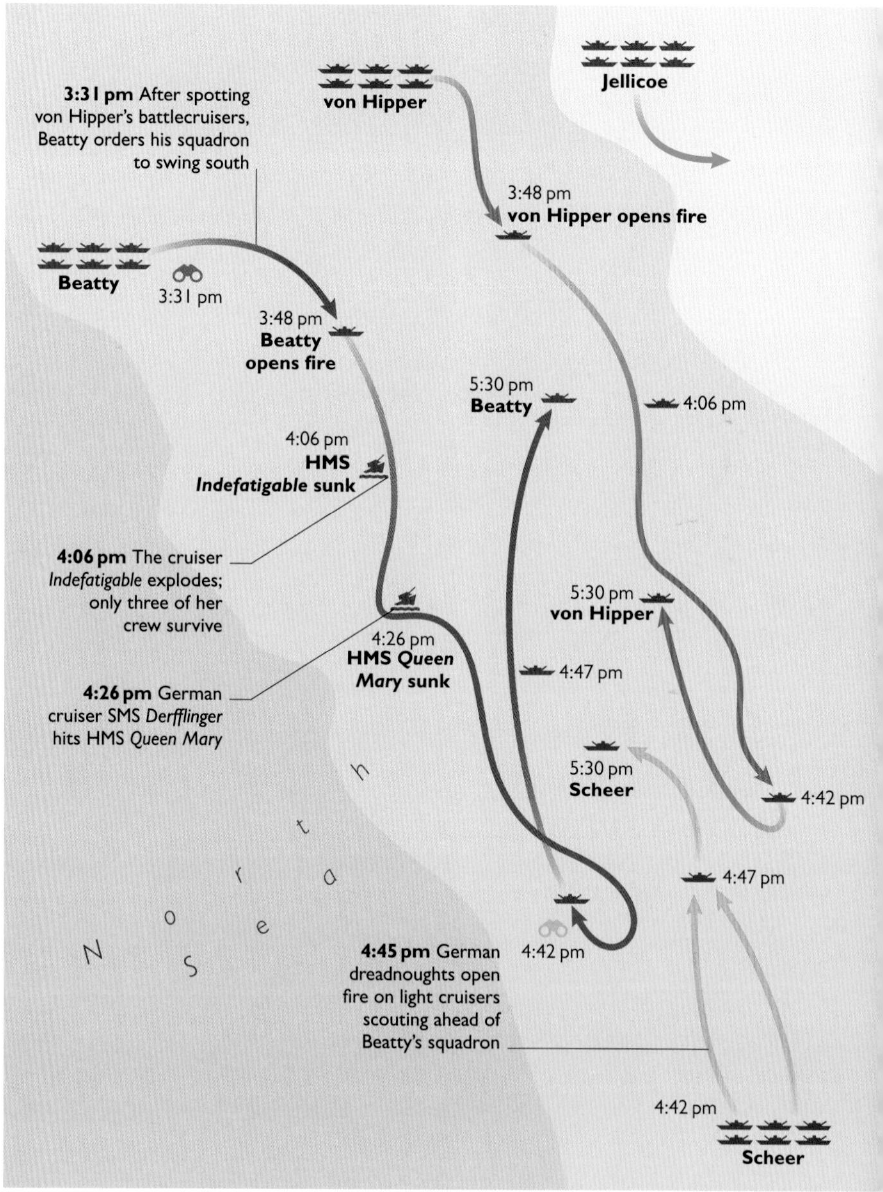
von Hipper
Jellicoe
3:31 pm After spotting von Hipper's battlecruisers, Beatty orders his squadron to swing south
3:48 pm von Hipper opens fire
Beatty
3:31 pm
3:48 pm Beatty opens fire
5:30 pm Beatty
4:06 pm
4:06 pm HMS *Indefatigable* sunk
4:06 pm The cruiser *Indefatigable* explodes; only three of her crew survive
5:30 pm von Hipper
4:26 pm HMS *Queen Mary* sunk
4:47 pm
4:26 pm German cruiser SMS *Derfflinger* hits HMS *Queen Mary*
5:30 pm Scheer
4:42 pm
4:47 pm
North Sea
4:45 pm German dreadnoughts open fire on light cruisers scouting ahead of Beatty's squadron
4:42 pm
4:42 pm
Scheer

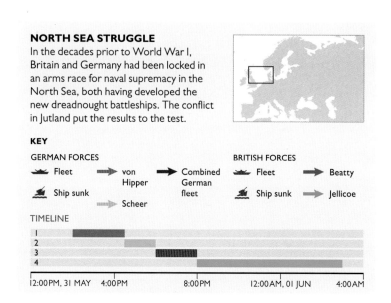

NORTH SEA STRUGGLE

In the decades prior to World War I, Britain and Germany had been locked in an arms race for naval supremacy in the North Sea, both having developed the new dreadnought battleships. The conflict in Jutland put the results to the test.

KEY

GERMAN FORCES: Fleet; Ship sunk; von Hipper; Scheer; Combined German fleet

BRITISH FORCES: Fleet; Ship sunk; Beatty; Jellicoe

TIMELINE

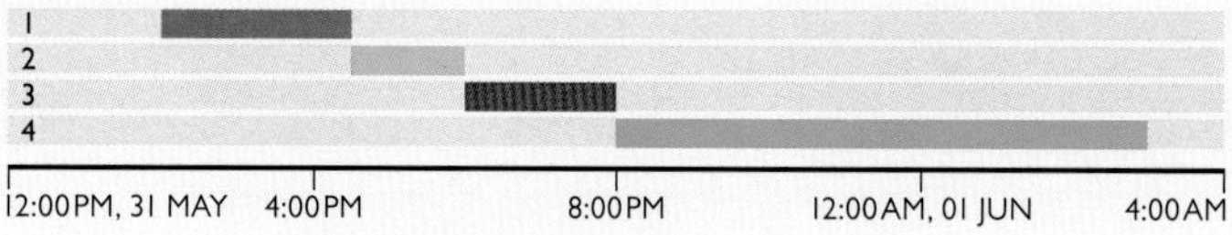
1
2
3
4
12:00PM, 31 MAY
4:00PM
8:00PM
12:00AM, 01 JUN
4:00AM

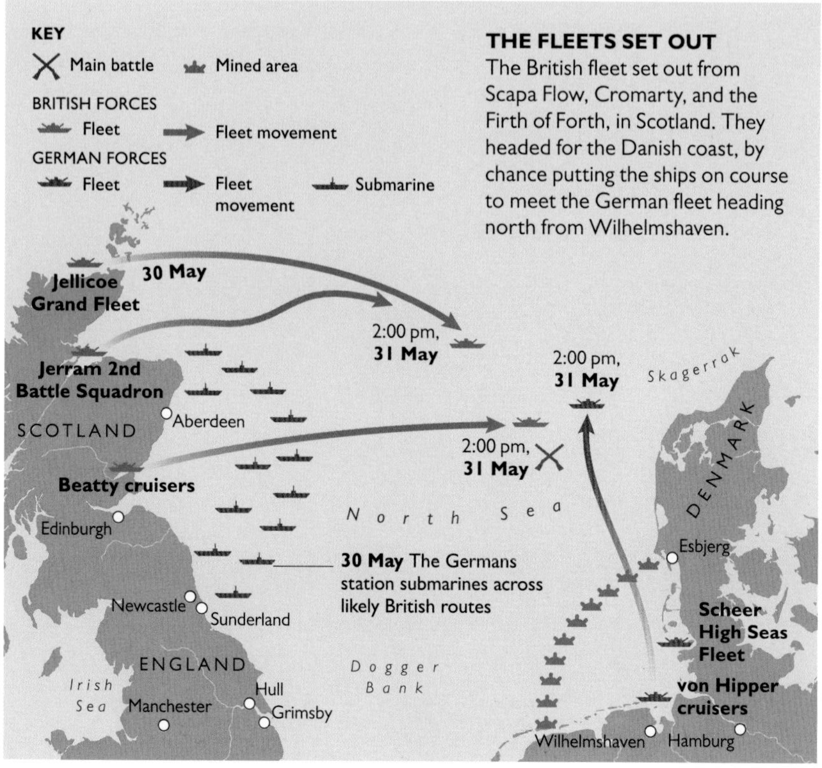
KEY
Main battle
Mined area
BRITISH FORCES
Fleet
Fleet movement
GERMAN FORCES
Fleet
Fleet movement
Submarine
Jellicoe Grand Fleet
30 May
2:00 pm, 31 May
Jerram 2nd Battle Squadron
2:00 pm, 31 May
Skagerrak
Aberdeen
SCOTLAND
2:00 pm, 31 May
DENMARK
Beatty cruisers
Edinburgh
North Sea
Esbjerg
30 May The Germans station submarines across likely British routes
Newcastle
Sunderland
Scheer High Seas Fleet
ENGLAND
Irish Sea
Dogger Bank
Hull
von Hipper cruisers
Manchester
Grimsby
Wilhelmshaven
Hamburg

THE FLEETS SET OUT

The British fleet set out from Scapa Flow, Cromarty, and the Firth of Forth, in Scotland. They headed for the Danish coast, by chance putting the ships on course to meet the German fleet heading north from Wilhelmshaven.

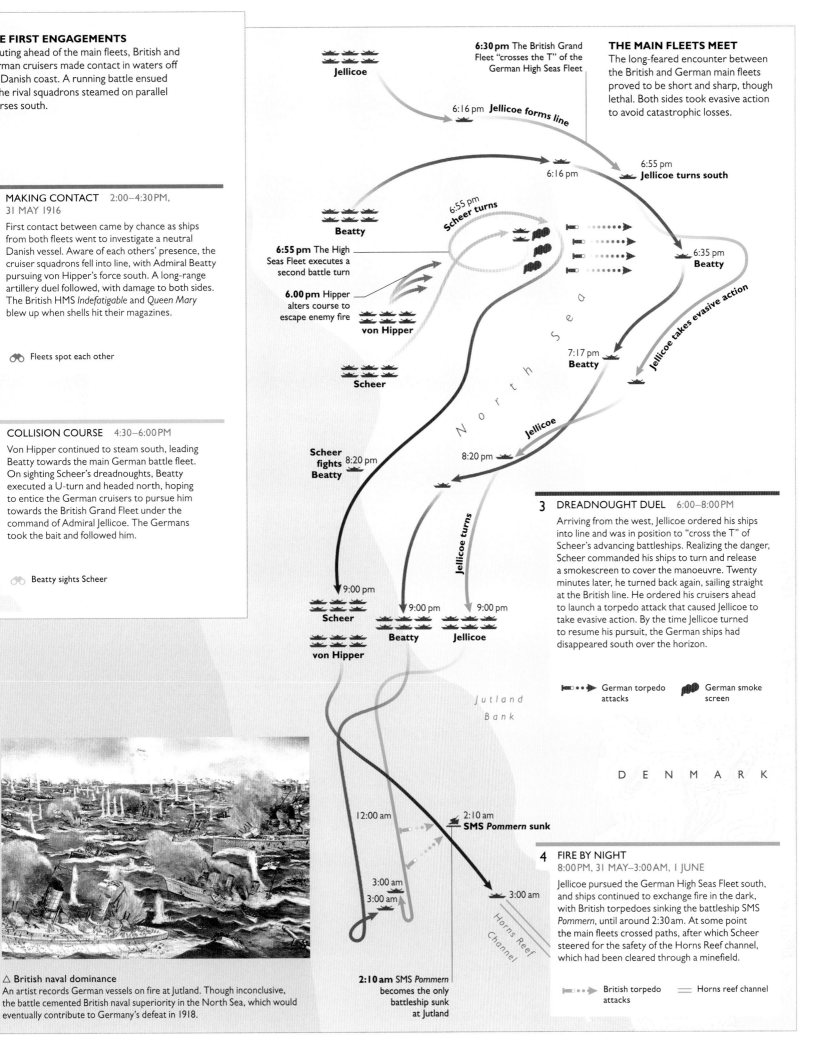

THE FIRST ENGAGEMENTS

Scouting ahead of the main fleets, British and German cruisers made contact in waters off the Danish coast. A running battle ensued as the rival squadrons steamed on parallel courses south.

1 MAKING CONTACT 2:00–4:30PM, 31 MAY 1916

First contact between came by chance as ships from both fleets went to investigate a neutral Danish vessel. Aware of each others' presence, the cruiser squadrons fell into line, with Admiral Beatty pursuing von Hipper's force south. A long-range artillery duel followed, with damage to both sides. The British HMS *Indefatigable* and *Queen Mary* blew up when shells hit their magazines.

Fleets spot each other

2 COLLISION COURSE 4:30–6:00PM

Von Hipper continued to steam south, leading Beatty towards the main German battle fleet. On sighting Scheer's dreadnoughts, Beatty executed a U-turn and headed north, hoping to entice the German cruisers to pursue him towards the British Grand Fleet under the command of Admiral Jellicoe. The Germans took the bait and followed him.

Beatty sights Scheer

THE MAIN FLEETS MEET

The long-feared encounter between the British and German main fleets proved to be short and sharp, though lethal. Both sides took evasive action to avoid catastrophic losses.

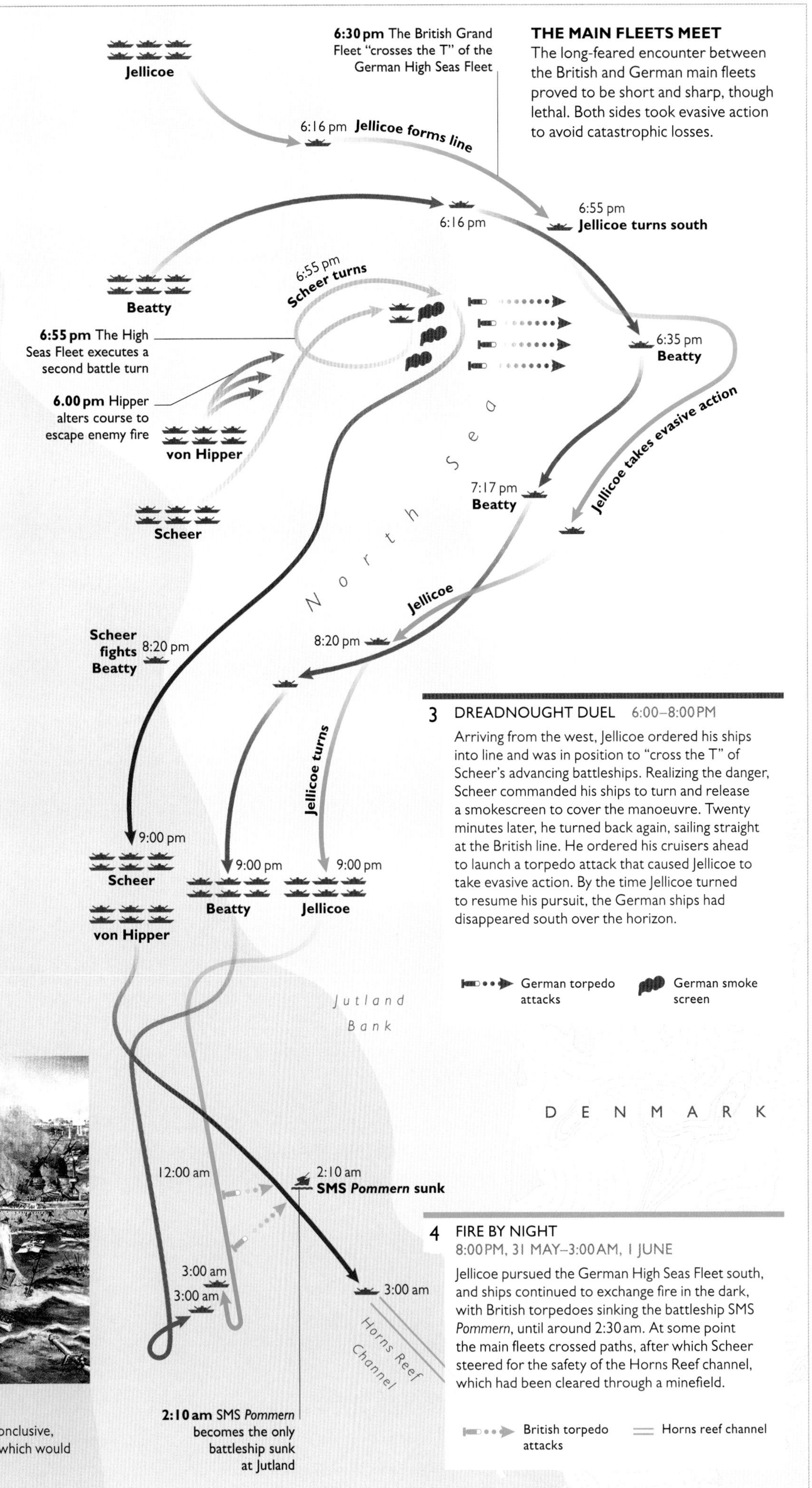

Jellicoe
6:30 pm The British Grand Fleet "crosses the T" of the German High Seas Fleet
6:16 pm **Jellicoe forms line**
6:16 pm
6:55 pm **Jellicoe turns south**
Beatty
6:55 pm Scheer turns
6:55 pm The High Seas Fleet executes a second battle turn
6.00 pm Hipper alters course to escape enemy fire
von Hipper
6:35 pm Beatty
Jellicoe takes evasive action
North Sea
7:17 pm Beatty
Scheer
Jellicoe
Scheer fights Beatty 8:20 pm
8:20 pm
Jellicoe turns
9:00 pm
Scheer
9:00 pm
9:00 pm
Beatty
Jellicoe
von Hipper
Jutland Bank
DENMARK
12:00 am
2:10 am
SMS Pommern sunk
3:00 am
3:00 am
3:00 am
Horns Reef Channel
2:10 am SMS *Pommern* becomes the only battleship sunk at Jutland
German torpedo attacks
German smoke screen
British torpedo attacks
Horns reef channel

3 DREADNOUGHT DUEL 6:00–8:00PM

Arriving from the west, Jellicoe ordered his ships into line and was in position to "cross the T" of Scheer's advancing battleships. Realizing the danger, Scheer commanded his ships to turn and release a smokescreen to cover the manoeuvre. Twenty minutes later, he turned back again, sailing straight at the British line. He ordered his cruisers ahead to launch a torpedo attack that caused Jellicoe to take evasive action. By the time Jellicoe turned to resume his pursuit, the German ships had disappeared south over the horizon.

4 FIRE BY NIGHT 8:00PM, 31 MAY–3:00AM, 1 JUNE

Jellicoe pursued the German High Seas Fleet south, and ships continued to exchange fire in the dark, with British torpedoes sinking the battleship SMS *Pommern*, until around 2:30am. At some point the main fleets crossed paths, after which Scheer steered for the safety of the Horns Reef channel, which had been cleared through a minefield.

△ **British naval dominance**
An artist records German vessels on fire at Jutland. Though inconclusive, the battle cemented British naval superiority in the North Sea, which would eventually contribute to Germany's defeat in 1918.

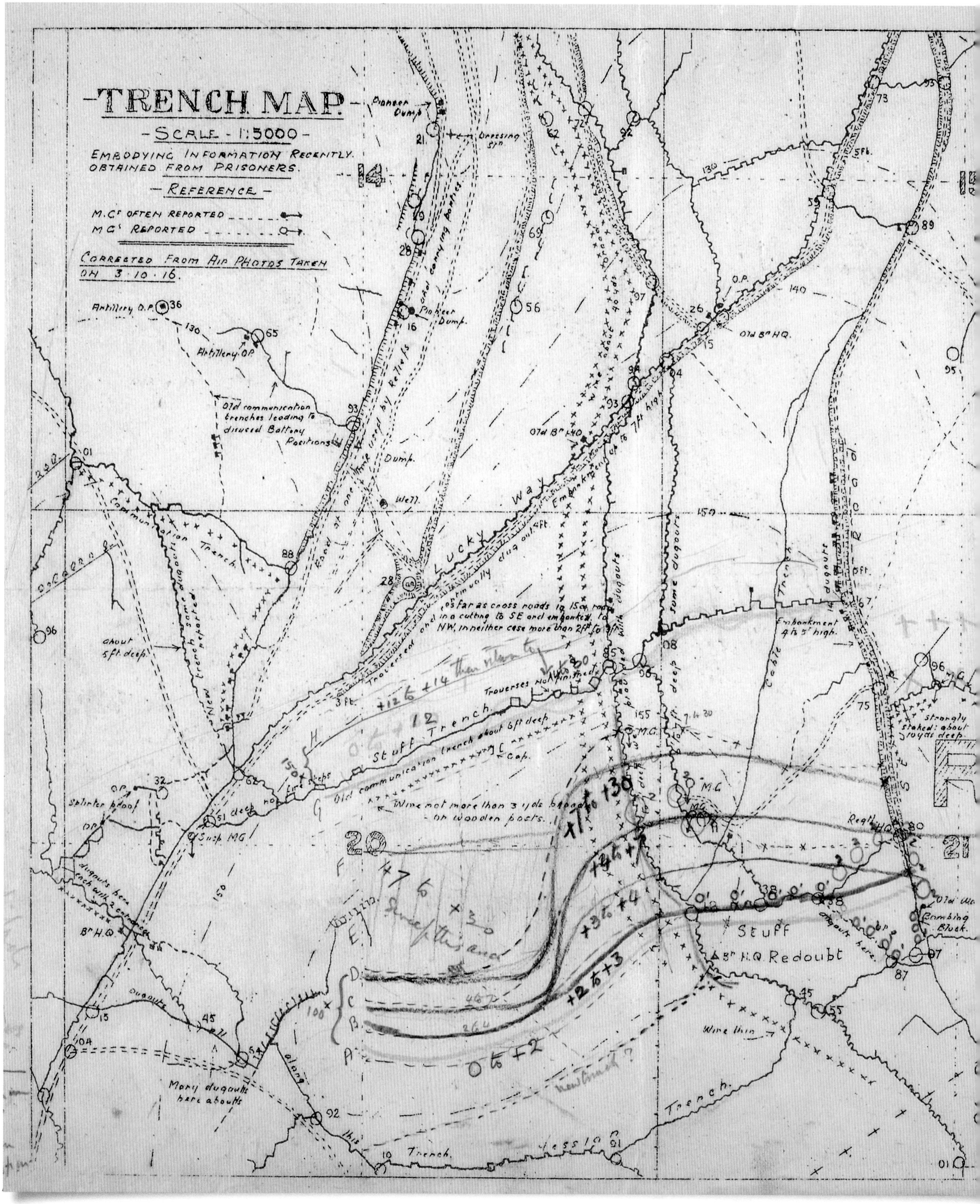
TRENCH MAP.
SCALE 1:5000
EMBODYING INFORMATION RECENTLY OBTAINED FROM PRISONERS.
REFERENCE
M.G's OFTEN REPORTED
M.G's REPORTED
CORRECTED FROM AIR PHOTOS TAKEN ON 3·10·16.
Pioneer Dump
Dressing Stn
Artillery O.P.
Old communication trenches leading to disused Battery Positions
Pioneer Dump.
Dump.
Well.
Communication Trench
Lucky Way
Stuff Trench
Old communication trench about 6ft deep
Wire not more than 3 yds broad on wooden posts.
Traverses not finished
Splinter proof
Susp. MG
Bn H.Q.
Many dugouts here abouts
Stuff Redoubt
Bn H.Q. Redoubt
Regtl H.Q.
Bombing Block.
Wire thin
Strongly staked: about 5 yds deep.
Embankment 4 to 5' high.
Cable Trench
Old Bn H.Q.
Hessian Trench

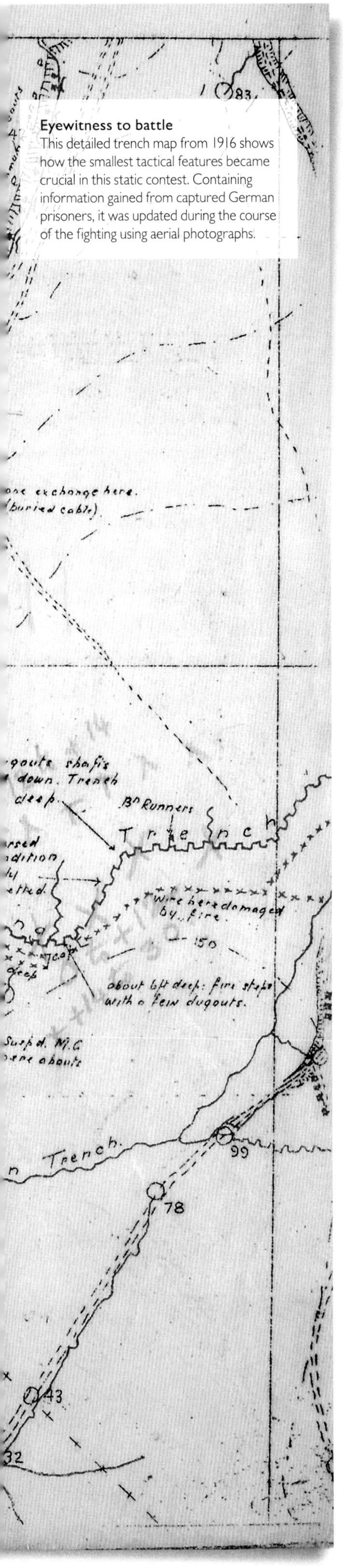
Trench
B^n Runners
Wire here damaged by fire
about 6ft deep: fire steps with a few dugouts.
150
99
78
43
32

Eyewitness to battle
This detailed trench map from 1916 shows how the smallest tactical features became crucial in this static contest. Containing information gained from captured German prisoners, it was updated during the course of the fighting using aerial photographs.

THE SOMME

Designed to force a breakthrough on the Western Front and to shatter German morale, the offensive launched by Allied forces on the River Somme in the summer of 1916 began with a bloodbath and gained little ground over several months. The battle came to symbolize the futility of combat in World War I.

The Allies originally planned an equally balanced Anglo-French attack on the Somme to coincide with pushes against Germany on the Russian and Italian fronts. However, in July 1916, Britain took the lead role in the attack to relieve pressure on the French caused by the German advance on Verdun (see pp.214–15).

Douglas Haig, commander of the mainly volunteer British Expeditionary Force (BEF), proposed using prolonged artillery barrages to punch paths through enemy lines, and even called up cavalry units to exploit the gaps he believed this would create. The reality was very different. Two-thirds of the 1.5 million shells fired in the week before the attack were shrapnel rather than high explosive, so did little to dislodge defenders in deep concrete-lined bunkers. Many shells were duds, built by unskilled labour. For over four months the muddy fields of the Somme valley became a killing ground with over a million casualties, including more than 300,000 dead. The Germans suffered nearly half of these terrible losses, but Allied territorial gains stood at only around 12km (7½ miles) of war-ravaged land. When the operation was called off in mid-November, the deadlock in northern France remained unbroken.

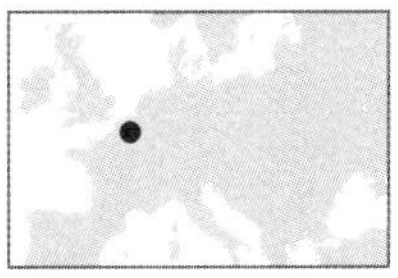

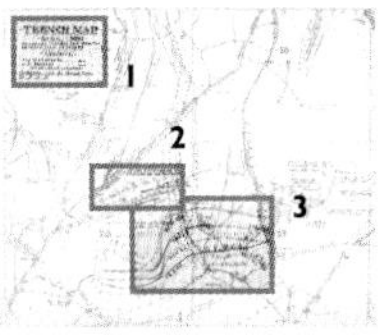
1
2
3

KEY

1 German machine gun positions are identified in the key (as "MG"); arrows indicate direction of fire.

2 Pencil annotations reflect updates made to the map during the battle.

3 German trenches are marked in red; hand-drawn numbered lines indicate the timings for the artillery barrage which would have supported an infantry assault.

"The results of the Somme fully justify confidence in our ability to master the enemy's power of resistance."

GENERAL DOUGLAS HAIG, 1916

A PITILESS FRONT

On July 1, Allied soldiers were ordered "over the top"; thousands were mowed down by machine-gun fire, with significant advances made only in the south. The BEF took almost 60,000 casualties, making this the bloodiest day in the history of the British Army. The French in the south were more successful and pushed over the Flaucourt plateau but were halted short of Peronne. Only a few advances, such as the capture of Pozières by Australian troops, were made by mid-September. The battlefront was then widened, and some modest and costly further gains were made before winter curtailed the battle.

KEY

British forces | French forces
British attacks | French attacks
Frontline 1 July 1916 | Frontline 18 Nov 1916
German forces

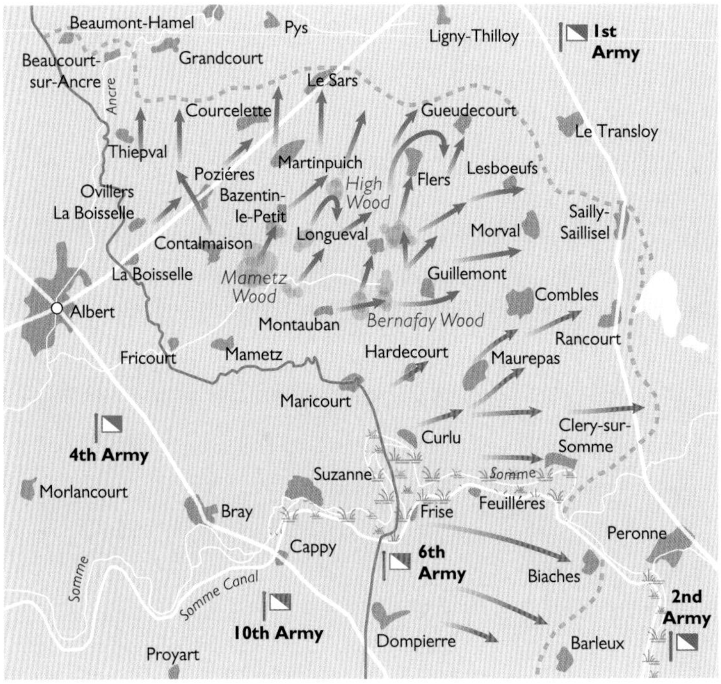
Beaumont-Hamel
Pys
Ligny-Thilloy
1st Army
Beaucourt-sur-Ancre
Grandcourt
Ancre
Le Sars
Courcelette
Gueudecourt
Le Transloy
Thiepval
Martinpuich
Pozières
High Wood
Flers
Lesboeufs
Ovillers
La Boisselle
Bazentin-le-Petit
Sailly-Saillisel
Contalmaison
Longueval
Morval
La Boisselle
Mametz Wood
Guillemont
Combles
Albert
Montauban
Bernafay Wood
Rancourt
Fricourt
Mametz
Hardecourt
Maurepas
Maricourt
4th Army
Curlu
Clery-sur-Somme
Suzanne
Somme
Morlancourt
Bray
Frise
Feuillères
Peronne
Cappy
6th Army
Somme
Somme Canal
Biaches
10th Army
2nd Army
Dompierre
Barleux
Proyart

1 OVER THE TOP 31 JULY–11 AUGUST 1917

After a ten-day bombardment, nine British divisions with support from a French First Army corps launched the offensive on an 18-km (11-mile) front. The German Fourth Army was deeply dug in, and the attackers made limited progress, mainly on the left of the line around the Pilckem Ridge, at a cost of some 27,000 casualties. Persistent rain delayed further attacks.

Allied attacks

2 SECOND STRIKE 12–16 AUGUST

General Gough of the British Fifth Army used the time to plan a new assault in improved weather conditions. Launched on 16 August, the attack succeeded in taking the village of Langemarck (beyond Pilckem). Elsewhere, the British made more limited progress, driven back by fierce German counter-attacks.

Battle of Langemarck

Village captured

3 A CHANGE OF STRATEGY 17 AUGUST–26 SEPTEMBER

Poor results from the first attacks prompted Haig to place General Plumer, rather than Gough, in the centre of the action. Instead of large-scale attacks, Plumer sought limited advances several days apart under the cover of rolling artillery barrages. His aim was to win control of the plateau east of Ypres with this "bite and hold" strategy. His first attack on 20 September along the Menin Road gained over 1 km (⅔ mile) of territory.

Allied advances, Battle of Menin Road

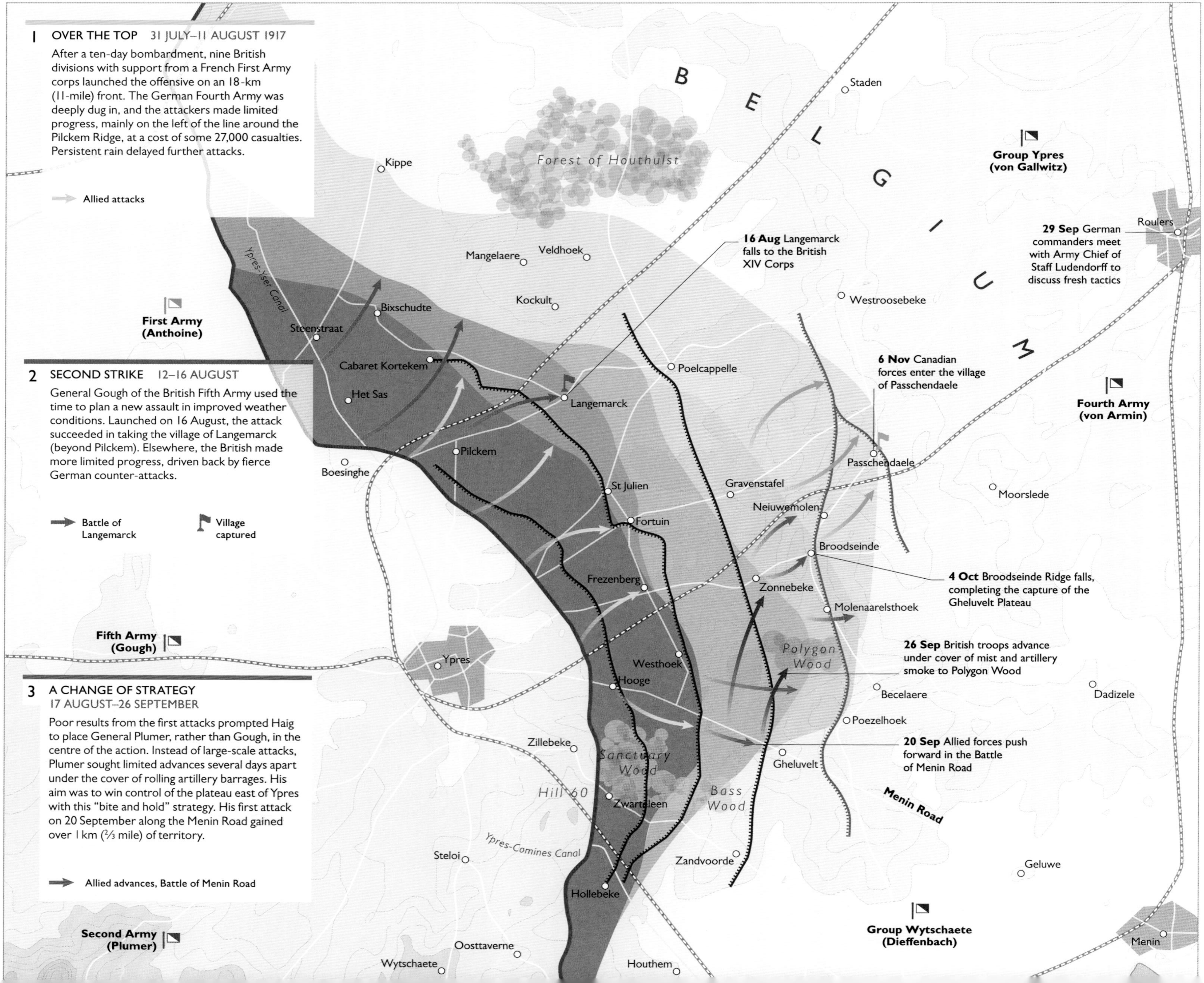

BELGIUM
Forest of Houthulst
Kippe
Staden
Group Ypres (von Gallwitz)
Roulers
29 Sep German commanders meet with Army Chief of Staff Ludendorff to discuss fresh tactics
Mangelaere
Veldhoek
Kockult
Westroosebeke
16 Aug Langemarck falls to the British XIV Corps
First Army (Anthoine)
Ypres-Yser Canal
Steenstraat
Bixschudte
Cabaret Kortekem
Het Sas
Poelcappelle
Langemarck
6 Nov Canadian forces enter the village of Passchendaele
Fourth Army (von Armin)
Pilckem
Boesinghe
Passchendaele
Moorslede
St Julien
Gravenstafel
Neiuwemolen
Fortuin
Broodseinde
4 Oct Broodseinde Ridge falls, completing the capture of the Gheluvelt Plateau
Frezenberg
Zonnebeke
Molenaarelsthoek
Fifth Army (Gough)
Ypres
Westhoek
Hooge
Polygon Wood
26 Sep British troops advance under cover of mist and artillery smoke to Polygon Wood
Becelaere
Dadizele
Poezelhoek
Zillebeke
Sanctuary Wood
Gheluvelt
20 Sep Allied forces push forward in the Battle of Menin Road
Hill 60
Zwartleen
Bass Wood
Menin Road
Ypres-Comines Canal
Steloi
Zandvoorde
Geluwe
Hollebeke
Group Wytschaete (Dieffenbach)
Second Army (Plumer)
Oosttaverne
Wytschaete
Houthem
Menin

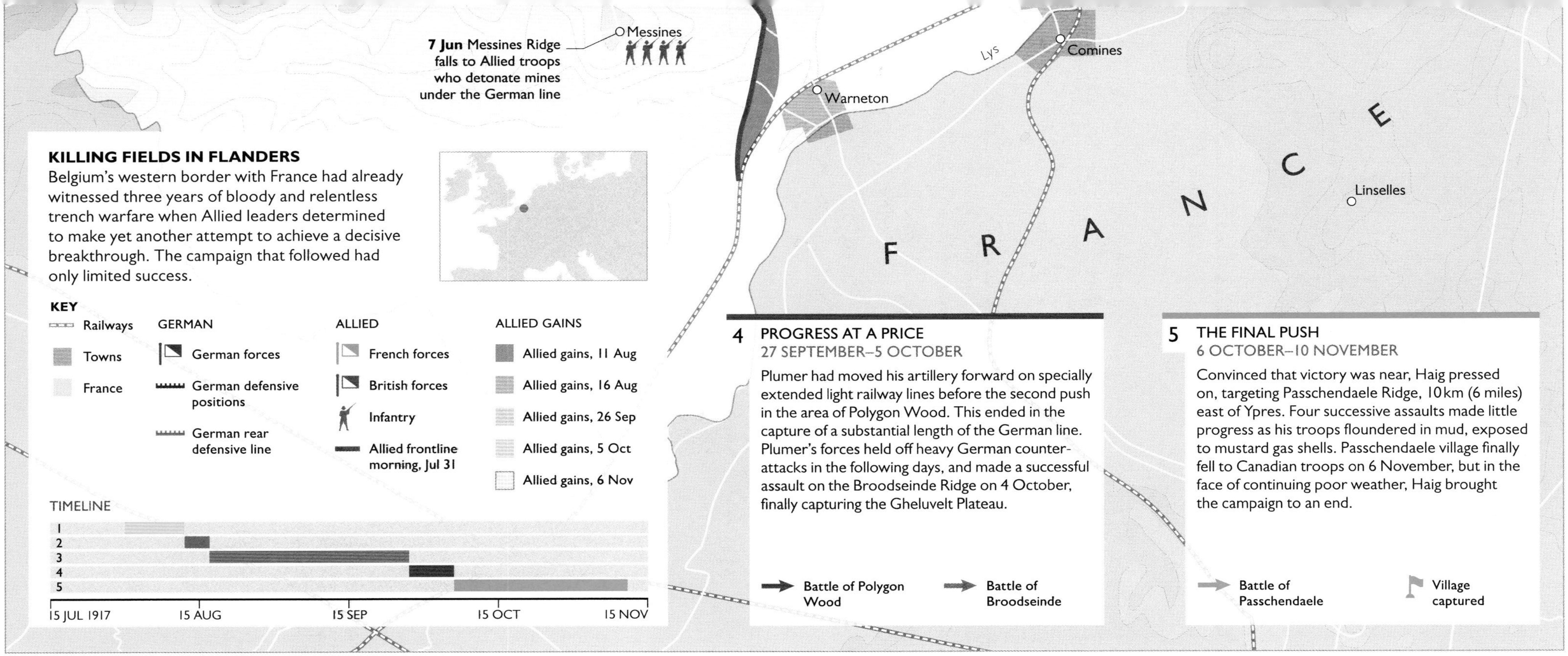
7 Jun Messines Ridge falls to Allied troops who detonate mines under the German line
Messines
Warneton
Lys
Comines
Linselles
F R A N C E
KEY
Railways
Towns
France
GERMAN
German forces
German defensive positions
German rear defensive line
ALLIED
French forces
British forces
Infantry
Allied frontline morning, Jul 31
ALLIED GAINS
Allied gains, 11 Aug
Allied gains, 16 Aug
Allied gains, 26 Sep
Allied gains, 5 Oct
Allied gains, 6 Nov
TIMELINE
1
2
3
4
5
15 JUL 1917
15 AUG
15 SEP
15 OCT
15 NOV
Battle of Polygon Wood
Battle of Broodseinde
Battle of Passchendaele
Village captured

KILLING FIELDS IN FLANDERS
Belgium's western border with France had already witnessed three years of bloody and relentless trench warfare when Allied leaders determined to make yet another attempt to achieve a decisive breakthrough. The campaign that followed had only limited success.

4 PROGRESS AT A PRICE
27 SEPTEMBER–5 OCTOBER
Plumer had moved his artillery forward on specially extended light railway lines before the second push in the area of Polygon Wood. This ended in the capture of a substantial length of the German line. Plumer's forces held off heavy German counter-attacks in the following days, and made a successful assault on the Broodseinde Ridge on 4 October, finally capturing the Gheluvelt Plateau.

5 THE FINAL PUSH
6 OCTOBER–10 NOVEMBER
Convinced that victory was near, Haig pressed on, targeting Passchendaele Ridge, 10 km (6 miles) east of Ypres. Four successive assaults made little progress as his troops floundered in mud, exposed to mustard gas shells. Passchendaele village finally fell to Canadian troops on 6 November, but in the face of continuing poor weather, Haig brought the campaign to an end.

PASSCHENDAELE

The Third Battle of Ypres – also known as Passchendaele, from the final objective captured – was another terrible battle of mutual attrition on World War I's Western Front. The Allies incurred a terrible death toll to make limited advances in the three-month campaign.

After France's Nivelle Offensive in spring 1917 failed, and caused a mutiny among the demoralized and exhausted French soldiers, there was understandable doubt about the wisdom of a similar British attack. Prime Minister David Lloyd George was sceptical, but British commander Field Marshal Sir Douglas Haig finally won approval for an offensive to improve the tactical situation in the long-contested salient at Ypres in Belgium, thereby also continuing to wear down the German army while the French recovered from their trauma.

> *"It's just not conceivable how human beings can exist in such a swamp, let alone fight in it."*
>
> ALLIED PILOT AFTER FLYING OVER THE BATTLEFIELD

The targets selected by Haig included the railway junction at Roulers (Roeselare) – some 20 km (12 miles) east of Ypres – that served as an important staging post for the German army. Success at Roulers may have permitted an Allied advance on the Belgian ports, which were used as forward bases for the U-boats that were threatening British shipping. A preparatory attack in June succeeded in taking the ridge at Messines, south of Ypres, raising Allied hopes of success.

The Allies failed in their main objectives. Unseasonably heavy rain and the destruction of drainage channels by shelling turned the plain around Ypres into a morass, making progress painfully slow. Moreover, the flatness of the terrain made stealthy attacks impossible. After three months, the Allied front had advanced by just a few kilometres. The price, in human lives, was high – around 250,000 casualties were sustained by each side.

△ **Fighting in a quagmire**
Torrential rain made parts of the battlefield impassible to vehicles, including tanks, and gave the Germans, who occupied higher ground, a tactical advantage.

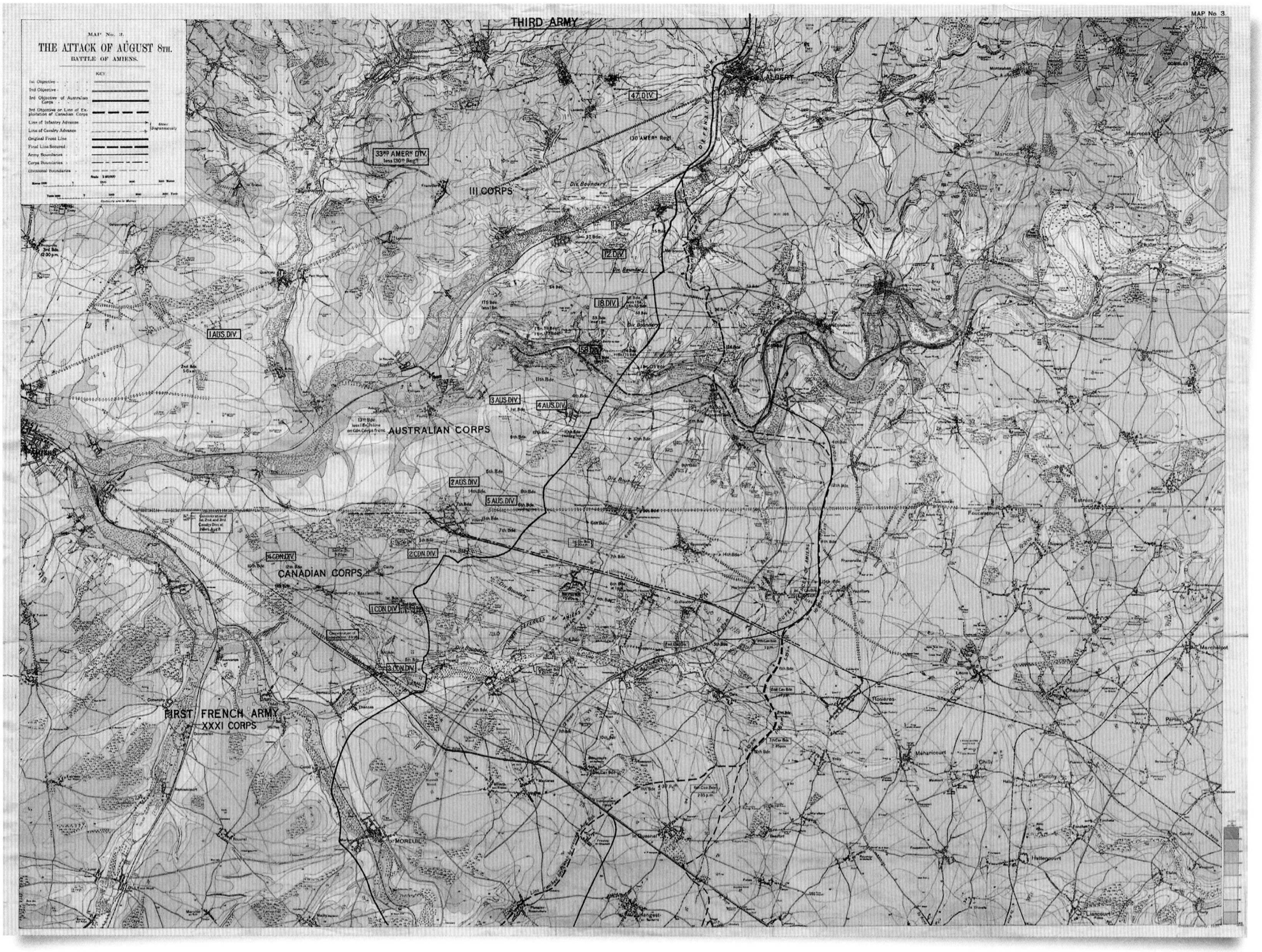
MAP No. 3
THE ATTACK OF AUGUST 8TH.
BATTLE OF AMIENS.
KEY
THIRD ARMY
47.DIV.
33RD AMERN DIV.
III CORPS
12.DIV.
18.DIV.
1 AUS. DIV.
58 DIV.
3 AUS. DIV.
4 AUS. DIV.
AUSTRALIAN CORPS
2 AUS. DIV.
5 AUS. DIV.
4 CDN. DIV.
2 CDN. DIV.
CANADIAN CORPS
1 CDN. DIV.
3 CDN. DIV.
FIRST FRENCH ARMY
XXXI CORPS
MOREUIL
ALBERT

△ **The first day of battle**
This post-war map of the Amiens battlefield, covering an area stretching 40km (25 miles) to the east of the city, shows the gains made on the first day of the clash when Allied forces drove overstretched German troops back more than 10km (6 miles).

AMIENS

In August 1918, the Allied powers launched a massive attack on German forces near Amiens, in northern France. It marked the start of the Hundred Days Offensive, which would finally break German morale and end World War I three months later.

In spring 1918, the situation for Germany looked hopeful: Russia had withdrawn from the conflict in March, allowing German strategists to concentrate their attention on the Western front. Erich Ludendorff, commanding the General Staff, pinned his hopes on a decisive breakthrough before the US (which had entered the war in 1917 on the side of the Allied Powers) sent large numbers of its troops to Europe.

Ludendorff's Spring Offensive initially made significant progress. At Saint-Quentin, British forces were driven back 60km (37 miles); on the River Aisne, French defences gave way, allowing a breakthrough to the River Marne that threatened Paris. Yet none of the assaults achieved the gains that Ludendorff needed.

By August, the Allies were ready to deliver a decisive blow. They chose the area east of Amiens, in northern France, where British, Australian, and Canadian units were flanked to the south by the French First Army. Tanks and infantry launched an assault through the mist at dawn on 8 August, achieving total surprise and causing the German troops to break and run. Around 30,000 of them were killed, wounded, or captured on what Ludendorff would call "the black day of the German army". What followed for the Germans was a fighting retreat, driven on by the arrival of battle-fresh US forces in their hundreds of thousands. By the end of that month, Ludendorff realized that there was no prospect of a German victory in the war.

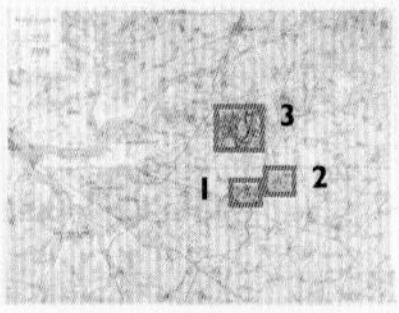
3
1
2

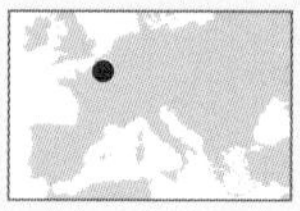

KEY

1 Australian forces managed to advance as far as Harbonnières by 11 am on the first day of fighting.

2 British armoured cars captured the headquarters of the German 11th Corps at Framerville at around noon

3 British forces met heavy resistance at Chipilly, on the north bank of the Somme.

WARSAW

To inhibit further Allied intervention in the Russian civil war, Lenin sent the Red Army westwards in the hope of spreading the revolution across Europe. In August 1920, outside Warsaw, capital of the newly independent Poland, the Red Army advance was brought to a halt.

As the Red Army gained the upper hand in the long civil war which followed the Bolshevik Revolution of 1917, Lenin sought to export Communism beyond Russia's borders and so undermine the Allied regimes which had intervened in favour of his "White" opponents. The revived Polish nation had occupied much of Belorussia and western Ukraine by May 1920, but by August the Red Army had driven Polish forces all the way back to their new capital, Warsaw. Polish leader Józef Piłsudski aimed to hold the invaders in a last-ditch defence outside the capital while also delivering a flank attack from the south on their weak left wing. The plan proved successful, and within a week, the Red Army was in headlong retreat. The setback effectively put an end to Lenin's hopes of spreading revolution by force of arms to Western Europe.

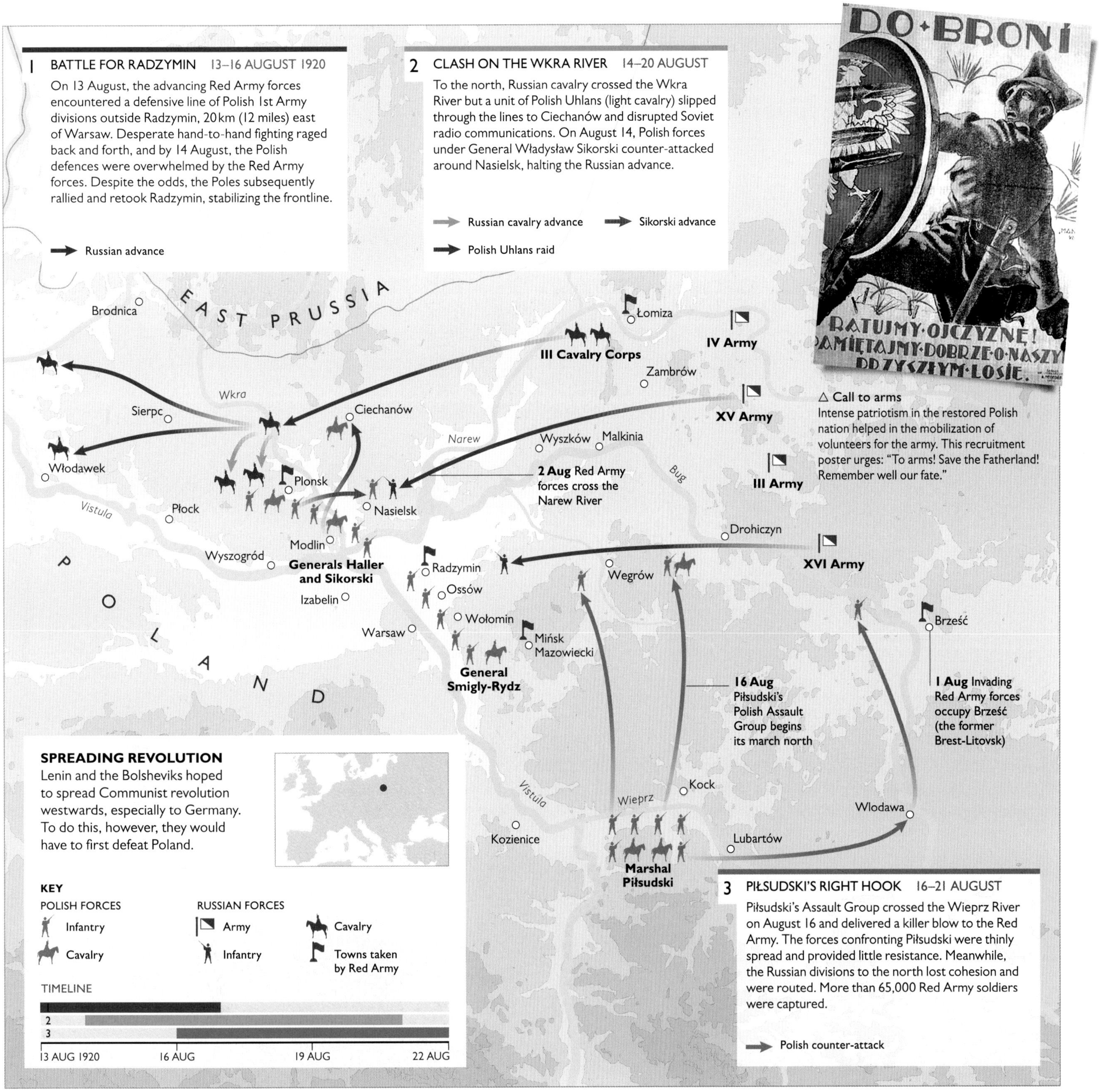
1 BATTLE FOR RADZYMIN 13–16 AUGUST 1920
On 13 August, the advancing Red Army forces encountered a defensive line of Polish 1st Army divisions outside Radzymin, 20 km (12 miles) east of Warsaw. Desperate hand-to-hand fighting raged back and forth, and by 14 August, the Polish defences were overwhelmed by the Red Army forces. Despite the odds, the Poles subsequently rallied and retook Radzymin, stabilizing the frontline.
Russian advance
2 CLASH ON THE WKRA RIVER 14–20 AUGUST
To the north, Russian cavalry crossed the Wkra River but a unit of Polish Uhlans (light cavalry) slipped through the lines to Ciechanów and disrupted Soviet radio communications. On August 14, Polish forces under General Władysław Sikorski counter-attacked around Nasielsk, halting the Russian advance.
Russian cavalry advance
Sikorski advance
Polish Uhlans raid
EAST PRUSSIA
Brodnica
Łomiza
IV Army
III Cavalry Corps
Zambrów
Wkra
Sierpc
Ciechanów
XV Army
Narew
Wyszków
Malkinia
Włodawek
Plonsk
2 Aug Red Army forces cross the Narew River
Bug
III Army
Vistula
Płock
Nasielsk
Drohiczyn
Modlin
Wyszogród
Generals Haller and Sikorski
Radzymin
XVI Army
Ossów
Wegrów
Izabelin
POLAND
Wołomin
Brześć
Warsaw
Mińsk Mazowiecki
General Smigly-Rydz
16 Aug Piłsudski's Polish Assault Group begins its march north
1 Aug Invading Red Army forces occupy Brześć (the former Brest-Litovsk)
SPREADING REVOLUTION
Lenin and the Bolsheviks hoped to spread Communist revolution westwards, especially to Germany. To do this, however, they would have to first defeat Poland.
Vistula
Kock
Wieprz
Wlodawa
Kozienice
Lubartów
Marshal Piłsudski
KEY
POLISH FORCES
Infantry
Cavalry
RUSSIAN FORCES
Army
Infantry
Cavalry
Towns taken by Red Army
TIMELINE
1
2
3
13 AUG 1920
16 AUG
19 AUG
22 AUG
3 PIŁSUDSKI'S RIGHT HOOK 16–21 AUGUST
Piłsudski's Assault Group crossed the Wieprz River on August 16 and delivered a killer blow to the Red Army. The forces confronting Piłsudski were thinly spread and provided little resistance. Meanwhile, the Russian divisions to the north lost cohesion and were routed. More than 65,000 Red Army soldiers were captured.
Polish counter-attack
DO·BRONI
RATUJMY·OJCZYZNĘ!
PAMIĘTAJMY·DOBRZE·O·NASZYM
PRZYSZŁYM·LOSIE.

△ **Call to arms**
Intense patriotism in the restored Polish nation helped in the mobilization of volunteers for the army. This recruitment poster urges: "To arms! Save the Fatherland! Remember well our fate."

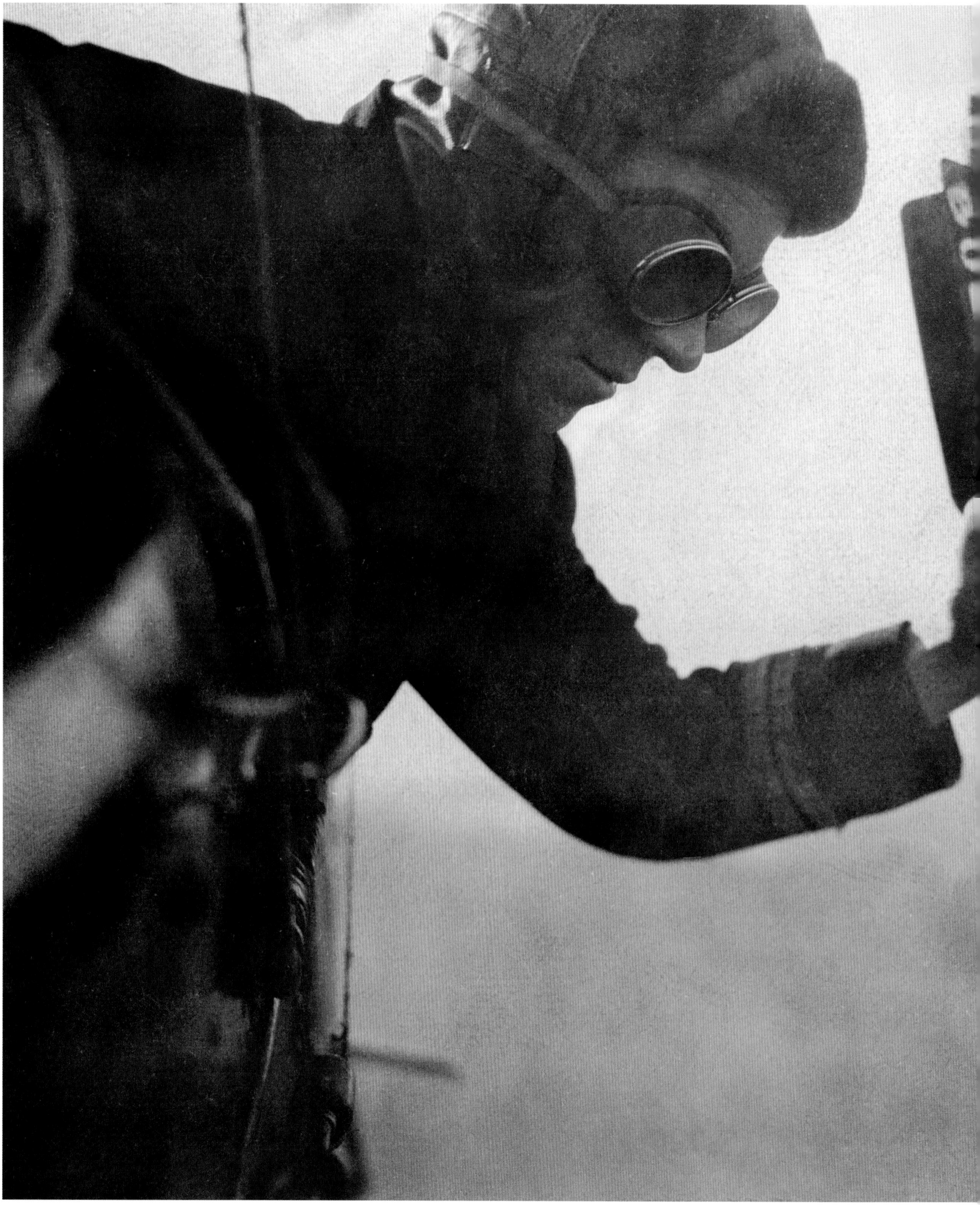

HUN

Bombing by hand
A British airman drops a small bomb by hand from his open cockpit. This primitive technique was used for tactical bombing early in World War I. Later in the war, larger bombs were dropped using mechanical release systems.

EARLY MILITARY AIRCRAFT

World War I was the first major conflict fought in the air as well as on land and sea. Military aircraft battled for control of the skies, attacked troops on the ground, and bombed civilians in cities.

▷ **German fighter**
The Fokker Dr.I triplane, introduced in 1917, is an example of a World War I aircraft specifically designed for air-to-air combat.

When the war began in 1914, all the combatants together fielded no more than 500 flimsy, unarmed reconnaissance aircraft. By the end of the war in 1918, Britain alone had more than 20,000 aircraft. These had diversified to include specialist fighters, armed with machine guns for air-to-air combat, and multi-engined bombers. The primary role of these aircraft was to support the army, photographing enemy lines to help artillery hit its targets or strafing and bombing ground forces. However, the "dogfights" between fighter aircraft attracted most attention. Propagandists praised fighter pilots as "knights of the air", making heroes of "aces" with high scores of enemy aircraft shot down.

Turning point

The bombing of cities was a controversial development that gave air power an independent role. Germany attacked London in 1915, first with its fleet of airships and then with bomber aircraft. Britain and France, in turn, bombed German cities. For the time, civilian casualties were relatively low – 1,400 killed in Britain. However, the arrival of strategic bombing was a turning point in modern warfare.

△ **Airships at war**
Germany deployed more than 50 Zeppelin and Schütte-Lanze airships between 1915 and 1918 to bomb London and Paris. They terrorized civilians, but being slow-moving and inflammable, they proved vulnerable to attacks by fighter aircraft.

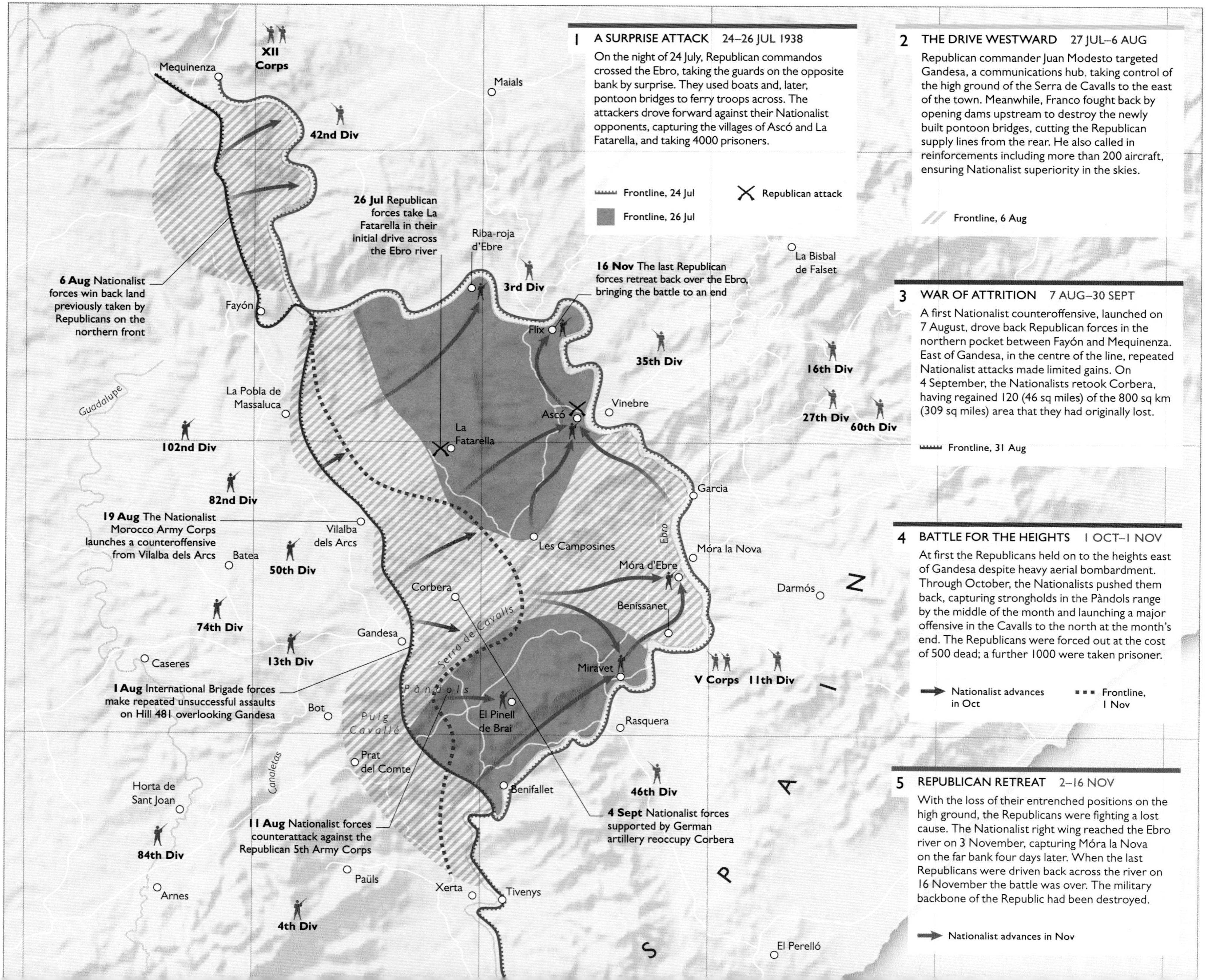
Mequinenza
XII Corps
42nd Div
Maials
6 Aug Nationalist forces win back land previously taken by Republicans on the northern front
Fayón
26 Jul Republican forces take La Fatarella in their initial drive across the Ebro river
Riba-roja d'Ebre
3rd Div
16 Nov The last Republican forces retreat back over the Ebro, bringing the battle to an end
La Bisbal de Falset
Flix
35th Div
16th Div
Guadalupe
La Pobla de Massaluca
102nd Div
La Fatarella
Ascó
Vinebre
27th Div
60th Div
82nd Div
Garcia
19 Aug The Nationalist Morocco Army Corps launches a counteroffensive from Vilalba dels Arcs
Vilalba dels Arcs
Batea
50th Div
Les Camposines
Ebro
Móra la Nova
Móra d'Ebre
Corbera
Darmós
Benissanet
74th Div
Gandesa
Serra de Cavalls
Caseres
13th Div
Miravet
V Corps
11th Div
1 Aug International Brigade forces make repeated unsuccessful assaults on Hill 481 overlooking Gandesa
Pàndols
Bot
Puig Cavallé
El Pinell de Brai
Rasquera
Prat del Comte
Candletas
Horta de Sant Joan
Benifallet
46th Div
11 Aug Nationalist forces counterattack against the Republican 5th Army Corps
4 Sept Nationalist forces supported by German artillery reoccupy Corbera
84th Div
Paüls
Xerta
Tivenys
Arnes
4th Div
El Perelló
S P A I N

1 A SURPRISE ATTACK 24–26 JUL 1938

On the night of 24 July, Republican commandos crossed the Ebro, taking the guards on the opposite bank by surprise. They used boats and, later, pontoon bridges to ferry troops across. The attackers drove forward against their Nationalist opponents, capturing the villages of Ascó and La Fatarella, and taking 4000 prisoners.

Frontline, 24 Jul
Frontline, 26 Jul
Republican attack

2 THE DRIVE WESTWARD 27 JUL–6 AUG

Republican commander Juan Modesto targeted Gandesa, a communications hub, taking control of the high ground of the Serra de Cavalls to the east of the town. Meanwhile, Franco fought back by opening dams upstream to destroy the newly built pontoon bridges, cutting the Republican supply lines from the rear. He also called in reinforcements including more than 200 aircraft, ensuring Nationalist superiority in the skies.

Frontline, 6 Aug

3 WAR OF ATTRITION 7 AUG–30 SEPT

A first Nationalist counteroffensive, launched on 7 August, drove back Republican forces in the northern pocket between Fayón and Mequinenza. East of Gandesa, in the centre of the line, repeated Nationalist attacks made limited gains. On 4 September, the Nationalists retook Corbera, having regained 120 (46 sq miles) of the 800 sq km (309 sq miles) area that they had originally lost.

Frontline, 31 Aug

4 BATTLE FOR THE HEIGHTS 1 OCT–1 NOV

At first the Republicans held on to the heights east of Gandesa despite heavy aerial bombardment. Through October, the Nationalists pushed them back, capturing strongholds in the Pàndols range by the middle of the month and launching a major offensive in the Cavalls to the north at the month's end. The Republicans were forced out at the cost of 500 dead; a further 1000 were taken prisoner.

Nationalist advances in Oct
Frontline, 1 Nov

5 REPUBLICAN RETREAT 2–16 NOV

With the loss of their entrenched positions on the high ground, the Republicans were fighting a lost cause. The Nationalist right wing reached the Ebro river on 3 November, capturing Móra la Nova on the far bank four days later. When the last Republicans were driven back across the river on 16 November the battle was over. The military backbone of the Republic had been destroyed.

Nationalist advances in Nov

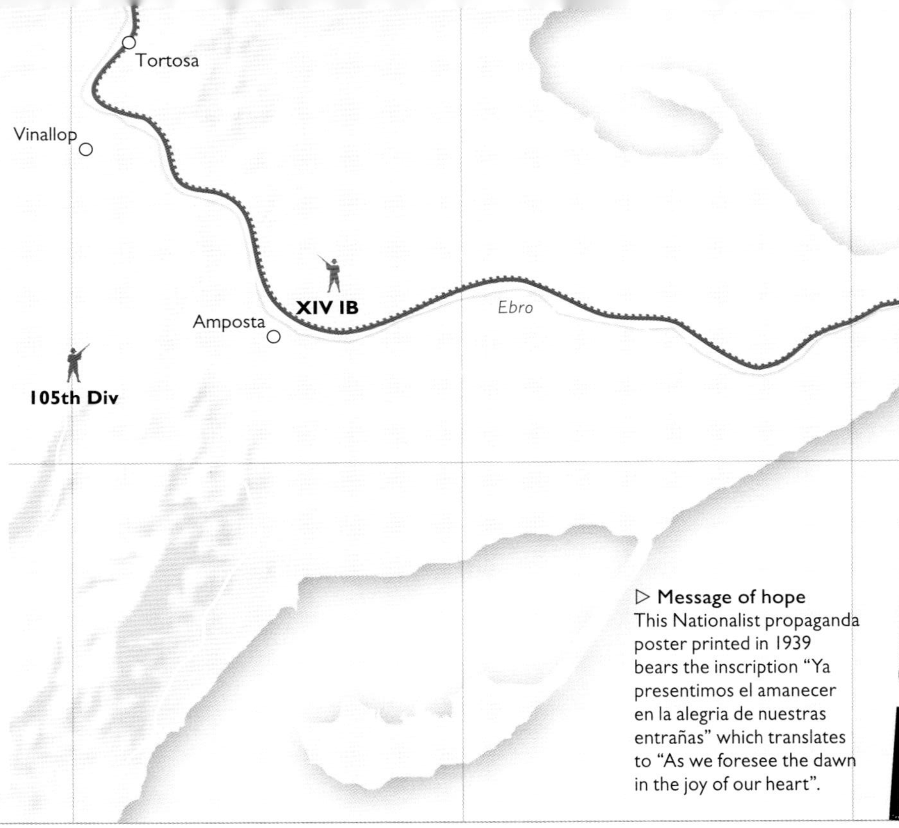
Sierra de Cardo
Tortosa
Vinallop
Amposta
XIV IB
105th Div
Ebro
Balearic Sea

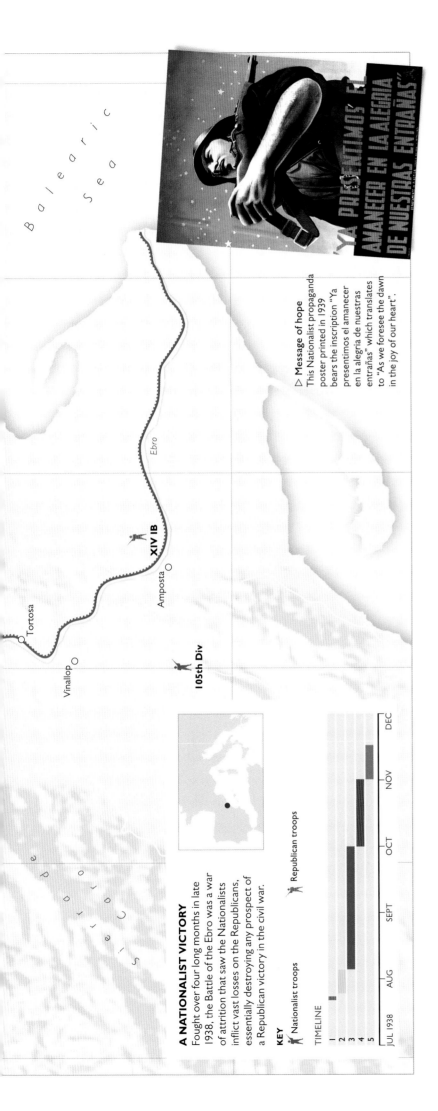

A NATIONALIST VICTORY
Fought over four long months in late 1938, the Battle of the Ebro was a war of attrition that saw the Nationalists inflict vast losses on the Republicans, essentially destroying any prospect of a Republican victory in the civil war.

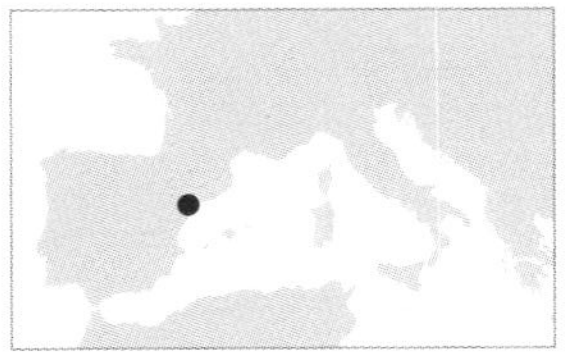

KEY
Nationalist troops
Republican troops

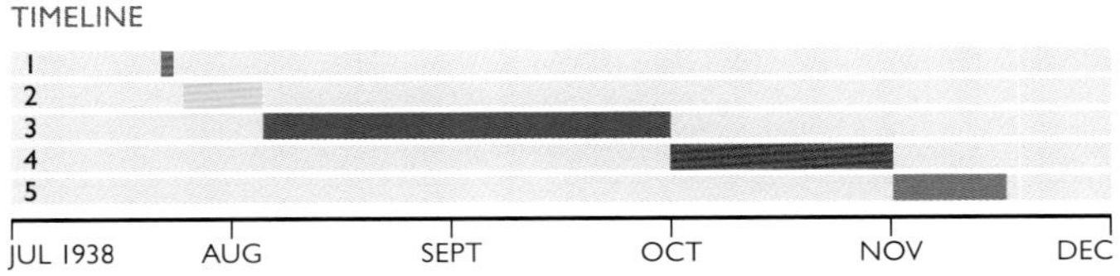
TIMELINE
1
2
3
4
5
JUL 1938
AUG
SEPT
OCT
NOV
DEC

"YA PRESENTIMOS EL AMANECER EN LA ALEGRIA DE NUESTRAS ENTRAÑAS"

▷ **Message of hope**
This Nationalist propaganda poster printed in 1939 bears the inscription "Ya presentimos el amanecer en la alegria de nuestras entrañas" which translates to "As we foresee the dawn in the joy of our heart".

THE EBRO

The climactic battle of the Spanish Civil War was fought on arid, hilly country on the west bank of the Ebro river. After making initial gains, the Republican forces were driven back by their Nationalist opponents, aided by German and Italian units. They never recovered from the setback.

Following a general election that had split the country between left- and right-wing ideologies, the Spanish Civil War broke out in 1936 when a section of Spain's armed forces launched a coup against the Republican Popular Front government. The Republicans fought back, plunging the country into three years of bloodshed. The war also had an international dimension: the Nationalist forces, led by General Francisco Franco, received aid from Hitler's Germany and Mussolini's Italy, while the Republicans were supported by the Soviet Union and by anti-Fascist volunteers from many countries in the International Brigades.

Despite fierce resistance, the Republicans lost ground in 1937 to Franco's better trained and well supplied forces. They suffered a major setback in April 1938 when the Nationalists advanced to the Mediterranean, cutting Catalonia off from the Republicans' remaining territory in southeastern Spain.

The Republican leadership responded with an all-out assault along the Ebro river, designed to reunite the two regions and protect their seat of government in Valencia. Initially the plan worked, raising Republican hopes, before relentless bombing by the German Condor Legion and the Italian Aviazione Legionaria turned the tables. The result was disastrous for the Republic; Barcelona was lost a couple of months later, and on April 1 1939, after Madrid fell, Franco was able to proclaim a Nationalist victory.

> *"Even if they bomb the bridge / You'll see me cross the Ebro / In a skiff or a canoe."*
>
> TRANSLATION FROM A REPUBLICAN SONG

A DIVIDED LAND
By spring 1938, Franco's Nationalist troops had driven a wedge between the two Republican-held areas of Spain. The Republican leadership decided on an all-out offensive as a final throw of the dice, choosing the Ebro river as the site of the confrontation.

KEY
Main battle
Rebel Nationalists
Republican Spain
FRANCE
ANDORRA
CATALONIA
Barcelona
Tortosa
Bilbao
Pamplona
Zaragoza
Valladolid
Madrid
Toledo
Valencia
Balearic Islands
Minorca
Majorca
Oporto
Coimbra
Lisbon
PORTUGAL
ATLANTIC OCEAN
Cordoba
Seville
Granada
Cartagena
Alicante
Cadiz
Malaga
Mediterranean Sea
Tangier
Melilla
ALGERIA
Fez
Casablanca
MOROCCO

EVACUATING DUNKIRK

In spring 1940, routed by the Germans in one of the opening campaigns of World War II, hundreds of thousands of soldiers of the British army and its allies were trapped on the French coast at Dunkirk. Their evacuation by sea was an epic feat of valour

After the British and French declared war on Nazi Germany at the start of World War II in September 1939, a British Expeditionary Force (BEF) was sent to France. It saw no fighting until 10 May 1940 when the Germans invaded the Netherlands, and Belgium, crossing into France two days later. Spearheaded by tanks operating with air support, German forces rapidly broke through the French defences at Sedan and swung northward towards the Channel coast. The BEF, which had advanced into Belgium, was threatened with being cut off from the rear. As the situation worsened, the Allies abandoned their plan to break through the German encirclement and join French forces to the south. Instead, the BEF fell back on Dunkirk, the only port within reach still in Allied hands, albeit precariously.

On 23 May, General Alan Brooke, a British corps commander, wrote: "Nothing but a miracle can save the BEF now". In the event, with the help of civilians (see below), almost 340,000 Allied soldiers were evacuated to Britain from the harbour and beaches of Dunkirk, two-thirds of them British, and nearly 200,000 more from operations at other French ports. The skill and courage of the evacuation enabled British propagandists to represent a crushing defeat as a triumphant escape, although Prime Minister Winston Churchill warned: "Wars are not won by evacuations". The evacuation left a legacy of bitterness in France, where many felt they had been abandoned by their British allies. After France surrendered on 22 June, Britain opted to fight on, encouraged in its defiance of Hitler by the "miracle of Dunkirk".

THE "LITTLE SHIPS" OF DUNKIRK

Most soldiers were evacuated to Britain on board Royal Navy destroyers and minesweepers, but a flotilla of small boats, some crewed by civilians, also played a crucial role in the evacuation. Most were already registered with the navy as part of its "small vessels pool". From trawlers and tug boats to lifeboats and private yachts, they sailed into shallow water to take men off the beaches, often ferrying them to warships further offshore. About 200 "little ships" were lost in the perilous operation.

A civilian "little ship" at Dunkirk

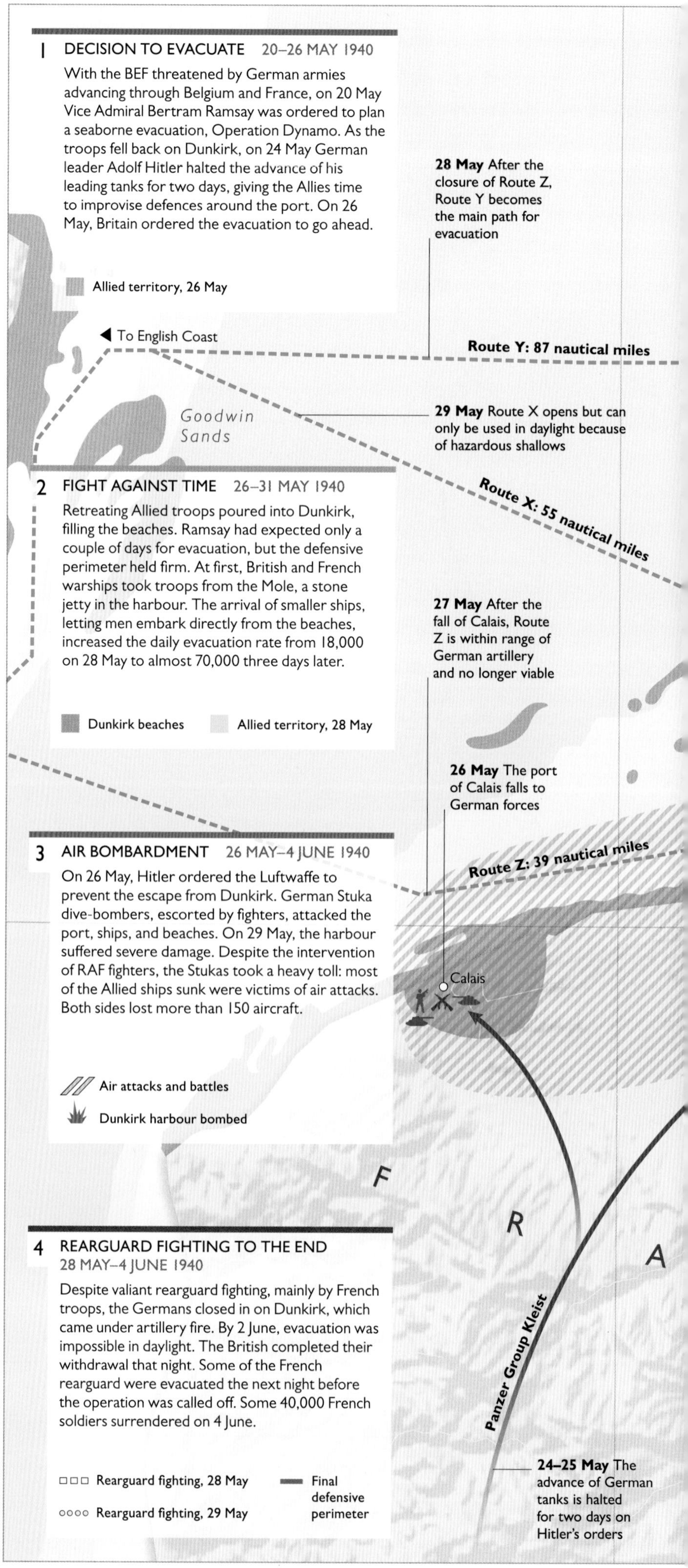

28 May After the closure of Route Z, Route Y becomes the main path for evacuation
To English Coast
Route Y: 87 nautical miles
Goodwin Sands
29 May Route X opens but can only be used in daylight because of hazardous shallows
Route X: 55 nautical miles
27 May After the fall of Calais, Route Z is within range of German artillery and no longer viable
26 May The port of Calais falls to German forces
Route Z: 39 nautical miles
Calais
F
R
A
Panzer Group Kleist
24–25 May The advance of German tanks is halted for two days on Hitler's orders

1 DECISION TO EVACUATE 20–26 MAY 1940

With the BEF threatened by German armies advancing through Belgium and France, on 20 May Vice Admiral Bertram Ramsay was ordered to plan a seaborne evacuation, Operation Dynamo. As the troops fell back on Dunkirk, on 24 May German leader Adolf Hitler halted the advance of his leading tanks for two days, giving the Allies time to improvise defences around the port. On 26 May, Britain ordered the evacuation to go ahead.

Allied territory, 26 May

2 FIGHT AGAINST TIME 26–31 MAY 1940

Retreating Allied troops poured into Dunkirk, filling the beaches. Ramsay had expected only a couple of days for evacuation, but the defensive perimeter held firm. At first, British and French warships took troops from the Mole, a stone jetty in the harbour. The arrival of smaller ships, letting men embark directly from the beaches, increased the daily evacuation rate from 18,000 on 28 May to almost 70,000 three days later.

Dunkirk beaches — Allied territory, 28 May

3 AIR BOMBARDMENT 26 MAY–4 JUNE 1940

On 26 May, Hitler ordered the Luftwaffe to prevent the escape from Dunkirk. German Stuka dive-bombers, escorted by fighters, attacked the port, ships, and beaches. On 29 May, the harbour suffered severe damage. Despite the intervention of RAF fighters, the Stukas took a heavy toll: most of the Allied ships sunk were victims of air attacks. Both sides lost more than 150 aircraft.

Air attacks and battles

Dunkirk harbour bombed

4 REARGUARD FIGHTING TO THE END 28 MAY–4 JUNE 1940

Despite valiant rearguard fighting, mainly by French troops, the Germans closed in on Dunkirk, which came under artillery fire. By 2 June, evacuation was impossible in daylight. The British completed their withdrawal that night. Some of the French rearguard were evacuated the next night before the operation was called off. Some 40,000 French soldiers surrendered on 4 June.

Rearguard fighting, 28 May — Final defensive perimeter

Rearguard fighting, 29 May

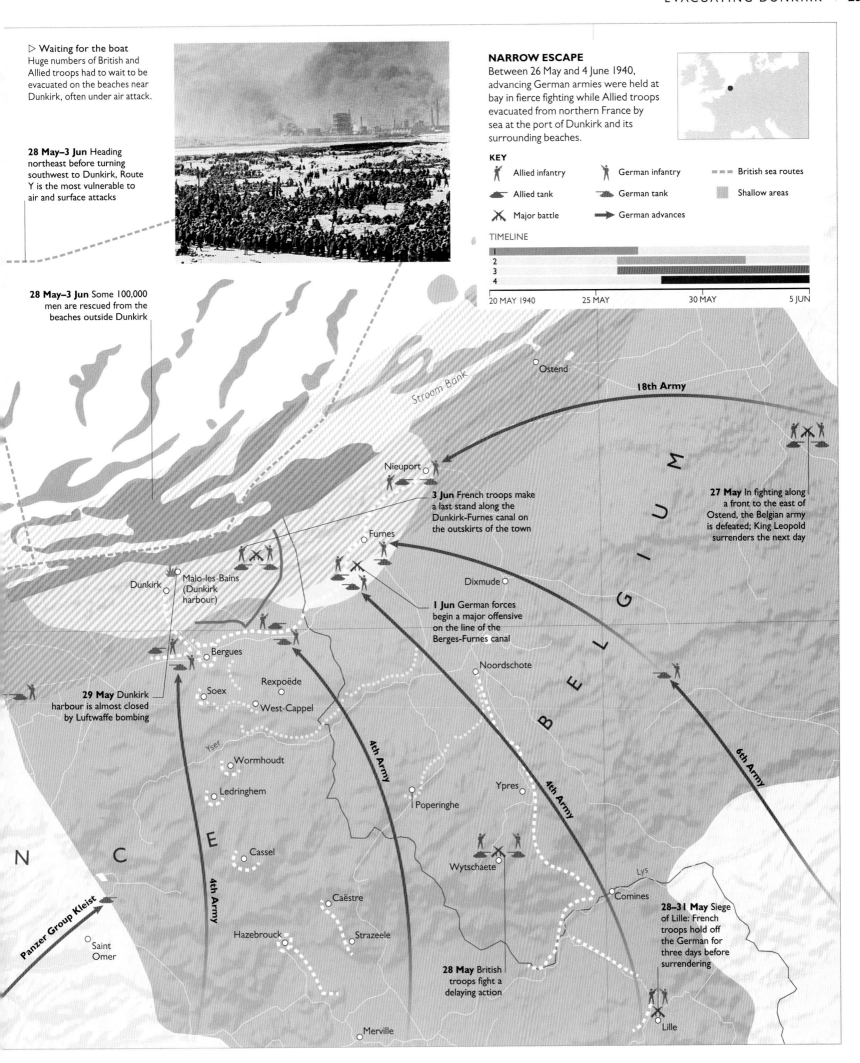

▷ Waiting for the boat
Huge numbers of British and Allied troops had to wait to be evacuated on the beaches near Dunkirk, often under air attack.

28 May–3 Jun Heading northeast before turning southwest to Dunkirk, Route Y is the most vulnerable to air and surface attacks

NARROW ESCAPE

Between 26 May and 4 June 1940, advancing German armies were held at bay in fierce fighting while Allied troops evacuated from northern France by sea at the port of Dunkirk and its surrounding beaches.

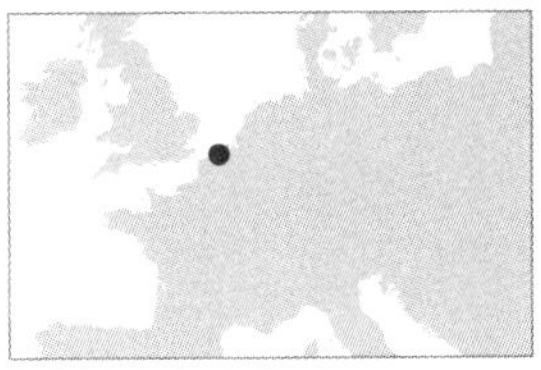

KEY

- Allied infantry
- Allied tank
- Major battle
- German infantry
- German tank
- German advances
- British sea routes
- Shallow areas

TIMELINE

1
2
3
4

20 MAY 1940 | 25 MAY | 30 MAY | 5 JUN

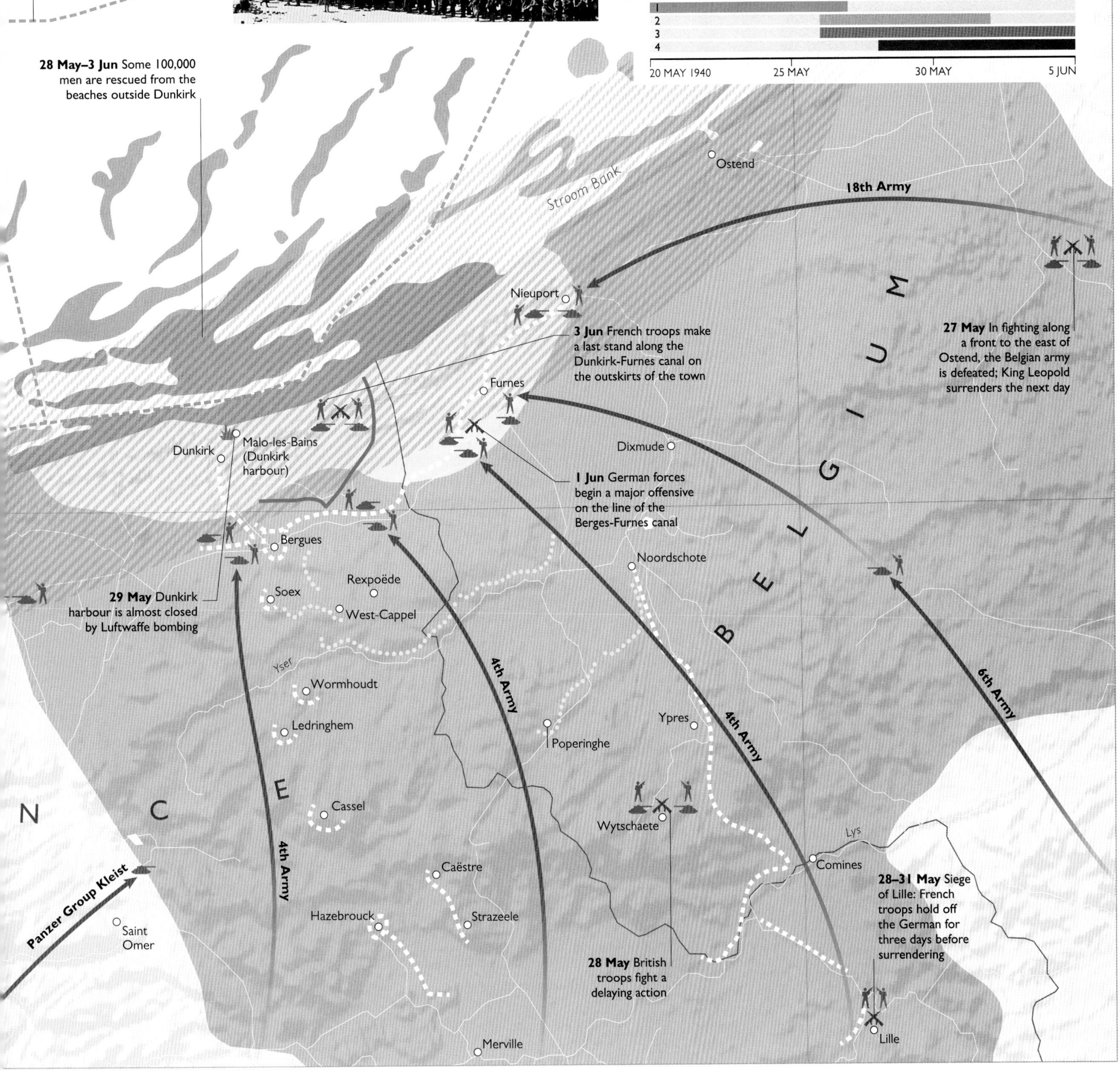
28 May–3 Jun Some 100,000 men are rescued from the beaches outside Dunkirk
Stroom Bank
Ostend
18th Army
Nieuport
3 Jun French troops make a last stand along the Dunkirk-Furnes canal on the outskirts of the town
27 May In fighting along a front to the east of Ostend, the Belgian army is defeated; King Leopold surrenders the next day
Furnes
Dunkirk
Malo-les-Bains (Dunkirk harbour)
Dixmude
1 Jun German forces begin a major offensive on the line of the Berges-Furnes canal
Bergues
Noordschote
Rexpoëde
Soex
West-Cappel
29 May Dunkirk harbour is almost closed by Luftwaffe bombing
B E L G I U M
Yser
Wormhoudt
4th Army
Ledringhem
Poperinghe
Ypres
4th Army
6th Army
N C E
Cassel
Wytschaete
Lys
Comines
Panzer Group Kleist
4th Army
Caëstre
28–31 May Siege of Lille: French troops hold off the German for three days before surrendering
Saint Omer
Hazebrouck
Strazeele
28 May British troops fight a delaying action
Merville
Lille

THE BATTLE OF BRITAIN

Fought between the British and German air forces, the Battle of Britain was a major turning point in World War II. The Royal Air Force (RAF) successfully resisted the Luftwaffe's bid to win command of the air, freeing Britain from the threat of a German invasion.

The Germans' victorious campaigns in spring 1940 (see pp.230–31) allowed the Luftwaffe to establish air bases within close range of southern England, in France and Belgium. Planning a seaborne invasion of Britain, Hitler needed to defeat the RAF to allow his planes to counter the superior Royal Navy. Luftwaffe commander Hermann Goering confidently predicted a swift victory. Britain's air defences, however, were well prepared. A chain of radar stations, aided by ground observers, provided early warning of enemy aircraft, and allowed radio-directed squadrons of fighter aircraft to intercept the intruders. Air Chief Marshal Hugh Dowding, head of RAF Fighter Command, conserved his resources in an attritional battle. While Britain's factories produced plentiful fighter aircraft, at times pilots were scarce. Commonwealth nations, Czechoslovakia, and Poland, all contributed fliers crucial to Britain's survival.

Faced with the unbroken resilience of the RAF, the German invasion plan was abandoned, and the Luftwaffe turned to nighttime bombing. London and other British cities were badly hit in the "Blitz" raids that lasted until May 1941. Nevertheless, in failing to defeat the RAF, Hitler had suffered his first serious setback of the war.

> *"Never in the field of human conflict was so much owed by so many to so few."*
>
> WINSTON CHURCHILL, 20 AUGUST 1940

HERMANN GOERING 1893–1946

After winning fame as a fighter pilot in World War I, Hermann Goering joined the Nazi Party in the 1920s and became one of Adolf Hitler's most powerful associates. Designated Reichsmarschall, the highest rank in the German armed forces, he took personal command of the air campaign against Britain in summer 1940. Its failure severely undermined his prestige. Prosecuted as a war criminal after Germany's defeat, he committed suicide to avoid execution.

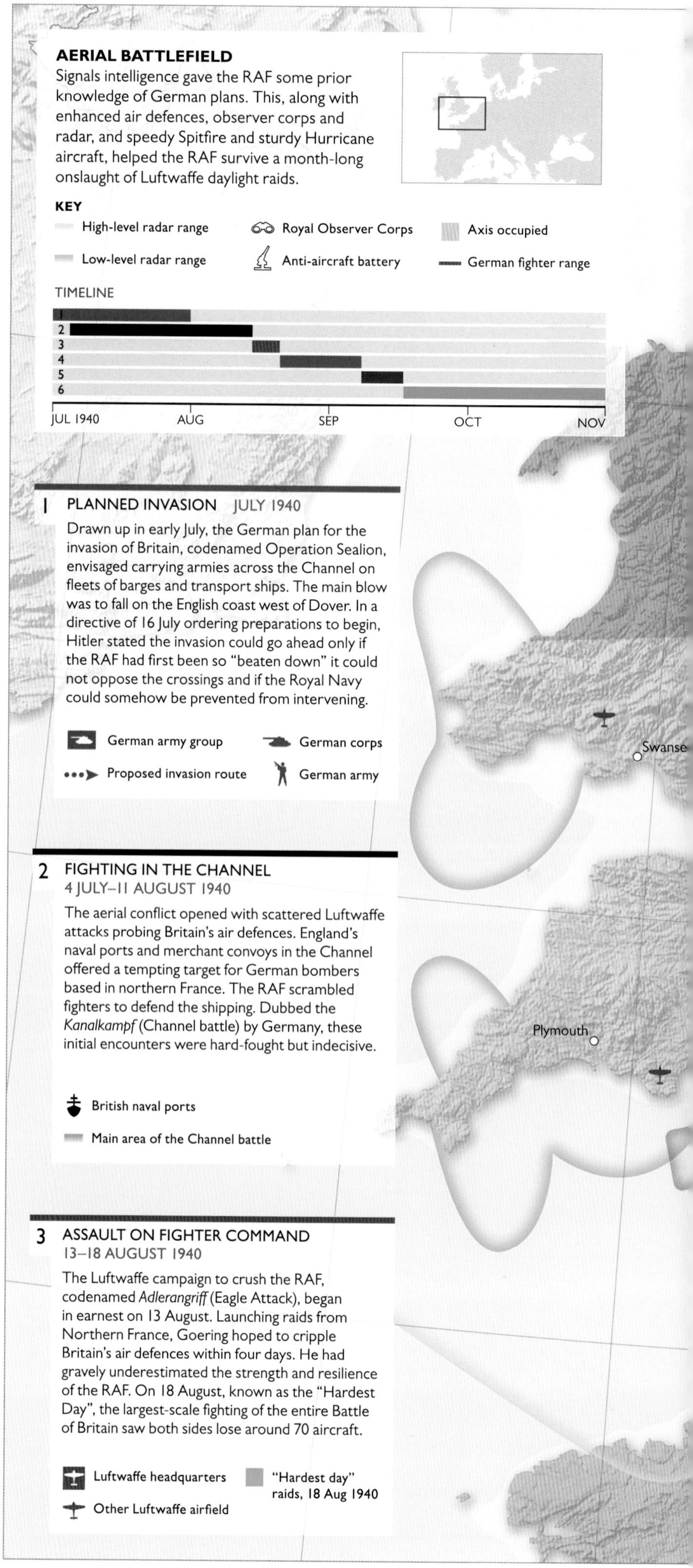
Swanse
Plymouth

AERIAL BATTLEFIELD

Signals intelligence gave the RAF some prior knowledge of German plans. This, along with enhanced air defences, observer corps and radar, and speedy Spitfire and sturdy Hurricane aircraft, helped the RAF survive a month-long onslaught of Luftwaffe daylight raids.

KEY

- High-level radar range
- Low-level radar range
- Royal Observer Corps
- Anti-aircraft battery
- Axis occupied
- German fighter range

TIMELINE

1 2 3 4 5 6

JUL 1940 AUG SEP OCT NOV

1 PLANNED INVASION JULY 1940

Drawn up in early July, the German plan for the invasion of Britain, codenamed Operation Sealion, envisaged carrying armies across the Channel on fleets of barges and transport ships. The main blow was to fall on the English coast west of Dover. In a directive of 16 July ordering preparations to begin, Hitler stated the invasion could go ahead only if the RAF had first been so "beaten down" it could not oppose the crossings and if the Royal Navy could somehow be prevented from intervening.

- German army group
- German corps
- Proposed invasion route
- German army

2 FIGHTING IN THE CHANNEL 4 JULY–11 AUGUST 1940

The aerial conflict opened with scattered Luftwaffe attacks probing Britain's air defences. England's naval ports and merchant convoys in the Channel offered a tempting target for German bombers based in northern France. The RAF scrambled fighters to defend the shipping. Dubbed the *Kanalkampf* (Channel battle) by Germany, these initial encounters were hard-fought but indecisive.

- British naval ports
- Main area of the Channel battle

3 ASSAULT ON FIGHTER COMMAND 13–18 AUGUST 1940

The Luftwaffe campaign to crush the RAF, codenamed *Adlerangriff* (Eagle Attack), began in earnest on 13 August. Launching raids from Northern France, Goering hoped to cripple Britain's air defences within four days. He had gravely underestimated the strength and resilience of the RAF. On 18 August, known as the "Hardest Day", the largest-scale fighting of the entire Battle of Britain saw both sides lose around 70 aircraft.

- Luftwaffe headquarters
- "Hardest day" raids, 18 Aug 1940
- Other Luftwaffe airfield

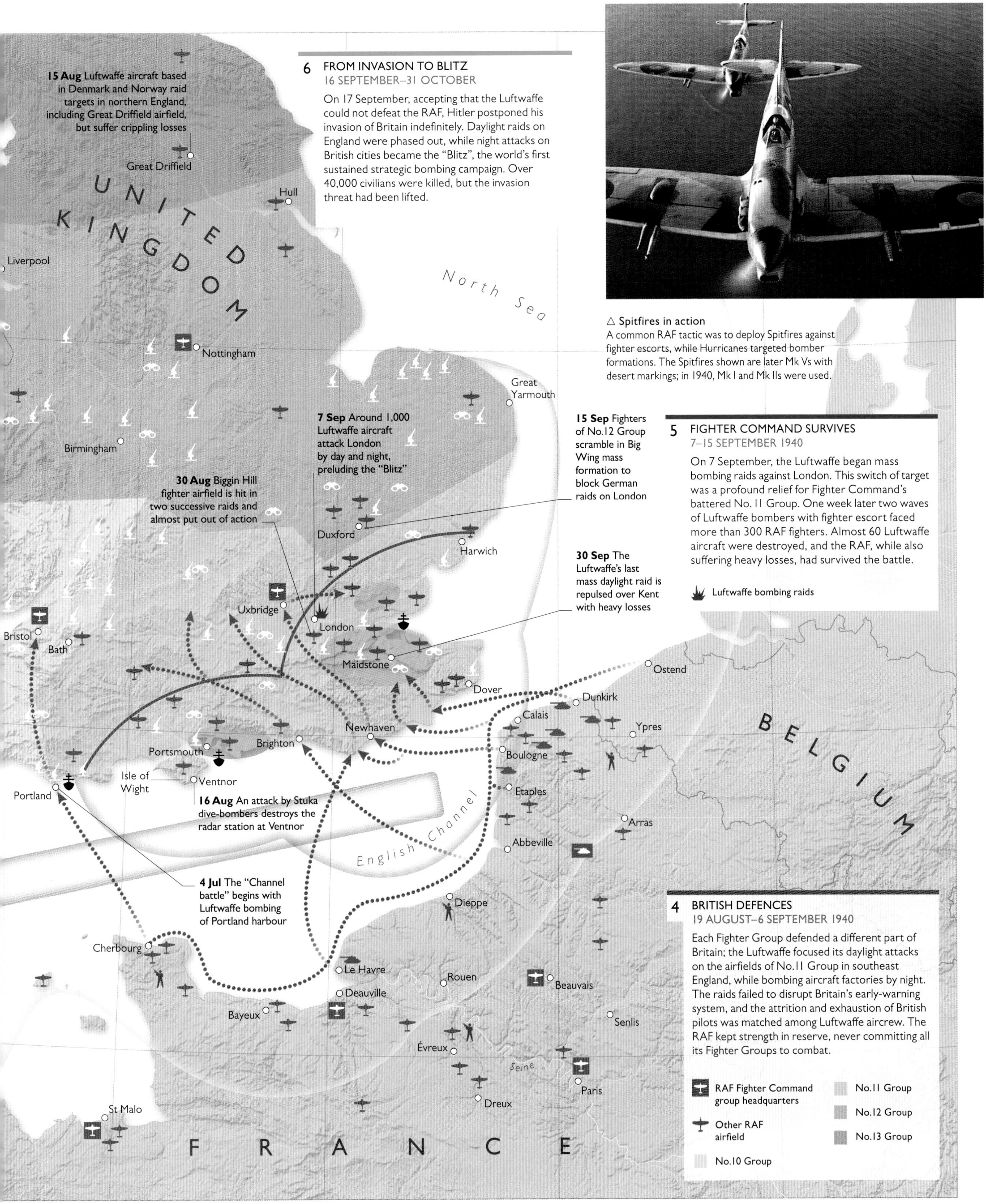
15 Aug Luftwaffe aircraft based in Denmark and Norway raid targets in northern England, including Great Driffield airfield, but suffer crippling losses
Great Driffield
UNITED KINGDOM
Hull
Liverpool
North Sea
Nottingham
Great Yarmouth
Birmingham
7 Sep Around 1,000 Luftwaffe aircraft attack London by day and night, preluding the "Blitz"
15 Sep Fighters of No.12 Group scramble in Big Wing mass formation to block German raids on London
30 Aug Biggin Hill fighter airfield is hit in two successive raids and almost put out of action
Duxford
Harwich
30 Sep The Luftwaffe's last mass daylight raid is repulsed over Kent with heavy losses
Uxbridge
London
Bristol
Bath
Maidstone
Ostend
Dover
Dunkirk
Calais
Ypres
BELGIUM
Newhaven
Brighton
Portsmouth
Boulogne
Isle of Wight
Ventnor
Portland
Etaples
16 Aug An attack by Stuka dive-bombers destroys the radar station at Ventnor
Arras
English Channel
Abbeville
4 Jul The "Channel battle" begins with Luftwaffe bombing of Portland harbour
Dieppe
Cherbourg
Le Havre
Rouen
Beauvais
Deauville
Bayeux
Senlis
Évreux
Seine
Paris
Dreux
St Malo
FRANCE
Luftwaffe bombing raids
RAF Fighter Command group headquarters
Other RAF airfield
No.10 Group
No.11 Group
No.12 Group
No.13 Group

6 FROM INVASION TO BLITZ

16 SEPTEMBER–31 OCTOBER

On 17 September, accepting that the Luftwaffe could not defeat the RAF, Hitler postponed his invasion of Britain indefinitely. Daylight raids on England were phased out, while night attacks on British cities became the "Blitz", the world's first sustained strategic bombing campaign. Over 40,000 civilians were killed, but the invasion threat had been lifted.

△ **Spitfires in action**
A common RAF tactic was to deploy Spitfires against fighter escorts, while Hurricanes targeted bomber formations. The Spitfires shown are later Mk Vs with desert markings; in 1940, Mk I and Mk IIs were used.

5 FIGHTER COMMAND SURVIVES

7–15 SEPTEMBER 1940

On 7 September, the Luftwaffe began mass bombing raids against London. This switch of target was a profound relief for Fighter Command's battered No. 11 Group. One week later two waves of Luftwaffe bombers with fighter escort faced more than 300 RAF fighters. Almost 60 Luftwaffe aircraft were destroyed, and the RAF, while also suffering heavy losses, had survived the battle.

4 BRITISH DEFENCES

19 AUGUST–6 SEPTEMBER 1940

Each Fighter Group defended a different part of Britain; the Luftwaffe focused its daylight attacks on the airfields of No.11 Group in southeast England, while bombing aircraft factories by night. The raids failed to disrupt Britain's early-warning system, and the attrition and exhaustion of British pilots was matched among Luftwaffe aircrew. The RAF kept strength in reserve, never committing all its Fighter Groups to combat.

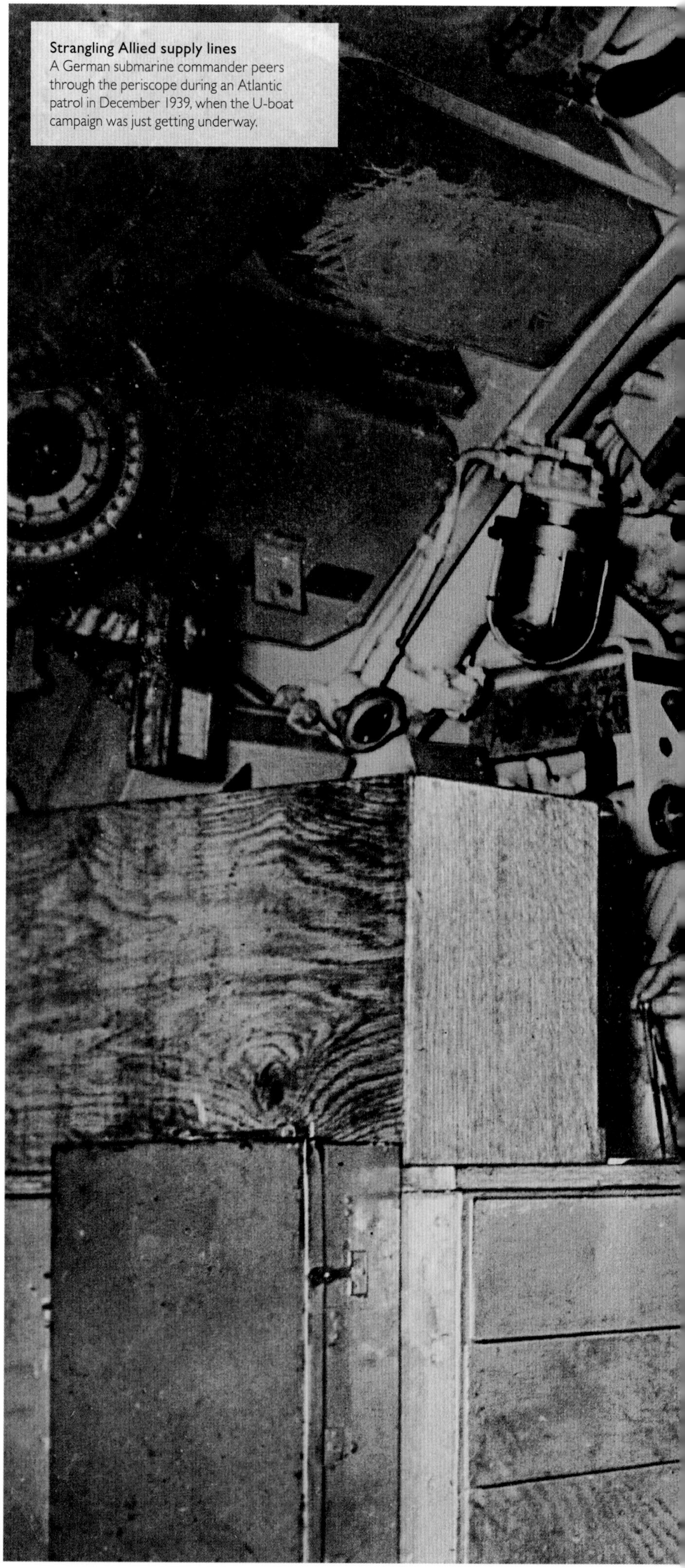

Strangling Allied supply lines
A German submarine commander peers through the periscope during an Atlantic patrol in December 1939, when the U-boat campaign was just getting underway.

STRATEGIC WARFARE

With land combat in northwest Europe blocked from 1940 to 1944 by the obstacle of the English Channel, and with the US even more detached on the other side of the Atlantic Ocean, both sides turned instead to strategic weaponry to try to overcome their opponents.

Der Feind sieht Dein Licht!
Verdunkeln!

△ **Allied retaliation**
This poster declares "the enemy sees your light", a warning to German civilians to maintain blackout to prevent Allied bombers from identifying their targets.

Germany's overall war strategy was dictated by Hitler's insistence on total victory, which worked well when its land forces achieved rapid success. However, this was not possible on all fronts. The Luftwaffe's attempts to knock Britain out of the war through the Battle of Britain (see pp.232–33) and the subsequent Blitz failed due to Britain's growing relative strength in the air. By 1942, British bombers were wreaking far greater havoc on German cities, and as they were joined by increasing numbers of US planes, Germany was forced to divert more and more scarce aircraft and guns from frontlines elsewhere to defend the homeland against increasingly heavy Allied bombing raids.

The U-boat war

The submarine campaign, led by German naval commander Karl Dönitz, was more effective, striking Atlantic convoys supplying Britain and the USSR. The U-boat fleet sank 2,600 Allied merchant ships, nearly bringing Britain to its knees. However, the tide turned after May 1943, thanks in part to US B-24 Liberators, whose long range could reach the "Atlantic Gap" where Allied convoys previously lacked air cover. Intelligence from British code-breakers reduced the strategic impact of the U-boats. The loss of French ports after the D-Day landings in 1944 (see pp.248–49) further neutralized the U-boats and swung the strategic advantage even more in the Allies' favour.

△ **B-24 Liberator bombers**
The B-24s' range allowed them to cover large swathes of the Atlantic for the first time. They helped dominate the U-boats after 1943 and also the Allied bombing of Germany itself.

4 AFTERMATH 9:45AM–5:30PM, 7 DECEMBER 1941

The aftermath saw a search for survivors on sunken ships. Only 29 Japanese aircraft failed to return to their carriers, and Japan considered, but did not attempt, a third wave of attacks. The US suffered 18 warships sunk or damaged, including all eight battleships, and severe casualties with 2,403 service personnel and civilians killed. Their carrier force, however, was away on missions, and six of the battleships returned to service, thanks to the shallow depth of the anchorage.

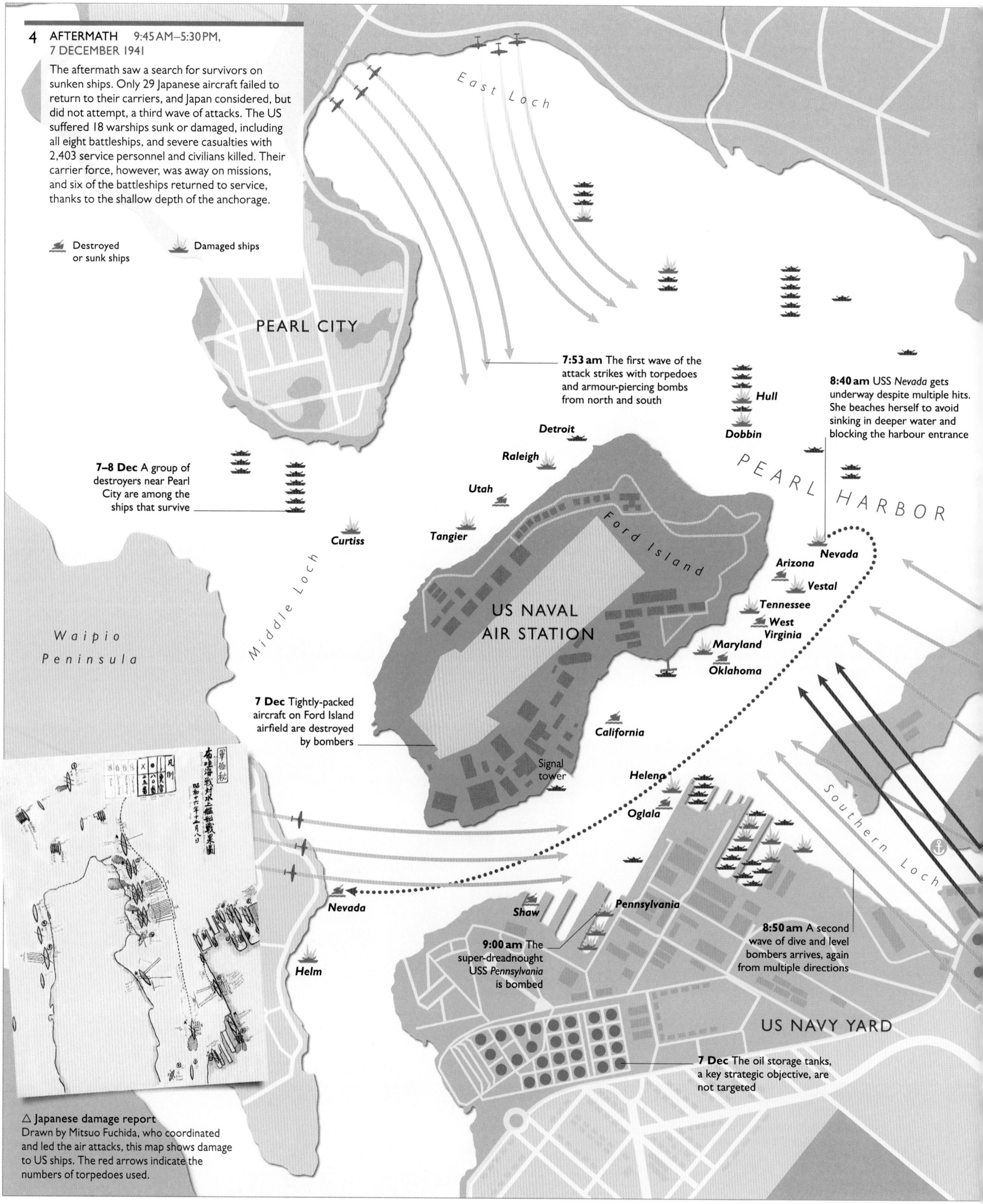

Destroyed or sunk ships
Damaged ships
East Loch
PEARL CITY
7:53 am The first wave of the attack strikes with torpedoes and armour-piercing bombs from north and south
Hull
Dobbin
8:40 am USS Nevada gets underway despite multiple hits. She beaches herself to avoid sinking in deeper water and blocking the harbour entrance
Detroit
Raleigh
PEARL HARBOR
7–8 Dec A group of destroyers near Pearl City are among the ships that survive
Utah
Tangier
Curtiss
Ford Island
Nevada
Arizona
Vestal
Tennessee
West Virginia
Maryland
Oklahoma
Middle Loch
US NAVAL AIR STATION
Waipio Peninsula
7 Dec Tightly-packed aircraft on Ford Island airfield are destroyed by bombers
California
Signal tower
Helena
Oglala
Southern Loch
Nevada
Shaw
Pennsylvania
9:00 am The super-dreadnought USS Pennsylvania is bombed
8:50 am A second wave of dive and level bombers arrives, again from multiple directions
Helm
US NAVY YARD
7 Dec The oil storage tanks, a key strategic objective, are not targeted

△ **Japanese damage report**
Drawn by Mitsuo Fuchida, who coordinated and led the air attacks, this map shows damage to US ships. The red arrows indicate the numbers of torpedoes used.

PEARL HARBOR

The Japanese air attack on the American naval base at Pearl Harbor, Hawaii, on 7 December 1941 brought the US into World War II. Brilliantly executed by Japan's carrier fleet, the raid took a heavy toll of American warships and began a brief period of runaway Japanese victories.

Japan's leaders nurtured ambitions to create an empire in Asia. In 1937, they embarked on a war of conquest in China, and from 1940 they began encroaching on European colonies in Southeast Asia. The US was alarmed by this expansionism, especially after Japan allied itself with Nazi Germany. To force Japan to halt its military adventures, the US eventually imposed a crippling economic blockade. Unwilling to abandon their bid for empire, Japan planned to go to war with the US.

The Japanese knew that, in the long term, they could not match American manpower or industrial strength. They gambled instead on winning swift victories that would give them a tactical stronghold in Asia and the Pacific: as well as Pearl Harbor, their forces attacked other targets including the Philippines, Hong Kong, and Malaya. The suprise raid at Pearl Harbor was launched before a declaration of war; it outraged the American public and shattered US isolationism.

On 11 December, German leader Adolf Hitler declared war on the US in support of Japan, and the lines were drawn for a truly global conflict. The Pearl Harbor attack succeeded in buying Japan time for its conquest of Southeast Asia, but it missed the US's aircraft carriers, which were not in port at the time and soon led the fight back. The slogan "Remember Pearl Harbor" inspired the US to strive for total victory over Japan.

> *"The moment has arrived. The rise or fall of our empire is at stake..."*
>
> ADMIRAL YAMAMOTO, MESSAGE TO THE JAPANESE FLEET, 7 DECEMBER 1941

DANGER FROM THE AIR

The Japanese Striking Force left Japan on 26 November and assembled north of Hawaii. The first attacks came at 7:53 am on 7 December, and the second wave at 8:50 am. The US declared war on Japan the following day.

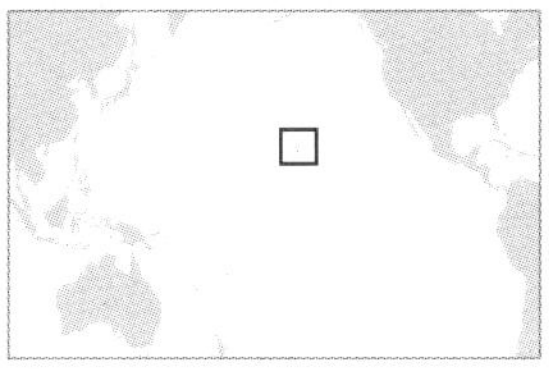

US ships at anchor or moored — Ford Island naval and air station

TIMELINE

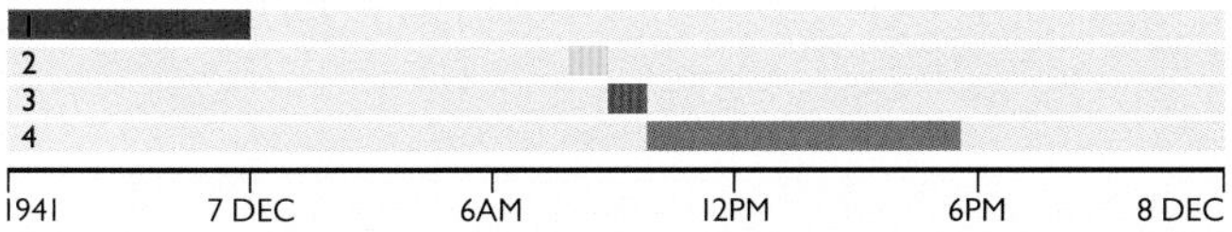
1
2
3
4
1941
7 DEC
6AM
12PM
6PM
8 DEC

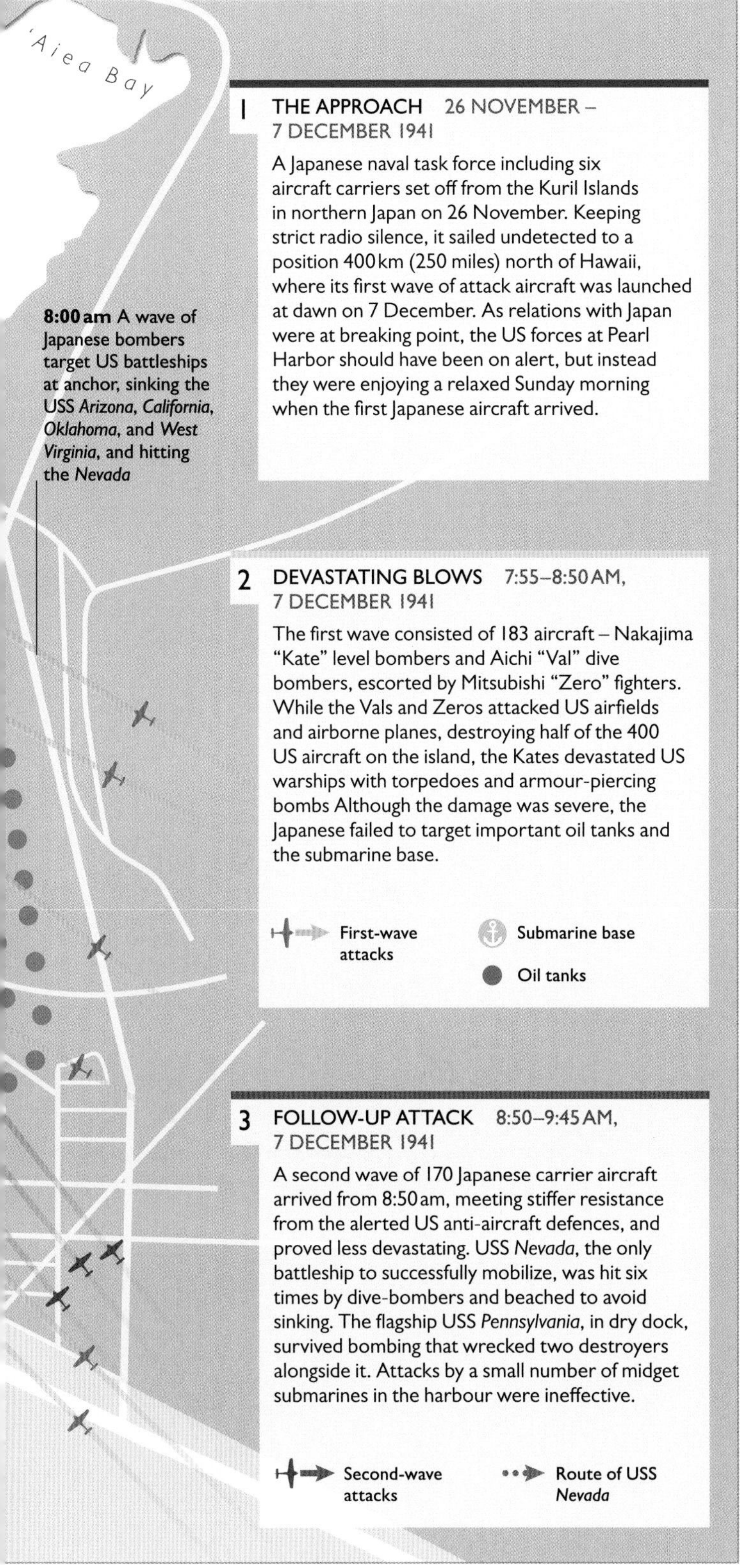
'Aiea Bay
8:00 am A wave of Japanese bombers target US battleships at anchor, sinking the USS *Arizona*, *California*, *Oklahoma*, and *West Virginia*, and hitting the *Nevada*

1 THE APPROACH 26 NOVEMBER – 7 DECEMBER 1941

A Japanese naval task force including six aircraft carriers set off from the Kuril Islands in northern Japan on 26 November. Keeping strict radio silence, it sailed undetected to a position 400 km (250 miles) north of Hawaii, where its first wave of attack aircraft was launched at dawn on 7 December. As relations with Japan were at breaking point, the US forces at Pearl Harbor should have been on alert, but instead they were enjoying a relaxed Sunday morning when the first Japanese aircraft arrived.

2 DEVASTATING BLOWS 7:55–8:50 AM, 7 DECEMBER 1941

The first wave consisted of 183 aircraft – Nakajima "Kate" level bombers and Aichi "Val" dive bombers, escorted by Mitsubishi "Zero" fighters. While the Vals and Zeros attacked US airfields and airborne planes, destroying half of the 400 US aircraft on the island, the Kates devastated US warships with torpedoes and armour-piercing bombs Although the damage was severe, the Japanese failed to target important oil tanks and the submarine base.

First-wave attacks — Submarine base — Oil tanks

3 FOLLOW-UP ATTACK 8:50–9:45 AM, 7 DECEMBER 1941

A second wave of 170 Japanese carrier aircraft arrived from 8:50 am, meeting stiffer resistance from the alerted US anti-aircraft defences, and proved less devastating. USS *Nevada*, the only battleship to successfully mobilize, was hit six times by dive-bombers and beached to avoid sinking. The flagship USS *Pennsylvania*, in dry dock, survived bombing that wrecked two destroyers alongside it. Attacks by a small number of midget submarines in the harbour were ineffective.

Second-wave attacks — Route of USS *Nevada*

ADMIRAL ISOROKU YAMAMOTO 1884–1943

The architect of the Pearl Harbor attack was Admiral Isoroku Yamamoto. Born Isoroku Takano, he lost two fingers fighting at the battle of Tsushima in 1905 (see p.205). Adopted by the Yamamoto samurai family in 1916, he studied at Harvard in the US and was twice naval attaché in Washington, gaining a great respect for the country. As an admiral in the 1930s, he became an advocate of naval aviation. Commander of the Combined Fleet from 1939, he regretted war with the US, but the strike on Pearl Harbor was his conception. He was killed when his aircraft was ambushed over New Guinea in April 1943.

Admiral Yamamoto in 1942

MIDWAY

At Midway Island, the Imperial Japanese Navy hoped to defeat the remnants of the US Pacific Fleet in its biggest operation in World War II. Instead, Japan suffered a naval defeat that cemented the importance of aircraft carriers in dominating the seas.

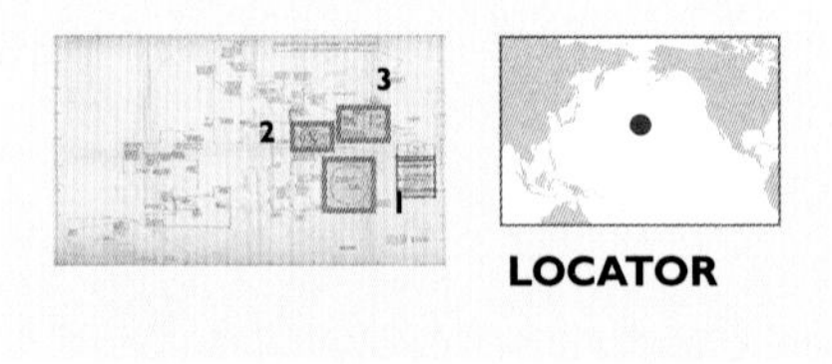
1
2
3
LOCATOR

The US's aircraft carriers survived Japan's raid on Pearl Harbor (see pp.236–37) and, as General MacArthur led the fightback in the Pacific in spring 1942, they became pivotal. This was proven when bombers from the USS *Hornet* bombed Japanese cities in April 1942, and when US and Japanese carriers engaged at Coral Sea in May 1942. As a result, the commander-in-chief of the Japanese fleet, Admiral Isoroku Yamamoto, aimed to destroy the US's carriers.

The island of Midway was the most westerly US base in the central Pacific. After luring part of the US fleet north with an attack on the Aleutian Islands, Yamamoto hoped to draw the US carrier fleet by attacking Midway. However, the US had cracked the Japanese cipher, JN-25, and knew of the plan. US admiral Chester Nimitz sent a force with three aircraft carriers northeast of Midway to wait for the Japanese.

The battle began early on 4 June when Japanese bombers raided the island. As they refuelled aboard their carriers, US dive bombers struck. Four Japanese carriers were damaged, two sank and two were scuttled. The Japanese managed to fatally damage the USS *Yorktown* before their last aircraft carrier, *Hiryū*, was crippled. The US victory marked the end of Japan's dominance in the Pacific.

TURNING POINT IN THE PACIFIC
Japan's failed raid on Midway began at dawn on 4 June. The Americans attacked the Japanese fleet when the Japanese strikeforce had landed back on the aircraft carriers, knocking out three of them by late morning. Planes from Japan's remaining carrier, *Hiryū*, did manage to fatally damage the USS *Yorktown*, before 40 US dive bombers set fire to the carrier shortly after 5:00 pm. By 5 June, the Japanese fleet was in retreat.

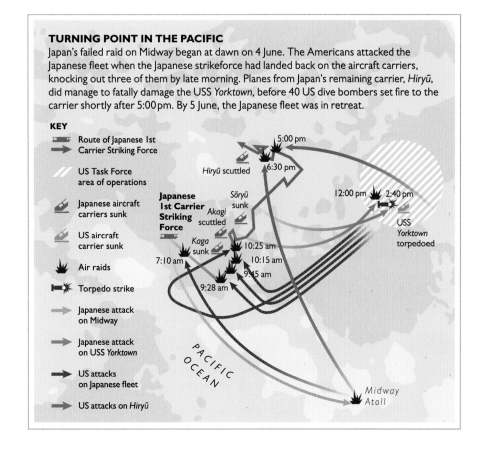

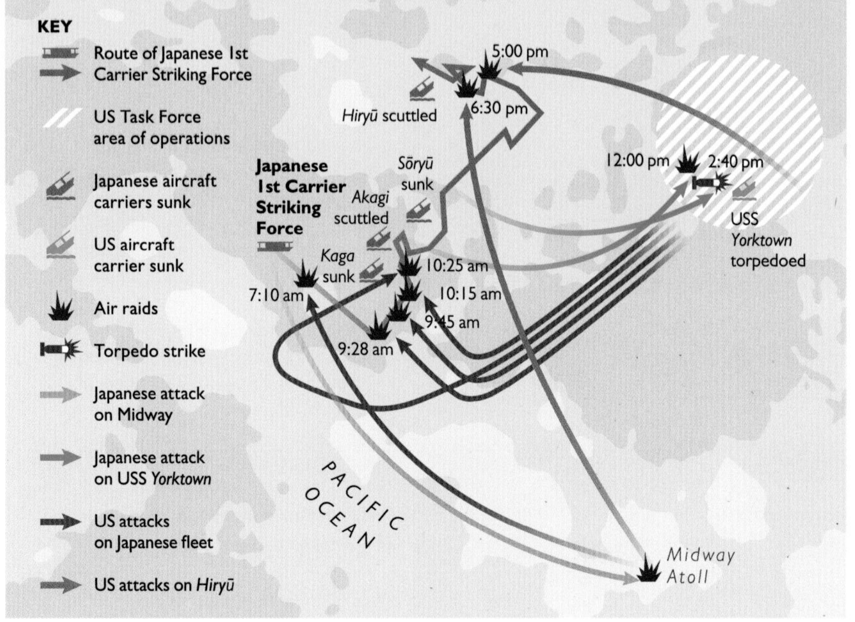
KEY
Route of Japanese 1st Carrier Striking Force
US Task Force area of operations
Japanese aircraft carriers sunk
US aircraft carrier sunk
Air raids
Torpedo strike
Japanese attack on Midway
Japanese attack on USS Yorktown
US attacks on Japanese fleet
US attacks on Hiryū
5:00 pm
6:30 pm
Hiryū scuttled
Japanese 1st Carrier Striking Force
Sōryū sunk
Akagi scuttled
Kaga sunk
12:00 pm
2:40 pm
USS Yorktown torpedoed
7:10 am
10:25 am
10:15 am
9:45 am
9:28 am
PACIFIC OCEAN
Midway Atoll

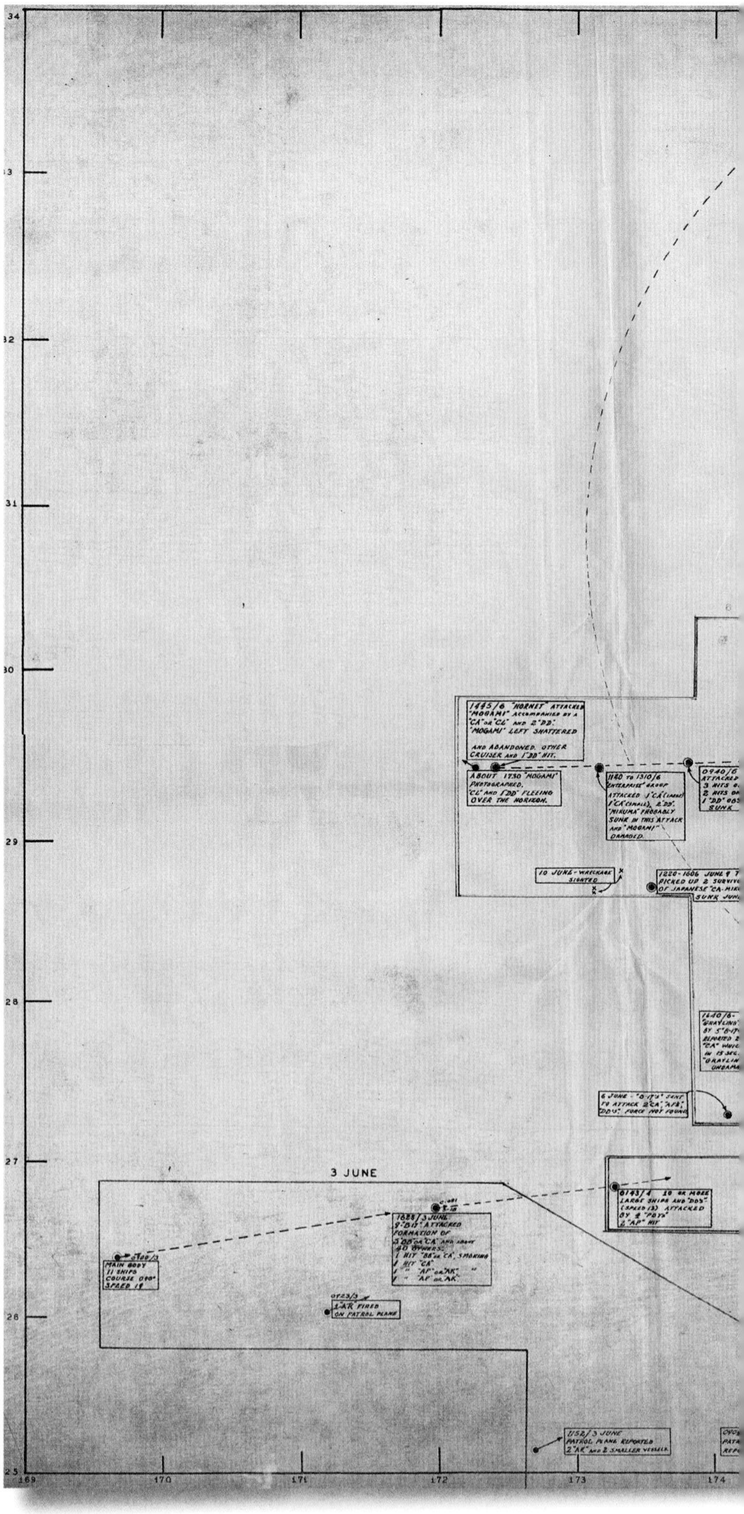
3 JUNE

△ **Mid-ocean manoeuvres**
Covering movements on 3–6 June 1942, this map shows the vast area over which the battle was fought and the radical changes in direction made by the Japanese fleet as it came under attack.

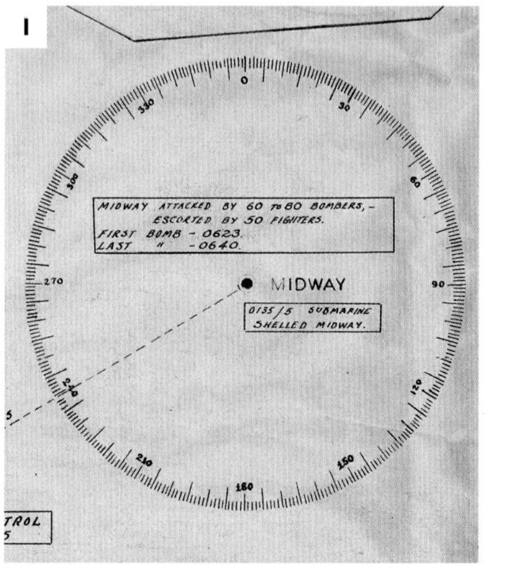
1
MIDWAY ATTACKED BY 60 TO 80 BOMBERS, -
ESCORTED BY 50 FIGHTERS.
FIRST BOMB - 0623.
LAST " -0640.
MIDWAY
0635/5 SUBMARINE
SHELLED MIDWAY.

▷ **A fierce encounter**
At dawn on 4 June, Japan's 1st Carrier Striking Force sent 108 aircraft to attack Midway. The raiders were intercepted and around one-third destroyed or damaged by US fighters and anti-aircraft fire from the island.

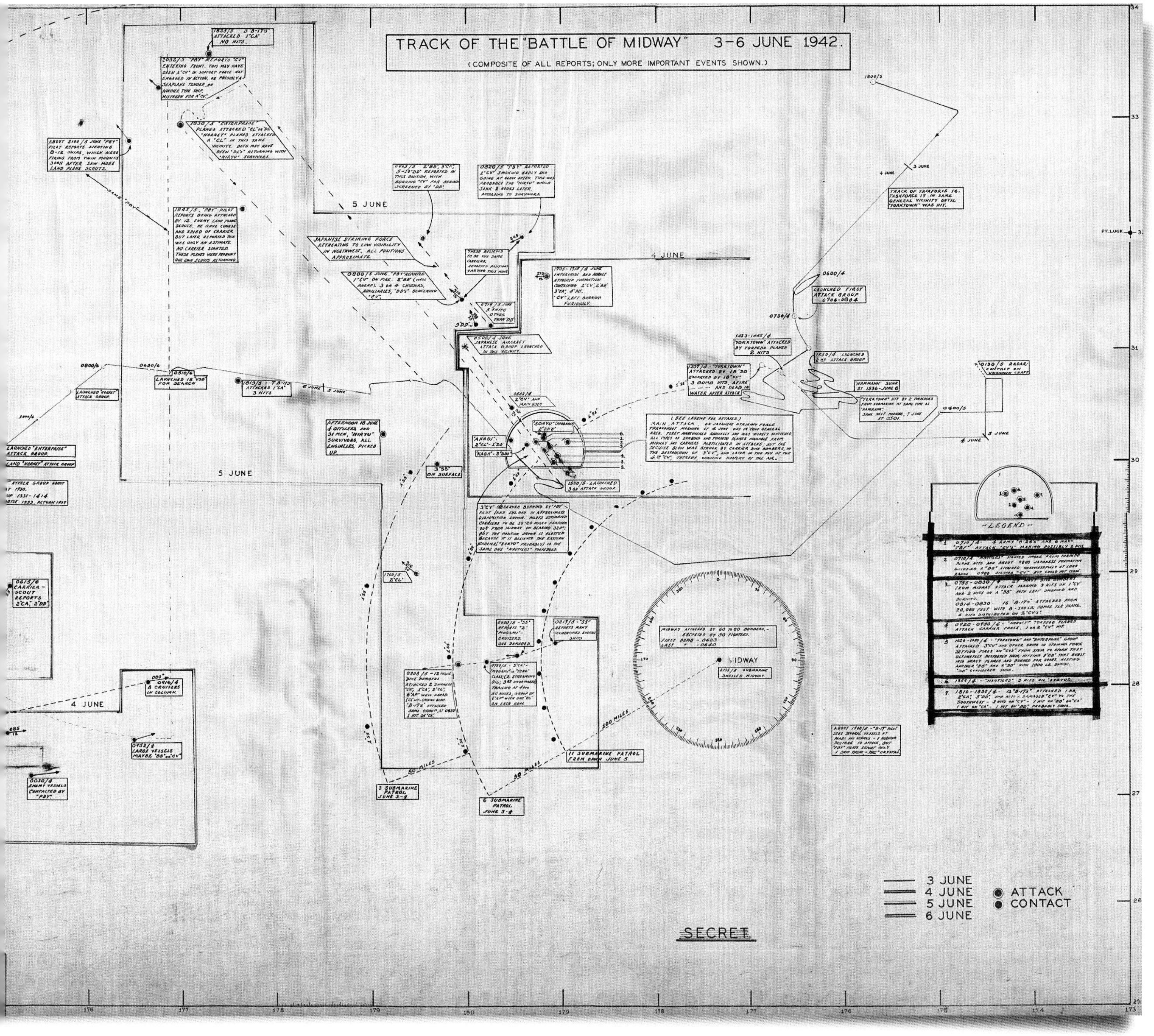

TRACK OF THE "BATTLE OF MIDWAY" 3-6 JUNE 1942.
(COMPOSITE OF ALL REPORTS; ONLY MORE IMPORTANT EVENTS SHOWN.)
5 JUNE
4 JUNE
MIDWAY
LEGEND
3 JUNE
4 JUNE
5 JUNE
6 JUNE
ATTACK
CONTACT
SECRET

2

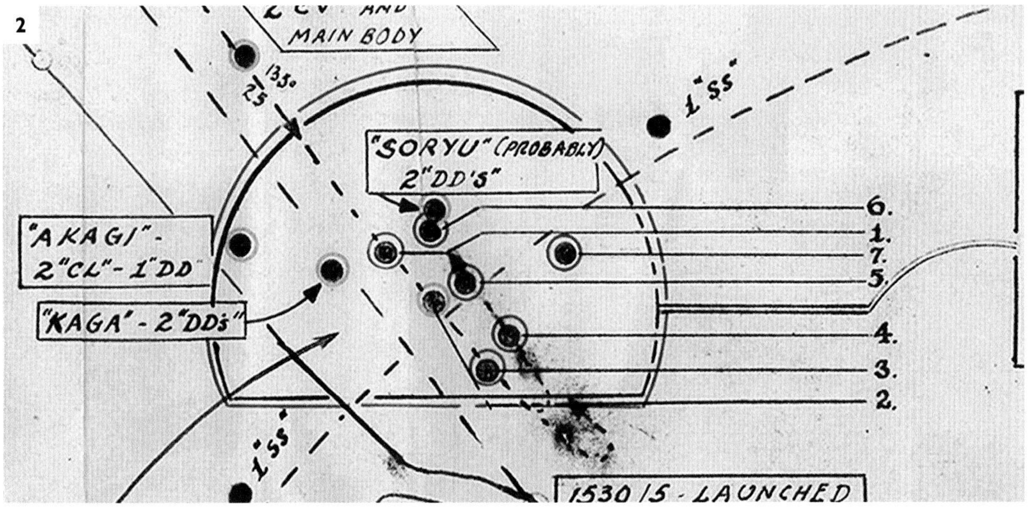

MAIN BODY
1"SS"
"SORYU" (PROBABLY)
2"DD'S"
"AKAGI"-
2"CL"-1"DD"
"KAGA"-2"DD's"
6.
1.
7.
5.
4.
3.
2.
1530/5 - LAUNCHED

3

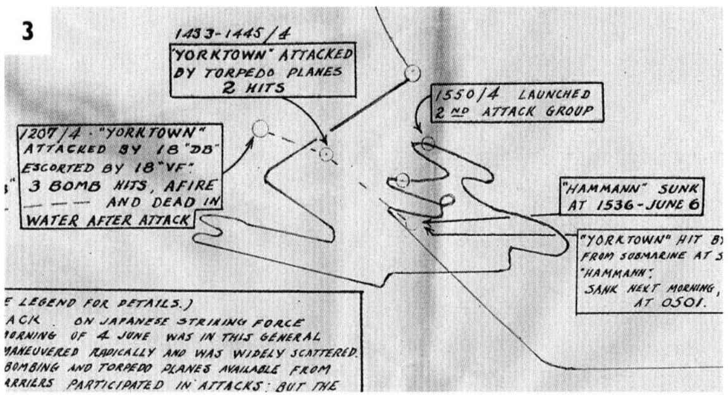

1433-1445/4
"YORKTOWN" ATTACKED
BY TORPEDO PLANES
2 HITS
1550/4 LAUNCHED
2ND ATTACK GROUP
1207/4 - "YORKTOWN"
ATTACKED BY 18 "DB"
ESCORTED BY 18 "VF".
3 BOMB HITS, AFIRE
AND DEAD IN
WATER AFTER ATTACK
"HAMMANN" SUNK
AT 1536-JUNE 6

◁ **US forces pounce**
Bombing aircraft from the US carriers and from Midway scattered the Japanese fleet and damaged Japanese ships including the carriers *Kaga* and *Sōryū*, and the flagship *Akagi*.

△ **Japan's final flourish**
Planes from the *Hiryū* broke through the US fighters to bomb USS *Yorktown* at around noon. Hit again by torpedo planes, *Yorktown* finally sunk on 7 June.

Preparing to land
Two Curtiss SB2C-3 Helldiver dive-bombers prepare to land on the USS *Hornet* after an anti-ship strike in January 1945. Nicknamed "the Beast", the Helldiver was the last dedicated operational dive-bomber of the US Navy.

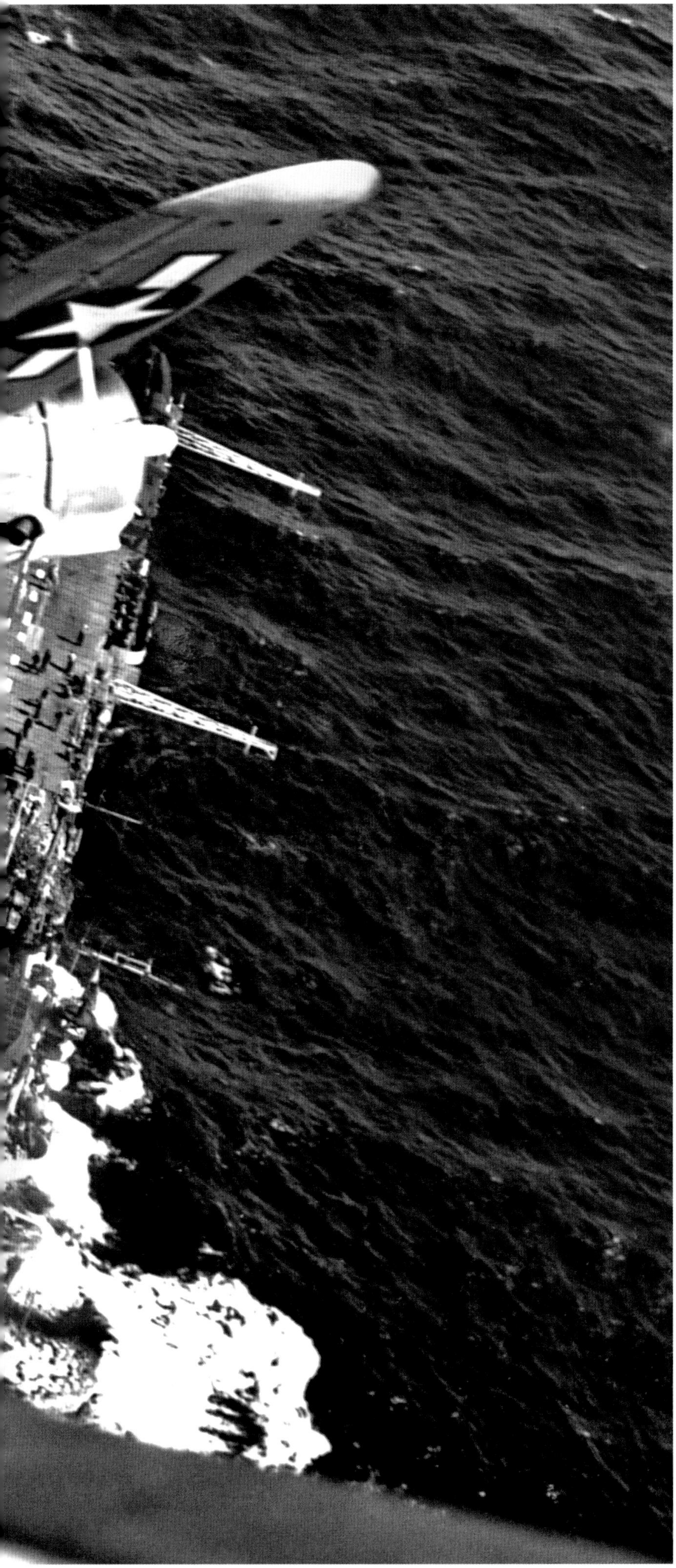

CARRIER WARFARE

Aircraft carriers and carrier planes made their first appearance in war in 1918. However, it was World War II that made them an essential part of modern warfare, transforming the way naval battles were fought.

JOIN
modern mobile mighty
NAVY

△ **Call for recruitment**
Three F-8 Crusader jets fly over a US Navy carrier in this recruitment poster from 1957. Aircraft carriers became the US Navy's *raison d'être* after 1945.

By 1939, Japan, Britain, and the US, separated by sea from potential adversaries, had recognized the utility of aircraft carriers and fielded significant carrier fleets. Other naval powers such as France, Italy, Germany, and the USSR prioritized land-based aircraft and did not create significant carrier forces during the conflict.

Despite its popularity, carrier warfare remained in its infancy during World War II, and navies gained practical experience of carrier combat by trial and error. Aircraft carriers became essential auxiliary vessels in European waters; however, in the Pacific Ocean, they reigned supreme. US–Japan carrier battles in 1942 at Coral Sea, Midway (see pp.238–39), the Eastern Solomons, and Santa Cruz became part of naval folklore. Although carriers were more vulnerable to attack than heavily armoured battleships, their speed and aircraft range allowed them to strike without coming into range of battleships' guns.

After World War II, aircraft carriers thrived due to their flexibility in deploying military force overseas, and projecting air power inland beyond the range of conventional naval shore bombardment. Conflicts in Korea (1950–53), the Suez Canal (1956), Vietnam (1964–73), the Falkland Islands (1982), and during Operation Desert Storm (see pp.266–67) all bore witness to the power of aircraft carriers.

△ **Modern carrier**
The USS *John C. Stennis* (CVN-74) sails through the Arabian Sea during a naval deployment in 2007. Part of her air wing can be seen on the deck, while an SH-60F Seahawk helicopter takes flight.

SECOND BATTLE OF EL ALAMEIN

The Allied victory at El Alamein in autumn 1942 was a major turning point in the fighting in the north African desert in World War II. Through a meticulously prepared, large-scale offensive, the British Eighth Army put German and Italian forces to flight, finally deciding the back and forth contest for north Africa.

From 1941, German general Erwin Rommel achieved notable victories over the British in north Africa in tank warfare. In July 1942, his Panzerarmee Afrika, advancing east into Egypt, was halted by the British at El Alamein, about 100km (60 miles) from the port of Alexandria. The next month, General Bernard Montgomery took command of Eighth Army, with orders to take the offensive. Montgomery was a cautious commander, and concentrated on building up his army's materiel and morale. While the Eighth Army grew in strength, adding new Sherman tanks, Rommel's forces faced growing supply problems and lacked reinforcements. An Axis attack from 30 August was defeated at Alam Halfa ridge. Rommel switched to static defence, fortifying his line with minefields and anti-tank guns.

Outnumbering Rommel's forces by nearly two to one, Montgomery engaged the Axis army in an attritional contest. After 12 days of costly fighting, Rommel retreated. Montgomery pursued the fleeing Axis troops west across Libya. Meanwhile, US and Allied forces had landed in Algeria and Morocco. Caught between the Eighth Army and these new Allied forces, the Axis forces surrendered in Tunisia in May 1943.

"This is not the end. It is not even the beginning of the end. But it is, perhaps, the end of the beginning."

WINSTON CHURCHILL ON SECOND EL ALAMEIN, 1942

MARSHAL ERWIN ROMMEL 1891–1944

Known as the "Desert Fox", Rommel was by training an infantry officer, serving with distinction in World War I. In 1937, he published a book on infantry tactics that attracted Hitler's attention. Enjoying the Führer's favour, he was given command of an armoured division for the invasion of France in 1940. He proved a success in this role and was sent to lead a German panzer force in north Africa – the Afrika Korps. Repeated victories in the Desert War raised his prestige to new heights. Recalled to Europe, he was placed in charge of the Atlantic Wall defences breached by the Allies on D-Day (see pp.248–49). After being implicated in a failed assassination attempt on Hitler in July 1944, he killed himself to shield his family from reprisals.

DESERT CONFRONTATION

The rival forces faced up along a 60km (40 mile) line south from El Alamein on the coast to the impassable Qattara Depression. The only way the battle could be fought was as a frontal assault

KEY

ALLIED FORCES

British, New Zealand, Indian, Australian, Greek, South African

AXIS FORCES

German, Italian

ALLIED TERRITORY

On 23 Oct, By 29 Oct, By 2 Nov, By 4 Nov

TIMELINE

1, 2, 3

15 OCT 1942 — 1 NOV — 15 NOV

2 CRUMBLING THE DEFENCES
25 OCTOBER–1 NOVEMBER 1942

Rommel returned from sick leave on 25 October. He moved his panzer divisions to counter-attack, but fuel shortages limited his ability to manoeuvre. Fiercest fighting occurred around Kidney Ridge and at the northern end of the line, where Australian troops pushed towards the coast road. Although Axis defences held, it was at a cost they could not sustain. Meanwhile, Montgomery prepared a new offensive – Operation Supercharge.

Allied amphibious feint attack — Axis movement

E G Y

3 BREAKING THROUGH 2–4 NOVEMBER 1942

After another massive night-time artillery barrage, British infantry armoured forces attacked towards Tel el Aqqaqir. Rommel counter-attacked in a large-scale tank battle that left more than a hundred German tanks destroyed. On 3 November, Rommel ordered a general retreat, only to be overruled by Hitler. The next night, Indian troops broke through at Kidney Ridge and the Axis position became untenable. The remnants of Rommel's force escaped to the west.

Aerial bombardment — Axis attacks

Allied attacks — Axis retreat

Major engagements

INTO THE MINEFIELDS 23–24 OCTOBER 1942

The Axis forces were outnumbered both in men and tanks, but they had created a formidable defensive position fronted by half a million mines – the "Devil's Gardens" – and an array of anti-tank guns. At 9:40 pm on 23 October, the Eighth Army launched its offensive. Under cover of a 1,000-gun artillery barrage, infantry advanced into the minefields to clear a path for the tanks. Progress was slow due to the depth of the minefields, and heavy losses were inflicted by Axis defensive fire.

LA DOMENICA DEL CORRIERE
Si pubblica a Milano ogni settimana
Supplemento illustrato del "Corriere della Sera"
Spedizione in abbonamento postale - Gruppo 2
Uffici del giornale: Via Solferino, 28 - Milano
Anno 44 – N. 44
1 Novembre 1942 XXI
Centesimi 50 la copia
La battaglia in Egitto. Un violento attacco dell'aviazione italo-germanica distrugge e disperde un gruppo di carri armati nemici.
(Disegno di A. Beltrame)

▷ **Armoured battle in the desert**
This Italian magazine cover from November 1942 depicts the Second Battle of El Alamein. A number of tanks were destroyed on both sides, but the outnumbered Axis armoured force was ground down first, forcing a headlong retreat.

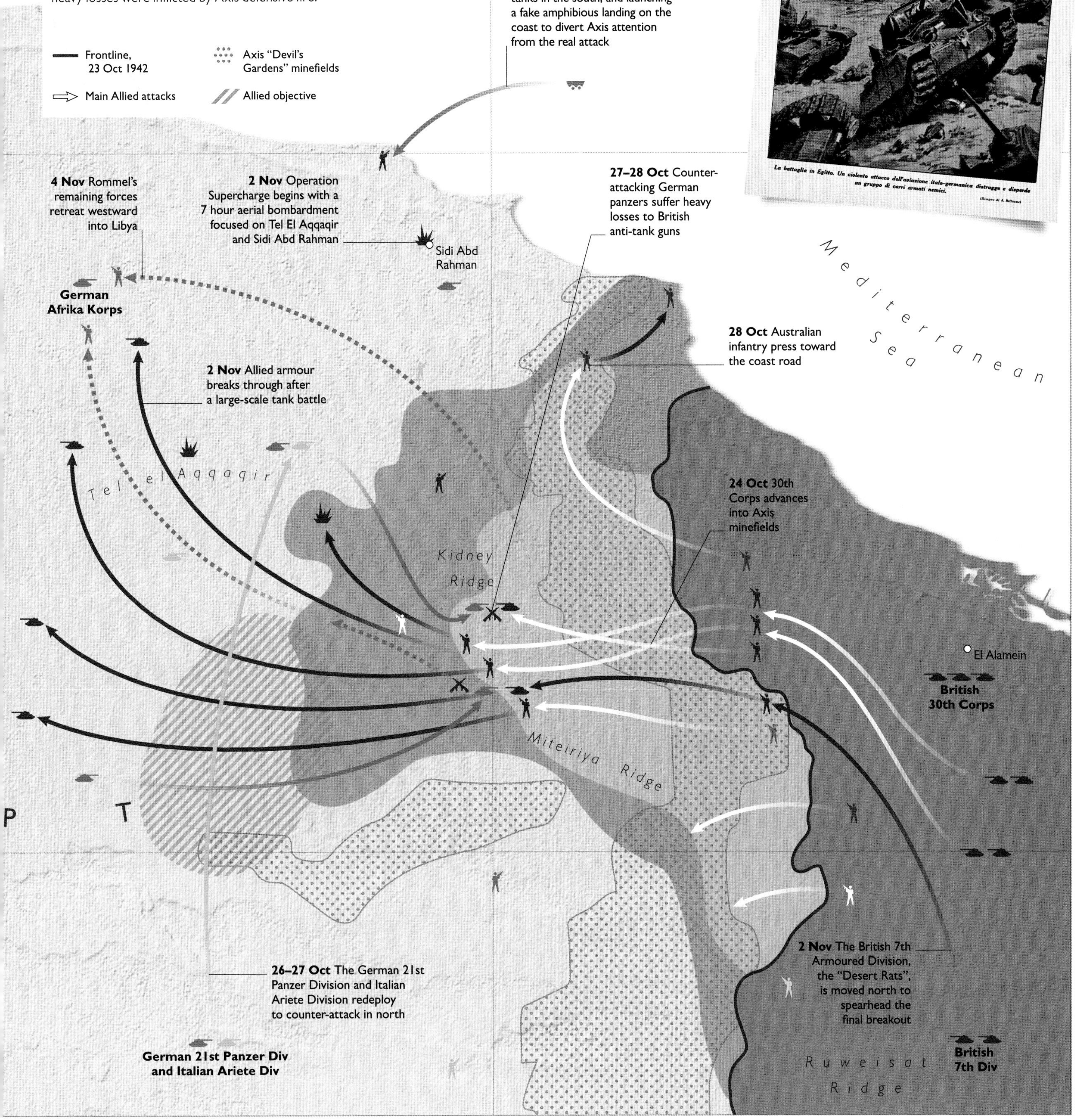
Frontline, 23 Oct 1942
Axis "Devil's Gardens" minefields
Main Allied attacks
Allied objective
Oct The Allies undertake extensive deception operations, deploying hundreds of dummy tanks in the south, and launching a fake amphibious landing on the coast to divert Axis attention from the real attack
4 Nov Rommel's remaining forces retreat westward into Libya
2 Nov Operation Supercharge begins with a 7 hour aerial bombardment focused on Tel El Aqqaqir and Sidi Abd Rahman
Sidi Abd Rahman
27–28 Oct Counter-attacking German panzers suffer heavy losses to British anti-tank guns
Mediterranean Sea
German Afrika Korps
28 Oct Australian infantry press toward the coast road
2 Nov Allied armour breaks through after a large-scale tank battle
Tel el Aqqaqir
24 Oct 30th Corps advances into Axis minefields
Kidney Ridge
El Alamein
British 30th Corps
Miteiriya Ridge
P T
2 Nov The British 7th Armoured Division, the "Desert Rats", is moved north to spearhead the final breakout
26–27 Oct The German 21st Panzer Division and Italian Ariete Division redeploy to counter-attack in north
German 21st Panzer Div and Italian Ariete Div
British 7th Div
Ruweisat Ridge

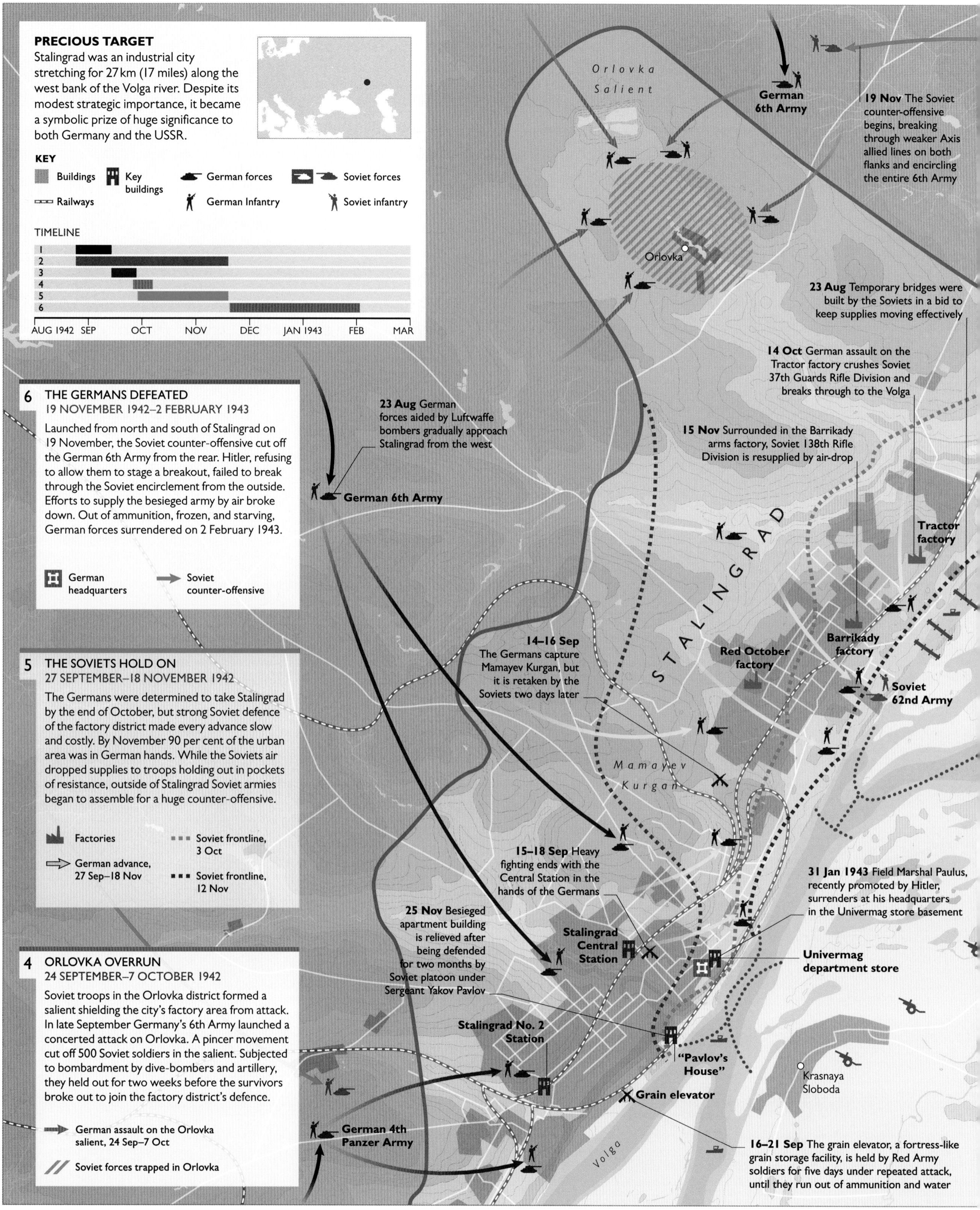
Orlovka Salient
German 6th Army
19 Nov The Soviet counter-offensive begins, breaking through weaker Axis allied lines on both flanks and encircling the entire 6th Army
Orlovka
23 Aug Temporary bridges were built by the Soviets in a bid to keep supplies moving effectively
14 Oct German assault on the Tractor factory crushes Soviet 37th Guards Rifle Division and breaks through to the Volga
23 Aug German forces aided by Luftwaffe bombers gradually approach Stalingrad from the west
15 Nov Surrounded in the Barrikady arms factory, Soviet 138th Rifle Division is resupplied by air-drop
German 6th Army
STALINGRAD
Tractor factory
Barrikady factory
Red October factory
14–16 Sep The Germans capture Mamayev Kurgan, but it is retaken by the Soviets two days later
Soviet 62nd Army
Mamayev Kurgan
15–18 Sep Heavy fighting ends with the Central Station in the hands of the Germans
31 Jan 1943 Field Marshal Paulus, recently promoted by Hitler, surrenders at his headquarters in the Univermag store basement
25 Nov Besieged apartment building is relieved after being defended for two months by Soviet platoon under Sergeant Yakov Pavlov
Stalingrad Central Station
Univermag department store
Stalingrad No. 2 Station
"Pavlov's House"
Krasnaya Sloboda
Grain elevator
German 4th Panzer Army
Volga
16–21 Sep The grain elevator, a fortress-like grain storage facility, is held by Red Army soldiers for five days under repeated attack, until they run out of ammunition and water

PRECIOUS TARGET

Stalingrad was an industrial city stretching for 27 km (17 miles) along the west bank of the Volga river. Despite its modest strategic importance, it became a symbolic prize of huge significance to both Germany and the USSR.

KEY

Buildings · Key buildings · German forces · Soviet forces · Railways · German Infantry · Soviet infantry

TIMELINE

1 2 3 4 5 6

AUG 1942 SEP OCT NOV DEC JAN 1943 FEB MAR

6 THE GERMANS DEFEATED

19 NOVEMBER 1942–2 FEBRUARY 1943

Launched from north and south of Stalingrad on 19 November, the Soviet counter-offensive cut off the German 6th Army from the rear. Hitler, refusing to allow them to stage a breakout, failed to break through the Soviet encirclement from the outside. Efforts to supply the besieged army by air broke down. Out of ammunition, frozen, and starving, German forces surrendered on 2 February 1943.

German headquarters · Soviet counter-offensive

5 THE SOVIETS HOLD ON

27 SEPTEMBER–18 NOVEMBER 1942

The Germans were determined to take Stalingrad by the end of October, but strong Soviet defence of the factory district made every advance slow and costly. By November 90 per cent of the urban area was in German hands. While the Soviets air dropped supplies to troops holding out in pockets of resistance, outside of Stalingrad Soviet armies began to assemble for a huge counter-offensive.

Factories · Soviet frontline, 3 Oct · German advance, 27 Sep–18 Nov · Soviet frontline, 12 Nov

4 ORLOVKA OVERRUN

24 SEPTEMBER–7 OCTOBER 1942

Soviet troops in the Orlovka district formed a salient shielding the city's factory area from attack. In late September Germany's 6th Army launched a concerted attack on Orlovka. A pincer movement cut off 500 Soviet soldiers in the salient. Subjected to bombardment by dive-bombers and artillery, they held out for two weeks before the survivors broke out to join the factory district's defence.

German assault on the Orlovka salient, 24 Sep–7 Oct · Soviet forces trapped in Orlovka

THE SIEGE OF STALINGRAD

Begun in the late summer of 1942, the five-month battle of Stalingrad halted the relentless progress of Axis forces invading the Soviet Union. Fiercely defended by Soviet troops and civilians alike, the city turned into a death trap for the German 6th Army.

By late summer 1942, German armies had seized the Crimea and penetrated the Caucasus, threatening the main Soviet source of oil supplies. Germany did not anticipate the capture of Stalingrad to pose a serious problem. Soviet dictator Joseph Stalin, however, soon prioritized the city's defence. After Luftwaffe bombing of Stalingrad began in late August, invading German ground forces in September met a city-wide fight raging from street to street, house to house, and even in the sewers; Germany dubbed the battle *Rattenkrieg* ("Rat war"). Both sides threw increasing resources into the battle.

While Soviet troops maintained a stubborn defence pressed back into small pockets along the west bank of the Volga, Stalin's most gifted general Georgy Zhukov prepared a masterly counter-offensive that cut off the German army from its supply lines to the rear. By the time the encircled Germans surrendered in February 1943, both sides had incurred vast losses. Germany's defeat at Stalingrad – the single largest in its army's history – marked a turning point in the war.

> *"There is only one way to hold the city, we must pay in lives. Time is blood!"*
>
> GENERAL VASILY CHUIKOV, SEPTEMBER 1942

VASILY CHUIKOV 1900–1982

Commander of the Soviet forces at Stalingrad, Vasily Ivanovich Chuikov was of peasant origins. He rose to be an officer through fighting on the revolutionary side in the Russian Civil War (1918–20). Sent to organize the defence of Stalingrad in September 1942, Chuikov brought a ruthless energy to the task, not hesitating to have his own soldiers shot if they showed signs of wavering. The defence of Stalingrad made him a Soviet hero. In spring 1945 he led Eighth Guards Army in the capture of Berlin. He was made a Marshal of the Soviet Union in 1955.

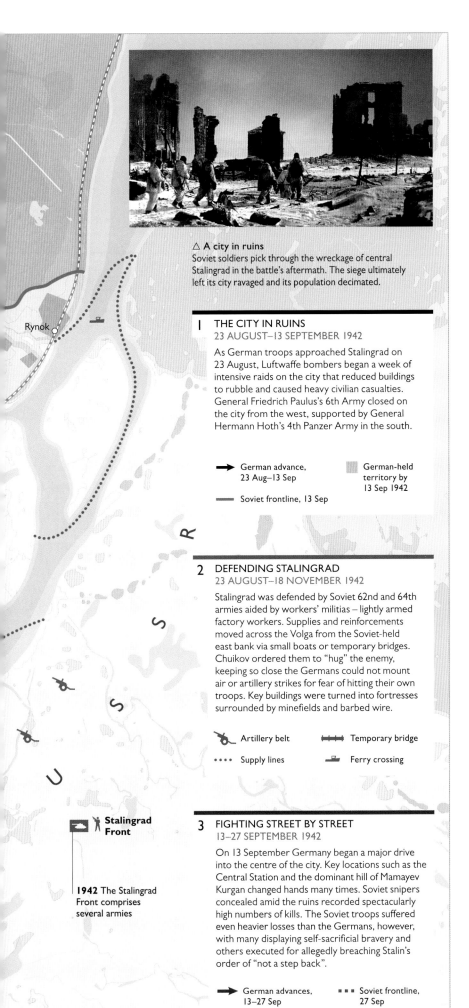

△ **A city in ruins**
Soviet soldiers pick through the wreckage of central Stalingrad in the battle's aftermath. The siege ultimately left its city ravaged and its population decimated.

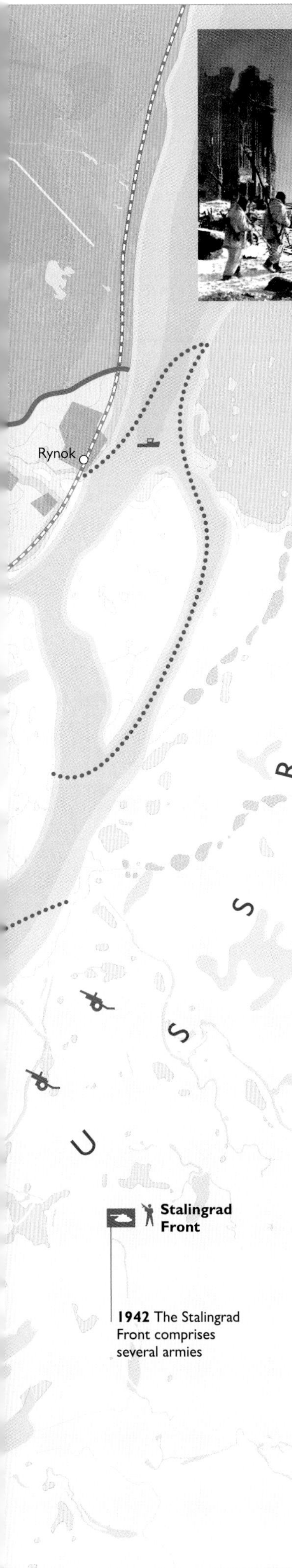
Rynok
U S S R
Stalingrad Front
1942 The Stalingrad Front comprises several armies

1 THE CITY IN RUINS
23 AUGUST–13 SEPTEMBER 1942

As German troops approached Stalingrad on 23 August, Luftwaffe bombers began a week of intensive raids on the city that reduced buildings to rubble and caused heavy civilian casualties. General Friedrich Paulus's 6th Army closed on the city from the west, supported by General Hermann Hoth's 4th Panzer Army in the south.

German advance, 23 Aug–13 Sep
German-held territory by 13 Sep 1942
Soviet frontline, 13 Sep

2 DEFENDING STALINGRAD
23 AUGUST–18 NOVEMBER 1942

Stalingrad was defended by Soviet 62nd and 64th armies aided by workers' militias – lightly armed factory workers. Supplies and reinforcements moved across the Volga from the Soviet-held east bank via small boats or temporary bridges. Chuikov ordered them to "hug" the enemy, keeping so close the Germans could not mount air or artillery strikes for fear of hitting their own troops. Key buildings were turned into fortresses surrounded by minefields and barbed wire.

Artillery belt
Temporary bridge
Supply lines
Ferry crossing

3 FIGHTING STREET BY STREET
13–27 SEPTEMBER 1942

On 13 September Germany began a major drive into the centre of the city. Key locations such as the Central Station and the dominant hill of Mamayev Kurgan changed hands many times. Soviet snipers concealed amid the ruins recorded spectacularly high numbers of kills. The Soviet troops suffered even heavier losses than the Germans, however, with many displaying self-sacrificial bravery and others executed for allegedly breaching Stalin's order of "not a step back".

German advances, 13–27 Sep
Soviet frontline, 27 Sep
Sites of key battles

TANKS IN WORLD WAR II

Tanks underwent rapid technological development during the course of World War II. Initially small and often underpowered and under-armed, by 1945 they had become massive, heavily armoured beasts.

△ **General Heinz Guderian** Guderian's methods of mobile armoured warfare played a major role in Germany's early victories in World War II.

In 1939, the warring nations fielded an array of specialized tanks for specific roles. Lightly armoured tanks were used for reconnaissance, fast tanks with medium armour carried out the cavalry's traditional role as shock troops, the heavier machines provided infantry support, and the heaviest ones were used to break through enemy fortifications.

The belligerents based their theories of armoured warfare on a mix of lessons learned in the later years of World War I (1917–18), the Spanish Civil War (1936–39), and the Second Sino–Japanese War (1937–45). Two main schools of thought emerged. In France, the meticulously planned "methodical battle" had armoured vehicles in rigid infantry support and reconnaissance roles. In Germany, however, some theorists proposed flexible, highly mobile, entirely motorized formations spearheaded by tanks.

The stunning German victory over the Western Allies in the spring of 1940 seemingly vindicated Germany's theorists, and at the same time exposed weaknesses in existing tank designs. By the following year, each country was racing to improve speed, armour, armament, and reliability. Germany focused its limited industrial capacity on size and new technology, while the Allies aimed for reliability, flexibility, and adaptability. By 1944–45, all armies were using mobile all-arms armoured divisions. Germany's emphasis on armour and firepower resulted in fearsome but underpowered tanks such as the Tiger I, fielded in limited numbers. The Allies' earlier single-role tanks were replaced by mass-produced, capable, and upgradable all-rounders such as the US M4 Sherman and the Soviet T-34.

ANTI-TANK WEAPONS

As armoured vehicles developed, so did anti-tank weapons. Early, relatively small single-shot rifles were replaced with portable but more unwieldy anti-tank rifles; mines and grenades were also used. Handheld, recoilless devices were developed during World War II. These, such as the German *Panzerfaust* ("tank fist", below), employed rocket-propelled grenades with "hollow charge" warheads. The most powerful and effective anti-tank weapons were anti-tank guns – dedicated anti-tank artillery.

Starker Feuerstrahl!
Starker Feuerstrahl!

Soviet tank attack
T-34-85 tanks with troops from the 3rd Ukrainian Front attack in the Odessa region in 1944. Infantry often rode directly on tanks, particularly in Soviet forces due to a lack of armoured personnel carriers.

THE D-DAY LANDINGS

One of the largest military operations of World War II, the Allied invasion of German-occupied France began on 6 June 1944, codenamed "D-Day". The success of the landings was a crucial step towards the liberation of France and the defeat of Nazi Germany.

A cross-Channel invasion of Occupied Europe from Britain was on the Allies' agenda from 1942, the US pressing for swift action while the British temporized, convinced of the extreme difficulty of such a venture. The Germans, meanwhile, fortified the coast from southwest France to Scandinavia with the Atlantic Wall, a formidable line of artillery emplacements, concrete bunkers and beach obstacles.

Planning for the invasion began in earnest in mid-1943, with US general Dwight D. Eisenhower as Supreme Commander and British general Bernard Montgomery commanding land forces. A vast build-up of troops and supplies in southern England could not be disguised, but a deception effort persuaded the Germans the invasion would strike the Pas-de-Calais instead of Normandy.

On D-Day itself, the Allies successfully landed more than 150,000 troops, forming a bridgehead they could reinforce and supply across the Channel. Casualties on the day were lighter than feared, with around 11,000 Allied soldiers killed or wounded. However, the Allies did not achieve many of their first-day objectives, and the German defenders fought fiercely. The Allies did not break out of their coastal toehold until late July; the battle for Normandy cost them more than 200,000 casualties. Paris was finally liberated on 25 August.

INVADING NORMANDY

The five target beaches were codenamed Utah, Omaha, Gold, Juno, and Sword. US and British airborne forces landed by parachute and glider during the night; the seaborne assault followed after dawn. All the beaches were taken, but stiff German resistance blocked Allied progress inland.

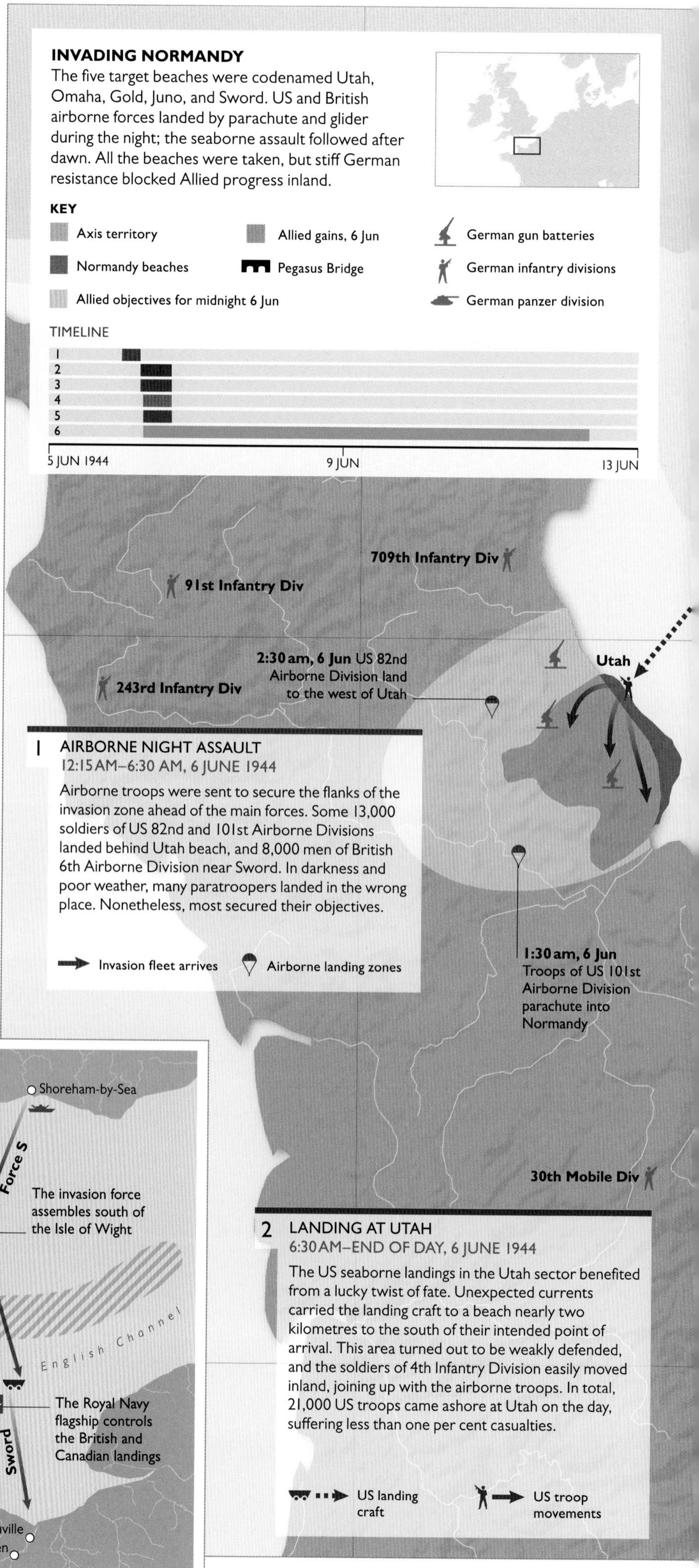
KEY
Axis territory
Allied gains, 6 Jun
German gun batteries
Normandy beaches
Pegasus Bridge
German infantry divisions
Allied objectives for midnight 6 Jun
German panzer division
TIMELINE
1
2
3
4
5
6
5 JUN 1944
9 JUN
13 JUN
709th Infantry Div
91st Infantry Div
2:30 am, 6 Jun US 82nd Airborne Division land to the west of Utah
243rd Infantry Div
Utah
1:30 am, 6 Jun Troops of US 101st Airborne Division parachute into Normandy
30th Mobile Div
Invasion fleet arrives
Airborne landing zones
US landing craft
US troop movements

1 AIRBORNE NIGHT ASSAULT

12:15 AM–6:30 AM, 6 JUNE 1944

Airborne troops were sent to secure the flanks of the invasion zone ahead of the main forces. Some 13,000 soldiers of US 82nd and 101st Airborne Divisions landed behind Utah beach, and 8,000 men of British 6th Airborne Division near Sword. In darkness and poor weather, many paratroopers landed in the wrong place. Nonetheless, most secured their objectives.

2 LANDING AT UTAH

6:30 AM–END OF DAY, 6 JUNE 1944

The US seaborne landings in the Utah sector benefited from a lucky twist of fate. Unexpected currents carried the landing craft to a beach nearly two kilometres to the south of their intended point of arrival. This area turned out to be weakly defended, and the soldiers of 4th Infantry Division easily moved inland, joining up with the airborne troops. In total, 21,000 US troops came ashore at Utah on the day, suffering less than one per cent casualties.

CHANNEL CROSSING

The largest amphibious operation in military history, D-Day involved more than 1,200 warships and 4,000 landing craft. These set sail from Britain on the night of 5–6 June, via lanes cleared in minefields. German defences were shelled by battleships and cruisers and bombed from the air; transport ships took men to landing craft for the final approach.

KEY
- Axis territory
- Allied territory
- Allied invasion
- Troop transports
- Minefield
- Landing craft
- Warships bombard coast

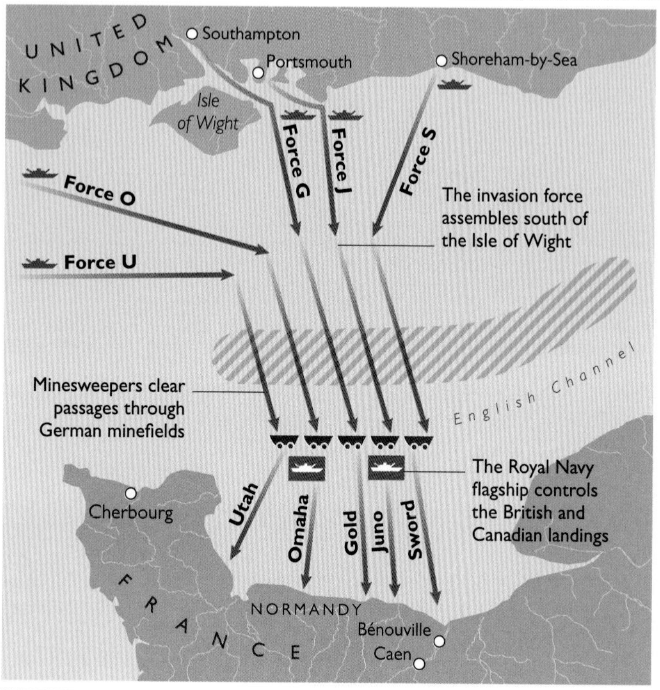
UNITED KINGDOM
Southampton
Portsmouth
Shoreham-by-Sea
Isle of Wight
Force G
Force J
Force S
Force O
Force U
The invasion force assembles south of the Isle of Wight
Minesweepers clear passages through German minefields
English Channel
The Royal Navy flagship controls the British and Canadian landings
Cherbourg
Utah
Omaha
Gold
Juno
Sword
NORMANDY
FRANCE
Bénouville
Caen

▷ **Armies assemble**
US Army Rangers are carried to a ship near Weymouth on the British south coast on 1st June 1944 as part of preparations for the D-Day invasions.

6 SETTLING IN 6–12 JUNE 1944

Field Marshal Erwin Rommel, in command of the Atlantic Wall defences, was on leave on 6 June. He arrived back late in the evening and began bringing in forces for a counter-offensive. However, the Allies made slow but definite progress. All the landing zones were joined up to form a single bridgehead by 12 June. "Mulberry" artificial harbours were built to allow a flow of supplies and reinforcements. Day by day, the Allied foothold became less precarious.

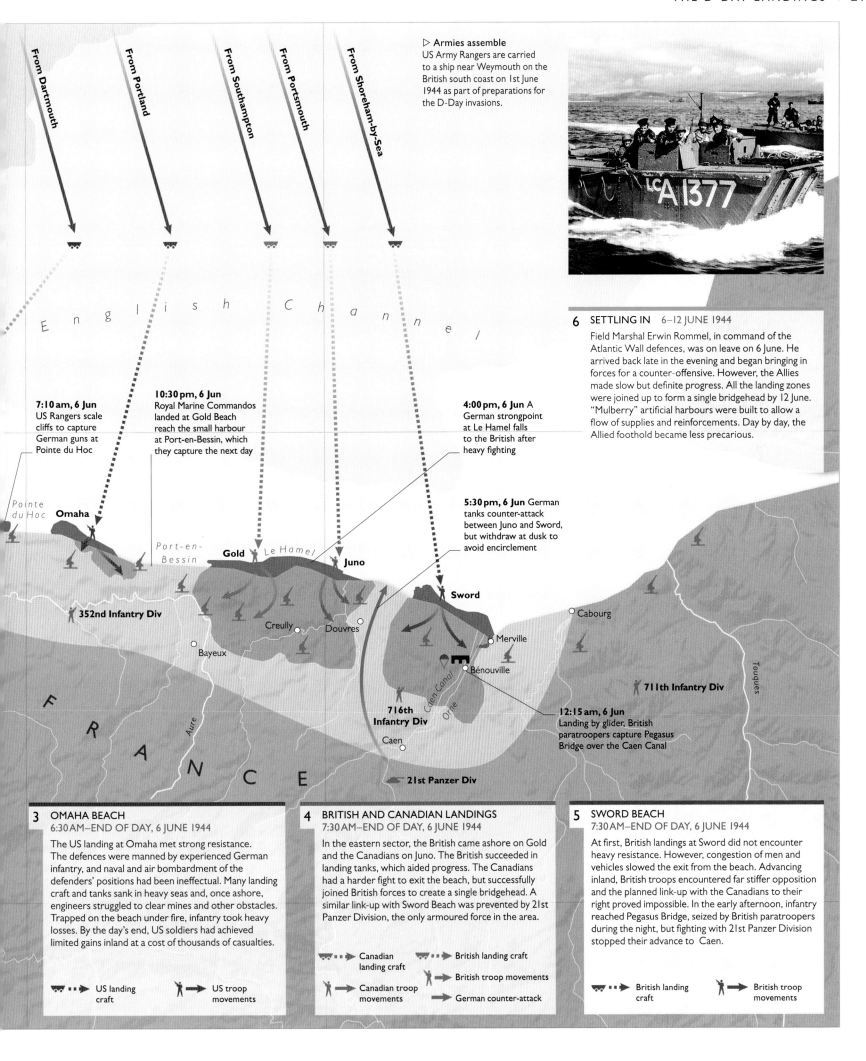

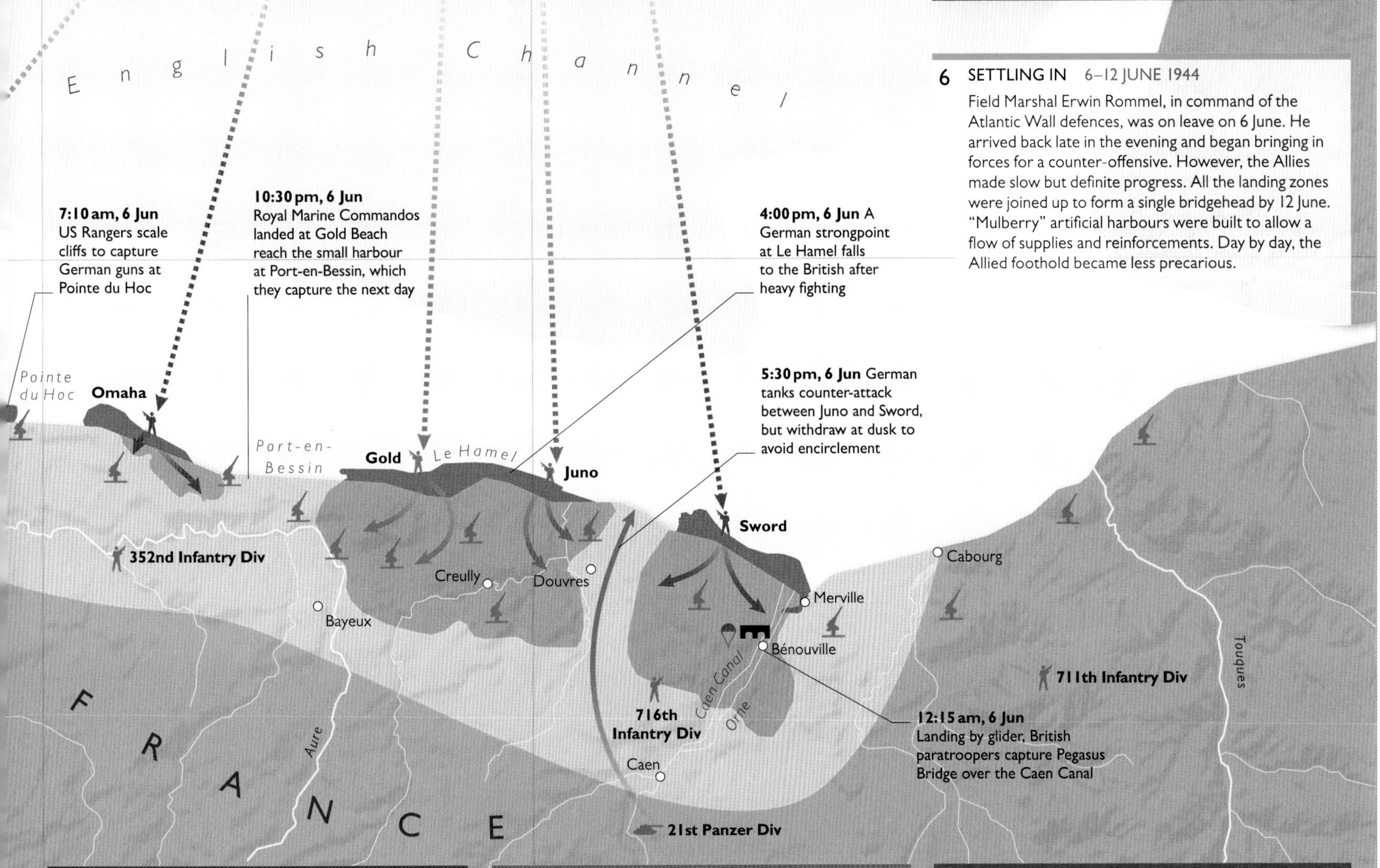
From Dartmouth
From Portland
From Southampton
From Portsmouth
From Shoreham-by-Sea
English Channel
7:10 am, 6 Jun US Rangers scale cliffs to capture German guns at Pointe du Hoc
10:30 pm, 6 Jun Royal Marine Commandos landed at Gold Beach reach the small harbour at Port-en-Bessin, which they capture the next day
4:00 pm, 6 Jun A German strongpoint at Le Hamel falls to the British after heavy fighting
5:30 pm, 6 Jun German tanks counter-attack between Juno and Sword, but withdraw at dusk to avoid encirclement
12:15 am, 6 Jun Landing by glider, British paratroopers capture Pegasus Bridge over the Caen Canal
Pointe du Hoc
Omaha
Port-en-Bessin
Gold
Le Hamel
Juno
Sword
352nd Infantry Div
Creully
Douvres
Bayeux
Merville
Cabourg
Bénouville
Caen Canal
Orne
716th Infantry Div
711th Infantry Div
Touques
Aure
Caen
21st Panzer Div
FRANCE

3 OMAHA BEACH
6:30AM–END OF DAY, 6 JUNE 1944

The US landing at Omaha met strong resistance. The defences were manned by experienced German infantry, and naval and air bombardment of the defenders' positions had been ineffectual. Many landing craft and tanks sank in heavy seas and, once ashore, engineers struggled to clear mines and other obstacles. Trapped on the beach under fire, infantry took heavy losses. By the day's end, US soldiers had achieved limited gains inland at a cost of thousands of casualties.

US landing craft
US troop movements

4 BRITISH AND CANADIAN LANDINGS
7:30AM–END OF DAY, 6 JUNE 1944

In the eastern sector, the British came ashore on Gold and the Canadians on Juno. The British succeeded in landing tanks, which aided progress. The Canadians had a harder fight to exit the beach, but successfully joined British forces to create a single bridgehead. A similar link-up with Sword Beach was prevented by 21st Panzer Division, the only armoured force in the area.

Canadian landing craft
British landing craft
British troop movements
Canadian troop movements
German counter-attack

5 SWORD BEACH
7:30AM–END OF DAY, 6 JUNE 1944

At first, British landings at Sword did not encounter heavy resistance. However, congestion of men and vehicles slowed the exit from the beach. Advancing inland, British troops encountered far stiffer opposition and the planned link-up with the Canadians to their right proved impossible. In the early afternoon, infantry reached Pegasus Bridge, seized by British paratroopers during the night, but fighting with 21st Panzer Division stopped their advance to Caen.

British landing craft
British troop movements

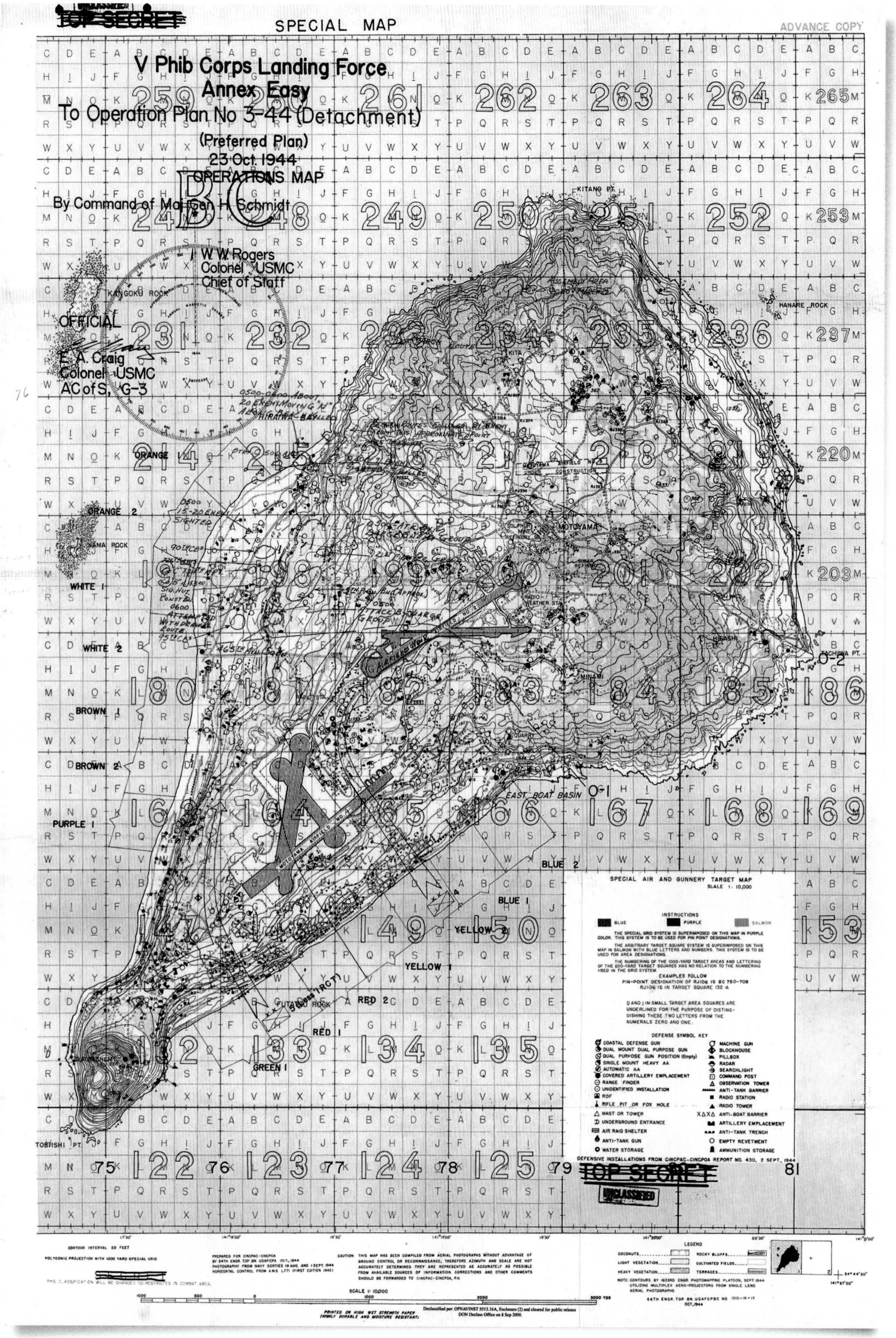
TOP SECRET
UNCLASSIFIED
SPECIAL MAP
ADVANCE COPY
V Phib Corps Landing Force
Annex Easy
To Operation Plan No 3-44 (Detachment)
(Preferred Plan)
23 Oct. 1944
OPERATIONS MAP
By Command of Maj Gen H Schmidt
W.W. Rogers
Colonel USMC
Chief of Staff
OFFICIAL
E. A. Craig
Colonel USMC
AC of S, G-3
KITANO PT.
KANGOKU ROCK
HANARE ROCK
KAMA ROCK
TACHIWA PT.
TOBISHI PT.
MOTOYAMA
MINAMI
HIGASHI
EAST BOAT BASIN
FUTATSU ROCK
O-1
O-2
ORANGE 1
ORANGE 2
WHITE 1
WHITE 2
BROWN 1
BROWN 2
PURPLE 1
BLUE 1
BLUE 2
YELLOW 1
YELLOW 2
RED 1
RED 2
GREEN 1
SPECIAL AIR AND GUNNERY TARGET MAP
SCALE 1: 10,000
INSTRUCTIONS
BLUE
PURPLE
SALMON
THE SPECIAL GRID SYSTEM IS SUPERIMPOSED ON THIS MAP IN PURPLE COLOR. THIS SYSTEM IS TO BE USED FOR PIN POINT DESIGNATIONS.
THE ARBITRARY TARGET SQUARE SYSTEM IS SUPERIMPOSED ON THIS MAP IN SALMON WITH BLUE LETTERS AND NUMBERS. THIS SYSTEM IS TO BE USED FOR AREA DESIGNATIONS.
THE NUMBERING OF THE 1000-YARD TARGET AREAS AND LETTERING OF THE 200-YARD TARGET SQUARES HAS NO RELATION TO THE NUMBERING USED IN THE GRID SYSTEM.
EXAMPLES FOLLOW
PIN-POINT DESIGNATION OF RJ106 IS BC 750-709
RJ106 IS IN TARGET SQUARE 132-A
Q AND I IN SMALL TARGET AREA SQUARES ARE UNDERLINED FOR THE PURPOSE OF DISTINGUISHING THESE TWO LETTERS FROM THE NUMERALS ZERO AND ONE.
DEFENSE SYMBOL KEY
COASTAL DEFENSE GUN
DUAL MOUNT DUAL PURPOSE GUN
DUAL PURPOSE GUN POSITION (Empty)
SINGLE MOUNT HEAVY AA
AUTOMATIC AA
COVERED ARTILLERY EMPLACEMENT
RANGE FINDER
UNIDENTIFIED INSTALLATION
RDF
RIFLE PIT OR FOX HOLE
MAST OR TOWER
UNDERGROUND ENTRANCE
AIR RAID SHELTER
ANTI-TANK GUN
WATER STORAGE
MACHINE GUN
BLOCKHOUSE
PILLBOX
RADAR
SEARCHLIGHT
COMMAND POST
OBSERVATION TOWER
ANTI-TANK BARRIER
RADIO STATION
RADIO TOWER
ANTI-BOAT BARRIER
ARTILLERY EMPLACEMENT
ANTI-TANK TRENCH
EMPTY REVETMENT
AMMUNITION STORAGE
DEFENSIVE INSTALLATIONS FROM CINCPAC-CINCPOA REPORT NO. 430, 2 SEPT., 1944
CONTOUR INTERVAL 20 FEET
POLYCONIC PROJECTION WITH 1000 YARD SPECIAL GRID
THIS CLASSIFICATION WILL BE CHANGED TO RESTRICTED IN COMBAT AREA
PREPARED FOR CINCPAC-CINCPOA
BY 64TH ENGR. TOP. BN. USAFICPA OCT., 1944
PHOTOGRAPHY FROM NAVY SORTIES 19 AUG. AND 1 SEPT. 1944
HORIZONTAL CONTROL FROM A.M.S. L771 (FIRST EDITION 1943)
CAUTION: THIS MAP HAS BEEN COMPILED FROM AERIAL PHOTOGRAPHS WITHOUT ADVANTAGE OF GROUND CONTROL OR RECONNAISSANCE; THEREFORE AZIMUTH AND SCALE ARE NOT ACCURATELY DETERMINED. THEY ARE REPRESENTED AS ACCURATELY AS POSSIBLE FROM AVAILABLE SOURCES OF INFORMATION. CORRECTIONS AND OTHER COMMENTS SHOULD BE FORWARDED TO CINCPAC-CINCPOA, P.H.
SCALE 1: 10,000
1000 500 0 1000 2000 3000 YDS
PRINTED ON HIGH WET STRENGTH PAPER (HIGHLY DURABLE AND MOISTURE RESISTANT)
Declassified per: OPNAVINST 5513.16A, Enclosure (2) and cleared for public release
DON Declass Office on 8 Sep 2000.
LEGEND
COCONUTS
LIGHT VEGETATION
HEAVY VEGETATION
ROCKY BLUFFS
CULTIVATED FIELDS
TERRACES
NOTE: CONTOURS BY 1633RD. ENGR. PHOTOMAPPING PLATOON, SEPT 1944 UTILIZING MULTIPLEX AERO-PROJECTORS FROM SINGLE LENS AERIAL PHOTOGRAPHS
64TH ENGR. TOP. BN. USAFCPBC NO. 1015-16-17
OCT., 1944

◁ An island stronghold
This US military map from October 1944 presents the preferred operations plan for the US landing. It includes all the Japanese gun emplacements and defensive installations on Iwo Jima.

▷ Early victory
Mount Suribachi – the highest point on the island – was protected by over 200 gun emplacements. The Marines raised the US flag on the summit on 23 February.

▽ The bloodiest battle
The battle among the hills concealing the Japanese communications system was so hard that the Americans nicknamed it the "Meatgrinder".

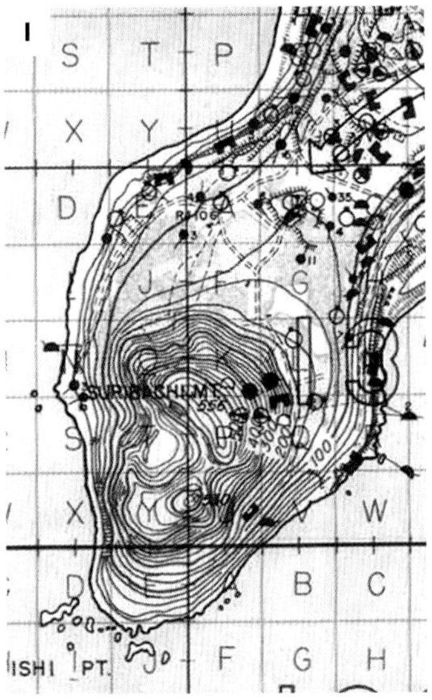

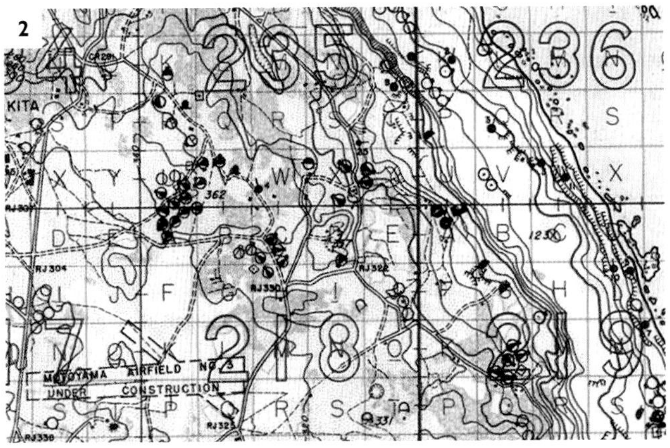

IWO JIMA

In early 1945, 110,000 US troops set out to take the tiny island of Iwo Jima from around 20,000 Japanese soldiers. In one of the bloodiest battles of the war, US forces cleared the Japanese from the network of defensive tunnels. After a month, they finally claimed a strategic and psychological victory.

After their success at Midway in 1942 (see pp.238–39), US forces went on the offensive, working their way west across the Pacific and causing terrible damage to the Japanese navy. In February 1945, the US launched an offensive on the tiny Japanese island of Iwo Jima, a vital strategic target that would provide the US with a base for Allied fighter planes and a refuge for damaged bombers.

The Japanese were well prepared for the invasion. General Tadamichi Kuribayashi had fortified the island, tunnelling into the island's rock to create a network of bunkers and rooms linked by 18km (11 miles) of tunnels that protected his men from naval and aerial bombardment.

The first of 110,000 US marines landed on 19 February. As they edged their way across the island, they found themselves exposed to a largely unseen enemy that would suddenly emerge from bunkers to attack. The advance was slow and costly – nearly 7,000 US troops were killed and over 19,000 wounded. A small Japanese force under Kuribayashi held out until 26 March, but almost all the defenders were killed; only around 1,000 were captured (many after staying hidden for months or even years).

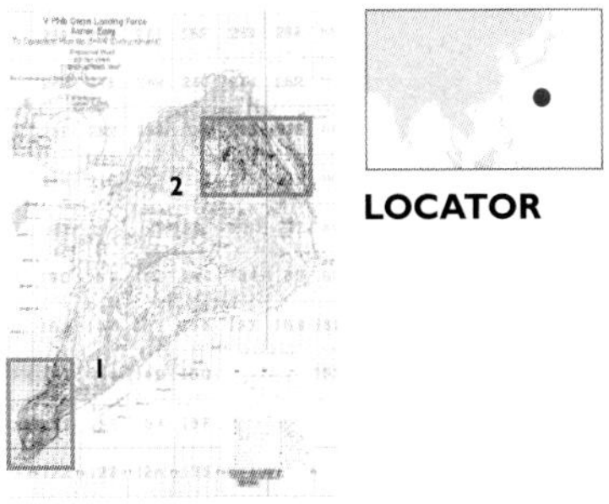
2
1
LOCATOR

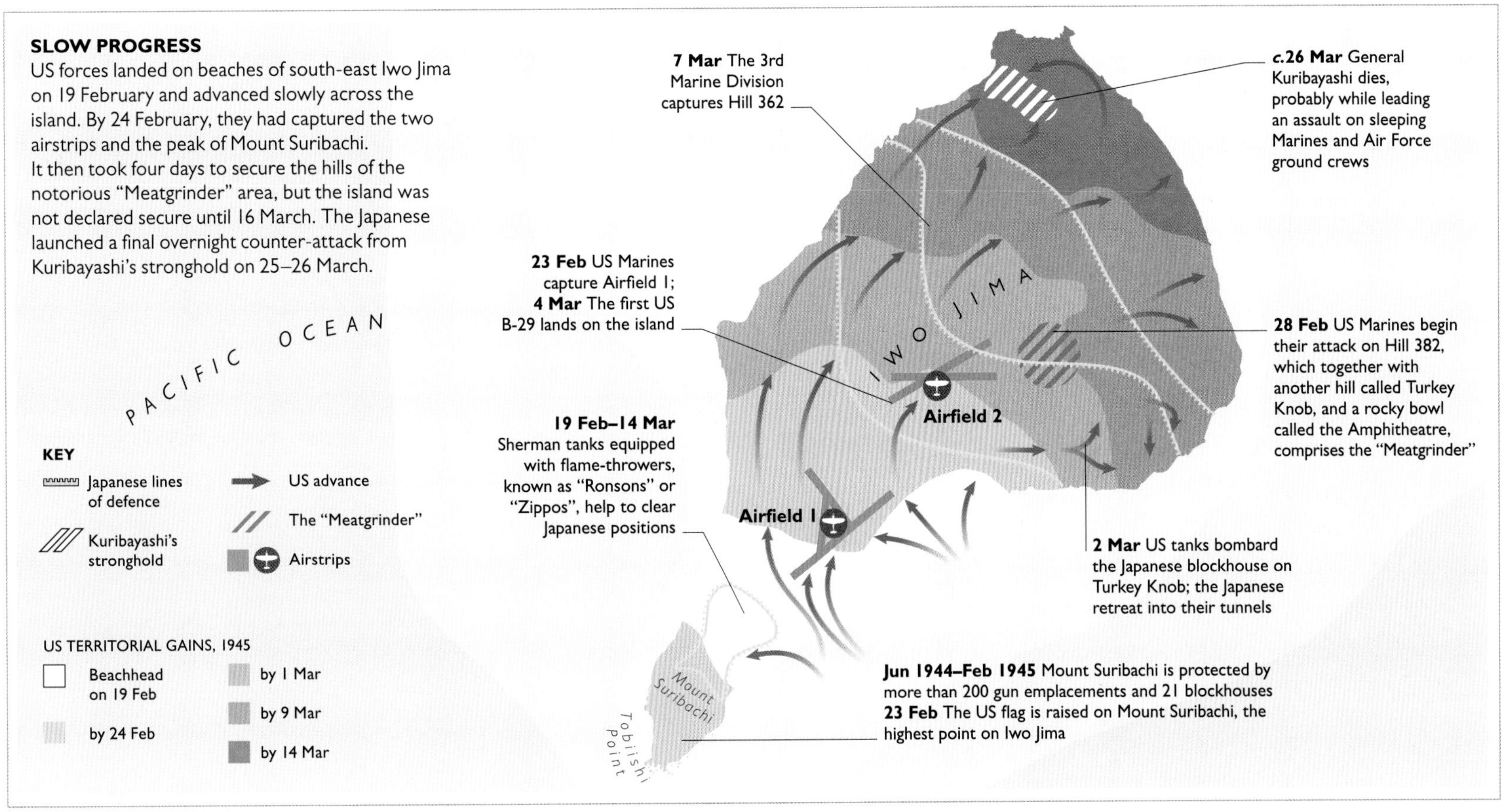
SLOW PROGRESS
US forces landed on beaches of south-east Iwo Jima on 19 February and advanced slowly across the island. By 24 February, they had captured the two airstrips and the peak of Mount Suribachi.
It then took four days to secure the hills of the notorious "Meatgrinder" area, but the island was not declared secure until 16 March. The Japanese launched a final overnight counter-attack from Kuribayashi's stronghold on 25–26 March.
PACIFIC OCEAN
IWO JIMA
7 Mar The 3rd Marine Division captures Hill 362
c.26 Mar General Kuribayashi dies, probably while leading an assault on sleeping Marines and Air Force ground crews
23 Feb US Marines capture Airfield 1; 4 Mar The first US B-29 lands on the island
28 Feb US Marines begin their attack on Hill 382, which together with another hill called Turkey Knob, and a rocky bowl called the Amphitheatre, comprises the "Meatgrinder"
19 Feb–14 Mar Sherman tanks equipped with flame-throwers, known as "Ronsons" or "Zippos", help to clear Japanese positions
Airfield 2
Airfield 1
2 Mar US tanks bombard the Japanese blockhouse on Turkey Knob; the Japanese retreat into their tunnels
Jun 1944–Feb 1945 Mount Suribachi is protected by more than 200 gun emplacements and 21 blockhouses
23 Feb The US flag is raised on Mount Suribachi, the highest point on Iwo Jima
Mount Suribachi
Tobiishi Point
KEY
Japanese lines of defence
US advance
Kuribayashi's stronghold
The "Meatgrinder"
Airstrips
US TERRITORIAL GAINS, 1945
Beachhead on 19 Feb
by 24 Feb
by 1 Mar
by 9 Mar
by 14 Mar

THE FALL OF BERLIN

The final battle of World War II in Europe saw Berlin face an overwhelming Red Army advance. Facing the end of his Third Reich, German leader Adolf Hitler nonetheless insisted his forces fight to the death, and the loss of life was vast on both sides.

After the invasion of Normandy by the Western Allies in summer 1944 (see pp.248–49), Hitler fought on stubbornly, even mounting a failed counter-offensive in the Ardennes at the Battle of the Bulge in December 1944–January 1945. In mid-January Soviet armies launched a vast offensive, invading Germany from the east. By March, the first US troops had crossed the Rhine from the west. In the air, British and US bombers laid waste German cities at will. His air force overwhelmed and his armies outnumbered, Hitler mobilized children and the elderly to die in defence of the Fatherland.

The question of whether the final Allied drive on Berlin would come from east or west was never disputed. US general Dwight D. Eisenhower was happy for the Soviets to take both the honour and the casualties. On 25 April, while fighting still raged in and around the German capital, Soviet and US troops met amicably at Torgau on the River Elbe. Anticipating humiliating defeat, as the battle raged on many leading Nazis, including Hitler, commited suicide. Berlin surrendered on 2 May, and five days later the war in Europe was over. Berlin was divided into Soviet and Western military occupation zones. These zones later hardened into a division between East and West Berlin that lasted until 1990.

1 May The German 12th Army and remnants of the 9th Army turn west to surrender to Allied forces
12th Army
Elbe
Dessau
1st US Army
Halle

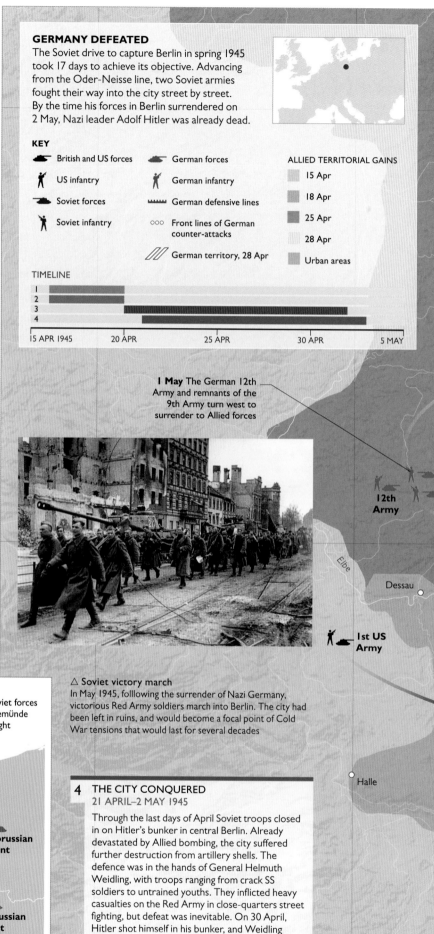

GERMANY DEFEATED

The Soviet drive to capture Berlin in spring 1945 took 17 days to achieve its objective. Advancing from the Oder-Neisse line, two Soviet armies fought their way into the city street by street. By the time his forces in Berlin surrendered on 2 May, Nazi leader Adolf Hitler was already dead.

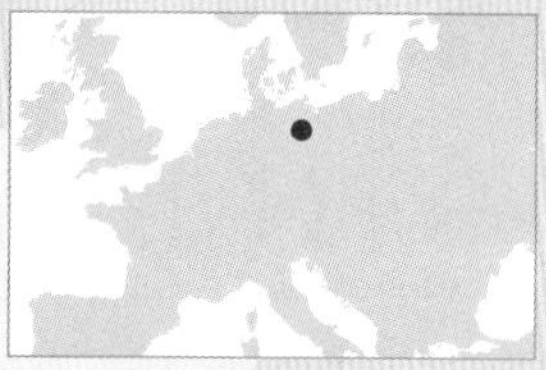

KEY

- British and US forces
- US infantry
- Soviet forces
- Soviet infantry
- German forces
- German infantry
- German defensive lines
- Front lines of German counter-attacks
- German territory, 28 Apr

ALLIED TERRITORIAL GAINS

- 15 Apr
- 18 Apr
- 25 Apr
- 28 Apr
- Urban areas

TIMELINE

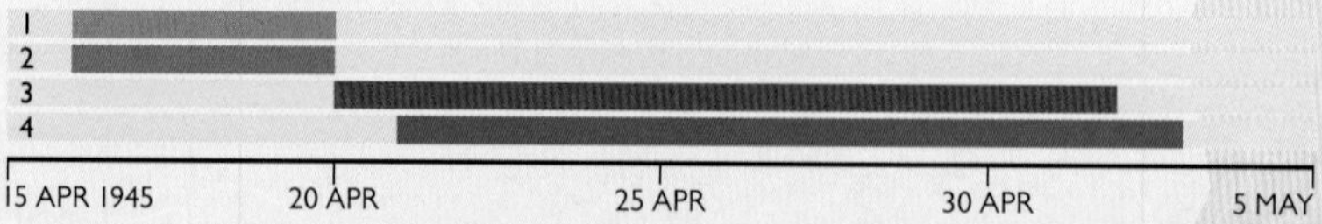
1
2
3
4
15 APR 1945
20 APR
25 APR
30 APR
5 MAY

△ **Soviet victory march**
In May 1945, folllowing the surrender of Nazi Germany, victorious Red Army soldiers march into Berlin. The city had been left in ruins, and would become a focal point of Cold War tensions that would last for several decades

4 THE CITY CONQUERED
21 APRIL–2 MAY 1945

Through the last days of April Soviet troops closed in on Hitler's bunker in central Berlin. Already devastated by Allied bombing, the city suffered further destruction from artillery shells. The defence was in the hands of General Helmuth Weidling, with troops ranging from crack SS soldiers to untrained youths. They inflicted heavy casualties on the Red Army in close-quarters street fighting, but defeat was inevitable. On 30 April, Hitler shot himself in his bunker, and Weidling negotiated the surrender of the city on 2 May.

Site of Hitler's bunker

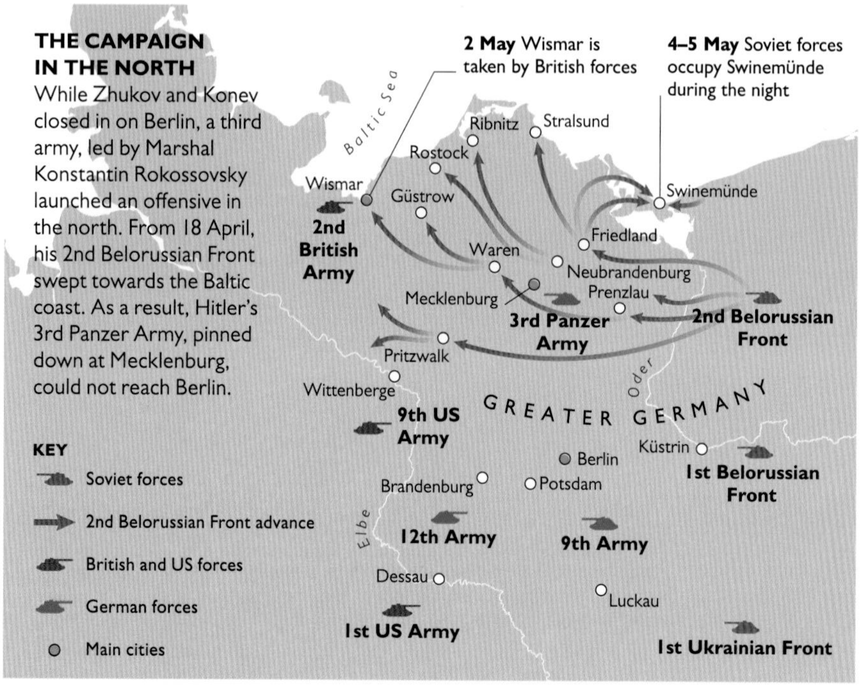
THE CAMPAIGN IN THE NORTH
While Zhukov and Konev closed in on Berlin, a third army, led by Marshal Konstantin Rokossovsky launched an offensive in the north. From 18 April, his 2nd Belorussian Front swept towards the Baltic coast. As a result, Hitler's 3rd Panzer Army, pinned down at Mecklenburg, could not reach Berlin.
2 May Wismar is taken by British forces
4–5 May Soviet forces occupy Swinemünde during the night
Baltic Sea
Ribnitz
Stralsund
Rostock
Wismar
Güstrow
Swinemünde
2nd British Army
Friedland
Waren
Neubrandenburg
Prenzlau
Mecklenburg
3rd Panzer Army
2nd Belorussian Front
Pritzwalk
Wittenberge
Oder
GREATER GERMANY
9th US Army
Berlin
Küstrin
Brandenburg
Potsdam
1st Belorussian Front
Elbe
12th Army
9th Army
Dessau
Luckau
1st US Army
1st Ukrainian Front
KEY
Soviet forces
2nd Belorussian Front advance
British and US forces
German forces
Main cities

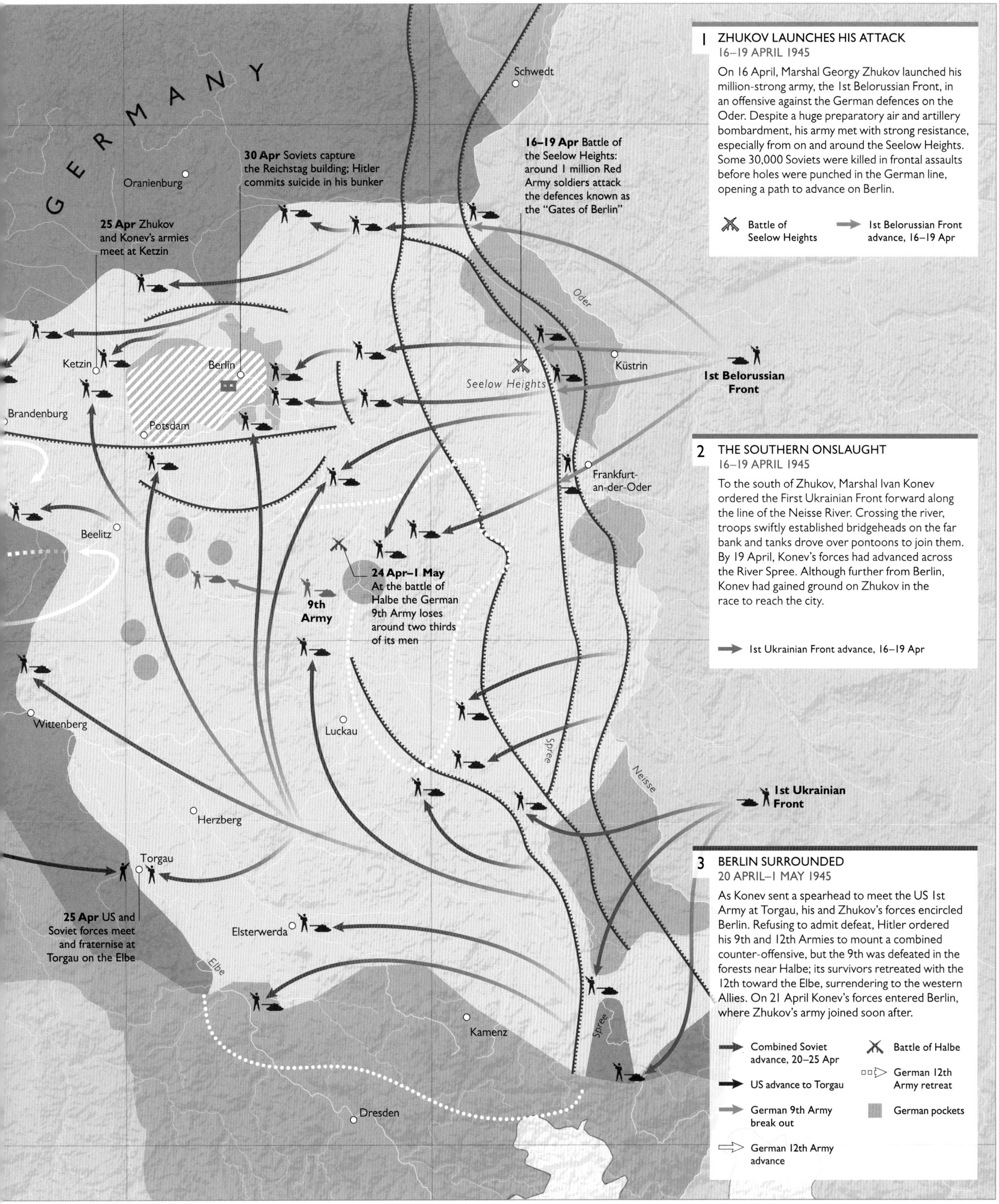
GERMANY
Schwedt
Oranienburg
30 Apr Soviets capture the Reichstag building; Hitler commits suicide in his bunker
16–19 Apr Battle of the Seelow Heights: around 1 million Red Army soldiers attack the defences known as the "Gates of Berlin"
25 Apr Zhukov and Konev's armies meet at Ketzin
Oder
Ketzin
Berlin
Küstrin
Seelow Heights
1st Belorussian Front
Brandenburg
Potsdam
Frankfurt-an-der-Oder
Beelitz
24 Apr–1 May At the battle of Halbe the German 9th Army loses around two thirds of its men
9th Army
Wittenberg
Luckau
Spree
Neisse
1st Ukrainian Front
Herzberg
Torgau
25 Apr US and Soviet forces meet and fraternise at Torgau on the Elbe
Elsterwerda
Elbe
Kamenz
Spree
Dresden

1 ZHUKOV LAUNCHES HIS ATTACK

16–19 APRIL 1945

On 16 April, Marshal Georgy Zhukov launched his million-strong army, the 1st Belorussian Front, in an offensive against the German defences on the Oder. Despite a huge preparatory air and artillery bombardment, his army met with strong resistance, especially from on and around the Seelow Heights. Some 30,000 Soviets were killed in frontal assaults before holes were punched in the German line, opening a path to advance on Berlin.

Battle of Seelow Heights

1st Belorussian Front advance, 16–19 Apr

2 THE SOUTHERN ONSLAUGHT

16–19 APRIL 1945

To the south of Zhukov, Marshal Ivan Konev ordered the First Ukrainian Front forward along the line of the Neisse River. Crossing the river, troops swiftly established bridgeheads on the far bank and tanks drove over pontoons to join them. By 19 April, Konev's forces had advanced across the River Spree. Although further from Berlin, Konev had gained ground on Zhukov in the race to reach the city.

1st Ukrainian Front advance, 16–19 Apr

3 BERLIN SURROUNDED

20 APRIL–1 MAY 1945

As Konev sent a spearhead to meet the US 1st Army at Torgau, his and Zhukov's forces encircled Berlin. Refusing to admit defeat, Hitler ordered his 9th and 12th Armies to mount a combined counter-offensive, but the 9th was defeated in the forests near Halbe; its survivors retreated with the 12th toward the Elbe, surrendering to the western Allies. On 21 April Konev's forces entered Berlin, where Zhukov's army joined soon after.

Combined Soviet advance, 20–25 Apr

US advance to Torgau

German 9th Army break out

German 12th Army advance

Battle of Halbe

German 12th Army retreat

German pockets

THE NUCLEAR AGE

After their first and only use over Japan in 1945, nuclear weapons inspired terror like no other military technology before them. They have not since been deployed in war, and are instead used as the ultimate deterrent.

△ **Atomic pioneer**
Born in 1904, American physicist J Robert Oppenheimer is renowned for spearheading the Manhattan Project, a US atomic weapons programme in the 1940s.

The world entered the nuclear age in August 1945, when the US bombed the Japanese cities of Hiroshima and Nagaski. The Soviet Union in turn developed its own nuclear capability in 1949, with Britain following suit in 1952.

Nuclear weapons were initially viewed as a special ordinance for strategic missions, but US president Harry S Truman's administration capitalized on their potential for deterrence to prevent direct clashes between the US and the Soviet Union. Across the world, massive expenditure was incurred in procuring and developing these weapons and their delivery systems, often overshadowing other elements of defence budgets. Ultimately, fission (atomic) bombs were supplanted by fusion (hydrogen) bombs. Strategic bombers were supplanted first by ground-based ballistic missiles, followed by submarine-launched ballistic missiles (SLBMs). Every advance in the field by a country was matched by its allies and competitors, and by the 1980s, the US and the Soviet Union wielded enough nuclear weapons to destroy the world many times over.

Present-day scenario

The Intermediate-Range Nuclear Forces (INF) Treaty, signed between the US and the Soviet Union in 1987, scaled down the tensions of this arms race. However, in the 21st century, nuclear arms continue to proliferate and are seen as important prestige weapons by nations.

INTERCONTINENTAL BALLISTIC MISSILES

Developed as strategic defense weapons, intercontinental ballistic missiles (ICBMs) are land-based, nuclear-armed ballistic missiles with a range of more than 5,600 km (3,500 miles). Russia, the US, China, France, India, the UK, and North Korea all currently hold operational ICBMs.

US Titan II ICBM

Cloud of fire
France entered the nuclear "arms race" in 1970 when it conducted Operation *Licorne* (Unicorn), an atmospheric nuclear test in the French Polynesia. A terrifying detonation of a nuclear device from the test can be seen here.

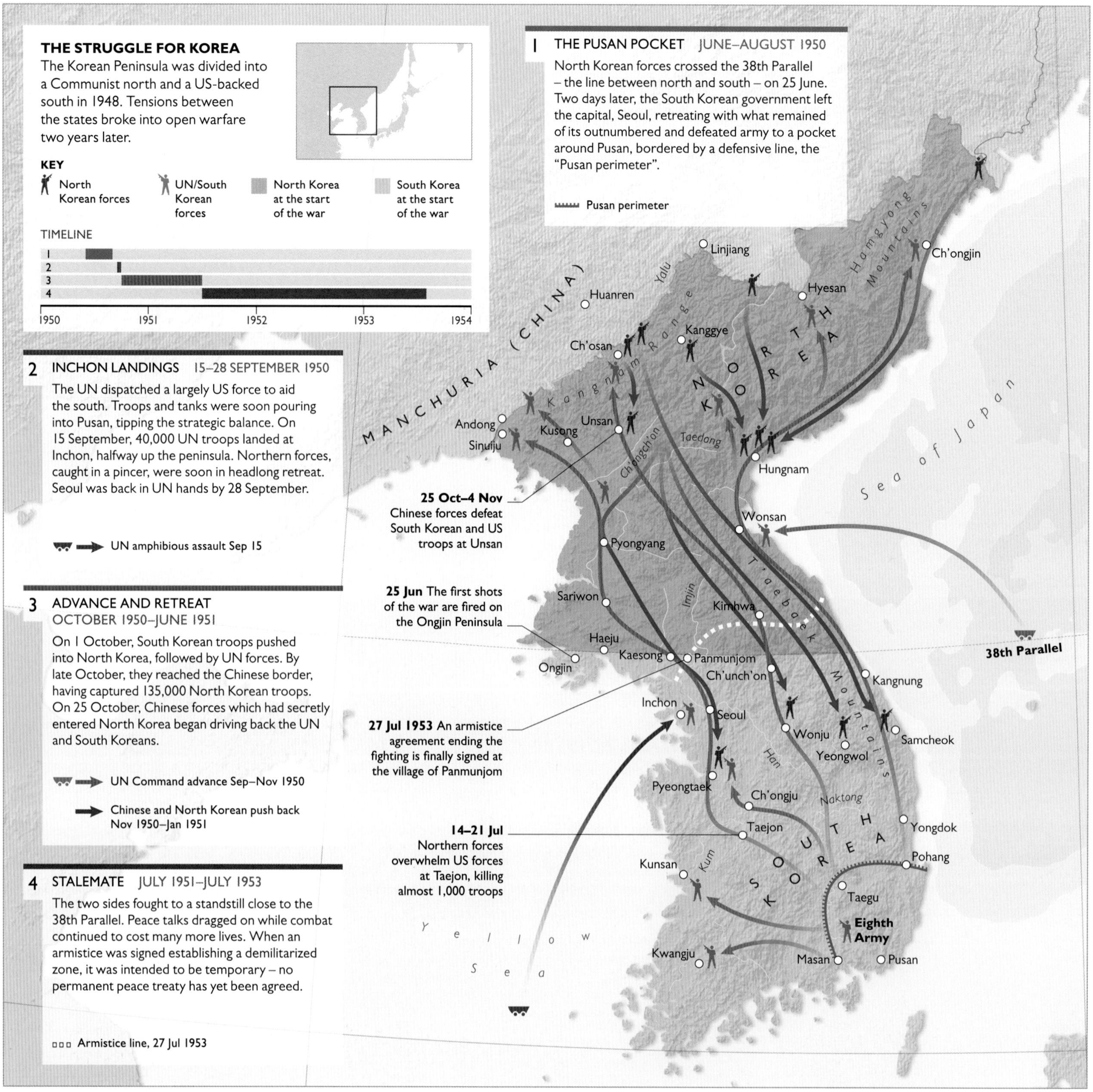
THE STRUGGLE FOR KOREA
The Korean Peninsula was divided into a Communist north and a US-backed south in 1948. Tensions between the states broke into open warfare two years later.
KEY
North Korean forces
UN/South Korean forces
North Korea at the start of the war
South Korea at the start of the war
TIMELINE
1
2
3
4
1950
1951
1952
1953
1954
1 THE PUSAN POCKET JUNE–AUGUST 1950
North Korean forces crossed the 38th Parallel – the line between north and south – on 25 June. Two days later, the South Korean government left the capital, Seoul, retreating with what remained of its outnumbered and defeated army to a pocket around Pusan, bordered by a defensive line, the "Pusan perimeter".
Pusan perimeter
2 INCHON LANDINGS 15–28 SEPTEMBER 1950
The UN dispatched a largely US force to aid the south. Troops and tanks were soon pouring into Pusan, tipping the strategic balance. On 15 September, 40,000 UN troops landed at Inchon, halfway up the peninsula. Northern forces, caught in a pincer, were soon in headlong retreat. Seoul was back in UN hands by 28 September.
UN amphibious assault Sep 15
3 ADVANCE AND RETREAT OCTOBER 1950–JUNE 1951
On 1 October, South Korean troops pushed into North Korea, followed by UN forces. By late October, they reached the Chinese border, having captured 135,000 North Korean troops. On 25 October, Chinese forces which had secretly entered North Korea began driving back the UN and South Koreans.
UN Command advance Sep–Nov 1950
Chinese and North Korean push back Nov 1950–Jan 1951
4 STALEMATE JULY 1951–JULY 1953
The two sides fought to a standstill close to the 38th Parallel. Peace talks dragged on while combat continued to cost many more lives. When an armistice was signed establishing a demilitarized zone, it was intended to be temporary – no permanent peace treaty has yet been agreed.
Armistice line, 27 Jul 1953
25 Oct–4 Nov Chinese forces defeat South Korean and US troops at Unsan
25 Jun The first shots of the war are fired on the Ongjin Peninsula
27 Jul 1953 An armistice agreement ending the fighting is finally signed at the village of Panmunjom
14–21 Jul Northern forces overwhelm US forces at Taejon, killing almost 1,000 troops
MANCHURIA (CHINA)
NORTH KOREA
SOUTH KOREA
Sea of Japan
Yellow Sea
38th Parallel
Hamgyong Mountains
Kangnam Range
Taebaek Mountains
Yalu
Taedong
Ch'ongch'on
Imjin
Han
Naktong
Kum
Linjiang
Ch'ongjin
Hyesan
Huanren
Kanggye
Ch'osan
Unsan
Kusong
Andong
Sinuiju
Hungnam
Wonsan
Pyongyang
Sariwon
Kimhwa
Haeju
Kaesong
Panmunjom
Ongjin
Ch'unch'on
Kangnung
Inchon
Seoul
Wonju
Samcheok
Yeongwol
Pyeongtaek
Ch'ongju
Taejon
Yongdok
Pohang
Kunsan
Taegu
Eighth Army
Kwangju
Masan
Pusan

INCHON

In the early months of the Korean War (1950–53), North Korean forces pushed the South Korean army and its allies back to a pocket in the southeast of the country. The amphibious landing of United Nations forces behind enemy lines at Inchon in 1950 marked the beginning of an ambitious counter-attack.

Liberated from Japanese rule at the end of World War II, Korea was divided into two republics: the Communist Democratic People's Republic of Korea in the north (supported by the USSR and China) and the Republic of Korea in the south (backed by the US). In June 1950, the north invaded the south, driving the southern army back to the southeast corner of the country, despite United Nations (UN) military support. UN Commander Douglas MacArthur planned a counter-offensive involving an amphibious landing 160km (100 miles) behind enemy lines at Inchon. The incursion was a success, and the UN forces rapidly won back the land they had lost. MacArthur attempted to pursue the enemy to the Chinese border – a move that triggered a Chinese intervention. This caused the UN forces to retreat, and by mid-1951 the two sides were back near where they had started at the beginning of the war.

DIEN BIEN PHU

At the end of World War II, France sought to re-establish control over its colonial possessions in Indochina. In Vietnam, the nationalist Viet Minh waged a lengthy guerrilla war of independence, finally defeating French forces in a bloody battle at Dien Bien Phu in May 1954.

French forces had been in conflict with the Viet Minh (who were fighting for an independent Vietnam) for more than seven years. Early in 1954, the French made plans to establish an outpost in the remote and mountainous northwest of Vietnam to break the deadlock. Supplied by air, this base would effectively cut the enemy's supply lines from neighbouring Laos. The French believed that the Viet Minh would not be able to move anti-aircraft guns and artillery into the area, but they underestimated the Viet Minh commander General Võ Nguyên Giáp, who spent months moving heavy weapons into virtually impregnable positions overlooking the French base. The French were taken by surprise when he attacked. Outlying positions fell fast, but the area around their airstrip held out for almost two months. When it fell in May 1954, the defeat was decisive, paving the way for the independence and partition of Vietnam.

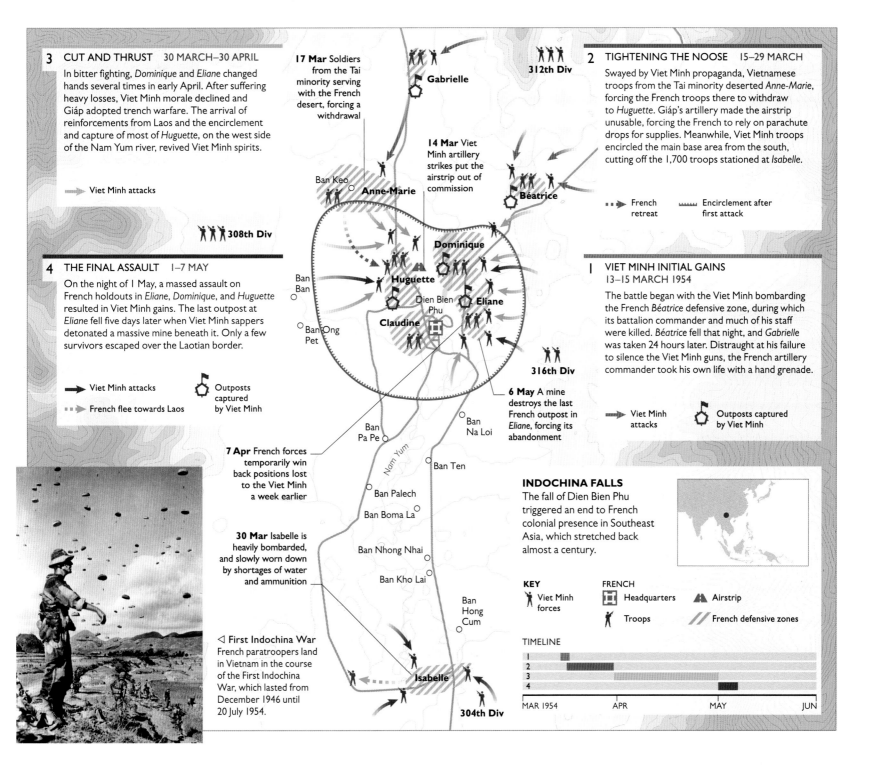

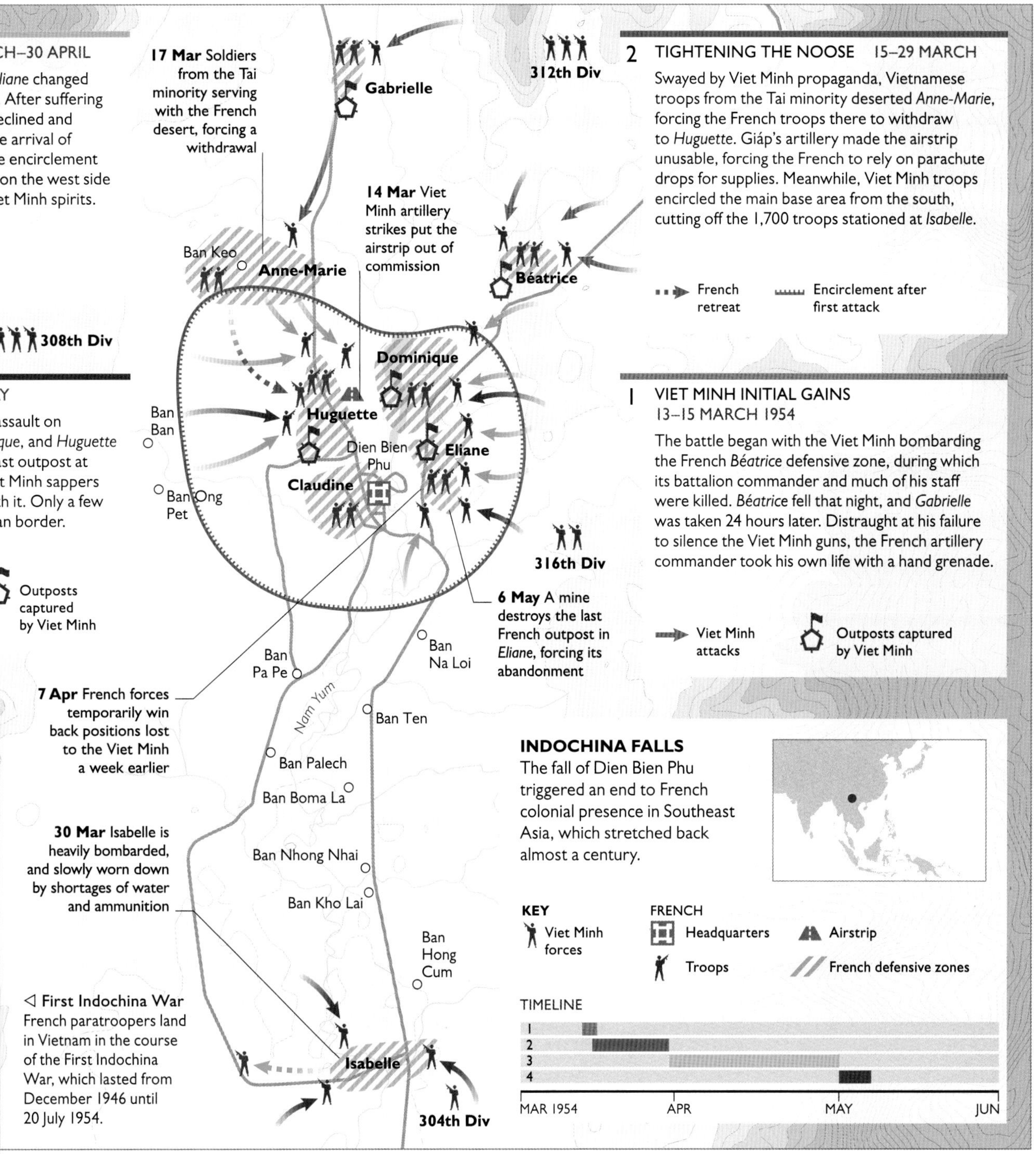
3 CUT AND THRUST 30 MARCH–30 APRIL
In bitter fighting, *Dominique* and *Eliane* changed hands several times in early April. After suffering heavy losses, Viet Minh morale declined and Giáp adopted trench warfare. The arrival of reinforcements from Laos and the encirclement and capture of most of *Huguette*, on the west side of the Nam Yum river, revived Viet Minh spirits.
Viet Minh attacks
308th Div
4 THE FINAL ASSAULT 1–7 MAY
On the night of 1 May, a massed assault on French holdouts in *Eliane*, *Dominique*, and *Huguette* resulted in Viet Minh gains. The last outpost at *Eliane* fell five days later when Viet Minh sappers detonated a massive mine beneath it. Only a few survivors escaped over the Laotian border.
Viet Minh attacks
French flee towards Laos
Outposts captured by Viet Minh
17 Mar Soldiers from the Tai minority serving with the French desert, forcing a withdrawal
Gabrielle
312th Div
14 Mar Viet Minh artillery strikes put the airstrip out of commission
Ban Keo
Anne-Marie
Béatrice
Dominique
Huguette
Eliane
Claudine
Dien Bien Phu
Ban Ban
Ban Ong Pet
316th Div
6 May A mine destroys the last French outpost in *Eliane*, forcing its abandonment
Ban Pa Pe
Ban Na Loi
Nam Yum
7 Apr French forces temporarily win back positions lost to the Viet Minh a week earlier
Ban Ten
Ban Palech
Ban Boma La
30 Mar Isabelle is heavily bombarded, and slowly worn down by shortages of water and ammunition
Ban Nhong Nhai
Ban Kho Lai
Ban Hong Cum
Isabelle
304th Div
2 TIGHTENING THE NOOSE 15–29 MARCH
Swayed by Viet Minh propaganda, Vietnamese troops from the Tai minority deserted *Anne-Marie*, forcing the French troops there to withdraw to *Huguette*. Giáp's artillery made the airstrip unusable, forcing the French to rely on parachute drops for supplies. Meanwhile, Viet Minh troops encircled the main base area from the south, cutting off the 1,700 troops stationed at *Isabelle*.
French retreat
Encirclement after first attack
1 VIET MINH INITIAL GAINS 13–15 MARCH 1954
The battle began with the Viet Minh bombarding the French *Béatrice* defensive zone, during which its battalion commander and much of his staff were killed. *Béatrice* fell that night, and *Gabrielle* was taken 24 hours later. Distraught at his failure to silence the Viet Minh guns, the French artillery commander took his own life with a hand grenade.
Viet Minh attacks
Outposts captured by Viet Minh
INDOCHINA FALLS
The fall of Dien Bien Phu triggered an end to French colonial presence in Southeast Asia, which stretched back almost a century.
KEY
Viet Minh forces
FRENCH
Headquarters
Troops
Airstrip
French defensive zones
TIMELINE
1
2
3
4
MAR 1954
APR
MAY
JUN

◁ **First Indochina War** French paratroopers land in Vietnam in the course of the First Indochina War, which lasted from December 1946 until 20 July 1954.

REVOLUTION AND WAR

After World War II, revolutionary and nationalist politics became linked with guerrilla warfare, resulting in insurgency movements. Many insurgents used guerrilla tactics, making it possible for weaker, less well equipped military forces to triumph over more powerful enemies.

LE THI HÔNG GÂM
TÂN CÔNG KIÊN QUYẾT QUẢ CẢM
BÁM TRỤ VỮNG CHẮC KIÊN CƯỜNG

△ **Fearless fighter**
This propaganda poster celebrates Le Thi Hong Gam, a Communist guerilla fighter killed in the Vietnam War.

Some of the most successful guerrilla campaigns in the 20th century took place in Vietnam. In 1946, the Viet Minh, a North Vietnamese nationalist group, launched an insurgency against the French colonial rulers. They followed the example of the Chinese Communist revolutionary Mao Zedong, who established guerrilla bases in the countryside and used propaganda to win popular support – a strategy that ultimately brought him to power in 1949. The Viet Minh's military tactics progressed from scattered raids, ambushes, and sabotage to full-scale military operations on the battlefield.

The success of the Viet Minh's campaign culminated in the defeat of the French at Dien Bien Phu (see p.257) and encouraged revolutionary movements worldwide. In Cuba, Fidel Castro's guerrillas overthrew the US-backed government in 1959, and the French faced a fresh guerrilla campaign in Algeria, leading to Algeria's independence in 1962. This was followed by guerrilla warfare resuming in South Vietnam, resulting in a full-blown war with the US (1965–73). In 1965, the Argentine Ernesto "Che" Guevara tried to spread the revolution, first in the Congo and then in South America. However, his efforts to unite anti-American forces failed. From the 1970s, urban guerrilla movements and international terrorism rose to equal prominence with the rural guerrilla tactics of the original revolutionaries.

△ **Armed patrol, 1966**
A communist Viet Cong guerrilla force patrols a river in South Vietnam. The soldier in the front is carrying an American M1918 Browning automatic rifle.

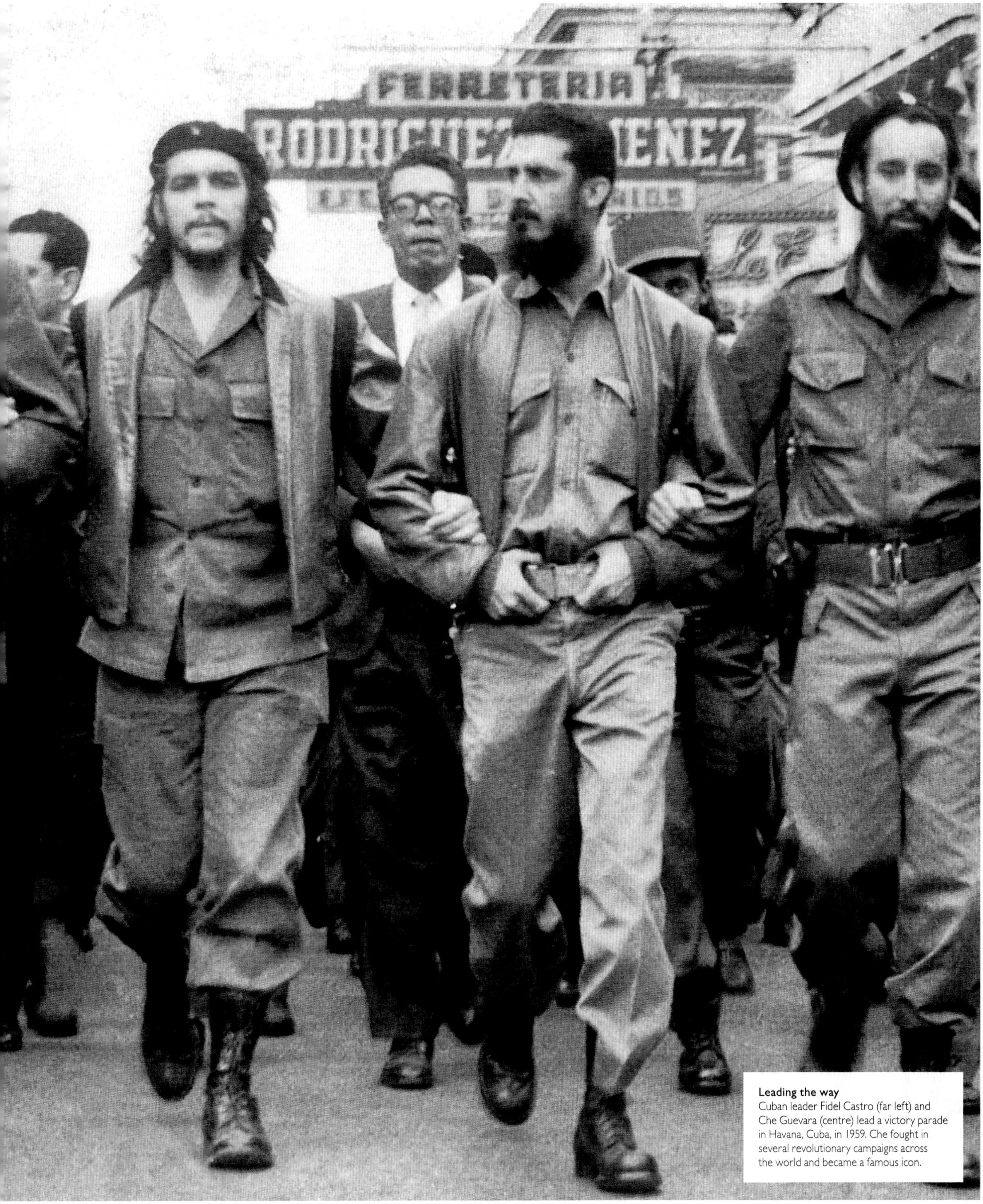
FERRETERIA

Leading the way
Cuban leader Fidel Castro (far left) and Che Guevara (centre) lead a victory parade in Havana, Cuba, in 1959. Che fought in several revolutionary campaigns across the world and became a famous icon.

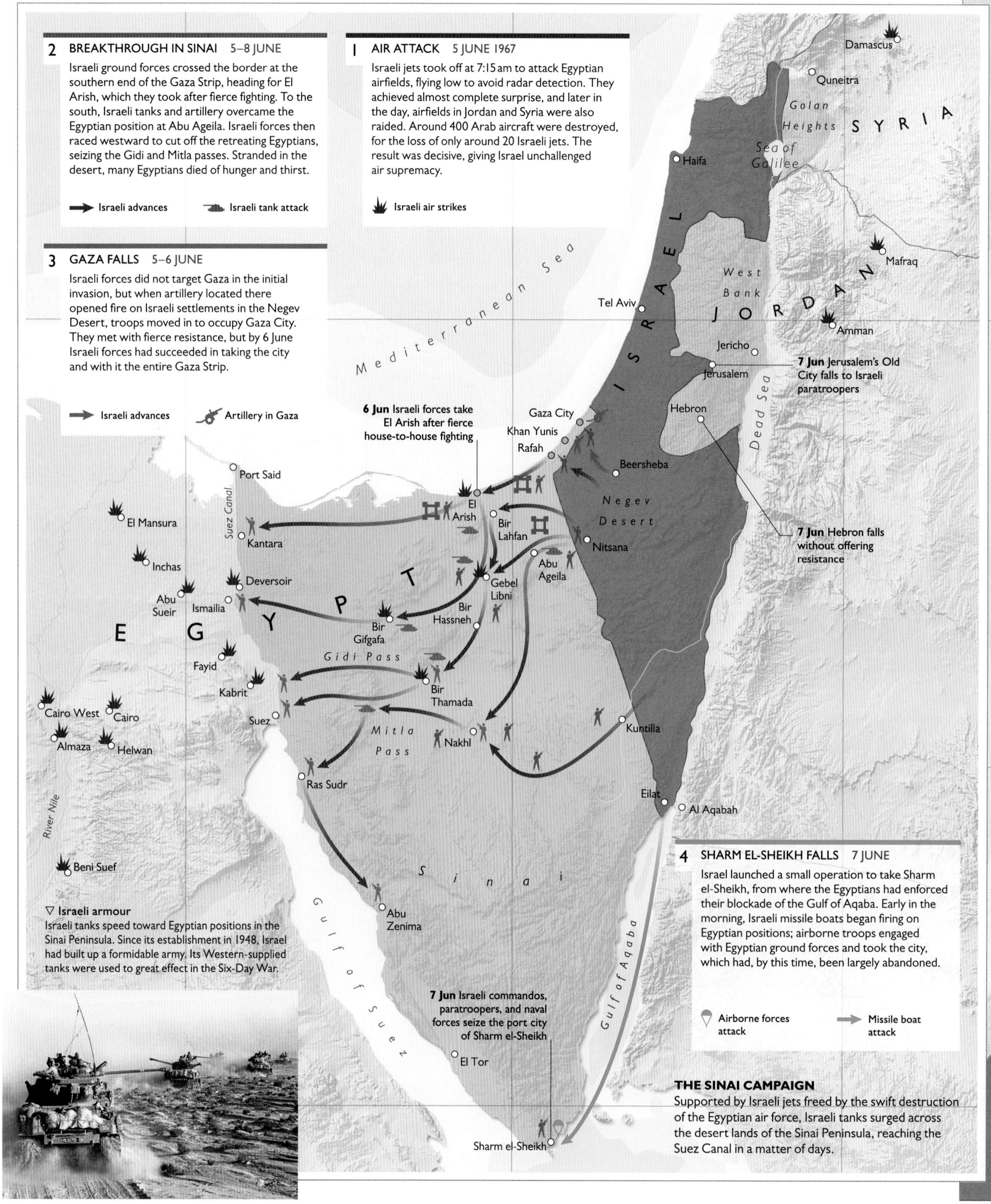

Damascus
Quneitra
Golan Heights
SYRIA
Sea of Galilee
Haifa
ISRAEL
Mediterranean Sea
West Bank
JORDAN
Mafraq
Tel Aviv
Amman
Jericho
Jerusalem
7 Jun Jerusalem's Old City falls to Israeli paratroopers
Dead Sea
Hebron
6 Jun Israeli forces take El Arish after fierce house-to-house fighting
Gaza City
Khan Yunis
Rafah
Beersheba
Port Said
Negev Desert
El Arish
Bir Lahfan
Nitsana
7 Jun Hebron falls without offering resistance
El Mansura
Suez Canal
Kantara
Abu Ageila
Inchas
Deversoir
Gebel Libni
Abu Sueir
Ismailia
EGYPT
Bir Hassneh
Bir Gifgafa
Gidi Pass
Fayid
Kabrit
Bir Thamada
Cairo West
Cairo
Suez
Almaza
Helwan
Mitla Pass
Nakhl
Kuntilla
Ras Sudr
Eilat
Al Aqabah
River Nile
Beni Suef
Sinai
Abu Zenima
Gulf of Suez
Gulf of Aqaba
7 Jun Israeli commandos, paratroopers, and naval forces seize the port city of Sharm el-Sheikh
El Tor
Sharm el-Sheikh

2 BREAKTHROUGH IN SINAI 5–8 JUNE

Israeli ground forces crossed the border at the southern end of the Gaza Strip, heading for El Arish, which they took after fierce fighting. To the south, Israeli tanks and artillery overcame the Egyptian position at Abu Ageila. Israeli forces then raced westward to cut off the retreating Egyptians, seizing the Gidi and Mitla passes. Stranded in the desert, many Egyptians died of hunger and thirst.

Israeli advances — Israeli tank attack

1 AIR ATTACK 5 JUNE 1967

Israeli jets took off at 7:15 am to attack Egyptian airfields, flying low to avoid radar detection. They achieved almost complete surprise, and later in the day, airfields in Jordan and Syria were also raided. Around 400 Arab aircraft were destroyed, for the loss of only around 20 Israeli jets. The result was decisive, giving Israel unchallenged air supremacy.

Israeli air strikes

3 GAZA FALLS 5–6 JUNE

Israeli forces did not target Gaza in the initial invasion, but when artillery located there opened fire on Israeli settlements in the Negev Desert, troops moved in to occupy Gaza City. They met with fierce resistance, but by 6 June Israeli forces had succeeded in taking the city and with it the entire Gaza Strip.

Israeli advances — Artillery in Gaza

4 SHARM EL-SHEIKH FALLS 7 JUNE

Israel launched a small operation to take Sharm el-Sheikh, from where the Egyptians had enforced their blockade of the Gulf of Aqaba. Early in the morning, Israeli missile boats began firing on Egyptian positions; airborne troops engaged with Egyptian ground forces and took the city, which had, by this time, been largely abandoned.

Airborne forces attack — Missile boat attack

▽ Israeli armour
Israeli tanks speed toward Egyptian positions in the Sinai Peninsula. Since its establishment in 1948, Israel had built up a formidable army. Its Western-supplied tanks were used to great effect in the Six-Day War.

THE SINAI CAMPAIGN
Supported by Israeli jets freed by the swift destruction of the Egyptian air force, Israeli tanks surged across the desert lands of the Sinai Peninsula, reaching the Suez Canal in a matter of days.

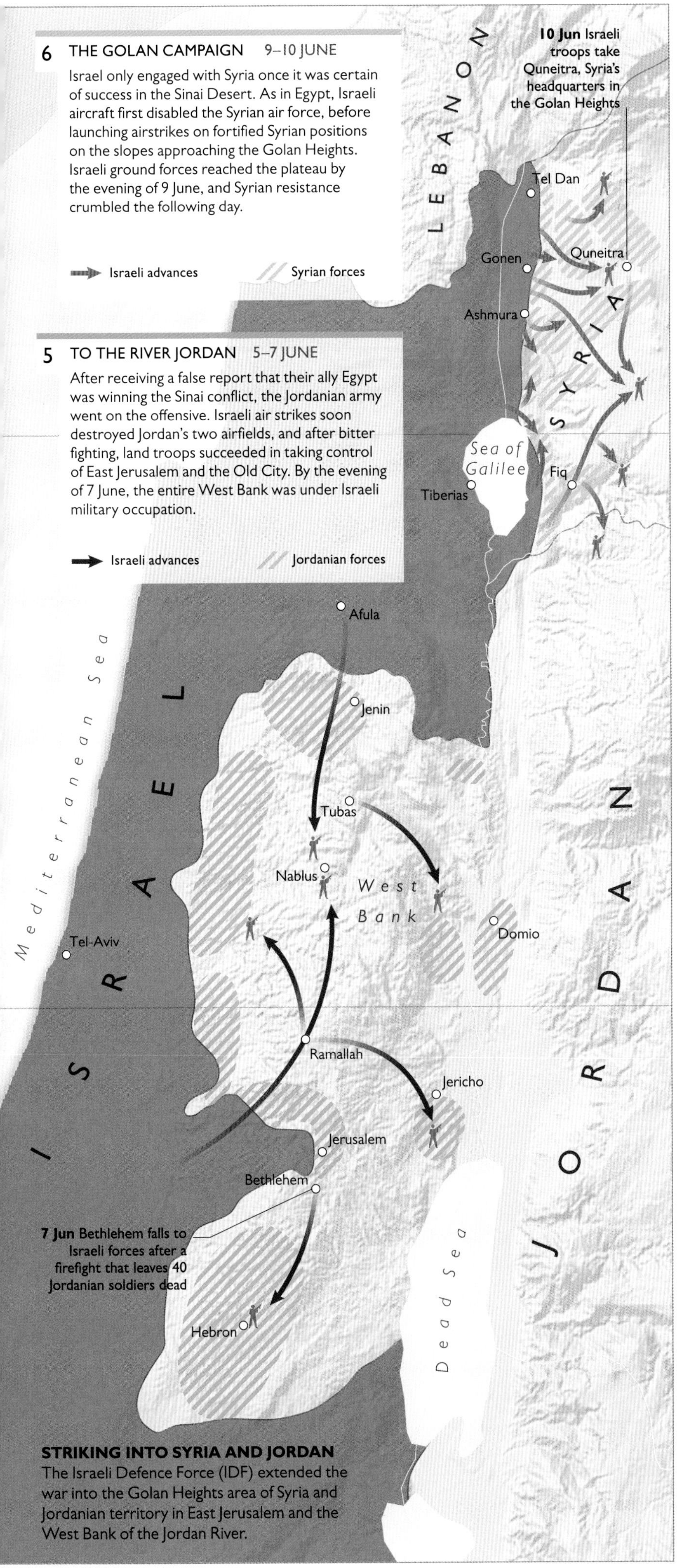
10 Jun Israeli troops take Quneitra, Syria's headquarters in the Golan Heights
LEBANON
SYRIA
ISRAEL
JORDAN
Mediterranean Sea
Dead Sea
Sea of Galilee
West Bank
Tel Dan
Quneitra
Gonen
Ashmura
Fiq
Tiberias
Afula
Jenin
Tubas
Nablus
Domio
Tel-Aviv
Ramallah
Jericho
Jerusalem
Bethlehem
Hebron
7 Jun Bethlehem falls to Israeli forces after a firefight that leaves 40 Jordanian soldiers dead
Israeli advances
Syrian forces
Israeli advances
Jordanian forces

6 THE GOLAN CAMPAIGN 9–10 JUNE

Israel only engaged with Syria once it was certain of success in the Sinai Desert. As in Egypt, Israeli aircraft first disabled the Syrian air force, before launching airstrikes on fortified Syrian positions on the slopes approaching the Golan Heights. Israeli ground forces reached the plateau by the evening of 9 June, and Syrian resistance crumbled the following day.

5 TO THE RIVER JORDAN 5–7 JUNE

After receiving a false report that their ally Egypt was winning the Sinai conflict, the Jordanian army went on the offensive. Israeli air strikes soon destroyed Jordan's two airfields, and after bitter fighting, land troops succeeded in taking control of East Jerusalem and the Old City. By the evening of 7 June, the entire West Bank was under Israeli military occupation.

STRIKING INTO SYRIA AND JORDAN

The Israeli Defence Force (IDF) extended the war into the Golan Heights area of Syria and Jordanian territory in East Jerusalem and the West Bank of the Jordan River.

SIX-DAY WAR

From its establishment in 1948, the state of Israel was in conflict with its Arab neighbours. When tensions rose to new heights in 1967, Israel launched a pre-emptive strike against Arab airfields, and sent its ground forces to occupy border territories and defeat the Arab armies.

The long-standing hostility between Israel and its Arab neighbours escalated in 1967 as tensions rose over Syrian support for Palestinian guerrillas. The crisis came to a head when Egypt's President Nasser mobilized his forces, blockaded Israeli shipping in the Gulf of Aqaba, and signed a defence pact with King Hussein of Jordan.

Convinced that the nation was under threat, the Israeli high command determined on pre-emptive action. On 5 June 1967, Israeli jets launched a series of attacks on Egyptian airfields that not only destroyed the bulk of the Egyptian air force on the ground but also made the airstrips themselves unusable. At the same time, ground forces embarked on a three-pronged invasion of the Sinai Peninsula, heading for the Suez Canal. In the fighting that ensued, air supremacy gave the invaders a decisive advantage.

When Jordan came to the aid of its Egyptian ally, its forces too were beaten back, placing East Jerusalem and the West Bank of the Jordan river under Israeli control. Buoyed by their success, Israeli forces then advanced over the Syrian border on the Golan Heights, taking that strategic stronghold before accepting a ceasefire as called for by the United Nations Security Council. In just six days, Israel had occupied almost 70,000sq km (27,000 sq miles) of land.

"Everyone must face the test and enter the battle to the end."

PRESIDENT NOUREDDIN AL-ATASSI OF SYRIA, 1967

DECISION IN THE DESERT

Simmering hostility between Israel and the surrounding Arab states broke into open warfare in June 1967. A pre-emptive strike by the Israeli air force gave Israel control of the air, paving the way for decisive gains by its land forces on three separate fronts.

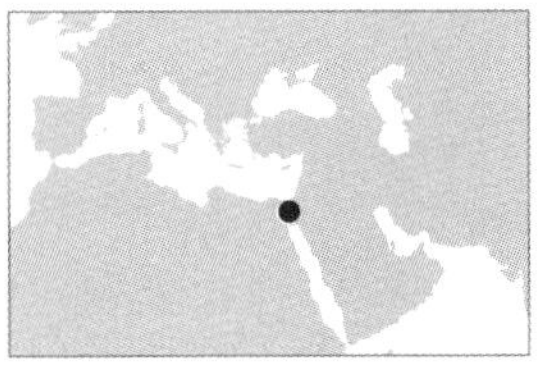

KEY

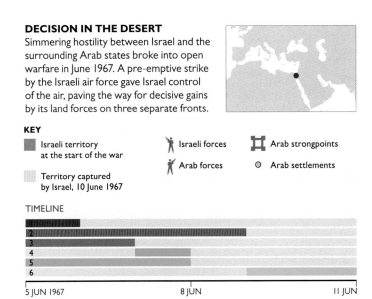

- Israeli territory at the start of the war
- Territory captured by Israel, 10 June 1967
- Israeli forces
- Arab forces
- Arab strongpoints
- Arab settlements

TIMELINE

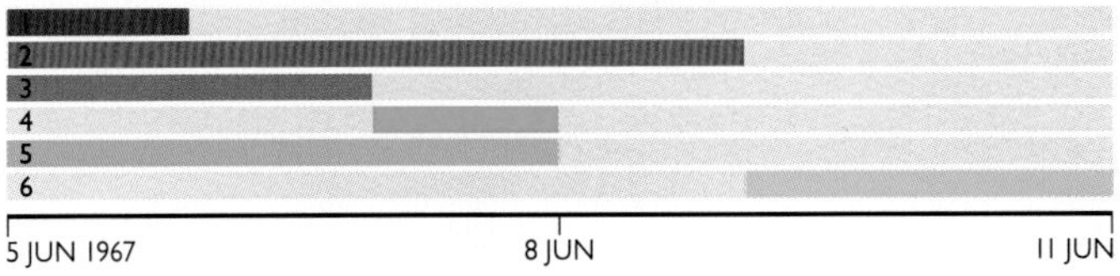
1
2
3
4
5
6
5 JUN 1967
8 JUN
11 JUN

THE TET OFFENSIVE

In 1967, US leaders sought to boost popular support for the Vietnam War. However, a series of attacks by Communist forces in 1968, known as the Tet Offensive, helped swing US opinion against the war, despite media coverage of the heavy losses suffered by the North Vietnamese and Viet Cong forces.

In 1954, the Geneva Conference divided Vietnam between a Communist north, supported by China and the USSR, and a Western-backed south. Hostilities between the two resulted in the US deploying active combat units in 1965; in the US, public opinion started to turn against such involvement.

In 1967, US commander General Westmoreland claimed that the Communist forces were "unable to mount a major offensive". In fact North Vietnam's leaders had been planning one since early that year. They timed their attack for the Tet New Year holiday, the biggest celebration of the year in Vietnam. Over three days in early 1968, they launched assaults in more than 100 cities. Most of the attackers were repulsed or killed within days, although fighting in the northern city of Hue lasted almost a month. The Viet Cong and the North Vietnamese People's Army of Vietnam (PAVN) lost tens of thousands of fighters. Yet the scope of the action disproved the notion that the war was almost won. Although North Vietnamese hopes of a decisive uprising proved to be misplaced, the battle helped turn US opinion against the war.

△ **US forces in Vietnam**
After the French withdrawal from Indochina (see p.257) Vietnam increasingly came under the influence of a US that wished to curb the spread of Communism. By 1962, there were some 10,000 US troops in the country.

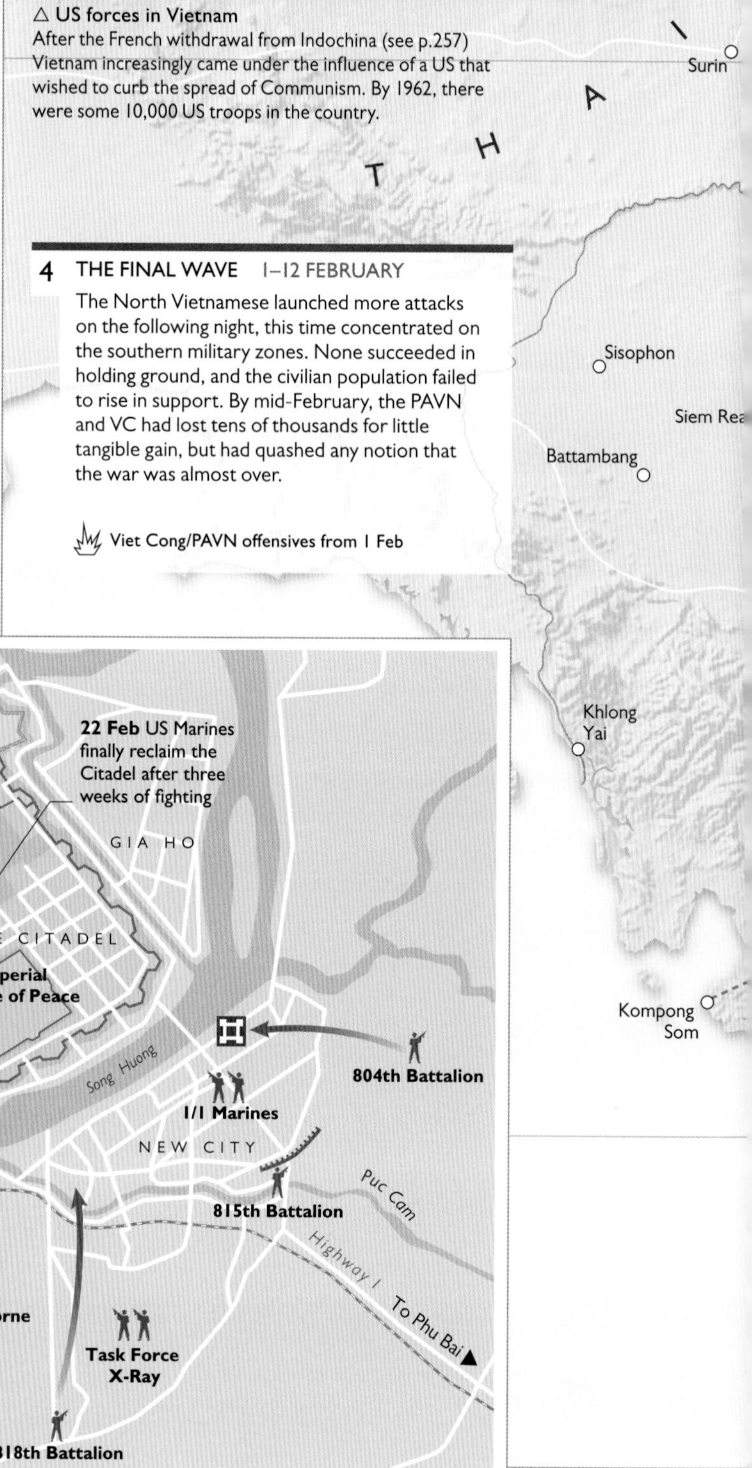

Surin
T H A
Sisophon
Siem Rea
Battambang
Khlong Yai
Kompong Som

4 THE FINAL WAVE 1–12 FEBRUARY

The North Vietnamese launched more attacks on the following night, this time concentrated on the southern military zones. None succeeded in holding ground, and the civilian population failed to rise in support. By mid-February, the PAVN and VC had lost tens of thousands for little tangible gain, but had quashed any notion that the war was almost over.

Viet Cong/PAVN offensives from 1 Feb

THE BATTLE FOR HUE
The longest battle of the Tet Offensive was fought in Hue. There, Vietnamese Army forces held out in parts of the Citadel while allied troops repelled attacks on the MACV (Military Assistance Command, Vietnam) headquarters south of the river. North Vietnamese insurgents occupied the rest of the city, which was only recaptured after weeks of fighting. By the end, most of the city was destroyed, and around 10,000 soldiers and civilians were dead.

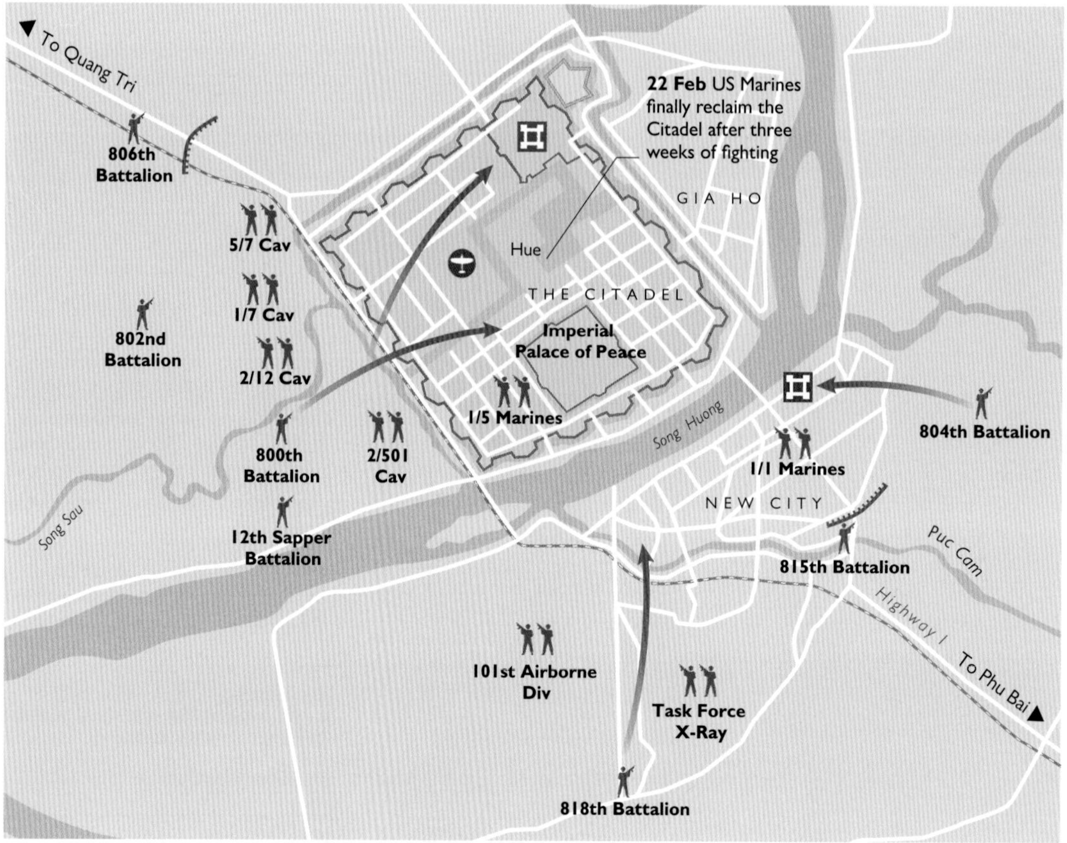

To Quang Tri
806th Battalion
5/7 Cav
1/7 Cav
802nd Battalion
2/12 Cav
800th Battalion
2/501 Cav
12th Sapper Battalion
Song Sau
22 Feb US Marines finally reclaim the Citadel after three weeks of fighting
GIA HO
Hue
THE CITADEL
Imperial Palace of Peace
1/5 Marines
Song Huong
1/1 Marines
804th Battalion
NEW CITY
815th Battalion
Puc Cam
Highway 1
To Phu Bai
101st Airborne Div
Task Force X-Ray
818th Battalion

KEY
- Communist forces
- US and ARVN forces
- Communist attacks
- Communist blocking positions
- ARVN Divisional HQ
- MACV command post
- Bach Ho railroad
- Tay Loc Airfield

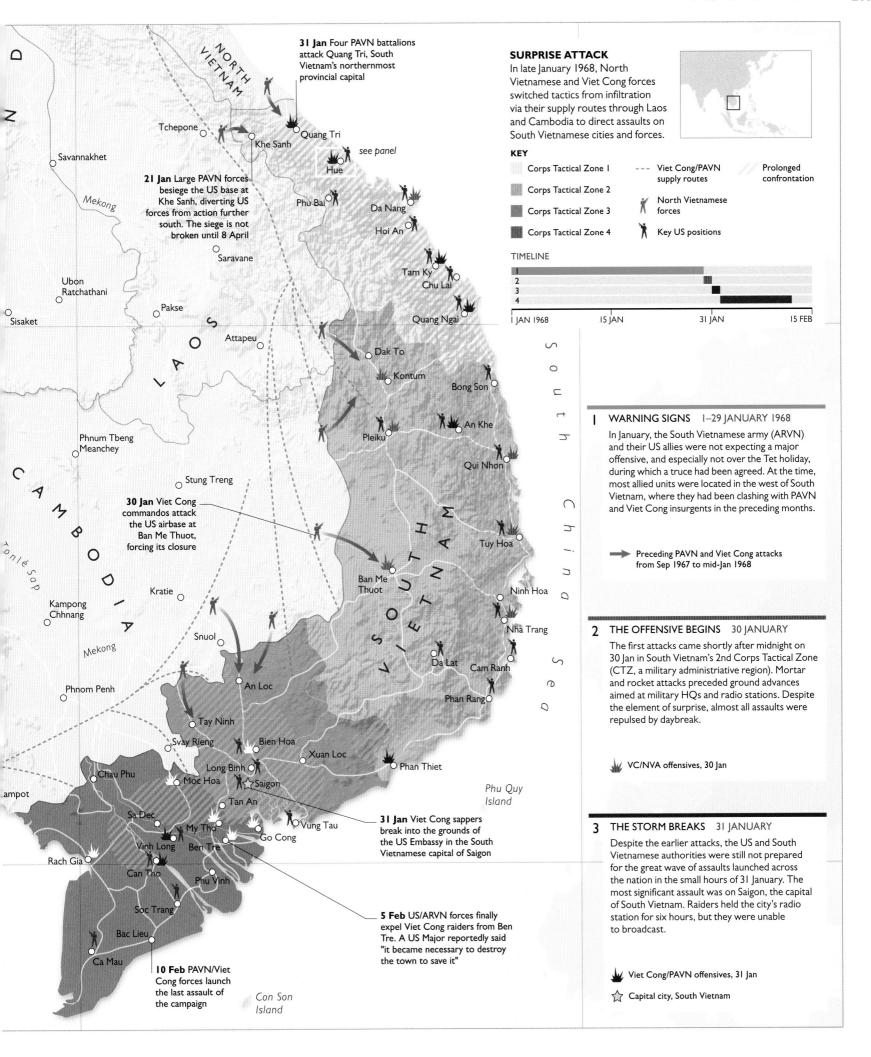

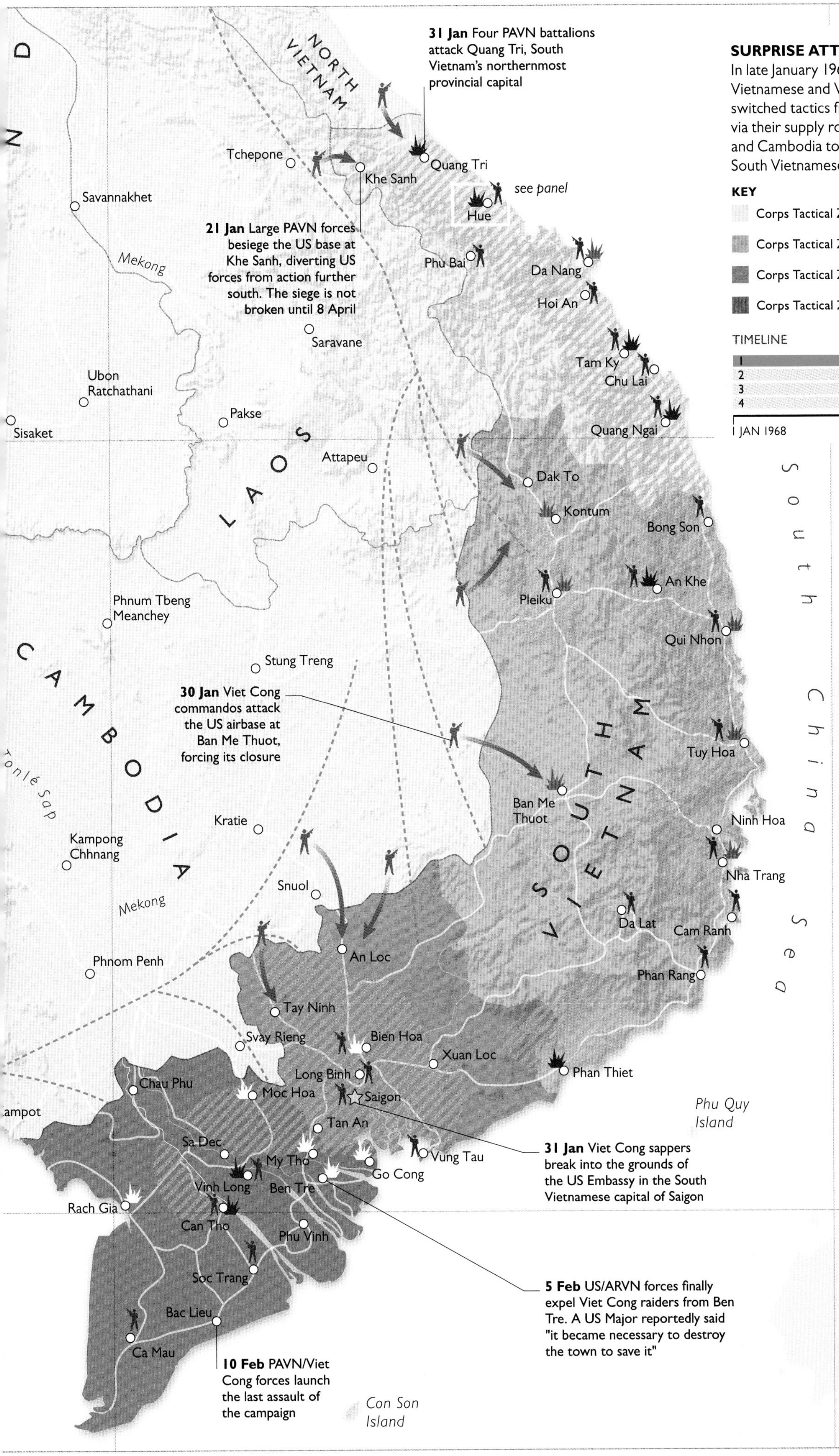
31 Jan Four PAVN battalions attack Quang Tri, South Vietnam's northernmost provincial capital
21 Jan Large PAVN forces besiege the US base at Khe Sanh, diverting US forces from action further south. The siege is not broken until 8 April
30 Jan Viet Cong commandos attack the US airbase at Ban Me Thuot, forcing its closure
31 Jan Viet Cong sappers break into the grounds of the US Embassy in the South Vietnamese capital of Saigon
5 Feb US/ARVN forces finally expel Viet Cong raiders from Ben Tre. A US Major reportedly said "it became necessary to destroy the town to save it"
10 Feb PAVN/Viet Cong forces launch the last assault of the campaign
see panel
NORTH VIETNAM
LAOS
CAMBODIA
SOUTH VIETNAM
South China Sea
Quang Tri
Khe Sanh
Tchepone
Hue
Savannakhet
Mekong
Phu Bai
Da Nang
Hoi An
Saravane
Tam Ky
Chu Lai
Ubon Ratchathani
Pakse
Sisaket
Quang Ngai
Attapeu
Dak To
Kontum
Bong Son
An Khe
Pleiku
Phnum Tbeng Meanchey
Qui Nhon
Stung Treng
Tuy Hoa
Tonlé Sap
Ban Me Thuot
Ninh Hoa
Kratie
Kampong Chhnang
Nha Trang
Snuol
Da Lat
Cam Ranh
An Loc
Phnom Penh
Phan Rang
Tay Ninh
Svay Rieng
Bien Hoa
Xuan Loc
Long Binh
Phan Thiet
Chau Phu
Moc Hoa
Saigon
Phu Quy Island
ampot
Tan An
Sa Dec
My Tho
Vung Tau
Go Cong
Vinh Long
Ben Tre
Rach Gia
Can Tho
Phu Vinh
Soc Trang
Bac Lieu
Ca Mau
Con Son Island

SURPRISE ATTACK

In late January 1968, North Vietnamese and Viet Cong forces switched tactics from infiltration via their supply routes through Laos and Cambodia to direct assaults on South Vietnamese cities and forces.

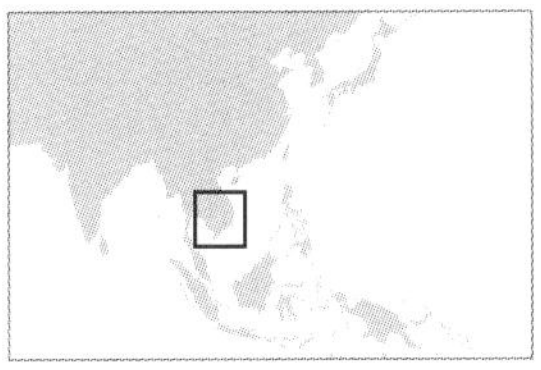

KEY

- Corps Tactical Zone 1
- Corps Tactical Zone 2
- Corps Tactical Zone 3
- Corps Tactical Zone 4
- Viet Cong/PAVN supply routes
- North Vietnamese forces
- Key US positions
- Prolonged confrontation

TIMELINE

1
2
3
4
1 JAN 1968
15 JAN
31 JAN
15 FEB

1 WARNING SIGNS 1–29 JANUARY 1968

In January, the South Vietnamese army (ARVN) and their US allies were not expecting a major offensive, and especially not over the Tet holiday, during which a truce had been agreed. At the time, most allied units were located in the west of South Vietnam, where they had been clashing with PAVN and Viet Cong insurgents in the preceding months.

Preceding PAVN and Viet Cong attacks from Sep 1967 to mid-Jan 1968

2 THE OFFENSIVE BEGINS 30 JANUARY

The first attacks came shortly after midnight on 30 Jan in South Vietnam's 2nd Corps Tactical Zone (CTZ, a military administriative region). Mortar and rocket attacks preceded ground advances aimed at military HQs and radio stations. Despite the element of surprise, almost all assaults were repulsed by daybreak.

VC/NVA offensives, 30 Jan

3 THE STORM BREAKS 31 JANUARY

Despite the earlier attacks, the US and South Vietnamese authorities were still not prepared for the great wave of assaults launched across the nation in the small hours of 31 January. The most significant assault was on Saigon, the capital of South Vietnam. Raiders held the city's radio station for six hours, but they were unable to broadcast.

Viet Cong/PAVN offensives, 31 Jan

Capital city, South Vietnam

YOM KIPPUR WAR

Launched on the Jewish holy day of Yom Kippur in October 1973, the surprise attack by Egypt and Syria on Israel sought to win back land occupied by Israel six years earlier. Despite early gains for Egypt and Syria, Israel counter-attacked, recapturing its lost territory.

Humiliated by their defeat in the 1967 Six-Day War (see pp.260–61), the leaders of Egypt and Syria sought an opportunity to reverse the gains made by Israel. They took their chance six years later, launching a surprise attack timed for the Jewish festival of Yom Kippur.

On 6 October, Egyptian forces crossed the Suez Canal to assault the fortified Bar-Lev Line, while Syrian tanks simultaneously stormed across the ceasefire line in the Golan Heights overlooking northern Israel. Initially, both co-belligerents made significant gains, causing shock in Israel. However, after the first four days of fighting, the tide of battle reversed and the Egyptian advance stalled. Alarmed by the war's geopolitical implications at a time when Cold War tensions remained high, the US and the USSR each put pressure on the two sides, and a ceasefire went into effect after 19 days of combat. Although neither side made significant gains, the diplomatic standoff between Israel and Egypt had been effectively broken, and in the years that followed a peace process got under way that led eventually to Egyptian recognition of the state of Israel and the return of Sinai to Egypt.

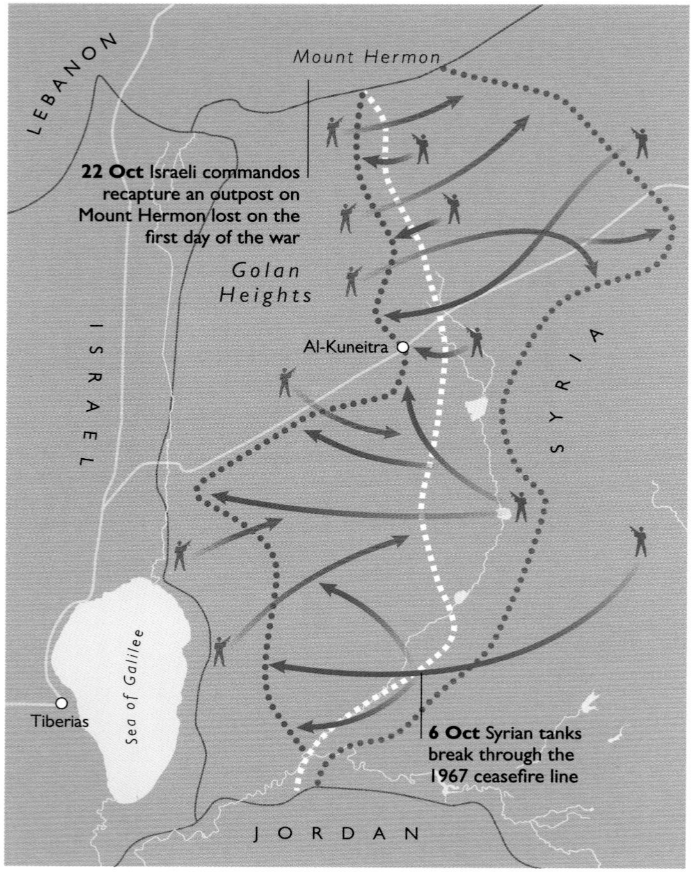
LEBANON
Mount Hermon
22 Oct Israeli commandos recapture an outpost on Mount Hermon lost on the first day of the war
Golan Heights
Al-Kuneitra
ISRAEL
SYRIA
Sea of Galilee
Tiberias
6 Oct Syrian tanks break through the 1967 ceasefire line
JORDAN

THE SYRIAN FRONT
On 6 October, in a move coordinated with its Egyptian allies, Syria sent five divisions to attack Israeli positions along the 1967 ceasefire line in the Golan Heights. In the north, they encountered strong resistance, but south of Al-Kuneitra, they achieved a breakthrough, threatening to invade Israeli territory around the Sea of Galilee. Israeli reserves rushed to confront the advancing forces, pushing them back to the old ceasefire line. On 11 October, the troops received orders to push on into Syrian territory, reaching within 40 km (25 miles) of the Syrian capital Damascus.

KEY
- Ceasefire line, 1967
- Syrian troops
- Syrian attacks
- Furthest Syrian advance
- Israeli troops
- Israeli counter-attack
- Furthest Israeli advance

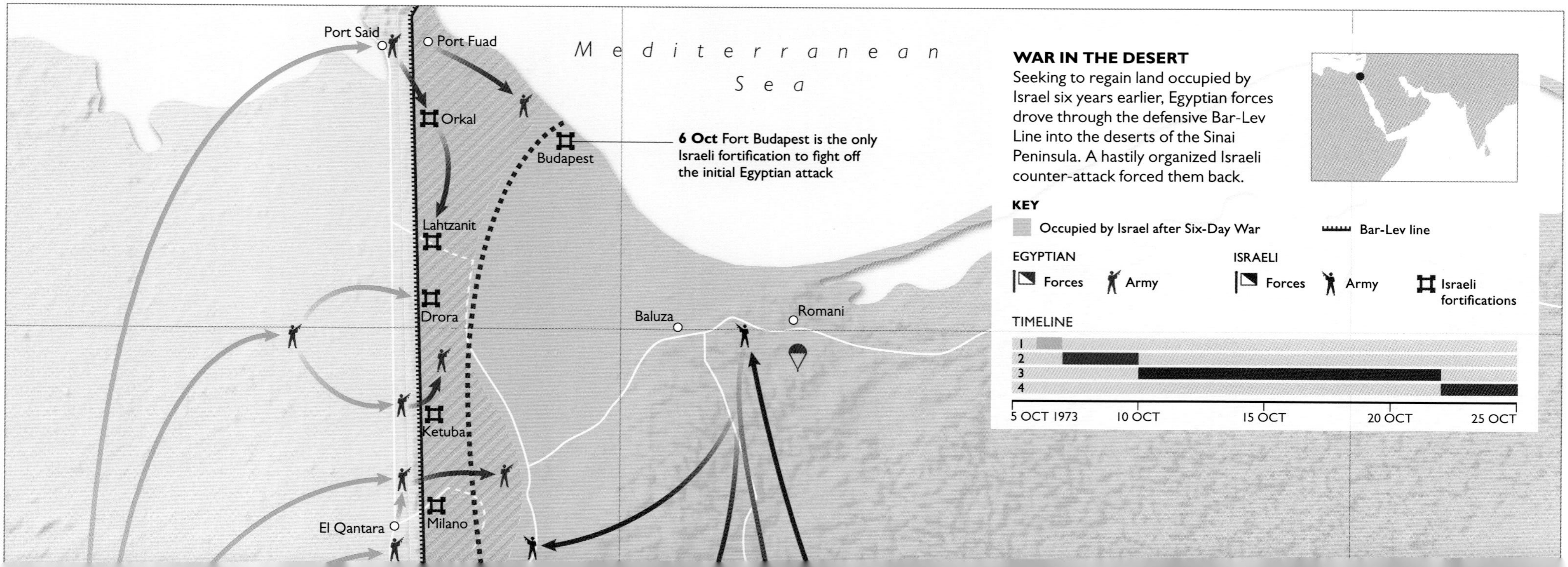
Port Said
Port Fuad
Mediterranean Sea
Orkal
Budapest
6 Oct Fort Budapest is the only Israeli fortification to fight off the initial Egyptian attack
Lahtzanit
Drora
Ketuba
Milano
El Qantara
Baluza
Romani
TIMELINE
1
2
3
4
5 OCT 1973
10 OCT
15 OCT
20 OCT
25 OCT

WAR IN THE DESERT
Seeking to regain land occupied by Israel six years earlier, Egyptian forces drove through the defensive Bar-Lev Line into the deserts of the Sinai Peninsula. A hastily organized Israeli counter-attack forced them back.

KEY
- Occupied by Israel after Six-Day War
- Bar-Lev line

EGYPTIAN: Forces, Army

ISRAELI: Forces, Army, Israeli fortifications

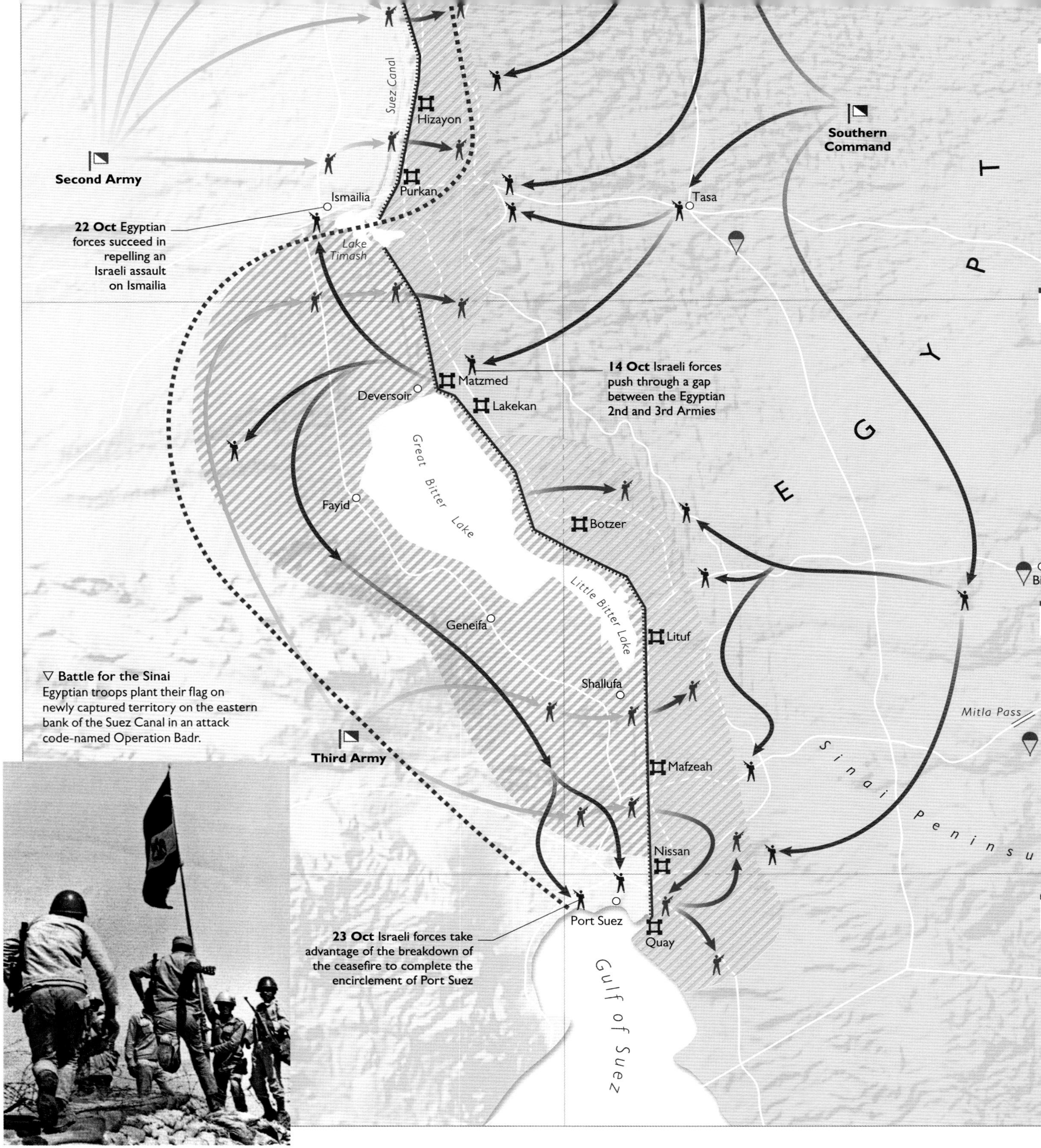
Second Army
Suez Canal
Hizayon
Purkan
Ismailia
Lake Timash
Southern Command
Tasa
E
G
Y
P
T
Matzmed
Lakekan
Deversoir
Great Bitter Lake
Fayid
Botzer
Little Bitter Lake
Bir Gidy
Geneifa
Lituf
Shallufa
Mitla Pass
Sinai Peninsula
Third Army
Mafzeah
Nissan
Port Suez
Quay
Gulf of Suez
22 Oct Egyptian forces succeed in repelling an Israeli assault on Ismailia
14 Oct Israeli forces push through a gap between the Egyptian 2nd and 3rd Armies
23 Oct Israeli forces take advantage of the breakdown of the ceasefire to complete the encirclement of Port Suez

▽ **Battle for the Sinai**
Egyptian troops plant their flag on newly captured territory on the eastern bank of the Suez Canal in an attack code-named Operation Badr.

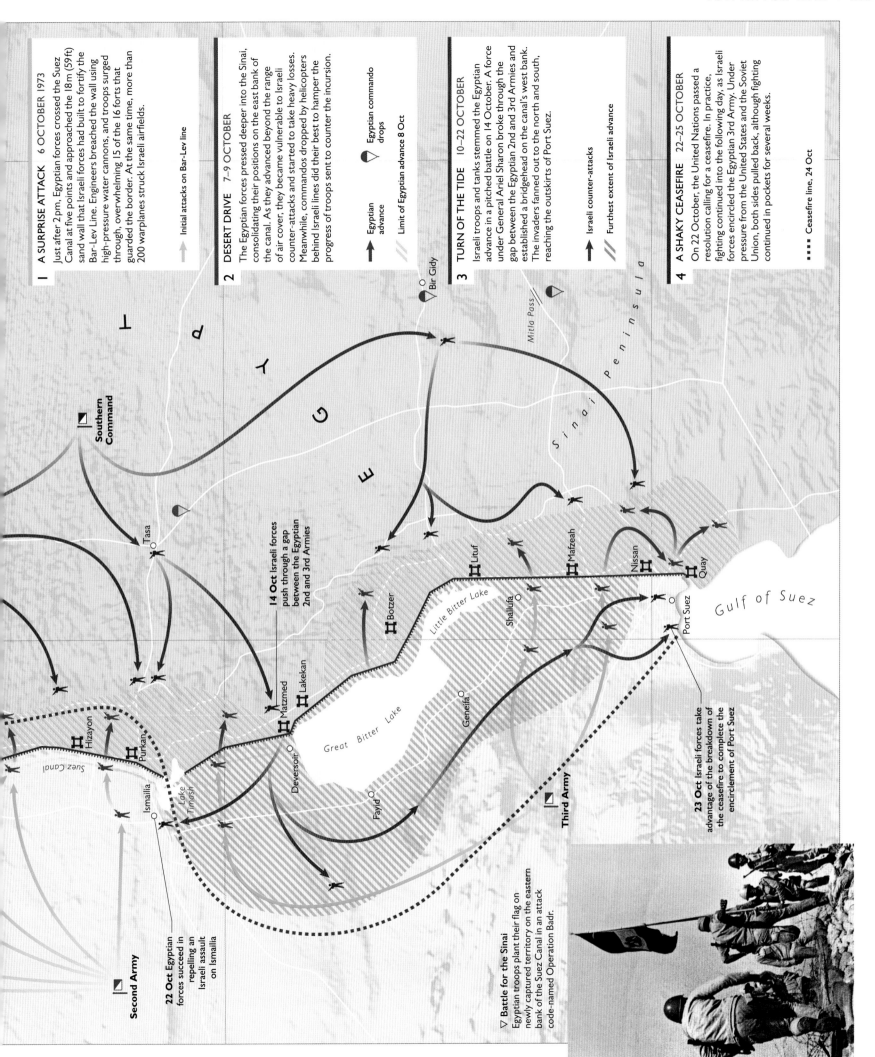

1 A SURPRISE ATTACK 6 OCTOBER 1973

Just after 2 pm, Egyptian forces crossed the Suez Canal at five points and approached the 18 m (59 ft) sand wall that Israeli forces had built to fortify the Bar-Lev Line. Engineers breached the wall using high-pressure water cannons, and troops surged through, overwhelming 15 of the 16 forts that guarded the border. At the same time, more than 200 warplanes struck Israeli airfields.

Initial attacks on Bar-Lev line

2 DESERT DRIVE 7–9 OCTOBER

The Egyptian forces pressed deeper into the Sinai, consolidating their positions on the east bank of the canal. As they advanced beyond the range of air cover, they became vulnerable to Israeli counter-attacks and started to take heavy losses. Meanwhile, commandos dropped by helicopters behind Israeli lines did their best to hamper the progress of troops sent to counter the incursion.

Egyptian advance
Egyptian commando drops
Limit of Egyptian advance 8 Oct

3 TURN OF THE TIDE 10–22 OCTOBER

Israeli troops and tanks stemmed the Egyptian advance in a pitched battle on 14 October. A force under General Ariel Sharon broke through the gap between the Egyptian 2nd and 3rd Armies and established a bridgehead on the canal's west bank. The invaders fanned out to the north and south, reaching the outskirts of Port Suez.

Israeli counter-attacks
Furthest extent of Israeli advance

4 A SHAKY CEASEFIRE 22–25 OCTOBER

On 22 October, the United Nations passed a resolution calling for a ceasefire. In practice, fighting continued into the following day, as Israeli forces encircled the Egyptian 3rd Army. Under pressure from the United States and the Soviet Union, both sides pulled back, although fighting continued in pockets for several weeks.

Ceasefire line, 24 Oct

DESERT STORM

In response to Iraq's invasion of Kuwait in 1990, the US brought together a coalition of nations to liberate the country. Following a protracted bombing campaign, their ground forces attacked in February 1991, meeting limited resistance. After four days' fighting, US President George Bush declared victory.

Following the end of the Iran-Iraq War in 1988, Iraq found itself deeply in debt to its neighbours Kuwait and Saudi Arabia. Disputes over this debt and over border oilfields soured relations, and in 1990, Iraqi president Saddam Hussein gave the order for an invasion of Kuwait, which took place on 2 August.

US president George Bush, appalled by this aggression and worried by the threat to global oil supplies, started moving troops to the Saudi-Iraq border and began a coalition of nations to resist Saddam; eventually 34 countries gave their support. The military build-up continued into early 1991 until over half a million troops were ready for action. The fighting started with an intensive allied bombing campaign, launched on 16 January. For the next six weeks, Iraq's military and civilian infrastructure was pounded day and night from the skies.

A ground invasion was finally launched on 24 February. As coalition forces headed into Kuwait and Iraq itself, Iraqi invaders retreated before them, leaving over 700 Kuwaiti oil wells on fire. After just three days, President Bush was able to declare the country liberated. On 28 February, with his troops within 240km (150 miles) of the Iraqi capital, Bush declared a ceasefire. The exiled Emir of Kuwait returned to his devastated country a fortnight later.

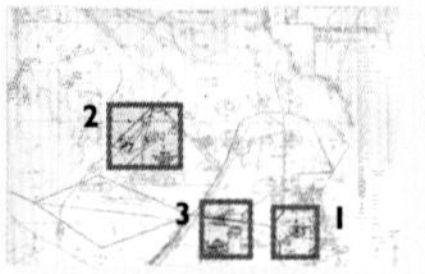
2
3
1

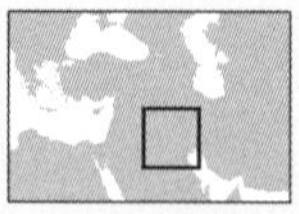

KEY

1 The main thrust into Kuwait moved north to liberate Kuwait City.

2 The US 7th Corps and the British 1st Armoured Division drove northeast into Iraq.

3 Saudi, Kuwaiti, and Egyptian forces moved into western Kuwait.

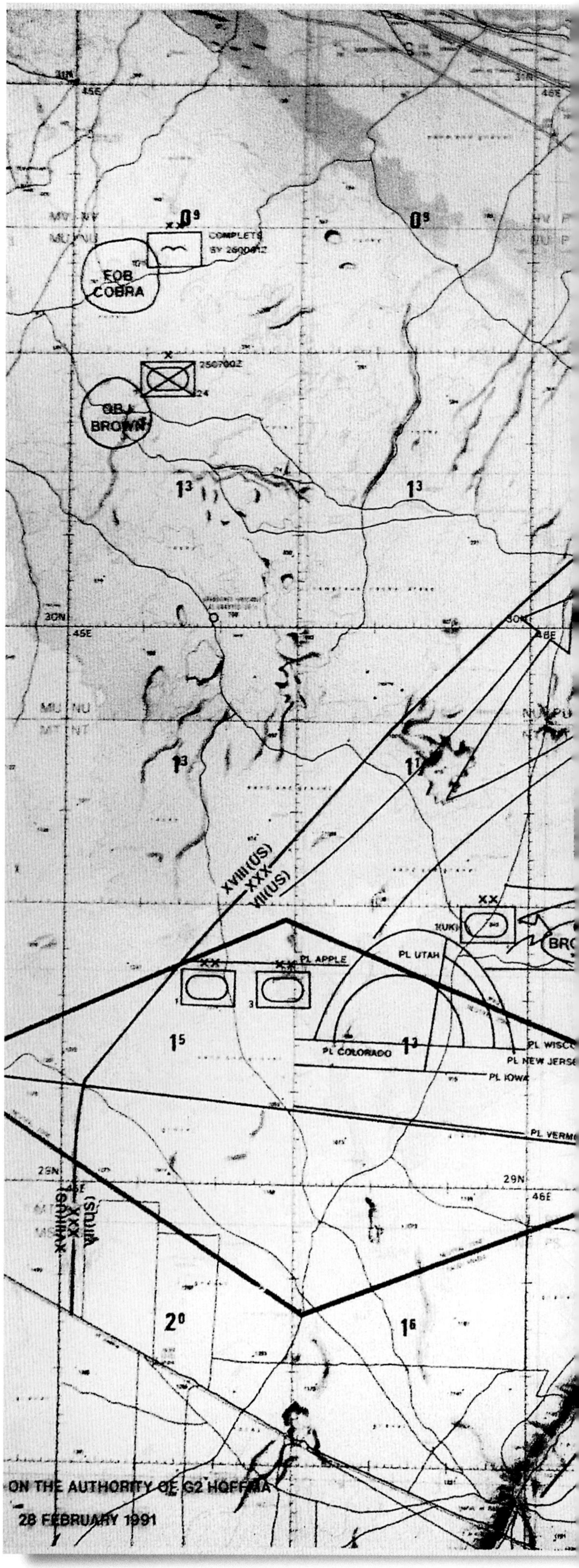
FOB COBRA
OBJ BROWN
PL APPLE
PL UTAH
PL COLORADO
PL NEW JERSEY
PL IOWA
XVIII(US)
XXX
VII(US)
ON THE AUTHORITY OF G2 HOFFMA
28 FEBRUARY 1991

▷ **Coalition plan of attack**
Dated 25 February 1991 and declassified three days later when the war ended, this initially secret situation report map shows movements at the start of the ground war. Blue arrows indicate the progress of coalition forces into Kuwait (to the right) and Iraq itself.

WAR IN THE SKIES
The coalition's strategic air campaign saw F-117 planes and Tomahawk missiles destroy much of Iraq's military and parts of its civilian infrastructure. Prime targets included command and communications installations, air force bases, and mobile missile launch pads. Although civilians suffered disruption due to these attacks, there was none of the massive loss of life caused by previous bombing campaigns.

KEY
- Allied airbase
- Coalition airstrike
- Iraqi airbase

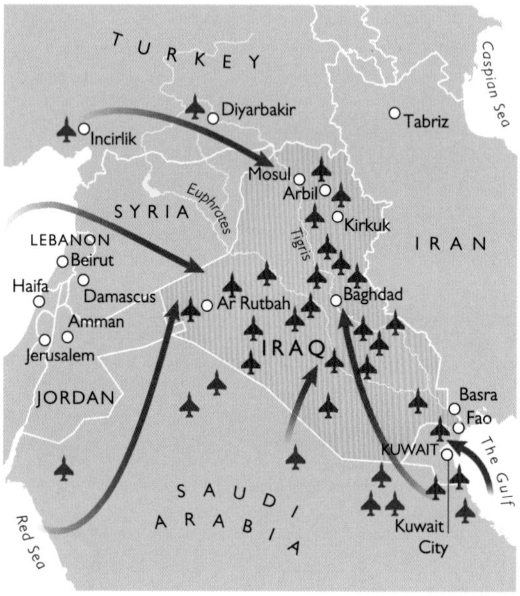
TURKEY
Caspian Sea
Diyarbakir
Incirlik
Tabriz
Mosul
Arbil
Euphrates
Tigris
SYRIA
Kirkuk
LEBANON
Beirut
IRAN
Haifa
Damascus
Ar Rutbah
Baghdad
Amman
Jerusalem
IRAQ
JORDAN
Basra
Fao
KUWAIT
The Gulf
SAUDI ARABIA
Kuwait City
Red Sea

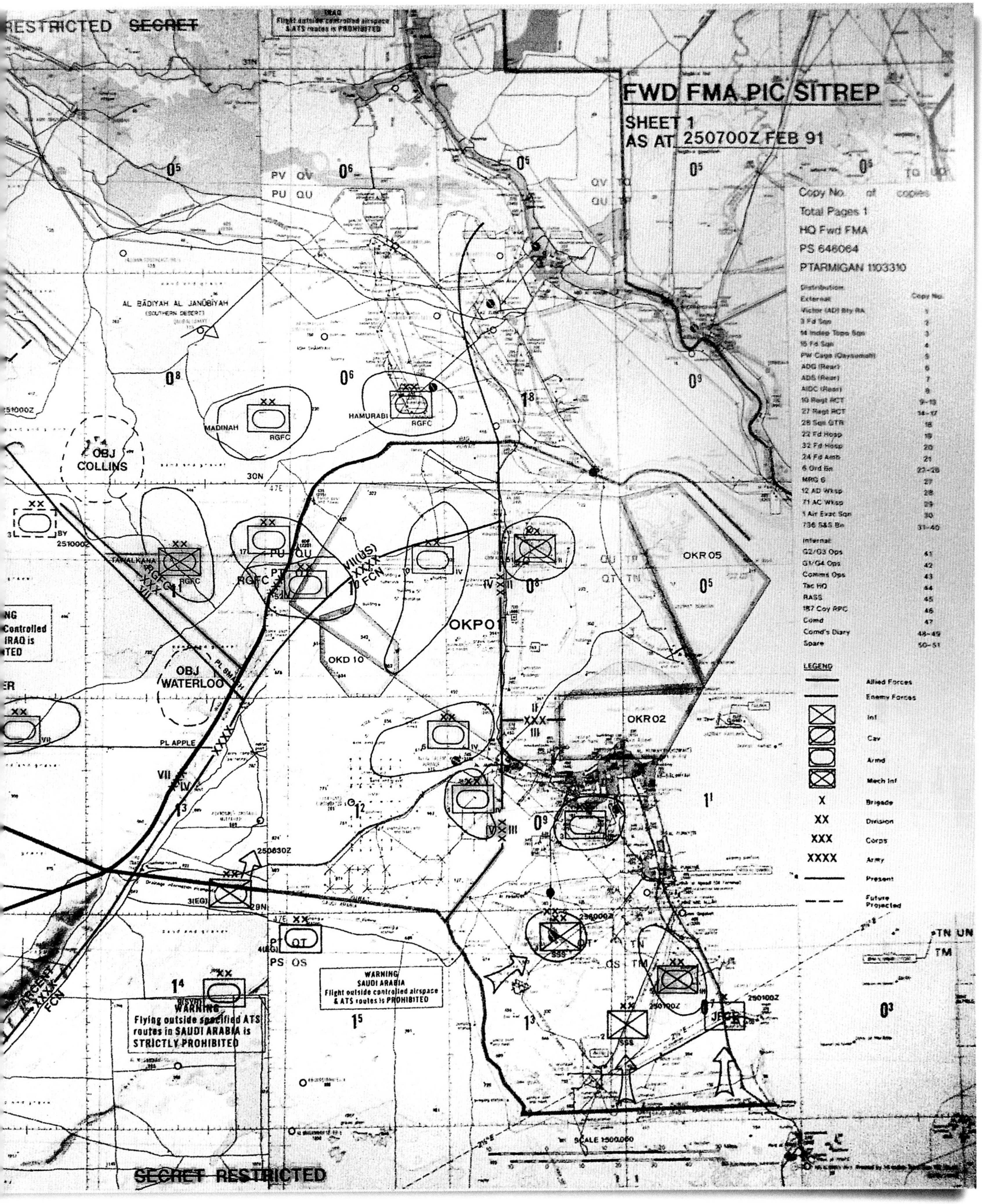
RESTRICTED SECRET
FWD FMA PIC SITREP
SHEET 1
AS AT 250700Z FEB 91
Copy No. of copies
Total Pages 1
HQ Fwd FMA
PS 646064
PTARMIGAN 1103310
Distribution
External
Copy No.
ADG (Rear) 6
ADS (Rear) 7
22 Fd Hosp 19
32 Fd Hosp 20
12 AD Wksp 28
71 AC Wksp 29
1 Air Evac Sqn 30
Internal
G2/G3 Ops 41
G1/G4 Ops 42
Comms Ops 43
Tac HQ 44
RASS 45
187 Coy RPC 46
Comd 47
Comd's Diary 48–49
Spare 50–51
LEGEND
Allied Forces
Enemy Forces
Inf
Cav
Armd
Mech Inf
X Brigade
XX Division
XXX Corps
XXXX Army
Present
Future Projected
AL BADIYAH AL JANUBIYAH
(SOUTHERN DESERT)
MADINAH
RGFC
HAMURABI
OBJ COLLINS
30N
TAWALKANA
OBJ WATERLOO
PL SMASH
PL APPLE
VII (US)
XXXX
OKP 01
OKD 10
OKR 05
OKR 02
250630Z
28N
3(EG)
4(EG)
WARNING
SAUDI ARABIA
Flight outside controlled airspace & ATS routes is PROHIBITED
WARNING
Flying outside specified ATS routes in SAUDI ARABIA is STRICTLY PROHIBITED
ARCENT
FCN
JFC-E
SCALE 1:500,000
SECRET RESTRICTED

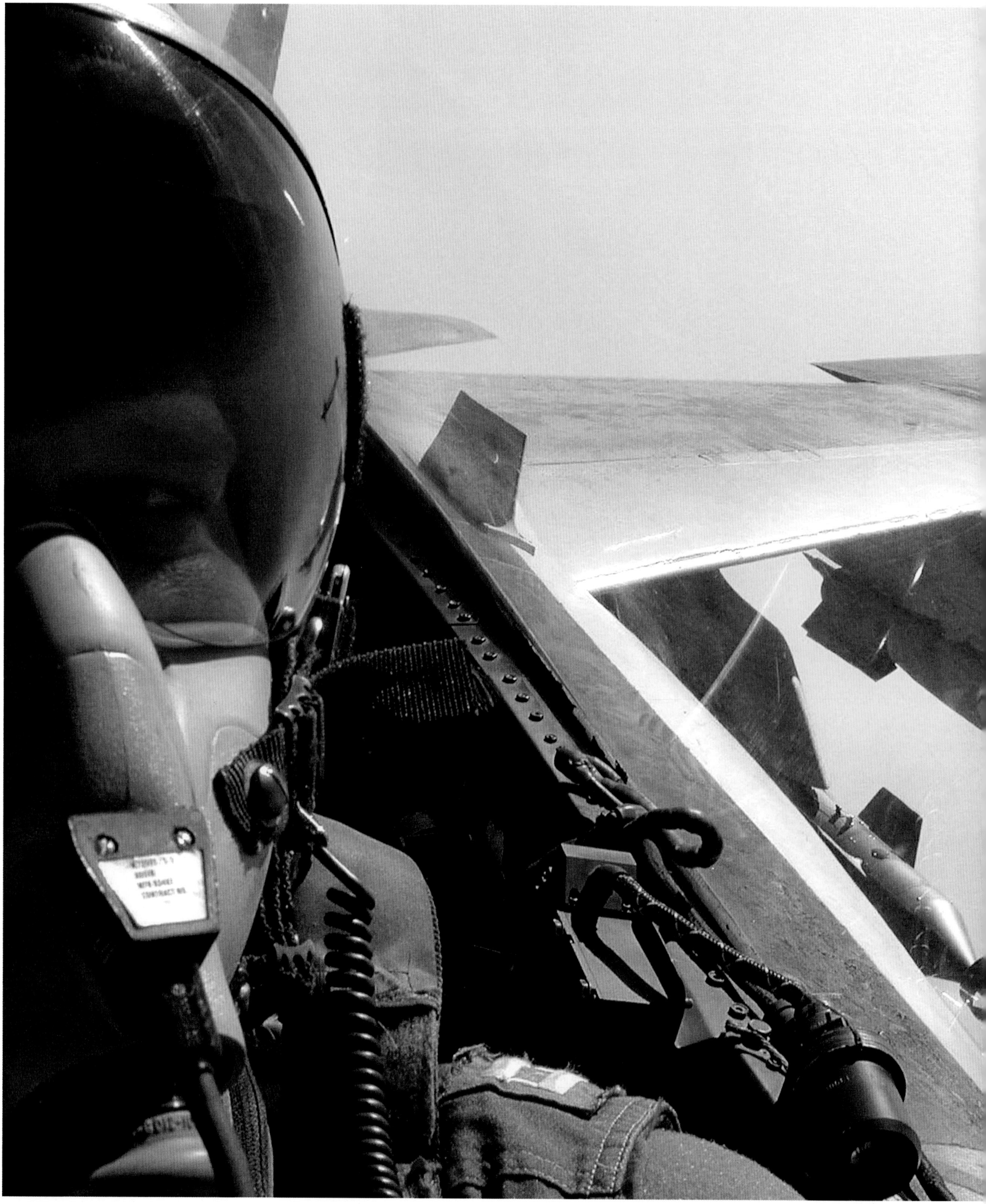

Flying above
A US Navy F-18C Hornet aircraft can be seen flying above Afghanistan. The aircraft is armed, from left to right, with two GBU-15 Paveway II laser-guided bombs and one AIM-9R infrared air-to-air missile.

SMART WEAPONS

The first operational use of smart weapons – munitions with guidance systems – dates back to 1943 when Germany deployed the Fritz X anti-ship guided bomb. Smart weapons are now a part of modern warfare.

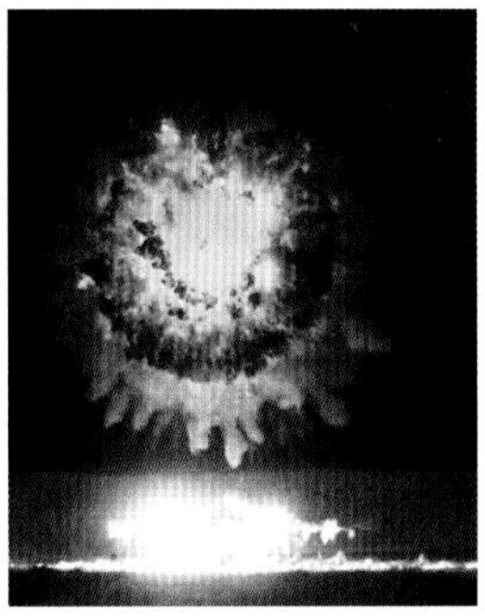

△ **Cloud of fire**
The warhead of a BGM-109 Tomahawk cruise missile, launched from a submarine, detonates over its test target.

The first precision-guided munitions were radio-controlled; subsequent technological advances saw the rise of laser-guided, radar-guided, infrared-guided, and GPS satellite-guided weapons. Although Germany was the first country to employ guided ordnance during World War II, the US and Britain also had research programmes. The US programme, which continued after the war, focused on ground and aerial targets, prioritizing air-to-air and surface-to-air missiles. By 1965, at the start of the sustained US air campaign against North Vietnam, air-to-air missiles were widespread. Early missiles, however, were unreliable, and misses were more common than hits. Air-to-ground guided ammunition, on the other hand, reached full-scale potential with Operation Linebacker in 1972, in which superior tactics, improved training, and guided weaponry allowed the US Air Force and US Navy to inflict heavy damage on the North Vietnamese Air Force from the skies.

Smart weapons became commonplace after their use by the US in Operation Desert Storm (see pp.266–67) – although only 9 per cent of US munitions used in the conflict were guided, they were found to be much more likely to hit their targets than non-guided weaponry.

△ **Work in progress**
US Air Force technicians work on an air-to-ground GBU-15 Paveway glide bomb in a hangar in Saudi Arabia. An EF-111A aircraft of the 390th Electronic Combat Squadron can be seen parked in the background.

THE IRAQ WAR

The 2003 invasion of Iraq by a US-led coalition of forces was a success in military terms, achieving its intended purpose of removing Saddam Hussein from power. However, widespread doubts over its justification increased further when it triggered enduring and bloody sectarian violence and political instability.

The Gulf War of 1990–91 left Iraq's defeated leader Saddam Hussein in charge of the country (see pp.266–67). Despite harsh sanctions imposed in its wake, US strategists viewed the regime as an ongoing threat, and accused it of colluding with terrorists and harbouring weapons of mass destruction.

In 2002, following the 2001 al-Qaeda destruction of the Twin Towers in New York, US Congress authorized President George W. Bush to use military force against Iraq. The US set about building a network of allies, including Britain, Australia, and Poland. When Saddam refused to give up power, troops of this "coalition of the willing" invaded the country across its southern border with Kuwait, while coalition air power began a bombing campaign against strategic targets. Meanwhile special forces co-operated with Kurdish Peshmerga guerrilla groups in the north despite Turkey's refusal to help (as in 1991).

Within three weeks, coalition forces reached Baghdad and Saddam went into hiding; he was captured eight months later, tried, and executed. However, no weapons of mass destruction were found, and far from transitioning to a peaceful democracy as hoped, Iraq fell victim to a long-running insurgency. The invasion served as a trigger for ongoing violence, and Western forces were tied down for many years trying to manage the turmoil.

"My name is Saddam Hussein. I am the president of Iraq, and I want to negotiate."

SADDAM HUSSEIN, SURRENDERING TO US TROOPS, 2003

INVADING IRAQ

Although the invasion of Iraq was well organized and effectively executed, the coalition did not make the necessary plans for occupying or reconstructing the country.

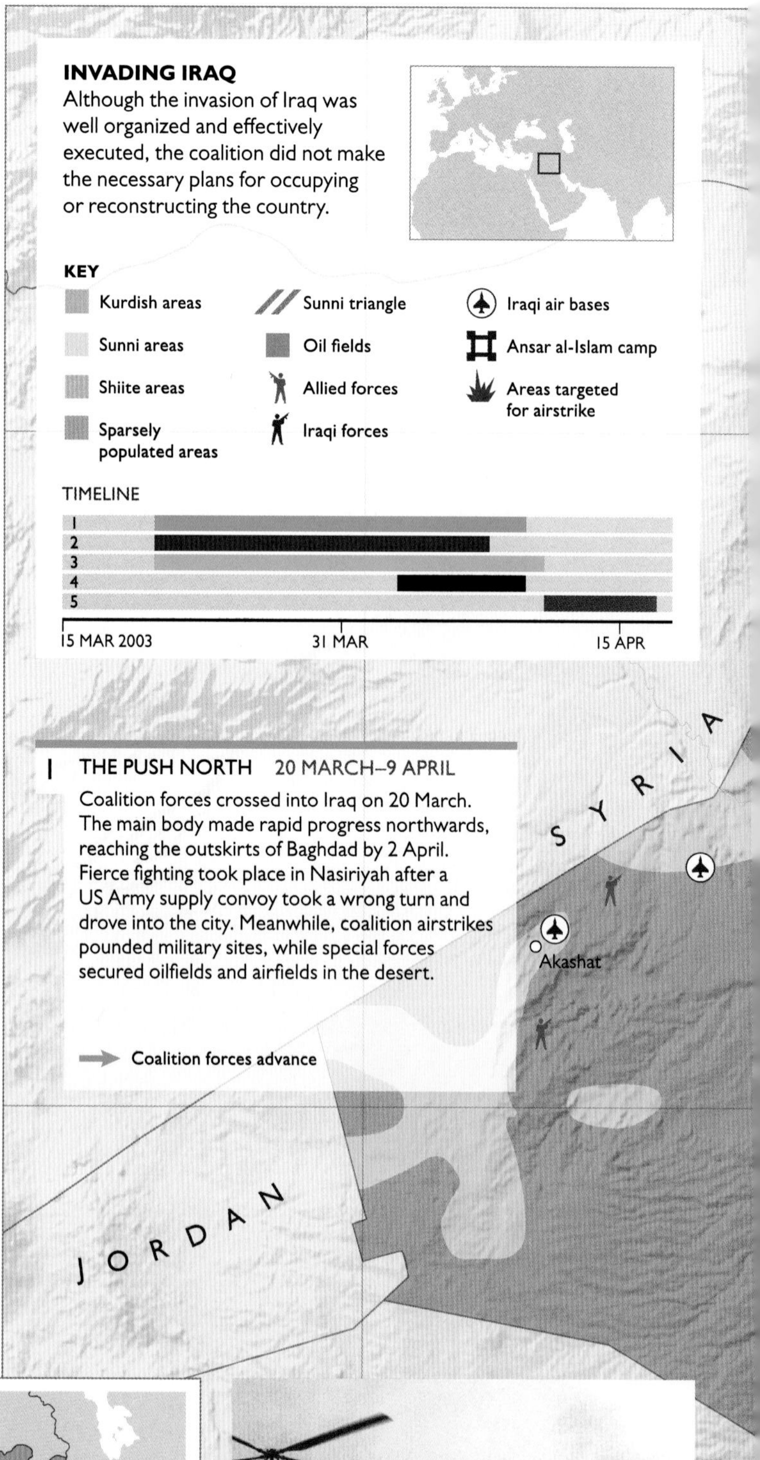
KEY
Kurdish areas
Sunni areas
Shiite areas
Sparsely populated areas
Sunni triangle
Oil fields
Allied forces
Iraqi forces
Iraqi air bases
Ansar al-Islam camp
Areas targeted for airstrike
TIMELINE
1
2
3
4
5
15 MAR 2003
31 MAR
15 APR
SYRIA
JORDAN
Akashat

1 THE PUSH NORTH 20 MARCH–9 APRIL

Coalition forces crossed into Iraq on 20 March. The main body made rapid progress northwards, reaching the outskirts of Baghdad by 2 April. Fierce fighting took place in Nasiriyah after a US Army supply convoy took a wrong turn and drove into the city. Meanwhile, coalition airstrikes pounded military sites, while special forces secured oilfields and airfields in the desert.

Coalition forces advance

SECTARIAN INSURGENCY

The fall of Saddam prompted Shia and Sunni militias, supported respectively by Iran and by al-Qaeda, to battle for power. After Western forces withdrew, a new militant group, the Islamic State in Iraq and the Levant (ISIL) seized most of northern and central Iraq in 2014. It proclaimed a global caliphate, and attracted many foreign jihadists, but was slowly rolled back by Western airstrikes, and Kurdish and government counter-attacks.

KEY

- Syrian and Iraqi Kurdish forces (2018)
- Islamic State group (2018)
- Iraqi government (2018)
- Syrian government (2018)
- Syrian rebel forces (2018)

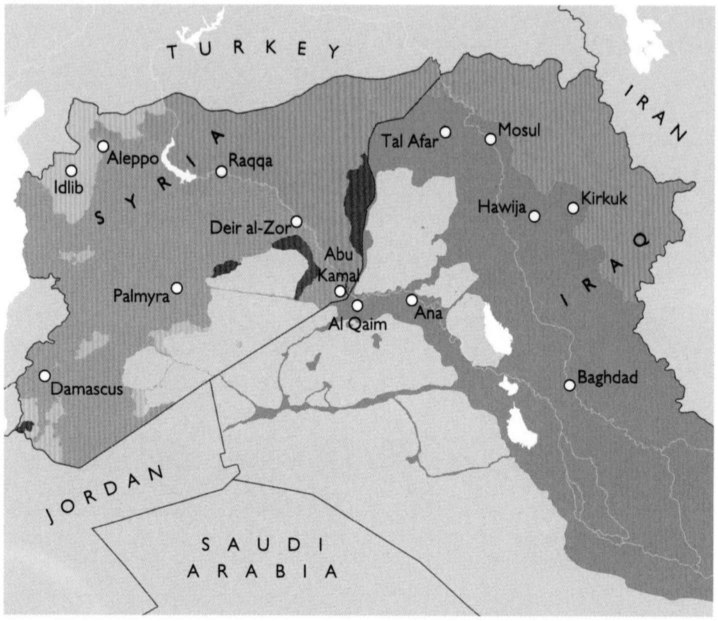
TURKEY
IRAN
SYRIA
IRAQ
JORDAN
SAUDI ARABIA
Aleppo
Idlib
Raqqa
Tal Afar
Mosul
Kirkuk
Hawija
Deir al-Zor
Abu Kamal
Palmyra
Al Qaim
Ana
Damascus
Baghdad

△ **Clearing a path**
Helicopter-borne troops of the British Army's Parachute Regiment prepare to carry out vehicle searches for weapons in southern Iraq.

TARGET BAGHDAD
The bombing of Baghdad signalled the start of the campaign to topple Saddam. During the invasion, coalition aircraft made around 1,000 bombing sorties a day against the city, targeting military and strategic installations, as well as members of the regime.

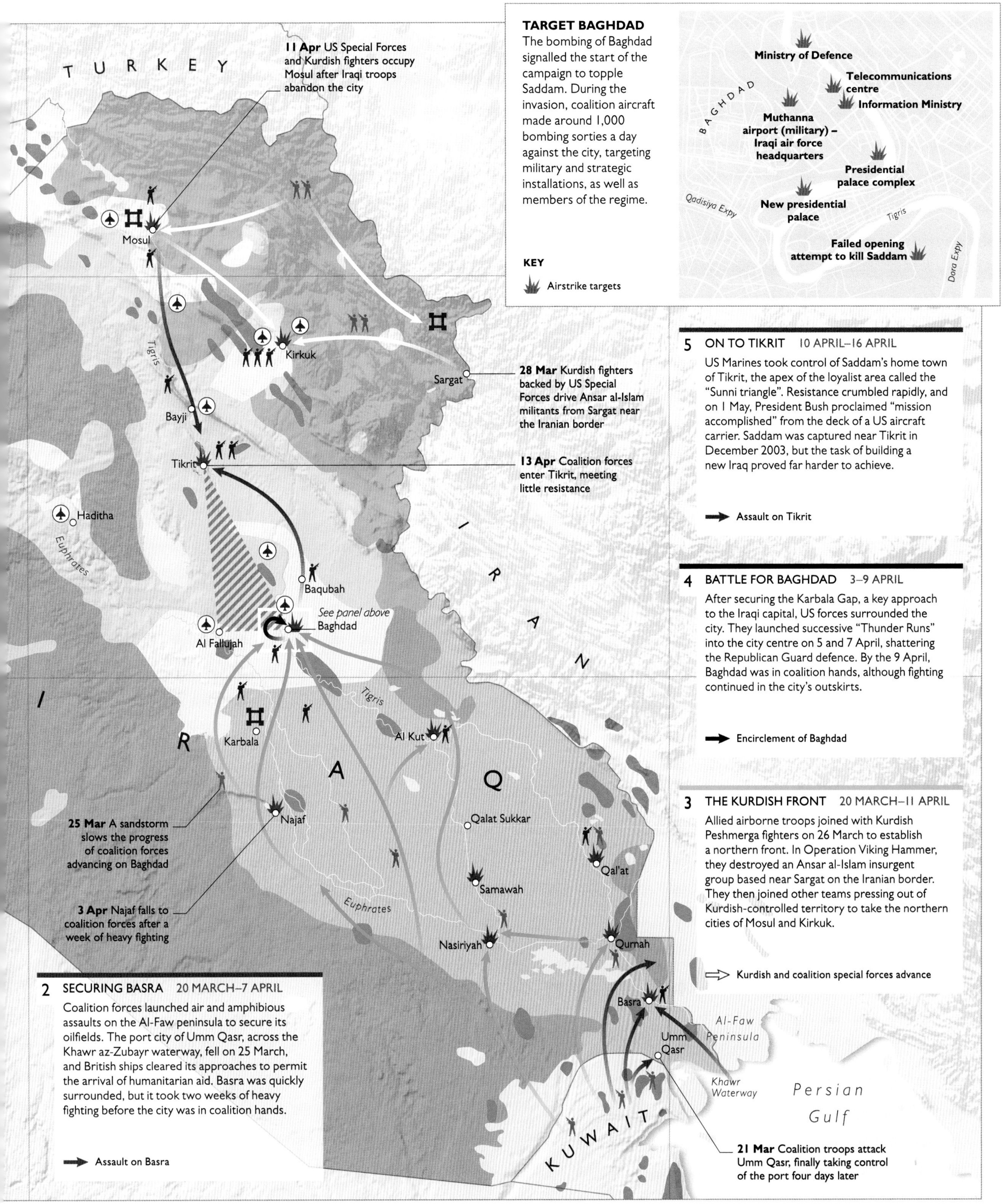
Ministry of Defence
Telecommunications centre
Information Ministry
BAGHDAD
Muthanna airport (military) – Iraqi air force headquarters
Presidential palace complex
Qadisiya Expy
New presidential palace
Tigris
Failed opening attempt to kill Saddam
Dora Expy

KEY

Airstrike targets

TURKEY
11 Apr US Special Forces and Kurdish fighters occupy Mosul after Iraqi troops abandon the city
Mosul
Kirkuk
Tigris
Sargat
28 Mar Kurdish fighters backed by US Special Forces drive Ansar al-Islam militants from Sargat near the Iranian border
Bayji
Tikrit
13 Apr Coalition forces enter Tikrit, meeting little resistance
Haditha
Euphrates
IRAN
Baquba
See panel above
Baghdad
Al Fallujah
IRAQ
Tigris
Karbala
Al Kut
Najaf
Qalat Sukkar
25 Mar A sandstorm slows the progress of coalition forces advancing on Baghdad
Samawah
Qal'at
3 Apr Najaf falls to coalition forces after a week of heavy fighting
Euphrates
Nasiriyah
Qurnah
Basra
Al-Faw Peninsula
Umm Qasr
Khawr Waterway
Persian Gulf
KUWAIT
21 Mar Coalition troops attack Umm Qasr, finally taking control of the port four days later

5 ON TO TIKRIT 10 APRIL–16 APRIL

US Marines took control of Saddam's home town of Tikrit, the apex of the loyalist area called the "Sunni triangle". Resistance crumbled rapidly, and on 1 May, President Bush proclaimed "mission accomplished" from the deck of a US aircraft carrier. Saddam was captured near Tikrit in December 2003, but the task of building a new Iraq proved far harder to achieve.

Assault on Tikrit

4 BATTLE FOR BAGHDAD 3–9 APRIL

After securing the Karbala Gap, a key approach to the Iraqi capital, US forces surrounded the city. They launched successive "Thunder Runs" into the city centre on 5 and 7 April, shattering the Republican Guard defence. By the 9 April, Baghdad was in coalition hands, although fighting continued in the city's outskirts.

Encirclement of Baghdad

3 THE KURDISH FRONT 20 MARCH–11 APRIL

Allied airborne troops joined with Kurdish Peshmerga fighters on 26 March to establish a northern front. In Operation Viking Hammer, they destroyed an Ansar al-Islam insurgent group based near Sargat on the Iranian border. They then joined other teams pressing out of Kurdish-controlled territory to take the northern cities of Mosul and Kirkuk.

Kurdish and coalition special forces advance

2 SECURING BASRA 20 MARCH–7 APRIL

Coalition forces launched air and amphibious assaults on the Al-Faw peninsula to secure its oilfields. The port city of Umm Qasr, across the Khawr az-Zubayr waterway, fell on 25 March, and British ships cleared its approaches to permit the arrival of humanitarian aid. Basra was quickly surrounded, but it took two weeks of heavy fighting before the city was in coalition hands.

Assault on Basra

DIRECTORY: 1900–PRESENT

RELIEF OF BEIJING

JUNE–AUGUST 1900

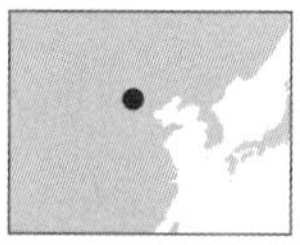

北京城總攻激之圖

△ In this illustration Japanese soldiers clash with Chinese forces in Beijing

The foreign occupation of Beijing in 1900 proved to be a decisive step towards the collapse of Imperial China. In the late 19th century, China was gripped by an anti-foreign movement, and the members of a nationalist society, known as Boxers, began to stir up dissent. The Empress Dowager Cixi declared support for the Boxer activists carrying out attacks on Christian missionaries and foreigners. The diplomatic quarter in Beijing, defended by some 400 foreign troops, was placed under siege on 20 June by the Boxers and the Chinese army. Soon after, a multinational force went to assist but was repulsed. On 4 August, a much larger force of Russian, Japanese, British, US, and French troops set out from Tianjin. Meanwhile, troops in the quarter fought off stiff attacks. On 14 August, the relief force scaled the city walls and stormed the gates. Fighting went on through 15 August, but the Chinese forces mostly fled. In the aftermath, foreign troops and civilians engaged in rampant looting and killed many suspected Boxers. Empress Cixi had to accept humiliating peace terms. The imperial system never recovered and was replaced by a republic in 1912.

MUKDEN

20 FEBRUARY–
10 MARCH 1905

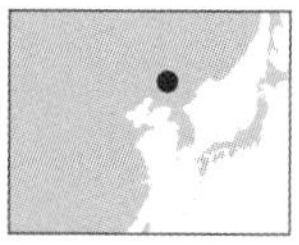

The Japanese defeat of the Russians at Mukden was the first major victory for an Asian power over a European power in the imperialist era. The Russo-Japanese War had started in 1904 over rival claims in Manchuria and Korea.

Russian General Alexei Kuropatkin established a defensive line over 80km (50 miles) long south of Manchurian capital Mukden (now Shenyang in China's Liaoning Province), facing a Japanese army under Marshal Oyama Iwao. Over 300,000 Russian soldiers were entrenched behind barbed wire. The Japanese, although lesser in numbers, were better equipped. Oyama launched an offensive against the left of the Russian line on 20 February. Fighting in ice and snow, the Japanese suffered heavy losses without a breakthrough. Oyama then switched the focus of his attack to the Russian right. Kuropatkin's fumbled attempt to move troops to meet this new threat reduced his army to chaos. As the Japanese succeeded in enveloping the enemy right, the Russians retreated in disorder, abandoning their equipment and the wounded. The Japanese forces occupied Mukden on 10 March. Although Japanese losses were as high as those of Russia, Kuropatkin withdrew his forces from the region and the defeat demoralized Russia's tsarist regime. The final decisive battle of the war was fought in the Tsushima Strait (see p.205), where the Russian fleet was defeated.

MEUSE–ARGONNE OFFENSIVE

26 SEPTEMBER–11 NOVEMBER 1918

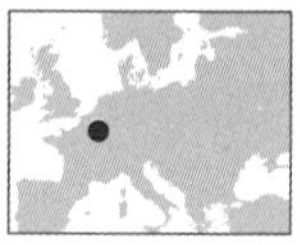

The Meuse–Argonne Offensive, involving 1.2 million US troops, was one of the largest battles ever fought by the US Army. It was a part of the Hundred Days Offensive (August–November 1918), a series of attacks with which the Allies ended World War I.

Commanded by General John Pershing, and supported by the French Fourth Army, the US First Army was to advance through the dense Argonne Forest to Sedan, a major rail junction in German-occupied eastern France. Hastily organized only two weeks after a US victory at the Saint-Mihiel salient, the initial attack yielded disappointing results. The terrain favoured defence, and the Germans had deep bunkers and fortified trenches. As a result, inexperienced US infantry suffered heavy losses for limited gains. Bogged down in heavy rain, the offensive was relaunched on 4 October. Pershing deployed fresh divisions to win the battle of attrition with the increasingly exhausted Germans. In late October, they broke through the Kriemhilde Stellung, a section of the fortified Hindenburg Line. The Americans approached their initial objective of Sedan just as the armistice ended the fighting on 11 November. The battle cost more than 26,000 American lives.

△ Troops of the US 369th Infantry Regiment fight in the Argonne forest

SHANGHAI

13 AUGUST–26 NOVEMBER, 1937

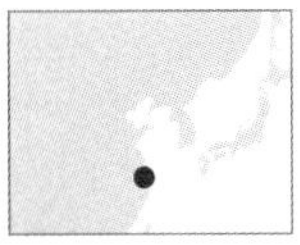

The battle between China and Japan in Shanghai in 1937 was the first major engagement of the Second Sino-Japanese War (1937–45). Starting in 1931, Japanese encroachments on Chinese territory had led to scattered outbreaks of fighting. Clashes escalated from July 1937, and on August 13 the fighting spread to Shanghai. Chinese nationalist leader Chiang Kai-Shek hoped to overwhelm the outnumbered Japanese garrison, but Japanese amphibious landings soon evened the odds. Prolonged street fighting, shelling, and air bombardments incurred huge civilian casualties. On 5 November the increasingly hard-pressed Chinese army finally withdrew from Shanghai, and on 26 November it was forced out of its final defence line before the capital, Nanjing. China lost many of its best-trained soldiers in battle, and, over the following years, Japan occupied much of the country. With US backing, Chinese resistance continued and became part of the wider World War II.

OPERATION BARBAROSSA

22 JUNE–2 OCTOBER 1941

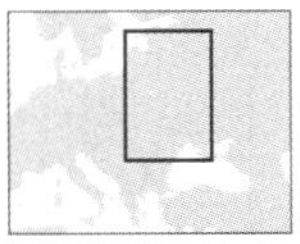

In June 1941, German leader Adolf Hitler amassed more than 3 million troops with thousands of tanks and aircraft to invade the USSR. On 22 June, the Axis forces poured across a front stretching from the Baltic to the Black Sea. Achieving total surprise, the Luftwaffe destroyed thousands of Soviet planes while the ground force advanced rapidly towards Leningrad (St Petersburg) in the north, Smolensk in the centre, and Kiev in the south. Hundreds of thousands of Soviet troops were trapped by encircling Axis forces, and Leningrad was besieged. However, mounting losses, stretched supply lines, and confused objectives slowed the Axis progress. A final push towards Moscow in autumnal rains and freezing weather was fruitless. Hitler's failure to achieve a quick victory in the USSR condemned him to a protracted war, which he had inadequate resources to win.

▽ German troops attack the Soviets

GUADALCANAL

7 AUGUST 1942–9 FEBRUARY 1943

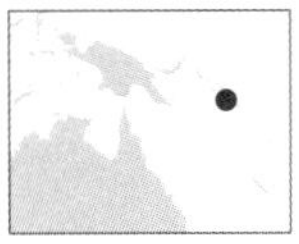

Guadalcanal island in the Solomons was the focus for some of the fiercest battles fought between Japan and the US and its allies. Japan occupied the island in May 1942, but the US Marines invaded in August and finished building the captured airstrip which they named Henderson Field. There followed months of intense fighting including three major land battles, two aircraft carrier battles, five nighttime surface naval battles off nearby Savo island, and almost daily air battles as both sides struggled to reinforce, resupply, and support their troops on Guadalcanal and eject their opponents. Growing US resource superiority finally prevailed and Japan began to withdraw its starving troops from the island in December, completing the evacuation by February 1943. The superiority of Allied forces in the Pacific was never again seriously in doubt.

MONTE CASSINO

17 JANUARY–18 MAY 1944

During World War II, the hill of Monte Cassino was a key location on the German Gustav Line that blocked Allied progress northwards to Rome during their invasion of Italy. Commanded by Generalfeldmarschall Albert Kesselring, the Germans made optimal use of the defensive potential of the mountainous terrain and fast-flowing rivers. The US 5th Army and British 8th Army were committed to breaking through the line. In January–March, the Allies made three failed assaults on the German position. US bombers destroyed the abbey at Cassino, mistakenly believing it to be occupied by German troops. The German forces went on to occupy the ruins left by the bombing, turning it into a formidable defensive strongpoint. A final Allied offensive, launched on 11 May, achieved the breakthrough. General Wladyslaw Anders' Polish corps planted its flag on the crest of the hill on 18 May. Rome fell to the Allies on 5 June, but the Germans escaped to block the Allies in northern Italy until April 1945.

INVASION OF SUEZ

29 OCTOBER– 7 NOVEMBER 1956

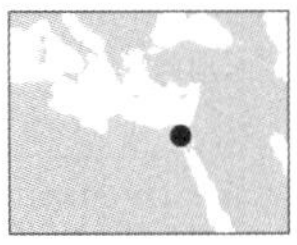

The coordinated attack on Egypt by Israel, Britain, and France in 1956 was a military success but a political disaster that hastened the end of European colonialism. The war was triggered by Egyptian leader Gamal Abdel Nasser's decision to nationalize the Suez Canal – a man-made waterway invaluable to international trade – which was owned by a Franco-British company. An aggressive Arab nationalist, Nasser was viewed as a threat not only to French and British interests but also to Israel. A plan was formulated in which Israel would invade Egypt's Sinai Peninsula, allowing Britain and France to justify military intervention with the excuse to defend the Suez Canal. The unavowed aim was to overthrow Nasser.

The Israeli forces attacked on 29 October, advancing with spectacular speed across the Sinai. On 5 November, after initial bombing attacks, British and French paratroopers jumped into the Suez Canal Zone and began occupying strategic points. The following day larger forces, accompanied with tanks, came ashore on landing craft while others were transported by helicopters. This was the first ever use of helicopters for assault landings. In response to the invasion, Egypt blocked the use of the Canal by sinking ships in the waterway – it remained closed to traffic for five months.

Key objectives of the plot were swiftly attained but the attack was met with heavy criticism in Britain and elsewhere. More importantly, diplomatic and financial pressure from the US, which had not been consulted, forced the military operations to a halt after only two days. Humiliated, Britain and France withdrew their forces, and Nasser emerged as a powerful hero in the Arab world.

△ Cargo ships line the Suez Canal, deliberately sunk by Egypt to block it

GLOSSARY

air wing A unit of command in military aviation comprising a number of squadrons. It originated in 1912 when the British Royal Flying Corps divided into a military wing and a naval wing.

archon Highest ranking official in Ancient Greece city-states, from the Greek word for ruler. Each city-state had several archons governing separate departments; the archon polemarchos was military commander.

armistice A formal agreement to suspend military operations between warring sides from different nations. Historically, a state of war may still have existed while an armistice was in place, but under contemporary international law an armistice means termination of war.

artillery Large-calibre weapons such as mounted shell-firing guns, howitzers, and missile launchers that can reach beyond the range of infantry firearms. The term is also used for the arm of the military service using these weapons, such as field artillery, coastal artillery, and anti-tank artillery.

auxiliaries (troops) Personnel providing support services to the military or police. They are often volunteers or do part-time paid work. In Ancient Rome, auxiliaries were non-citizens drafted for an average 25 years' service, after which they received citizenship.

bar shot A cannon shot, or projectile, formed of two iron balls connected with a bar, resembling the shape of dumbbell. The weighted ends cause the shot to spin through the air when fired, making it very effective at cutting the masts of sailing ships and tearing through their spars and rigging.

bastion The bulwark projecting from the curtain wall of a fortification. Shaped like an arrow head, this style of outcrop was designed to eliminate the blind spot just below the parapet wall and protect soldiers as they fired on invaders below.

battlecruiser A large armed warship equipped with battleship armaments, but lighter and faster than a battleship. The first battlecruisers were the three *Invincible*-class vessels that entered into the service of the Royal Navy in 1908.

battleship The largest and heaviest type of warship equipped with large-calibre guns and thick armour. Battleships were the centrepiece of naval fleets in the first decades of the 20th century.

beachhead An area close to the sea or a river that, when captured by attacking troops, is the foundation for a subsequent advance deeper into enemy-held territory.

Blitzkrieg Meaning "lightning war" in German, this World War II military tactic was used in the invasion of Poland in 1939. It consists of mass tank formations, supported by dive-bombers and motorized artillery, making a thrust forwards on a narrow front.

bombard (n) Late medieval cannon of the 15th century. Mostly used during sieges for smashing stronghold walls, they developed into a super gun of the era, made from iron and using gunpowder to fire mortar and granite balls. Examples include Russia's 1586 Tsar Cannon and the Ottoman Empire Dardanelles gun of 1464.

bridgehead Strategic site at a bridge or water crossing where defensive units set up military lines to provide cover for crossing troops.

brigade Military formation, typically consisting of three to six battalions, plus supporting reconnaissance, artillery, engineers, supply, and transport elements.

brigantine Two-masted sailing vessel from the 16th century, square-rigged but with fore-and-aft rigging on the main mast. Its name comes from the two-masted sailing ships of brigands, or pirates, on the Mediterranean Sea.

broadside The cannon battery installed on both sides of side of a warship, a feature of naval ships from the 16th to mid-19th centuries. The term also means the act of firing the guns from the side of the ship.

cannister shot Artillery ammunition in the form of a metal cylinder filled with metal balls. The canisters disintegrate when fired from a cannon and deliver a shotgun-like blast. Very common in the 18th and 19th centuries, cannister shot remains in use to this day.

caravel Fast, manoeuverable sailing vessel invented in Portugal in the 15th century for long-distance travel across the Atlantic. Used by Christopher Columbus on his journeys to South America, the caravel was rigged with lateen sails designed for sailing windward.

carbine Lightweight, rifle-like gun with a short barrel, usually less than 51 cm (20 in) long. The original carbine was used by soldiers on horseback but has since developed into a gas-operated semi-automatic.

carrack Portuguese-designed ocean-going sailing vessel with three masts, widely used by European naval powers between the 14th and 17th centuries. Henry VIII's *Mary Rose* is one of the best known surviving examples.

cataphract Heavily armoured cavalry of Persia and other ancient kingdoms of the Middle East; later adopted by the Romans and Byzantines. Cataphracts are considered precursors of the medieval knight.

ceasefire Temporary or partial cessation of military hostilities – for the purposes of collecting the dead, for example, or to stage peace talks.

chevauchée From the French "to ride", a medieval warfare tactic of conducting an armed raid on horseback into enemy territory to destroy property and pillage. Civilians were also often targeted.

Companions (Greek) Elite cavalry of the Macedonian army from the time of King Phillip II. Recruited from nobility, the Companions were the most senior regiment. Under Phillip's son, Alexander the Great, they were the key to victory over the Persian army in 331 BCE.

Confederacy (American Civil War) An association of 11 Southern states that broke away from the United States in 1860–61 with the aim of forming a new nation in which slavery would be legal. Also known as the Confederate States of America, or the Southern Confederacy.

corps An army unit made of two or more divisions. Napoleon is credited with devising the corps formation, with each corps self-sufficient and able to fight on its own or join together with other corps. This structure made the army more flexible and maneuverable.

crossing the T Naval warfare tactic prevalent from the late 19th to mid-20th century in which a line of warships crosses perpendicular to an enemy's line of ships. This allows the crossing line to use all of their guns to fire at the enemy, while their enemy can only use their forward guns. This technique was often used to great effect, such as in 1905 by Japan in the Battle of Tsushima (see p.205).

cuirassier A cavalry solider wearing a cuirass (breastplate armour designed to protect the torso), and carrying a sword or saber and pistol. Cuirassier regiments rose to prominence in the 18th century and played an important role in Napoleonic armies.

daimyo Feudal lords who controlled most of Japan under the shoguns, from the 10th century to the mid-19th century. They maintained power by hiring samurai warriors to protect their interests.

dive bomber Military aircraft that dives straight at its target until it reaches a low altitude before dropping its bomb load, levelling off and flying away. This increases the accuracy of the hit. The tactic was used during the Spanish Civil War and World War II.

division Large military formation comprising several regiments or brigades that fight as an independent unit. A division numbers between 10,000 and 20,000 soldiers on average.

dragoon Mounted infantry who would use horses for mobility and fight on foot. Originating in 16th century Europe, gradually dragoons became an accepted military unit. They take their name from the type of short muskets they used.

dreadnought / super-dreadnought British battleship named after the Royal Navy's revolutionary steam propulsion HMS *Dreadnought* of 1906, with a main armament of up to 14 guns, more than double that of previous models (see pp.206–207). The second-generation super-dreadnoughts were phased in from 1914 and were the flagships of several nations up until World War II.

drone Remote aerial surveillance device, also called a UAV (unmanned or uncrewed aerial vehicle), automated or piloted remotely. Developed during World War I, drones were widely deployed during the Vietnam War for reconnaissance, as combat decoys, and in leaflet drops.

fire lance (*Huo qiang*) Chinese spear-like weapon with a gunpowder charge, used in battle from the 12th century.

fire ship A ship filled with combustible material, set on fire, and steered, or set adrift to float into an enemy fleet, with the intention of causing panic and forcing the fleet to break formation.

flank The far left or right side of troops in battle, a point vulnerable to enemy attack and a weakness used by military tacticians since ancient times.

fleche (fortification) Defensive architectural structure shaped like an arrow and attached to the exterior of a fortress to face the enemy. It was built with a parapet to provide a firing vantage point.

flintlock A firearm mechanism that employs a flint striking against iron to create a spark, which lights the gunpower inside the barrel and fires the gun.

frigate Square-rigged war vessel developed in the late 18th century for speed and maneuverability. In the 20th century, the Royal Navy gave the name frigate to a class of small escort ships, which later expanded to include fully equipped antiaircraft vessels.

fyrd Anglo Saxon tribal-style army originating in the 7th century CE with ranks filled by conscripted freemen. It was compulsory to enlist and fight in a campaign when called upon by the king or local rulers.

galleass Large fighting galley, heavily equipped with firepower and used in warfare in the Mediterranean Sea in the 15th–18th centuries. It was propelled by 50–200 oarsmen.

galliot Narrow, shallow-draft Dutch or Flemish merchant galley with a main mast and mizen, often with oars. Used between the 17th and 19th centuries, its precursor was the Mediterranean half-galley with oars, as favoured by the Barbary pirates. A variation was the French naval *galiote*.

garrison Group of soldiers stationed at a strategic location such as a fortress, island, or town in order to defend it.

Gatling gun Hand-driven machine gun with multiple rapid-firing barrels rotated by a crank around a central axle. It was invented in 1861–62 by Richard Jordan Gatling during the American Civil War.

gendarmes Historically a heavy cavalry troop in the armies of France, by the late 18th century the gendarmes had become a military police force for protecting French royalty and officials and keeping law and order during civil unrest.

grenadier From the French word for grenade, grenadiers were specialized soldiers who carried and threw grenades during attacks. From the mid-17th century onwards grenadiers formed elite companies within battalions.

guerrilla Fighter in an irregular military force engaging in targeted raids and ambushes against a conventional military force. The term was first applied to the Spanish-Portuguese guerrilleros, or partisans, in the 1807–14 Peninsular War who drove French forces from the Iberian peninsula.

harquebusier European cavalry soldier armed with a harequebus (or arquebus), a type of long-barrelled firearm, and a sword. Harquebusiers are noted for their tactical role in both the Thirty Years War and the English Civil War during the 17th century.

Holy Roman Empire Group of territories in western and central Europe ruled over by Frankish and Germanic kings from 800 CE under Charlemagne until 1806, when it was abolished by Napoleon.

howitzer Long-range cannon used to fire shots into the air at an angle calculated to hit a target under cover or in a trench. Howitzers were first used in the 16th century and became a critical piece of artillery in trench warfare during World War I.

huscarl Professional elite bodyguards of medieval Viking and Anglo-Saxon kings. Huscarls made up Canute's invading forces in the Danish occupation of Anglo-Saxon England in 1015, and the core of Harold's army at Hastings in 1066 (see pp.58–59).

Janissary Elite professional infantry soldier of the Ottoman Empire army from the late 14th to early 19th centuries. They are considered the first modern standing army, meaning they were permanently on duty in their barracks when not engaged in military action.

Knights Templar Catholic Christian military order founded around 1119 by French knights with the aim of defending Christian pilgrims in Jerusalem and the Holy Lands from Muslim attack.

knot (nautical speed measurement) Equivalent to one nautical mile (1.852 km or 1⅙ land miles) per hour. The term dates from the 17th century when sailors measured the speed of their ship using a coil of rope with evenly spaced knots, which they dropped over the stern.

legate (Roman) High-ranking officer in the army of the Roman Empire, equivalent to a modern general. The legate commanded a legion, the army's largest unit, comprising around 5,000 soldiers.

level bomber Attack aircraft used in both World War I and World War II for bombing raids. They maintained a level flight attitude from which bombs were dropped over the target. The development of bombsights enabled level bombers to perform more accurately.

Manhattan Project Codename for the US program to develop the atomic bomb in 1942–45. The project was spread across several locations, including various sites in Los Alamos, New Mexico, Oak Ridge, Tennessee, and Hanford, Washington.

matchlock First mechanism for firing a hand-held gun. When the lever or trigger was pulled, a clamp dropped a lit match into the weapon's flashpan to ignite a charge of shot and gunpowder in the barrel.

metallurgy The scientific study of the physical and chemical properties of metals, how to extract metals from ore, and how to modify them to create alloys.

Minié ball Bullet for rifled muskets invented by Claude-Étienne Minié around 1849. Quick and easy to load by simply dropping it down the rifle barrel, the bullet expanded when fired creating a tight fit and increased accuracy.

mortar Lightweight, portable muzzle-loaded weapon, constructed from a barrel, baseplate, and bipod support. It is limited to indirect firing at angles above 45 degrees.

musket Muzzle-loading shoulder firearm with a long barrel firing either a musket ball or minié ball. The first muskets were produced in 16th century Spain and evolved over time with matchlocks, then flintlocks, and finally percussion locks. Muskets were superseded by breechloading rifles in the late 19th century.

mustard gas Or sulfur mustard, a chemical agent causing severe burning of the skin, eyes and respiratory tract. German forces introduced it as a weapon in 1917 during World War I, where they fired it into enemy trenches in projectiles.

onager Catapult-like device for firing stones powered by torsion and used in Ancient Roman warfare. Its name derives from the Roman word for a wild donkey, so called because the weapon would tend to kick up at the back when fired.

palisade Defensive wall constructed from wooden or iron stakes, or tree trunks. Also known as a stakewall, its early use has been documented in Ancient Greece, Ancient Rome, and pre-colonial America.

phalanx Rectangular mass military formation of heavy infantry armed with spears, pikes, sarissas, or similar weapons. Originating in Ancient Sumeria and Greece, it was used to efficiently attack and intimidate the enemy.

raid Quick attack by an armed force on a location intended to cause damage or achieve a specific strategic mission without capturing the location.

redoubt Temporary fortification or satellite defensive structure outside a permanent fort or fortress. A redoubt can range from basic earthworks and no flanking protection to a substantial building.

rifling Spiral grooves inside the barrel of a gun designed to put spin on the bullet as it exits and lend it greater accuracy.

rearguard Detachment of soldiers positioned at the rear of the main body of troops to defend them from attack, typically during a retreat.

regiment Permanent organizational unit of an army, adopting a distinct identity, including its uniform and insignia, and usually commanded by a colonel.

sarissa Pike up to 7 m (23 feet) long used in the Macedonian army in a phalanx formation with shields. The sarissa was introduced by Phillip II of Macedon in the 4th century BCE and used by Alexander the Great's infantry.

satrap Provincial governor in the Persian Empire, presiding over the economy (especially tax collection) and overseeing law and order. Satraps had the power to act as judge and jury.

sepoy Professional armed soldiers under the Mughal emperors of India. The term was later used to refer to Indian soldiers who served under British or European forces in the 1800s.

ship of the line Largest navy warships of the 17th and 18th centuries, carrying 100 guns or more across three decks. In battle they formed a line to broadside their enemies.

Sixth Coalition Victorious combined forces in the War of the Sixth Coalition (1813–14) against Napoleon. The coalition was formed of Great Britain, Russia, Sweden, Spain, Prussia, Portugal, and Austria.

star fort Also called *trace italienne* from the 16th century (because they had been designed in Italy), these fortifications were built with angled walls to deflect the impact of cannons, which did most damage when they hit perpendicular to a wall.

sue for peace A term for when forces on the losing side of a battle would petition those with the upper hand to stop a full-scale rout in hopes of good terms and fewer losses.

Teutonic Knights Created in the late 12th century as a hospital of volunteers and mercenaries near Jerusalem, the German military Teutonic Order adopted a white tunic with a black cross.

U-boat German submarine first used in World War I. The *Unterseeboot* was far more advanced than other nations' submarines, and notoriously hard to sink.

Union (American Civil War) The northern states of America, forming the Federal Government of the United States during the American Civil War (1861–65).

vanguard Advance forces securing ground and seeking out the enemy ahead of an offensive. They were referred to as the avant-guard in medieval times.

wheellock Style of gun lock dating from the 16th century, and preceding the flintlock. It has a friction-wheel mechanism to generate a spark for firing.

Zeppelin Famous for the Hindenburg disaster and the bombing of London in World War I, Zeppelins were launched as civilian airships in the early 1900s. They were made with a rigid steel frame covered by a waterproof membrane, and stayed aloft with hydrogen. The German military adopted them during World War I.

INDEX

Page numbers in **bold** indicate main entries

C

D

E

F

G

H

T

U

ACKNOWLEDGMENTS

Dorling Kindersley would like to thank the following people for their help in the preparation of this book: Philip Parker for additional consulting; Alexandra Black for glossary text; Jessica Tapolcai for design assistance; Helen Peters for indexing; Joy Evatt for proofreading. DK India would like to thank Arpita Dasgupta, Ankita Gupta, Sonali Jindal, Devangana Ojha, Kanika Praharaj, and Anuroop Sanwalia for editorial assistance; Nobina Chakravorty, Sanjay Chauhan, and Meenal Goel for design assistance; Ashutosh Ranjan Bharti, Rajesh Chhibber, Zafar-ul-Islam Khan, Animesh Pathak, and Mohd Zishan for cartography assistance; and Priyanka Sharma and Saloni Singh for jackets assistance.

The publisher would like to thank the following for their kind permission to reproduce their photographs:

(Key: a-above; b-below/bottom; c-centre; f-far; l-left; r-right; t-top)

2 Dorling Kindersley: © The Trustees of the British Museum / Nick Nicholls. **4 Alamy Stock Photo:** Peter Horree (t). **4-5 Getty Images:** DEA / G. DAGLI ORTI (b). **5 Alamy Stock Photo:** Fine Art Images / Heritage Images (tl); Prisma Archivo (tr). **6 Alamy Stock Photo:** GL Archive (t). **6-7 Getty Images:** Popperfoto / Rolls Press (b). **7 Getty Images:** Corbis Historical / Hulton Deutsch (t). **8-9 Getty Images:** Archive Photos / Buyenlarge. **10-11 Alamy Stock Photo:** Peter Horree. **12 Alamy Stock Photo:** The Picture Art Collection (c). **Dorling Kindersley:** University of Pennsylvania Museum of Archaeology and Anthropology / Angela Coppola (tl). **13 Alamy Stock Photo:** Adam Eastland (cr); FALKENSTEINFOTO (tl). **14 Alamy Stock Photo:** Album (tl). **15 Dorling Kindersley:** University of Pennsylvania Museum of Archaeology and Anthropology / Gary Ombler (tr). **16 Getty Images:** Hulton Archive / Print Collector (cla); Science & Society Picture Library (bl). **16-17 Getty Images:** DEA / A. JEMOLO. **19 Alamy Stock Photo:** World History Archive (tr). **20 Alamy Stock Photo:** Panagiotis Karapanagiotis (bc). **Bridgeman Images:** (bl). **23 Alamy Stock Photo:** Cola Images (tc). **24 Alamy Stock Photo:** Artokoloro (c); Chronicle (bl). **24-25 Getty Images:** DE AGOSTINI PICTURE LIBRARY. **26 Alamy Stock Photo:** adam eastland (cr). **27 Alamy Stock Photo:** INTERFOTO / Fine Arts (crb). **29 Alamy Stock Photo:** Cultural Archive (tl). **30-31 Getty Images:** DEA / G. Dagli Orti. **31 Alamy Stock Photo:** Erin Babnik (bc); Science History Images (cr). **32 Getty Images:** DEA / A. DAGLI ORTI (cla). **33 Alamy Stock Photo:** The Granger Collection (cr). **35 Alamy Stock Photo:** Heritage Image Partnership Ltd (br). **36-37 Alamy Stock Photo:** Prisma Archiv (all images). **38-39 Getty Images:** Universal Images Group / Independent Picture Service. **39 Dreamstime.com:** Chris Hill / Ca2hil (cra). **Getty Images:** DEA / ICAS94 (br). **41 Bridgeman Images:** (tr). **43 Getty Images:** Corbis Historical / John Stevenson (br). **44-45 Getty Images:** LightRocket / Wolfgang Kaehler. **44 Dorling Kindersley:** Durham University Oriental Museum / Gary Ombler (cl). **Getty Images:** S3studio (bc). **46 Alamy Stock Photo:** Album (cr). **49 Alamy Stock Photo:** Ancient Art and Architecture (br). **50 Bridgeman Images:** Tallandier (tr). **52 akg-images:** Erich Lessing (c, br). **53 Alamy Stock Photo:** Niday Picture Library (br); www.BibleLandPictures.com / Zev rad (c). **54-55 Alamy Stock Photo:** Fine Art Images / Heritage Images. **56 Bridgeman Images:** (cl). **57 Bridgeman Images:** Pictures from History / Woodbury & Page (cr). **Dorling Kindersley:** Wallace Collection, London / Geoff Dann (tr). **59 Alamy Stock Photo:** Forget Patrick (br). **60-61 Alamy Stock Photo:** Vintage Book Collection. **60 Dorling Kindersley:** Gary Ombler (cla). **Getty Images:** Bridgeman Art Library / Hulton Fine Art Collection (bl). **62 akg-images**: Erich Lessing (bc). **Alamy Stock Photo:** Science History Images (tr). **64 Alamy Stock Photo:** Album (tl). **66 Bridgeman Images:** (br). **Getty Images:** DEA / A. DAGLI ORTI (bl). **68 Bridgeman Images:** (cr). **71 Alamy Stock Photo:** Album (tr). **72 Alamy Stock Photo:** Granger Historical Picture Archive (bl). **Dorling Kindersley:** Gary Ombler / © The Board of Trustees of the Armouries (cl). **72-73 Alamy Stock Photo:** World History Archive. **75 Alamy Stock Photo:** The Picture Art Collection (ca). **76 Alamy Stock Photo:** Heritage Images / Fine Art Images (cr). **78 Alamy Stock Photo:** World History Archive (tl). **Dorling Kindersley:** University Museum of Archaeology and Anthropology, Cambridge / Ranald MacKechnie (c). **78-79 Alamy Stock Photo:** Werner Forman Archive / Gulistan Library, Teheran / Heritage Images. **80 Getty Images:** Hulton

Archive / Heritage Images (cl). **83 Alamy Stock Photo:** Granger Historical Picture Archive (tl). **84 Alamy Stock Photo:** Everett Collection Inc (tl). **Dorling Kindersley:** Wallace Collection London / Geoff Dann (ca). **84-85 akg-images:** Erich Lessing. **86-87 Christie's Images Ltd:** (all map images). **89 akg-images:** jh-Lightbox_Ltd. / John Hios (cr). **90 Getty Images:** DEA PICTURE LIBRARY (cr). **92-93 akg-images:** François Guénet (all map images). **94-95 Getty Images:** DEA / G. DAGLI ORTI. **95 Alamy Stock Photo:** Classic Image (br). **Dorling Kindersley:** Royal Artillery, Woolwich / Gary Ombler (ca). 9**8 Alamy Stock Photo:** Science History Images (cr). **99 Alamy Stock Photo:** Heritage Image Partnership Ltd / Fine Art Image (bl). **Getty Images:** Hulton Archive / Culture Club (br); Universal Images Group / Leemage (tr). **100-101 Alamy Stock Photo:** Prisma Archivo. **102 Dorling Kindersley:** © The Board of Trustees of the Armouries / Gary Ombler (tl). **Getty Images:** Hulton Fine Art Collection / Heritage Images (cl). **103 Alamy Stock Photo:** GL Archive (tl). **Getty Images:** DEA / A. DAGLI ORTI (tr). **104 Getty Images:** Hulton Archive / Print Collector (tl). **106-107 Rex by Shutterstock:** Harper Collins Publishers. **107 Alamy Stock Photo:** Granger Historical Picture Archive (br). **Dorling Kindersley:** CONACULTA-INAH-MEX / Michel Zabe (c). **109 Dorling Kindersley:** © The Board of Trustees of the Armouries / Gary Ombler (tr). **Getty Images:** DEA / ARCHIVIO J. LANGE (br). **111 Alamy Stock Photo:** Science History Images (cl). **112 Bridgeman Images:** Granger (cra). **113 Getty Images:** DEA / A. DAGLI ORTI (cr). **114-115 Getty Images:** Universal Images Group / Leemage. **115 Alamy Stock Photo:** World History Archive (br). **Dorling Kindersley:** © The Board of Trustees of the Armouries / Gary Ombler (ca). **116 SuperStock:** gustavo tomsich / Marka (br). **118-119 akg-images:** (all images). **121 Alamy Stock Photo:** Photo12 / Ann Ronan Picture Library (bl). **122-123 Alamy Stock Photo:** Prisma Archivo. **123 Alamy Stock Photo:** Album (br). 1**24 Alamy Stock Photo:** Stephen Bay (crb). **126-127 Alamy Stock Photo:** CPA Media Pte Ltd. **127 Alamy Stock Photo:** World History Archive (br). **Dorling Kindersley:** © The Board of Trustees of the Armouries / Tim Ridley (cra). **128 Alamy Stock Photo:** The Picture Art Collection (all map images). **129 Alamy Stock Photo:** The History Collection (b). **131 akg-images:** Col. copper engr. by Matthaeus Merian the Eld. (1593–1650) Theatrum Europaeum 1637.; Berlin, Sammlung Archiv für Kunst und Geschichte. (tr). **132 Bridgeman Images:** G. Dagli Orti / De Agostini Picture Library (bc). **Dorling Kindersley:** Combined Military Services Museum / Gary Ombler (c). **132-133 akg-images:** Rabatti & Domingie. **134 Alamy Stock Photo:** Digital Image Library (bc). **135 Alamy Stock Photo:** World History Archive (tr). **136-137 Alamy Stock Photo:** CPA Media Pte Ltd. **138 Bridgeman Images:** (cl). **139 Alamy Stock Photo:** GL Archive / Mr Finnbarr Webster (bl). **Bridgeman Images:** (crb). **Getty Images:** Bettmann (c). **140-141 Alamy Stock Photo:** GL Archive. **142 Alamy Stock Photo:** INTERFOTO (tl). **Bridgeman Images:** (cl). **143 Alamy Stock Photo:** Niday Picture Library / James Nesterwitz (cr). **Getty Images:** Bettmann (tc). **145 Getty Images:** Photo 12 / Universal Images Group Editorial (br). **146 Getty Images / iStock:** duncan1890 (br). **148-149 Getty Images:** DEA / G. DAGLI ORTI. **148 Alamy Stock Photo:** Juan Aunion (bl); The Picture Art Collection (cl). **150 Alamy Stock Photo:** Chronicle (tr). **152 Alamy Stock Photo:** Granger Historical Picture Archive. **155 Alamy Stock Photo:** North Wind Picture Archives (cr). **156-157 Library of Congress, Washington, D.C.:** Mondhare (Firm). **157 Getty Images:** Hulton Fine Art Collection / Mondadori Portfolio (bc). **158 Alamy Stock Photo:** Antiqua Print Gallery. **159 akg-images:** Anonymous Person (all map images). **160 Bridgeman Images:** Look and Learn (cr). **162 Alamy Stock Photo:** World History Archive (crb). **163 Alamy Stock Photo:** World History Archive (tr). **164 Alamy Stock Photo:** The Picture Art Collection (bc). **164-165 Alamy Stock Photo:** GL Archive. **167 Dreamstime.com:** Mccool (br). **168-169 Alamy Stock Photo:** Antiqua Print Gallery. **170 Bridgeman Images:** (tr). **172 Bridgeman Images:** (bl). **Dorling Kindersley:** ina Chambers and James Stevenson / Musee de l'Emperi, Salon-de-Provence (cla). **172-173 Getty Images:** DEA / G. DAGLI ORTI. **175 Alamy Stock Photo:** Austrian National Library / Interfoto (tr). **177 Alamy Stock Photo:** Classic Image (br). **179 Bridgeman Images:** (tc); Heath, William (1795-1840) (after) / English (br). **180 Bridgeman Images:** British School, (19th century) / British (cr). **182 Bridgeman Images:** Troiani, Don (b.1949) / American (cr). **184 Alamy Stock Photo:** Vernon Lewis Gallery / Stocktrek Images (bl). **Getty Images / iStock:** duncan1890 (cla).

184-185 Alamy Stock Photo: Granger Historical Picture Archive. **187 Bridgeman Images:** Troiani, Don (b.1949) / American (br). **188-189 akg-images:** Anonymous Person (all map images). **190 Dorling Kindersley:** Fort Nelson / Gary Ombler (bl). **191 Alamy Stock Photo:** Chronicle (tr). **192 Barry Lawrence Ruderman Antique Maps Inc:** (all map images). **194 Alamy Stock Photo:** Balfore Archive Images (all map images). **195 Alamy Stock Photo:** Historic Collection (all map images). **196-197 Getty Images:** DEA PICTURE LIBRARY. **196 Alamy Stock Photo:** Lordprice Collection (bc). **Dorling Kindersley:** Peter Chadwick / Courtesy of the Royal Artillery Historical Trust (cla). **198 Getty Images:** Hulton Fine Art Collection / Print Collector (cra); UniversalImagesGroup (bl). **199 Alamy Stock Photo:** Niday Picture Library (cr); Ken Welsh (bl). **200-201 Getty Images:** Corbis Historical / Hulton Deutsch. **202 Getty Images:** Hulton Archive / Fototeca Storica Nazionale. (cr). **203 Alamy Stock Photo:** Everett Collection Inc (tl); PA Images / Dan Chung, The Guardian, MOD Pool (cr). **204 Bridgeman Images:** Look and Lear (crb). **206 Alamy Stock Photo:** The Reading Room (cl); The Keasbury-Gordon Photograph Archive (bl). **206-207 Alamy Stock Photo:** Scherl / Süddeutsche Zeitung Photo. **208 Alamy Stock Photo:** Pictorial Press Ltd (bc). **209 Alamy Stock Photo:** Scherl / Süddeutsche Zeitung Photo (tr). **210 Alamy Stock Photo:** Photo12 / Archives Snark (bl). **213 Getty Images:** Fotosearch (tr). **214 Alamy Stock Photo:** World History Archive (bc). **215 Alamy Stock Photo:** Lebrecht Music & Arts (bc). **216-217 Getty Images:** Mirrorpix. **216 Dorling Kindersley:** By kind permission of The Trustees of the Imperial War Museum, London / Gary Ombler (c, cr). **Getty Images:** Imperial War Museums (bl). **219 Alamy Stock Photo:** Chronicl (bl). **220-221 Mary Evans Picture Library:** The National Archives, London. England. **223 Getty Images:** ullstein bild Dtl. (tr). **224 123RF. com:** Serhii Kamshylin. **225 Alamy Stock Photo:** Historic Collection (cra). **226-227 Alamy Stock Photo:** Chronicle. **227 Dorling Kindersley:** Gary Ombler / Flugausstellung (cr). **Getty Images:** Popperfoto (br). **229 Alamy Stock Photo:** World History Archive (tc). **230 www. mediadrumworld.com:** Royston Leonard (bc). **231 Alamy Stock Photo:** Vintage_Spac (tc). **232 Getty Images:** Bettmann (bc). **233 www.mediadrumworld.com:** Paul Reynolds (tr). **234-235 Getty Images:** ullstein bild Dtl. **234 Alamy Stock Photo:** Photo12 / Collection Bernard Crochet (bl); Pictorial Press Ltd (c). **236 Alamy Stock Photo:** Andrew Fare (clb). **237 Getty Images:** Universal History Archive (bc). **238-239 Battle Archives:** (all maps). **240-241 Getty Images:** Corbis Historical. **241 Alamy Stock Photo:** PJF Military Collection (br); Vernon Lewis Gallery / Stocktrek Images (cr). **242 Alamy Stock Photo:** Historic Images (bl). **243 akg-images:** Fototeca Gilardi (tr). **245 Getty Images:** Hulton Archive / Laski Diffusion (tc); Universal Images Group / Sovfoto (br). **246-247 Getty Images:** Universal Images Group / Sovfoto. **246 Alamy Stock Photo:** Scherl / Süddeutsche Zeitung Photo (cl). **Dorling Kindersley:** The Tank Museum, Bovington / Gary Ombler (bl). **249 Getty Images:** Hulton Archive / Galerie Bilderwelt (tr). **250-251 Getty Images:** Corbis Historical (all map images). **252 akg-images:** (cr). **254 Alamy Stock Photo:** GL Archive (cl). **Getty Images:** The Image Bank / Michael Dunning (bc). **254-255 Alamy Stock Photo:** Science History Images. **257 Alamy Stock Photo:** Keystone Pres (bl). **258-259 Alamy Stock Photo:** World History Archive. **258 Bridgeman Images:** Pictures from History (cl). **Getty Images:** Hulton Archive / Keystone (bl). **260 Alamy Stock Photo:** Photo12 / Ann Ronan Picture Library (bl). **262 Getty Images:** The LIFE Picture Collection / Larry Burrows (tr). **265 Getty Images:** Popperfoto / Bride Lane Librar (br). **266-267 Dominic Winter Auctioneers Ltd**. **268-269 Getty Images:** The LIFE Images Collection / Mai. **269 Getty Images:** Corbis Historical (cr); The LIFE Picture Collection / Greg Mathieson (br). **270 Alamy Stock Photo:** PA Images / Chris Ison (br). **272 Alamy Stock Photo:** ClassicStock / Nawrock (br); INTERFOTO (cla). **273 Getty Images:** Corbis Historical / Hulton Deutsc (br); Universal History Archive (clb)

Endpaper images:
Front: **Getty Images:** DEA / G. DAGLI ORTI
Back: **Getty Images:** Universal Images Group

For further information see: www.dkimages.com